SELECT LETTERS

OF

TIPPOO SULTAN

TO

VARIOUS PUBLIC FUNCTIONARIES.

SELECT LETTERS

OF

TIPPOO SULTAN

TO

VARIOUS PUBLIC FUNCTIONARIES:

INCLUDING HIS

PRINCIPAL MILITARY COMMANDERS; GOVERNORS OF FORTS AND PROVINCES;
DIPLOMATIC AND COMMERCIAL AGENTS

ARRANGED AND TRANSLATED BY

WILLIAM KIRKPATRICK

GYAN

Published by

GYAN

Gyan Publishing House
5, Ansari Road
Daryaganj, New Delhi-110002
Phone: 011-47034999, 9811692060
E-mail: books@gyanbooks.com

Distribution Network
gyanbooks.com
India, USA, Canada, UK, Australia, France

ISBN: 978-81-212-7186-8 (PB)
First Published, 1811

2nd Impression 2024

Printed at: Gyan Press, Delhi.

SELECT LETTERS OF TIPPOO SULTAN TO VARIOUS PUBLIC FUNCTIONARIES
Author: TIPPOO SULTAN, Translator: WILLIAM KIRKPATRICK

SELECT LETTERS

OF

TIPPOO SULTAN

TO

VARIOUS PUBLIC FUNCTIONARIES.

SELECT LETTERS

OF

TIPPOO SULTAN

TO

VARIOUS PUBLIC FUNCTIONARIES:

INCLUDING HIS

PRINCIPAL MILITARY COMMANDERS; GOVERNORS OF FORTS AND PROVINCES;
DIPLOMATIC AND COMMERCIAL AGENTS;
&c. &c. &c.

TOGETHER WITH SOME ADDRESSED TO THE

TRIBUTARY CHIEFTAINS OF SHÂNOOR, KURNOOL, AND CANNANORE,

AND

SUNDRY OTHER PERSONS.

ARRANGED AND TRANSLATED BY

WILLIAM KIRKPATRICK,

Colonel in the Service of the Honorable East-India Company.

With NOTES and OBSERVATIONS, and an

APPENDIX,

CONTAINING SEVERAL ORIGINAL DOCUMENTS NEVER BEFORE PUBLISHED.

London:

Printed for Black, Parry, and Kingsbury, Booksellers to the Honorable East-India Company, Leadenhall Street; and for John Booth, Duke Street, Portland Place.

1811.

TO THE MOST NOBLE

RICHARD, MARQUIS WELLESLEY,

KNIGHT OF THE MOST NOBLE ORDER OF THE GARTER;

ONE OF HIS MAJESTY'S PRINCIPAL SECRETARIES OF STATE;

FORMERLY

GOVERNOR-GENERAL OF THE BRITISH POSSESSIONS,

AND

CAPTAIN-GENERAL OF THE BRITISH FORCES, IN INDIA,

&c. &c. &c. &c.

My Lord:

It is neither for the ostentatious purpose of gracing the front of my book with an illustrious name, nor, by thus giving it the apparent stamp of your approbation, to promote its favourable reception with the public, that the present work is dedicated to your Lordship. It is equally remote from my intention, either to offer it as a tribute of gratitude for former, or to employ it as a passport to future obligations. The first of these objects would be but feebly answered, and the latter could not, in any degree, be advanced, by such inadequate means. It is a principle of justice, and of justice alone, which has prompted me to address it to your Lordship.

I am

I am far from the vanity or presumption of imagining, that the introduction of your name, on this occasion, can be in the least flattering to your Lordship. No, my Lord; I am only anxious to avoid the manifest impropriety of which I should be guilty, if I were to dedicate to any but your Lordship, a work, which, in truth, owes its existence to you.

This is no compliment, my Lord, but a mere historical fact: for who does not know that it was your Lordship's political sagacity which penetrated, and your prompt and energetic measures which defeated, the hostile designs of Tippoo Sultan against the British Dominions in India? Who is ignorant, that it was those measures which led to the rapid annihilation of the most formidable power with whom we ever had to cope in that quarter of the globe, and which substituted in its place an order of things, redounding no less to the glory, than conducing to the solid interests, of your country?

To the complete success which, under Divine Providence, crowned the wise and vigorous conduct of your Lordship, in this short but arduous contest, is the public indebted, among other inestimable advantages of the most important and durable nature, for the possession of the archives of *Seringapatam*. To whom, therefore, can a work, compiled from those archives, be so appropriately addressed, as to him who procured us access to whatever information they contain?

Having thus, I presume, satisfactorily established your Lordship's public claim to the present humble tribute, it only remains for me to

shew,

shew, that you possess still another title to it, which though of a private nature, is equally imperative upon me, as the compiler of the following sheets: for if that tribute would have been due to your Lordship from any person whatsoever, who might have casually obtained possession of the documents composing this work, and have anticipated me in the publication of them, how much more is your Lordship entitled to receive such an acknowledgement from one, who is, in fact, indebted for his materials to the official situations in which he had the honor of being employed under your Lordship's administration in India?

I have the honor to be,

With the highest respect,

My LORD,

Your Lordship's most obedient

and most faithful servant,

WILLIAM KIRKPATRICK.

Exeter,
1st February, 1811.

ADVERTISEMENT.

It is already generally known, that upon the reduction of Seringapatam, in the year 1799, *all the public records of the then existing Government of Mysore passed into the possession of the captors. It is also, however, but too certain, that many of these precious documents were accidentally burnt, or otherwise destroyed, in the confusion and disorder which unavoidably ensued upon the assault of the fort: nor is it improbable, that some portion of them has disappeared, in consequence of falling, on the same occasion, into the hands of private persons, ignorant of the value, and indifferent to the preservation of their prize. But whatever loss may have arisen from the last mentioned cause, it is, nevertheless, owing to the active care, and intelligent research, of an individual, that several of the most important of the Mysore papers, now remaining, have been rescued from oblivion; and, among the rest, the very Register of public Letters, from which the correspondence, contained in the present volume, has been extracted. The gentleman here alluded to is Lieutenant-Colonel Ogg, of the East-India Company's Madras Establishment,* to whose kindness the Translator is indebted for the chief part of the interesting materials relative to Tippoo Sultan, of which he is in possession.*

Of

b

* Lieutenant-Colonel (then Captain) Ogg held, at the period in question, an official situation under Viscount Wellington, at that time Commandant of Seringapatam.

Of the state papers discovered at Seringapatam, immediately after the capture of that place, many have been already communicated to the Public, through official and other channels. Those, in particular, which served to develope the more recent intrigues of Tippoo Sultan with the enemies of Great-Britain, were published, soon after his overthrow, by authority of the Supreme Government of India, and subsequently in this country. A report of the general nature of these documents was drawn up, at an early period, in pursuance of directions from Marquis Wellesley, by the present writer, who had been employed to examine them, and who suggested, at the time, the expediency of having the whole translated, preparatory to a proper selection being made from them, for the information of the public.† The great pressure of business in the Persian Department, prevented, however, the adoption of this recommendation, when first submitted to the Governor General; and the same cause has probably continued to operate, to the disappointment of the expectation which may be presumed to have been excited on the occasion. By none can this disappointment be more severely felt or regretted, than by the compiler of these sheets, who is too well acquainted with the eminent talents of the gentleman‡ then at the head of the Persian Office in Bengal, not to appreciate duly the heavy loss sustained by the literary world at large, but more especially by such as are fond of enquiries into the Modern History of India, in consequence of his having been precluded, by his official avocations, from undertaking the task alluded to.*

But it may still, perhaps, be permitted us to hope, that this object has not been absolutely relinquished; and that some portion, at least, of the extensive and valuable

* Vide Asiatic Register for 1799, and Lieutenant-Colonel Beatson's "View of the Origin "and Conduct of the War with Tippoo Sultan."

† The substance of the report, here referred to, may be seen at page 179 of Colonel Beatson's publication.

‡ N. B. Edmondstone, Esq.

valuable documents, enumerated in the report just referred to, may at no distant period, be submitted to the public eye, which, in the mean while, may possibly view with indulgence, the present specimen of the less copious, but equally curious and interesting materials, discovered subsequently to the date of that report. Of those materials, (or, rather, such of them as have reached the Translator's hands) the following sheets constitute only a part. The remaining letters of Tippoo Sultan, to say nothing of other documents in the writer's possession, would, after due selection, furnish abundant matter for another volume: but enough, probably, is here done, for the immediate gratification of the public curiosity. It must rest on the reception given to the present work, and on the state of the Translator's health, whether he shall hereafter attempt a continuation of it. However this may be, as the other materials, alluded to, have no necessary dependence, either upon those employed in the ensuing pages, or upon one another, no inconvenience can result to the reader or purchaser from their separate publication.

The Translator will probably have reason to regret, that he has allowed so long a period to intervene, between the publication of the present volume and his acquisition of the materials which principally compose it. It would, no doubt, have excited a stronger interest than it can now be hoped to do, if it had appeared, while the public curiosity, with regard to whatever related to Tippoo Sultan, was still eager, and while the memory of the events connected with his name was yet recent. But various circumstances, with which it is unnecessary to trouble the Reader, combined to prevent the Translator, till within the last twelvemonth, from undertaking to arrange the documents in his possession for the press. He will only mention one; which is, that during the whole of the intermediate time, he was constantly in expectation that the work in his contemplation (for he confesses to have always had it in view) would be anticipated from some other quarter.

Notwithstanding,

Notwithstanding, however, the unfavourable effect, but too likely to be produced by the delay which has occurred, the Translator is willing to flatter himself, that, even at this late period, the attempt to illustrate a character, so conspicuous in modern days as that of Tippoo Sultan, and to throw light on transactions, so closely connected, as those of his reign are, with the history of the British Empire in India, is in little danger of being deemed entirely destitute, either of interest or utility. In this humble confidence are the following sheets now presented to the Public, whose judgment concerning them will be awaited by the Translator with no inconsiderable anxiety.

PREFACE.

THE Register from which the following letters have been taken, and which has been cursorily noticed in the Advertisement, is the fragment, only, of a record, which, if it had reached us in a perfect state, would probably have exhibited copies of all the public or official correspondence of Tippoo Sultan, from the commencement to the close of his reign. Unfortunately, however, the portion of these highly interesting documents which has been preserved, or, at least, hitherto discovered, is not so extensive as could have been wished; the correspondence, in question, not beginning till February 1785, and ending with November 1793. But, even in this period, considerable chasms occur; while, from 1794 to 1799, is an absolute blank. In short, we are, at present, in possession of little more than a third part of the correspondence, which may reasonably be supposed to have taken place within the time spoken of: in which account, however, I do not include such detached letters of the *Sultan* as have come to us through other channels, and all of which are of a subsequent date to the latest of those recorded in the Register.

But whatever cause we may have to regret the actual deficiency of our present materials, we ought not, perhaps, absolutely to despair of its being yet supplied by the successful diligence of future enquirers. Adverting to the extreme regularity observed by the *Sultan* in the registry of his official correspondence, little doubt can be entertained of the existence of the now missing part of it, at the time of his death. Supposing it, therefore, to have escaped the destruotion, which, as was stated in the Advertisement, swept away but too many of the archives of his government, it is still possible, that it may be recovered, out of the private hands into which it has probably fallen. In the mean while, the value of the portion actually preserved, is not, perhaps, essentially diminished, by the loss that appears to have been sustained. Enough remains, if not to elucidate every transaction of the *Sultan's* reign, at least to develope his singular character in the most satisfactory manner. The importance of these letters, indeed, does not consist so much in the light which they are calculated to shed on several material occurrences of the period they relate to (though, in this respect, they will certainly be found a useful guide to the future historian of *Mysore)* as in the vivid illustration which they afford of the genius, talents, and disposition of their extraordinary author, who is here successively and repeatedly delineated, in colors from his own pencil, as the cruel and relentless enemy; the intolerant bigot or furious fanatic; the oppressive and unjust ruler; the harsh and rigid master; the sanguinary tyrant; the perfidious negociator; the frivolous and capricious innovator; the mean and minute economist; the peddling trader; and even the retail shop-keeper. The painter will not be suspected of overcharging the unfavorable traits of the picture, when it is considered that that picture is his own.

In making the present selection from about a thousand letters,* I have confined myself, almost entirely, to such as either appeared to exhibit the *Sultan* in some new light; to unfold some of his political, financial, or commercial views; or to elucidate some historical fact. Those which merely related to the details of ordinary business, without eliciting any thing peculiarly characteristic of the writer, have been passed over. I have also judged it unnecessary to insert any part of the *Sultan's* correspondence

* The Register comprises altogether about two thousand letters; of which number I have not yet arrainged above half.

respondence with the several British Governors of India, as most of these documents are already in the possession of the Public.

I will now proceed to give some account of the rules, by which I have, in general, been guided in the course of the present translation.

My principal object, in this work, being to present as striking a likeness of Tippoo, as the nature of my materials, and the extent of my ability to employ them advantageously, would admit, I thought it essential to this end, to render his sentiments, on all occasions, as closely as the different idioms of the two languages would allow, without involving the sense in difficulty or obscurity. In short, what I wished, but cannot hope to have attained, is, that the reader, losing sight entirely of the translator, should fancy himself in presence of the *Sultan*, listening to the latter, while dictating to one or other of the different secretaries by whom he was usually attended.

Proceeding on this principle, I have, for the most part, adhered more strictly to the phraseology or diction of my original, than is usually deemed necessary, or expedient, in translations from a foreign language; and I am ready to admit, that my unwillingness to relinquish the slightest turn of expression, appearing particularly to denote the feeling which suggested it, may have sometimes led me too far. Still, however, my translation is not absolutely a verbal one; since I have not scrupled to exercise a certain license, as often as either our language could not be easily bent to the form of the Persian, or ambiguity was likely to result from the attempt. There are, indeed, two points, in which I acknowledge to have uniformly deviated from the *strict* letter of the original, and on which it may not be improper, in this place, to submit a few observations to the notice of the Reader.

One of the points alluded to consists in my making the writer of these letters almost constantly use the first person *plural*, when speaking of himself: but though it is true, that the precise words, corresponding to

 we,

we, *our*, and *us*, are not employed by the *Sultan*, yet are the latter entirely agreeable to the genius of the language, in which nothing is more common than the substitution of the plural for the singular pronouns, unless it be that of the third for both the first and second.* In these letters, however, the pronoun of the first person, whether singular or plural, scarcely ever occurs,† the words حضور *Hūzoor* (Presence), and سرکار *Sircar* (state or government), being every where used instead of them. As, therefore, the perpetual recurrence of such terms would have had a very awkward appearance in English, if it would not, also, have sometimes embarrassed the sense, I did not hesitate at converting them generally into pronouns. It may be further urged, in justification of the liberty I have taken, that while, on the one hand, the style of majesty, thus assigned to the *Sultan*, is in perfect conformity with the usage of the East, it is also the best suited to the mandatory nature of the chief part of the letters, and to the actual rank of the writer. In a few instances, where the persons addressed are of a different description from the generality of his correspondents, I have judged it right to make the *Sultan* descend (as, indeed, he more or less does himself in the original) to the customary style of equality.

The second point, in which I have ventured to depart pretty constantly from the manuscript, respects the *tense*, as the preceding one does the *person*. Instead of the perfect, or preterpluperfect tense, in which the letters of his correspondents are always spoken of by the *Sultan*, I have adopted,

* Thus the third person is very commonly put for both the first and second (governing the verb accordingly) in such phrases as the following : اینجانب or مخلص or دوستدار منتظر رسیدن ایشان or تشریف اوردن آن مهربان or سامي نشسته‌اند *i. e.* "this side, or person, or friend, (*i. e.* I) is seated in expectation of *their*, or *that friend's* (*i. e. your*) arrival." Where, اینجانب &c. standing for the pronoun of the third person, takes the verb accordingly in the third person نشسته‌اند

† I have not met with more than two or three instances in the course of the following letters.

adopted, as more agreeable to the idiom of our language, the use of the present and compound preterite: thus, for نوشته بود *it was written* (by you), or *you wrote*, I have put, *you write*. In the same manner I have rendered ازنظر گذشت *passed under view*, by, *has passed under (our) view;** and so in other similar cases.

With the exceptions which have been stated, and scarcely with any other, my general rule has been, to retain, as nearly as possible, every word and thought, that seemed to mark, in any prominent degree, the peculiar cast of the writer's mind.

Tippoo Sultan, indeed, rarely took up his pen, without its laying open some recess or other of his various and irregular mind. He seldom issues an order, that does not bespeak, either the general tone of his nature, or the particular impulse of the moment. He seems to have felt no hesitation in avowing, in the course of the letters which follow, the most flagitious sentiments; and this may be accounted for on one or other, or on both, of these principles. The letters being, in the first place, addressed, with few exceptions, to persons in absolute dependence on him, he consequently would be wholly free from that sort of reserve, which arises from the fear of incurring the censure or reproach of the world. He knew his will to be a law, the propriety of which, as it might concern others, would never be canvassed or doubted by any of his slaves. In the next place, he probably measured the sentiments in question, by a different standard from that with which we estimate them. Thus, the various murders and acts of treachery, which we see him directing to be carried into execution, were not criminal, but, on the contrary, just, and even meritorious, in his eyes. They might, and most likely did, in a great degree, proceed from a disposition naturally cruel and sanguinary: but, perhaps, an intolerant religious zeal and

c bigotry

* To avoid tiring the eye or the ear, by the perpetual recurrence of this metaphor, I have sometimes substituted, in its place, the simple phrase, *has been received.*

bigotry were not less active motives to them. The *Koran* taught him, that it was not necessary to keep faith with infidels, or the enemies of the true religion, in which class it was not difficult for him to persuade himself that it was right to include all who opposed, or refused to co-operate in, his views, for the extension of that religion; or, in other words, for his own aggrandisement. Hence it was, that our Musulman allies and subjects were scarcely less obnoxious to his hatred and vengeance than ourselves. With regard to the secret murder of his English prisoners, his dreadful slaughter of the Koorgs and Nairs, and his forcible conversion of so many thousands of the two latter tribes to the Mahommedan faith, he most probably thought such enormities no less warranted, both by the example and precepts of the founder of his religion, than the infraction of oaths and engagements in transactions with unbelievers.

It may be thought, that admitting the propriety of a close adherence, in general, to the original of a work of the peculiar nature of the present, still there was no necessity for retaining, so scrupulously as I may seem to have done, its numerous pleonasms and tautologies, both in matter and expression. With respect, however, to the former of these defects, (namely, the perpetual reiteration of the same opinion or direction) I confess I did not deem it right to retrench superfluities, which did not appear as such to their author; who, though he undoubtedly too often wearies us with a repetition of the same thing, might, nevertheless, in so doing, have had it in view to stimulate the diligence and zeal of his servants: and where the fault may not seem to have proceeded from this cause, it at least marks an earnest solicitude of mind, for the accomplishment of the objects so incessantly impressed on the attention of the persons addressed. These observations will be found, perhaps, more especially applicable to the letters written to Kumrûddeen Khân, to Bûrhânûddeen, and to the diplomatic agents at *Poonah*.

With

With regard to the mere verbal tautologies, I am ready to admit that they might have been considerably abridged, without any injury to the general sense of the original, and certainly with advantage to the style. As, however, they appeared to me, in many instances, strongly characteristic of the genius and temper of the writer, I have, on such occasions, thought it right to preserve them in the translation, though somewhat at the expence of good taste and brevity. On the other hand, where the perpetual recurrence of an unmeaning form of speech would have become grating to the ear, or tiresome to the eye, I have not scrupled to vary it occasionally. I shall be found to have exercised this liberty most frequently in the introductory part of these letters, where, instead of "*your humble address has passed under view, and the circumstances set forth therein are manifest, or duly comprehended, &c.*" with which, or similar words, they usually begin, I have generally contented myself with a simple notification of the receipt of the letter referred to. Now and then, only, for the sake of variety, I have retained the circuitous phraseology of the original. On the whole, however, I have no where, for the mere sake of improving the general style of the translation, or of infusing more spirit into any particular passage or expression, deviated intentionally from my manuscript, of which my endeavour has been to give as faithful a version as was compatible with a due regard to perspicuity. If I have not always succeeded in this object, I am willing that the failure should, for the most part, be attributed to my incompetency. At the same time, I owe it to myself to observe, and trust my readers will believe, that it has sometimes proceeded entirely from the obscurity of the original, occasioned either by the carelessness of my author, or by the errors of transcribers.

Notwithstanding the few redundancies of style which have been noticed as pervading the following letters, their general characteristic is certainly brevity, which, perhaps, might proceed, in some degree, from a notion of the writer, that the laconic manner was the one best suited to the authoritative nature of his dispatches, as well as to the relative situation of the persons to whom they were chiefly addressed. It was certainly, too, well adapted, if not absolutely necessary, to the purpose of one who had his pen for ever in his hand, and who himself (whether from inclination, or from an universal distrust of all whom he employed, or from a passion to be thought, not only the principal, but the sole originator, of every thing) directed, either by writing or orally, the most minute details of his government. Such a one could not have had leisure to compose long letters, had they been necessary; which, however, would rarely be the case. But be this as it might, the *Sultan* does not appear to have possessed a sufficient stretch of thought upon any subject (even those that he most delighted in or affected) to enable him to discuss it, either with logical force or precision. A consecutive train of argument was a thing of which he no where seems to have had an idea: yet some of the occasions, on which he wrote or dictated, certainly afforded ample scope for the display of the reasoning faculty. His writings, however, furnish as little proof of his having possessed this faculty, as his actions in general did. Even in his own Memoirs, which he did not begin to compose till he was past forty, we meet with nothing indicating capacity of any kind. He did not even write with facility. This is clearly shewn, by various memorandums in his hand-writing, which, though very short, and on subjects of no difficulty, abound in erasures and corrections. One, in particular, relating to the question, whether Major Doveton should be allowed to accompany the hostage princes, on their return from Madras? is nearly unintelligible, in consequence of the interlineations which disfigure, and the general confusion of ideas and dates which pervades it. As this curious document, besides serving to establish the truth of the position just advanced, is, in some other respects, extremely interesting, the Persian reader

reader may not be displeased to see a *fac simile* of it, which has been engraved for this work, and forms Appendix A.

Although the authenticity of these letters will hardly be disputed, even by the most sceptical, yet the reader may hesitate to believe, that, with the exception, perhaps, of those addressed to the Emperor of Hindostan (the late Shah Allum), and a few others of the more elaborate or finished kind, if any of them may be so considered, they were either dictated by the *Sultan*, or actually proceeded from his pen. Nor, indeed, does this notion admit, at present, of any direct or positive proof. Its probability only can be contended for; and that, I think, sufficiently deducible from the internal evidence afforded by these documents themselves. Their laconic and abrupt style, their commanding and peremptory tone, and the asperity of language which distinguishes so many of them, all abundantly indicate their origin. No *Munshy*, or secretary, in short, can be reasonably supposed to have drafted such letters; while, as to the labour attending the composition or dictation of so many dispatches, as sometimes appear under the same date, it will scarcely be thought to constitute any objection to the present hypothesis, in the case of one so addicted to writing, and so indefatigable in business, as the *Sultan* was.

To return from this digression, to the account I proposed giving of the plan of the following translation. The notes which I have annexed to it are of two kinds: those merely explanatory of a single word, or phrase, or referring to other letters, or relating to dates, appear at the bottom of the page. When, on the other hand, a particular letter or passage has suggested to me any reflections, to which I wished to draw the reader's attention, I have, instead of encumbering the page with them, placed them under the title of "OBSERVATIONS," at the end of the letter giving rise to them. Upon this commentary, if I may so call those observations, I have taken occasion to engraft, besides other original matter, a considerable portion of a highly interesting manuscript, purporting to be a

Memoir

Memoir of Tippoo Sultan, written by himself. This curious document was among the numerous papers discovered by Colonel Ogg. The copy with which that gentleman favored me was entitled *Tareekhe Khodâdâdy*, *i. e.* the *Khodâdâdy* Annals, or History of the *Khodâdâd Sircar*. The work was, from the beginning, in an imperfect state; the narrative being brought down to no later a period than the termination of the Mahrattah war, or the month of February 1787. My copy, however, has been rendered still more incomplete, by an unfortunate accident, which occasioned the destruction of several leaves of it. The original Memoir evidently formed, as far as it went, the ground-work of the more diffuse and elaborate history of Zynûl Aabideen Shoostry, mentioned by Colonel Wilks, and called by its author, in allusion to his master's name, "the "Sultan of History." I am not enabled to say, whether the copy of the fragment found by Colonel Ogg was in the actual hand-writing of the *Sultan*: but, however this may be, I venture to think, that no just doubt can be entertained of its genuineness. It was discovered in the palace of the *Sultan*, and along with other documents of unquestioned authenticity. The style and matter of it, moreover, abundantly support its claim to credit. It is written throughout in the first person; and while it states some facts which could be known only to the *Sultan*, it every where breathes the same over-weening spirit, which so strongly distinguishes almost every production of his pen. The Persian scholar, however, who may wish to judge on this point for himself, will have it in his power to do so, by inspecting the manuscript in question; which, together with the original of the following letters, will be deposited in the East-India Company's Library.*

Such

* Though the *Sultan's* own account of his operations against General Matthews, in *Bidnore*, and of the subsequent siege of *Mangalore*, belongs to a period antecedent to the commencement of the following correspondence, and could not conveniently be incorporated with the Observations, in the manner that great part of his Memoirs has been, I have thought it too curious andinteresting a document to be omitted in the present work, and have therefore given a translation of it in article B. of the Appendix.

Such technical terms (and especially the names of offices and employments) as I could not render into English, with perfect reliance on the fidelity of my interpretation, I have retained in the original, and subjoined, by the way of notes, the best explanation of them in my power to give. I may add here, that whenever I have been in any doubt, with respect to the sense of a particular word or phrase, I have usually noticed it, offering, at the same time, the interpretation that seemed to me to be nearest the truth, and not unfrequently putting the original Persian at the bottom of the page. Where the meaning, on the other hand, owing to some error in the manuscript, or to my insufficiency, has appeared utterly inexplicable, I have thought it best to pass over the unintelligible part altogether, but never without announcing the omission.

This seems the proper place for apprizing the reader, that the words enclosed in hooks, or crotchets, are not strictly warranted by the original, but have been supplied, in order to complete the sense, and prevent the obscurity which their omission would have been liable to produce: for, however diffuse or exuberant the usual style of Persian composition may be, that language abounds in phrases and modes of expression, which, owing to their concise structure, leave much to be understood, and which can be rendered intelligible in English, only by such means as I have occasionally adopted.

I could have wished it had been in my power to have elucidated the geography of the present work, in a more satisfactory manner than has been done. In fact, I have been enabled to afford the reader little or no additional information on this subject, in aid of what is to be obtained from the latest maps of *Mysore*, of which I consider the one, given in Colonel Wilks's valuable History of that state, as the best. What has increased my difficulty, on this occasion, is, that the names of many places, occurring in the Persian manuscript, are written so indistinctly, that I could only guess at them; which, however, I have never done, without

without noticing the circumstance. Besides this, there are several forts and towns mentioned in the following pages, which would be sought for in vain in any map or gazetteer, hitherto published; because, in the rage for innovation, which never ceased to actuate the *Sultan*, he was led, among other reforms of a similar nature, to change their ancient and still generally prevalent names. Thus, to *Chittledoorg* he gave the name of *Furrúkh-yáb Hisár;* to *Gooty*, that of *Fyze-Hisár*, &c. Some of these innovations are officially announced, in the course of the present work. It appears somewhat singular, that in his childish eagerness to give new denominations to every thing, he should have suffered *Seringapatam* and *Bangalore* to retain their old names; especially as the former appellation, having been derived from an idol, might, on that account, be supposed to have been particularly offensive to a bigotted Musulman. It is not, therefore, improbable, that some superstitious notion may have restrained him in these instances, and saved those ancient cities from the transformation experienced by so many others.

On the subject of the oriental orthography of the present work, it is the more necessary to submit a few remarks to the reader's consideration, as these letters abound so greatly in proper names, and other Persian or Hindivi words. Such a diversity of opinion and practice prevails in this respect, that it would not be possible to adopt any scheme entirely acceptable to all. That which I have, for the most part, endeavoured to follow, is the one introduced at the College of Fort William, on the first establishment of that admirable institution, which appears to me better adapted than any other, to convey to the English reader an accurate notion of the pronunciation of the Persian language, as spoken in India. I have not, however, rigidly adhered to the scheme in question, having, for instance, rarely followed it, in opposition to any very prevalent or general practice, however incorrect the latter might be. Thus I have always, in compliance with the common usage, written *Mahommed*, in-

stead

stead of *Muhummed*; *Mysore*, instead of *Mysoor*; *Bangalore*, instead of *Bungloor*; *Seringapatam*, instead of *Sri-rung-putn*, &c. On the same principle, I have preferred *Tippoo Sultan* to the more correct spelling of *Tipoo Sûltaun* or *Sûltân*; though I observe that the latter mode of writing the word *Sultan* has been adopted by Major Stewart and others. Still, however, as the short, or quick sound, of the last of the two syllables composing it, is almost in universal use, I have thought it right to preserve the spelling which best expresses that sound.*

d

Before

* The following is a brief exposition of the plan on which I have *usually* expressed in Roman characters, the different Persian, Arabic, and Hindoostâny sounds, or letters, composing the proper names, &c. which occur in the present work. I say *usually*, because, as already acknowledged, I have, in some cases, purposely deviated from the rule here exhibited, in deference to long established usage; while, in others, I have done so through inadvertency or oversight. It is hoped, however, that the instances of the latter kind will not be found numerous, no pains having been spared by the reviser to correct such as had escaped the writer.

There being no such sound in Persian or Arabic, or (I believe) in Hindoostâny, as that of our *a*, in *hat*, *cat*, &c. I have, in consequence, rarely employed plain or unaccented *a*, confining the use of it to such words as *Ahmed* and *Mahommed*; which orthography, as being the most familiar to English readers, I have preferred to the more correct one of *Uhmud* and *Muhummud*.

A with a circumflex *(â)* invariably stands for آ or *alif mumdoodeh*, and is always to be sounded like *a*, in the words *ball*, *call*, &c. It also represents the *alif* long by position, as in تاب *tâb*, which differs nothing in sound from the *alif mumdoodeh* in آب *âb*.

Double *a*, or *aa*, represents ع medial, as *baad* for بعد; also ع ending a syllable or word, as in جمعدار written *jumaadâr*, and جمع written *jumaa*. It likewise expresses ع followed by ا as in شاہ عالم which written correctly should be, according to my scheme, *Shah Aalum*. I have, nevertheless, followed the more usual orthography of *Shâh Allum*.

I no where use *c* to express ق or ک or the corresponding Hindoostâny letter; excepting in a few instances, as *Calicut*, *Sircar*, &c. where I have preserved the *c*, in conformity with general practice. With these exceptions, both ق and ک as well as the Hindoostâny or Nâgry letter क corresponding to the latter, are expressed by *k*.

Ch, which represents the چ of the Persian, and the corresponding sound in the Hindoostâny, is to be constantly sounded as in *church*.

I think the sound of our *e*, in *pen*, *hen*, &c. is equally unknown to the Persian and Arabic, as that of our *a*, in *hat*, *cat*, &c.: when, therefore, I employ a single *e*, it is either in compliance

Before I conclude these introductory remarks it may be proper to state, that my chief trouble, in the present work, has arisen from the difficulty I have had in adjusting the Kalendar introduced by the *Sultan*. On this subject I have found it necessary to enter into a distinct discussion, which, accordingly, immediately follows the Preface. It may here suffice to say, that though I am, by no means, confident of having completely succeeded

compliance with established custom, or because I am uncertain whether the short vowel of the Persian and Arabic, which it represents, is a *kusr* or *futha*. The former I have generally expressed by *i* (having the sound of *i* in *sin*); the latter by *u* (to be uniformly sounded as *u* in *gun*). The *e*, in *hen*, is a sound between the two.

Double *e*, or *ee*, denotes the long ي of the Persian and Arabic (as well as the corresponding Hindoostany *mâtra*, or vowel) whether so by position, or by having *kusr* or *zair*.

The ي at the end of a word, as in احمدي, حيدري &c. having nearly the same short sound as our *y*, in *needy*, *hairy*, &c. I have, for the most part, expressed it by that letter, which, at the end of a word, is accordingly to be always pronounced as the *y* in *needy*. The proper name علي I have, nevertheless, written *Ali*, in conformity with general usage. When *y*, on the other hand, occurs at the beginning of a word or syllable, it is to be sounded like *y* in *yore*, *yes*, &c. as, in such cases, it represents initial ي In all other situations, *y* (as representing the ي preceded by *futha*) is to be pronounced as *y* in *dying*: thus the months بياضي and حيدري are written *Byâzy* and *Hydury*.

Double *o*, or *oo*, constantly represents و preceded by *zum*, or *paish*, which has always the sound of *oo*, in *doom*, *room*, &c.

U with a circumflex (û) invariably stands for the short vowel *zum* or *paish*, and is always to be sounded like *u* in *ruby*. *U* without the circumflex, or plain *u*, constantly denotes *futha* or *zubr*, and is invariably to be sounded like *u* in *fun*. Thus دور *(far)* is written *door*; دُر *(a pearl) dûr*; and در *(in) dur*.

Ow, sounded as in *gown*, expresses و with *futha* or *zubr* before it. Thus دولت is written *Dowlut*.

Kh uniformly denotes the خ of the Persian and Arabic; and *gh* the غ *Th* denotes the Arabic ث as in عثمان which I write *Othman*, though the ث is usually pronounced in India as an *s*. *G* is always hard.

The remaining letters require no particular remark, as they are to be always sounded as in English. Some writers distinguish between the س and the ص; the ط and the ت; the ض the ز and the ذ; the ق and the ک; the ع and the ء; but I have not thought it necessary to do so.

It is only requisite to add, that I express the ي *mujhool* by our diphthong *ai*, as sounded in *daily*; and the و *mujhool* by open *o* or *ô*, sounded as in *open*.

succeeded in my endeavors on this occasion, I nevertheless trust, that none of my dates will be found materially wrong. I also deem it requisite to observe, that notwithstanding the pains which I have taken to arrange these letters in the regular order of time, I am apprehensive that some of them will be found out of their proper place. The reason of this is, that with a view to dispatch, the original was distributed, for copying, among several transcribers; and that, on the completion of the work, the different portions of the copy, instead of being carefully disposed, according to their respective dates, were bound up promiscuously together. Owing to this inadvertency, I constantly found, when I came to examine them in a collected form, that two letters which, agreeably to their dates, should have stood together, were separated, perhaps, by a hundred pages: consequently, before I could proceed satisfactorily with my translation, I was obliged to reduce this chaos to some order; and if I have not been entirely successful in the attempt, the indulgent reader will make due allowance for the difficulty and irksomeness of my task.

Besides the extensive obligations which I have declared myself to be under to the liberal kindness of Colonel Ogg, it is incumbent upon me to acknowledge, on the present occasion, the great assistance I have derived, in several instances, from another source. I here allude to various valuable communications with which I have, at different times, been favoured, by my very able friend, Lieutenant Colonel Colin M'Kenzie, of the Madras Engineers; to whose indefatigable and laudable researches, respecting the History and Antiquities of the South of India, such just and honorable testimony has been borne by Colonel Wilks, in the valuable work which that accomplished writer has lately presented to the public.

The list of those, however, to whom I owe the humble tribute of my

d 2 thanks

thanks on the present occasion is not yet closed. I am proud to add to it the name of Dr. Wilkins, the learned and ingenious Librarian of the East India Company, to whose friendly assistance and advice, at the outset of my undertaking in particular, I consider myself to be much indebted. I am also eager to acknowledge my obligations to Charles Stewart, Esq. the learned Professor of Arabic, Persian, and Hindostâny, at the East-India Company's College at Hertford; and to Sir Charles Warre Malet, Bart., who filled with distinguished reputation, during a period of ten years, the important station of Resident at the Court of *Poonah.* The nature of the communications with which I have been favored by the two latter gentlemen, will appear more fully in the sequel.

But to none of my literary friends do I feel more deeply indebted, for aid afforded me in the conduct of the present work, than to John Shakespear, Esq. of the Honorable East-India Company's Military Institution at Croydon, in Surry; for if that able Orientalist had not most kindly undertaken to superintend it in its progress through the press, I must, of necessity, on account of my unavoidable absence from town, have postponed its publication to an indefinite period, if I had not even been induced, by the difficulties arising from this circumstance, to relinquish my design altogether. I would fain, therefore, enlarge, in this place, on the advantages which my book has derived, from the indefatigable care bestowed upon its revision; but I am restrained from indulging my inclination, in this respect, by knowing that I shall best consult the satisfaction of the gentleman in question, by abstaining, on the present occasion, from any more particular acknowledgement of my obligations to him.

To the names of the persons already announced, as having contributed, by their communications, to whatever value the present work may be thought to possess, I am bound to add those of Lieutenant Colonel Thomas

Thomas Munro and Lieutenant Colonel Mariott, both of the Madras establishment. I must, at the same time, lament, that circumstances should not have admitted of my profiting by their extensive information, in the degree which an earlier application to them might have enabled me to do.

REMARKS

EXPLANATORY OF THE KALENDAR OF

TIPPOO SULTAN.

BEFORE I could proceed in the translation of the following letters, it was necessary that I should acquire some insight into the construction of the Kalendar instituted by Tippoo Sultan, and always employed by him, excepting in his correspondence with persons not subjected to his authority, when he condescended to use the common Mahommedan reckoning. Till I could attain this knowledge, it would neither be possible for me to rectify the confusion in the arrangement of the manuscript, occasioned by the accident noticed in the Preface, nor to convert the *Sultan's* dates into the corresponding English dates. Of the necessity of the first of these operations, or the classing of the letters in the order of time, there could be no doubt, since this was absolutely necessary to the right understanding of many of them; while the utility of others, in an historical view, depended, in some measure, on the degree of accuracy with which the dates of the original might be reduced to our chronology.

When, however, I came to examine the means I possessed for this purpose, I found that they were much more scanty than I had supposed them to be: nor have I been so fortunate as to supply the deficiency, by such enquiries as it has been in my power to make in this country. No doubt, the requisite information might have been obtained from India; but the fact is, that it was not until very lately that I discovered the want of any. As it is, I trust that I have, at least, made such an approximation to the truth (if I have not actually arrived at it), as will sufficiently answer the main ends in view.

I have no means of ascertaining with precision, at what period of his reign Tippoo Sultan introduced his first innovation in the Kalendar; but there is good reason to believe, that it was about a year after his accession to the *Musnud.* The earliest document in my possession, dated according to his new Kalendar, is an edict, or regulation, of the

15th

15th *Jaafury* of the year *Ual* (or thirty-eighth of the cycle hereafter explained), corresponding, as I reckon, to the 10th of June 1784: but another, issued about six months anterior to this, or in January 1784, shows that the reformed Kalendar was not in use at the latter period, since the edict in question bears no other date than the Mahommedan one of *Zilhijjeh*, A.H. 1197.(1) From these data it may be inferred, that the new Kalendar was established some time between January and June 1784.

There is no doubt, that this Kalendar was founded on the reckoning in common use in *Mysore*, which was that of the Malabar cycle of sixty years. To the years composing this cycle, the *Sultan* gave new names; as he did to the months of the year. But though he took the Hindoo computation for his ground-work, he would not appear to have adhered strictly to it, since disagreements between the two reckonings sometimes occur. Thus the 14th *Tûlooey* (or 9th month of Tippoo Sultan's year), which was the *Sultan's* birth-day, did not coincide with the 14th, but with the 17th of *Mârgaiser* or *Ughun* (9th month of the Hindoo year). The cause of this discrepancy may probably be traced in the following division of the year, according to the *Sultan's* first regulation of it.

Order of the Month.	Name.	Number of Days.	Corresponding with the Hindoo Month, ... and	...... Zodiacal Sign.
1st	احمدي *Ahmedy*, ..	29	*Choiter*, ...	*Aries.*
2d	بهاري *Behâry*, ..	30	*Bysâk*, ...	*Taurus.*
3d	جعفري *Jaafury*, ..	30	*Joister (Jait)*, ...	*Gemini.*
4th	داراي *Dârdey*, ..	29	*Âsâr*, ...	*Cancer.*
5th	هاشمي *Hâshimy*,..	29	*Sâwun* or *Srâwun*, ..	*Leo.*
6th	واسعي *Wâsaaey*,..	30	*Bhâdon* or *Bhâder*, ..	*Virgo.*
7th	زبرجدي *Zuburjudy*,	29	*Âsin*, ...	*Libra.*
8th	حيدري *Hydery*, ...	30	*Kârtic*, ...	*Scorpio.*
9th	طلوعي *Tûlooey*, ..	29	*Mârgaiser* or *Ughun*,..	*Sagittarius.*
10th	يوسفي *Yoosûfy*, ..	30	*Poos*, ...	*Capricornus.*
11th	ايزدي *Eezidy*, ...	29	*Mâgh*, ...	*Aquarius.*
12th	بياضي *Byâzy*,(2) ..	30	*Phâgûn*, ...	*Pisces.*

Though

(1) Hyder Ali died on the 1st of *Mohurrem* of this year.

(2) Should any disagreement occur between the orthography adopted in these remarks and that used in the body of the work, the former may be regarded as the most correct.

Though the foregoing names are not absolutely unmeaning, yet they would not appear to have had any appropriate signification attached to them; with the exception of the first, called by one of the names of Mahommed, and of the eighth, or *Hydery*, which might possibly have been so denominated in honor of the *Sultan's* father, as *Túlooey* might likewise have been, in allusion to its being the month in which the *Sultan* himself *arose*, or was born. Whether *Beháry* had any reference to the spring, in which season it always occurred, is uncertain. Of the whole of these months it is, however, to be observed, that the initial letter of each denotes its place in the Kalendar, according to the well-known notation called ابجد or *Ubjud*, which assigns a certain numerical power to every letter in the alphabet.(2) There being no single letter to express either 11, or 12, the two first letters of *Eezidy* and *Byázy*, added together, denote the place of each, respectively, in the order of months, *viz.* $1 + 10 = 11$. $2 + 10 = 12$.

I cannot state positively, whether or not these months invariably consisted of the same number of days; but, as far as the documents in *my* possession enable me to judge, it would not appear that any fluctuation took place in this respect. It is here, however, proper to notice, that in the Appendix to Colonel Beatson's book, a memorandum of the *Sultan's* appears (respecting the battle of Suddasir), according to which the month of *Rázy* would seem to have consisted of thirty, whereas my table assigns to it only twenty-nine days. I have not the means, at present, of consulting the original document; but it occurs to me as being possible, that the *Sultan* may have written سلخ *Sulkh*, or, "the last day," and that the translator may have supposed the thirtieth to be meant. If this should not be the case, it will not be easy to reconcile the disagreement in question.

The names given to the years of the cycle were formed also on the principle of the *Ubjud* notation, with the exception of the two first years, which were denominated احد *Ahd* (one or unity), and احمد *Ahmed* (Mahommed), in honor of God and the Prophet; and implying that

(2) The nonsense verse (after the first word of which this notation is called) as well as the numerical power assigned severally to the letters composing it, may be seen in Richardson's dictionary, under the word ابجد

that the latter was the *second*, as the Almighty was the *first* object of veneration. The rest of the names, though like those of the months, not entirely destitute of meaning, had no specific import. They merely denoted the order of each year in the cycle, which was found by adding together the numerical powers of the several letters composing the name, the amount being the number of the year. Thus ازل *Uzl* (the name of the year with which the following correspondence commences) is equivalent to 38 (1 + 7 + 30), and denotes that the year, so called, is the thirty-eighth of the cycle (corresponding to A.D. 1784-5.)

But this arrangement was, after some time, superseded by another; the *Sultan* having, as there is reason to believe, made a second reform of the Kalendar, in the forty-first year of the cycle (or A.D. 1787-8). The latter alteration, however, would not appear to have extended further than to the substitution of new names to the months and years, in the place of those first assigned to them. These new names possessed the same property as the old; namely, that of severally indicating the number of the year, and the order of the month, by virtue of their numerical power. The notation, however, now used was different from the *Ubjud*, and has been called by some *Ubtus* (an unmeaning word, formed by a combination of the first four letters of the alphabet (3)); but is, by the *Sultan* himself, in one of the letters of the present collection, denominated (if there be no error in the manuscript) زر *Zur*, and derived by him, but I do not distinctly understand *how*, from the *Koran*. The difference between the two schemes consists in this: in the *Ubjud*, the numerical powers of the letters depend on the order of the latter in the arbitrary verse already referred to; whereas, in the *Ubtus*, or *Zur*, they depend on the order of the letters of the alphabet: as

1000 900 800 700 600 500 400 300 200 100 90 80 70 60 50 40 30 20 10 9 8 7 6 5 4 3 2 1

ابتث جحخد ذرزس شصضط ظعغف تكلم نوهي

If, as there is reason to think, and as I shall presently endeavour to show, the new era invented by the *Sultan*, and which he sometimes called

e the

(3) The Persian letter پ *(pé)* being excluded from this scheme, as well as from the *Ubjud*. The Persian letters, گ *(gáf)*, چ *(ché)*, and ژ *(zhé)*, are, in like manner, omitted in both.

the era of Mahommed, and sometimes the *Mowloody*, or era of the birth (*i. e.* of Mahommed), was introduced at the same time with the change in the names of the years and months, just described; his motive for the latter innovation was not, perhaps, entirely capricious, but may be safely referred, in some measure, to his zeal for the glory of his religion. As the new epoch was, no doubt, designed to do honor to the Prophet, whom he seems to have thought degraded by the designation given to that in common use,(4) so, probably, were the new names of the years and months, which, instead of being formed upon a vulgar or profane practice, were now constituted upon a principle, sanctified, as it would seem, by the word of the law. Be this, however, as it may, there are good grounds for believing, that the new era, and the second regulation respecting the names of the years and months, took place together, and that the use of both commenced with the forty-first year of the Malabar cycle.

It happens unfortunately, that one of the chasms in the following correspondence occurs at that very period; there not being a single letter of the forty-first year in the collection, nor any document whatever, of that date, among the papers in my possession. But though we are, by this means, deprived of any direct or positive proof on the subject, yet there are not wanting circumstances that afford, what will probably be deemed a sufficient presumption in favor of the opinion I have offered.

1st. In a letter to his diplomatic agents at *Dehli*, dated in *Hydery* (or eighth month) of the fortieth year (*Dullo*), the *Sultan* enumerated the names of the years and months, according to the second or new arrangement, which he had then probably determined on, but which he certainly did not carry into effect during the remainder of the fortieth year, as abundantly appears from existing documents. The letter here referred to is manifestly imperfect; otherwise we might have learnt from it, why the arrangement in question was announced so long before the period of its actual adoption. Possibly the great distance of *Dehli* may have suggested the expediency of an anticipated communication.

2d. It

(4) *Higera* signifies *flight*. See the *Sultan's* letter, referred to in the subsequent page.

2d. It is established by a variety of documents, that both the new nomenclature and the new era were in use in the forty-second year of the cycle, which was accordingly called *Sárá;* whereas, under the preceding arrangement, it would have been named *Kubk.*

3d. It is improbable, that the *Jultan*, after announcing the new nomenclature, so early as *Hydery* of the fortieth year, should have delayed the introduction of it till the forty-second year, or *Sárá*: it is, therefore, most likely, that it commenced with the forty-first year, which, in this case, would be called *Shá*, while, according to the former rule, it would be *Má*.

4th. In a letter, dated the 29th *Eezidy* (eleventh month) of *Dullo*, or the fortieth year, the *Sultan* directs an enquiry to be instituted among the learned men in different parts of his dominions, for the purpose of ascertaining, with exactness, the respective dates of the birth, mission, and flight of the Prophet. An explanation of the cause of the *Higera*, or flight, is also required by this letter. This investigation seems to have been preparatory to the establishment of the epoch under consideration.

5th. But the most unequivocal proof of the *Mowloody* era having been established in the forty-first year, is furnished by a decree, or regulation, of the year *Rásikh*, or forty-eighth of the cycle (corresponding to the 1209th year of the *Higera)*, to which a seal is affixed, bearing the date 1215.(5) Now as this date could not be meant for the *Higera*, it must, of necessity, have been intended to denote the year of Mahommed. The 1215th year of Mahommed co-incided with the forty-first of the cycle: and as we know that the *Mowloody* era was not in use during the fortieth of the cycle (or *Dullo*), it necessarily follows, that the seal in question was engraved in the *first* year of the institution of that epoch.

I will add here the few remaining observations that I have to make on the subject of the *Mowloody* era, and then return to the consideration of the Kalendar.

e 2 As

(5) It is usual in India to insert in the seal the year in which it is engraved.

As this era was not adopted till after the time to which the letters in the present volume reach, it was not absolutely necessary to my immediate purpose, to have offered any explanation of it: but being upon the subject of the *Sultan's* Kalendar, I thought it right to state what I knew, respecting so prominent an article of it. Even in the later documents, wherein it pretty constantly occurs, it is of little or no use in fixing the date of any letter, regulation, or transaction; since it is generally, if not invariably, accompanied by the year of the cycle. The first time that I meet with it is in an edict of the year *Särd*, or forty-second of the cycle (and 1216 of Mahommed). It is continually employed, however, in the *Sultan's* Memoir of his own reign, where it is applied even to events which took place many years before its actual introduction. Thus, among other instances, Hyder Ali Khân is said to have died on Saturday, the 3d of *Zäkiry* "of the year of Mahommed 1209." But of these Memoirs it is to be observed, that they bear internal evidence of having been composed subsequently to the peace of *Seringapatam*, in 1792.

The term *Mowloody*, strictly considered, is certainly not applicable to the era in question; according to which there would appear to have been no more than an interval of thirteen years between the birth and flight of Mahommed. It has been conjectured, that, instead of the birth, this era was, in fact, reckoned from the mission of Mahommed, or the period when he first announced himself as the messenger of God: and this notion receives some countenance, from the tenor of the enquiry spoken of above, which strongly implies a dislike of the term *Higera*, and an intention to sink the event it alludes to, in a reference to one of a more dignified and memorable kind. But, even in this view of the matter, it is difficult to account for the new era being called *Mowloody*, rather than *Nüboowet;* unless it be supposed, that the *birth* was put as a metonymy for the regeneration of the Prophet, which might be reckoned from the commencement of his mission.

I now resume my account of the Kalendar, which was interrupted by this digression concerning the *Mowloody* era.

The names of the months, according to the second and latest arrangement, became as follows:

1st month

1st month	احمدي	*Ahmedy*	} being the same as in the former scheme.
2d.......	بهاري	*Behåry*	
3d.......	تقي	*Tuky.*	
4th......	ثمري	*Sumry.*	
5th......	جعفري	*Jaafury,*	being the third month of the former scheme.
6th......	حيدري	*Hydery,*	being the eighth do. of...... do.
7th......	خسروي	*Khůsrowy.*	
8th......	ديني	*Deeny.*	
9th......	ذاكري	*Zåkiry.*(6)	
10th.....	رحماني	*Rehmåny.*	
11th.....	رازي	*Råzy.*	
12th....	رباني	*Rubbåny.*	

The eleventh and twelfth months are here indicated, as in the former scheme, by the first two letters of their respective names, را *(rå)*, being 10+1; and رب *r(u)b*, 10+2.

Although I could present the reader with a table, exhibiting the names of every year in the cycle, according to both the schemes which have been described, yet it would answer no useful purpose, that will not be equally accomplished by the following abridgement, including only the years of Tippoo Sultan's reign.

Year of the Cycle.	Name according to the First Scheme.	Name according to the Second Scheme.	Corresponding with A.D.
36	جبال *Jebål*........	رب‌تاز *Rub-tåz*.....	1782-3.
37	زكي *Zuky*........	سخ *Sukh*.........	1783-4.
38	ازل *Uzl*..........	سخا *Sukhå*.......	1784-5.
39	جلو *Jullo*.........	دراز *Duråz*.......	1785-6.
40	دلو *Dullo*........	بسد *Busd*........	1786-7.
41	ما *Må*..........	شا *Shå*.........	1787-8.
42	كبك *Kubk*........	سارا *Sårå*........	1788-9.
43	جم *Jum*.........	سراب *Suråb*.......	1789-90.
44	جام *Jåm*.........	شتا *Shetå*.......	1790-1.
45	آدم *Adam*........	زبرجد *Zuburjud*....	1791-2.
46	ولي *Wuly*........	سحر *Sehr*........	1792-3.

(6). Whatever allusion there might be to the *Sultan's* birth in the name of the ninth month of the former nomenclature, nothing of the kind is discoverable in the word *Zåkiry*.

Year of the Cycle.	Name according to the First Scheme.	Name according to the Second Scheme.	Corresponding with A.D.
47	والي *Wály*	ساحر *Sáhir*	1793-4.
48	كوكب *Kaukub*	راسخ *Rásikh*	1794-5.
49	كواكب *Kuwákib*	شاد *Shád*	1795-6.
50	يم *Yum*	حراست *Hirást*	1796-7.
51	دوام *Duwám*	ساز *Sáz*	1797-8.
52	حمد *Humd*	شاداب *Shádáb*	1798-9.
53	حامد *Hámid*	بارش *Bárish*	1799.

It is worthy of remark, that the name of the last of these years, or *Bárish*, signifying *rain*, was changed by the *Sultan*, only a short time before his death, to *Báshir*;(7) which meaning *joyful*, or *auspicious*, he thought a word of better omen than the other. But it did not prove such to him; for on the last day of *Ahmedy* (first month) of that very year, he lost his life, and the sovereignty of *Mysore* passed away from the *Khodádád Sircar*,(8) to the hands of those, towards whom he ever cherished the most deep and irreconcileable hatred; paralleled, perhaps, only by that borne, in ancient times, by Hannibal against the Romans.

It will be seen, by the table of months inserted at page xxvii, that the *Sultan's* year, though considered by him as solar, consisted of no more than three hundred and fifty-four days. In order, therefore, to correct this reckoning, and to approximate it to the true solar time, he occasionally added a *thirteenth* month to the year. I say, *occasionally*: because I have not been able to discover (if, as is probable, there existed) any fixed rule for determining either the return of the leap year, or the period of such year, at which the intercalary or supplementary month was to be introduced. It is stated in some of my notes, collected at *Seringapatam*, that every third year was considered as embolismal, and that the supplementary month was always inserted, according to one account, after the tenth, and, according to another, after the eleventh month.

(7) *Báshir* consisting of the same letters as *Bárish*, has the same numerical power, both words standing for fifty-three.

(8) *i. e.* "the State or Government bestowed by God," which was one of the terms by which the *Sultan* designated his government. The *Ahmedy Sircar* was another. In some places he calls it the *Hydery Sircar*, and in others the *Usud-Ilhye*; the former of which might refer to his father's name: but it might, also, like that of *Usud-Ilhye*, allude to *Ali*, one of whose appellations was *Hyder*.

month. But each of these statements is clearly proved to be wrong by a variety of authentic documents, showing that the thirty-ninth, forty-fourth, forty-seventh, forty-ninth and fifty-second of the cycle were leap years. On what year, between thirty-nine and forty-four, leap year fell is not known, owing to the want of documents for that period: but whether we suppose it to have been the forty-first or forty-second year, it will be equally manifest, that the embolismal year did not uniformly occur every third year. The same thing is shown by the fact of the forty-seventh and forty-ninth years having both been leap years.

It is a known rule, that to make the solar and lunar years accord, *seven* returns of the intercalary, or supplementary month, are required in the course of *nineteen* years, Now from the thirty-fifth to the fifty-third year of the cycle (both inclusive) is a period of nineteen years, in the course of which seven leap years occur, (*viz.* five which are clearly ascertained, and two which have been assumed). But, notwithstanding this apparent conformity, the two reckonings do not co-incide, when, according to this rule, they might be expected to do so. The reason of this disagreement, no doubt, is, that though the months established by Tippoo were ordinarily called *lunar*, they were not strictly so; six of the twelve months of the year having consisted of thirty, and the other six of twenty-nine days each: the common year, therefore, comprizing three hundred and fifty-four days, was, in fact, neither *lunar* nor *solar*.

The documents abundantly prove, that the intercalary, or supplementary month, called by the *Sultan* زاید *Zâid* (as *zâid Ahmedy; zâid Behâry*, &c. according to the month *before*[9] which it was inserted) was not added at any fixed or regulated period of the year, but, apparently, according to his fancy: at least I have not met with any clue to the principle (if principle there was) on which it was arranged. All that is certain is, that in the thirty-ninth year the *Zâid*, or adscititious month, was *Ahmedy*; in the forty-fourth year, *Sumry*; in the forty-seventh year, *Behâry*; in the forty-ninth year, *Hydery*; and in the fifty-second year, *Jaafury*: by which unquestionable facts it appears, that in no one

(9) The extra, or supplementary month, always preceded the regular month of the same name, for what reason does not appear. Its natural place one would suppose to have been *after*, and not *before*, the month whose name it took.

one instance, in so many years, did it happen to fall either on the tenth or eleventh month.

But although so much uncertainty prevails on this article, yet being apprized, as we are, that the first day of the fifty-third year co-incided with the 6th April 1799, and knowing, also, both the names of the leap-years, and of the supplementary months which occurred between that time and the forty-fourth year, inclusive, we are fortunately enabled to convert the *Sultan's* dates, during that period, with sufficient accuracy, into our own. It is after passing, in a retrogade progression, the forty-fourth year, that the principal difficulty commences; since there are, at present, no means of ascertaining in what year, between that and the thirty-ninth, the leap-year occurred, or at what period of such year the intercalary month was added.

In this difficulty I could only arrive at the fortieth and thirty-ninth years (so essential to my immediate purpose, on account of the principal portion of the following letters belonging to those years) by assuming, at a venture, one of the intervening years, between forty-four and thirty-nine, as the leap-year. I therefore fixed upon *Sárá*, or the forty-second year, by which means something like system and regularity is made to appear in the recurrence of the embolism; which, by this distribution, would seem to have returned (as far as our materials enable us to judge) alternately, every third and every second year: that is to say, in the thirty-ninth, forty-second, forty-fourth, forty-seventh, forty-ninth, and fifty-second. With regard to the supplementary month of the assumed leap-year, I was obliged to resort to the same expedient; and, accordingly, fixed on the third month, or *Tuky*. By this means, each of the first six months of the year (though not in regular succession) will appear to have served as the intercalary months, three of them being months of thirty days, and the three others months of twenty-nine days. Hence the leap years, thirty-nine, forty-four, and fifty-two, are made to contain each three hundred and eighty-three days; and the leap years, forty-two, forty-seven, and forty-nine, each three hundred and eighty-four days.(10)

Having

(10) According to this arrangement, it is evident that, though the *Sultan's* year was in general eleven days shorter than the common year in use with us, yet, owing to the frequent recurrence of his intercalary month (making his leap-year three hundred and eighty-three, or three hundred and eighty-four days) his reckoning must, in a series of years, have gained considerably upon ours; apparently no less than at the rate of three days in five years.

Having constructed my table of corresponding dates in the best manner I could, with the imperfect materials in my possession, I was, fortunately, enabled to verify or correct the same, by means of a practice occasionally observed by the *Sultan*, of giving the day of the week along with the day of the month. An instance of this kind occurs in Letter CCCIV, which led to the discovery of an error I had committed, in converting the 18th of *Jaafury* of the year *Dullo* into our reckoning. I had made it agree with the 20th *June*, which fell on a Tuesday; while the 18th of *Jaafury* being expressly stated to have been a Wednesday, must, of course, have co-incided with the 21st June 1786. The detection of this mistake necessarily led to an alteration of the whole series of my dates for the two years comprized in the present volume, every one of which it became requisite to advance *one* day. This correction leaves scarcely any doubt of the perfect accuracy of the dates as now adjusted. The only point in which any mistake can have occurred, is in the number of days assigned to *extra Ahmedy* of the year *Jullo:* for though it is known, that regular *Ahmedy* consisted of twenty-nine days, it is not *certain*, (however probable) that the extra, or supplementary month, always had the same number of days as the regular month of the like name.

This is all that it has been in my power to do, with a view to the attainment of the accuracy so desirable on the present occasion. I trust I have not fallen into any material error. For the rest, I rely on the indulgence of the reader.

CONTENTS.

Where the spelling adopted here, and in the Index, differs from that used in the body of the work, the former may be considered as the most systematical and correct.

CONTENTS.

g

APPENDIX.

SELECT LETTERS,

&c. &c

LETTER I.

To MIRZA MAHOMMED ALI, *Superintendant of the Elephant Stables at* NUGR;[1] *dated* PUTN *(or Seringapatam)*, 2d *of* BYÁZY, *Year* UZL. (17*th February* 1785.)

THE humble address [you] sent [us] has passed under [our] view, and the circumstances submitted [therein] are duly comprehended.[2] You write, "that the *Mŭtusuddies*[3] attached to you have adopted habits "of ease and of lounging in *Nugr*, pretending that it is necessary for "them to see and confer with the *Taalŭkdar*[4] of *Nugr;* the conse- "quence of which is, that fifteen days are consumed in preparing the "accounts of one,[5] and that nothing is done excepting at *Nugr*, "though

(1) i. e. *Bidnore.*

(2) This may serve as a sample of the manner in which most of these letters commence: in those that follow, I shall either abridge, or entirely omit, the introductory part.

(3) Clerks or Accountants.

(4) The Manager of a District.

(5) Or the meaning may be, "neglect their ledger for fifteen days at a time."

B

"though a *Kunry Mútusuddy*[(6)] (agreeably to our orders) attends on the "part of Nursia[(7)] to assist in the business."

This [representation] has caused [us] the utmost surprize. Whenever the *Mútusuddies* belonging to your department cease to yield you proper obedience, you must give them a severe flogging;[(8)] and making them prepare, with the greatest dispatch, the lists and other papers required by our former orders, transmit the same duly to the Presence.[(9)]

OBSERVATIONS.

To understand the foregoing letter properly, it is necessary to suppose, what, indeed, is most probable, that the Elephant Mews, or Stables, were situated at some distance from the town of *Nugr*.

This letter furnishes a proper occasion for cautioning the reader, who may not be conversant in the history, or acquainted with the genius, or frame, of the native governments of India, against hastily drawing any general conclusions, with respect to the latter point, from the particular practice, or maxims, of Tippoo Sultan. The conduct of this prince was too commonly governed by caprice, and was too often the mere result of individual feelings and character, to afford a just criterion of the generality of Asiatic sovereigns, or Asiatic states. Thus, any one who should be led to infer, from the punishment here directed to be inflicted on the idle clerks of the elephant department, that it is customary in India (as in China and Russia) to flog any but the menial servants of government for neglect of duty, would be greatly mistaken: as he would, also, if he supposed that castration was no uncommon penalty in that country, for corruption, or other misdemeanors

(6) A Canarese Clerk.

(7) The name of the Manager.

(8) Original تازیانه‌کاری *táziáneh-kāry.*

(9) There is considerable obscurity in that passage of the original, which I have rendered, "though a *Kunry-Mútusuddy* attends, &c." I am, therefore, not certain of having understood it rightly.

misdemeanors in the administration of public affairs, because the *Sultan* sometimes thought proper to threaten official delinquents with that punishment. The fact is, that all his *Hookm-námehs,* or instructions to the governors of provinces, and others, conclude with a denunciation of the penalties to which they will be liable, in case of disobedience or disregard of the orders contained in them. Sometimes these are generally stated, under the vague, but emphatic, term of " the worst of punishments : " at others, they are specifically named ; as crucifixion, in one or two instances, and emasculation, in others. Whether or not the latter menace was ever, in any case, actually executed, I am not able to determine ; but there is nothing in the character of Tippoo Sultan to render the affirmative unlikely. Colonel Munro assures me, that it is an absolute fact that on one occasion he ordered all the male population of a particular village, which had given him offence, to be castrated.

What the practice of Hyder Ali was on similar occasions, I have not the means of stating ; but there is sufficient reason to suspect, that the example of the father was not much calculated to restrain the severity, or cruelty, of the son. It is certain, indeed, as I learn from Colonel Wilks, that Tippoo himself was once publicly bambooed (or caned) by order of Hyder, in whose good graces he would never appear to have stood very high. This opinion is strongly confirmed, by a most curious original document, which I met with at *Seringapatam,* in the year 1799, while employed in examining the mass of papers discovered more immediately after the capture of the place. I found it amongst a variety of other papers of the time of Hyder, deposited in a basket or box, where it had probably remained undisturbed and forgotten ever since his death. It is a narrow slip, about twelve inches in length : is entitled, at top, اقرارنامه or " an agreement ;" beneath which words is the impression, in ink, of a small square seal, resembling, in all respects, the usual signet, or ring-seal, of the *Sultan,* and bearing, together with the name " Tippoo Sultan," the date " 1184 " *(Higera).*(10) The instrument itself is without date ; but it must, of course, have been

B 2

(10) The existence of this seal satisfactorily proves that *Sultan* was not a title assumed by Tippoo (as commonly supposed) upon succeeding his father, but made part of the name given him, probably, at his birth.

been executed some time between the year 1769 (the period when the seal was engraved) and 1782, in which last year Hyder died. On the back of this paper is a short endorsement of two or three words, in *Canarese*, which, I am sorry to say, I cannot explain.

I am equally unable to determine, whether this interesting document is in the hand-writing of the *Sultan.* It certainly bears but little resemblance to the specimens exhibited in a great variety of notes and memorandums, written by him in the latter part of his life. But his hand-writing might well undergo a material change in a period of twenty or thirty years : besides which, I suspect that most of the articles of his writing which happen to be in my possession, were written with a gold or silver pen, which he was much in the practice of using, and of which I obtained two or three at *Seringapatam* that had belonged to him. This occasioned his later writing (at least what I have seen of it) to have an air of stiffness and crabbedness, of which there is not near so great an appearance in the document under consideration.

But it is not essential to the authenticity of this paper that it should have been written in the *Sultan's* own hand. The place in which it was discovered, joined to the seal and internal evidence furnished by its extraordinary tenor, sufficiently establishes its genuineness ; but whether the engagement it contains was voluntarily entered into by the *Sultan,* or exacted by Hyder, does not appear. The latter, however, is not unlikely to have been the case, notwithstanding what the writer himself declares in the eighth article. After this general account of the document in question, I proceed to present the reader with a translation of it ; and, for the satisfaction of those conversant in the language of the original, a fac-simile of it is given in article C. of the Appendix.

" AGREEMENT.

" 1.(11) I will not do [any] one thing without the pleasure of your blessed Ma-
" jesty, Lord of Benefits [or my bountiful Lord] : if I do, let me be punished, in
" whatever manner may seem fitting to your auspicious mind.—— One article.(12)

" 2. If

(11) The articles are not numbered in the original, but divided by lines drawn under each of them.

(12) Original يكـ قلم which is repeated at the end of each article.

" 2. If, in the affairs of the *Sircar*, I should commit theft, or be guilty of " fraud, great or small, let me, as the due punishment thereof, be strangled.[13] " —— One article.

" 3. If I be guilty of prevarication, or misrepresentation, or of deceit, the " due punishment thereof is this same strangulation.—— One article.

" 4. Without the orders of the Presence, I will not receive from any one, " *Nuzzers*, &c.; neither will I take things from any one [meaning perhaps for- " cibly]: if I do, let my nose be cut off, and let me be driven out from the city. " —— One article.

" 5. If, excepting on the affairs of the *Sircar*, I should hold conversation " [probably *cabal* or *intrigue*] with any person, or be guilty of deceit, &c., let " me, in punishment thereof, be stretched on a cross.—— One article.

" 6. Whenever a country shall be committed to my charge by the *Sircar*, " and an army be placed under my command, I will carry on all business regard- " ing the same, with the advice, and through the medium of such confidential " persons as may be appointed [for the purpose] by the *Sircar*; and if I transact " such affairs through any other channel than this, let me be strangled.—— One " article.

" 7. If there should be any occasion for correspondence by writing, or to buy " or give [away] any thing, or any letters should arrive from any place, I will do " nothing [in such matters] without the concurrence and advice of the person " appointed by the *Sircar*.—— One article.

" 8. I have written and delivered these few articles of my own free will: " keeping the contents whereof in my heart's remembrance, I will act in each " article accordingly. If I forget this, and act in any other [or different] manner, " let me be punished, agreeably to the foregoing writing."

It will not, perhaps, be wondered at, that one, to whom the idea of corporal punishment, even in his own person, would seem, from the preceding instrument, as

(13) Original كل بايدداد of the meaning of which expression I am far from being certain. It may possibly signify, " to extinguish," and hence, figuratively, " to put to death."

as well as from Colonel Wilks's report, to have been familiar, before his accession to the *Musnud*, should, after that event, have applied the practice, with similar disregard to the rank or station of offenders, to those then subjected to his authority.

Before I dismiss this subject it may be proper to notice, that the style of the foregoing document (and especially of the seventh article) is extremely perplexed and indistinct: but, even at a more advanced period of the *Sultan's* life, most of the productions of his pen (as was observed on a former occasion) were characterized by the same involved structure of sentences, frequently creating considerable obscurity in the sense.

LETTER II.

To MEER KÂZIM, *Commercial Consul, or Chief of the Factory at* MUSCAT; *written* in the Night *of the* 5th *of* BYÂZY. (20*th February.*)

PROPOSE to the merchants of *Muscat*, (and get the *Imaum*(1) to issue orders to the same effect,) to bring hither, on the empty *Dingies*,(2) such horses as they may have for sale; which being sold to us, the owners can carry back the produce in rice.

OBSERVATIONS.

Several letters in this collection, as well as the present one, are dated *at night*, a circumstance that does not denote them to be of any urgency or particular importance

(1) The Prince, or Sovereign, of *Muscat*.

(2) A small vessel employed in the trade between the *Malabar* Coast and the Gulfs of *Persia* and *Arabia*: the same name is given to a kind of canoe used on the *Ganges*. By empty *Dingies*, may be meant either *Dingies* of *Muscat*, proceeding in ballast to the Coast of *Malabar*; or *Dingies* belonging to the ports of *Mangalore* or *Calicut*, and returning thither from *Muscat*, after discharging their cargoes at the latter place: but it is most probable that the former are intended.

importance (as one might be led to suppose), but merely shows the diligent application of the *Sultan* to business; the word *night* here implying some time after midnight.(3) Its insertion in such a dispatch as the preceding one, certainly carries with it an air of affectation.

Tippoo Sultan was very desirous of establishing a commercial intercourse with *Muscat*; not, perhaps, without some ulterior view to a political connexion with that petty state. The encouragement which he held out, for this purpose, to the merchants of *Muscat*, as well as his own particular notions of trade, will appear in the sequel.

LETTER III.

To Mahommed Ghyâs; *dated 6th of Byâzy.* (21*st February.*)

Your letter of the 19th of *Eezudy* [5th of February] has been received, and the whole of its contents are comprehended. The *fixed* or *regulated* money is ready. Whenever the chiefs of that place [*Poonah*] demand it, bankers' bills to the amount shall be forwarded.

Representations of the contumacious conduct of the *Zemindâr* of *Nergûnd* were frequently transmitted [by us], in the course of last year, to Noor Mahommed Khân, who, no doubt, communicated the same to all the chiefs there [*Poonah*]. If a petty *Zemindâr*, and a subject of our government, like this, may not be punished, how shall our authority be maintained? The justice of this argument was admitted, even by Râo Râsta.(1) Thus the chastisement of this *Zemindâr* became necessary. If he is brought to reason from thence [*i. e.* by the Mahrattah chiefs] it will be well; otherwise he will be exterminated.

Let

(3) For some further account of the manner of dividing the night, see Letter CCCLXII.

(1) For an account of this personage, see Letter VIII.

Let the *Gúmáshteh* (2) of Apâjee Rào receive a monthly stipend of four *pagodas*.

You must not admit the *Brahmens* (3) to a participation in the conduct of any secret negotiation. You and Noor Mahommed Khân [alone] are jointly to transact [all such affairs].

If the chiefs of that place, forgetting our past favors, should dispatch an army to the assistance of the *Zemindár* of *Nergúnd*, what will it signify? We have, under the divine blessing, sent a strong force to reduce *Nergúnd*, and are in no fear of its suffering any misfortune from their army.

N.B. A letter, to the same effect as the above, and of the same date, was written to Noor Mahommed Khân (the colleague of Mahommed Ghyâs) with an immaterial addition, respecting some bills of exchange.

OBSERVATIONS.

Mahommed Ghyâs Khân and Noor Mahommed Khân were, at this time, the diplomatic agents of Tippoo Sultan, at *Poonah*. The former of them was, probably, at the head of the mission, since many of the letters are addressed singly to him, and in all of them his name stands first. Noor Mahommed Khân, however, would seem to have resided longest at the Mahrattah court, to which, there is reason to believe, he had been originally deputed by Hyder Ali.

The present correspondence commences just at the period when the war of 1785 broke out between the *Sultan* and the Mahrattahs; the latter of whom were, after some time, joined by Nizâm Ali Khân, who sent a considerable body of troops to act with their army.

The

(2) An Agent. Apâjee Rào was probably a Mahrattah Chief, in the interest of Tippoo Sultan.

(3) *i. e.* the *Brahmens* attached to the Mission. For further particulars respecting whom, see Letters CLXV. and CLXVII.

The ostensible, or more immediate cause of the present rupture, is to be traced, on the one hand, to the right which the *Sultan* assumed of chastising a contumacious tributary; and, on the other, to the protection which the Mahrattah Government thought, or affected to think, it incumbent on them to extend to this offender; who was, perhaps, a feudatory of the Mahrattah Empire, in like manner with many other *Zemindárs* and *Polygárs*, who depend, in various shapes, and at the same time, on different superiors; rendering to one *Paishcush*, or tribute, and to another military service.(4)

But it was not merely, or perhaps principally, for the purpose of supporting the *Zemindár* of *Nergúnd*, that the Mahrattah Government took up arms against the *Sultan*. They had claims on him for considerable arrears of tribute, the discharge of which he had hitherto refused or evaded; and it was, probably, less with a view of befriending the obnoxious *Zemindár*, than of enforcing these claims, that they appealed to the sword.

It will be seen in the sequel, that though the *Sultan* succeeded in inflicting a signal chastisement on his rebellious tributary, he was, nevertheless, obliged to pay the Mahrattahs a considerable sum of money; not less, according to some accounts, than forty *lacks* of *rupees*.(5) Whether this was the whole, or only part of the arrears of tribute claimed by them, is unknown to the translator, who has never met with the treaty concluded between the belligerent powers, about the beginning of the year 1787. The *Nizám*, during this war, lost *Adoni*; which, however, was restored to him by the peace.

By the *fixed*, or *regulated sum*, spoken of by the *Sultan* in the present letter, he means the *Paishcush*, or tribute, which he was bound by former treaties to pay to the Government of *Poonah*; but which he does not think proper to recognize, or designate, by any term denotive of inferiority, which the word *Paishcush* certainly is. Those who negociated our first treaty with the court of *Hyderabad* were less nice, since they agreed to pay an annual *Paishcush* to the *Nizám*: by which concession they virtually, but, no doubt, unconsciously, placed the East-India Company in the situation of a vassal to that chieftain; the term *Paishcush*, in

C

(4) The *Sultan's* own Memoirs are entirely silent on the subject of *Nergúnd*.

(5) The *Sultan* himself, in his Memoirs, states the sum at twelve *lacks* of *rupees*.

in its restrained sense, and as used in India, signifying *tribute;* and in no case being applied to *presents,* excepting to those of a subject to his lord, or from an inferior to a superior. It might be difficult now, and may be deemed needless, to obtain the suppression of this degrading appellation. The usurpers of this, and similar vain distinctions and marks of preeminence,[6] in proportion as they have lost, in the revolutions of time, the substance, may be more safely indulged in the possession of this shadow of power. There is, happily, no longer any danger of the abuse being extended: this is equally precluded by our increased political consideration throughout India, and by our improved knowledge of its languages and usages. The time is past, when the general ignorance that prevailed, in these respects, among the Company's servants, placed the interests and the honor of their employers and of the nation, but too much at the mercy of native agents and interpreters.

There is only one more remark suggested by the preceding letter. If the *Sultan* be allowed credit for sincerity, when he declares himself ready to pay the arrears due by him to the Mahrattahs, immediately on demand, it will necessarily follow, that the question of tribute was not the principal one with that state, any more than with its ally the *Nizâm,* whom, indeed, it could only remotely concern. Both governments, possibly, thought to oppose some check to the rising power of the *Sultan,* whose ambitious views had begun to develope themselves, in a manner that might well awaken the jealousy, and excite the fears of his neighbours. In this case, it will be easy to account for the Mahrattahs not being satisfied with the *Sultan's* professed readiness to discharge their pecuniary demands (however sincere they might think him in that respect), but insisting on his relinquishing his designs against *Nergûnd.* On the whole, it seems highly probable, that he would have avoided a war at this time, if he could have done so.

(6) Amongst these, the modes of address employed by many of the Pseudo-princes of India, in writing even to the English governors, and other persons in high official situations under the British Government, deserve to be particularly noticed; some of them being such as would not now be tolerated, if attempted to be introduced for the first time. The same advantage was taken of our inexperience in other matters of a ceremonial kind; with regard to many of which, I am inclined to think, we do not occupy the station to which we are entitled.

so consistently with the "maintenance of his authority" (as he himself expresses it), or without submitting to the disgrace of being prescribed to by a foreign power. His favorite object, and most ardent desire, was to resume, at the earliest possible moment, hostilities against the English; and though he might think himself equal, without the help of the Mahrattahs and *Nizâm*, to the successful prosecution of that design, yet he would, at least, wish for the neutrality of those powers during its progress. With a view to the undertaking alluded to, he had already resolved upon reverting to his former alliance with the French; and he cherished the hope of being soon enabled, by the renewal of his connexion with that nation, to give vent to his always ill-concealed hatred of their rivals. To this ever-predominating bias of his mind, and to his eager anticipation of the period, when the successful termination of his negociations with France would put him in a condition to execute his projects against the English, may, perhaps, in a great measure, be ascribed the advantageous peace which he granted to the courts of *Poonah* and *Hyderabad*, at the end of a war, in which he certainly gave such proofs of military superiority, as made his enemies very willing to retire from the contest. The reader already knows, that his expectations from France, and his hopes of conciliating his neighbours, proved alike fallacious; and that, in the end, he was compelled, prematurely and single-handed, to commit his fortunes in an unequal struggle with the combined forces of all the powers of the Peninsula.

LETTER IV.

To TURBIYUT ALI KHÂN *and* RÂJAH RÂM CHUNDUR;(1) *dated* 12*th of* BYÂZY. (27*th February*.)

YOUR letter has been received. You write, "that the European "[formerly] taken prisoner in the *Pâyen-ghaut*,(2) and whose original "allowance

(1) These were officers at *Bangalore*. Râm Chundur was the *Dewân* of the *Kuchurry*: Turbiyut Ali Khân (who, I believe, was a grandson of the Murtuza Ali of *Arcot*, mentioned in Orme's History) appears to have been the Chief Collector of the District.

(2) The country below the *Ghauts*.

"allowance of two *fanams*[3] a day had been, in consequence of his "misbehaviour, reduced to one, being skilled in the mortar practice,[4] "you proposed converting him to the faith, and wished for our orders "on the subject." It is known (or understood).

Admitting the aforesaid to the honor of Islâmism, you will continue to pay him, as before, two *fanams* a day. Let him also be employed in firing at the flag.[5] We have ourselves, however, brought the mortar practice to that degree of perfection, that children, of ten and eleven years of age, are taught to hit the point of a spear.

You may, as you propose, engage a sweeper, at the monthly wages of ten or twelve *fanams*, and employ him in sweeping out the *Rung-mahl*,[6] and the public halls of the *Dewâny* and *Ehshâm*.[7]

OBSERVATIONS.

The European here spoken of was, no doubt, one of those unhappy British soldiers who had the misfortune to fall into the hands of this cruel enemy; and numbers of whom he forcibly detained, in spite of the stipulations of the treaty of *Mangalore*. It is not quite clear, whether the subject of the present letter was to be compelled to embrace Mahommedanism, or had expressed a readiness to do so. The latter, however, is not so likely as the former; though there is reason to believe, that some few of our wretched countrymen were induced to apostatize, with the view of alleviating the intolerable hardships of their situation.

The

(3) A *fanam* is equal to about eight-pence.

(4) Original فن نشانه اندازی گرنال *i. e.* The art of firing at a flag [with] mortar shells (or bombs).

(5) It is not distinctly said that he was to be employed in *teaching* the mortar-practice, but this was probably meant.

(6) A painted apartment. Most palaces, as well as that at *Bangalore*, contain one.

(7) *Dewâny* is the revenue department. The *Ehshâm* were a description of guards, or state retinue, as the term implies.

The reader will be amused by the ostentatious boast made by the *Sultan*, of the perfection to which he had brought the practice of gunnery: but though there is, probably, some exaggeration in his statement, it cannot be denied, that he had accomplished much in this respect.

The directions, relative to the sweeper, show to what low and minute objects, particularly in matters of economy, the mind of the *Sultan* was accustomed to stoop. Other instances, of the same kind, will appear in the course of these letters; but a still greater number are omitted.

It may seem rather extraordinary, that a Hindoo (as Râjah Râm Chundur was) should be joined with a Mahommedan, in a commission for converting a Christian to the Mussulman faith: but this proceeding, however strange, will probably be thought much less so, than another of a somewhat similar nature, noticed under Letter CCCXXXIII.

LETTER V.

To the Governor of Pondicherry, *dated* 19*th Byázy.* (6*th March.*)

We have had the pleasure to receive your agreeable letter, informing us that peace has lately been concluded in Europe, between the King of France and the English, in consequence of which the port of *Pondicherry* has been restored to the French. This information has afforded us much satisfaction. You must let us know [what you learn] respecting the [expected] arrival of ships belonging to you [*i. e.* your nation], as well as how far Monsieur Suffrein is advanced in his voyage.

OBSERVATIONS.

I believe this letter contains almost the only instance in which the title of *Bádsháh*, or King, is bestowed upon any European sovereign by Tippoo Sultan, who appears, on all other occasions, to have thought as if this designation would be be degraded, by being applied to any but a prince professing the Mahommedan faith; he, therefore, generally affected to call, not only the King of England, but his own friend and ally, the King of France, *Râjah*; intending, by this ingenious contrivance, to intimate (though, of course, not to those so addressed), that he considered them as nothing superior to the petty Hindoo *Râjahs* of India, and, in fact, as Idolators. What rendered this appellation the more insulting was, that though originally, and strictly, signifying a King, it had now become extremely common, the title being borne, as has been seen, by one Hindoo, at least, in the service of the Sultan himself, and being frequently bestowed on their subjects of that religion, by the different upstart rulers of the dismembered empire of *Hindostan.*

For a more distinct view of the sentiments entertained by Tippoo Sultan, with respect to Christians in general, the reader is referred to the Preface to Colonel Wilks's History of *Mysore,* where they are exhibited in the most undisguised manner, in an extraordinary letter from the *Sultan* to the late General Macleod. The same letter occurs, with very little variation from Zynûl Aabideen's copy, in the *Sultan's* own Memoirs.

LETTER VI.

To MAHOMMED USHRUF, *DAROGHA*(1) *of the DEWANY KUCHURRY of GOOTY; dated* 16*th of* BYÂZY. (3*d March.*)

YOUR letter has been received, and its contents are duly understood. You write, "that the *Bâzâr* price of *Kûrg pagodas* was thirteen "*fanams* and three-quarters, but that you had advanced the same one "*fanam* and four *annas,* and issued them, at this rate, to the *Piâdehs* "of the *Ehshâm.*"(2) It is known. You will fix the value of the *pagoda*

(1) A superintendant or overseer.

(2) See Note 7 of Letter IV. *Piâdeh* means a foot soldier; but the term is almost exclusively applied to infantry, or foot soldiers formed on the irregular plan of the natives.

pagoda at one *fanam* above the market price, or exchange, and issue it, at that rate, to the servants of the State. There is no necessity for raising the exchange higher than this standard; and, accordingly, this has been heretofore repeatedly signified to you. It surprises us extremely, that you should nevertheless pursue the suggestions of your own fancy.

OBSERVATIONS.

No prospect of advantage could tempt the *Sultan* to wink at any contravention of his positive orders. The financial operation, here spoken of, is not an uncommon one in India. The *Sultan's* displeasure was not occasioned by the oppression, but by the disobedience, of which the *Darogha* had been guilty.

LETTER VII.

To Shah Noorûllah; *dated 22d of Byâzy.* (*9th March.*)

Enclosed is a letter which has been received from Othmân Khân, &c. reporting their arrival at *Bussorah*, and subsequent departure from thence for the presence of the King.(1) You will learn [further] from its perusal. The Governor of *Bussorah* has likewise written an answer to our letter to him, saying that he had sent forward the aforesaid *Khân* and the others [*i. e.* his colleagues] to the Court of the King.

Such being the case, that eminent person(2) must use the utmost expedition, agreeably to our former orders, in docking the ship *Fukhurûlmûbâruk*, and giving it such repairs as may be required.

(1) I suppose the Grand Signior to be here meant.

(2) Original آن رفعت نشان meaning Shâh Noorûllah.

OBSERVATIONS.

The embassy, here alluded to, was that which the *Sultan* dispatched to Constantinople, some time in the year 1784. At the head of it was Mahommed Othmân Khân, who had formerly filled the station of Hyder Ali Khân's *Vakeel* at *Madras,* and was afterwards associated with Mahommed Durwaish Khân, and the other ambassadors, sent in the year 1787, by sea, to France. What was the object of his mission to Constantinople, I am not able to state, having met with no documents regarding it. On the return, or recall, of Othmân Khân, Ghûlâm Ali Khân, together with Shah Noorûllah, was dispatched ostensibly to supply his place; but, in fact, with instructions to proceed from Constantinople to France. This design, however, was subsequently relinquished by the *Sultan,* who substituted, in its stead, the more direct mission by sea, noticed above.[3]

LETTER VIII.

To Mahommed Ghyâs *and* Noor Mahommed Khân; *dated* 1*st of Extra* Ahmedy, *Year* Jullo. (18*th March.*)

In consequence of the chiefs of that place [*Poonah*] forgetting their obligations to us, we have come to the positive determination of taking possession of the territory situated on the banks of the *Kishna.*[1] It is therefore written, that if your negociation proceeds according to our heart's desire, it is well: if not, you and Noor Mahommed Khân, taking leave of Râo Râsta, must repair to the Presence.

The

(3) Major Stuart relates, on the authority of a French writer, that Othmân Khân, and one of his colleagues, were put to death by the *Sultan* on their return from France. A great part, if not the whole of the correspondence of Othmân Khân, during his residence at *Madras,* was found at *Seringapatam,* amongst the records of Hyder Ali's time. These letters would throw considerable light on many of the political transactions of that period.

(1) That is, all the country *as far* as the *Kishna.*

The 14th of *Ahmedy*(2) is fixed on for our marching; in case, therefore, of ungraciousness(3) [on their part], you will proceed with all haste to our Presence.

You write, that Peer Mahommed Mûnshy (who, when he accompanied the Mahrattah minister in the field received sixty *rupees*) being now reduced to forty *rupees* a month, and having the incumbrance of a large family, finds his salary inadequate to their support. It is known. If the aforesaid should intend to accompany you to the Presence, let him be paid sixty *rupees* a month; but, otherwise, forty *rupees* is sufficient.(4)

OBSERVATIONS.

The *Sultan's* instructions to his envoys at *Poonah* will be found to be marked throughout with considerable indecision. In speaking of the Mahrattah Government, he assumes, in general, a very lofty and menacing tone; it is, notwithstanding, pretty evident, that he is not averse to reconciliation. He frequently betrays the irritation of his mind, and, in these moods, issues the most peremptory orders to his agents to quit *Poonah*. They, nevertheless, remain at their post, where they appear to have continued till the month of May of the following year (1786), or during the greatest part of the war. The reason of this fluctuation in the conduct of the *Sultan*, would, no doubt, be more intelligible than it is, if we were in possession of the dispatches of the envoys, as well as those of their master. It is true, that the substance, and perhaps the entire contents of many of the former, is (agreeably to the common practice in the epistolary correspondence of India) recited in the answers to them; but still it is reasonable to suppose, that many

D

(2) *i. e.* Of the second, or ensuing *Ahmedy*. Yet he would not appear to have followed up this resolution.

(3) Original عدم لطف also incivility, unkindness, &c.

(4) The *Sultan* was at all times desirous of drawing Mussulmans, of every description, to his court; but not equally liberal of pecuniary aid to such adventurers, as will be seen, on more occasions than one, in the course of these letters.

many particulars are unnoticed in these brief capitulations, or summaries, the knowledge of which would materially elucidate the transactions in question.

The Râstas are a family of considerable eminence and weight in the Mahrattah empire, being nearly allied to the *Paishwa*. They have, generally, been distinguished for their favourable disposition towards the Mysore ruler, in consequence of which, it was usual for most negociations between the latter and the government of *Poonah* to be conducted through them.

The obligations of the Mahrattah state to Hyder Ali Khân and his successor, are often alluded to in the course of the following letters. They are more particularly stated in his letter to the King of France;(5) and he thus expresses himself, on the subject, in his Memoirs.

" Previously to the resolution of making war against the Nazarenes (i. e. before " the commencement of hostilities against the English by Hyder Ali Khân) the " Mahrattahs being reduced to great straits, and defeated by the English, had " [actually] filled their houses with straw, and prepared to burn the city of *Poonah*. " In this situation they dispatched four of their principal and confidential people " to our late father, with letters, accompanied by oaths and deceitful engagements, " soliciting the grant of a fort within our dominions, wherein they might lodge " their chief (more worthless, in truth, than a horse keeper).(6) Accordingly these " trusty persons (who, in fact, were not to be trusted) arriving in the presence of " our deceased father (whose place is in Paradise) represented, that being broken " down [or discomfited] by the English, they were on the point of abandoning their " country, within eight *coss* of [the capital of] which the Nazarenes were arrived: " that, in these circumstances, they could look for help to no one but his High- " ness; that their master was a child, the preservation of whose life, honor, " country, and wealth, by the *Ussud Ilhye*(7) state, would confer an obligation, " which

(5) See Letter CCCXXXVI.

(6) In the original بنا برگذاشتن رئیس خود که در حقیقت بدتر از سایس بود where the word *Syse* (or horse-keeper) is introduced for the sake of a jingle with the word *Ryse* (a chief or leader).

(7) The Sultan gave various denominations to his government or state. It was sometimes, as in this place, the *Ussud Ilhye Sircar*: at others, the *Hydery*, the *Ahmedy*, and the *Khodâdâd Sircar*.

" which would continue to be acknowledged, as long as any of the Mâdho Râos " existed; and, finally, imploring his Highness to consider their chief in the light " of a son. These representations were seconded, on the part of Nizâm Ali " Khân,(8) whose country had also been threatened by the English, and whom " the Mahrattahs had prevailed on, by promises and engagements, to espouse " their cause, and to interest himself in their favour (with our late father); in " consequence of which he, accordingly (through the Mahrattah *Vakeels*), made " certain proposals, ratified on the *Koran*, to his Highness, our father. Hereupon " our father (who reposes in Paradise) agreed to their propositions, and resolved " on war with the English, notwithstanding the opposition made to the measure " by the chiefs of the state, who represented that the war would prove arduous " and tedious; that there was no necessity for his drawing the misfortunes of " another's house upon himself; that these two impure ones (namely Mâdho Râo " and Nizâm Ali) were both of spurious origin, and neither their words nor actions " entitled to the least credit or faith. Our illustrious father replied, ' that it was " ' a traditionary saying of the Prophet:—" Verily only by deeds, and not by " ' " thoughts, [shall ye judge]." We lay them under this obligation: if they " ' have any evil designs in their hearts, the Almighty will requite them with evil:' " and, so saying, he prepared for war.

" It was further stipulated by the treaty concluded [on this occasion] between " *these two bastards* and the Hydery state, that no peace should be entered into " with the English, except with the knowledge of all three. Accordingly, while " Sadlier was still on his way, we wrote to the chiefs who accompanied him, " desiring that his progress might be retarded, by amusements and entertainments " at every stage. In the interim, we wrote ten or twelve letters to Mâdho Râo, " the chief of the Mahrattahs, stating, that though he had, upwards of a year " ago, and during the life-time of our illustrious father (who reposes in Paradise) " secretly, and without our knowledge, concluded a separate peace with the Eng- " lish, yet he had not, to that moment, made any communication on the subject " to us. ' It is well [we proceeded]: our pleasure is yours. The confidential

D 2 " ' agents

(8) Called, in the original, Hujjâm Nully Khân: for an explanation of which see Letter CCCLI.

" 'agents of the English are on the way from their own country to our Presence, " 'to solicit peace: if such be your pleasure, signify your demands to us by " 'letter, that we may treat for you at the same time that we treat for ourselves. " 'If, on the other hand, you should have actually concluded a separate peace " 'without our knowledge, let us be informed thereof, in order that we may set " 'about a peace for the Hydery Sircar.' To no one of our letters was any answer " sent: neither did they write a word to their own *Vakeel*, residing with us, " though he was a kinsman of theirs [*i. e.* of the *Paishwas*].[9]

" In this manner did we, for six months, contrive to put off the arrival " of the English ambassador; at the end of which we wrote to the Mahrattah " *Vakeel* at our court to this effect: 'We have, by different means, managed " 'to detain the English ambassador six months on the road; in which period " 'we have written about fifteen letters, on the subject of peace, to your " 'master. You, also, have repeatedly written; but to neither has any answer been " 'given. Now that the English ambassador is at hand, what would you advise " 'to be done? Let us know your opinion.' To this the Mahrattah *Vakeel*, who " was among the nearest of [the] relatives [of the *Paishwa*], replied by letter: " 'that his master was an infant; that his ministers, &c. were whoresons,[10] on " 'whose words and actions no reliance was to be placed; and that six months " 'had already passed, in expectation [of hearing from thence]. 'How much " 'longer [continued he] are you to wait? Conclude your peace with the " 'English; and, dismissing me, let me proceed to those good-for-nothing " 'fellows,[11] in order that I may be enabled to deal with them personally, either " 'by reproaches or a sound bastinade;[12] and, by this means, bring forward " 'some person, who shall prevent, for the future, the recurrence of snch " 'shameful conduct.' "

" After this, we protracted the negociations for peace with the English for two " months longer, during which time we again wrote [to *Poonah*], but without any " better

(9) This *Vakeel* was probably one of the Râsta family.

(10) Original مادر بي نكاح پدر مشخص‌هستند and ولد الحرام

(11) Original نابيكاران

(12) Original شلاق‌واقعي

" better success than before: whereupon we proceeded to conclude the treaty with " the English, &c."

Such, according to his own account, were the grounds of Tippoo Sultan's complaints against the Mahrattah Government, at the period of the treaty of *Mangalore*, and it would not appear that any attempts were subsequently made, either by the court of *Poonah*, or by that of *Hyderabad*, to appease him. At this rate, it would be difficult to acquit these courts, and especially the former, of the charge of bad faith towards their ally: but we must not, too hastily, give credit to the *Sultan's* statement of facts. Some of these are manifestly exaggerated, and others may be misrepresented: but however this may be, it is pretty clear, that the *Sultan* really thought himself the aggrieved party; and this being the case, it is not, perhaps, so much to be wondered at, that he should have taken up the question concerning the *Zemindâr* of *Nergûnd* in the manner he did, as that he should have so long repressed the resentment he appears to have felt at the conduct of his late allies.

I abstain from many other reflections, naturally suggested by the curious extract just given from the *Sultan's* own Memoirs; both because a fitter opportunity than the present may hereafter offer for them, and because it is time to proceed with the correspondence.

LETTER IX.

To the same; dated 6th of Extra AHMEDY*, Year* JULLO*.*
(23d March.)

Two letters from you have passed under our view. The note containing sundry propositions, which you addressed to Râo Râsta, and of which you transmitted a copy [for our information], was highly proper, and is much approved by us. Both of you are experienced in the business, and in the paths [of politics]; and we are persuaded that there is no point, however minute, that will be neglected by you.

LETTER X.

To BÛRHÂNÛDDEEN, *dated* ——[1] *Extra* AHMEDY.

[AFTER some immaterial directions, the letter proceeds as follows:]— If you should receive intelligence of the approach of any considerable force of the enemy, you must raise the siege of the fort, and taking your heavy ordnance with you, proceed and encamp near *Dhárwár*. With the will of God the helper, we also shall march on the 14th of *Ahmedy*, and soon arrive there, when what may be proper shall be done. Nobody is going to lift the hill of *Nergúnd* to [his] head and carry it away: it is where it is. [*i. e.* it will remain where it is.][2]

OBSERVATIONS.

Bûrhânûddeen was the brother-in-law of Tippoo Sultan, who had married a sister of his. He appears to have possessed a great share of the confidence of the *Sultan*, who frequently intrusted him with important military commands, but not without placing him (at least at this period) in a certain degree of tutelage. He lost his life in the battle of *Sattimungalam*, in the year 1790. Of that battle the *Sultan* has given a partial and exaggerated account in one or two letters; in which it is remarkable, that he speaks of the death of this gallant commander without a single expression of regard or regret.

The fort, the siege of which is here provisionally directed to be relinquished, was no doubt *Nergúnd*.

(1) The day of the month is uncertain.

(2) Original كوه نرگندرا كسي بر سر برداشته نميبرد جاي‌كه هست هست

LETTER XI.

To Meer Kumrûddeen Ali Khân; *dated* 11th *Extra Ahmedy*, (*28th March.*)

Your letter, informing us of your arrival at *Chekry*,(1) and applying for a supply of gun-flints, powder, &c., has been received, and its contents are duly understood. Send to Bûrhânûddeen for gun-flints, powder, and whatever else you may want. The *Sipahdâr*(2) Mahommed Ali, has no doubt joined you by this time with the troops under his command, orders for this purpose having been repeatedly dispatched to him. That part of your forces which was at *Kurpah* (3) has also marched from thence, and will soon join your army. What more?

OBSERVATIONS.

Meer Kumrûddeen Ali Khân was the son of Meer Ali Rizâ Sâheb, commonly called Meer Sâheb, who fell at the battle of *Porto Novo*, in the year 1781. Hyder Ali Khân, who was married to his sister (the mother of Tippoo Sultan), is reported to have immediately conferred all the honors and appointments enjoyed by his brother-in-law upon his son, Kumrûddeen, then a young man, whom he, at the same time, committed in a very public manner to the especial care and favor of his cousin, Tippoo Sultan. The latter, however, would not appear to have had much confidence in him at any period of his reign. He was sometimes, indeed, ostensibly placed at the head of an army; but he was always under the direction of some more experienced person. Upon the death of the *Sultan*, the British Government, in conjunction with the *Nizâm*, provided for Kumrûddeen Khân

(1) Name uncertain.

(2) The commander of a *Kushoon*, or brigade.

(3) A town and district bordering on the *Carnatic*, ceded in 1792, by Tippoo Sultan, to the *Nizâm*, and by the latter to the East-India Company, in 1800.

Khân in the most liberal manner. He did not, however, long survive his cousin and master, dying very soon after he had taken possession of the *Jagire* bestowed upon him.

LETTER XII.

To Turbiyut Ali Khân; *dated* 11*th Extra* Ahmedy. (28*th March.*)

It has been represented to us, that Tumanâ Nâikwâry,(1) the warden of the *Kurbnâth* Pass, receiving bribes [for his connivance], suffers people to proceed to the *Pâyen-Ghaut:* we therefore write, to desire you will station two respectable and sensible men, with some trustworthy *Piddehs*,(2) in one of the forts [commanding the said pass] for the proper care and regulation of the same. This guard must be relieved every three months.

OBSERVATIONS.

This letter furnishes one among numerous proofs, of the unceasing jealousy and dislike, with which the *Sultan* viewed any sort of communication between his territories and those of the British Government, or of the Nabob of the Carnatic. He anxiously laboured to keep all his neighbours (but particularly the English) in as complete ignorance as possible of every thing that passed in *Mysore:* and to this object he unreluctantly sacrificed whatever advantages, either his subjects or himself might have derived, from a free commercial intercourse between the countries.

(1) Those at the head of the *Kundachâr*, or militia, were called *Nâikwâries.*

(2) A sort of irregular foot soldiers, armed usually with a matchlock and *Tulwâr*, or sabre.

LETTER XIII.

To MAHOMMED GHYÂS; *dated* 18*th Extra* AHMEDY. (4*th April.*)

You wrote stating, "that Râo Râsta had said, 'that if the design "'against *Nergûnd* were relinquished, the *Vakeel*[1] of the *Zemindâr* "'of that place was empowered to pay us a certain fine; by which "'mode of adjustment we should not only be the gainer, but "'appearances would likewise be saved with the world.'" It is known. You must say, in answer to Râo Râsta, that what we demand is, that not only the *Paishcush* due by the said *Zemindâr* be discharged, but that he shall also make due compensation for the ravages he has committed within our dominions; and that, on this condition, we will wave our purpose of reducing the place.

You further write, "that Râo Râsta had told you, 'that you must "'apply to have the amount of the arrears due for past years remitted "'in specie, as bills would not be accepted by the bankers there.'" It is understood. We wrote before, and we now write again, to desire that Noor Mahommed Khân, who is well acquainted with all matters in that quarter, may be dispatched to the Presence. A verbal communication from him will best enable us to judge of the truth of their professions, and the rectitude of their proceedings, as well as to ascertain the extent of the *Durbâr charges;* after which we can consider what is to be done. What more?

OBSERVATIONS.

By "*Durbâr charges*" is here meant the *douceur* to be paid to the Mahrattah ministers upon the conclusion of a settlement. This is a matter of course in the negociation

E

(1) Ambassador or Envoy: diplomatic agent.

negociation of all treaties, and in the adjustment of differences between the native powers of India. Sometimes the presents, or largesses, made on these occasions, are, to a certain degree, reciprocal; but it is generally on the weaker, or yielding party of the two, that the chief burthen falls.

LETTER XIV.

To KUMRÛDDEEN KHÂN; *dated* 19*th Extra* AHMEDY. (5*th April.*)

YOUR two letters, dated the 14th and 16th instant, informing us of the junction of the *Sipahdâr*, Mahommed Ali, with his *Kushoon*, have been received. What you write, respecting the audacity and contumacious conduct of the *Zemindâr* of *Surhutty*, and your receipt of letters from Ghûlâm Hûsain and Ghûlâm Mohyûddeen, the *Kilaadâr* of *Lukhmaiser*, on the subject of chastising the said *Zemindâr*, is comprehended.

Notwithstanding the said fort is situated in your road, yet as you have no heavy [or battering] ordnance with you, it is to be apprehended, that if you were to attack it, you might be detained before it, and thereby prevented from advancing. We write, therefore, to desire our dear Son (1) will merely encamp his army near the fort, and endeavour, by striking an awe into the garrison, or by stratagem, to get possession of it. If this should not appear to be practicable, you must proceed straight forward, without making any delay.

(1) In the original, اقبال نشان *Ukbâl-nishán*, "of happy or fortunate mark," "giving "or containing signs of prosperity:" a term of endearment, exclusively applied to one's own children or younger relatives.

LETTER XV.

To MAHOMMED GHYÂS *and* NOOR MAHOMMED KHÂN; *dated* 21*st* *Extra* AHMEDY. (7*th April.*)

YOUR letter of the 9th instant was received this day, and the whole of its contents are understood. The translation of our Persian letter,(1) which that friend,(2) of his own suggestion, made and sent to Râo Râsta, and a copy of which was enclosed for our information, was a highly judicious and commendable proceeding. What you say in so much detail, respecting the communications of Râo Râsta on the subject of *Nergùnd*, and [particularly] of his proposal that we should, for the present, accept, in the way of mulct, and as an adjustment [of the past], eighty thousand *rupees*, with an assurance of being paid hereafter, year by year, the established *Paishcush* of former times, is understood; and, together with your account of his importunate instances for our raising the siege of the place, has been duly considered.

The friendship we bear Râo Râsta makes us willing to remit the proposed mulct on the aforesaid *Zemindâr*; but let the latter make due compensation for the ravages he has committed within our dominions, and let him pay up the arrears of *Paishcush* due to us: we will then send the necessary order to our commanders for raising the siege of *Nergùnd*, which, by the divine favour, is on the point of being reduced.(3)

You must not communicate *in writing* to Râo Râsta every proposition you may have to make to him, or transmit to him copies of our dispatches to you. On such occasions you are to send for Râo Râsta's

E 2 *Mùtusuddy*,

(1) *i. e.* its translation into the *Mahrattah* or *Hindivy* dialect.

(2) Original آں مہربان On this passage see the second paragraph of the following observations.

(3) Yet it was not reduced till July following.

Mútusuddy, and make him commit to paper whatever may be proper to be written: by this means you will avoid pledging yourself under your own hand.(4)

You judged right, in keeping back the letter which we enclosed for Râo Râsta, and which you must return to us. We now send [instead of that letter] one framed agreeably to your suggestion, which you will deliver to him.

What you have stated so much at length, by desire of Râo Râsta, on the subject of our remitting specie [and not *bills*], in discharge of the *yearly money*,(5) and for the *Durbâr* charges, is understood. As Noor Mahommed Khân is well acquainted with all the circumstances of that quarter, as well as with whatever relates to the subject of *Durbâr* charges, he must be dispatched to us; in order that, ascertaining from him the true state of things, we may pursue such measures as shall be necessary. (6)

We hear that eight or ten thousand of their horse have crossed the *Kishna*, with hostile intentions against our army. Hitherto, notwithstanding their forgetting what they owe to our kindness, we have not in a single article broken the treaty [subsisting between the two governments]; but if, in spite of the numberless favours we have bestowed upon them, and contrary to their solemn engagements, they become the aggressors, and proceed to improper lengths, it will then behove us to repel such aggression. After repulse and chastisement, there will no longer remain any appearances of good-will or amity.(7)

(4) Or, "to the end that nothing under your hand may remain in their possession." Original تادست آویزآن مهربان بدست شان نباشد

(5) This is the same as the *fixed* or *regulated* money spoken of in Letter III.

(6) Or, "that, after understanding all matters from him, we may provide accordingly." Original که همه مراتب دریافته فکرآن بعمل آید

(7) Or, "after repulse and chastisement, there will be an end to all relations of courtesy "and amicable intercourse." Original بعد دفعیه و تنبیه هیچ لطف نخواهد ماند

OBSERVATIONS.

It is not very clear what *translation* of the envoy's is alluded to in the beginning of the present dispatch (whether a letter to themselves, or of one to the address of Râo Râsta); nor is it worth while to offer any conjectures on this subject.

It is rarely that the *Sultan* condescends to bestow the title of *Mehrbân*, or *friend*, upon any of his servants, however high in his confidence; yet he has applied it, no less than three times, in the present letter, to Mahommed Ghyâs. It is probable, that the envoy knew his master too well to exult much in this uncommon mark of favour; but if he was weak enough to do so, he was not suffered to enjoy the dream of honour long.(8)

The directions here given to the envoys, respecting the mode in which they were to communicate with Râo Râsta, will prepare the reader for the still further developement of the *Sultan's* crooked and unprincipled politics in his subsequent correspondence, as well with his agents at *Poonah*, as with others of his servants.(9)

The Mahrattah government and Tippoo Sultan differed too widely, on the subject of *Nergûnd*, to afford any prospect of amicable agreement between them. Of this both parties were probably equally satisfied; and therefore neither of them is to be supposed to have been very serious in the discussions which took place, relative to the *mode* in which the money, claimed by the Mahrattahs, should be paid. The fact was, that neither the latter expected, nor the *Sultan* intended, any payment at all, as long as the question regarding *Nergûnd* remained at issue.

LETTER XVI.

To ABDÛL HUKEEM KHÂN, *NABOB of SANORE; dated 24th Extra AHMEDY.* (*10th April.*)

BÂBOO RÂO, RÂM RÂO, and the other *Mûtusuddies*, whom you deputed hither for the purpose of adjusting the accounts of your

eonditional

(8) See Letter CLXVII, and also Letter CCXCVII.

(9) See particularly Letters LIII, LXVI, LXIX.

conditional *Jagire*,[1] have accordingly come to a settlement, by which it appears that there is justly due to us the sum of 38,40,785 *rupees*. Of this amount we have excused [you] (or abated) two *lacks* of *rupees*: for the remaining 36,40,785 *rupees* we have received the engagements of the aforesaid *Mútusuddies*, which we have lodged with our bankers, who are now, together with the said *Mútusuddies*, dispatched to you. Be expeditious in putting the payment of this money in train, and in sending back the bankers to us. It will not be well, that any delay, or procrastination, should take place in this matter. You must likewise discharge the separate obligation for ten *lacks* of *rupees*, entered into by that friend's *Mútusuddies* and ratified by you.

OBSERVATIONS.

Abdûl Hukeem Khân was a *Patan* chief, who possessed the principality of *Sánore*, *Shánoor*, or *Savanore*,[2] called here by Tippoo Sultan a *Jagire Mushrooteh*; by which is meant, a *Jagire* held under specific stipulations, to distinguish it from a free *Jagire* or *Jagire* in ordinary. This principality was compelled to submit to the superior power of Hyder Ali Khân in the year 1764, when Abdûl Hukeem agreed to pay to the *Mysore* chieftain a certain proportion of his annual revenue. A double alliance by marriage was, at the same time, concluded between them; Hyder bestowing one of his daughters upon the eldest son of the *Patan*, who, in his turn, gave one of his to Kureem Saheb, the second son of Hyder. This connexion, however, was not productive of any advantage to the *Patan*; who, at length, revolted from Tippoo, and sought the protection of the Mahrattahs, to whom the district of *Shánoor*, including *Bankypoor*, was finally ceded, by the partition treaty of 1792; when its dispossessed chieftain became wholly dependent on the government of *Poonah*.[3]

(1) Original جاگیرمشروطه

(2) It is thus variously written: I believe *Shánoor* is the most common pronunciation.

(3) For an historical sketch of this *Patan* dynasty, extracted from documents furnished by Lieutenant Colonel Colin M'Kenzie, see Appendix D.

LETTER XVII.

To BURHÂNÛDDEEN ; *dated 22d Extra* AHMEDY. (*8th April.*)

YOUR letter has been received, and its contents are duly understood. You write, " that having reduced your baggage as much as you " could, you were prepared, with the victorious army [under your " command], to chastise the enemy, and that, if the latter made their " appearance in force, it was your intention to raise the siege,(1) and " send off your heavy ordnance to *Dhârwâr*." It is well : be it done as you propose. In the mean while, being careful to procure constant information of the enemy's motions, you will act as circumstances may render expedient, taking counsel herein from the three commanders [attached to you], whose opinions being committed to writing, must regulate your proceedings. We have here the fullest intelligence regarding the enemy's forces, which we are persuaded dare not look at our army : caution and vigilance are nevertheless necessary. Agreeably to your desire, letters have been written to Dileer Dil Khân, &c. Doubtless they will discharge the obligations of fidelity and devotedness ; and you will all, in conformity with our instructions, conduct matters in concert, and after mutual consultation. Hereafter, what is behind the veil of invisibility will be displayed.(2)

OBSERVATIONS.

It appears from this, and several other letters, that Bûrhânûddeen (as well as Kumrûddeen), had a council of war assigned him, without whose advice and concurrence he was not at liberty to take any material step. His council, at this time,

(1) *i. e.* the siege of *Nergûnd*.

(2) Original منبعد آنچه در پرده باشد جلوه‌گر خواهد شد

time, was composed of Dileer Dil Khân, Syed Humeed, and Syed Ghûfâr, three *Sipahdârs*, or commanders of *Kushoons*, whose military reputation stood very high, and who possessed a considerable share of the *Sultan's* confidence. Syed Ghûfâr fell with his master in defending *Seringapatam*. Of the fate of the other two commanders I am uninformed.

LETTER XVIII.

To Dileer Dil Khân, Syed Humeed, *and* Syed Ghûfâr ; *same date. (8th April.)*

Consulting together on the contents of our written instructions to you, committing the result of your deliberations to writing, and confiding in the divine goodness, you will prepare to approve your fidelity and devotion to us. You must do nothing without holding counsel of each other. Hereafter, what is at present concealed by the curtain of invisibility will be displayed. In this matter there is no room for hesitation or remissness.(1)

LETTER XIX.

To Râjah Râm Chundur ; *dated 23d Extra* Ahmedy. *(9th April.)*

Two letters from you have been received. You write, " that vermil-" lion is not procurable within our dominions, and is only to be got at " Pondicherry, &c." This being the case, you must send money, and buying it at those ports, dispatch it to the Presence. There is no necessity for sending [thither] goods [or merchandize] to barter for it.

You

(1) Literally " there is no necessity or occasion." The passage may also be rendered, " hesitation or remissness is not to be admitted."

You further write, "that the *Serishtedárs*[1] of ——,[2] incited "thereto by others, have preferred various complaints against you, with "the intention of bringing upon you our displeasure." It is known. You have had instructions given to you. Acting in conformity therewith, and attending diligently to the business of the state, you may rest perfectly confident and easy in your mind: if, however, complaints and accusations should be preferred against you, they will not be regarded or meet our approbation. Esteeming you to be intelligent and solicitous for our prosperity, we have entrusted you with an important office, in which we have no doubt of your proving your attachment and zeal for our service.

OBSERVATIONS.

The preceding letter affords a fresh proof of the unremitting jealousy and dislike with which the *Sultan*, at this time, viewed any intercourse between his subjects and those of the neighbouring countries, but particularly the English possessions. He here objects to the exportation of the produce of *Mysore* even to *Pondicherry*; not so much, probably, on account of its being an European settlement, as because no trade could be carried on with it, that would not almost necessarily lead to some commercial intercourse with the *Carnatic*, through part of which the trade in question must unavoidably pass. Rather than incur this risk, we see him sending away the specie of his dominions for the purchase of the commodities he required, and which he could, no doubt, have obtained on more advantageous terms by barter. At a subsequent period he would appear to have acquired rather juster notions of what was essential to the prosperity of his country; having, in the year 1794, issued some commercial regulations, tending to encourage a limited trade with his neighbours. Still, however, his natural distrust of

F those

(1) A revenue officer.

(2) This word, in the original, is not perfectly legible.

those neighbours predominated; ultimately superseding, or rendering null, the expectations which seemed to have been held out by the edicts referred to.(3)

My information does not enable me to say, how far the *Sultan* fulfilled the promises made in the present dispatch to Râjah Râm Chundur. I think there is a passage in a subsequent letter to another of the *Sultan's* officers, that points at some secret impeachment of the *Râjah's* integrity, and encourages the informer to pursue his inquiries. Colonel Munro, indeed, acquaints me, that being a native of *Arcot*, he finally became suspected of disaffection to the *Sultan*, who put him to death. However this may be, it is certain, that he continued in office, and apparently in the full possession of his master's confidence, as late as the year 1791.

LETTER XX.

To KUMRÛDDEEN KHÂN; *same date.* (*9th April.*)

YOUR letter, informing us of your arrival at *Koodry-hâl*,(1) together with its enclosure, has been received, and its contents are understood. You must proceed with the force under your command, and encamp near Bûrhânûddeen. Last night, whatever was necessary to be written, was fully written: to that dispatch we therefore refer you.(2) The enemy's force is inconsiderable. It is not to be supposed that they will presume to look at our army.(3*)

LETTER XXI.

To the GOVERNOR *of* PONDICHERRY; *same date.* (*9th April.*)

[AFTER compliments]. You write "that the *Bouparies*(1*) of the port "of *Pondicherry*, who come into our dominions to purchase articles of "merchandize,

(3) See Appendix E.

(1) Name uncertain.

(2) Literally, "the perusal of these will inform you."

(3*) Literally, "what power have they to look at the army of the *Sircar*?"

(1*) Travelling traders.

" merchandize, are, on their return with their goods, molested by the " *Taalúkdár* of *Selim*, who will not suffer them to proceed; in conse- " quence of which, you request of us to direct him to let the aforesaid " merchandize pass." It is known: and, agreeably to your desire, we enclose an order to the *Taalúkdár* of *Selim*, commanding him to release the goods in question. Let the same be forwarded to him.

In future, when you dispatch *Bouparies* into our dominions to purchase goods, you must give them a letter from yourself to the *Taalúkdár*, written either in *Urwy*(2) or *Telingy*;(3) when he will, in conformity with your desire, suffer the specified articles to pass. The reason of the orders which we have issued on this subject is, that of late certain *strangers* have come into our dominions; where borrowing money of the *Ryots*(4) and others, they have been guilty of various unwarrantable practices. Always continue to delight and rejoice us with accounts of your welfare.

OBSERVATIONS.

As a personal compliment to the Governor of *Pondicherry* (whom he probably, at this time, wished to conciliate) we here see the *Sultan* relaxing, in some degree, the severity of the regulations spoken of under the nineteenth letter. It is most likely, however, that the concession was only temporary, and that the French governor was frequently obliged to renew his present application.

The allusion to *strangers* is, no doubt, pointed at the English, and the subjects of the *Carnatic*. It is not equally certain, that the cause here assigned by the *Sultan* for the prohibition in question was the real one, or that the accusation, thus made, had any foundation in truth.

F 2

(2) The Malabar language.

(3) Properly, the dialect spoken in *Telingana*; but not strictly confined to the ancient limits of the kingdom so called.

(4) Subjects, in general; but, in a restrained sense, the peasantry.

LETTER XXII.

To KUMRÛDDEEN KHÂN; *dated 24th Extra* AHMEDY. (*10th April.*)

YOUR letter, filled with complaints and accusations against the *Kushoon* of the *Sipahdâr*, Mahommed Ali, has passed under our view. The particulars therein set forth are distinctly perceived. The aforesaid *Sipahdâr* is still *ignorant* [of many parts of his duty], and but imperfectly acquainted with the manner in which the business of our government is conducted. Hence it is, that although employed on [actual] service, he has neglected the proper equipment of his *Kushoon*, and, in this manner, shown his worthlessness.(1) Bearing in mind the expediency of the moment, you must issue the necessary orders for his being supplied with such stores as may be requisite, and then employ him [as you may think fit].

The *Kurpah* troops have reached *Gooty*, and will soon join you. You are not, however, to wait their arrival, but to proceed straight to *Nergûnd*, and there unite yourself to the army of the *Sircar*.(2)

You did right in purchasing the iron, and other articles you mention, for the use of the aforesaid *Sipahdâr's Kushoon*. You will furthermore furnish whatever stores may be required, for repairing any damages which his gun-carriages may have sustained.

You write that the enemy, to the number of sixteen thousand horse and sixteen thousand foot, with five pieces of light artillery,(3) are encamped at the distance of sixteen *coss* from the fort of *Nergûnd*. It is revealed. By the favor of God, the force appointed for the reduction of that

(1) Original وسليقه ناكاركي خود باينقسم ظاهر نمود

(2) *i. e.* the army already in advance under Bûrhânûddeen.

(3) Original توپ لمچهر I am not quite clear with respect to the meaning of *Lumchhur*: it may signify a long field-piece.

that fortress is so strong,[4] that though there should be fifty thousand horse of the enemy, it will suffice for their effectual chastisement. This being the case, how will they dare to look at our army? Let that beloved son, then, hasten with his corps to join [the rest of] our forces: and if the army of the enemy should show itself in your way, take counsel of each other, and with one accord inflict due punishment upon them. What more needs proceed from our pen?

OBSERVATIONS.

The lenity with which the *Sultan* here notices the remissness of the *Sipahdár*, Mahommed Ali, is the more remarkable, as it was his general practice to animadvert, with the greatest severity, on every instance of neglect or disobedience of his orders, and particularly of his military regulations. His moderation, on the present occasion, might possibly have arisen from something like a personal partiality towards the offending officer; but it may also have had no other foundation than caprice. From whatever cause it proceeded, similar instances will be rarely met with. It is true, that the conduct of the *Sipahdár* is spoken of with strong disapprobation; but this still falls very short of the usual measure of the *Sultan's* anger on such occasions. The *inexperience* imputed to the officer in question, rather countenances the idea of his having been prematurely raised, through private favor, to the important command he enjoyed. In the regular course, a *Sipahdár*, or brigadier (and especially in an army so actively employed as Tippoo Sultan's generally was) could not be *inexperienced.* Still, however, no distinct traces are observable in the written documents, nor did I ever hear a report of the *Sultan's* being influenced by favorites of any kind.

(4) Original سنگین weighty; heavy.

LETTER XXIII.

To RÂJAH RÂM CHUNDUR; *dated 24th Extra* AHMEDY. (10*th April.*)

Two letters have been received from you, and their contents are understood.

[After some directions on certain trivial points, like those remarked on under Letter IV. page 13, the letter proceeds:]

You write, "that wishing to marry your daughter,(1) and there being "none of her cast in this country to contract her to, there is a necessity "of sending for a proper person for the purpose from the *Pâyen-Ghaut*: "and you therefore solicit passports for the ingress and egress of parties, "whom it will be requisite to invite on the occasion, according to the "list which you have enclosed."(2)

It is known. A passport for the persons who are to come from the *Pâyen-Ghaut* to *Bangalore*, on this occasion, is enclosed: you will, therefore send for some person of your cast, and giving your daughter in marriage to him, detain him near you. Where is the necessity for sending him back to the *Pâyen-Ghaut?* If this, however, should not be practicable, you must seek for one of your own cast in this country to betroth her to; when [having found such a one] you will celebrate their nuptials. What more?

OBSERVATIONS.

The *Sultan* would not appear to have had any objections to the entrance of strangers into *Mysore*, provided they came thither for the purpose of settling;

(1) I am doubtful whether the daughter of Râm Chundur, or of some other person (a kinsman of his) be meant.

(2) This passage confirms the report (noticed before) of Râm Chundur's having been a native of *Arcot*.

settling; but it was extremely difficult for any, who had found admission into his dominions, to quit them again. That he should have insisted on the detention of Râm Chundur's intended son-in-law, in the event of the latter being brought from the *Carnatic*, is not to be wondered at, considering the distrust with which he habitually viewed all intercourse between that country and his own. To have allowed the son-in-law, and perhaps the daughter, of a person of the rank and authority of Râm Chundur, to reside in the territories, and be liable to the influence, of the power of whom he was most jealous and apprehensive, would have been entirely at variance with those maxims of policy, which constantly governed his conduct in regard to the English.

LETTER XXIV.

To Kumrûddeen Khân; *dated 26th Extra Ahmedy.* (*12th April.*)

Your letter has passed under our view; and what you have written, respecting your having withdrawn from before *Nergûnd*, and of Bûrhânûddeen's having occupied, with his army, a position on the banks of the *Pundhileh*,(1) is understood. It is fit that you also speedily join the army; and, according to our former directions, apply yourself to the chastisement of the enemy

What you say, regarding the reduction you have made in the baggage of your troops, is revealed, and meets with our approbation.

LETTER XXV.

To Bûrhânûddeen; *same date.* (*12th April.*)

Your letter has been received. What you state, respecting your having withdrawn from the trenches,(1*) and taken up a position with your army on the banks of the *Pundhileh*, is understood.

You

(1) Or, perhaps, *Bundhileh.*

(1*) *i. e.* having raised the siege of *Nergûnd.*

You must give orders to the predatory cavalry to harass the front and rear of the enemy, and to seize on all the horses they can; the present being the proper time for collecting together and obtaining horses.

Nursia, the *Taalûkdâr* of *Nugr*, has sent you, by our direction, forty thousand *Behâdury pagodas*,(2) for the pay of your army, which you will, of course, have received. What more?

LETTER XXVI.

To Kumrûddeen Khân; *dated 28th Extra* Ahmedy. (*14th April.*)

Your letter of the 25th Extra *Ahmedy*, (11th April), informing us of your arrival, with the forces under your command, at *Nergûnd*, and of your interview with Bûrhânûddeen, has passed under our view, and the particulars contained in it are fully revealed to us. Uniting yourself to the division belonging to Bûrhânûddeen, you must advance in open day against the enemy, and attacking them with vigour, chastise them in a manner that shall deter them from confronting you again.

LETTER XXVII.

To Mahommed Ghyâs *and* Noor Mahommed Khân; *same date* (*14th April.*)

We have received your letter, and its contents are understood. In conformity with the wishes of Râo Râsta, the siege of *Nergûnd* has been relinquished, and our victorious army has encamped at the distance of two or three *Coss* from thence. You must state to Râo Râsta, that a mulct

(2) The *Behâdury pagoda* was a gold coin, exceeding the value of the *Kunterâi pagoda* about thirty per cent.

mulct is not what we want from the *Zemindár*, but due compensation for the injury sustained by our dominions [in consequence of his depredations], and payment of the arrears due by him for [several] years past.

OBSERVATIONS.

The movements and near approach of the Mahrattah army, which had now advanced in considerable force to the support of the *Zemindár* of *Nergúnd*, appear to have rendered it inexpedient to prosecute the siege of that place, which was, therefore, relinquished for the present; the *Sultan*, at the same time, taking credit for having, in this instance, yielded to the wishes of Râo Rásta; who, however, was not to be so easily duped, as may be seen by Letter XXXVII to Mahommed Ghyâs. No material progress could have been made in the siege at the time it was relinquished.

LETTER XXVIII.

To Búrhánúddeen; *dated 2d Regular* Ahmedy. (*17th April*).

Your encamping at *Misrycótah*, as well as your dispatching of the *Kázy* of *Toorkul* to the Presence, was proper. According to your request, *Purwánehs*(1) are enclosed for the *Aumils*(2) of the several *Taalúks*, and for the *Kilaadárs*, directing them to furnish you with intelligence of the enemy.

Let loose the plundering cavalry, and other predatory troops, upon the enemy's army, with orders to seize and bring in horses *without number*.(3) Take care, also, of your own army, and be always prepared.

G

(1) Written orders, or mandates.

(2) Governors or collectors of districts.

(3) Original اسپان بیشمار

LETTER XXIX.

To KUMRÛDDEEN KHÂN; *dated 4th Regular* AHMEDY. (*19th April*).

YOUR letter, proposing "to open[1] trenches against *Nergând*, and "applying for *Purwâنehs* to the *Aumils* in the vicinity [of your camp] "to collect fascines and scaling ladders,[2] for the attack and reduction of "*Râmdoorg*, and the other forts situated on that road," has been received, and is understood. You must not, at present, lay siege to *Nergând*; but pursuing the army of the enemy wherever it may be, drive it beyond the *Kishna*, and deal with it in such a manner, as shall deter it from facing our troops again.

Purwânehs are enclosed for the *Aumils* of *Dhârwâr*, *Biddâmy*, and *Gujunder-ghur*, directing them to supply the necessary materials for scaling ladders, &c. When these things are wanted, forward the orders, and apply for what you require.

Describe particularly, for our information, what sort of a place *Râmdoorg* is.

LETTER XXX.

To BÛRHÂNÛDDEEN; *dated 8th Regular* AHMEDY. (*23d April*).

The army of the enemy is encamped at the distance of a gun-shot from *Râmdoorg*. In conjunction with Meer Kumrûddeen Ali Khân, lead our victorious army against it, and chastise it in such a manner, as shall *break*

(1) If the date assigned to this letter be right, the meaning must be to resume the siege of *Nergúnd*.

(2) Some of the terms here employed are of doubtful meaning.

break its loins, and render it incapable of facing you again. You must take fifteen days' grain with you. The aforesaid *Khân* is indisposed; you will, therefore, dispatch *Kishna Pundit*, the physician attached to that dear son,(1) to administer to him. What more?

LETTER XXXI.

To the same; dated 9th Regular AHMEDY. *(24th April.)*

Do you, our dear son, repair to our beloved son, Meer Kumrûddeen Ali Khân, and, consulting together, act according to your united judgment; pressing the enemy in such a manner, that they may not be able to take breath on this side the *Kishna*. Having accomplished the chastisement of the enemy, you will resume your position before *Râmdoorg*.

OBSERVATIONS.

Although the authority vested in Bûrhânûddeen, on the present occasion, appears to have been very limited (Kumrûddeen, even when actually united with him, receiving his orders, on various occasions, directly from the *Sultan* himself) yet there is some reason to believe, that he was considered as the principal commander of the forces opposed, at the commencement of this war, to the Mahrattah army.(1*) The circumstance of his being directed, in the foregoing letter, to repair to the camp of Kumrûddeen, for the purpose of consulting with the latter on the operations of the campaign,

G 2

(1) That is, Bûrhânûddeen. In the original it is نور چشم *Noor-chushm*, "light of my "eyes;" an expression of endearment, applied in the same manner as *Ukbâl-nishân*: for which see Note 1, Letter XIV.

(1*) It no where appears, by what official designation Bûrhânûddeen was distinguished. The rank next above that of *Sipahdâr* is, in some places, stated to have been that of *Meer Bukhshy*: in others, the *Sipahdâr's* immediate superior is called *Sipah-sâlâr*. It is probable, that this last was the title of Bûrhânûddeen.

campaign, does not at all invalidate this opinion; since the order in question is sufficiently accounted for by the indisposition of Kumrûddeen, noticed in Letter XXX: besides which, it will be seen, by the following Letter, that it was the express wish of the *Sultan*, that they should keep up an intercourse of mutual visits. But, however this may have been, it is certain, that a considerable jealousy subsisted between these two commanders, of which some proofs will appear in the sequel.

LETTER XXXII.

To KUMRÛDDEEN; *dated 9th Regular* AHMEDY. (*24th April.*)

WHAT you write, respecting the flight of the enemy's army, and of horses taken by our troops, as also your application for *Purwâneh*s to Ibrâheem Ali Khân and Râjoo Pundit, directing them to dispatch supplies to you,(1) is understood. With regard to the horses, you must take them [from the captors,] at a valuation;(2) and, after placing such as are strong and in good condition in our stables, distribute the rest among the *Silahdârs*,(3) to be mounted by men out of employ. You will, in conjunction with Bûrhânûddeen and the other [commanders], chastise the enemy in such a manner, that they may not be suffered to take breath before they reach the river *Kishna*. Having thus soundly beaten them, you will again encamp before *Râmdoorg*. You are also, from time to time, to repair to the quarters of Bûrhânûddeen; and to act in concert with him, and all the rest of the commanders, in whatsoever

(1) In the original, رسد زر *rusd e zur*, and زررسد *zur e rusd*, both of which mean a supply of money in *specie*, in contradistinction to *bills*. I am indebted for this explanation to Lieutenant Colonel Munro.

(2) In the original اردل *urdul*: my interpretation of which (*valuation*) is entirely conjectural, as I am unacquainted with the word.

(3) Cavalry, whose horses belong to the riders.

whatsoever relates to occupying the necessary positions, and to the opening of the trenches. On the other hand, if you should, upon any occasion, find it necessary to do so, you will send to Bûrhânûddeen to come to you. The latter, as well as the *Sipahdârs* attached to him, has been instructed to the same effect.(4) Ibrâheem Ali Khân and Râjoo Pundit have likewise been written to, according to your desire.

LETTER XXXIII.

To Bûrhânûddeen ; *dated* 10*th Regular* Ahmedy. (25*th April.*)

Your letter, reporting the sickness of Meer Kumrûddeen Ali Khân, and containing an application for two *Yoonâny* (or Greek) physicians,(1) and some *Telingy* doctors, to attend him, has been received, and is understood. Let the said Khân be attended by the physician Kishna Pundit, who is with you ; and write to Abdûl Hukeem Khân,(2) to desire he will send a doctor from thence.(3) These two, being appointed to administer to the said Khân, must be so strictly enjoined on the occasion, that his restoration to health may speedily be effected.(4*)

Enclosed is an order to the *Kilaadâr* of *Dhârwâr*, where there are a number of gun-bullocks, directing him to dispatch them to you : you will, accordingly, send for them, and, on their arrival, select such as are stout and young, and most fit for the draught of artillery, and deliver them over to the *Sipahdâr*, Syed Ghûfâr.

(4) If so, the letter does not appear ; the preceding one to Bûrhânûddeen speaking only of a single specific visit to be paid by him to Kumrûddeen.

(1) *i. e.* Physicians practising according to the rules of Hippocrates, Galen, &c.

(2) The Chief of *Shanoor*, or *Savanore*.

(3) *i. e. Shanoor.*

(4*) That is, " they are to be particularly desired to exert their skill to effect his early " recovery."

LETTER XXXIV.

To Kumrûddeen ; *dated* 14*th Regular* Ahmedy. (29*th April.*)

Your letter has been received, and its contents are understood. What you say, respecting your having left the *Kushoon* of the *Sipahdâr* Syed Ghûfâr for the guard of the baggage, and taken the *Kushoon* of the *Sipahdâr* Mahommed Ali along with yourself, is known. With the exception of tents and *pawls*(1) and other articles of indispensable necessity, there is no baggage attached either to you or to the division of Bûrhânûddeen ; therefore the leaving the *Kushoon* of the said *Sipahdâr* for their protection is absolutely superfluous. Besides, adverting to [the near approach of] the rainy season, it is of importance, on the score of health, that you should have your tents and *pawls* along with you. Such being the case, you will take the *Kushoon* of Syed Ghûfâr also with you, as well as your tents and *pawls*.

You and Bûrhânûddeen must live together in harmony, and not thwart or oppose one another in the conduct of our affairs, but apply yourselves to the chastisement of the enemy. It will also be suitable to the friendship [which should subsist between you,] and will contribute to the success of our affairs, if you sometimes visit his quarters : nor will it be amiss if you occasionally invite him to yours.

OBSERVATIONS.

It is abundantly evident from the foregoing letter (and will appear still more from some others that follow) that no very good understanding subsisted between the cousin and brother-in-law of the *Sultan ;* whose admonitions, on the occasion, being mostly addressed to Kumrûddeen, it may, from thence, be inferred, that the fault was chiefly on the side of the latter ; who might probably think that his nearer affinity to the *Sultan*, as well as the services of his father, gave him a claim to superior consideration.

(1) *Pawls* are small tents, used by the inferior officers and privates.

LETTER XXXV.

To Râjah Râm Chundur ; *same date.* (*29th April.*)

Your two letters have been received. What you write, respecting the excuses made by the manufacturers of the district [under you] for declining to weave the stuffs we require, has excited our astonishment ; we therefore direct, that they be compelled, by menaces, to prepare the number of pieces required, with the utmost expedition, and agreeably to the pattern [heretofore] sent. If, notwithstanding your injunctions and menaces, they persist in their false pretexts and disobedience, they must be well flogged.

What you write, regarding the affair of the *Hurkâreh*(1) Râmâ, who has been propagating false reports to the prejudice of the people of *Punganore*,(2) is understood. Let the said *Hurkâreh* be put in irons and confined ; and after taking security from the bankers of *Punganore*, let them be released, as their further detention would be idle.

OBSERVATIONS.

Revolting as the idea of *flogging* a body of weavers, for being averse to undertake a fabric, with which they were probably unacquainted, or which they might not be able to execute without detriment to their ordinary occupations, must appear to every English reader, we are obliged, in fairness to Tippoo Sultan, to acknowledge, that similar acts of oppression and violence are, by no means, uncommon, under the native governments of India. Still, however, such acts usually proceed from subordinate officers, or persons exercising, and perhaps abusing, delegated power ;

(1) A servant employed in carrying messages and letters, running before a *palankeen*, and various other services. The term literally signifies a *factotum*.

(2) The particular persons are specified in the original, but the passage is illegible. They were, probably, the bankers mentioned immediately afterwards.

power; and rarely, if ever, distinctly and immediately, as in the instance before us, from the sovereign himself. Thus the evil, generally speaking, is to be traced to the despotic nature of the government; while, in the case under consideration, it may justly be referred, in a great measure, to the personal character of the ruler.

It is impossible not to be struck, in the foregoing letter, by the sudden transition which it exhibits, from flagrant oppression to rigorous justice. Imprisonment and chains are not thought too severe a punishment for calumny by the man, who in the same breath, as may be said, consigns a numerous class of industrious artisans to the scourge, for refusing to relinquish their accustomed pursuits, in order to administer to his caprice. But such inconsistencies are constantly presenting themselves in the conduct of Tippoo Sultan; whose irregular mind was, at no time, under the influence of any fixed principle, if bigotry, and still more, hatred of the English, be excepted. To humanity of disposition, or to a love of justice, in the abstract, he certainly could lay no claim; and, therefore, in punishing the *Hurkâreh* Râmâ as he did, it is much more probable that he was actuated by resentment, at the imposition attempted to be practised upon him by that informer, than by any feeling for the injury which his slander might have done to the objects of it.

LETTER XXXVI.

To Meer Kumrûddeen *and* Bûrhânûddeen; *dated* 16*th Regular* *Ahmedy.* (1*st May.*)

Two letters from you have passed under our view, and the particulars therein stated are duly perceived. With respect to the war which you two are conducting in conjunction with the three *Sipahdârs,* (that is to say, Syed Humeed, Syed Ghûfâr, and Shaikh Unser), all of them prudent and intelligent men, our desire is, that acting in concert together, you should pursue the object of chastising the enemy with the utmost vigor and sagacity, and in an effectual and glorious manner: accordingly, we we have transmitted strict orders to this effect to the aforesaid *Sipahdârs*; who will, in consequence, be obedient to you, and co-operate on all occasions with you.

What you say of the scarcity of grain [in your army,] notwithstanding your having a *Cutwâl*(1) and [so many] *Lumbânehs*(2) with you, has astonished us; you must, therefore, denounce the heaviest threats against the said *Cutwal*, and make him provide abundance of grain, agreeably to our regulations on this head, to the end that your people may suffer no distress for that article.

By the Divine favor your health(3) is now re-established, and it is, consequently, no longer proper that you should have a physician attending you, or that you should take any more medicines; let him, therefore, be sent back to *Shahnoor*.

After chastising the enemy in a signal manner, and driving him to the other side of the *Kishna*, you will take up a position for the attack of *Nergûnd*.

Your sending away your baggage is a proceeding in no respect proper: you must keep it with you. Indeed, where is the great quantity of baggage belonging to you, seeing that you have nothing besides tents, *pawls*, and other such necessary articles?

The cavalry attached to you have been very remiss in skirmishing and marauding, and in having suffered the enemy to flee without making booty of any of their horses, and finally to escape by the pass of *Râm-*

H *doorg*,

(1) *Cutwâl* is the chief police officer of a town. Every army is also provided with one, whose principal duty it is to see that the *Bâzârs*, or markets, are properly supplied.

(2) *Lumbâuehs*, or *Lumbâdehs*, otherwise called *Bunjârehs*, are a particular tribe of *Hindoos*, who occupy themselves in supplying armies in the field with grain and other provisions. They transport the articles they deal in on bullocks; are, in general, armed with match-locks, swords, and spears; and travelling, for the most part, in numerous bodies, occasionally render themselves very formidable to the countries they pass through.

(3) This passage is, of course, individually addressed to Kumrûddeen.

doorg, although they might have taken numberless horses. It is well. You must now give the most peremptory orders to the *Risâladârs* of cavalry to go forth on separate parties, and exert themselves properly to make prize of the enemy's horses; the present being a favorable opportunity for getting together a great number of horses. Scouring, likewise, the enemy's country, they must seize on all the grain, &c. they can discover.

OBSERVATIONS.

The present letter is somewhat at variance with the thirty-second, on the subject of horses captured from the Mahrattahs; since, from the latter, it would appear, as if some success had attended the *Sultan's* army in this respect, whereas he here complains of the enemy's having been suffered to escape, without "any horses" having been taken from them. It is probable, that the first report of the commanders, on this head, did not descend to particulars; and that, when they subsequently stated the specific number of horses actually taken, the *Sultan* might have been disappointed at the result; and, under this impression, have been led to under-rate the little that had been done. The great solicitude which he betrays for procuring horses, would, of course, enhance his disappointment on the occasion.

LETTER XXXVII.

To MAHOMMED GHYÂS; *same date.* (1*st May.*)

YOUR letter, dated the last day [or 29th] of Extra *Ahmedy*,(1) has passed under our view, and its purport is duly understood. An answer has been written, on all points, in our *Hindivy* letter, to which you are referred for particulars.

The

(1) Or 15th of April.

The villainy and bad faith which *they*[2] have manifested, in spite of the most solemn engagements, is abundantly well known. Upon what grounds then, [or, with what confidence,] can we, all at once, send thither a large sum of money? Noor Mahommed Khân has been sent for by us, merely for the purpose of our ascertaining [through him] their treaties and engagements, and with no other view. You must state this matter distinctly to Râo Râsta, and, removing all suspicions of a different tendency from his mind, dispatch Noor Mahommed Khân to the Presence; and if [at the same time] they should [think proper to] be very urgent for your departure also, assuredly you, too, must repair hither.

You write, "that Râo Râsta observed to you, on occasion of the "siege of *Nergúnd* having been raised, that if the orders for that mea-"sure had been previously communicated to his government, according "to his suggestion, such a proceeding would have had the best effect, as "it would have tended to strengthen his hands in the management of "the negociation; but as things had happened, they bore a very ungra-"cious appearance, inasmuch as he had been led to declare repeatedly "to the minister,[3] in the most positive manner, that if the Mahrattah "army ventured to meet ours they would inevitably be put to shame; "whereas, in fact, the very reverse of all this had taken place, to his "great disturbance and confusion."

It is known. We have not deviated a hair's breadth from the suggestions of Râo Râsta: nor, though we have raised the siege [of *Nergúnd*,] has there been any deficiency,[4] on our part, in chastising the enemy's army. This is a fact of such abundant notoriety as not to require any other evidence. What more?

H 2

(2) The court of *Poonah*.

(3) Nana Furnaveese.

(4) Or *remissness*.

OBSERVATIONS.

It is not easy to conceive, what motive the *Sultan* could have for addressing his agents on any occasion in the *Hindivy*, rather than in the *Persian* language; in which last, it may be safely presumed that he usually conveyed his written orders to such of his servants as understood it. It could not be with a view to secrecy; since a *Hindivy* letter, supposing it to fall into improper hands, would at least be as generally intelligible as a *Persian* one. Possibly the *Hindivy* letter, referred to in the present instance, might have been dispatched, for the express purpose of being communicated to Râo Râsta; though, in this case, some intimation of that design would, it may be thought, have been given in the *Persian* letter. But whatever the reason of the proceeding under consideration might be, it is proper to observe, that it was not confined to the present occasion, or to the persons of the envoys at *Poonah;* since other examples of the practise in question will be met with in the course of this work.

It would seem, by the second paragraph of the foregoing letter, that some sinister interpretation had been put by the court of *Poonah*, or at least by Râo Râsta, upon the desire expressed by the *Sultan* for the return of Noor Mahommed Khân. What the particular nature of the suspicions entertained on this occasion by the Mahrattahs was, does not appear; but it is not improbable, that, they may have apprehended the real object of the envoy's recal to be connected with some secret intrigue of the *Sultan's* at *Poonah*: nor is it likely, that the latter's disavowal of any improper view in the matter would have the effect of removing those doubts or fears; especially, as the two states were now at open war. Be this as it may, it is certain that Noor Mahommed Khân did not, at this time, obtain leave to obey the summons of his master; and that, both he and his colleague, were detained at *Poonah*, till the month of May in the following year.

I am not sufficiently acquainted with the details of this war, to be enabled to decide between the opposite pretensions of Râo Râsta and of Tippoo Sultan, respecting the success of the earlier operations of it. It is clear, however, that the *Sultan* had, at this period, been compelled to relinquish the siege of *Nergûnd*, by the

the menacing position of the Mahrattah army, and that Rão Râsta was not to be persuaded, that the measure had been adopted purely at his instance. The truth, indeed, would appear to be, that, hitherto, no material advantage had been obtained by either side.

LETTER XXXVIII.

To the same; same date. (1*st May.*)

WHAT you write, regarding the variations of the temperature(1) in your quarter, is revealed. Our physicians have thoroughly ascertained the proper mode of treating(2) the diseases in question. The first thing to be done is, to draw off, by bleeding, all the corrupt humours; by which means an effectual improvement will be produced in the general constitution of the patient. The body of the diseased party being thus completely brought under subjection,(3) the next step must be to expel from it every remaining seed of the distemper, administering, in the meanwhile, whatever medicines may be found necessary. What more?

OBSERVATIONS.

This curious enigmatical letter is sufficiently intelligible. The unwholesome *temperature* of *Poonah,* alludes to the hostile disposition towards the *Sultan,* which had latterly superseded at that Court the amicable sentiments, formerly entertained for himself and his father by the Mahrattah rulers. By his *physicians,* the *Sultan* means his counsellors, or perhaps, the commanders of his army. The *disease* to be *cured* is, of course, the enmity of the Mahrattahs; and the *mode* of *cure,* that

(1) Original اختلاف آب و هواي آنجا "unhealthiness of the air, or climate, of that place."

(2) Literally "curing."

(3) Original برهمه بدن مريض حاكم گشته

that which he had begun to pursue; namely, an active war against them. The remaining allusions are equally obvious; and, indeed, so much so, that it can hardly be imagined that the *Sultan* proposed to disguise his instructions under this metaphorical cypher, which could not fail to be immediately understood by any person, knowing who the writer, or even the party addressed, was: it is, therefore, most probable, that nothing more was intended by it, than a display of the writer's ingenuity.

LETTER XXXIX.

To Noor Mahommed Khân; *same date.* (1*st May.*)

The letter you sent us has passed under our view, and its contents are understood. Whatever was necessary to be said, has been written at length to Mahommed Ghyâs; our letter to whom will inform you [of our sentiments], agreeably to which you will act.

LETTER XL.

To Bûrhânûddeen; *dated* 19*th Regular* Ahmedy. (4*th May.*)

It has been represented to us, that the garrison of *Râmdoorg* proposed to capitulate, but that you intimidated them [by your answer], and thereby threw away the favorable opportunity [or the advantage thus offered]. Where was the propriety of this [proceeding]? It is well. You must still encamp before the said fortress; and sending for battering guns from *Dhârwâr*, and collecting together the materials for trenches, by these means strike such a terror into the garrison as may induce them to submit: upon their doing which, you may permit them to march out of the fort with their arms. After putting a proper garrison in the place, you

you are to direct such of the enemy as are included in the capitulation, to be conducted, with their arms, beyond the *Kishna.*

Nursia, the *Taalûkdâr* of *Nugr*, has, of course, sent you, in pursuance of our orders, two hundred *Coolies.*(1) Let their arrival be reported to us.

You and Meer Kumrûddeen Khân must keep united, both in word and thought, and execute every business of the *Sircar* in an able and creditable manner,(2) agreeably to what we have formerly and repeatedly written on this subject.

N. B. A letter of the same tenor and date was written to Kumrûddeen.

OBSERVATIONS.

The foregoing letter furnishes a clear proof, that whatever the degree of general confidence reposed in Bûrhânûddeen by the *Sultan* might be, the latter, nevertheless, kept spies upon his brother-in-law; who were encouraged to animadvert freely on his conduct; and to whose representations considerable attention was paid. Indeed it appears, from several of the documents among the state papers found at *Seringapatam*, that the *Sultan* had organized a very extensive system of *espionage* throughout his dominions, and in almost every department of his government.

His envoys at foreign courts, his military commanders, his governors of forts and districts, were all diligently watched; or, at least, ordered to be so: but as the spies, thus employed, were, in general, very well known, it may be safely presumed, that their integrity was often corrupted, and their vigilance as often eluded. The practice of placing spies over public functionaries is, no doubt, very common under all the governments of *India:* but I am inclined to think, that few of them have carried it so far as was done by Tippoo Sultan; of whose regulations,

(1) *Coolies* are labourers, and carriers of burthens.

(2) In the original برونق or "splendidly."

tions for this department an outline (consisting of a short edict on the subject), will be found in Appendix F.

LETTER XLI.

To the same; dated 20th Regular Ahmedy. *(5th May.)*

Your letter has been received; and your account of the reduction of *Râmdoorg*, and of your having placed a garrison therein, is understood.

Sending for the battering guns from *Dhârwâr*, and collecting together the necessary materials for the erection of batteries, &c. you will proceed against *Nergûnd*, and lose no time in reducing it.

Nursia, the *Taalûkdâr* of *Nugr*, has, by our order, sent you two hundred *Coolies*, who have most probably joined you. You will report their arrival. The *Coolies* belonging to *Kopul* and *Bâdâmy* are already with you: be expeditious, therefore, in collecting together every thing necessary [for the early siege of *Nergûnd*]. A *Hindivy* order has been sent, for placing two *Jowks*,(1) &c., in garrison at *Râmdoorg*, agreeably to which you will act.

You and Kumrûddeen Khân, agreeing in word and thought, must execute the business of the *Sircar* in a splendid [or creditable] manner.

N. B. A letter of the same tenor and date was dispatched to Kumrûddeen.

LETTER XLII.

To Ghûlâm Ahmed, *Kâzy of* Nugr; *dated 24th Regular* Ahmedy. *(9th May.)*

Your letter has been received. You have written, that nine Frenchmen, together with their captain, had embraced the faith, and that

(1) A *Jowk* was a subdivision of a *Risâla* or *Kushoon*, answering to our company: consequently, a *Jowkdâr* was the captain of a company.

that the said captain humbly hoped to be honored with the command of of a *Risála* of [1] *Ahmedies.* It is known: and our pleasure is, that ten *rupees* be given to each of them, and that they be all dispatched, under an escort [a safeguard], to the Presence, where, on their arrival, the aforesaid captain shall receive the honor he solicits. Peremptory orders for the payment of the above stipends, and for furnishing the necessary escort, have been sent to the *Kilaadár* of *Nugr*.

OBSERVATIONS.

The *Ahmedies* here mentioned were a military corps, composed of the converts (whether forced or voluntary) to the Mahommedan religion. It was instituted by Tippoo Sultan, with whom it seems to have been a favorite establishment; of the origin of which he himself gives the following curious account in the Memoirs already referred to:

" The Portuguese Nazarenes[2] established themselves, about three hundred " years ago, in a factory situated near the sea shore, and on the banks of a large " river. This place they obtained of the *Rájah* of *Soondah*, under the pretext of " trading [with his subjects][3]: and here, availing themselves of the opportunities " which arose in the course of time, they acquired possession of a territory, " yielding a yearly revenue of three or four *lacks* of *rupees*, throughout which they " equally prohibited fasts and prayers among the Musulman inhabitants, and the " worship of idols among the Hindoos; finally expelling from thence all who refused " to embrace their religion, which the Hindoos were required to do within three days,

I " under

(1) *Risála* usually denotes a body of cavalry of an indefinite number, but, for the most part, corresponding to the strength of a regiment: the term, however, is sometimes applied to infantry, and occasionally to a mixed corps of horse and foot. The commander of a *Risála* is called a *Risáladár*.

(2) The *Sultan* applies this name to Christians in general; but it sometimes denotes the English in particular.

(3) *Goa* is, no doubt, meant here.

" under pain, if they remained in the country after that time, of being forcibly " converted to it. Some of the people, alarmed at this proceeding, abandoned " their property and homes, and took refuge in other countries: but the greater " part, considering the threatened danger as improbable, and not possessing the " means of removing their effects, preferred remaining; whereupon these infidel " Nazarenes, at the end of the appointed time, obliged them all to embrace their " false religion. Sometime after this, by means of gifts and presents distributed " among the *Rájahs* and *Aumils* of that quarter, they were suffered to erect " from eighty to a hundred idol temples,(4) in the countries of *Nugr*, *Soonda*, and " *Kúriál-Bundur*;(5) in each of which they placed a *Pádre* or two, whose religion, " in fact, was that of the *Guebres*;(6) and by whose means they prevailed, partly " by artifice, and partly by tempting the avarice [of the poorer classes], on vast " numbers of the inhabitants to adopt their faith. [Such was the state of things " here] when, by the divine favor, and through the aid of the Asylum of Prophecy,(7) " and with the help of the conquering Lion of God,(8) the port of *Kúriál* fell " into our hands; on which occasion the odious proceedings of these accursed " *Pádries* becoming fully known to us, and causing our zeal for the faith to boil " over, we instantly directed the *Dewán* of the *Húzoor Kuchurry*(9) to prepare a " list of all houses occupied by the Christians, taking care not to omit a single " habitation. The officers of the *Kuchurry*, accordingly, employing the " *Mútusuddies* of *Soonda*, *Nugr*, *Kúriál*, &c. for this purpose, soon prepared " and delivered to us a detailed report on the subject. After this, we caused an " officer and some soldiers to be stationed in every place inhabited by the " Christians,

(4) Meaning, of course, *churches*.

(5) *Mangalore*: *Bundur* signifies a sea port.

(6) The ancient *Parsees*, or worshippers of fire.

(7) *Mahommed*.

(8) Original اسدالله الغالب *Usudúllah ulghálib*, viz. of the Caliph Ali, and was adopted by Tippoo Sultan as a sort of motto, which he sometimes inscribed on his weapons and other articles.

(9) A *Dewán* is a minister or officer, superintending the revenues of a state or province. The *Húzoor Kuchurry* was the revenue board at *Seringapatam*, or that attending the *Presence*.

" Christians; signifying to them, that, at the end of a certain time, they should " receive further orders, which they were then to carry into full effect. These " men and officers being all arrived at their respective posts, the following orders " were transmitted to them, viz. 'On such a day of the week and month, and " 'at the hour of morning prayer, let all the Christians, whatever their number " 'may be, together with their women and children, be made prisoners and " 'dispatched to our Presence.' And on the sealed cover, or superscription, of each " of these dispatches, was specified the day of the week and month on which " it was to be opened and read. Accordingly our orders were every where opened " at the same moment; and at the same hour (namely, that of morning prayer) " were the whole of the Christians, male and female, without the exception of a " single individual, to the number of sixty thousand, made prisoners, and " dispatched to our Presence; from whence we caused them, after furnishing " them duly with provisions, to be conveyed, under proper guards, to *Se-* " *ringapatam*: (10) to the *Taalúkdárs* of which place we sent orders, directing that " [the said Christians] should be divided into *Risálas*, or corps, of five hundred " men, and a person of reputable and upright character placed, as *Risáladár*, " at the head of each. Of these *Risálas*, four (together with their women " and children) were directed to be stationed at each of the following places,(11) " where they were duly fed and clothed, and ultimately admitted to the honor of " Islamism; and the appellation of *Ahmedy*(12) was bestowed upon the collective " body." (13)

Thus far the *Sultan*. Of these sixty thousand Christians, fifteen thousand may be supposed to have been capable of bearing arms, which number would form

I 2 " thirty

(10) The *Sultan*, at the time here spoken of, was in the neighbourhood of *Mangalore*.

(11) *Seringapatam* is here named, but the rest of the passage I do not clearly understand.

(12) *Ahmed* is one of the names of Mahommed.

(13) The date of this institution is indicated (the *Sultan* adds) by the following couplet:

" God is the defender of the *Ahmedy* religion;
" The light of the firmament is derived from the *Ahmedy* religion," (or people.)

where the letters comprising the last line, or hemistich, in the original, give the year of the *Higera* 1197.

thirty *Risálas*. But this corps was not composed exclusively of converts from Christianity. Soon after its establishment, it received a considerable accession of strength in the captives of the Kûrg or Koorg nation; all the males among whom, being compelled to embrace the Mahommedan faith, were afterwards enrolled in the *Ahmedy* corps, to the number (according to the *Sultan's* own account in a subsequent part of this Memoir) of from sixty to seventy thousand men.(14) The united corps were distributed throughout the garrisons and districts of *Mysore*; and every where the strictest orders (says the *Sultan*) were issued, commanding those in authority to treat these new Mahommedans with the greatest tenderness, and, in short, to consider them " as more precious even than their own souls."

LETTER XLIII.

To MEER KUMRÛDDEEN KHÂN; *dated 25th Regular* AHMEDY. (*10th May.*)

YOUR letter has passed under our view, and its contents are understood. You write, " that the *Byde horse*,(1) out of employ, have " committed great excesses and depredations in the *Sircar's* dominions." It is known. You must issue the most peremptory orders [to these people] to carry their ravages into the Mahrattah territories, bringing away

(14) That is, as I suppose, that the total number of *Koorg* prisoners, including women and children, were between sixty and seventy thousand; giving, probably, about the same number of soldiers, as the sixty thousand Christians mentioned in the text. The *Koorg* converts were formed into *Risálas* of a thousand men each. (Memoir.)

(1) The horse, here called *Byde*, are the same as those denominated *Pindárehs*, *Looties*, and *Kuzzáks*. They are predatory troops receiving no regular pay, but maintaining themselves by plunder; in pursuit of which they sometimes make equally free with friends and foes. By *Bydes* " out of employ," is to be understood such as had not been formally engaged by the *Sultan*, but followed the army spontaneously, which it is very common for many of them to do.

away from thence all the horses they can make booty of, and desisting [for the future] from their depredations in our country.

You and Bûrhânûddeen must remain united in your councils; and collecting together the necessary materials for opening trenches against *Nergûnd*, lose no time in reducing that place. In short, you must, in all affairs, agree in word and thought.

Turrokul belongs to the *Zemindâr* of *Kolapoor*, and the said *Zemindâr* is well disposed towards us: you must, therefore, never mention his name, but attend to what we heretofore particularly and strictly enjoined on this head. What more shall be written?

OBSERVATIONS.

If some disagreement had not recently arisen between Bûrhânûddeen and Kumrûddeen, it may, at least, be inferred from the second paragraph of the foregoing letter, that the *Sultan* was in apprehension of it, and, therefore, judged it necessary to repeat so soon his former exhortations to harmony. It may be doubted, however, whether these admonitions produced the desired effect; since, not long after the date of the present dispatch, fresh symptoms of discord between the rival commanders are manifested.

It is not very clear, what the *Sultan* means, by enjoining Kumrûddeen "never "to mention the name" of the *Zemindâr* of *Kolapoor*. *Kolapoor* is a district situated near *Soonda* and *Goa*, and in the possession of a chieftain, who acknowledges the authority of the government of *Poonah*, and pays, I believe, a tribute to the *Paishwa*. It would seem, that a good understanding secretly subsisted between this chieftain and the *Sultan*; and that the latter, on this account, had determined to treat him as a neutral, notwithstanding his connexion with the Mahrattah empire. It is also not improbable, that Kumrûddeen (ignorant, perhaps, of the friendly disposition of the *Zemindâr* towards the *Sultan*) may have proposed to take possession of *Tûrkûl* or *Turrokul*; in which case, the purport of the expression under consideration might have been, that the *Zemindâr* of *Kolapoor* was

was not to be considered or spoken of in a hostile manner, or his territory treated as that of an enemy.

LETTER XLIV.

To Mahommed Ghyâs *and* Noor Mahommed Khân; *dated 29th Regular* Ahmedy. (*14th May.*)

Your two letters, of the 11th and 15th of *Ahmedy*, have been received, and the account of your conferences with the *Paishkâr*(1) of Râo Râsta is understood.

The Mahrattah army has come and laid waste our dominions, to the amount of eight *lacks* of *pagodas*,(2) and otherwise proceeded in an unwarrantable manner: the commanders of our forces have, in consequence, been reduced to the necessity of attacking that army, which, after sustaining a severe defeat, has been driven across the *Kishna*. On their return [from the pursuit of the enemy] our commanders seized on *Râmdoorg*, and have since opened trenches against *Nergûnd*. We still, however, are willing to relinquish the attack upon the latter place, on condition that the arrears of the usual *Paishcush* be discharged, and due satisfaction be made to us for the injury done to our country. We shall otherwise soon reduce the place.

You must return to us by the post all the bills of exchange in your possession and in the possession of Noor Mahommed Khân.(3) If the chiefs of that place consent to the dismission of the said *Khân*, and to his

(1) A *Paishkâr* is a manager or conductor of business, whether public or private.

(2) Or twenty *lacks*: for the manuscript is here so illegible, that either reading may be adopted.

(3) The bills, here spoken of, had probably been sent to the envoys, for the purpose of being paid over to the Mahrattah government, in satisfaction of its pecuniary claims on the *Sultan*.

his being dispatched hither, we shall then be enabled to ascertain from him every particular respecting that quarter, and to consider the means of remitting the money [due or claimed].

Your account of receipts and disbursements is duly arrived. A remittance will, hereafter, be made to you, for defraying the expences of your mission.(4)

LETTER XLV.

To Kumrûddeen Khân; *dated* 1*st Behâry.* (15*th May*).

You have represented, " that notwithstanding the peremptory com-
" mands issued by us for the purpose, the necessary articles for enabling
" you to open trenches [against *Nergûnd*] have not yet been sent to you
" by any of the *Aumils*; to whom you, in consequence, request we will
" repeat our orders." It is known.

That light of our eyes(1) has always been a mere child: (2) but now his senses must absolutely have forsaken him, as otherwise he could not write to us so often to repeat our orders. One peremptory order from us is [in all cases] sufficient. Where is the *Aumil*, who dares to be remiss in dispatching the articles [directed to be furnished by us]? If there be any who has disregarded our commands, let him be put to death: or(3) let the *Purwâunehs*,(4*) so slighted, be returned to the Presence.

The

(4) Literally " of the people attached to you."

(1) See Note 1, Letter XXX.

(2) It is thus I understand the words ازسابق که ان نورچشم طفل بود

(3) A slight alteration in the reading (namely با *bá* for یا *yá*) will admit of the passage being rendered " *and* let the *Purwâneh* so slighted, &c."

(4*) A written mandate or order.

The workmen[5] who arrive from the different *Taalûks* for the service of the trenches, as well as those already with Bûrhânûddeen, are to be divided between you. Taking half of them, therefore, you must immediately commence the business of the trenches: seeing that the rainy season approaches, and that, when that sets in,[6] the siege cannot any longer be prosecuted with vigour. For this reason, you are to proceed with the utmost dispatch in the attack and reduction of *Nergûnd.*

OBSERVATIONS.

The foregoing letter, at the same time that it affords a pretty strong proof of the slight estimation in which the *Sultan* held the talents of Kumrûddeen, also shews (what is further evinced in many other instances) that in the occasional expression of his disapprobation, he was not apt to be restrained by any consideration for the rank of the person incurring it; dealing out the same measure of asperity to the highest as to the lowest officer or servant, and making no distinction, in this respect, in favour even of his own near relation. The lofty tone, which he assumes in speaking of his orders, is likewise highly illustrative of his imperious temper, and of his quick sensibility of whatever affected his authority; which, it is difficult to believe, should have been actually insulted, in the manner that would seem to be indicated by the close of the second paragraph. Daring, indeed, must the *Aumil* have been, who could, on any pretext, not simply refuse or with-hold obedience to a *Purwâneh* of this prince, but contumaciously *return* it to the person delivering or sending it: for such is the construction to which the passage in question is liable. But whatever the fact may have been, no farther trace of, or allusion to it, is to be met with in the correspondence.

(5) There is a specification of these in the original, but the terms employed are either miswritten or unknown to me.

(6) The periodical rains in *Mysore*, and the elevated countries adjoining it, usually set in the beginning of June.

LETTER XLVI.

To the same; dated 3d Behâry. (17*th May.*)

Your letter, informing us of the molestation given by the cavalry and *Kushoons* attached to the division under Bûrhânûddeen to the labourers(1) coming from *Dhârwâr* [to your camp,] has been received, and its contents are understood.

You write also [in the same letter,] "that the quantity of powder, as "well as of eighteen and twenty-four pounds shot, with Bûrhânûddeen's "army, is inadequate [to the service going forward,] and request us to "send orders to the *Kilaadâr* of *Dhârwâr*, to dispatch a further supply "of those articles." It is known. We have already written, and now again write, to say, that all stores arriving from the *Taalûks* of the *Sircar* are to be divided equally between you and Bûrhânûddeen.

We enclose an order for the shot, &c. required, to the *Kilaadâr* of *Dhârwâr*, to whom you will forward it. On receiving this supply, deliver half of it to Bûrhânûddeen In like manner, take the half of all other supplies that arrive; and attacking *Nergûnd* from one side, while Bûrhânûddeen attacks it from the other, let the fortress be speedily reduced.

LETTER XLVII.

To Mahommed Ushruf; *same date.* (17*th May.*)

Your letter, accompanied by a statement of the receipts, disbursements, and balances of the *Taalûks* of *Gooty*, *Bulhâry*, *Ouk*, and *Hindi-Ununtpoor*,

K

(1) The original is either *Bégâries* or *Pykâries*. The former is a *Hindivy* word, signifying a day labourer, or pressed *Cooley*. *Pykâr* is a Persian word, signifying war or fighting, and, of course, is not applicable here: I am, therefore, inclined to read *Bégâry*.

Unnuntpoor, has been received, and the particulars set forth [therein] are understood.

You write, "that there are large balances outstanding in the *Taalûks* "of the *Sircar*, and particularly in *Gooty* and *Bulhâry*, where only a "thousand pagodas have been collected, notwitstanding four horsemen "have been employed as *Suzâwuls*;(1) and you therefore desire, that "peremptory orders may be issued [on the occasion] from the Presence."

You must scourge the defaulters severely, and [by this means] speedily realize the dues of the *Sircar*. What more?

LETTER XLVIII.

To KUMRÛDDEEN; *dated* 11*th* BEHÂRY. (25*th May*.)

YOUR letter, mentioning that you had nearly completed your first two approaches, and that Bûrhânûddeen's batteries were still unfinished, has passed under our view, and the contents are comprehended. This is an affair of a hill-fort. Without approaching very close to the place, and making a very wide and effectual breach, it will never be advisable or proper to attempt an assault: you must, therefore, wait until Bûrhânûddeen's batteries are completed; keeping up, in the mean while, such a fire on the place, as shall utterly destroy the wall on your side. Bûrhânûddeen has been written to, directing him to deliver to you half of the guns and labourers [he has recently received]; with the help of which you must continue to push on your approaches, and speedily reduce this fort.

(1) *Suzâwuls* are a kind of bailiffs, or duns, employed to enforce payments due on account of revenue. They are maintained, while they are employed, at the expence of the creditor.

LETTER XLIX.

To Bûrhanûddeen; *same date.* (25*th May.*)

Your letter, requesting our authority for engaging in your service a *Mûnshy*, for the purpose of making out passports and writing letters, has been received. Agreeably to your desire, you may hire a *Kunry* writer for the purposes you mention.[1]

You are to deliver to Kumrûddeen Khân half the guns and labourers [that join you.]

Kâlâ Pundit, it seems, together with his family, has fled from *Nergûnd*. Make enquiries, and let us know who now commands that place.

OBSERVATIONS.

I have been unable to ascertain whether Kâlâ Pundit was the *Zemindâr* of *Nergûnd*, or only an officer intrusted by him with the defence of the place. The report here noticed of his flight proved to be unfounded.

LETTER L.

To Mahommed Kâzim (*Brother of the deceased* Zynûl Aabideen, *late* Buktshy *of the* Jyshe Kuchurry); *dated* 12*th* Behâry. (26*th May.*)

It has, at this time, pleased God that your brother should die. This event has caused us much concern. Having it in view to provide for you, we desire you will repair speedily to our Presence, and consider yourself as secure of our favor.

K 2

(1) But not a *Múnshy*, or Persian writer, as Bûrhânûddeen had proposed. A *Kunry* writer would be less chargeable than a *Múnshy*.

LETTER LI.

To Zynûl Aabideen; *dated* 19*th* Behâry. (2*d June.*)

Your letter, enclosing an account of the receipts and disbursements of the *Taalûk* of *Loll-ghurry*, has been received, and what you have therein stated is understood. You say, "that the *Aumil* of the aforesaid "*Ghurry* has absconded, and desire that a new *Aumil* and *Kilaadâr* may "be sent from the Presence." It is known. But how is it, that the said *Aumil* should have absconded *without cause or motive?*(1) You must enquire very particularly into this matter, and report the result to us.

LETTER LII.

To Bûrhânûddeen; *dated* 21*st* Behâry. (4*th June.*)

You have represented to us, "that you had proposed to Kumrûddeen "Khân to make over to him the *Kushoon* of Shaikh Unser, and to take, "in its place, the *Kushoon* of the commandant Mahommed Ali; but "that the aforesaid *Khân* had given for answer, that it was not proper, "at this time, to make such an exchange." Well! what does it signify? Let the *Kushoon* of Mahommed Ali remain there (*i. e.* with Kumrûddeen.)(1*)

You write also, "that you purposed transferring to Kumrûddeen half "of the great guns, of the labourers, *Coolies*, &c. and keeping the "other half yourself." It is well: and you will continue to make the same division hereafter.

You

(1) The *Sultan* seems to have suspected some collusion in this transaction.

(1*) The exchange here declined by Kumrûddeen nevertheless took place at a subsequent period.

You say, "that the *Vakeel*(2) of *Kittoor* had been with you, and "represented to you, that if his master were allowed a week or two, he "would, at the end of that time, wait upon you, and perform such "services for the *Sircar* as should be required of him." It is known. At the expiration of the specified period, you will, accordingly, send for him, and employ him in our service.(3)

LETTER LIII.

To MAHOMMED GHYÂS; *dated* 22*d* BEHÁRY. (5*th June.*)

FIVE letters(1) from you, dated the 22d and 25th of *Ahmedy* [7th and 10th of May], and 1st and 4th of *Behâry* [15th and 18th May], have been received, and every particle of their contents is understood.

You observe, "that we have said in our letter to Râo Râsta (of "which a copy was sent to you, 'that he, (Râo Râsta) having told "'Mahommed Ghyâs and Noor Mahommed Khân, for our information, "'that he was willing to engage that his government should make good "'to us the *Paishcush* due to us by the *Nergünd* man, as well as make "'us compensation for the ravages committed in our country, we had, "'in consequence, made known our sentiments to the aforesaid *Khân*, "'who would accordingly communicate the same to him.'" You then add, "that this was not the purport of your letters to us; and request "us to refer to them again, when it will appear that what you stated "was, that Râo Râsta had proposed that eighty thousand *rupees* should "be

(2) A *Vakeel* is a representative: and the term is applied to almost every kind of agent, acting for or in the name of another, from an ambassador to a petty attorney. See Letter XIII.

(3) It will hereafter be seen, that the *Sultan*, at this very time, probably meditated the seizure of *Kittoor*.

(1) But only *four* are mentioned. Possibly two might have been of the same date.

"be paid to us by way of fine, and ten thousand *rupees* for *Durbâr* "charges; and that, for the future, the payment of the *Paishcush* "should be secured to us, in the same manner as when it used to be "paid through Apâjee Râm. Such being the case, you wish to know "what answer you are to give to Râo Râsta, if he should demand "of you at what time he had ever made the communication ascribed "to him."

It is known. Whenever letters are received from you, the proper answers to them are deliberated on, and written accordingly. *Thus, in the present case, our writing in the manner we have done* [to Râo Râsta,] *was the result of expediency; and sometime hereafter the utility of the proceeding will appear.*

What you write of the death of Anund, Râo Râsta's son, is known. You will deliver to the aforesaid Râo the dress of condolence, and the letter which we have sent for him on the occasion.

If your longer stay at *Poonah* should be marked with incivility [or be attended with any circumstances derogatory to our dignity,](2) it can be productive of no advantage; and, in this case, you will demand your dismission, and repair hither, declaring yourself plainly at your departure [to the following effect.]

"Notwithstanding the favors you have received at the hands of my "master, you have afforded assistance to a *Polygâr*,(3) belonging [or "subject] to him: and forgetting the boundless kindness of the *Sircar*, "you have sent your army, and laid waste his country, to the amount "of [many] *lacks* of *rupees*; while [on the other hand] my master, in "conformity with the wishes of Râo Râsta, expressed, both verbally "and by writing, directed the siege of *Nergúnd* to be raised, and his "forces

(2) In the original it is اگر بي لطف نمايد *i. e.* "if it should look, or appear, ungracious "or unkindly."

(3) A *Polygár* is the same as a *Zemindár*.

" forces to withdraw to a distance from thence. The army of Purserâm " Bhow, nevertheless, attacked that of the *Sircar;* the issue of which " [act of aggression], however, was, that the *Bhow* was completely " worsted, and compelled to flee beyond the *Kishna.* In spite, however, " of all this, Râo Râsta continues to require of my master to relinquish " the siege of *Nergûnd;* and accepting a mulct of eighty thousand " *rupees,* and a farther sum of ten thousand *rupees* for *Durbâr* charges, " to agree, for the future, to receive the *Paishcush* in the manner it was " heretofore paid by Apâjee Râm. Now my master only wishes, that " you yourselves would fairly consider this matter, and bear in mind the " repeated declaration he has made to you [through us], regarding the " contributions levied on his subjects, to the amount of ten *lacks* of " *pagodas,* by the *Nergûnd* man, as well as the ravages committed by " him in the *Sircar's* territories: [all which being duly weighed] he " leaves you to judge how far it is possible for him to consent to an " arrangement, so entirely inadequate to the losses he has sustained, " through the aggressions of this *Polygâr.*"

You mention, " that Râo Râsta had represented to the minister,(4) " that having caused the latter's sentiments to be repeatedly conveyed " to us, through our confidential servants (meaning yourselves), and " having moreover himself communicated them to us by letter, he could " not be justly blamed, because we had not sent a suitable answer to the " same."

To which you say, the minister had replied, " that he had always " declared it to be his opinion, that as, notwithstanding his (Râsta's) " constant importunity, no money had been sent from hence, it was " become perfectly clear, that we no longer wished to maintain the " relations of amity with them; seeing that, otherwise, such procras-" tination

(4) *i. e.* Nana Furnaveese.

" tination and evasion in dispatching the money [due] could never have " taken place; and that, this being the case, he now thought proper " plainly to desire that we might be informed, through you, ' that if " ' we had it in view duly to strengthen the foundations of harmony, " ' we would [immediately] send the arrears due for the three [last] " ' years, together with [the necessary sum on account of] *Durbâr* " ' charges: and that, with respect to the *Nergûnd* business, we must " ' consent to what was heretofore settled [on that point.'] He con-" cluded, as you report, by saying, ' that if we did not wish for the " ' preservation of their friendship, and were determined to persist in " ' withholding the money [due], he could see no use in your remaining " ' there.' "

It is known. No doubt, our bad faith, and our disinclination to cultivate their friendship, are manifest, in the same manner as their performance of their strong and solemn engagements is as clear as the light of the sun. What pleasure can there be in reiterating these things? It is a common saying, " that if any body be at home, one word is " sufficient." But, notwithstanding all this, we wrote, desiring Noor Mahommed Khân to be sent to us, in order that we might the better ascertain the views of the rulers there, and obtain the necessary explanations on the subject of their engagements, preparatory to our setting about the transmission of the stipulated money.(5) If the aforesaid *Khân* had accordingly been sent hither, this would have been carried into effect. It is still our desire, that he should be dispatched to us, and that you [Mahommed Ghyâs] should remain there; but if *your* departure also should appear to be desired by that government, or if they should [openly] insist upon it, then you, as well as Noor Mahommed, taking leave of them, will immediately repair hither.

Instead

(5) Meaning the usual tribute claimed by the Mahrattahs

Instead of denoting the name of the *friend* of the *Sircar*, as you propose doing, by the number 20; and the name of the *well-wisher* of the *Sircar*, by the number 60 (these being the numerical powers of the initial letters of their respective names), you must, in future, call the former, whose name begins with a *Gawf*, Gûlâb Khân; and the latter, whose name begins with a *Seen*, Surdâr Khân; this last cypher being *neat* and *clean;* and the names to be employed not at all leading to a knowledge of the real ones. What more?

OBSERVATIONS.

This is a very curious and interesting document; as, besides exposing the chicanery, and even downright falshood, to which the *Sultan* never scrupled to resort in his diplomatic transactions, when he thought he could thereby advance his purposes, it throws considerable light on the grounds of the quarrel subsisting between him and the government of *Poonah;* and discloses, in particular, the opinion entertained of the conduct and views of Tippoo by Nana Furnaveese, who, at this period, presided over the affairs of the Mahrattah empire.

It is not the least remarkable circumstance in the foregoing letter, that to the natural question of the ambassadors, "what answer they were to give to Râo "Râsta, if he should demand of them at what time he had made the communi-"cation ascribed to him," the *Sultan* makes no reply, but leaves it to the ingenuity of his agents to extricate themselves from the difficulty in which he had placed them, in the best manner they could.

The cypher which appears to have been proposed by Mahommed Ghyâs is a very common one in *Hindostan*, being founded on the numerical powers assigned to the letters of the alphabet by the *Ubjud* scheme, as explained in the Introduction; and, according to which, 20 stands for ك *(gawf* or *kawf)*; and 60 for س *(Seen)*. Now, while to this cypher it is justly objectionable, that it expressly declares the initial letters of the names intended to be disguised, and so far furnishes a clue to the latter, it must be admitted, that the one substituted by

L the

the *Sultan* was not quite so liable to detection; since it conveyed no clear or absolute indication of the initials of the concealed names. Thus *Surdar Khân* would not so easily suggest the idea of *Saindiah,* as would the saying "he whose "name begins with 60, or S;" since no positive or necessary reason existed, for supposing that the initial letters of the feigned and concealed names were the same.

Still, however, the *Sultan's* cypher did not possess any great advantage over that of Mahommed Ghyâs; and still less did it merit the praise of being "neat "and clean;" because, like the latter, it is so much in use, that the generality of readers would be very apt to suspect the principle of its construction. At a subsequent period, the *Sultan* appears to have improved somewhat in the art of cyphering; for the *Vakeels,* who accompanied the hostage princes to *Madras,* in 1792, were in possession of a figure-cypher, in which a descriptive account of the works of Fort St. George, written throughout in cypher, was discovered among the papers found *at Seringapatam* on the capture of that place. Even this, however, was but an indifferent contrivance, and, in consequence, was not difficult of detection.

It is not possible, at this time, to say, who were meant by Gûlâb Khân and Surdâr Khân; but it is sufficiently evident, from the epithets by which each is distinguished, that the former was a person of consideration, and the latter some one of inferior rank.

LETTER LIV.

To Chishty Yâr Khân; *dated* 23d *Behâry.* (*6th June.*)

Mahommed Ushruf, the Superintendant of the *Dewâny Kuchurry* of *Gooty,* wrote to you, by our direction, desiring you to send to him Buswunt Râo, the *Aumil* of *Beiginpilly;* in order to his examining the accounts of the said *Aumil,* and ascertaining his malversations. Instead, however, of complying with this requisition, it appears, to our great astonishment, that you exhibited, on this occasion, the most senseless

senseless and extravagant behaviour; tearing the letter of the superintendant in pieces, and returning it to him in that condition. Such conduct is very remote from what we expected from your good sense: you must instantly, therefore, on receipt of this letter, dispatch the said *Aumil* to Mahommed Ushruf; and take care not to be guilty again of the like improper and rude behaviour, as such proceedings are contrary to our pleasure.

OBSERVATIONS.

The reproof conveyed in this letter, considering the magnitude of the offence which gave rise to it, and the usual severity of the *Sultan* in similar cases, is so remarkably moderate, as almost to warrant a suspicion, that he occasionally suffered himself to be actuated, in his treatment of his servants, by motives of a personal and private nature, partaking, in some degree, of the character of partiality, not to say favouritism. The tearing in pieces, and returning in that condition, a letter written by the express direction of the *Sultan*, and most probably announcing it to be so, was hardly a less contempt of his authority, than the conduct of the *Aumil* mentioned in Letter XLV., whose crime was declared to merit death. It is possible, however, that the *Sultan* might not have viewed the transaction in this light; but have considered it as a mere personal affront to Mahommed Ushruf, which would be sufficiently punished by the bare manifestation of his displeasure.

LETTER LV.

To Kumrûddeen Khân; *dated* 25*th* Behâry. (8*th June.*)

You write, " that it is not advisable, until the reduction of *Nergünd*, " that the *Sipahdâr*, Mahommed Ali, should be relieved, as you propose

L 2 that

"th at his *Kushoon* should continue to occupy its present post in the "trenches." It is known

As the aforesaid *Sipahdár* is an officer of no experience, and as his *Kushoon* consists of ignorant and new raised troops, we directed that you should send for, and keep with you, Shaikh Unser and his *Kushoon*, and station Mahommed Ali and his *Kushoon* with Bûrhânûddeen; by which means you would have the services of old soldiers, while the others would be more in the way of acquiring instruction. The fact is, that the instruction of the aforesaid *Sipahdár*, and the improvement of the men composing his *Risála*, is our object [in this arrangement], and not his exchange or supercession: you will, therefore, after speaking in an encouraging manner to him, send him to join Bûrhânûddeen.

What you say respecting the *Risála* of Mahommed Nâsir (part of which you have incorporated into Mahommed Ali's *Kushoon*, and made over the remainder to Bûrhânûddeen) is understood. The men belonging to the aforesaid *Risála* are to be considered by you in the light of a loan or deposit,(1) and are neither to be made over to Bûrhânûddeen, nor to be incorporated into Mahommed Ali's *Kushoon*; but are to be dispatched to the Presence, whenever our orders, for that purpose, shall be issued.

With regard to your sending away the stable horses, &c.(2) on account of the scarcity of grain and forage, it is to be observed; that the war you are just now carrying on is against a fort; and that field operations being [for the present] out of the question, there can, of course, be no call for cavalry. You will, therefore, dispatch all the stable horses, &c. to *Kuppood-ghur*, where there is abundance of forage and good pasturage. This, indeed, was formerly signified to you; and it is a matter

(1) Original امانت

(2) The *stable* horses were the property of the *Sircar*; whereas the horses of the *Silahdár* cavalry belonged to the men and officers composing it.

matter of extreme astonishment to us, that you should perpetually write and apply for orders in such plain and easy cases as this.

OBSERVATIONS.

The foregoing letter clearly shows, that if the *Sultan* did not place unlimited confidence in the military talents or experience of Bûrhânûddeen, he at least considered the camp of that commander as a better school for the young and inexperienced soldier than that of Kumrûddeen. There is reason to believe, however, that the professional merits of Bûrhânûddeen were duly appreciated by his master; since we shall hereafter see him entrusted with the important charge of a wing of the united army of *Mysore,* in a general action with the Mahrattahs, near *Shahnoor.*

LETTER LVI.

To MAHOMMED GHYÂS *and* NOOR MAHOMMED KHÂN; *dated* 26*th* BEHÂRY. (9*th June.*)

YOUR three letters (two of them dated the 9th of *Behâry*, and the other the 13th of *Behâry)* accompanied by five bills of exchange,(1) namely, four from yourself, and one from Noor Mahommed Khân, have been received. The detail you have entered into, regarding the insolent conduct of Suddashoo, the *Hurkâreh,* is understood. The aforesaid [person] is only an *Hurkâreh*: what question or debate [therefore] can arise with him, and why should he be made privy to any secret affairs? You must require of him those services which it is his duty to perform [and no other]; and when you may have any thing of a particularly secret

(1) These were probably the bills directed to be returned to the *Sultan* in Letter LXIV. Besides the bills mentioned, these dispatches enclosed what is called in the original two *Lâkût-lukoteh,* the meaning of which I am unable to discover.

secret nature to communicate, you must do it in the couplet cypher which is enclosed.(2)

If the [Mahrattah] minister, *and the rest of them*, will dismiss Noor Mahommed Khân, and allow him to return hither, it will be well; and, in the event of their being urgent for the return of you both, it will be better still: you will, in that case, set out together for the Presence.

LETTER LVII.

To RÂJAH RÂM CHUNDUR; *dated 27th* BEHÂRY. (10*th June.*)

IT has been represented to us, that a balance of fifteen or sixteen thousand *pagodas* is still due from some of the *Taalûks*, under the charge of Meer Futah Ali, the *Taalûkdâr* of *Chuck-Bâldpoor* (from which amount, however, certain deductions remain to be made), and that you have taken very rigid measures for enforcing payment of the same. Now, as the aforesaid *Taalûkdâr* has never before exercised the functions of that office, and as he is, moreover, a stranger, and inexperienced in business, it is our pleasure, that you desist from those rigorous proceedings, and be content with gradually realizing the balance due. You will therefore recall your *Suzâwuls* [bailiffs], to the end that the aforesaid *Aumil* may be relieved from his present dismay.

N.B. The remainder of this letter is on an uninteresting subject.

OBSERVATIONS.

The preceding letter affords another exception to the usual severity of the *Sultan* on similar occasions. The motives assigned for his lenity, in the present instance are,

(2) The cypher here referred to does not appear. It is called a couplet cypher, because the key to it was comprehended in a *Bite*, or *Distich*.

are, no doubt, satisfactory and creditable to his justice; though, as in the case of the *Sipahdâr*, Mahommed Ali, they necessarily bring in question the prudence of the *Sultan;* whom we see placing men in trusts, to which he knew them to be unequal. The following letter will be found to breathe a very different spirit.

LETTER LVIII.

To Mohyûddeen Ali Khân; *dated* 28*th* Behâry. (11*th June.*)

Your letter, on the subject of the revenue accounts of the *Huwaily*(1) and *Taalûk* of *Ali-Nugr* (depending on *Guramcoondah*), has passed under our view, and is duly understood. You must examine the accounts of the said *Taalûks* in the strictest manner, and apply yourself diligently to the realization of the revenue. On this occasion, you must flog, without favour or partiality to any, all such persons as, adopting the practice of ingratitude, have defrauded the *Sircar*. By this means, let the payment of our dues be enforced.

N.B. The rest of this letter is omitted as immaterial.

LETTER LIX.

To Kumrûddeen Khân; *dated* 29*th* Behâry. (12*th June.*)

Your letter has been received. We highly approve of your having placed the *Kushoon* of the *Sipahdâr*, Mahommed Ali, with Bûrhânûddeen: in the room of which you must take Shaikh Unser [and his corps]; that commander and his men being intelligent and well instructed.

You should open a negociation with the garrison of *Nergûnd*, through the *Kilaadâr* of *Bâdâmy*, or the *Kâzy* of *Tûrkul*, or through any other

(1) The *Huwaily* is the principal division of a *Sircar*, or district; the chief town of which is always included in it.

other channel; and endeavour, by some means or other, to obtain speedy possession of the fort.

OBSERVATIONS.

The reader will recollect, that the measure, for the execution of which Kumrûddeen is here commended, did not originate with him, but had been directed by the *Sultan*, and a compliance with it evaded, in the first instance, by the *Meer*.

I am inclined to infer, from the instructions here given to Kumrûddeen for opening a negociation with the garrison of *Nergûnd*, that the *Sultan* sometimes addressed his orders to one, and sometimes to another of the two commanders employed against that place, and that they were in the habit of communicating such orders to each other. It would be difficult, indeed, on any other supposition, to account for such an order as the present one being apparently addressed to Kumrûddeen exclusively; since there can be very little doubt that Bûrhânûddeen took the lead, at least, in all political, if not also in all military movements, connected with the general command of the army now advanced towards the Mahrattah frontier. It is, on the other hand, possible, that similar instructions to those under consideration may have been addressed directly to Bûrhânûddeen, although no entry, to that effect, appears in the correspondence.

LETTER LX.

To BÛRHÂNÛDDEEN; *dated* 3d JAAFURY (16*th June*.)

YOUR letter, containing an application for money to enable you to make up some clothes, has been received. You may take three hundred *rupees* from the *Tosheh-khâneh*,(1) and apply that sum to the purposes of furnishing yourself with apparel.

Muster

(1) For an explanation of this term, see the observations on this letter.

Muster returns of the whole of the troops under your command, whether cavalry, regular infantry, or other description, as well as a statement of [your] receipts and disbursements, must be sent to us.

A month has elapsed since Kumrûddeen's batteries were established close to the fort; but you have not advanced so far from your side, although you commenced your approaches so much sooner than he did. This is what we do not understand. It is necessary, that you should be more expeditious in the prosecution of this business; and that, by properly battering the walls of the place, you should effect such a plain and practicable breach, as may enable you to storm it with success. In this affair you must be brisk and active.

OBSERVATIONS.

Parsimony, or perhaps, more strictly speaking, a rigid economy in his general expenditure, was always known to be a prominent feature in the character of Tippoo Sultan; and we have here a curious and striking proof of the fact. One of his principal generals, and his brother-in-law, is obliged to apply to him for the means of providing himself with wearing apparel; and the *Sultan,* although he complies with the request, is so far from leaving any thing on the occasion to the discretion of Bûrhânûddeen, that he restricts him to the disbursement of a specific sum, in fixing of which he certainly has displayed none of the munificence of a sovereign prince.

The *Tosheh-khâneh* is distinguished by Tippoo himself (in one of the letters of the present collection) into two kinds, *viz.* the *Nukdy* and *Jinsy.* The former I take to have been the *Treasury,* properly so called, or office in which the current specie, and, perhaps, bullion were deposited. The latter would appear to have comprehended a great variety of articles besides the wardrobe; to which, however, the term *Tosheh-khâneh* is, I believe, usually restrained in the northern parts of *Hindostan.* Where this word occurs by itself (that is, without its being joined to the words *Nukdy* or *Jinsy,* which is in general the case) it is not easy to determine

M its

its precise sense. In some places, as in the present letter, it appears to signify the treasury in its strictest sense; in others, the wardrobe; and, occasionally, a general storehouse or magazine. The *Jinsy*, in some parts of *Hindostan*, includes ordnance and ordnance stores; but I am unable to say, whether the term was, on any occasion, applied in the same manner by Tippoo Sultan.

It would be a difficult matter to judge, how far the censure here passed on the conduct of Bûrhânûddeen before *Nergûnd*, was justly merited, without a much fuller knowledge of the circumstances and operations of the siege than we possess. It may be presumed, however, that it was upon such a knowledge that the judgment of the *Sultan* was formed; and that, consequently, there was actually some remissness manifested by Bûrhânûddeen on this occasion.

LETTER LXI.

To the same; dated 2d Jaafury. (15*th June.*)

The *Piddehs* from the [adjacent] *Taalûks* of the *Sircar*, [at present] stationed with your army, are distressed for want of [the usual] means of subsistence; we therefore write to desire, that, in order to remove their difficulties, you will make them a monthly allowance of ten *fanams* per man.

LETTER LXII.

To Râjah Râm Chundur; *same date.* (15*th June*)

Your letter, together with the *Hindivy* enclosure, addressed to the *Aumil* of *Vencatigeery*, has been received, and the particulars therein stated are become known.

Write to the aforesaid *Aumil*, that he must address Bâboo Râo, the renter of *Vellore*, to this effect, *viz.* " that it is not the custom of the

" *Taalûks*,

" *Taalûks* belonging to our *Sircar* to allow the residence of robbers " therein; and that, upon the discovery of any such, they are imme- " diately put to death." What more?

OBSERVATIONS.

The *Hindivy* enclosure, here referred to, was probably from the renter of *Vellore* (in the *Carnatic)*, requiring some robbers, supposed to have taken refuge in the *Vencatigeery* district, to be delivered up. The answer ordered to be sent to this demand is a sufficient proof of the little disposition which the *Sultan* had to maintain an amicable, or even civil, intercourse with the existing government of the *Carnatic.*

LETTER LXIII.

To CHISHTY YÂR KHÂN;[1] *dated* 5*th* JAAFURY. (18*th June.*)

YOUR letter has been received, and its contents are duly understood. What you write, respecting the rigorous proceeding of Mahommed Ushruf, the *Darogha* of *Gooty*, in sending five horsemen to enforce payment of the third instalment of the revenue of your district, is revealed.

Esteeming you to be intelligent in business, a person of integrity, and a well-wisher of our government, we appointed you to your present charge; and we confidently trust, that you will use your utmost exertions to promote the interest of the *Sircar*, the prosperity of your *Taalûk*, and the increase of its revenue; and [especially] that you will, according

M 2 to

(1) This is the same person to whom Letter LIV is addressed; and who, perhaps, owed the mortification of having a *Suzâwul* placed over him by Mahommed Ushruf, to the affront he had lately put upon the latter. See Letter LIV.

to your written engagement, discharge the whole of the third *Kist* within the period of a month, paying the amount thereof into our treasury. In this persuasion, we transmit you a *Purwâneh*, to the address of the aforesaid(9) [*Darogha*], directing him to withdraw his horsemen, which you will accordingly forward to him. You must, at the same time, labour most diligently in the improvement of your *Taalûk*, and in the collection and augmentation of its revenues.

LETTER LXIV.

To MOHYÛDDEEN ALI KHÂN, *DEWÂN of KURPAH: an Extract; dated 6th JAAFURY.* (19*th June.*)

WHAT you have stated to us, respecting the pay of four men belonging to [the garrison of] *Guramcoondah*, who have been some time dead, having been appropriated to their own use by the officers of that place, is revealed. We desire you will enquire very particularly into this transaction; and having ascertained the time that the aforesaid officers have been in possession [or receipt] of this money, make them refund the same.

OBSERVATIONS.

I am not clear, whether it be here meant that the officers continued to draw and receive the pay of the deceased men after their death, or that they had only possessed

(9) This *Purwâneh* accordingly appears, but I have not thought it necessary to translate it. It is sufficient to mention, that after bearing testimony to the qualifications of Chishty Yâr Khân, as an officer of revenue, the *Sultan* observes, that if the *Taalûkdâr* in question should not discharge the *Kist* due at the stipulated time (which, on this occasion, he states at a *month and a half*, though, in the letter to Chishty Yâr Khân, it is said to be a *month*), there will be no impropriety in placing *Suzâwuls* over him, to enforce payment of the same.

possessed themselves of the pay due to them at their decease. In either case, the notice taken of the offence by the *Sultan* appears extremely slight.

LETTER LXV.

To Mahommed Ushruf, *Dewân of the Kuchurry of Gooty; dated 7th Jaafury. (20th June.)*

Directing the name of Fyze Hisâr to be substituted for that of Gooty.

Similar orders were issued, under the same date, directing *Bulhâry* to be in future called *Sumrputn,* and *Chittledoorg* to be named *Furkhyâb Hisâr.*

OBSERVATIONS.

Some of the letters in this collection, instead of being complete transcripts of those dispatched, are only, as it were, *notes* of the originals. These heads, or memorandums of dispatches, are titled and dated like the entire entries, but are distinguished by beginning always with the words درباب or درماده that is to say, " on the subject of——" followed by a brief abstract of the subject.

The present letter is the first of this description that has occurred. I propose, in every future case of the kind in question, to render the introductory words just quoted, in the same way I have done on the present occasion, namely, by the word " directing," or other suitable participle; which will sufficiently distinguish this portion of the correspondence from the more complete part.

LETTER LXVI.

To MAHOMMED GHYÂS; *dated* SERINGAPATAM, *5th* JAAFURY.
(*18th June.*)

IF they(1) should allow Noor Mahommed Khân to depart, then you must dispatch him hither, and practising procrastination, you will yourself remain behind for some time, writing us occasionally the news [of that quarter]. In the event, however, of their not giving the aforesaid *Khân* his audience of leave, you must both of you continue there; and contrive, by one means or another, to amuse them for a certain time, and to deceive them by speeches, calculated to flatter their selfish views(2) [or to work upon their avariciousness].

OBSERVATIONS.

The real situation of these envoys at *Poonah,* as well as their continuance there so long, is enveloped in a good deal of obscurity. At one time it is intimated, that the Mahrattah government have objections to the departure of Noor Mahommed Khân; at another, Nana Furnaveese is seen to hint an intention of dismissing both envoys. The *Sultan's* wishes and intentions respecting them are, at least, equally inexplicable; and will appear still more so, as we proceed in the correspondence. The only conclusion to be distinctly drawn from the present dispatch is, that if the agents remained at *Poonah,* it was to be with no other objects than those of transmitting intelligence, and of *amusing* and *deceiving* the Mahrattah government. This is clearly and explicitly expressed; and abundantly proves, that he thought of nothing less, at this time, than of affording any satisfaction whatsoever

(1) *i. e.* the government of *Poonah.*

(2) Original سخنان طمع آمیز

whatsoever to that government. Whether by "speeches calculated to flatter their "selfish views," it was meant, that the envoys should hold out the temptation of bribes to the Mahrattah ministers, or only that they should continue to profess his readiness to discharge the arrears of *Paishcush* due by him, is doubtful; but it is by no means so, that the *Sultan* had no serious intention of parting with his money for either purpose.

LETTER LXVII.

To Mahommed Ghous; *same date.* (18*th June.*)

Some time since, a *Distich*, according to the *Juml* form or rule,(1) was communicated to you, and has, no doubt, been comprehended by you. A scroll, exhibiting the details of that rule, and which will make you completely acquainted with the subject, is now enclosed. Nobody besides yourself is to be admitted to a knowledge of it; and when you have any thing of a particular or secret nature to communicate, you must write in this cypher.

N. B. At the end of the foregoing letter a *Distich* is added, which I take to be the *Distich* referred to in the beginning of it, though that would seem to have been transmitted on a former occasion. Of the scroll spoken of, nothing appears. I omit the *Distich*, because I am, at present, unable to make out the meaning of it.

OBSERVATIONS.

The title of this letter assigns it to Mahommed *Ghous:* but I incline to think that *Ghous* is an error of my transcriber, for *Ghyds*. If not, I am unable to say who

(1) *Juml* is the arithmetical rule of *addition*, upon the principle of which the cypher in question (which I do not at present comprehend) may possibly have been founded.

who Mahommed *Ghous* was, or what diplomatic situation he filled; for such, it is reasonable to suppose, must have been his employment, from the injunction given him to write occasionally in cypher.

LETTER LXVIII.

To KUMRÛDDEEN KHÂN; *dated* 6*th* JAAFURY. (19*th June.*)

YOUR letter, advising us of your having detached a *Risâla* to *Kunnek-geery*, has been received, and we approve of what you have done. We desire [however] that you will particularly state, whose *Risâla* you have sent [on this service], as well as what number of cavalry it consists of. Your are to send the pay abstracts(1) of this cavalry to Mohyûddeen Ali Khân, the *Dewân* of *Kurpah.*

Having erected batteries close to the walls of the fort, and well breached the same, you will, with the concurrence of the *Sipahdârs* and other commanders with you, assault and reduce the place. It will be better, however, to endeavour, to the utmost of your power, to gain possession of it by *management*,(2) and by striking an awe into the garrison. It must be stormed only in case of absolute necessity.

OBSERVATIONS.

The kind of *management* here recommended to Kumrûddeen Khân will more fully appear in subsequent letters. It consisted in the practice of every unprincipled art that might tend to circumvent the garrison, and induce them to submit to terms.

(1) In the original تصديق *Tusdeek.* I am not certain that I have rendered the term rightly.

(2) In the original حكمت عملي *Hikmut-iumly*, which signifies, *finesse, trick, stratagem, circumvention, &c.*

LETTER LXIX.

To the same; dated SERINGAPATAM, 8*th* JAAFURY. (21*st June.*)

YOUR letter has passed under our view, and its contents are duly understood.

We notice what you state, respecting the mortality prevailing among the *Jyshe*,[1] in consequence of the unhealthiness[2] of your position, and approve of your having dispatched the commanders of companies[3] into the adjacent districts, in search of recruits to fill up the vacancies [which have occurred]. You must, furthermore, order additional levies, for the purpose of completing your own *Kushoon*, as well as to enable you to send a supply to the Presence.

There are physicians attached to your *Kushoon:* let them be strictly enjoined to attend diligently to the care of your sick. The officers, also, of the said *Kushoon*, must be peremptorily directed to prevent desertion among their men. The horses and cattle belonging to your baggage should be dispatched to some place abounding in forage, and the *Risâladârs*, having charge of them, must be instructed accordingly.

Agreeably to our former directions, let a capitulation be granted to the besieged, allowing them to depart with their arms and accoutrements. Kâlâ Pundit, with his family and kindred, and the principal bankers, must also be induced, by *engagements*,[4] to descend from the fort, upon doing which they are to be placed under a guard, and ten *lacks* of *pagodas* to be demanded of them, for the ravages committed in our territories.

N

(1) Or that part of the army composed of irregular infantry.

(2) Original اختلاف آب وهوا "badness of the air and water."

(3) Original سرخيلان *Sur-kheelân*; literally the *heads of tribes*. A company of irregulars appears to have been called a *Kheel*, while a company of regulars was called a *Jowk*.

(4) Original قول *Kowl.*

tories. If they pay this sum, it will be well; otherwise they must be kept in confinement. In short, you are, by finesse, to get the aforesaid *Pundit*, together with his kindred and the bankers, out of the fort, and *then* to secure their persons.

[A few lines, containing other directions of no consequence, are here omitted.]

When your batteries are erected close to the walls of the fort, and the ditch is completely filled, you will, if the measure be approved of by the *Sipahdárs*, advance to the assault: otherwise the attempt will not be proper, inasmuch as this is a *hill-fort affair*.(5)

N.B. A letter, of the same tenor and date, but less in detail, was dispatched to Bûrhânûddeen.

LETTER LXX.

To the same; dated 10th Jaafury. *(23d June.)*

We have received your letter, acknowledging the receipt of twenty-one thousand *pagodas;* and representing that, so far from that sum sufficing for the payment of all your troops, it is inadequate even to the payment of the regular infantry. It is understood. Adverting to this very circumstance, we some time since wrote to you, desiring you to transmit to us a full and distinct statement of the monthly disbursements of the troops under your command, in order that we might make you the necessary remittances. We now repeat those directions; upon your complying with which we will take your report into consideration, and supply you with money [according as may appear requisite to us].

N.B. There follows here another short passage, respecting the pay of the troops, which I suspect to have been miscopied, but which is, at any rate, unintelligible to me.

(5) Original مقدمه قلعه كوهي

LETTER LXXI.

To the BÂDSHÂH ;[1] *dated* 10*th* JAAFURY. (23*d June.*)

UPON receipt of the Imperial Mandate, [my] glorified head touched the summit of honour. The special gifts of ennobling quality [or virtue], which your Majesty, in your boundless favour, graciously bestowed [on me], by the hands of Râo Bâl Mukn Doss, also arrived in the most auspicious conjuncture, and put [me] in possession of the wealth of distinction and pre-eminence. In acknowledgment of this magnificent donation, [I] respectfully offer [my] most humble obeisance.

This stedfast believer, with a view to the support of the firm religion of Mahommed, undertook [some time since] the chastisement of the Nazarene tribe; who, unable to maintain the war [I] waged against them, solicited peace [of me] in the most abject manner. This is so notorious a fact, as not to require to be enlarged on. With the divine aid and blessing of God, it is now again [my] steady determination to set about the total extirpation and destruction of the enemies of the faith.

In token of [my] sincere attachment [or devotion] to your Majesty, [I] send, *by way of Nuzr*, a hundred and twenty-one gold *Mohrs* to your resplendent Presence: let them be [or may they be] honoured by [your Majesty's] acceptance. [I] am humbly hopeful, that [I] may continue to be honoured and distinguished by the receipt of your ennobling commands. More would exceed the bounds of respect.

N 2

(1) That is, the reigning emperor, or sovereign, of *Dehli*, Shâh Allum. This letter is entitled an "*Urzdásht*," i. e. a petition, memorial, or humble address.

OBSERVATIONS.

Notwithstanding the apparent air of humility, which may be thought to pervade the first paragraph, in particular, of the foregoing letter, it is nevertheless remarkably deficient in the forms of respect, invariably observed in all addresses to the Emperor of *Hindostan* (even though " fallen from his high estate") from those acknowledging him as their sovereign. The writer here does not once style himself, as is customary, " the slave," " the devoted servant," or even " the dependent" (in any respect) of Shâh Allum. The very manner in which he offers his *Nuzr* is lofty, and unsuitable to the occasion; but is still less offensive and affronting than the *Nuzr* itself, as will be seen by the following letter. In short, the address is marked throughout with a strong and visible repugnance to any direct or express acknowledgment of the imperial authority. This is more especially shown in the studied omission of the nominative case, the use of which would have reduced him to the necessity of employing some of the ordinary terms of respect appropriate to similar occasions; such as, " this slave," or the like. The nominative, in fact, occurs but once in the course of the letter; and then it is not " this devoted " servant," but " this stedfast believer" in Mahommed.

There can be no doubt, that by the Nazarenes, mentioned in the second paragraph, the English are meant; and that the peace alluded to is that of *Mangalore*, concluded in March 1784, or about fifteen months previously to the date of the letter under consideration. Here, then, we have an indisputable proof, that it was " the steady determination" of the *Sultan*, as early, *at least*, as June 1785, to seize the first favourable occasion of " utterly extirpating and " destroying" us. It is highly probable, however, that this resolution was taken long before it was announced to Shâh Allum, and, in short, that it was coeval with the very treaty by which he bound himself to maintain the relations of amity with us. Unfortunately, his instructions to the first embassy which he dispatched to *Europe* (via *Constantinople*) and which I conceive to be that alluded to in Letter VII, have not been preserved, or, at least discovered; otherwise, there is abundant reason to suppose, that this document would have fully shown, that a

vigorous

vigorous prosecution of the war against us, was an object which never ceased to occupy his chief attention, from the moment of his accession to the *Musnud.* Subsequent events, indeed, compelled him to suspend, for some time, but not to abandon, his hostile purposes; nor would he seem to have ever taken any particular pains to conceal them. In his own *Durbár* he certainly did not: and there is sufficient ground for concluding, that he was not more reserved on the subject, in his occasional communications to other foreign or independent powers, than tothe Emperor of *Dehli.* It is not unlikely, indeed, that he *wrote* with less freedom than he *spoke* of his intentions, or than he authorized his diplomatic agents to speak of them. Oral declarations could be easily disclaimed, and would be difficult to prove; while written ones, unless very cautiously expressed, might lead to premature discovery. Accordingly he has not, in the present letter, distinctly and explicitly stated, that the English were " the enemies of the faith," whom he was determined " to extirpate;" although few persons will entertain any doubt on the subject. Still, however, if the letter had been intercepted, or communicated to the British government, and he had been questioned regarding it, he might have pretended that he meant the *Koorgs,* or *Nairs,* or *Mahrattahs;* all of whom being infidels, as well as the English, might be equally considered as " enemies of the faith." It is not to be denied, that the *Sultan,* all this while, kept up a cold and formal intercourse, by letter, with the British government in *India;* but there can be little question that this was a constraint, to which he submitted with reluctance; and only because he could not have waved such a correspondence, without manifesting, thereby, to that government itself, and in a manner more direct and explicit than he was yet prepared to do, the hostile spirit by which he was actuated towards it. In fine, though he either did not deem it necessary, or was unable, from the violence of his hatred, to conceal his designs against us from his own dependents, or from some of the foreign princes and states with whom he was in correspondence, still it is not to be supposed, that he was absolutely indifferent to our being apprized of them; since, no doubt, he would rather have taken us by surprise, than have found us prepared to resist him: he, therefore, continued to maintain an outward show of distant civility towards us, till weary of waiting for the assistance he had been led to expect from

from the French, and no longer able, perhaps, to restrain the rancour which animated him against us, he at length gave full vent to it; and by an open attack on our ally, the *Rájah* of *Travancore*, plunged into that war from which he had hitherto abstained, only because he hoped, by delay, to prosecute it to greater advantage. But with his impetuous feelings, delay, beyond a certain point, was intolerable; and, therefore, yielding to those feelings, he willingly incurred the hazards of a contest, to which, though standing alone, he doubtlessly thought himself more equal than the event proved him to be.

The only remaining observation, suggested by the foregoing letter, relates to the professed object of the last war waged by Hyder Ali Khân against the English; for the war alluded to in the second paragraph must, of course, have been that of 1780, though the *Sultan*, on this occasion, has thought proper to sink the name of his father. This war is said to have been undertaken "with a "view to the support of the Mahommedan religion." This may serve as a clue to the real, however covert, meaning of Mahommedans, and particularly bigotted ones, whenever they talk of "holy wars," of "wars entered into for the advance-"ment or security of *Islám*," and of "the extirpation of the enemies of the "faith." This language is susceptible, no doubt, of being applied to other infidels besides the Nazarenes; but the time and occasion of its use, to say nothing of other circumstances, always sufficiently indicate who are actually intended. Thus, in the present case, the context so plainly points at the English, that we will venture to say, it would be difficult to find a candid and intelligent Mussulman, who would hesitate, for an instant, to declare his conviction, that they, and they alone, were alluded to in the passage in question. Indeed, it may be farther remarked, in confirmation of this opinion, that the "extirpation" of the Mahrattahs would never seem to have been an object in the contemplation of the *Sultan*; whose hatred to that nation was far less virulent than that which he bore to the English; nor was their power viewed by him with the same fear or jealousy. In his disputes with them, the acquisition of some fort or district, or the relinquishment of some pecuniary demand, was probably all that he at any time contended for.

LETTER LXXII.

To Munzoor Ali Khân ;[1] *same Date.* (23d *June.*)

Having heard, from Râo Bâl Mukn Doss, of the many excellencies and virtues which distinguish your character, the information has been productive of the greatest satisfaction to me. A bag,[2] containing an *Urz-dâsht,*[3] addressed to the resplendent Presence, and accompained by a *Nuzr*[4] of a hundred and twenty-one gold *Mohrs,* is herewith dispatched; and I trust to your friendship and kindness, for presenting the same to his Majesty's blessed notice.

Many Mussulmans are in the habit of carrying about their persons (in pockets and the like) for their convenience [or to answer occasional calls] gold *Mohrs* and *Rupees.* But, inasmuch as the gold and silver coins, stamped with the names of the rulers of the age, contravene the prescriptions of our liturgy, I have, on this account, devised and coined, and caused to be circulated, a new and superior kind of gold *Mohr;* in which the names of God, of the Holy Prophet, and of the august Prince of Sanctity and of Sages,[5] are introduced. Of this new coinage is my *Nuzr* to his Majesty composed; and I have likewise sent, in token of friendship, twenty-five of the same sort of gold *Mohrs* for your acceptance.

Considering

(1) Munzoor Ali Khân was the chief of the eunuchs at the court of *Dehli,* and at this period the principal confidential servant of Shâh Allum. He was, in fact, the minister of the day.

(2) Letters to persons of any distinction are usually enclosed in bags, called *Khureeta.* The materials with which these bags are made are regulated by the rank of the person addressed.

(3) An *Urz,* or humble address; a petition.

(4) A present, or offering, from an inferior to a superior.

(5) Meaning Ali.

Considering me to be always anxious to hear of your welfare, you must occasionally make me happy by your friendly letters. Other particulars will be made known to you, by the letter addressed to you by Bâl Mukn Doss. For the rest, may content and gladness attend you.

OBSERVATIONS.

Though the various pseudo-sovereigns, who sprung up on the dissolution or dismemberment of the Mogul Empire, in different parts of *Hindostan*, soon threw off the authority of the Court of *Dehli* in all material points, they, nevertheless, continued to observe towards it some of the external forms of homage and dependence; such as styling themselves, in their addresses to the reigning representative of the house of Timur, "his faithful slave" or "devoted subject;" presenting him on certain festivals, and on other occasions, with the *Nuzrs* appropriate to royalty, and soliciting or accepting titles of honour from him. But the chief symbol, or vestige, of the nominal power, thus conceded to him, consisted in the general practice which had obtained among these upstart rulers, of continuing to stamp the current coins of their respective territories with the usual legend of the imperial coinage; by which means the Emperor, for the time being, became every where ostensibly recognized as the legitimate sovereign; and his name, at least, rescued from oblivion, and even rendered familiar to the people in general. Of this empty honour, Tippoo Sultan was, I believe, the first, and, indeed, the only one(6) of these self-created princes, who thought fit to divest him. Not content, however, with putting this affront upon the aged monarch, he had the temerity to aggravate it in the highest degree, by sending the latter a *Nuzr*, consisting of a coin, from the inscription on which the name and titles of Shâh Allum

(6) For I do not (with Captain Moor) consider the *Abdalli*, or King of *Cábúl*, as forming an exception, that country having been formally ceded by the Emperor, Mahommed Shâh, to the Persians, from whom it was wrested by Ahmed Shâh Abdalli, otherwise called *Dúrány*.

Allum were entirely excluded. The argument, by which he attempted to justify this innovation, was sufficiently curious and frivolous, but was little calculated to reconcile, even a Mahommedan court to it: accordingly, as will hereafter be seen, it was not submitted to in silence.

Never having seen a gold *Mohr*, of the specific coinage employed by the *Sultan* on this occasion, I am, of course, not enabled to say to what degree he adhered, in the legend impressed upon it, to the sanctimonious principle by which he professed to regulate it. The gold *Mohr*, of which a representation is given by Captain Moor, in his Narrative of Little's Campaign,(7) happens to be of the year *Zubrjud*,(8) or six years posterior to the date of the two preceding letters; and in this interval, the *Sultan*, no doubt, might have made some alteration in the inscription.

There is, however, in the publication just referred to, the figure of a double *Rupee*, struck in the same year (namely *Jullo*) in which Tippoo dispatched his *Nuzr* to *Dehli*; and it is probable that the inscription on the gold *Mohrs*, of which the latter consisted, differed little, or perhaps nothing, from that which appears on the *Rupee* of the same year. Assuming this for the fact, let us examine how far the inscription in question corresponds with the description given of it by the *Sultan*, in the foregoing letter.

On one side is the following legend, written here in the order in which I suppose it intended to be read:

١١٩٩

دين احمد درجهان روشن است ز فتح حيدر ضرب پتن سال جلوس سنه هجري

which may be translated, " the religion, or faith, of Ahmed [*i. e.* of Mahommed] " is rendered luminous on earth by the victories of Hyder.(9) Struck at *Putn* " [*i. e. Seringapatam*] in the year *Jullo*(10) [or] *Higera* 1199."

O Here

(7) Vide fig. 4, plate I, page 465.

(8) Captain Moor not being acquainted with the *Sultan's* Kalendar, was not aware that *Zubrjud* was the name of a particular year, *viz.* the forty-fifth of the *Mysore Cycle*, and corresponding with A. D. 1791.

(9) Or, " derives its [present] lustre on earth from the victories of Hyder."

(10) *Jullo* (which, like *Zubrjud*, was not understood by the author of the Narrative) was the 39th year of the *Mysore Cycle*, and coincides with A. D. 1785.

Here *Hyder*, though ostensibly standing for the *Caliph* Ali (one of whose names or titles it was) was, in all probability, intended by the *Sultan* to suggest the idea of his own father; whose name is, by this contrivance, introduced into the legend, without any direct or open deviation from the rule proposed to be followed. In like manner, the word *Futah*, though apparently conveying no other meaning than its usual and obvious one, viz. *victory*, may be safely supposed as designed to shadow out either his own original name, or that of his paternal grandfather, *viz.* Futah Ali Khân. Here, then, in two words, seemingly employed for a different purpose, has he ingeniously managed to impress his coin, not only with one of his own names, but also with those of his father and grandfather; and so far, without any verbal breach of the law he had imposed upon himself.

We will now enquire, how he has succeeded in the exergue, or reverse, of the coin under consideration?

The legend is as follows:

٣
هو السلطان الوحيد العادل سيوم بهاري سال جلو سنه جلوس

That is, "He [*i. e.* God] is the only *Sultan* [or Lord] and dispenser of justice. "3d [of the month] *Behâry*, year *Jullo*, and third of the reign."

It is very remarkable, that the first word in this inscription (or هو) and, consequently, that which immediately precedes the word *Sultan*, is so impressed, as to be susceptible, without any extraordinary licence or exercise of the fancy, of being read Tippoo. For the tail, or lower part of the ه does not appear in its usual form, but assumes something like the figure of a crescent, and might, therefore, be very easily taken for an ornament, instead of a component part of a character. Omitting, then, the tail (as if it were nothing but a flourish) the rest of the word will be exactly the same as if it were the proper name Tippoo, written without the diacritical points, the omission of which, though certainly unusual in coins, is common enough on other occasions. Supposing this, therefore, to have been the *Sultan's* design, the sense would be, "Tippoo, the only *Sultan*, the just."

On the whole, then, it may be observed, that with the help of a few equivoques (of which he seems, on many occasions, to have been very fond) he has contrived, while fulfilling his promise of inserting in his coin none but the names of God, of

the

the Prophet, and of Ali, to impress it also, without actually appearing to do so, with the names of at least "two rulers of the age."

The date on the reverse of the rupee which we have been considering, shows that it was struck on the anniversary of his *Júloos*, or enthronement, which took place on the 3d of *Behâry* of the year *Sukh*;[11] corresponding, as nearly as I can calculate, to the 10th of May 1783; and being, therefore, somewhat more than five months subsequent to the death of Hyder.[12]

It would not be easy to assign any consistent or rational motive for the conduct of the *Sultan*, with respect to the court of *Dehli*. If he thought it capable of promoting any of the objects of his ambition, and was, on this account, desirous of cultivating a good understanding with it, it is rather extraordinary, that he should have adopted the measure of rendering such a *Nuzr* to the Emperor, as a very little reflection might have satisfied him, was but ill calculated to conciliate the favour of that court towards him. If, on the other hand, he neither expected nor desired any thing from it, it is equally strange, that he should have put himself to any trouble or expence, in maintaining an intercouse with it. The mere news of the place (that, too, transmitted to him only at distant intervals) could prove very little interesting, and still less useful to him.

O 2

(11) See the Introduction. This is the word occurring in the reverse of the impression of Tippoo's gold *Mohr* given by Captain Moor; (fig. 4. plate I.) but which he, owing to the misplacing of the diacritical points, was led to read *Sunh.*

(12) If *Sukh*, however, should have been a leap year (a doubt that I have not the means of clearing up) then its commencement would coincide with the 10th or 11th of March (instead of the 9th of April) 1783; and, consequently, the 3d of *Behâry* would be thrown back to the 10th or 11th of April. What leads me to prefer the 10th of May is, that Tippoo, in his Memoirs, fixes the death of his father on the 3d of *Zákiry*. Now from the 3d of *Zákiry* (corresponding to the 1st *Mohurrem*, A. H. 1147) to the 3d of *Behâry*, is exactly five months: so that, if Hyder died in December 1782, it follows that the *Júloos* of his son must have taken place in May, and not in April.

LETTER LXXIII.

To MOAL CHUND *and* SÛJÂN RÂE[1]; *same Date.* (*23d June.*)

YOUR letter, with the newspapers which accompanied it, has passed under our view, and the contents thereof are understood.

A bag, enclosing an address [from us] to the resplendent Presence,[2] together with a hundred and twenty-one gold *Mohrs* of a new coinage, [designed] in the way of *Nuzr*, as likewise a separate bag, to the address of Munzoor Ali Khân, and twenty-five of the same kind of gold *Mohrs*, as a token of [our] friendship [for the said *Khân*], are sent herewith. For the greater security, the gold *Mohrs* have been sewed up in the garments[3] of the messengers. You will, therefore, on their arrival, take the gold *Mohrs* from their garments, and, through the medium of Munzoor Ali Khân, present a hundred and twenty-one of them, with our *Urz-dásht* [or humble address], to his Majesty, delivering the remaining twenty-five to the aforesaid *Khân*.

A bill of exchange for one thousand *rupees* is sent herewith. Out of the amount [when realized] you are to take for yourselves sixteen months' arrears of wages, at thirty *rupees* per month, making four hundred and eighty *rupees*; and a twelvemonth's wages, at the same rate, in advance, being three hundred and sixty *rupees*; or, together, eight hundred and forty *rupees*. Eighteen *rupees*, which are to be paid to the *Hurkâréhs* [or messengers, on their arrival at *Dehli*] being added to this sum, there will remain one hundred and forty-two *rupees*, which you

(1) These persons were the *Sultan's* agents and news-writers at *Dehli*.

(2) Tippoo, in several of his letters, has applied this phrase (حضورپرنور) to himself.

(3) Original حوغدها possibly meant for خرقدها If not, I can make nothing of the word.

you will apply to the payment of the [regular] wages of our *Hurkârehs.* Of the two pair now dispatched, one of them, named Tolârâm and Mhâdâjee, are to receive, the first ten, the other nine *rupees* per month. The second pair, named Kishnajee and Suntajee, are to receive each nine *rupees* per month. Both sets have received from us their wages, at the above rate, for three months; namely, from the beginning of *Rujub* to the end of *Rumuzân* 1199 (A.H.). While they continue with you, they are to be paid at the specified rate, commencing from the month of *Shuvwâl.* When they are dispatched, two months' wages are to be advanced to each pair.

You must [from time to time] faithfully and accurately communicate [to us] the intelligence of that quarter.

You wrote, that you had dispatched to us, by a pair of hired *Hurkârehs,* two baskets of *Bai-dâneh* pomegranates,[4] together with a letter from yourselves. The said *Hurkârehs,* with the letter and baskets, have not [hitherto] arrived.

According to your desire, seventy-two *rupees* have been paid here *to* the last pair of hired *Hurkârehs* dispatched by you. Further particulars will be communicated to you by Râo Bâl Mukn Doss.

OBSERVATIONS.

These two agents would seem to have been natives of *Hindostan,* and personally unknown to the *Sultan;* by whom they were probably employed, on the recommendation of the Bâl Mukn Doss, mentioned in this and the preceding letter.[5]

This

(4) This is the pomegranate without stones. It is not the produce of *Hindostan,* but is brought, together with grapes, apples, and other fruit, from *Câbûl* and the adjacent countries, by the horse merchants.

(5) Various dispatches from these two agents to the *Sultan* were contained among the papers found at *Seringapatam.*

This letter furnishes another instance of the minuteness to which the *Sultan* was accustomed to descend in all matters of disbursement. Another sovereign, in his situation, would have left such details to one of his secretaries, or to the proper officers of the department to which they naturally belonged. But either this was a degree of confidence, which it was foreign to the character of Tippoo to repose in any of his servants, or he was ambitious of appearing to be equally attentive to the most trivial, as well as to the most important affairs of his government: nor can it be denied, that a general impression, to this effect, would tend, in some degree, to secure the fidelity and diligence of those whom he employed.

LETTER LXXIV.

To Kumrûddeen Khân; *dated* 12*th* Jaafury. (25*th June.*)

Your letter has been received, and your account of the batteries of Bûrhânûddeen being completed is understood. We have repeatedly written before now, desiring you to advance your batteries close to the walls of the fort; to destroy these effectually; to fill the ditch; and [finally] with the concurrence and advice of the *Sipahdârs*, to proceed to the assault of the place. Such being the case, it is astonishing that you should still wait, and continually apply to us for fresh orders for storming. [We repeat, however, once more]: In case the walls are destroyed, and the ditch is filled, you must, with the advice and concurrence of the commanders with you, proceed to the assault and reduction of the place.

OBSERVATIONS.

The justice of the reproof contained in the preceding letter may be very fairly questioned: for though it is certain, that the *Sultan* had expressed considerable impatience to obtain possession of *Nergûnd*, yet his orders, relative to the means by by which that object was to be pursued, could not be said to have been so explicit and distinct, as to leave no doubt of his real wishes and intentions; for in Letter LIX he directs a negociation to be opened with the garrison for the surrender of the place, and about a week after (Letter LXVIII) he suggests the expediency of getting possession of it, by what he calls *management*, plainly saying, at the same time, "that it was not to be stormed, excepting in case of absolute necessity." The letter immediately following the last (or Letter LXIX) is not more decisive or explicit than the others. Thus it appears, that it was not without reason that Kumrûddeen was desirous of receiving more precise and positive instructions for his guidance.

LETTER LXXV.

To MAHOMMED GHYÂS *and* NOOR MAHOMMED KHÂN; *dated* 14*th* JAAFURY. (27*th June.*)

IF the chiefs of that place consent to Noor Mahommed Khân's repairing hither, it will be well: and if they should dismiss you both, you must both, after formally declaring them to be responsible for the consequences,(1) set out for our Presence.

LETTER LXXVI.

To SHAIKH AHMED, *son of* MAHOMMED MUKRUM, *the Merchant; dated* 15*th* JAAFURY, *and endorsed* "KOWL-NÂMEH."(1*) (28*th June.*)

HAVING received a full account of you from the verbal report of Meer Mahommed

(1) In the original, "after fixing all blame upon them."

(1*) A *Kowl-námeh* is a written engagement, whereby the person executing it promises to grant protection, or some particular favors or immunities, to the party receiving it. *Kowl* means also a capitulation.

Mahommed Rizâ,[2] as well as from the representation of Mahommed Mukrum, we, in consequence, write to desire, that you will, immediately on receipt of this our bounteous mandate, set out with the utmost confidence of mind for our Presence, accompanied by your family, and such other persons as may be disposed to come with you. On your arrival here, you shall in all things experience our care and protection, agreeably to your wishes, and be appointed to the charge of the mercantile concerns, &c.[3] A proper place shall be assigned you for a factory; and such advances of money be made you, as may be requisite for enabling you to carry on your trade [advantageously], all the profits of which shall rest with you for the term of two years: during which time, also, we promise to grant you an exemption from all duties on your merchandize. Repair, therefore, to our Presence, without fear or distrust. All remaining particulars will be explained to you by the letter of Mahommed Mukrum, and the verbal communications of Meer Ali Rizâ.[4]

OBSERVATIONS.

The encouragement here held out to Shaikh Ahmed, seems to have been abundantly liberal, and shows how much the *Sultan* had it at heart to open a trade with those countries, of which he had no jealousy. It does not appear at what place Shaikh Ahmed was a resident, or whether he accepted the offers of the *Sultan*.

(2) Literally, " by the tongue of."

(3) I am doubtful whether the charge, or superintendance, of the *Sultan's* own commercial concerns is meant to be included.

(4) Most probably the same person as the Meer Mahommed Rizâ, mentioned in the beginning of the letter.

LETTER LXXVII.

To BÛRHÂNÛDDEEN ; *dated* 16*th* JAAFURY. (29*th June.*)

You write, that " the besieged have solicited a capitulation, through " the *Aumil* of *Bâdâmy*, stipulating only for their lives and honour,(1) " but requiring the guarantee of the *Mâgrycotah* man." In answer to this proposal, they must be told, that if they are willing to treat with the commanders of our army, you are ready to grant them a capitulation, but that the *Mâgrycotah* man, not being a servant [a subject] of ours, his agency in the affair cannot be admitted.

We formerly issued orders for your dispatching your cavalry to graze [or forage], and we now repeat those orders. We also direct, that strict injunctions be given to the baggage department, for sending all the lean *Tatoos*,(2) bullocks, &c. to grass, the rainy season being now *at hand.*(3)

OBSERVATIONS.

The *Sultan* would not, for reasons sufficiently obvious, agree to any guarantee which he could not subsequently violate with perfect impunity. The garrison of *Nergând* knew whom they had to deal with; and, therefore, naturally sought to obtain a better pledge for their security, than they could receive from the " commanders of his army," or any other person depending upon him. They were, in the end, however, compelled to trust to the good faith of the commanders, and the event was such as they seem to have anticipated.

P

(1) In the original جان وآبرو where by *âbroo* is usually meant, more particularly, the sanctity of the *Harem*, or female part of a family.

(2) A kind of poney, or small degenerate horse.

(3) Such I take to be the strict meaning of دربيش است though I think it might also be rendered *set in* : and this last sense would, no doubt, better agree with the time of the year, (*viz.* the end of June.)

LETTER LXXVIII.

To the SÂNORE Man ;[1] *dated* 18*th* JAAFURY. (1*st July.*)

YOUR letter, containing an account of your welfare, adorned the face of arrival, and imparted joy and pleasure to us. What the pen of friendship has traced, in excuse for past offences, is comprehended. Of this matter not the slightest impression remains on the mind of this friend : the only fault (or failure) imputable to that friend being, that he did not examine with care and diligence into the state of his revenue accounts ; the consequence of which has been, a heavy deficiency in the amount realized. Our accomptants have made themselves thoroughly acquainted with the details of the territory held *conditionally* by you ;[2] and after making every fair and proper deduction for military charges, have ascertained the balance justly due to us from you.[3] You must, therefore, agreeably to your former promises, speedily pay the amount into the hands of the bankers, and dispatch the latter to us. You must not suffer any delay to take place in this matter. With respect to the accomptants and others in your employ, who have been guilty of the malversations [in question], you should compel them, by rigorous proceedings, to make restitution of the sums of which they have plundered you.

In regard to the servants and *Taalûkdârs* of that friend, we assure him that no interruption or disturbance shall be given to them by any one.

(1) It is Abdûl Hakeem Khân, the *Nabob* of *Shanoor*, that is here meant by this slighting designation ; which, though (no doubt) confined to the record, or entry, is no unequivocal mark of the little account he was held in at *Seringapatam*.

(2) See Letter XVI.

(3) This balance was stated, in Letter XVI, at about thirty-eight *lacks* of *rupees*.

LETTER LXXIX.

To Mahommed Ghyâs *and* Noor Mahommed Khân; *same Date.* (1*st July.*)

Your letter of the 9th of *Jaafury*, was received on the 18th of the same month [or this day]. You write, "that in the course of a con-"ference which you had had with Râo Râsta, Hurry Pundit [1] being "present gave a licence to his tongue, of a nature that tended to lower "and disgrace you; and that, in consequence, you thought it utterly "inexpedient to remain there any longer.

It is known. Such being the ungracious and unpalatable state of things, what advantage can arise from it? That friend, therefore, together with Noor Mahommed Khân, must, at any rate, and without leaving a single individual of your mission behind you, set out for our Presence, nor wait for any farther orders.

OBSERVATIONS.

It might be supposed, from the recital here made by the *Sultan* of the letter of the envoys, that the latter had not communicated the offensive observations of Hurry Pundit in detail, but satisfied themselves with stating, that they had been of the most affronting nature. Be this as it may, it is clear that the *Sultan's* warmest indignation was excited on the occasion: nor did it immediately subside, since we shall presently see him repeating his order for the return of the envoys, in a still more peremptory tone than in the foregoing dispatch. But however wounded his pride might have been at first, by the injurious language imputed to

P 2 Hurry

(1) Hurry Pundit was at the head of the army of the Mahrattah empire; and, at a subsequent period, commanded the army sent by the government of *Poonah* to co-operate with Lord Cornwallis.

Hurry Pundit, he seems ultimately to have subdued, or at least to have repressed, his anger; inasmuch as he thought proper, at no great distance of time, to change his mind with regard to the recall of his agents.

LETTER LXXX.

To Meer Moaalla Khân, *Kilaadâr of Mudgul; dated 20th Jaafury.* (*3d July.*)

[After compliments]....... We have just learned, from the report of the Deputy Governor of *Gujunder-ghur*, that that friend, having collected together a body of troops, maintains himself with great firmness in the fort of *Mudgul;* soliciting, however, at the same time, our assistance: we therefore write, to desire that you will, without any reserve or ceremony, state to us what succours you require, when, with the blessing of God, the same shall be effectually furnished.

OBSERVATIONS.

I am not quite certain with regard to the real name of the fort here mentioned, since, in the original, it is written both *Mudgul* and *Nudgul.* From the style and general tenor of this letter it might be concluded, that it was not addressed to any person in the service of the *Sultan,* but rather to the governor of a fort (belonging either to the Mahrattahs or to the *Nizâm*) who had entertained a traiterous correspondence with the *Sultan.* I am not, at present, sufficiently informed on the subject to clear up this point satisfactorily; but if, in the course of this work, I should meet with any new light respecting it, I will communicate it in the Appendix.

LETTER LXXXI.

To BÛRHÂNÛDDEEN ; *dated* 23*d* JAAFURY. (6*th July*.)

You write " that the *Piâdehs* from *Surhutty*, who were stationed " with Kumrûddeen Khân, have run away, and that light of our eyes(1) " has placed a *Dalwâr*(2) and a *Vakeel* in custody of a guard." It is known. Furnish Kumrûddeen Khân with other *Piâdehs*, in the room of those who have deserted; keep the two persons you mention in irons; and seize, for the use of the *Sircar*, the horses and camels belonging to them.

OBSERVATIONS.

The context would, in this place, seem to imply, that the *Dalwâr* and *Vakeel*, here mentioned, belonged to *Surhutty*, and were seized and confined by Bûrhânûddeen, as a sort of hostages for the fugitive *Piâdehs*. If this was not the case, it is impossible to say, at this time, who the persons in question were. The rigorous proceeding against them, here directed, may seem to exceed the measure of justice; but it is probable, that it was not designed so much as a punishment, as a means of accomplishing the recovery of the deserters, Such expedients are but too common, in similar cases, throughout *Hindostan*; the East-India Company's possessions excepted.

(1) Meaning Bûrhânûddeen, See Note 1, Letter XXX.

(2) This term, I believe, denotes a minister, or principal manager; as the *Dalwâr* of *Mysore*. *Vakeel* has been already explained, at Note 1, Letter XIII.

LETTER LXXXII.

To MAHOMMED GHYÂS *and* NOOR MAHOMMED KHÂN; *dated 27th* JAAFURY. (*10th July.*)

YOUR two letters, of the 12th and 14th of *Jaafury* [25th and 27th June] have been received. You write, "that what Hurry Pundit and "the rest of them propose is, to dispatch Noor Mahommed Khân to us, "and to take an engagement from you to pay down the money [claimed "of us], if, after his departure, there should be any delay in the trans-"mission of the same from hence." It is known. If any message, to the above effect, should be actually sent to you, your answer must be, "that you are our servants, and therefore dare not enter into any "engagement whatsoever without our orders; but that *it was most pro-"bable*, that after Noor Mahommed Khân's arrival, and *when we "should have ascertained from him the* [*true*] *state of things, we should "consider the means of transmitting the money.*"

You moreover write, "that Râo Râsta has desired you to represent to "us, that the *Zemindâr* of *Nergûnd*, having been brought to agree to "the payment of a lack and seventy-five thousand *rupees*, by way of "amercement, it is wished that we would direct the siege of *Nergûnd* "to be discontinued." It is known. The aforesaid *Zemindâr* has collected from our dominions ten *lacks* of *pagodas*: waving, therefore, all consideration of an amercement, let him make restitution of what he has levied from our dominions, and then we will certainly raise the siege of *Nergûnd*.

OBSERVATIONS.

It is observable, that, in the present dispatch, the *Sultan* is far from repeating his orders of the 1st July, for the immediate departure of both his agents from *Poonah:* on the contrary, he seems satisfied with the idea of Noor Mahommed Khân's return singly, and thereby tacitly approves of the continuance of Mahommed Ghyâs at his post. His indignation at the behaviour of Hurry Pundit had probably cooled in the interval; but it was soon revived, as we shall see, by a fresh affront from the same quarter. It must be allowed, that the answer directed in the foregoing letter to be returned to the expected message, or proposal, from the Mahrattah ministers, was not much calculated to produce any favorable change in the department, either of Hurry Pundit or of his colleagues.

LETTER LXXXIII.

To BÛRHÂNÛDDEEN; *dated 1st Dârâey. (14th July.)*

You write, "that you never buy caravan horses." It is known. But though you never purchase any, you must direct the *Silahdârs* to do so.

You further write, "that the labourers with you receive their daily "subsistence from the *Aumils* of the districts which have supplied "them." But there is no necessity for this. Let them be paid by you, from the day on which they joined you, and as long as they may remain with you.

We have learnt from our beloved son,(1) Meer Kumrûddeen, that a camel-courier, belonging to Râo Râsta, has arrived with a letter addressed

(1) Original برخوردار "happy, prosperous." It is most commonly applied as a term of endearment by parents to children, in the same manner as نورچشم and اقبال نشان

addressed to you and him. Having duly considered the contents thereof, you will dispatch such an answer by the courier, as you shall judge proper.

OBSERVATIONS.

I was in some doubt, respecting the meaning of *Caravan* horses, till Colonel Wilks, the author of the admirable History of *Mysore*, recently published, informed me, that the strings of horses brought for sale by the northern merchants, and others to the south of *India*, were so called. It would not be easy to guess why Bûrhânûddeen made it a rule (as he would appear to have done) never to buy horses from these dealers. But whatever objection that commander might have to such purchases, the *Sultan* appears to have had none; as otherwise it is not probable that the merchants would have resorted to his dominions, or that he should have been desirous that the *Silahdârs* should deal with them.

What is said here of the letter from Râo Râsta, seems to confirm, in some measure, the idea suggested on a former occasion,(2) *viz.* that Bûrhânûddeen exercised the chief authority in the army employed at this period on the Mahrattah frontier. His name probably stood foremost in the superscription of Hurry Pundit's letter; which, on that account, or because he was generally considered as commander-in-chief, was, in the first instance, carried and delivered to him.

The authority given to Bûrhânûddeen, by the last paragraph of the foregoing letter, seems to exceed the usual measure of the *Sultan's* confidence in his servants, of whatever rank they might be.

LETTER LXXXIV.

To Bûrhânûddeen; *dated 2d Dáráey.* (15*th July.*)

By a letter from Ibrâheem Ali Khân it appears to us, that the *Risáladârs*, Syed Humeed, Bubi Ali Baig, and Ibrâheem Khân, have received

(2) See observations on Letter XXXI.

received bribes, &c.(1) from various persons. A copy of this letter, the original of which has been deposited in the *Kuchurry* of the *Jyshe*, is enclosed. We, in consequence, direct, that the aforesaid *Risâladârs* be divested of their commands,(2) that they be confronted [with their accusers], obliged to refund to the *Sircar* the money [they have corruptly obtained], and finally, that they be kept under restraint, and the matter reported to us; when we will send other *Risâladârs* from hence [to supply their places].

OBSERVATIONS.

This letter does not afford a very favorable specimen of the *Sultan's* notions of justice, or of his mode of proceeding against persons charged with crimes or misdemeanors. He acts upon the bare information of Ibrâheem Ali Khân, as if the truth of the charge preferred by the latter were already undeniably established, inflicting every penalty upon the accused before trial, that could be inflicted, in the event of their guilt being completely proved. It is true, that he directs a kind of trial to be instituted; but the possibility of the innocence of the accused is neither contemplated nor provided for. The result is to be communicated to the *Sultan;* not in order that he may, in case of the acquittal of the accused, give directions for their restoration to their rank, liberty, and property, but only that he may immediately send new officers to supply their vacant places. All this is at variance, not only with common justice, but even with the usual mode of proceeding against military offenders of the rank of officers, prescribed by the *Sultan's* own regulations; one of which appears to have directed, that "the sword "of the accused officer to be taken from him, and deposited in the guard-room, there "to be kept during the trial of the accused, and till ordered to be restored to him "by the *Sultan*." On the other hand, it must be acknowledged that the enquiry

Q commanded

(1) In the original رشوت وغیره What the "*&c.*" refers to, it is not possible to guess.

(2) Literally, "be turned out of their *Risâlas*."

commanded to be made, and the postponement of the appointment of successors to the accused till the result was known, are circumstances, which seem to show that the *Sultan*, notwithstanding the precipitancy and irregularity of his proceeding, on this occasion, did not deem it absolutely impossible that the *Risáladárs* might be able to clear themselves; in which case it is, perhaps, only fair to suppose, that he would have made them suitable reparation for the injury they had suffered.

LETTER LXXXV.

To the same; *dated* 3d *Dáráey*. (16*th July*.)

We have learned, by a letter from the *Sipahdár*, Mahommed Ali, " that he has carried his approaches to the edge of the ditch; that " the walls and batteries on his side are levelled to the ground; and " that the ditch only remains to be filled." That, then, is a trifling affair. Let the ditch be filled, and, *with the consent and concurrence of all*, let the place be stormed and taken. If, however, the garrison will capitulate, it will be well: and [in this case] with the exception of Kâlâ Pundit, the rest may be allowed their lives and arms; but the *Pundit's* person must be secured. In the event, however, of [your being obliged to proceed to] the assault of the place, *every living creature in it, whether man or woman, old or young, child, dog, cat, or any thing else, must be put to the sword*, with the single exception of Kâlâ Pundit. What more?

OBSERVATIONS.

The sanguinary and ferocious disposition of Tippoo Sultan is here displayed in the most glaring and odious colours. The spirit of Nâdir Shâh appears to breathe through

through every line of the concluding sentence of this memorable letter. Kâlâ Pundit was, most probably, reserved for some signal punishment; or, perhaps, he was exempted from the general carnage here directed, because his immediate death might have frustrated the *Sultan's* views to pecuniary indemnification. It is rather extraordinary, that this last consideration did not also lead him to make an exception, in his exterminating mandate, in favor of the wealthy merchants and bankers of the place; to secure whose persons he was subsequently extremely anxious.

LETTER LXXXVI.

To Kumrûddeen Khân; *dated* 3d *Dârâey.* (*16th July.*)

You write, "that, in conformity with our orders, you have trans-"ferred the *Sipahdâr* Mahommed Ali and his *Kushoon* to Bûrhânûd-"deen, and in his place have taken Shaikh Unser and his *Kushoon*, "which you have posted in the trenches." It is known and approved. You will cause the pay abstracts of Shaikh Unser's *Kushoon* to be made out, and issue the amount. Bûrhânûddeen will issue the pay of Mahommed Ali's *Kushoon.*

You further state, "that Syed Meerân, the *Kilaadâr* of *Dhârwâr*, "has replied to your letter to him, 'that all the powder and shot at that "'place had been dispatched to Bûrhânûddeen, and that it would not "'be in his power to furnish another ball or grain of powder, till a "'fresh supply reached him from *Nugr*.'" It is known. Orders, both to Syed Meerân and to the *Taalûkdâr* of *Nugr*, are gone from us, to send you powder and shot, which will reach you in due time.

You have also written, "that the works on your attack are com-"pleted, but that those on the side of Bûrhânûddeen want two or "four days[1] of being finished: at the end of which time, after due "consultation with the *Sipahdârs* and other commanders of the army, "an assault would be made, and the fort of *Nergûnd* be conquered." It is known. If the garrison will surrender the place upon terms, it will be well, as, in this case, the loss of men will be avoided. You must, otherwise, advancing your works on every side, breaching the walls, and filling up the ditch, proceed, with the advice and concurrence of the *Sipahdârs* and commanders of the army, to storm the place; which should be done the first favorable opportunity, either at day-break or at noon.

The tank-diggers[2] must, on their arrival from *Shânoor*, be placed under a guard, and dispatched to the Presence.

You write, "that a camel-courier, belonging to Râo Râsta, had "arrived with a letter, addressed to you and Bûrhânûddeen, who, you "conclude, had forwarded the same to us." It is known. The letter in question has not been received: had it reached us, we should immediately have replied to it. You and Bûrhânûddeen [therefore] after [duly] considering the contents of the aforesaid letter, must dispatch such an answer to Râo Râsta, by his courier, as you shall judge to be proper.

(1) This is a peculiarity of the Persian idiom, in which it is, at least, as usual to say *two or four*, *ten or twelve*, as two or three, ten or eleven, &c.

(2) Original ورديواران my translation of which is on the authority of Colonel Munro, the term being entirely unknown to me.

LETTER LXXXVII.

To the SIPAHDÁR, MAHOMMED ALI; *same Date.* (16*th July.*)

YOU write, "that you have carried on your approaches to the edge of "the ditch, the filling of which is the only thing remaining to be "done." It is known. Where is the great difficulty of filling the ditch? That, therefore, being done, let the place *(every one concurring in the propriety of the measure)* be stormed and taken.

OBSERVATIONS.

It might almost be inferred, from the tenor of this letter, that Mahommed Ali, though a raw and inexperienced officer, was co-ordinate in authority with Bûrhânûddeen and Kumrûddeen. But the only conclusion to be justly drawn from this document is, that the *Sultan* was in the habit of corresponding, separately, with the superior officers of his army, who probably acted as so many spies upon the chief commanders. Such a wretched system would be naturally enough suggested, by the characteristic jealousy and distrust of the *Sultan.*

LETTER LXXXVIII.

To KUMRÛDDEEN; *dated* 5*th* DÁRÁEY. (18*th July.*)

[AFTER an immaterial passage, respecting a supply of money, the letter thus proceeds:]—

All the operations of the siege are completed, and the walls of the place

place demolished: why, then, this delay? If the garrison will evacuate the fort on terms, it will be well; otherwise, watching a suitable opportunity, *and acting with the concurrence* of the *Sipahdárs*, and other commanders of the army, you must take the place by assault.

LETTER LXXXIX.

To the SIPAHDÁR, MAHOMMED ALI; *same Date.* (18*th July.*)

You write, "that placing yourself at the head of five companies[1] "from the *Jyshe-Risálas*, you advanced into the ditch; from whence, "after putting to the sword every man of the enemy found there, some "of your *Kushoon* pushed on, and ascending the walls, planted their "colours on one of the towers [or bastions]. Here, however, the "enemy's people, assembling in great numbers, and assailing ours with "musquetry, hand-granades,[2] &c. you [thought proper to] recall "your men from the tower, [and to content yourself with] making a "lodgement in advance.[3]"

It is known. Your duty is to perform such services as you are ordered to execute, and not to act according to the suggestions of your own mind. You must not again proceed in this idle manner, but regulate your conduct by the general opinion.

(1) In the original جوق *jowk*.

(2) Original حقه وبتي with the precise meaning of which I am unacquainted.

(3) This is not the precise sense of درمرحله قايم كردم Perhaps the *Murhuleh* (*i. e.* stage or halting place) may here mean the covert-way.

OBSERVATIONS.

If Mahommed Ali was a raw and inexperienced soldier,[4] he seems, at least, to have been a bold and enterprising one. The action here described would appear to have been performed without the knowledge, or orders, of his superiors; and is, therefore, very properly condemned by the *Sultan*, whose reproof on the occasion was, perhaps, sufficiently mild.

LETTER XC.

To Bûrhânûddeen; *dated 6th Dárâey.* (*19th July.*)

You write, "that your approaches are carried to the foot of the wall, "and that it is determined to storm the place in two or three days; that "Dileer Dil Khân says, he must go and forage with his people; that a "numerous force is required for the approaching assault; and that, "with our permission, you will detain the said Khân, together with the "dismounted men of the cavalry *Kuchurry*, until the conclusion of the "business." It is known: and we, in consequence, direct that you detain the aforesaid Khân, as well as the men you have mentioned, till the period you propose; when you will allow them to go and forage.

OBSERVATIONS.

The two preceding letters satisfactorily prove, how independently the superior officers of the army sometimes acted, and how feeble Bûrhânûddeen's authority over

(4) See Letter XXII.

over them was. But this is an evil inherent in the constitution of all Indian armies: and, perhaps, it was less prevalent in that of *Mysore,* than in any other native army of *Hindostan.*

It might at first view, and on general principles, be supposed, that it was much easier to introduce strict military discipline into the armies of arbitrary states, like those of the East, than into any other: and so, no doubt, it would be, if it were not for the distrust and jealousy natural to the rulers of such states, who fear to invest their commanders with the powers necessary to the due maintenance of subordination, lest the latter should, on any occasion, be tempted to employ them for traiterous purposes. Instead, therefore, of strengthening the hands of their generals, by concentrating in them the powers which they are compelled to delegate (but which they circumscribe as much as possible), they judge it expedient, with a view to their own security, to divide and parcel them out among the different commanders; and, in fine, to establish in their armies such a system of checks, as leaves but little efficient or useful authority any where. To this more general and remote cause of the great insubordination observable in the armies of the East, may be added another, more particular and immediate (arising, as it were, necessarily out of the former); and that is, the total want of fixed or written rules for their government: the consequence of which, of course, is, that disorder and confusion pervade the whole body, almost every thing relating to which, is made to depend on the caprice and partial views of individuals.

Tippoo Sultan, as if sensible of this last defect in the constitution of his army, in common with those of his neighbours, would appear to have aimed at correcting it in some measure; and for this purpose (though, probably, not with any very deep or accurate views of the subject) caused to be compiled and disseminated a military code, or treatise, which he entitled *Futhŭl' Mŭjăhideen,* or, " the " Triumph of the holy Warriors." I have not, hitherto, had an opportunity of examining this work, with attention; but the impression made on me by a cursory inspection of it, some years ago, inclines me to think, that it treated chiefly of the manual exercise, evolutions, and similar details, and contained but few regulations,

lations, calculated to ascertain and uphold the authority of the superior, or to inculcate and enforce the obedience of the inferior ranks of the army.[1]

LETTER XCI.

To MAHOMMED GHYÂS *and* NOOR MAHOMMED KHÂN; *dated* 8*th* DÂRÂEY. (21*st July*.)

YOUR letter of the 23d of *Jaafury* has been received. You write, "that Hurry Pundit sent a message to you, through Râo Râsta, "desiring you to send away the musqueteers[1*] with you, as it was not "proper that they should remain at *Poonah*."

It is known. We have already repeatedly written, and we now again write to say, that the hostile intentions of the chiefs in that quarter are evident; that the longer residence of *that friend* and of Noor Mahommed Khân there, is consequently in the highest degree improper;[2] and that you must, therefore, both set out for our Presence, with the whole of your retinue. *This order is accordingly to be considered by you of equal force with a hundred orders.* You must not wait for any other; but, immediately on receipt of our present commands, proceed with Noor Mahommed Khân, and all the people attached to you, to the Presence. *We shall write no more on this subject.*

R

(1) Since writing the above, Lieutenant-Colonel Marriot has obligingly lent me a copy of this curious work, of which some further account will be found in the Appendix. The extracts there given from it, will show the exact extent to which the *Sultan* provided for the maintenance of subordination.

(1*) In the original مردم بار which was the name, as Colonel Wilks informs me, by which Hyder Ali distinguished his regular infantry.

(2) In the original موجب کمال بي لطفي است *i. e.* "leads to perfect unkindness" or "un-"graciousness:" or "must carry with it the most unfavourable appearance."

OBSERVATIONS.

The only remark necessary to be made on this letter is, that notwithstanding the apparently inflexible resolution of the *Sultan,* to withdraw his agents from *Poonah* immediately, they both appear to have continued there till the month of May in the following year (1786), or nearly a whole year after these peremptory orders for their recall.

LETTER XCII.

To Bûrhânûddeen; *dated 9th* Dârâey. *(22d July.)*

It has been reported to us, that the besieged are desirous of capitulating, and have opened a negociation for the purpose: it is therefore written, that if they will surrender on terms, there is no use in an assault. You and Kumrûddeen must jointly treat with the besieged on the occasion, and, by every practicable means, induce them to deliver up the place. Failing in this, you will, with the concurrence of all the *Sipahdârs* and commanders[1] of the army, (after having ascertained from what point the attempt can be made with the least loss of men) seize the proper moment for proceeding to the capture of the place by open assault.

We

(1) *Sipahdârs* and commanders. I take this to be a mere pleonasm; for I do not suppose that any officers, below the rank of a *Sipahdâr,* were meant to be consulted; and with the exception of Bûrhânûddeen and Kumrûddeen, there would not appear to have been any with the army of superior designation. I wish, however, to be understood, as speaking with great diffidence on this point; since I have only a superficial knowledge of the constitution, or formation, of the *Sultan's* army, at this period.

We are here likewise prepared to move at the head of our forces,(2) and shall shortly arrive in that quarter. In the mean while, you must *temporize*, and employ every means, *fair or foul*,(3) which may induce the besieged to surrender the fort: because, in an assault, many lives would be lost; while a long detention before the place would also prove extremely destructive to the army. It is, moreover, in our blessed contemplation, to engage, after the rainy season, in a certain *weighty* enterprize; you must, therefore, try every means of effecting the [early] evacuation of the place; acting at the same time, in all our affairs, in [perfect] concert with each other.

OBSERVATIONS.

The fluctuating orders of the *Sultan*, respecting *Nergúnd*, as well as his impatience to obtain speedy possession of the place, have appeared in several of the foregoing letters. It has also been seen, that his solicitude, on this occasion, led him, more than once, to authorize, and even to direct, in sufficiently explicit terms, the adoption of the most unjustifiable measures for the attainment of his object. But it was reserved for the present dispatch, to display, in the most glaring colours, his unprincipled and profligate policy. He is no longer satisfied with vague and distant intimations of his wishes; but here, throwing off all reserve and disguise, openly and boldly declares, that there is no act of treachery, deception, or perjury, by means whereof the conquest of *Nergúnd* could be achieved, to which he was not ready to give an unqualified sanction.

The *weighty enterprize*, alluded to in this letter, can, at this time, only be guessed. It could hardly be the surprize of *Adoni*; which, though it might possibly

R 2

(2) Original درانیجا هم سواری خاص حاضر است literally "here, too, the special cavalcade is ready or prepared.

(3) Original بهر طرح راست ودروغ زمانه سازی نموده "by every way, true and false, and by temporizing."

bly be in his contemplation at this juncture, he did not attempt till the month of May of the following year (1786).[4] Neither could he well mean a sudden attack of the Mahrattah army, to be conducted in person by himself; as this was not carried into effect till a still later period: and, consequently, both events were considerably posterior to the "*close of the rainy season.*" There remains, therefore, no other *known* occurrence, to which the expression in question can be so well referred, as to his short expedition against the *Koorgs*, in the following month of November; when he marched suddenly and rapidly to *Zuferâbâd*, in which quarter the *Koorgs* had recently appeared in open revolt; and owing to the incapacity of the officer whom he had left in charge of that ever turbulent and never completely settled portion of his territories,[5] had obtained some advantages over the *Sultan's* troops.

LETTER XCIII.

To KUMRÛDDEEN KHÂN; *dated* 10*th* DÂRÂEY. (23*d July.*)

AGREEABLY to your desire, we have transmitted to Bûrhânûddeen an answer to the *Urz*[1*] which he forwarded to us from Kâlâ Pundit. The aforesaid *Pundit*, for his complete satisfaction [or security] demands the sanction of oaths, &c. [to our engagements]. But where is the necessity for oaths and the like, in an affair of this kind? You and Bûrhânûddeen must, *by every possible artifice and deception*, get the garrison to quit the place.

We have written a letter to Shaikh Unser, which is enclosed.

(4) See on this subject the observations on Letter CXXXVIII.

(5) See Letter CXVII.

(1*) An humble address or petition.

OBSERVATIONS.

The true meaning of what the *Sultan* here says is, that as he depends on his generals for circumventing the garrison, he sees no necessity for personally perjuring himself for the purpose: he thinks the end in view may be sufficiently answered by *their* doing so, and is therefore averse to a waste of perfidy. But although he did not think proper to pledge himself to the extent required by Kâlâ Pundit, it is highly probable that, in his letter to that person (referred to above), he was not at all backward in giving him such assurances, as would be best calculated to dispel any fears he might entertain for his personal safety and honour.[2]

LETTER XCIV.

To Bûrhânûddeen; *same Date.* (*23d July.*)

Your letter, enclosing a paper, containing the demands of the people of the fort, has been received; and, in consequence thereof, we now transmit to you, in answer to these demands, an engagement from us to Kâlâ Pundit.[1] We also enclose three letters for Mahommed Ali and the other *Sipahdârs.*

The aforesaid *Pundit* has, for his greater satisfaction [or security], demanded the sanction of oaths, &c. [to our engagements]. But what is the use of oaths on this occasion? You must, conjointly with Kumrûddeen, *by every possible artifice and deceit*, persuade the besieged to evacuate the fort.

(2) See the following letter.

(1) The letter or engagement, here referred to, was most probably in the *Canarese* language, and therefore does not appear.

LETTER XCV.

To JUSÂRETÛDDOWLAH, MEER ABÛL MAANA KHAN, BEHÂDÛR JUSÂRET JUNG; *dated* 13*th* DÂRÂEY. (25*th July.*)

[After compliments]......... You write, "that in obedience to the "dictates of honor, you shall exert yourself, to the best of your power, "in chastising the seditious." It is comprehended. Verily, such is the obligation of honor, and such the true character of courage. If you should be desirous of obtaining any assistance, we request you will not scruple or hesitate to consider our *Sircar* [state] as your own, but [freely] signify to us your wishes, which you may depend upon our fulfilling to your satisfaction.

N.B. A letter, of the same tenor and date, was written to Mukhun Zaal (probably the agent of Jusâret Jung.)

OBSERVATIONS.

I am not enabled to say who this Jusâretûddowlah was; but there can be little or no doubt of his having been a subject of the *Nizâm*, and (to judge by his titles) a person of distinction. He was, most probably, an immediate dependent of Busâlet Jung, the brother of the *Nizâm*, and the *Jagiredâr* of *Adoni*.

LETTER XCVI.

To MAHOMMED GHYÂS *and* NOOR MAHOMMED KHÂN; *dated* 14*th* DÂRÂEY. (27*th July.*)

YOUR two letters, of the 23d and 28th of *Jaafury* [6th and 11th July] have been received. You write, "that they are about to require "of

" of you to send away your escort, and that their ungracious deport-
" ment towards you is beyond measure."

It is known. You and Noor Mahommed Khân must repair to the house of Râo Râsta, and, placing yourselves opposite to him, say to him, " that you have nothing to do with the minister (Nana Furnaveese) " or any one else, and that all you have to desire is, that he will procure " you the necessary passports, in order that you may return to us." In short, let them be pleased or displeased, you must, at any rate, get passports, and set out with all your retinue for our Presence. *This order must be considered as if it were a hundred orders.* Two letters for Kishen Râo Nârâin and Râo Râsta, on the subject of your dismission, are enclosed. You must bring Syed Zynûl Aabideen Khân along with you.

You write for a supply of money, and represent the dearness of every thing there. Now that you are about to return hither, where is the necessity of making you a remittance for your expences?

Let us know the name and rank of the *Hâkim* [ruler] of *Cambay*, as we purpose writing to him.

We, also, are prepared for war. Fear not, but speedily commence your journey hither, and bring the *Mûnshy*, Peer Mahommed, as well as ——,(1) with you.

OBSERVATIONS.

The former part of this letter is in substance, and indeed nearly in terms, the same as Letter XCI. In fact, the envoy's dispatch of the 23d *Jaafury* is acknowledged in both; and, probably, that of the 28th of the same month (which

(1) The original here is either miswritten, or I do not understand it. A *writer*, however, of some kind, is intended.

(which would seem to have led to the present letter) did not differ materially from it.

The letter to the *Nabob* of *Cambay* (his intention of writing which is here announced) will be further noticed under Letter CXVIII.

LETTER XCVII.

To MEER MOYENÛDDEEN KHÂN; *dated* 19*th* DÂRÂEY. (1*st August.*)

YOUR letter, written in the *Hindivy* character, and informing us that there was a prospect of Budl Nâig's coming in to you, has been received and understood. When the said *Nâig* arrives, you must confront him with Tummycoor,[1] and after establishing his guilt, and placing him under a guard, tell him, "that you will release him, provided he sends "for his family." Having induced him, *by means of this artifice*, to send for his family, you must put the whole of them in confinement, and make a report of the circumstances to us.

OBSERVATIONS.

The instances of the *Sultan's* treacherous and unprincipled conduct, in his negociations, multiply so fast, as to make it difficult to avoid the appearance of sameness and repetition, in the remarks to which they naturally give rise; I shall, in future, therefore, instead of obtruding my sentiments, leave the reader to his own reflections on such occasions.

(1) Name uncertain.

LETTER XCVIII.

To Râjah Râm Chundur; *dated* 20*th* Dârâey. (2*d August.*)

You write, "that, in conformity with our orders, you have esta- " blished shops, on our behalf, in every *Taalûk* [under your authority], " and engaged in our service a *Surrâf*[1] and accountant, for conducting " the concerns of each: but that, in some districts, the object of profit " is completely frustrated; while, in others, the gains are so very small " as to be even inadequate to the monthly pay of the *Surrâfs* and " accountants; owing (as you say) to the more considerable towns, " where, heretofore, gold and silver, bullion and specie, to the amount " of thousands of *pagodas*, used to be brought for the purposes of " traffic, being now forsaken by the traders, who taking alarm at the " establishment of our shops [or warehouses] resort, in consequence, " to other places; none but the poorer classes, in short, ever dealing " with them, and then only to the amount, perhaps, of six or seven " *fanams*."

It is known. Admitting that the profits, for instance, are only *seven pagodas*, and that the expence, on account of the wages of the *Surrâf* and accountants, amount to *ten*, how long can this last, or the dealers continue to carry their money and bullion to other places? They will, finally, come and make their purchases at our warehouses: you will, therefore, [proceed to] establish *Surrâfs* and accountants in every *Taalûk*, according to the amount of its [saleable] produce.

You suggest the establishment of banking-houses on the part of the *Sircar*, and the appointment of a banker, with a salary, to superintend them. You also propose, with our permission, to open warehouses for

S the

(1) By Europeans usually miscalled *Shroffs*. A *Surrâf* is a money-changer or broker.

the sale of cloths at *Bangalore, Ouscottah,* and other places. It is comprehended. *There is no regulation issued by us, that does not cost us, in the framing of it, the deliberation of five hundred years.* This being the case, do you perform exactly what we order; neither exceeding our directions, nor suggesting any thing further from yourself.

OBSERVATIONS.

The fact of Tippoo Sultan having established such shops, or warehouses, as those mentioned in the foregoing letter, was, I believe, very well known, before the commencement of the last war, to those persons most intelligent in the affairs of *Mysore.* The present dispatch, by fortunately reciting at so much length the representation of Râjah Râm Chundur on the subject, furnishes a tolerably clear idea of the institution, of which I have no where else met with any account. Till I saw this document, however, I had supposed, that the *Sultan's* views in this scheme embraced nothing more than a monopoly of the *wholesale* trade of his dominions; but it is evident, from Râm Chundur's statement, that the *retail* trade also was proposed to be engrossed. "None but the poorer classes," says the *Râjah*, "deal at our shops; and then only to the amount, perhaps, of six "or seven *fanams*."(1)

I do not clearly know what the result of this extraordinary project was, or whether the establishment, which has been described, continued in existence at the period of its founder's death. I rather think, however, that Râm Chundur's prognostic regarding it was verified, and that, though framed "with the delibe-"ration of five hundred years," it was soon found impracticable, and ultimately abandoned.

Râm Chundur certainly could not have chosen a more unpropitious occasion for submitting his own project of banking-houses, than the one he embraced: nor would he seem to have at all adverted to the character of his master, when he could

(1) *i. e.* about a *shilling.*

could have the temerity, in one and the same moment, to condemn pretty plainly a favorite scheme of the *Sultan*, and to offer to his acceptance another of his own devising. The result was such as he might have expected. The *Sultan* would, at no time, have been likely to listen with complacency to the uninvited suggestions of any of his servants; but least of all, when proceeding from one, who had ventured to question the policy of a measure, on which he would seem to have plumed himself in no small degree.

LETTER XCIX.

To Kumrûddeen; *dated 25th Dârâey. (7th August.)*

You write, " that in concert with Bûrhânûddeen, you are treating " with the besieged for the surrender of the place, which you expect " will submit in two or three days." You must, by any means, whether by engagements or by artifice, get the garrison to evacuate the fort, in order that our troops may obtain a little respite from fatigue, as we have it in contemplation to employ them, ere long, *on a weighty service.*(1)

You state, " that yourself and Bûrhânûddeen labour diligently toge- " ther, and in perfect concert, in the conduct of our affairs; but that, " possibly, some envious persons, incapable of viewing things clearly, " may have made a different representation to us." It is understood. How shall any one [presume to] represent to us, that any disagreement subsists between *that light of our eyes* and Bûrhânûddeen, since both are

S 2 our

(1) This passage does not apply (as suggested under Letter XCII) to the subsequent expedition against the Koorgs, as the *Sultan* could hardly have had it in contemplation to employ Bûrhânûddeen's forces on that occasion, to which, according to his own account, the troops immediately at his disposal were more than adequate. The *weighty service* alluded to must, therefore, have been some enterprize of a more arduous nature.

our beloved sons, and have been brought up alike under our care: we therefore entertain a confident persuasion, that you will both, with *one heart*, exert yourselves earnestly in the service of the *Sircar*.

OBSERVATIONS.

A letter of the same date, and nearly of the same tenor as the preceding one, was addressed to Bûrhânûddeen, who likewise appears to have assured the *Sultan*, "that he conducted all affairs in concert with Kumrûddeen." But though the *Sultan* thought fit to intimate to these commanders his belief that a proper harmony really subsisted between them, it appears, I think, sufficiently clear, from the tenor of his letters, that he was far from being entirely satisfied of the fact; and it may, at least, be confidently assumed, that there were those who thought otherwise, and who endeavoured to impress him with their opinions.

LETTER C.

To KUMRÛDDEEN; *dated 26th* DÂRÂEY. (*8th August.*)

YOU write, "that on the day following [the date of your letter], "or the 22d of *Dârâey*, the enemy were to evacuate the place, when, "having put a garrison of ours into it, you would report the same to "us."

Having got the besieged to evacuate the fort *on terms*, and having placed a garrison of our troops in it, let the *Piâdehs*, &c. who composed the enemy's garrison, be set at liberty, *according to the capitulation*: but Kâlâ Pundit, and three of the most opulent bankers, together with all the *Brahmens* and *Mûtusuddies* of any consideration (to whatever class

class or description they may belong) *must be placed in confinement, and most carefully guarded,* and the same be reported to us.

LETTER CI.

To the same; dated 27th Dáráey. (9th August.)

You write, under date of the 22d *Dárdey* [4th August], "that on "that day our colours were hoisted on the walls of the fort, and a party "of our troops admitted into the place, which was to be evacuated by "the garrison on the following day."

It is known. Kâlâ Pundit, with his family and kindred, *four*[1] of the most opulent bankers, and the most distinguished of the commanders of cavalry, as well as of every other class or department, must be placed under guard: the remaining persons, of inferior description, are to be set free, *according to the capitulation.*[2]

You must dispatch *Doolies*[3] to *Dhárwár*, to bring back the wounded men who were sent thither [during the siege]; in order that, being placed, together with the wounded now with your division, under the care of their respective relations, they may be the more at their ease. The wounds of these men must also be carefully attended to, and properly treated. The army likewise, with horses, cattle, &c., must be encamped in some good spot, abounding with water and grass, and where

(1) *Three* only were ordered to be detained in the letter of the preceding day.

(2) *i. e.* the capitulation was to be observed *only* in regard to the inferior classes, possessing no property.

(3) *Doolies* are a sort of humble conveyance, constructed on the same principle as a *Palenkeen.* They frequently consist of nothing but a common bedstead or cot, suspended to a *Bamboo*, with or without curtains. They are generally appropriated to the use of sick persons and of women.

where but little rain lies. Having undergone such fatigue, let them now enjoy some repose.

You write, "that you had dispatched one *Risâla* of *Sair*(4) cavalry, "and the horses of one stable,(5) towards *Kunnekgeery*, &c., and given "an order for their pay upon Mohyûddeen Ali Khân, the *Dewân* of "*Kurpah*, who, however, had returned the same." We have, therefore, signified our pleasure to the aforesaid *Khân*, who will, in consequence, furnish the pay of the cavalry, and the subsistence of the horses, &c., agreeably to your requisition.

We, some time since, dispatched money for the payment of your army: it has, probably, reached you before now. The returns which you sent of the troops have been received. To-morrow we purpose sending you an additional supply of money.

OBSERVATIONS.

The orders here given, respecting the *wounded*, as well as the consideration which the *Sultan* appears to have had for the ease and comfort of the army at large, are creditable to his character as a military commander. They would have been still more so, had they comprehended *the sick* in general.

(4) The *Sair* cavalry were, I believe, what were otherwise called the *stable horse*; but I am by no means confident that this was the case.

(5) I am not quite certain how many horses composed a stable; but in a memorandum of the military establishments, written by the *Sultan* himself, some time in the year 1793, the number appears to be stated at twenty-two.

LETTER CII.

To the NABOB RUNMUST KHÂN; *dated* ———.[1]

[AFTER compliments]....... Your letter, informing me of your welfare, was delivered by Khâjeh Lûtfûllah, and afforded me much pleasure. I have also learned, from the said *Khâjeh*, the particulars which you entrusted to his verbal communication. Of the eleven *lacks of rupees*, to which I had a just claim, I have been induced, by consideration for the attachment which that friend has so long borne to me, as well as for the sake of the true faith, and on account of the eminence of your family,[2] to remit four *lacks*: you must, therefore, put the remaining seven *lacks of rupees* in a speedy course of payment, by which means our mutual regard and friendship will be augmented. Further particulars will be imparted to you by the above-named *Khâjeh*. Continue always to afford me the satisfaction of hearing of your welfare. For the rest, may you be joyful!

OBSERVATIONS.

Runmust Khân was a *Patan* chieftain, who possessed the district of *Kurnool*.[3] Hyder Ali compelled him to agree to an annual tribute; though he was, at the same time, a feudatory of the *Nizâm*, to whom, when required, he was bound to render military service. By the partition treaty of 1792, his son and successor, Alif Khân, was released from his dependence on Tippoo Sultan, and the tribute payable

(1) This letter is without date: I have given it the place which it occupies in my manuscript.

(2) Original خاندان

(3) Frequently, but improperly, written *Canoul* and *Canoade*.

payable to the latter transferred to the *Nizâm*; by whom (if I mistake not) it was ceded to the East-India Company, by the treaty of 1800. For a more particular account of the dynasty the reader is referred to Appendix, G.

LETTER CIII.

To Mahommed Ghyâs *and* Noor Mahommed Khân; *dated* 3d *Hâshimy.* (14*th August.*)

Your letter has been received. You may pass twenty days or a month longer there, in *an evasive* and *procrastinating way*;[1] but, at the end of that time, you must, in whatever manner may be [necessary], set out for the Presence, since your remaining there is incompatible with our dignity.

LETTER CIV.

To the same; dated 4*th Hâshimy.* (15*th August.*)

Your longer continuance there is destitute of graciousness [or dignity].[1*] The dishonour arising from your residing there, upon this unhandsome footing,[2] is now become manifest: you must, therefore, at any rate, repair to the Presence.

(1) Original بليت ولعل گذرانده

(1*) Original بي لطف است

(2) Original بي لطفي ماندن

OBSERVATIONS.

As the *Sultan* would not appear to have received any fresh dispatch from the envoys, between the 3d and 4th of *Háshimy*, it may be supposed, that the directions contained in the present letter (revoking, in a certain degree, those of the former day) arose from a reconsideration of the subject; which probably, for a moment, revived his indignation at the behaviour of the Mahrattah ministers. I say, *for a moment*, in reference to the counter-orders which soon followed.

LETTER CV.

To Kumrûddeen Khân; *dated* 9*th* Háshimy. (20*th August.*)

Directing him to repair, with the troops under his command, to the Presence, and to leave Shaikh Unser's *Kushoon* with Bûrhânûddeen.

LETTER CVI.

To Râjah Râm Chundur; *dated* 11*th* Háshimy. (22*d August.*)

We have received your letter, wherein you write, "that Tâj Khân "and Abdûl Ghufoor Khân, the *Kilaadârs*(1) of *Kishngeery*, have sent a "requisition to Wunkut Râo, the *Aumil* of the *Bâreh-mehâl*,(2) for five "hundred hired bullocks and five hundred labourers." We have consi-

T dered

(1) Many of the fortresses in *Mysore*, as well as *Kishngeery*, had two *Kilaadârs*, or governors.

(2) In the original دوازده محال which is the Persian for *Bâreh-mehâl*, or the twelve districts.

dered your letter, as well as that of Wunkut Râo, which was enclosed in it. No other bullocks, besides those belonging to the *Sircar*, are wanted, excepting on urgent occasions, when it may be proper to hire additional ones. In fact, the public establishment of bullocks is not large, and our service sometimes demands more than it can provide: in such cases it is allowable to hire bullocks, as otherwise our service might suffer by delay. We have accordingly written, and enclose a letter to the above-named [*Kilaadârs*], which you will forward to them. This will prevent them from making any further demand for hired bullocks.

LETTER CVII.

To MOHYÛDDEEN ALI KHÂN; *dated 20th HÂSHIMY.* (31*st August.*)

[AFTER some minute directions, respecting the fabric of *Bubry* cloths for the use of the troops (patterns of the kinds required being enclosed)(1) the letter proceeds thus:]—

It has been reported to us, that you sit constantly at home, without ever appearing at the *Kuchurry.* This is not well. You must pass [a proper portion of] your time [daily] in the *Kuchurry*, and there diligently apply to the affairs of the *Sircar*, without suffering any one to come to you at your own house [on public business]. It would appear, that you never look into the [written] instructions which you received from us. If you act in conformity with our orders, it will be well: otherwise, you will assuredly incur the penalty therein specified.(2)

(1) The *Bubry* cloth was a sort of *Chintz*, manufactured in *Mysore.* The pattern was of the *Sultan's* invention, and consisted in the Tyger stripe, from which it received its name. This stripe was adapted by Tippoo as a kind of crest, which was stamped on his books, his plate, and almost every thing belonging to him.

(2) See observations on Letter I.

LETTER CVIII.

To Monsieur Souliac,[1] *Governor of Pondicherry; dated 23d Háshimy.* (*3d September.*)

[After compliments]....... The letter which you sent us, by the hands of the *Vakeel*, Râm Râo, containing accounts of your welfare, and informing us of your arrival at *Pondicherry*, for the administration of the affairs of that place, was duly received by us; and an answer thereto (accompanied by a dress) was dispatched some time since, and will, of course, have reached you.

Our earnest wish and object is, that the strong and sincere friendship which has, from former times, subsisted between us and the *Rájah* of the French, should daily increase; and that, by the divine favour, the affairs of France should attain fresh splendour and prosperity. It is most manifest, that the *Rájah* of the French is lying in wait for a favourable opportunity;[2] and as that eminent person[3] is a leader of political experience, we assure ourselves that the means of attaining this object will not have failed to engage your attention.

At a former period, when the English army had advanced within eight *Coss* of *Poonah*, and the Mahrattah chiefs, not finding themselves able to cope with the enemy, meditated on setting fire to their houses, and taking to flight; in this crisis they humbly solicited our aid and support, which, relying on their engagements and promises, we afforded, by waging

T 2

(1) I am not certain that this name is written correctly, and have not, just now, the means of ascertaining the point. This letter was accompanied by a complimentary dress, consisting of five pieces of *Kárchóby*; a sort of brocade or gold and slver tissue.

(2) Original بقابوطلبي هستند

(3) Meaning M. Souliac.

waging war [against the English] in the *Carnatic* for some years, during which period their lives and property, their country and honour, remained in safety. These facts are more manifest, even than the sun. Nevertheless, a certain *Zemindár* (among the *Zemindárs* subject to our authority) having lately been instigated, by a contumacious and insolent disposition, to lay waste our country, and we having, in consequence, sent our army to chastise him and to reduce his place, the aforesaid Mahrattahs, forgetting the numberless obligations conferred on them by us, dispatched their army to the assistance of the said *Zemindár*. Hostilities have accordingly taken place between the two armies, and the Mahrattahs are meditating further mischief against us. With the blessing of God, however, you shall [soon] hear in what manner we have chastised these people. Further particulars will be detailed to you by the *Vakeel*, Râm Râo. We have sent, as a token of friendship, a few pieces of cloth.

OBSERVATIONS.

It is observable, that the *Sultan*, in this letter, entirely sinks the name of his father, whose actions he applies to himself. Whether such a mode of expression was absolutely warranted by custom, or by the idiom of the language, may be doubted: but, however this might be, there is no reason to suppose that any slight was intended by it to the memory of Hyder; of whom he has, on many occasions, spoken with suitable demonstrations of filial regard and respect.

Having already had occasion to remark on the studied but disguised affront put upon the King of France, by stiling him a *Rájah*,(4) it is unnecessary to say any thing, in this place, on the instance of it afforded by the foregoing letter. We shall hereafter see this degrading title applied to the French King, in an epistle addressed directly to himself.

There

(4) See observations on Letter V.

There can be little or no doubt, that a renewal of the war with the English is alluded to, in the second paragraph of the present letter. No other satisfactory explanation can be given of the "opportunity" which the French monarch is represented to be "waiting for," or of "the attention" which Monsieur Souliac is presumed to have bestowed on "the means" of promoting his sovereign's views. In short, except for the purpose of aiding his hostile designs against the English, what motive could the *Sultan* possibly have for cultivating the friendship of the French?

LETTER CIX.

To KUMRÛDDEEN KHÂN; *dated 24th HÂSHIMY. (4th September.)*

WE approve of your having sent Shaikh Unser's *Kushoon* to join Bûrhânûddeen.

You write respecting a supply of money for the pay of your troops. At present we have taken up our residence, with a small retinue,(1) at *Bangalore*: we are, consequently, unable to supply you from hence;(2) but have sent necessary orders for the purpose to our treasury at *Seringapatam*...........(3) We enclose a *Purwâneh* to the *Zemindâr* of *Annagoondy*, directing him to supply you with baskets(4) and boat-men, and otherwise to assist you in crossing your army at the *Kûmply Ghaut*.(5)

Another

(1) Original جریده *jureedeh*, which literally signifies single; alone. This is the only intimation we have of the *Sultan's* departure from his capital and visit to *Bangalore*.

(2) So I understand the words زردرتوشه خانه رکاب معمور though their obvious import is quite the reverse; معمور signifying *full*.

(3) There is here a hiatus of a word or two in the original, which renders the line following it rather unintelligible.

(4) For a description of these baskets (used instead of boats, for the passage of rivers) see Captain Moor's Narrative.

(5) I am not quite clear that I have given the name of this *Ghaut*, or passage, of the *Tungbudra*, correctly.

Another *Purwâneh* is enclosed for the *Aumil* of *Hurriâl*, directing him also to send baskets and boatmen for you to the same *Ghaut*. Join us speedily with your army, and make no delay.

LETTER CX.

To the same; dated 26th Hâshimy. (6th September.)

You write, " that having collected together some baskets, you have " begun the passage of the *Tungbudra*, and daily cross some part of " your army." You also mention, " that a *Vakeel* and *Hurkâreh* " belonging to the *Kunnek-geery* man, accompanied by a banker's " *Gomâshteh*,(1) had waited on you, and acknowledged the justice of our " claims upon that *Zemindâr*: [in consequence of which] you had [at " their desire] detached a *Risâla* of *Jyshe*, and a *Risâla* of *Sair* cavalry, " to chastise Eeri Nâik, a *Polygar* dependant on the said *Zemindâr*, but " who had [recently] revolted against his authority."

It is known. We approve of your having made this detachment, and direct that, on its return, the troops composing it be likewise made to cross the river, and proceed [hither] with you.

We some time ago dispatched money for the payment of the troops commanded by that light of our eyes. This money is arrived at *Dhârwâr*, whither you must send an escort to bring it to you.

(1) An Agent.

LETTER CXI.

To Mahommed Ghyâs *and* Noor Mahommed Khân ; *dated 28th Háshimy.* (*8th September.*)

Three letters have been received from you. You write, "that the "minister manifests an inclination to procrastinate, with respect to "your dismission." It does not signify. You must remain there as long as he is disposed to detain you, and not precipitate your departure. Whenever he dismisses you, you will proceed to the Presence.

LETTER CXII.

To the same; dated 29th Háshimy. (*9th September.*)

Whatever circumstances we judged it necessary to communicate to you, have been written at great length and distinctly in *Hindivy:* the perusal of it [*i. e.* of the *Hindivy* dispatch] will make you acquainted [with every thing].(1) You must ascertain its contents by means of a secret and trust-worthy *Múnshy:* one in all respects entitled to credit and belief, and who shall be incapable of revealing the secrets [entrusted to him.]

OBSERVATIONS.

It has been already seen, that Tippoo Sultan occasionally sent his orders in the *Hindivy* language, even to persons whom he usually addressed in *Persian.* Here we

(1) In the original ازرویش خواهد دریافت literally "from the face of it you will understand."

we have another example of this extraordinary and unaccountable practice, but still more striking and embarrassing than the former one; in which we were at liberty to suppose, that the envoys could read a *Hindivy* as well as a *Persian* letter, and only left to wonder why the *Sultan* should, at any time, prefer writing in the *Hindivy*. But it now appears, that his ambassadors were ignorant of that character; and that, in order to possess themselves of their master's instructions, it was necessary for them to have recourse to an interpreter. It might have been expected, that under these circumstances, the envoys would, at least, have been spared the trouble and responsibility of procuring such a person, by having one of that description regularly attached to their mission. But this was evidently not the case: nor is it ev enabsolutely certain, that the person to be employed on this occasion was to be found among the servants of the embassy; though we must either assume this as the fact, or adopt the monstrous supposition of the envoys being obliged to seek, in the capital of their master's enemy, for an interpreter of his most secret and important orders. To conclude, I must acknowledge that there is nothing in the whole correspondence, which appears to me so completely inexplicable as this matter we have been considering: nor can I help regretting, that the difficulty did not occur to me before my departure from *India*, where I might possibly have been able to obtain a solution of it.

LETTER CXIII.

To KUMRÛDDEEN KHÂN; *dated* 2d *WÂSAAEY*. (11*th September*.)

YOUR letter, stating the distress of your troops for money, has been received. Previously to your writing, we had, in contemplation of this distress, dispatched a supply to you, which is, accordingly, now lying at *Dhârwâr*, to which place you must send a party of horse to escort it to you. Besides this money, we have now sent you from hence a further supply

supply of twenty thousand *pagodas*. When the whole amount shall have reached you, distribute it among your people, and report the same to us

LETTER CXIV.

To Meer Mahommed Sâdik; *same Date.* (11*th September.*)

It has been represented to us, that Owbultia,[1] a *Mûtusuddy* belonging to the *Tosheh-khâneh*, is on the point of death, and that his brother-in-law is at *Oussoor*: we therefore write to direct, that you cause guards to be placed over his brother-in-law and *Gomâshtehs*; and that, having made enquiries respecting his substance[2] and property, you proceed, by means of scourging [the parties], to obtain possession of the same. Let the utmost diligence and exertions be employed in this business.

Lutchmun, another *Mûtusuddy* of the *Tosheh-khâneh*, possesses a full knowledge of the particulars of Owbultia's substance: you must, therefore, make enquiry of him also; and send and secure the goods and property [in question] wherever they may be.

You and others formerly represented to us, that [this man] possessed property to the amount of a *lack* of *pagodas*. Let the same be sought after and discovered, and the whole be brought to the account of the *Sircar*. What more?

U

(1) Name uncertain.

(2) The word which I have translated *substance* is in the original زندگي which commonly enough denotes subsistence or livelihood; but I do not recollect to have met with it before, in the sense in which it is here used.

OBSERVATIONS.

It does not appear, from any thing contained in this document, that Owbultia was a public defaulter, or stood charged with any malversations; and yet, considering the rigour of the proceedings directed, it is difficult to believe otherwise. There is a pretty plain hint in the concluding paragraph, that Meer Sâdik would be held responsible for the realization of the supposed amount of Owbultia's property. Perhaps, however, this was only meant as a stimulus to the *Dewân's* exertions in the business.

Meer Mahommed Sâdik was the *Sultan's* principal *Dewân*, and, in that character, presided over the revenue department of *Mysore*. Europeans commonly considered him as Tippoo's prime minister; but Tippoo's government recognized no such officer. For a curious engagement which the *Sultan* made this person enter into, toward the end of the year 1798, the reader is referred to the Appendix, H. Meer Sâdik lost his life in the assault of *Seringapatam*. He was believed by many persons to have been a son of the celebrated Bussy; nor was the uncommon fairness of his complexion the only circumstance that gave weight to the report, of which more particular mention is made in the Appendix.

LETTER CXV.

To Syed Mahommed, *Kilaadâr of Seringapatam; dated 3d Wâsaaey. (12th September.)*

It has been reported to us, that the *Mûtusuddy* of the *Jyshe*, Kishn Râo, has been bitten by a mad dog: we therefore write to desire that you will give the aforesaid [*Mûtusuddy*] in particular charge to the physician, Mahommed Baig, who must administer to him the proper medicines

medicines in such cases, and restore him to health. He must also be told *not to let the discharge from the wound stop, but to keep it open for six months.*

N.B. A letter, to the above effect, was likewise written to the physician, Mahommed Baig.

OBSERVATIONS.

This is not the only letter in which the *Sultan* has exhibited himself in the character of a physician. A still more curious instance of the same kind will appear hereafter. It would be well, if we could attribute his interference in such matters to any particular solicitude for the welfare of the patients. This motive would, at least, be creditable to his humanity: but humanity, or sympathy in the sufferings of others, was not, it may be safely affirmed, among the *Sultan's* virtues. His conduct, therefore, on the occasions in question, can only be referred to the vanity, which made him desirous of appearing to know, as well as to direct, every thing.

The Syed Mahommed Khân, to whom this letter is addressed, continued to be *Kilaadâr* of *Seringapatam,* to the period of the capture of that place by the English; and was among the few persons of distinction who survived its fall. He stood high in the confidence of the *Sultan,* who speaking, in his Memoirs, of the manner in which he disposed of some of the principal offices of state on his accession to the *Musnud,* says: " the *Kilaadâry* of *Putn* I consigned to Syed " Mahommed, a man long distinguished for his fidelity and courage, and one of " [our] most ancient adherents." The situation held for so long a period by this person, must necessarily have made him a participator in many, or most, of the cruelties committed within the walls of *Seringapatam,* by order of his master: he has, nevertheless, obtained credit, for having often granted to the English prisoners confined there, at different times, indulgencies by no means authorized by the *Sultan's* instructions.

LETTER CXVI.

To Noor Mahommed Khân *and* Mahommed Ghyâs; *dated from* Bangalore, *5th Wâsaaey.* (*14th September.*)

We have, of late, repeatedly heard, that Râo Râsta having sent for you, you declined waiting upon him, on account of a dispute that had arisen respecting a woman belonging to some Musulman; returning for answer to his message, " that if they would let the woman in " question go,(1) you would attend him." This account has occasioned us the utmost surprise and astonishment. This is a domestic disturbance among the inhabitants of their own country. Where was the necessity of your interfering in this matter, or of your refusing to wait upon Râo Râsta when he sent for you? thereby throwing our affairs into confusion. It seems to us, *that old age*(2) *must have produced this deviation*(3) [or change] in your conduct [character or disposition], and rendered you *thus unmindful of your lives and honor.* It would have been most consonant to the state of the times, and to the regard you owed to our interests, if, considering their dissensions as beneficial to *Islâm*, you had [secretly] encouraged [or excited] the Musulmans [in their proceedings], while you [apparently] looked on as [unconcerned] spectators, instead of interposing with such an extraordinary recommendation(4) as you did; and which was, indeed, altogether, unworthy of your

(1) Or, " would release, or deliver her up." Original خواهد گذاشت

(2) Original كبرسن و پيرانه سري literally " *great years* and *old heads*; or, still more strictly, " *old headedness.*

(3) Original تفاوت در مزاج افتاده

(4) Original سفارش

your understandings.[5] When the Nazarenes seized upon hundreds of Musulman women, where was the zeal for the support [or honour] of Islamism, which you are now so desirous of manifesting *there?*

For the future, it will be proper that you should never take any share in their domestic concerns, but attend [exclusively] to whatever may promote the success of our affairs. Let the fire of discord, therefore, be again kindled amongst them, to the end that they may, in this manner, waste [their strength upon] each other.

OBSERVATIONS.

If I understand the foregoing letter rightly (of which, however, I must confess myself to have some doubts) the *Sultan's* meaning was, that both his own personal interests, and those of Islâmism, would have been better promoted, by a continuance of the feuds and animosities which seem to have arisen between the Musulman and Hindoo inhabitants of *Poonah*, in consequence, apparently, of some female intrigue, than by the interposition of the envoys; which, if it succeeded, would have the effect of terminating the disputes in question. Instead of this, he would have had his agents secretly foment and encourage them, and therefore concludes his dispatch, by broadly desiring them "to rekindle the fire "of discord," in order that his enemies may be consumed therein: that is to say, to measure back the false steps they had taken, and let the quarrel which had sprung up take its natural course. At the same time, he seems to have thought, that the interference of the envoys, besides being impolitic, was indecorous and presumptuous, as encroaching on the rights of an independent state. "It is a "domestic difference, (says he) concerning only the inhabitants of their own "country."

It is uncertain to what particular transaction the *Sultan* alludes, in the passage mentioning the Nazarenes, or English. The violence, however, here imputed to them, is mentioned on other occasions, as well as the present.

(5) I am far from being satisfied that I have rendered this passage correctly.

LETTER CXVII.

To Meer Zynûl Aabideen, *Sipahdâr of a Kushoon; dated 8th Wâsaaey. (17th September.)*

It has lately been represented to us, that the *Koorgs* have committed some excesses[1] at *Zuferâbâd*. We have, in consequence, written to the *Buktshy* of the *Jyshe*, to dispatch you with two guns and your *Kushoon* to that place. He is also ordered to advance you two thousand *Behâdury pagodas*, on account of the pay of your *Kushoon;* as well as a thousand *rupees*, to be applied in compensations to the wounded.[2] After leaving a guard over such of Othman Khân's *Kushoon* as are not to be trusted,[3] you will proceed, as above directed, to *Zuferâbâd;* to the *Foujdâr* of which place, Zynûl Aabideen, we have addressed another letter, which is enclosed. You are, in conjunction with him, to make a general attack on the *Koorgs;*[4] when, having put to the sword, or made prisoners of, the whole of them, *both the slain and the prisoners* are to be made Musulmans.[5] In short, you must so manage matters, as [effectually] to prevent them from exciting any further sedition or disturbance.

Obtaining from the treasury a copy of our regulations respecting the wounded, let your wounded be paid in conformity thereto. Rewards to those

(1) Original شرارت

(2) *i. e.* to such as may be wounded in the course of the service ordered.

(3) Probably men impressed into the army, and suspected of an intention to desert.

(4) In the original it is قتل عام or a *general slaughter;* but as *prisoners* are afterwards supposed to be made, I have, to avoid the apparent contradiction, given a different turn to the translation.

(5) *i. e.* "circumcised." If this conjecture were well founded, it would follow that Zynûl Aabideen Shoostry was a *Sipahdâr*, or a commander of a *Kushoon*, which, however, I have no authority for supposing him to have been.

those men, who may be entitled to them, must also be given from the money in your hands; from which you must, likewise, make such advances [of pay] to your *Kushoon*, as shall seem proper to you.

OBSERVATIONS.

I am doubtful, whether by the Zynûl Aabideen, mentioned in the title of this letter, is meant Zynûl Aabideen Shoostry (to whom Letter CXXVIII is unquestionably addressed) or a distinct person, bearing the same name. Though the former is usually distinguished by the addition of *Shoostry* (denoting him to be a native of *Shuster* or *Suza*, in *Persia*) yet the appellation might have been accidentally omitted in the present letter, as it most clearly appears to have been in the title of Letter CXLV.

The زخم پتي *Zukhm-putty*, or *compensation to wounded soldiers*, is a custom pretty general in the native armies of India. Having never seen Tippoo Sultan's regulations on this head, I am unable to give any information respecting them. As, however, all the *Sultan's* establishments were formed on the most economical, if not the most parsimonious scale, it is not probable, that his donations to the wounded were regulated by a different spirit. The rewards occasionally bestowed on men, distinguishing themselves in battle or otherwise, usually consisted of gold or silver chains, or of rings for the wrists, according to the rank of the person receiving them.

The reader will probably be startled at the order contained in the foregoing letter, for making Musulmans, not only of the living, but of the *dead* Koorgs, who might fall into the hands of the *Sipahdâr*; and the extravagance of the proceeding may even lead him to suspect, either the correctness of the manuscript, or the fidelity of the translation. With respect to the former, it will be sufficient to say that there is not the slightest ground for supposing any error of the manuscript in this passage; and as to the latter, I will only observe, that nothing can be expressed with more plainness, or freedom from ambiguity, than the original, which,

which, for the satisfaction of the oriental reader, at least, shall be inserted at the bottom of the page.[6]

LETTER CXVIII.

To MAHOMMED GHYÂS KHÂN *and* NOOR MAHOMMED KHÂN; *same Date.* (*17th September.*)

YOU write, "that a very great intimacy and friendship subsisted "between Syed Zynûl Aabideen Khân and Noorûddeen Hûsain Khân, "the latter of whom is come there [*i. e.* to *Poonah*] on a mission from "Mr. Boddam, the Governor of *Bombay*; and that the aforesaid Syed, "actuated by his attachment to our *Sircar*, furnishes you, privately, "with the secret intelligence of that quarter, and is furthermore ready, "if it meets our approbation, to take steps towards establishing a friend-"ship between us and the said Governor." It is well. We have no objection to your agitating this affair, as you propose, with the *Syed*. You must also obtain the most accurate intelligence from thence, and regularly communicate the same to us. You will, likewise, take the same occasion to represent,[1] that our territories and those of the English are contiguous to each other;[2] and that, at the time of the treaty concluded between us and the English, it was stipulated, that no assistance should be afforded, either openly or secretly, to our enemies: and, accordingly, we are in possession of copies of the said treaty, containing the aforesaid stipulations, under the respective seals of the Governors of *Bengal,*

(6) كورگ‌هارا تهیه تیغ آورده و قتل عام نموده و دستگیر ساخته کسانیکه کشته شدند و کسانیکه اسیر شوند معه زن و بچه همه‌هارا مسلمان نمایند

(1) *i. e.* to Syed Zynûl Abideen, for the ultimate information of Mr. Boddam.

(2) Literally, "are under the same shade."

Bengal, *Madras*, and *Bombay*. This being the case, it is unsuitable to the rules of friendship, and is even a violation of good faith, that notwithstanding his delivery [to us] of a treaty under his own seal, the Governor of *Bombay* should afford assistance to our enemies. Such conduct is abundantly remote from the usages and conduct of great chiefs.

Agreeably to your suggestion, we enclose a letter to the address of Nujmûd' Dowlah Behâdûr,(3) which you will forward [to him].

OBSERVATIONS.

I believe that the Zynûl Aabideen, mentioned in the foregoing letter, was an agent employed at the court of *Poonah* by the *Nabob* of *Cambay*. The *Sûltan's* letter to the latter, being merely complimentary, and only designed to lead to a further intercourse, is omitted.

The treaties with the English, spoken of in this letter, must, of course, refer to the separate treaties concluded at different times between Hyder Ali and the respective British presidencies. The treaty of *Mangalore*, likewise, contains a stipulation to the same effect as that so much insisted on here by the *Sultan*. The Governor of *Bombay* was not, however, a subscribing party to that treaty.

I am ignorant to what circumstance the *Sultan* alludes, where he charges the Governor of *Bombay* with affording assistance, at this period, to the Mahrattahs.

LETTER CXIX.

To Mâh Mirzâ Khân; *dated 7th Wâsaaey.* (16*th September.*)

We have, at this time, thought proper to employ you, and the troops under your command, in the reduction of the fort of *Oalpilly*.(1) The

X *Sipahdâr*,

(3) The *Nabob* of *Cambay*.

(1) This fort is, I believe, situated in a district of the same name, which is adjoining to *Punganoor*.

Sipahdár, Shaikh Omar,[2] with the troops belonging to him, is already before that place, where you will be joined by him, as well as by four thousand *Kuchurry Piádehs* from *Bangalore.* Part of this force is already arrived at its destination, and the remainder is on its way. On your arrival at *Oalpilly*, you must, in conjunction with the said *Sipahdár*, proceed to dislodge and chastise the *Piádehs* of the *Zemindár* of *Punganoor;* who have posted themselves in the neighbouring woods, from whence they [issue forth and] commit depredations. Having cleared these woods, you must move forward, and taking up a position near *Oalpilly*, open trenches against that place.

Shaikh Omar has with him four large guns, two field-pieces,[3] and two howitzers.[4] If any more heavy guns should be wanted, Turbiyut Ali Khân, the *Buktshy* of *Ehshám*,[5] has been instructed to dispatch them upon your requisition. Mounting these guns in the batteries, you must open a fire upon the fort; which being taken, you will put into it a garrison of our troops. In the fort is the *Zemindár*, Chukra Mull, together with several *Náigwáries*[6] of note. You must take especial care that these persons are made prisoners, and report to us all the particulars respecting them. If, however, the above named persons should escape through the woods, and take refuge in the districts of *Chundrageery*, *Chittoor*, or other *Polygars* depending on the *Fringy*,[7] you must write to the *Taalúkdár* of such district, informing him that the fugitives are robbers

(2) A letter to this officer, dated 24th *Háshimy* (4th September) is given in the correspondence; but as it contains nothing material that does not appear in the present dispatch, I have not thought it necessary to translate it.

(3) Original توپ حلوي } I am not quite certain that I have rendered these terms rightly.
(4) Original قنبارہ }

(5) At *Bangalore.* In a note to Letter IV, I have erroneously called him the collector of the district.

(6) Officers of the *Kundachár*, or militia.

(7) *i. e.* the *Frank*, meaning the English.

robbers of our *Sircar*,(8) and requiring of him not to protect but to deliver them up. You are, at the same time, to report these circumstances to us, in order that we may make a representation of the matter to the Governor of *Madras*, and endeavour to obtain possession of the person of the aforesaid *Polygar*.

If any of the *Piddehs* of the *Polygar* of *Punganoor* should be still concealed in the adjacent woods, you must contrive to discover their haunts, and to make prisoners of them.

You have with you fifty bullock-loads of gunpowder, each load being a hundred and twenty *seers*, making together six thousand *seers*.(9) You have been also furnished with twelve thousand *seers* of *Carnatic* lead, and four thousand gun-flints: these articles you will preserve carefully, expending them [only] in battle. If you should be in want of more lead, powder, or shot, apply to the aforesaid *Buktshy*, who has our orders to supply you; and when such supplies reach you, you must transmit to him a receipt for the same.

Mohyûddeen Ali Khân, the *Dewân* of *Kurpah*, and Râjah Râm Chundur, have been directed to supply you with gram(10) for the consumption of the horses of your *Kuchurry*. They will, at the same time, each send a *Mûtusuddy* in charge of the gram, who will remain with you, and serve out the gram as it may be wanted. Receipts for the same, under your seal and signature, must be regularly given by you to the aforesaid *Mûtusuddies*, who will deliver them to their respective principals.

The country of *Punganoor* appertains to our *Sircar*, and we have appointed

X 2

(8) This expression may mean either *robbers* from the *Sultan's* territories, or public defaulters, men who had defrauded his government.

(9) *i. e.* about 12,000 lb. weight.

(10) This is a species of pulse, with which they feed cattle, and especially horses, in *India*. The term is unknown to the natives, by whom it is called *chunnah*. I do not know from what language the English have adopted it.

appointed Dâsiâ to collect the revenues of it; you will, therefore, issue strict orders to your people not to commit any ravages or depredations there; *nor are you to make any incursions into the country of the Fringy, which adjoins to Punganoor, or to give it any disturbance.* On this head you must be very strict: and if the *Aumils* of the *Fringy* should write to you, to desire you not to make any incursions in their country, or to give it any molestation, you will send such an answer as may be proper, and at the same time report the circumstances to us.

The pay of the troops under you and Shaikh Omar, will be sent to each of you respectively. *You* will distribute the pay of your own people, *man by man;* and *he* will distribute the pay of the *Jyshe* under *his* command. Such *Piâdehs*, or others, as may be wounded, you will remunerate according to the separate regulations on this head, with which you have been furnished. You must also apply yourself to the procuring of secret intelligence from the *Ryots* and others, in that quarter, giving to those who communicate it *from five to ten rupees*, as you may judge proper.

Dâsiâ is the *Umldâr* of that place [*i. e. Punganoor*]: you will, therefore, afford him every [necessary] encouragement and countenance, and make yourself acquainted, by his means, with the [different] roads leading through the hills of *Oalpilly*. The country of the *Fringy* adjoins to *Oalpilly;* so that, in order to satisfy or tranquilize the *Fringy Taalûkdârs*, you must, immediately on your arrival there, write to them saying, "that the *Polygar* of *Punganoor* having contumaciously raised his head, "you have been sent by us to chastise him; and therefore request that, "if he should take refuge in their country, he may not receive protection."

Let a reward of five *rupees* be given to every man of our people bringing in the head of a *Piâdeh* belonging to the rebel *Polygar;* and let the same reward be granted for every prisoner brought in alive.

OBSERVATIONS.

The foregoing document is denominated in the original a *Hûkm-nâmeh,* or " mandate;" by which name all the *formal* or *set orders,* with which public functionaries were furnished, either at the time of their appointment to office, or subsequent thereto, were usually called, to distinguish them from the current and occasional instructions transmitted to them. They were sometimes divided into articles which were regularly numbered; and, as observed on a former occasion, generally concluded with a denunciation of the punishment appointed for a neglect or disobedience of the directions contained in them.

The term *Fringy,* applied in this dispatch to the English, is generally used (by the superior classes among the natives of India, at least) in contempt; as *Nusâra,* or *Nazarene,* also is for a Christian. Strictly speaking, however, there is nothing reproachful or degrading in the former appellation, as it properly means nothing more than a *Frank,* or European.

LETTER CXX

To Bûrhânûddeen; *dated* 8*th Wâsaaey.* (17*th September.*)

What you have written, relating to Kâlâ Pundit, is duly understood. A letter to him, framed in the manner suggested by you, is sent herewith. Let it be delivered to him: and if, notwithstanding this letter, he should still prove disinclined to repair to our Presence, and persist in his contumacy, an hundred men of the *Uskur,*(1) armed with swords and daggers, but without firelocks, must be sent, with orders to approach him gradually, while he is held in conversation [by persons to be instructed for the purpose]. They must then suddenly rush forward,

ten

(1) The regular troops were distinguished by this name.

ten men upon every *one* of his[2] : and, disarming the *Pundit* and all his party, bind them hand and foot, put the whole in irons, and [in this manner] dispatch them to the Presence. We enclose a letter of the above tenor to Syed Ghuffâr.[3] to whom you will deliver it.

LETTER CXXI.

To MOHYÛDDEEN ALI KHÂN, *DEWÂN of KURPAH ; dated 9th WÂSAAEY.* (18*th September.*)

IT has been represented to us, that you have, in a most rigorous and peremptory manner, required of several of our servants at *Kurpah* to evacuate houses which they have occupied for years past, and in the erection of which they have expended considerable sums of money. Such improper proceedings are of evil tendency, and directly contrary to our pleasure : you must, therefore, desist from them, nor again require of any of our servants to quit their habitations. Act according to the instructions which have been delivered to you, and do not pursue the suggestions of your own fancy.

LETTER CXXII.

To KUMRÛDDEEN ; *dated 9th WÂSAAEY.* (18*th September.*)

AGREEABLY to your request, we have written, and enclose an order to Mohyûddeen Ali Khân, the *Dewân* of *Kurpah*, directing him to desist

(2) Kâlâ Pundit and his party, or attendants, consisted, according to this passage, of ten persons. (See Letter CXXV.)

(3) Syed Ghuffâr was selected by the *Sultan* to execute this notable piece of treachery.

desist from disturbing our servants in the possession of their houses. You must forward the same to him.

What you write, respecting your desire to proceed unattended [or by yourself][1] to pay your respects to us, is understood. Repair straight, yourself and army, to *Seringapatam*,[2] whither we ourselves are proceeding.

LETTER CXXIII.

To BUDEEA ÛZ ZUMÂN, *TAALÚKDÂR of HÚSCOTAH; dated 6th WÂSAAEY.* (15*th September.*)

YOU write, "that in consequence of the *Cutwâl* being included in "the pay abstracts of the *Kundachâr*, the *Kilaadâr* of *Húscotah* "[conceiving the office to be in his disposal] had placed a very low "and improper person in the *Cutwâly*, to the great detriment of the "business of your department." It is known. The appointment and removal of the *Cutwâl* rests with you: you will, therefore, replace [as you propose] the former *Cutwâl*, and taking the payment of his monthly stipend upon yourself, see that he applies himself with diligence to the business of the *Sircar*. We have written to the aforesaid *Kilaadâr* on the subject of the *Cutwâl*, whose appointment, we have told him, is to depend upon you.

(1) Original جریده which has been already explained.

(2) Though the name of this city is most commonly written *Putn* throughout the correspondence, yet it is sometimes, as in the present instance, written سریرنگ پتن *Sirirung-putn.* Tippoo was at this time at *Bangalore*, to which place he had repaired (for what purpose does not appear) in the beginning of September.

LETTER CXXIV.

To ALI RÂJAH BEEBY; *dated 9th WÂSAAEY.* (*18th September.*)

WHAT you have written, relative to your having paid twenty thousand *rupees* to Meer Zynûl Aabideen, the *Foujdâr* of *Zuferâbâd*, is understood, and meets our approbation. You must, in like manner, discharge the remaining balance due by you. Upon your arrival at the Presence, we will personally state all matters to you. *Tillicherry* is situated near the *Taalûk* of *that refuge of chastity*:(1) you will, therefore, regularly transmit to us whatever intelligence you may [from time to time] be able to procure from thence.

OBSERVATIONS.

Ali Râjah Beeby was the same person, whom the English, in the west of *India*, sometimes dignified with the title of Queen of *Cannanore*, of which petty state she was the hereditary ruler. I am ignorant, at what period *Cannanore* became tributary to the *Mysore* chief: but it continued so till the cession of *Malabar* to the English, by the partition treaty of 1792; when all the rights and authority claimed by Tippoo Sultan in that province, were transferred to the East-India Company.

Ali Râjah Beeby was a Mahommedan; and on this account, perhaps, was treated by the *Sultan* with somewhat more distinction and lenity, than he was accustomed to show to his other tributaries in *Malabar*. He would not seem, however, to have succeeded in his endeavours to conciliate her good-will, or to inspire her with confidence in him. This fact is deducible from the constant repugnance, which she evinced to complying with his desire of seeing her at *Seringapatam*; and which will appear, on more than one occasion, in the course of the subsequent correspondence.

(1) Original عفت پناه which as well as عصمت پناه is a common form of address to women.

LETTER CXXV.

To Bûrhanûddeen; *dated* 10*th* *Wâsaaey*. (19*th September.*)

[After authorizing him to entertain in his service a *Hindivy Mûnshy*, the letter proceeds as follows] :—

It appears, that Kâlâ Pundit is attended by ten or twelve [armed] followers: let [therefore] a hundred men of the *Uskur*, armed with swords and shields, be sent [to his habitation or quarters], with instructions to close in with the party, and, overpowering, seize on the whole. The aforesaid *Pundit*, together with his adherents, must then be dispatched to the Presence, as before directed.

OBSERVATIONS.

This letter is little more than a repetition of Letter CXX, addressed to the same person, and written only two days before. Such an early re-iteration of his orders on the subject, strongly marks the impatience of the *Sultan* to get possession of his victim.

LETTER CXXVI.

To Mahommed Ghyâs *and* Noor Mahommed Khân; *dated* 14*th* *Wâsaaey*. (23*d September.*)

You will proceed from thence to the Presence, whenever the minister shall give you your dismission.

Y On

On the anniversary of the *Dusharrah*,(1) you will distribute among the Hindoos, composing your escort, a goat to every ten men; and on the anniversary of the festival of *Zilhijjeh*,(2) the like number of goats among the Musulmans of your party.

LETTER CXXVII.

To SYED GHUFFÂR; *dated from* SERINGAPATAM, *27th* WÂSAAEY. (*6th October.*)

YOUR letter, inclosing a list of the arms of Kâlâ Pundit, &c. has been received. What you write, respecting the seizure and confinement in irons of the said *Pundit* and his adherents, is understood and approved. We shall shortly direct you to repair to our Presence: be quick, therefore, in dispatching what business you have there.

OBSERVATIONS.

This is the last occasion on which Kâlâ Pundit is mentioned. Of his ultimate fate I know nothing: but it may be safely conjectured, that it was not a mild one.

(1) A Hindoo festival, occurring at the close of the rainy season. It is at this period that the native armies of *India* usually take the field. The Mahrattahs are said to celebrate this festival in a manner peculiar to themselves; which is, by destroying a village, to denote that the campaign is opened.

(2) This is a Mahommedan festival, celebrated on the tenth of *Zilhijjeh*, and commonly called *Bukr-eed* and *Eedûz-zohd*. It is commemorative of the sacrifice of Isaac.

LETTER CXXVIII.

To ZYNÛL AABIDEEN SHOOSTRY; *same Date.* (*6th October.*)

YOUR letter has been received. How came it, that notwithstanding your knowledge of the rainy season, you did not take *Kûndilehs*(1) with you? This circumstance occasions us great surprize. Let the grain, furnished by such of the *Ryots* as have submitted to your authority, be paid for. On the other hand, let that belonging to those *Ryots* who have adopted a rebellious course, be plundered, and applied to the use of your army.

Let assistance be afforded to Lucherâm, the *Huzâry*.

OBSERVATIONS.

The person to whom the foregoing letter is addressed was a brother of Meer Allum, so well known as minister for English affairs at the court of *Hyderabad.* I do not know at what period he engaged in the service of Tippoo Sultan; but I believe, that no intercourse, of any kind, subsisted between the brothers. Zynûl Aabideen, though occasionally employed by the *Sultan* in situations of trust, would appear to have been principally esteemed for his supposed literary qualifications. He it was who composed the *Futhûl Mûjâhideen,*(2) under the immediate direction of the *Sultan* himself. He was also the author of the *Sûltâne Tuwâreekh,* mentioned by Colonel Wilks, in the Preface to his valuable

Y 2 History

(1) In the original کندلها a term of which I can obtain no explanation. I am inclined, however, to think, that some description of tents is meant: perhaps bell-tents, or store-tents. The word frequently occurs, and the context every where seems to warrant the construction I have hinted at.

(2) See observations on Letter XC, where some account of this work is given.

History of Mysore: but this work appears to have been little more than a rhetorical amplification of the *Sultan's* own Memoirs, as far as the latter went. The reproof given to Zynûl Aabideen, in the present dispatch, is mild in the extreme, compared with the invectives which we shall hereafter see bestowed upon him.

LETTER CXXIX.

To KUMRÛDDEEN ; *dated* 29*th* *WÁSAAEY, from* SERINGAPATAM.
(8*th October.*)

YOUR letter, informing us of your arrival with your army on the banks of the *Tungbudrah*,(1) and of your intention to repair speedily to the Presence, has been received. You must hasten your arrival here; and order things in such a manner [on your march], that no desertion may take place from your army, which [you know] is composed of men from all the four quarters, ——— as *Kurpah*, &c. You must, therefore, employ some of the *Jyshe* troops to look after them, so that no desertions may happen, but the whole join us in safety. On this head the utmost care and strictness are necessary.

OBSERVATIONS.

It would appear, from this and other letters in the present collection, that desertions were frequent in the armies of the *Sultan*: but so they are in all the native armies of *India*. It is probable, however, that the evil might be experienced

(1) I am at a loss how to reconcile this letter with Letter CX, by which it would appear that Kumrûddeen had begun to cross the *Tungbudra*, on his way to *Seringapatam*, so early as the beginning of September.

rienced, in a peculiar degree, by Tippoo Sultan, since he would seem to have been in the habit of occasionally recruiting his ranks by forced levies; a practice, of which I am not aware that any other example is to be found among the princes or states of *India.*

LETTER CXXX.

To ZYNÛL AABIDEEN, *BUKTSHY*[1] *of EHSHÂM, at FURRÚKH-YÂB HISÂR*;[2] *same Date.* (8*th October.*)

YOUR letter, stating the insolvency of the late postmaster[3] of *Mânâ-yâr*,[4] &c., has been received. What was necessary to be said, regarding the above-mentioned postmaster, as well as the postmasters of *Runhully*,[5] was heretofore written at the greatest length. It is wonderful that you should not have acted conformably [to those directions:] but that, instead of doing so, you should repeatedly address us on the subject, and pursue [in this manner] your own fancies. For the future, you must not write to us on such matters, but conduct yourself agreeably to our former orders.

(1) There appear to have been different descriptions of *Buktshies.* The *Buktshies* of *Kushoons* were a sort of commissaries and paymasters, and were subordinate to the *Sipahdár*, if not to the *Risáladár*, or commander of a battalion. The *Meer Buktshy*, however, took rank of the *Sipahdár.* The *Buktshies* of the *Ehshám* and *Jyshe* were, I believe, the superior officers of those corps, respectively.

(2) *Chittledoorg.*

(3) Original اخبار والہ which I conjecture to mean a postmaster.

(4) I do not understand this term, or proper name, whichever it may be: but the meaning may be, the " late postmaster of *Malabar.*"

(5) This may be intended for *Hurpunhully.*

LETTER CXXXI.

To ZYNÛL AABIDEEN SHOOSTRY; *dated* SERINGAPATAM, *1st* ZUBURJUDY. (*10th October.*)

AHMED BAIG has been dispatched [to you], and other troops will shortly follow. In the mean while, you must not remain idle, but pursue, exterminate, or make prisoners of the rebels, wheresoever they may take refuge. You must also quickly inform us of the state of the rains in that quarter.

LETTER CXXXII.

To the same; dated 3d ZUBURJUDY. (*12th October.*)

YOUR letter has been received, and its contents are duly understood. What you write, concerning your operations [against the enemy]; your want of gunpowder and grain; the violence of the rains; and, lastly, your opinion, that though ten more *Kushoons* were to be sent thither nothing could be effected, unless we ourselves should proceed in person to that quarter, in which case, you think, that every thing would be speedily accomplished. All this is known.

You have with you fifteen hundred bundles of gunpowder, thirty rounds of ammunition, and two thousand men of the *Jyshe*. That you should not, with such a force, have made any effort to chastise the enemy, but should be waiting for our arrival, occasions us the utmost amazement, is utterly irreconcileable with [every idea of] courage, and warrants a strong suspicion of absolute cowardice [in you]. If this were not the case, two hundred *Jyshe* would be fully adequate to the suppression of this revolt.(1)

We

(1) The original has it, "*the chastisement of the enemy:*" but I have rendered it as above, to avoid the perpetual recurrence of the same phrase.

We therefore order, that, uniting your force with that of Meer Zynûl Aabideen, the *Foujdár*,(2) you do together exert yourselves in the signal chastisement of the *Koorgs.* You must, in particular, be careful, that your people do not disperse, and, by this means, expose themselves to be cut off. That country is populous. Collect together such of the inhabitants as are well disposed to our government, and giving them encouraging assurances, buy their grain, and distribute it among your troops. As to the rebels among them, you must pursue them wheresoever they can be found, and chastise them effectually.

OBSERVATIONS.

Strong as the censure, conveyed in the preceding letter, undoubtedly is, it will presently be seen, that the full measure of the *Sultan's* anger against this unfortunate commander was not yet dealt out. Vide Letters CXXXVI and CXXXVII.

LETTER CXXXIII.

To Mahommed Ghyâs *and* Noor Mahommed Khân; *same Date.* (12*th October.*)

Your letter has been received. What you write, respecting your having made up and delivered to your followers new flags, banners, &c., is understood, and meets our approbation. You must take care, that the [regular] infantry, attached to your escort, perform their exercise regularly. *You must not, however, expend any powder on these occasions*

Noor

(2) The appointment of this Zynûl Aabideen to the *Foujdáry* of *Zuferâbâd* is mentioned by the *Sultan* himself in his Memoirs. It took place on the first subjugation and settlement of that district, in the year 1784.

Noor Mahommed Khân being indisposed, it would be highly improper that you should, at such a time, be separated. Under these circumstances, you must take up your residence in the same place with him, and exert yourself for his recovery. In fine, you must, conjointly, discharge all the duties of attachment and fidelity that you owe to us.

LETTER CXXXIV.

To Ghûlâm Hyder; *same Date.* (12*th October.*)

You write for instructions, with regard to the prices at which you should buy certain articles for our use,(1) in order that you may regulate your purchases accordingly. Old age has certainly made havock on your understanding, otherwise you would have known that the *Mûtusuddies here* are not the proper persons to determine the market prices *there.* It is the *Mûtusuddies* there, and the instructions given to them on this head, which should be referred to on this occasion. Seek the necessary information from the *Dewâny Kuchurry*, and act accordingly.

LETTER CXXXV.

To Bûrhânûddeen; *dated* 4*th* Zuburjudy. (13*th October.*)

Your letter has been received. Your longer continuance at *Nergûnd*, is needless; while it is also productive of the ruin and destruction of your army: we therefore write, to desire(1*) you will remove with your forces into the country of *Kittoor*, where forage and gram will be found in abundance. Let orders be given to the *Kilaadâr* of *Nergûnd,* to make the necessary repairs to the fort.

The

(1) The articles are specified in the original, but I cannot make them out.

(1*) Literally, " it is therefore written that you," &c.

The troops of the *Uskur*,(2) and others which have been sent [ostensibly] to forage at *Dhárwár*, are, in fact, stationed there only to create disorder and disputes: these men must, therefore, be recalled. The place in question appertains to the cavalry foragers, and not to you [or to your people.]

What you say, of the assembling of the enemy's forces, is known. Do you keep your mind collected, and entertain no apprehensions. *Thousands of this kind of people are [constantly] coming and going.*

OBSERVATIONS.

It will be seen, hereafter, that the real object of the *Sultan*, in directing Búrhânûddeen to remove his camp to *Kittoor*, was not to facilitate the procuring of supplies, but to obtain possession of that place.

The indifference, if not contempt, with which the *Sultan* here speaks of the movements of the Mahrattah army, is strongly expressive of the low estimation in which he always either actually held, or affected to hold, the military character of that nation. Of the *Nizám's* troops he certainly did not entertain a more favorable opinion. With respect to the English, it is hardly credible that, with the impression which the successes obtained over him by Lord Cornwallis must necessarily have produced, he should really have thought so meanly of them, as, to judge by the sentiments he has left on record, he would appear to have done, even at a period posterior to the war of 1791-2. Spleen, arising from disappointed hopes, from baffled ambition, or even from a narrow policy, such as usually regulated his conduct, might have led him to write, and perhaps also to speak, in a more disparaging strain of his European neighbour and antagonist, than accorded strictly with his inward conviction or feeling. Arrogance and vanity were, undoubtedly, among the most prominent features of the *Sultan's* mind: but however those passions, seconded by the flattery of the people surrounding him, might encourage

Z him

(2) عسکر is the Arabic of لشکر and both words signify an army in general: but Tippoo Sultan applied the former term, exclusively, to his regular troops. The *Suwár-uskur* were the regular cavalry, and the *Piádeh-uskur* the regular infantry.

him to believe himself superior in military skill and prowess to the English, it seems impossible that his infatuation should have been so great, as to inspire him, in reality, with that contempt, which he occasionally professed to entertain for them as rivals in arms.

LETTER CXXXVI.

To ZYNÛL AABIDEEN SHOOSTRY; *dated* 5*th* ZUBURJUDY.
(14*th October*.)

YOUR letter has been received, and the particulars therein stated are fully revealed.

It appears, from the tenor of all the letters which have successively reached us from you, that you have conceived a mortal dread of the accursed tribe [to which you are opposed]. This being the case, neither the chastisement of the worthless crew, nor the proper settlement of our affairs [in that quarter], can be expected from you: we therefore direct, that you proceed, with the force under your command to *Periapatam*, and there remain [till further orders].

LETTER CXXXVII.

To the same; dated from SERINGAPATAM, 6*th* ZUBURJUDY.
(15*th October*.)

YOUR two letters, of the 2d and 5th of *Zuburjudy*,(1) have been received, and their contents are duly understood. We enclose two *Purwânehs*, one for the *Aumil* of *Hybutpoor*, the other for the *Aumil* of *Koondnoor*,

(1) If there is no mistake in these dates, the communication between *Seringapatam* and the scene of Zynûl Aabideen's operations must have been quick and uninterrupted, and the distance not considerable.

Koondnoor, directing them each to dispatch a thousand *goonies* of grain[2] to that person of mighty degree.[3] You will forward these *Purwáneks* to their address; and, on receiving the two thousand *goonies* of grain, dispatch the same to *Zuferábád*. Your wounded you are to send to *Hybutpoor*, the *Aumil* of which place has been written to respecting them. Of the two surgeons with you, one must accompany the wounded to *Hybutpoor*: the other will remain with you.

A hundred *Clashies*[4] have been sent to you from the Presence: a thousand bundles of cartridges have likewise been dispatched. Your detachment took with it, in their cartridge-boxes, forty-eight thousand musket-cartridges, besides fifteen thousand spare cartridges, making together sixty-three thousand cartridges. You write, "that you have "not remaining more than from fifteen to twenty cartridges in each "cartouch-box:" at this rate, the expenditure of cartridges has been very great. *We are curious to know, and desire you will inform us, how many of the enemy have been sent to hell*, by the expenditure of *such a number of cartridges*. We also desire to be informed of the amount of the rebel force. One hundred of your men being wounded, no doubt great numbers of the enemy must have been killed and wounded.

It is truly wonderful, that you, whose pen was employed in describing, in the *Futhúl' Mújáhideen*, the mode of making war in a close and woody country, should, at the moment of your being yourself engaged in conducting a similar warfare, have forgotten the rules there laid down. If you had carried on your operations according to those rules, you would never have sustained the loss you have done.[5]

Z 2 With

(2) I do not know the amount of this weight or measure: the *Goonies*, or *Gunnies*, are bags made of a sort of hempen cloth.

(3) This title would appear to have been applied, in this place, rather sneeringly.

(4) Men employed about tents, &c.

(5) For an extract from the *Futhúl' Mújáhideen*, containing the rules here spoken of, the reader is referred to Appendix, I.

With respect to your reiterated representations of the expediency of our repairing, in person, to that quarter, we answer, that (God willing) we shall shortly arrive there with an *inconsiderable* force, with which we trust we shall be enabled utterly to kill and destroy the enemy.

Now that you are about to proceed with grain, and other supplies, to *Zuferâbâd*, be mindful to regulate your march according to the rules laid down in the *Futhûl' Mûjâhideen* for operations in a close country; and to conduct the convoy, with circumspection, to its destination.

OBSERVATIONS.

It may be inferred, from the foregoing dispatch, that Zynûl Aabideen had received rather a serious check from the *Koorgs*. This conjecture derives the more support, from the circumstance of the *Sultan's* judging it necessary to proceed in person against the insurgents. I have, at this time, no means of ascertaining what force he actually took with him on this occasion; but though he affected to make so light of the business, it is not probable that he would put any thing to hazard, by proceeding against such a determined enemy with a *very* inconsiderable force. I am ignorant of the sequel of Zynûl Aabideen's history. It is, however, probable, that the *Sultan* did not again entrust him with the management of the sword, but confined him, for the future, to the exercise of his pen.

It seems impossible, that any thing, like that nice sense of honour which usually distinguishes persons of a liberal education, and particularly those of the military profession, should have existed in an army (or indeed in any other branch of a government) the superior officers of which were accustomed to be addressed by their sovereign in such coarse and degrading language, as that adopted by Tippoo Sultan in expressing his occasional disapprobation of their conduct; accordingly, few, if any, men of superior birth or elevated sentiments were ever known to have appeared amongst the higher classes of his subjects. These classes, in fact, were almost exclusively composed of persons of humble origin, and mere adventurers; who having been trained in implicit submission to the will of a cruel and unprincipled

unprincipled tyrant, could not be expected to exhibit any portion of that loftiness of spirit or generosity of disposition, which still adorn many of the genuine descendants of the ancient nobility of the Moghul empire; and would still make them spurn at any action, by whomsoever commanded, which they thought incompatible with their habitual notions of honour, or with the obligations of family pride. It was not so with the nobles (if nobles they might be called) of Tippoo Sultan's court. They were, on all occasions, the passive instruments of the irmaster; at whose nod they were used to murder, betray, and pillage, certainly without remonstrance, and, most probably, equally without repugnance.

But however deficient this order of men may have been in the species of spirit and honor which we have been considering, they would not appear to have been wanting in fidelity to his government, not to say attachment to his person. With this last sentiment, it was not, perhaps, in the nature of things, that a man of his harsh and unconciliating disposition should be capable of inspiring them:(6) but their general character of loyalty must be allowed to have been unimpeachable. To what degree this adherence to him might proceed from a real sense of duty and gratitude, is a question not easy of decision. No doubt, some of his principal servants might have been, and probably were, influenced by such motives: yet, I confess, I am of opinion, that it was owing less to considerations of this kind, than to the precautions adopted by the *Sultan* for its prevention, that so few instances of defection occurred among them, during the different wars in which he was engaged. It was his practice to oblige all the chief officers of state, and others holding employments of material trust, to fix the residence of their families permanently in *Seringapatam;* from whence their removal, without his knowledge and concurrence, became impossible. This expedient may be easily conceived to have had the effect of confirming the fidelity of many, who might otherwise have been prompted, by discontent, or other reasons, to quit *Mysore.* But if this miserable policy answered the *Sultan's* immediate purpose, it also promoted one, which

(6) It has been affirmed by some, that Tippoo Sultan was in conversation "remarkably "lively and entertaining;" but I have strong doubts of the correctness of this statement. It very ill accords with his general character, and is, in some measure, contradicted by himself in one of his "Dreams," where he distinctly says, "that it was not his custom to "enter into playful discourse with any one."

which he little contemplated at the period of its adoption. The final conquest and settlement of Tippoo Sultan's dominions by the English, was facilitated by nothing so much, as the circumstance of the families of most of the principal men of the country having fallen into their hands, along with the fortress of *Seringapatam*.

LETTER CXXXVIII.

To KUMRÛDDEEN KHÂN; *dated* 9*th* ZUBURJUDY. (18*th October*.)

DESIRING him to repair with his army, as expeditiously as possible, to the Presence: and signifying, *that the design of reducing Adoni was dropped*.

OBSERVATIONS.

This dispatch was not in my recollection, at the time of my writing my observations on Letter XCII, or I should have been inclined to refer the *weighty enterprize*, there spoken of by the *Sultan*, to a meditated attack upon *Adoni*, with more confidence than I then thought it right to do. It now clearly appears, that this enterprize had certainly been in his contemplation, previously to the date of the foregoing letter, and very probably as far back as the end of July. Why the attempt was dropped at this time, cannot now be satisfactorily shown: but it is not improbable, that the necessity which arose, for his directing his attention to the *Koorg* quarter, might have obliged the *Sultan* to suspend the execution of his purpose for some time longer.

LETTER CXXXIX.

To ZYNÛL AABIDEEN SHOOSTRY; *dated* 10*th* ZUBURJUDY. (19*th October*.)

ANNOUNCING to him the intended arrival of the *Sultan*, in person, [at *Zuferâbâd*], after the festival of *Zilhijjeh*; but desiring that the circumstance should not be made public.

LETTER CXL.

To Mahommed Ghyâs and Noor Mahommed Khân; *dated* 7*th* *Zuburjudy.* (16*th October.*)

What you write, on the subject of having made up and delivered new flags and banners to your people, is understood and approved. You and Noor Mahommed Khân must reside together in the same place, and display your zeal in our service on all occasions. What more? You must see, that your men regularly perform their exercise, but without using gunpowder.

OBSERVATIONS.

This letter is nearly a transcript of letter CXXXIII, written only four days before. Other instances of the like repetition occur in the course of this correspondence.

The injunction against expending powder on the field days of the escort, may have proceeded either from an economical motive, or from an apprehension that the use of it, in the city of *Poonah*, might have given umbrage to the Mahrattahs. There can be little doubt, that this would have been the consequence of such a military display, in the present humour of that government: and as, notwithstanding all his orders to the contrary, it is very certain that he wished his agents to remain at *Poonah*, it behoved him the more to beware of furnishing the ruling power there with any fresh ground of complaint or irritation.

LETTER CXLI.

To Bûrhânûddeen; *dated* 13*th* *Zuburjudy.* (22*d October.*)

Directing him again (1) to remove with his army into the *Kittoor* country, and to report to the *Sultan* the state of affairs in that quarter. Telling

(1) See Letter CXXXV.

Telling him, also, *that after receiving an order from the Presence, he must be careful to act in conformity with it.*

OBSERVATIONS.

The concluding sentence of the foregoing abridged dispatch is somewhat ambiguously expressed in the original. It might either have been meant as a rebuke, for the general's not having marched to *Kittoor,* in pursuance of the former orders for that purpose; or it may have signified, that he was to be prepared to execute such future directions as the *Sultan* might send him immediately upon the receipt of the same, (contemplating, probably, the subsequent orders of the subject of *Kittoor.*)(1) I incline to prefer the latter interpretation.

LETTER CXLII.

To Mâh Mirzâ Khân; *dated* 14*th* Zuburjudy. (23*d October.*)

The Governor of *Madras* has written to us, "that, agreeably to our "desire, he has sent strict orders to the *Taalúkdárs* of *Sátghur* not to "afford protection to the *Zemindár* of *Punganoor,* or to any people "of the latter district." We *therefore* direct, that you give no disturbance to the country of the English, but pursue the business you have been sent upon. You will be speedily joined by the *Sipahdár,* Imâm Khân, who has been sent with his *Kushoon* to reinforce you.

OBSERVATIONS.

The *Sultan* would appear to have been put into better humour than usual with the English, by the ready compliance of the government of Fort St. George with the application he had made to it, respecting the *Zemindár* of *Punganoor.* He drops,

(1) See Letter CXLVII.

drops, in the present letter, the disrespectful appellation of *Fringy*, and (grounding his order, as it were,[1] on the British governor's amicable conduct) directs Mâh Mirzâ Khân not to give any disturbance to the English territory. It will be recollected, however, that the same order was issued to this officer, on his first appointment to proceed against *Oalpilly*. (See Letter CXIX.)

LETTER CXLIII.

To Ehsânûllah Khân; *dated* 18*th* Zuburjudy (27*th October.*)

You will put into [or enroll in the corps of] *Usud-Ilhyes*, as many Hindoos, *male and female*, as are willing, of their own accord, to enter into the same: and you will then transmit a return of them to us, it being our intention to augment their pay.

OBSERVATIONS.

Whether the *Usud-Ilhyes*, here mentioned, were a distinct body from the *Ahmedies*, spoken of in Letter XLII, or whether this was only another appellation for the latter corps, I am unable to say. I rather think, however, that they were separate institutions; but that both were military, and both composed of proselytes to the Mahommedan faith, though of different descriptions. It is true, that there is nothing distinctly said of the conversion of the Hindoos, mentioned in the text, to *Islâmism*: but I think the context, as well as the name given them, sufficiently shows, that their embracing the Mahommedan religion, was a necessary condition of their incorporation with the *Usud-Ilhyes*. This term signifies *the Divine Lion*, or *the Lion of God*, and was one of the appellations bestowed on Ali. It has been already seen, that Tippoo sometimes designated his own state, or country, by this name; calling it, occasionally, the *Sircar Ussud-Ilhye*; as well as *Ahmedy*, *Hydery*, and *Khodâdâd*.

2 A It

(1) "We therefore direct," &c.

It has struck me as possible, that the *Ahmedies* might have consisted exclusively of Christian converts (including the native Christians of *Malabar* or *Canara*), and the *Usud-Ilhyes* of Hindoo proselytes only. It will be easy for any of my Indian readers to ascertain what grounds there are for this conjecture.

With respect to the order for enrolling *women* among the *Usud-Ilhyes,* I conclude that it referred to the *wives* of such men as might qualify themselves for admission into the corps: but why they should have been *enrolled,* as if constituting part of the corps, it is not easy to comprehend. No one ever heard, I believe, of a female regiment in the service of Tippoo Sultan; though it is a certain fact, that the late *Nizâm* had a body guard composed of women, armed with muskets, and partly clothed in the manner of *Sepoys.*

LETTER CXLIV.

To Râjah Râm Chundur; *dated* 19*th* Zuburjudy. (28*th October.*)

That which is contained in our instructions, respecting the transactions of the *Surrâfs* [or money-brokers,] is to be considered as an absolute [or irrevocable] decree,(1) according to which you must act in all matters, great or small.(2)

LETTER CXLV.

To the Governor *of* Pondicherry; *dated* 21*st* Zuburjudy. (30*th October.*)

Desiring him to send back to *Madras* [*i. e.* to dismiss] the *Brahmen* news-writer residing at *Pondicherry* [on the part either of the *Nabob* of *Arcot,*

(1) Original حکم محکمه

(2) Original جزوکل "particular and general."

Arcot, or the English government]; and signifying the *Sultan's* wish, to purchase [at *Pondicherry*] seven or eight thousand firelocks.

OBSERVATIONS.

The objection taken by the *Sultan* to the residence of a news-writer from *Madras* at *Pondicherry*, could proceed only from an anxiety to prevent the English Government from obtaining information, from the latter place, of the correspondence he was at this time carrying on with the French. If such an application, as the one here recorded, had come to the knowledge of the British government at the period it was made, it would certainly have justified, and probably have led to, the gravest suspicions of the *Sultan's* designs. Yet it would not appear, that any doubts were entertained, at the period in question, of his disposition to maintain the peace, which he had not long before concluded with us.

I have no means of ascertaining, whether the *Sultan's* request to the French governor, respecting the news-writer, was complied with or not. It is not, however, likely that it was; since the governor could have assigned no plausible reason for a proceeding, so unusual among friendly powers in *India*.

LETTER CXLVI.

To MEER ZYNÛL AABIDEEN, *and* AHMED BAIG, *SIPAHDÂR; dated* 22d *ZUBURJUDY*. (31*st October*.)

DIRECTING them to dispatch four hundred *Goonies* of grain to *Zuferâbâd*; and to leave a gun and guard(1) from each of their divisions at *Hybutpoor*, from whence the *Sultan* would bring them on, when he arrived there, which would be soon, as he had that day [*viz.* the 22d *Zuburjudy*]

(1) Original یزک *(yuzuk)* which likewise signifies a division, consisting of six rank and file. یزکدار *(yuzukdár)* was the term employed by Tippoo to denote a sentry.

Zuburjudy] entered his tents, for the purpose of proceeding against the rebels.

OBSERVATIONS.

Meer Zynûl Aabideen *Shoostry,* was informed, in Letter CXXXI, that Ahmed Baig had been sent to join him ; so that it is probable, that he is meant by the Zynûl Aabideen, named in the title of the present letter, though the usual addition to his name, or *Shoostry,* has been omitted. If omitted in this instance, it may also have been omitted in the title of Letter CXVII, which see.

LETTER CXLVII.

To BÛRHÂNÛDDEEN ; *dated 29th* ZUBURJUDY. (*7th November.*)

YOUR letter, informing us of the arrival of yourself and army near the fort of *Kittoor,* has been received. You must, in the first instance, *send and invite the* Daisye (1) *of that place to an interview, and give encouraging assurances to his managing servants.* You will next dispatch some rocket-men for the protection(2) of the country. *After the aforesaid* Daisye *shall have arrived at your quarters, let the fort be occupied by a party of the* Sircar's *troops.*

OBSERVATIONS.

If the reader should be at any loss to comprehend the drift of the *Sultan* in the preceding letter, his difficulty will be entirely removed, on a perusal of Letter CLVII.

I am

(1) I am not acquainted with the etymology, or proper meaning, of this word; but I conceive it to have the same import as *Zemindâr* or *Polygar.* Perhaps the term may be derived from *Daise,* the *Hindivy* for a country.

(2) In the original جامداري *Jámdáry,* which is a guard posted for the protection of villages, cultivated fields, &c. from the depredations of the followers of an army.

I am ignorant of the situation of *Kittoor*, if I rightly read the name, which, however, is extremely doubtful; the characters, in which it is written, being susceptible of at least a dozen different readings. It may be the *Kittoor* of Captain Moor's map, which is placed north-west of *Dhárwár*, about twenty miles. The *Polygar*, or *Zemindár*, of *Kittoor*, is mentioned in the tenth article of the treaty of *Poonah* (concluded between the British government and the Mahrattahs, in June 1790) as one of those feudatories, dependent, at the same time, both on the courts of *Poonah* and *Hyderabad*. It is very possible, that he might also have been among the tributaries of Tippoo Sultan; as the *Nabob* of *Sháhnoor* certainly was, though declared in the treaty, just referred to, to be " subject to service with both " the *Nizám* and the *Paishwa*.

LETTER CXLVIII.

To the Imaum *of* Muscat; *dated* 4*th* Hydery. (11*th November.*)

[After compliments]........ A *Dow*, the property of Rutn Jee and Jeewun Doss, merchants of *Muscat*, having in these days [*i. e.* lately] been dismasted in a storm, came into *Byte-Koal*,(1) a sea-port, belonging to the *Sircar*. Although, in such cases, it is customary for the prince, or ruler of the place, where a ship happens to be wrecked, to take possession of it, and whatever it contains; yet, as there is no distinction between the country of the *Sircar* and *Muscat*, and as the above mentioned merchants declared themselves to be your subjects, the vessel in question, together with all the stores contained in it, has been restored to the aforesaid merchants, and is, accordingly, now dispatched to you, along with this friendly epistle. For the rest, peace be with you.

(1) Name uncertain; perhaps *Batcole*, on the coast of *Canara*.

OBSERVATIONS.

The word, which I have rendered *wrecked*, is in the original شكست *(shikust)* and such, I believe, is its usual acceptation, when applied to a ship. But this interpretation does not well agree with the argument of the text, since the vessel in question was only *damaged*, not *wrecked*. Then, whatever the custom may be in some countries, with respect to wrecks (properly so called), it is no where, I believe, usual to consider vessels, merely dismasted, or otherwise damaged, as wrecks: consequently, the *Sultan* has here pretended to confer a favor, where nothing more than a right was rendered (for we are not told that the repairs were made at his expence), and laid claim to a credit for having released a ship, which he was not authorized, by the practice of any civilized country, to confiscate, or detain.

LETTER CXLIX.

To Mahommed Ghyâs *and* Noor Mahommed Khân; *dated 7th* Hydery. *(14th November.)*

Agreeably to your suggestion, we have written to Bûrhânûddeen, desiring him, in the event of the hat-wearer,(1) Monsieur Tuvias,(2) passing over to our army from the forces under *Kishn Pundit*, to advance the aforesaid [hat-wearer] something to defray his expences [on the road], and dispatch him to the Presence.

N. B. A letter, of the same tenor and date, was written to Bûrhânûddeen.

OBSERVATIONS.

The person here spoken of was probably some French adventurer in the Mahrattah service, who may have made overtures to the Mysore envoys at *Poonah* for deserting

(1) Original كلاه پوش for which term the people of *Hindostan* substitute *Topy-wâleh*, from whence, perhaps, the word *Topaz* and *Topazes*.

(2) Name uncertain.

deserting to their master, or may have been tampered with by them for that purpose.

Kishn Râo, I believe, commanded the division of the Mahrattah army, which passing the river *Kishna*, had advanced, towards the end of February of this year (1785), with the ostensible view of supporting the *Zemindár* of *Nergúnd;* but which would appear to have very soon retired again, leaving Bûrhânûddeen at liberty to resume the siege of that place, and subsequently to reduce both it and *Ramdoorg*, as well as to seize upon *Kittoor*, without offering him any interruption. I am unable to account for the apparent inactivity of the Mahrattahs during so many months. They were, probably, waiting to concert a plan of operations with the *Nizám*. In the mean while, the *Sultan* seems to have contented himself with acting on the defensive. It was not, accordingly, till the month of October in the following year (1786), that the main armies of the contending powers could be said to have come into contact with each other, or to have entered upon offensive operations, on a large or general scale. What had preceded, was considered mere skirmishing; and, indeed, Tippoo himself appears, in his Memoirs (as will hereafter be seen), to have dated the actual commencement of the present war, from the period when the Mahrattahs, in conjunction with the *Nizám*, proceeded to the attack of *Báddmy*.

LETTER CL.

To Hukeem *Khán of Sháhnoor; dated 9th Hyderí.*
(16th November.)

Your agreeable letter has been received. You write, "that you have "discharged to the amount of eighteen *lacks* of *rupees* [of our claim "upon you] by bankers' accepted bills, and request that we will either "excuse you the remaining eight *lacks* [due to us] or allow the payment "of it to be postponed to next year."

It

It is known. A statement of the sums, of which that friend was, through his own negligence, defrauded by his servants, specifying the amount of each individual's malversations, was submitted to him. Where, then, was the difficulty of making the several plunderers refund their plunder, and of paying the same to us [in discharge of our claims]? We desire you will also raise the remaining eight *lacks* of *rupees*, and transmit the amount, in bankers' bills, by the hands of our bankers, whom we wish you to send back to us immediately.(1)

LETTER CLI.

To the SHÂHNOOR WÂLEH *(i. e. the* NABOB *of* SHÂHNOOR*); dated* 10*th* HYDERY. (17*th November.*)

DISPATCH to Nursia, the *Dewân* of *Nugr*, one *lack* of *pagodas*, on account of annual *Paishcush* for the year *Jullo*,(1*) and take his receipt for the same.

OBSERVATIONS.

The year *Jullo* had still more than four months to run; consequently, so far from granting Abdûl Hukeem any indulgence of the kind he had solicited, the *Sultan* appears determined to make him pay his *Paishcush in advance*, or, at least, before it was fairly due.

The

(1) My construction of this passage is, that the bankers in question had been sent from *Seringapatam*, for the purpose of settling this account with Abdûl Hukeem Khân, and of procuring the payment of the amount due to the *Sultan*

(1*) The name of the Malabar year, corresponding with *Jullo*, is likewise given in the original; but as I am doubtful of its being written accurately, and as it is not of any consequence, I omit it.

The style of Letter CL was tolerably civil: that of the present letter (written only the day after) is abrupt, and rudely peremptory. I cannot account for so sudden and striking a change in the *Sultan's* mode of address in any other manner, than by supposing that he might, in the interval (though only a single day), have received some information, tending to excite a suspicion of Abdûl Hakeem's attachment to the Mahrattah interests; which that chieftain certainly not long after embraced openly, though, probably, driven to do so by the rigorous proceedings of his brother-in-law.

LETTER CLII.

To TURBIYUT ALI KHÂN; *dated* 10*th* *HYDERY*, *from near* *ZUFERABÂD.* (17*th November.*)

ORDERING the *Hydery* and *Kuntarâey fanams* to be put in circulation, throughout all the districts depending on *Bangalore*.

LETTER CLIII.

To RÂJAH RÂM CHUNDUR; *same Date.* (17*th November.*)

To the same effect as the preceding letter; with this addition, *viz.* "that no other but the *Kuntarâey* and *Hydery fanams* shall be allowed "to pass current"

LETTER CLIV.

To MEER KÂZIM, *DÂROGHA, or* COMMERCIAL CONSUL; *dated* 10*th* *HYDERY*, *at* *MUSCAT.* (17*th November.*)

DIRECTING him not to dispose, hastily or immediately, of the black pepper and *sandal* wood [in his charge], but to wait till they had attained a desirable price. [Literally, " till the selling price of them " equalled his *heart's desire*."]

N.B. The *Sultan*, not thinking, perhaps, the preceding orders sufficiently explicit, repeated them two days after, in Letter CLVI.

LETTER CLV.

To the same; dated 11*th* HYDERY. (18*th November*.)

JUZEERAH DIRÂZ [or *Long Island*] is in that quarter.(1) Silk-worms *and their eggs* are produced there. We wish you to procure some of both, and to dispatch them to us, together with five or six men, acquainted with the proper mode of rearing them.

We direct, that such of our vessels as import at *Muscat* be unloaded in two days; and that their export lading of sulphur, lead, copper, &c., be also completed in two days, and the vessels dispatched to *Mangalore*. If more than four days be consumed in lading and unlading the vessels, *you shall be responsible for the extra expence* [that may be incurred in consequence]. You must regularly report to us the day each vessel arrives at *Muscat*, and also the day on which it is dispatched from thence.

N.B. A separate letter to the same person, and of the same date, directs him to engage as servants, and dispatch to *Mangalore*, ten persons experienced in the pearl fishery.

OBSERVATIONS.

The *Sultan's* distrust of the integrity or diligence of his agent is here strongly manifested; as is also his own want of reflection, in attempting to regulate, with such

(1) *Juzeerah Dirâz* (or *Long Island*) is the *Kismish* of our maps, and situated in the Gulf of *Persia*.

such strictness and precision, the business of loading and unloading vessels, which must necessarily have depended, in a great degree, on the state of the weather and other circumstances, which it might not be in the power of the consul to controul.

The *Sultan's* anxiety to establish a pearl fishery on the Coast of *Malabar*, as well as to introduce the culture of the silk-worm into his dominions, appears to have been very considerable; but I believe that he failed entirely in both attempts.

LETTER CLVI.

To the same; dated 12*th* HYDERY. (19*th November.*)

YOU must not be in haste to dispose of the cinnamon, *sandal* wood, black pepper, and rice, imported at *Muscat* from *Mangalore* and *Khooshhâlpoor*. Keep them carefully, till they become dear, and will yield a [good] profit, and then sell them.

LETTER CLVII.

To BÛRHÂNÛDDEEN; *dated* 15*th* HYDERY. (22*d November.*)

WE sometime since wrote, to desire that possession might be obtained of the fort of *Kittoor*. You must (no matter by what contrivance or pretext) get possession of it for the *Sircar*. *If some degree of violence even* should be requisite for the purpose, let it be employed: and let the present be considered as a most urgent injunction.

N.B. Two letters, to the same effect as the foregoing one, were written to Syed Humeed and Syed Ghuffâr, both of them belonging to Bûrhânûddeen's army.

2 B 2

LETTER CLVIII.

To the same; dated 16th Hydery. *(23d November.)*

Your letter has been received. Keeping a strict watch[1] upon Luchmun Râo, the brother of Sumâjee Pundit,[2] you must encamp with your army within gunshot of the fort of *Kittoor*, and send for the *Daisye* and Sumâjee Pundit. If they should come [to you] it will be well; otherwise you must, with the advice of Syed Humeed and Syed Ghuffâr, contrive, by some means or other,[3] to obtain possession of the said fortress for the *Sircar*.

LETTER CLIX.

To Meer Kâzim, *and the other Commercial Agents at* Muscat, *dated 18th* Hydery. *(25th November.)*

Having ascertained in what part of that country saffron is cultivated,[1*] engage two persons in our service, and send them thither to purchase one or two *maunds*[2*] of the seed, which [when procured] is to be dispatched to us. You must also procure silk-worms, and send them hither, together with some men acquainted with the mode of managing them, to whom you will make an advance of money for their support.

N.B. A letter, to the same effect, was written to the *Dulâl* (or public broker) at *Muscat*.

(1) Original در نظر بند داشته to keep in sight; to place in arrest; to put under restraint.

(2) Name uncertain. It may be *Tumâjee*.

(3) Original بهر طور

(1*) Literally, "where the seed of saffron is procurable."

(2*) A *maund* is a weight or measure varying in different countries. In *Hindostan* it consists of forty *seers*, or about eighty pounds averdupoise.

LETTER CLX.

To Meer Kâzim; *same Date.* (*25th November.*)

You are to buy yearly, and send to the *Aumil* of *Mangalore*, a hundred *Utls*(1) of almonds, and thirty *Utls* of pistachio-nuts.

You have still [on hand], of former importations, both *Sandal* wood and black pepper: you will now receive more of each. This stock you must not [immediately] expose to sale; but give out, that you have received our orders to discontinue the sale thereof [at *Muscat*], and to dispatch it to *Juddah* (where also we have a factory), and that you are, in consequence, about to do so. Having circulated this report, you must keep the goods by you, till the price of them advances twenty-five or thirty *pagodas* [the *candy*,] when you will sell them [without further delay].

LETTER CLXI.

To Budrûz Zumân Khân; *same Date.* (*25th November.*)

You have done well in making prisoners of the turbulent and seditious, including Kurry-tummah,(1*) with their women and children. These last must be detained. With respect to Kurry-tummah, if he be one of the insurgents he must be suspended on a tree.

[A verse.] " The head of an enemy is best when hurled from the " point of a javelin: as a path-way is best, from whence the bramble " has been rooted out."

After

(1) Original اطل which I am at present unable to explain. I am inclined to think, however, that it is a term of the *Sultan's* invention, and that it may have been intended to express a *Maund*. See, in support of this conjecture, Letter CLXXII, where a similar order to the present one is given, and where the word *Maund* seems substituted for *Utl*.

(1*) Name extremely uncertain.

After properly securing the passes, you must proceed, with your collected force, in quest of the rebels, making prisoners of as many of them as possible. We some time ago wrote to you, desiring you would contrive some means of getting possession of the person of Moona Kool;(2) and we now again write, to say that *he must be secured, by stratagem or deceit.* Let a roll, moreover, of the number of men and women already made captives, be transmitted to us.

OBSERVATIONS.

The foregoing letter commences with three or four words, of which I am not able to make any sense. The transcriber may, probably, have miswritten them. They appear thus in my manuscript: الاحي نغاي بايد داشت which may, no doubt, be so read as to be interpreted, "You must put [or keep] the *cardamums* in a pit." The writer then proceeds to say, "You have done well, &c." But if the foregoing passage be understood literally, it will appear to be a strange and very unintelligible order, to be addressed to an officer at the head of a body of troops employed on active service. On the other hand, if it be taken in a metaphorical sense, it will be no easy matter to assign a plausible meaning to it. *Cardamums,* I believe, are a principal article of the natural produce of the country in which Budrûz Zumân Khân was, at this period, stationed, and which I suppose to have been *Bidnore,* and the districts situated between that and the sea coast: possibly, then, by the word *cardamums,* the *Sultan* (who sometimes affected to express himself enigmatically) might intend to designate some particular individuals, or class, among the refractory inhabitants of that quarter, whom he wished to be disposed of *under ground.* It must be owned, however, that this conjecture is too slightly supported to be entitled to much consideration; and I shall, therefore, being unable to suggest a better, leave the difficulty to exercise the ingenuity of some of my oriental readers.

With

(2) Name uncertain.

With respect to the Kurry-tummah (as I have written it) mentioned in this letter, I am not clear whether it is the proper name of an individual, or an official designation. However this may be, it seems extraordinary that the *Sultan* should be under any uncertainty with regard to his being one of the seditious, or insurgents; a doubt of which would seem to be implied, by the qualifying word, *if.* The meaning, however, might be, that *if* Budrûz Zumân Khân had any reason to believe him to have been *particularly forward or active* in the insurrection, he was, *in that case,* to be hanged.

Budrûz Zumân Khân was one of the principal men at the court of Tippoo Sultan, and seems to have possessed the confidence and esteem of his master in a considerable degree.(3) He commanded at *Dhârwâr,* when that place was besieged by the united English and Mahrattah forces, in 1791; and though it appears, by the correspondence of that period, that the *Sultan* was not perfectly satisfied with his defence of that place, yet it may be inferred, from subsequent events, that no permanent impression to his disadvantage was produced on the occasion. Budrûz Zumân Khân, and his son, Mirza Bâkir, were among the chiefs of *Mysore* who survived their sovereign; and who, submitting to the British authority, were liberally pensioned by the Company's government.

We have, in the present letter, another example of the flagitious policy which the *Sultan* was, at all times, ready to pursue, for the accomplishment of his views. Provided Moona Kool was seized, he did not care by what atrocity that object was effected.

LETTER CLXII.

To the same; same Date. (25th November.)

Write a letter to Moona Kool, inviting him to come to you, *and then seize upon his person.*

(3) He entered into the service of Hyder Ali (according to Colonel Wilks) in A.D. 1762.

LETTER CLXIII.

To KHÂJEH SETH, KHÂJEH HERÂTOON,[1] *and two others, (names illegible); dated* 19*th* HYDERY. (26*th November.*)

We have lately learned from Khâjeh ——, "that you have it in con-"templation to come, with ships laden with merchandize, to our ports, "for the purpose of trading; and that you wish to sail under English "or Portuguese colours, and to obtain our special license[2] for these "purposes." We highly approve of your intention, and desire you will repair, in the utmost confidence, with your merchandize, either to the port of *Mangalore* or to the port of *Calicut;* where landing your goods, you shall, in the first instance, supply us, at a fair price, with such articles as we may want, after which you shall be at liberty to sell the remainder at your pleasure, and to take your departure when you like.

We have accordingly written, and herewith enclose, two *Purwâneh*s to the above effect: one of them to Urshud Baig Khân, the *Foujdâr* of *Calicut*, and the other to Ghûlâm Hyder, the *Aumil* of *Mangalore;* to either of which ports you may resort, as you shall think proper.

N.B. Then follow the two *Purwâneh*s, referred to in the foregoing letter. In these, the *Sultan* directs an invoice, or list, of the goods imported, to be transmitted to him on the arrival of the ships; in order that he may signify his pleasure respecting the articles which he may wish to purchase, previously to a free and general sale of the cargoes taking place. It does not appear by the subsequent correspondence, whether or not the merchants, in question, thought proper to open a trade with *Mysore,* on the discouraging condition stipulated by the *Sultan.*

(1) These were Armenian merchants; but it does not appear in what country they were settled. The word خواجه which I have written *Khâjeh,* is usually written and pronounced *Cojah;* but improperly, *Khojah,* or *Cojah,* signifying an Eunuch, whereas *Khâjeh* answers to Sir, Master, &c.

(2) Original قول *Kowl.*

LETTER CLXIV.

To RÂJAH RÂM CHUNDUR; *dated* 20*th* HYDERY. (27*th November.*)

RESPECTING a manufactory of musquets to be established in the Fort of *Khân-Khân-hully*: for which purpose, if it should be necessary to pull down forty or fifty houses belonging to poor people, *it will not signify*, as they will erect other habitations in their room, within the *Paith* [or outer town].

OBSERVATIONS.

No mention being made of any compensation to the poor inhabitants for the demolition of their houses, it may be concluded that none was authorized. It is probable, indeed, that the houses in question were of very little value: but that consideration does not lessen the injustice of the present order, whatever may be the case as to the actual hardships which it inflicted.

LETTER CLXV.

To MAHOMMED GHYÂS *and* NOOR MAHOMMED KHÂN; *dated* 21*st* HYDERY. (28*th November.*)

YOU write, " that the *Brahmens* attached to your mission cabal or " intrigue [privately] with the managers [ministers] there, indepen- " dently of you, and, by this means, occasion prejudice to our affairs." It excites our astonishment, that such unwarrantable proceedings should take place, notwithstanding your being on the spot. What is the reason that you do not flog and [otherwise] severely punish the offenders? Let us be informed what person has been guilty of this offence.

You write for a supply of money. Bills or money shall be hereafter transmitted to you.

We have already replied to the letter from Râo Râsta, as well as to that from yourselves, which you sent to us by Inkut Râo.

LETTER CLXVI.

To Budrûz Zumân Khân ; *dated* 22d *Hydery.* (*29th November.*)

Your letter, containing an inventory, or memorandum, of plundered cattle, money, and goods,(1) has been received. You must load the money and goods upon five hundred of the aforesaid cattle ; and placing a strong guard over them, send them to Ghûlâm Ali, at *Pálindg-tár*,(2) from whence a thousand *Piádehs* are about to be dispatched to the Presence. Your party having joined these, the whole will proceed hither together. You must [continue to] make diligent search for, and get possession of, more [of the property of the rebels].

LETTER CLXVII.

To Mahommed Ghyâs *and* Noor Mahommed Khân ; *dated* 25*th* *Hydery.* (*2d December.*)

Your letter has been received. We approve of the offerings you have made at the two *Durgáhs* [or shrines]. You also did well, in presenting a *Búrhánpoory* dress and a *Fuzee* to Râo Râsta the day he visited you.

You write, " that it is the intention of Râo Râsta to dispatch a " confidential person hither with letters for us." It is known, and it

(1) That is, of booty made from the insurgents.

(2) Name uncertain.

it is well. Let Râo Râsta send his confidential servant in charge of his secret communications. We must attribute this proceeding to motives of friendship. An answer to the before mentioned Râo's [former] letter was forwarded some time ago. A bill for money to defray the expences of the people attached to you shall be sent hereafter.

You moreover write, "that the *Mûtusuddies*(1) with you have [of "late] assumed a most presumptuous [or impudent] mode of be-"haviour;(2) holding separate conferences [or carrying on intrigues] "with the minister and Hurry Pundit, without your knowledge, and "to the prejudice of our affairs." You add, "that you have heard "this, both from Râo Râsta and from other quarters." It is comprehended. All this arises from your neglect. That your people should act in this improper manner, and that you, instead of punishing them for so doing, should complain of them to us, is to be attributed to your great age, and to the climate of that place [*Poonah*]. Communicate to us the names of the several persons who have been guilty of this shameful conduct..

OBSERVATIONS.

The offerings, here spoken of, were directed to be made in a former letter, (which it has not been thought necessary to give), and consisted of a coverlid, or counterpane, of *Kemkhâb*, and fifty *rupees* in money. The *Durgâhs* (or shrines) in question, where those of *Hûsâmûddeen* and *Sulâhûddeen*, situated, I conclude, somewhere in the vicinity of *Poonah*, or at least in the Mahrattah territory.

It would appear, from the circumstances of Râo Râsta's determining to communicate with Tippoo, through the medium of an agent or messenger of his own,

2 C 2 that

(1) In Letter CXLV they were designated the *Brahmens*. The *Mûtusuddies* in the *Decan* are usually of that class.

(2) Original خبرگي اختيار کرده

that he was not disposed to open himself freely to the *Sultan's* envoys; and indeed, theweakness which the latter had recently manifested, in regard to the *Mútusuddies* attached to their mission, was but little calculated to inspire him with confidence, either in their ability or discretion.

LETTER CLXVIII.

To BUDRÛZ ZUMÂN KHÂN; *dated 26th* HYDERY. (3d *December.*)

DIRECTING him to stop for four days at *Tul-Kauvery*, and to wait for further orders from the Presence, previously to his proceeding to the *Páyen-Ghaut.* Also, to seize upon as many of the rebels and their cattle as possible; and, cutting the rice [around him], to feed his own cattle upon it. The closing paragraph of this dispatch is given entire, and is as follows:

A *Purwáneh* for Moona Kool is enclosed. Let the same be conveyed to him, and consider on some way of getting him to come to you [*i. e.* of getting him into your possession].

LETTER CLXIX.

To BÛRHÂNÛDDEEN; *same Date.* (3d *December.*)

THE letter you sent us has passed under our view, and its contents are duly perceived.

You write, " that seizing on the *Vakeel* of the *Kittoor* man, and " detaining him in custody, under you own eye, you had dispatched " Syed Ghuffâr and Syed Humeed with some troops into the *Paith* " [or outer town], where the *Daisye* and Goornâth Pundit, the ma- " nager, immediately came and presented them with the keys of both " castles, of which, as well as of the *Paith,* instant possession was " taken

"taken by our troops." [You proceed to state,] "That the *Daisye*, "and Tumsâjee Pundit, and some others of superior distinction, were "afterwards brought into the victorious camp, and there placed under "guards." You further report, "that five *hat-wearers* [*i. e.* Eu-"ropeans], one of whom rides in a *Palankeen*, as well as the *Ramdoorg* "man, and one called *Pedro*, have been made prisoners: that, for the "protection of the town, *ryots*, and inhabitants of the districts in "general, you had stationed rocket-men, horse, and also some infantry "guards, in different places: that, for the present, you had put seals "on the store-houses, such as the *Tosheh-khâneh* belonging to the "*Daisye*, and placed *Jyshe* guards over them: that you had commis-"sioned Yunkut Runjia, the *Aumil* of *Dhârwâr*, to take the necessary "measures for collecting together and encouraging the *Ryots* and "others: and that, as soon as our pleasure on the subject should be "communicated to you, it was your intention to take an inventory of "all the effects, horses, &c. belonging to the *Daisye*, under the in-"spection of the managers of the *Daisye*, and to transmit the same to "us for our information."

It is known and approved. In the town and fort [of *Kittoor*] are many wealthy persons, possessing *lacks* [of *rupees*]; some of them proper inhabitants of the place, and others belonging to *Poonah*, from which last city there are several *Mûtusuddies* established at *Kittoor*, in whose hands considerable property has been deposited. You must, therefore, by offering pecuniary rewards to the inhabitants of the place, endeavour, through their means, to discover the individuals alluded to; and having done so, you must put *them*, likewise in confinement. It is the custom of that country, for the most opulent bankers to assume the habit of *Fakeers*, and to make their escape in that disguise.(1) Pay particular

(1) That is, whenever driven to the extremity by the violence of the times, or the injustice of their rulers; which, according to the context, must have been *customary* or usual events.

particular attention to this point: and having duly identified the principal inhabitants of the class in question, secure their persons, and take care that their effects are not embezzled, as a strict account of this matter will hereafter be required of you.

Whosoever among the former managers of the *Daisye* has been removed from office, and incurred the displeasure of the *Daisye*, let *him* be encouraged, and some mark of favor be bestowed upon him; and, with the exception of the town and fort, let him be appointed to superintend the collections (2) of the country: then ascertaining, through his means, the circumstances of the great ones and bankers, you will keep the latter in custody. You must, also, through the same channel, obtain an account of the property (3) of the *Daisye*, as well as that of the principal men and other inhabitants of the place, and having discovered where it is, send for and secure the same. You are, moreover, to station a guard from Shaikh Unser's corps, and another from Syed Ghuffâr's, in the town and fort, and over the *Tosheh-khâneh* and other store-houses of the *Daisye*, to the end that no part of the effects of the latter, or of the inhabitants, may, in the disorder of the moment, be made away with. Rocket-men must also be stationed in proper places, for the protection of the *Paith* [or outer town.]

Sending then, in the *first* instance, for the managers of the *Daisye*, you must tell them, that you propose making an humble application to us, to reinstate the *Daisye* in the possession of his country: but that, to enable you to do this, it will be necessary that a contribution should be [previously] paid down; and that if they will, accordingly, agree to raise fifty *lacks* of *rupees*, and give you [due] security for the same, you will represent the case to us; and obtaining a *Purwâneh* of confirmation in their

(2) Original معاملات *Moamulut.*

(3) Original زندگي *Zindugy.*

their name [*i. e.* the *Daisye's* name] restore the place to them. You may, at the same time, observe, that such care has been taken of their country, that no injury whatever has been sustained by it. Addressing them, *at first*, in words calculated like these to excite [or humour] their avarice, and to inspire them with confidence, you will bring them, after some altercation, to agree to pay a *Paishcush;* the amount of which being settled, as well as the manner of discharging it [*i. e.* whether in money, goods, or bankers' bills], *you will next*, by their means, send for the concealed bankers,(4) and ascertain from these the assets in their hands; a statement of which, specifying the several bankers' names, must be transmitted to us, to the end that the requisite orders for the restoration of the place [to the *Daisye*] may be subsequently dispatched to you.

In the mean while, you must affix both the seal of the *Daisye* and your own on the *Tosheh-khâneh*, and other storehouses of the *Daisye*, as well as on all such places as contain money or goods in deposit: in addition to which, some of the most trusty men of Syed Unser's and Syed Ghuffâr's *Kushoons* must be placed as guards over the whole. In regard to the horses, camels, and elephants, belonging to the *Daisye*, you are to cause an exact account of them to be taken, in conjunction with the latter's managers, and then to have them removed from the *Paith*, and placed in front of, but at some distance from, the *Daisye's* quarters; where they are to be accompanied by their usual attendants, with the exception of horsemen, or other military persons. Here they are, moreover, to be provided with grain and fodder, and otherwise taken proper care of, at our charge. The family of the *Daisye*, as also all his managing servants, are to be permitted to remain in their houses; over which, however, guards are to be placed, to prevent the egress of the persons in question from thence.

Let

(4) The original is here so obscurely expressed, that I am very doubtful of having rendered it rightly.

Let the two forts and the ditch be examined by yourself in person, conjointly with the *Sipahdárs*, and let a report of their present condition be made to us. Transmit, likewise, a detailed account of the magazines and artillery, and state your opinion with respect to the place [that is, as to its importance or its strength].

You will repeat to the *Daisye* and to his managers, that if they quickly agree to a heavy composition or contribution,(5) and put the same in an [immediate] train of payment, their place shall be restored to them.

Enquire of the *Daisye's* servants, and let us know, the extent of *Kittoor*, and what number of forts it contains. Write letters of encouragement to the actual *Aumils*, and continue them in office. Send to the present *Kilaadárs* [or governors of forts], desiring them to wait upon you; and [then] superseding them in their commands by servants of our own, let the forts be garrisoned by *Piádehs* from your army.

Obtain from the *Daisye's* managers lists of all the *Daisye's* servants, menials and others, and then have them mustered. The *Buktshy* of your cavalry must be directed to take a muster of the *Daisye's* cavalry, in the presence of the *Daisye's* manager. This being done, the cavalry in question are to be placed in charge of a particular *Risáladár* [of your army], along with whose own corps they must be encamped. The *Piádehs* [or foot soldiers] must, after being mustered, be consigned to the charge of Syed Humeed, and be encamped on his line.(6) They must not have guards openly placed over them, but a strict watch is to be secretly kept on them.

Next send for the commanders of [the *Daisye's*] horse and foot, and hold an encouraging language to them, by intimating your expectation of shortly receiving our orders for restoring the place [to the *Daisye*.]

You

(5) Original كهندني سنگين

(6) Original مثل *misl.*

You will then proceed to tell them, that, in the mean while, they must infuse confidence into their people, and get them to take up their quarters in your camp. This point being gained, and the troops in question encamped with your own, let guards be placed over all the aforesaid commanders, independent of, and separate from those [previously] posted over the *Daisye* and the others. They must not be suffered to go among their brethren [or comrades];(7) and you must supply them with such provisions and other necessaries as they may require.

You will take particular care, that no horses are allowed to be kept near that part of the camp occupied by the *Daisye* and his managers;(8) nor must any of his people be suffered to pass backward and forward, without your authority.

Several persons of consideration, and opulent bankers, reside at *Shâhpoor*, *Pulkawum*,(9) and *Gokauk*, all three dependencies of *Kittoor*. Shaikh Unser with his *Kushoon*, two *Mûtusuddies*, and two intelligent *Hurkârehs* from the cavalry *Kuchurry*, together with two *Risâlas* of horse, and some *Piâdehs* [foot], must be dispatched to take possession of these places. The principal men and bankers being ascertained, must then be sent for, and the *Aumils* of the aforesaid places be continued in their offices: for which purpose, you will transmit to them the necessary letters of confirmation from yourself and the *Daisye*.

Shaikh Unser must be instructed to obtain from the *Aumils* of the before-mentioned three *Taalûks* written engagements, purporting that they will be responsible for the flight of any of the inhabitants of their respective districts.

2 D We

(7) Original برادري

(8) The object of this order was probably to guard against the danger of the *Daisye's* effecting his escape on horseback.

(9) Name uncertain; but probably meant for the *Bulgong*, mentioned in Letter CLXXXVI.

We shall ourself shortly arrive in that quarter; inasmuch as we have, by the blessing of God, completely settled all the affairs of *Zuferâbâd.*

OBSERVATIONS.

The foregoing dispatch forms one of the few exceptions, afforded by the present collection, to the usually concise style of the *Sultan's* mandates. It is diffuse and minute in the extreme: from which circumstance may be inferred the importance which he attached to the acquisition of *Kittoor*, and his solicitude to turn it to the best account.

We hear little more of *Kittoor*, or of its *Daisye*,(10) for a month after the date of the present Letter. The interval was probably employed in negociations with that chieftain, or *Polygar*, the result of which may be collected from the tenor of Letter CCXVII.

The *Sultan* would appear to have returned, soon after the date of the preceding letter, to his capital. The only notice I have any where met with of his proceedings, during his stay at *Zuferâbâd*, or of the manner in which he "settled the "affairs" of that quarter, is contained in the brief account he has himself given of the business, in a subsequent letter to the *Patan* chief of *Kurnool*.(11) The following extract, however from his Memoirs, as it relates to a previous settlement of the country in question, soon after his accession to the *Musnud*, may not be unacceptable to the reader.

After a brief, but curious, account of the reduction of the *Bul* country,(12) where he caused a new fortress to be erected, to which he gave the name of *Munzirâbâd*,(13) the *Sultan* proceeds thus in his narrative :—

"From

(10) With the exception of the short Letter CLXX, immediately following.

(11) See Letter CXCVI.

(12) Called also *Bullam*.

(13) This fortress was erected (according to the *Sultan's* own account) on the scite of one which had been raised about twenty-five years before (or A.D. 1764), by Hybut Jung (a distinguished officer in the service of Hyder Ali Khân, better known by the name of Fuzloollah Khân) but which had been subsequently demolished by the *Râjah* of *Bul*. "I "directed,"

"From hence [*i. e.* from *Munzirábád*] I proceeded towards *Koorg*, some of "the principal men of which country seeing that they were without any chief or "leader, had, at the time that we were moving against the *Nazarenes*,(14) chosen "and placed at their head one of their own body; to whom, investing him with "absolute power, they became obedient. After this, they set about raising dis-"turbances in that quarter, and laid siege to a fort newly erected by the *Sircar*,(15) "and in which the governor [of the district] resided. The garrison being "reduced to great straits, surrendered on capitulation; but were all massacred, "on marching out of the place. The fort was completely demolished by the "rebels, who *through enmity* [*i. e.* to mark their hatred the more strongly] con-"veyed away every stone belonging to it, and threw the whole into the quarry "from which it had been originally taken. Elated with this success, they "continued to occupy the position they had assumed.(16) When this occurrence "came to our blessed hearing,(17) we dispatched a commander, named Hyder Ali "Baig, with a suitable force, to reduce the *Koorg* country. The aforesaid com-"mander proceeding to the borders of *Koorg*, had arrived near the fort of *Peria-"patam*, when the rebels collecting together advanced to meet him. One or two "battles ensued: but the aforesaid commander was not able to settle the affairs "of that quarter. In this conjuncture, I was proceeding in person from the "country of *Arcot* towards the country of *Nugr*, and had got about half way.

2 D 2 Hereupon

"directed," says the Sultan, "that it should be constructed with nine sides, than which "there is no better figure" for a fortification. He called it *Munzirábád*, because the numerical powers of the several letters composing that word, when added together (according to the *Ubjee* diagram), indicate the year of the *Higera* in which the place was conquered, *viz.* 1198.

(14) In the original it is سواري خاص by which the *Sultan* appears, from the context, to have meant his father's *retinue*; so that the period, here referred to, must have been that of the invasion of the *Carnatic* in 1780.

(15) The name of this fort is not given in this place, but I conclude, from the context, that it was the *Merkerrah*, afterwards mentioned.

(16) The original has it همهها خود سر شده بجاي خودها نشستند literally, "they all, becoming "self-headed, continued in their places."

(17) Original بسمع مبارك

" Hereupon I detached another army, under the direction of the *Rájah* of *Kunnik-*
" *geery*, to the aid of the aforesaid commander, and pursued my march to *Nugr*;
" after the recapture of which, the victorious army was engaged in the reduction
" of *Mangalore*. It was during this period, that the two before mentioned com-
" manders, having advanced, for the purpose of subduing *Koorg*, two or three
" *coss* into the woods, were attacked from all quarters by the *Koorgs*, who closed
" up every avenue [to their camp or position]. For three successive days was the
" conflict maintained; at the end of which time, my base commanders, consult-
" ing only the safety of their worthless lives,(18) took to flight, leaving behind them
" their troops and guns. The *Rájah* of *Kunnikgeery*, however, with a few men,
" maintained their ground [for some time]; and after amply discharging the
" obligations of valor, and sending numbers of the enemy to hell, made an
" offering of their lives for the service of the *Usud Ilhye Sircar*.(19)

" In consequence of these events, I proceeded, after the reduction [or subjuga-
" tion] of *Bul*, as above related, towards *Koorg*. From *Periapatam* the army
" advanced in two divisions, by different roads, and in two days, by rapid
" marches, reached the residence(20) of the governor [of the district], where the
" infidels had taken post. Here I made a great number of prisoners. Kutty Nâik,
" however, the no-chief(21) of the *Koorgs*, effecting his escape, with his family
" and children, through the woods and adjacent hills, concealed himself and
" followers in a glen, or valley,(22) of the *Eláichy* mountains, which was inaccessible
" both to wild beasts and birds. Hither the *Hydery* army pursued the fugitives,
" and after some search discovering the entrance of the before mentioned glen,
" encamped

(18) Original جان نا پاک literally, " *impure* souls or lives."

(19) I am not quite clear, whether the *single death* of the *Rájah*, or the sacrifice of his *whole party*, is here meant to be recorded by the *Sultan*.

(20) *i. e.* The place which the *Koorgs* are said, in the beginning of this extract, to have seized and demolished.

(21) Original ناسردار or *Sirdar*, with the privative نا prefixed: a term of contempt very usual with the *Sultan*. The name of the *Koorg* chief is doubtful.

(22) In the original غار which strictly means a cavern or cavity: but the context requires the interpretation I have adopted.

" encamped there [for the night]. The following day, taking two *Risdlas* of " *Jyshe*, about five hundred *Piádehs*, and two guns with me, and leaving the " two guns at the mouth of the glen, I formed an advanced guard of a *Jowk* [or " company] and two hundred *Piádehs*, which after firing two or three guns, I " directed to proceed [into the glen], under the command of a *Jowkdár*. I " followed myself with the two *Risálas*, and three or four hundred *Piádehs*, and " accompanied by a few select persons. Though it was now mid-day, the glen, " owing to the prodigious lofty trees which overhung it, was so excessively dark, " that it was with difficulty a man could see the ground; while no one could make " a step [in advance] till he had cleared his way, by removing with his sword the " small trees [bushes] which obstructed it.

" When we had, in this manner, proceeded about half way through the glen, " the darkness was such, that there was no distinguishing on which side the sun " was.[23] In this distress, great were the efforts which were made to obtain a sight " of the sun, as being essential to the discovery of a passage through the glen: " but, notwithstanding several men ascended the trees, and [from their tops] " looked out for the sun, they were not [for a long while] able to obtain the least " glimpse of it. At length a man, who had mounted a tree at some distance " from the troops, having seen the sun, came and pointed out to me the western " quarter, stating, at the same time, that there remained three hours of day. By " knowing the quarter, we were enabled to advance two or three *coss* further " through the glen; at the opposite extremity [or side] of which we at length " arrived. Beyond this end of the glen was a small plain, where three houses of " Kutty Nâik stood. When we reached the spot it was sun-set; so I took up my " quarters in those houses, drawing up and encamping my followers on each side " of Kutty Nâik's dwelling. Here, telling my people that the enemy would " approach in the night, and after discharging their muskets at a great distance, " would set up a howl or noise, in the manner of dogs, swine, and jackals, I " strictly forbad their standing to their arms on that account, directing them to " sit still, and satisfy themselves with frightening the dogs away.[24] Accordingly, towards

(23) That is, they could not ascertain in what direction they were moving.

(24) Original نهیب به سگان باید داد or it may be نهیت " groaning at."

" towards the morning, the aforesaid dogs and jackals, approaching on every side, " fired their muskets, and set up a great cry; of which, however, my people, " agreeably to orders, took no other notice than by frightening the dogs away: " the noise for which purpose was no sooner made, than all the dogs of the desert " fled.

" When morning came, I set the pioneers and others to work upon making a " road, fifty yards[25] wide, through the glen, which was accordingly completed by " the evening. The following day I sent for the whole army, with which I pro- " ceeded in three marches to the passes,[26] spreading detachments, as I advanced, " over the country, for the purpose of seizing on the thieves. The aforesaid " *Nâik*, fleeing into the woods, escaped with his family, by another road over " the passes, to *Tillicherry* a sea-port belonging to the English. Here dying a " natural death, at the end of two or three days, *he made his entry into hell:* " whereupon orders were sent to his followers from the Presence, directing them " to bring his family and effects to the Presence; and accordingly *the thieves*, who " had accompanied him, leaving *Tillicherry*, repaired with his family, two or " three elephants, and his other effects, to the Presence.

" The special retinue[27] returning from hence through the glen and other places " [by which it had advanced], reached, after some marches, the fort of " *Merkerrah*,[28] which the infidels had demolished. Here I halted for two or " three

(25) Original ذرع *Ziraa* or *guz*, measuring from two and a half to three feet, according to the standard used.

(26) Original کتل a height over which a road is conducted.

(27) Original سواري خاص. By " the special retinue," the writer here means his own. This mode of expression is common.

(28) In the original it is uniformly written *Meprkerrah:* but as I take the *Merkerrah* of our maps to be the place meant, I conclude the *p* to have been an accidental interpolation. In new naming this place, according to the fantastical mode adopted by the *Sultan*, he was obliged to call it *Zufeerâbâd* instead of *Zuferâbâd* (the more proper appellation), as otherwise the chronogram would have been defective, *Zuferâbâd*, or ظفراباد yielding only 1188, whereas the number required was 1198, and therefore *Zufeerâbâd* became necessary. *Merkerrah*, I fancy, did not long retain its new name of *Zuferâbâd*, which, in the month of December 1786, was transferred to *Gurramcoondah*. See Letter CXC.

" three days, during which I examined the spot very carefully, and then issued " orders for rebuilding the fort; to which I nominated a *Kilaadár*, &c. appointing " Meer Zynûl Aabideen [at the same time] to be *Foujdár* of the district. " Proceeding from *Merkerrah*, I marched ten *coss* to the residence of the aforesaid " *Náik*, where there was a small fort, in which I put a garrison, and directed the " *Foujdár* to abide till the conclusion of the rainy season; which being now very " near, I hastened, by successive marches, to *Periapatam*, and I gave to the " [new] fort of *Merkerrah* the name of *Zufeerábád*; from which name may be " deduced, without any ambiguity, the date of the conquest of the place. From " *Periapatam* I detached a respectable force to the assistance of the *Foujdár* of " *Zufeerábád*; and then our elevated standards proceeded in the direction of the " seat of the *Sultan* at *Putn*."

The *Sultan* has added to the preceding narrative the following curious and important notice:—

" When I arrived at *Zufeerábád*, I sent for all the leaders of the rebels, and " delivered into their hands written mandates to the following effect:—

" It is the custom with you, for the eldest of five brothers to marry, and for the " wife of such brother to be common to all five: hence there cannot be the slightest " or remotest doubt of your being all bastards and whoresons. This is *about* the " seventh time that you have acted treasonably towards the *Sircar*, and plundered " our armies: I have now [therefore] vowed to the true God, that if you ever " again conduct yourselves traiterously or wickedly, I will not revile or molest a " single individual among you, but making *Ahmedies* (29) [*i. e. Musulmans*] of the " whole of you, transplant you all from this country to some other; by which " means, from being illegitimate, your progeny or descendants may become " legitimate, and the epithet of whoresons (30) may no longer belong to your tribe."

(29) It is clear from this passage, that the term *Ahmedy* was not confined to Christian converts to the Mahommedan faith.

(30) The term which is here, and in one or two other places, rendered *whoreson*, is in the original مادر خطائي *i. e.* a sinful mother," or " one with or having a sinful mother."

LETTER CLXX.

To Syed Humeed *and* Syed Ghuffâr; *dated from* Zuferâbâd, *28th* Hydery. (*5th December.*)

The humble address sent by you has been received, and the particulars of the occupation of the fort of *Kittoor*, by a garrison of our troops, are comprehended.

You must place guards, composed of trust-worthy men, at different points, which must be most carefully watched, in order that a single blade of grass may neither be dispersed nor pillaged. Let not the property be plundered, as, owing to the want of suitable precautions,(1) was the case at *Nergând*. On this head you must issue and enforce the strictest orders, as otherwise you will be held responsible for the consequence.

LETTER CLXXI.

To Urshud Baig Khân, *Foujdâr of* Calicut; *dated* 1st Tûlqory. (*8th December.*)

You must, on some pretence or other, send to Worm-râj, the *Râjah* of *Kurtinâd*, to his brother Sabbâbut, and to Unnund Kurp, his manager,(1*) to come and visit you; upon their doing which you are to secure their persons, and to report the same to us. You must keep this matter secret, and make no delay [in the execution thereof.]

(1) Original ازبي تشفي which rendered literally would be "from (or owing to) discou- "ragement," *i. e.* perhaps "from due encouragement not being given to the inhabitants." But though this should be the sense of the passage (which however is very doubtful) it would not follow that the *Sultan* meant any other than delusive encouragement. Possibly, however, the transcriber may have inadvertently written بي تشفي instead of بي تشفي "want of en- "couragement," which would render the passage perfectly intelligible.

(1*) All these names are somewhat doubtful. A fourth person is mentioned, but his name is perfectly illigible.

LETTER CLXXII.

To Meer Kâzim; *dated 2d Tûlooey.* (*9th December.*)

The first sort of *sandal* wood you must sell at the rate of one hundred and twenty *pagodas* the *candy;* the second sort at one hundred *pagodas;* the third sort at ninety *pagodas;* the fourth sort at eighty *pagodas;* and black pepper at eighty *pagodas* the *candy.* You must not sell them at any other [*i. e.* not at less] prices than these. If you should have to keep them even for a year or two, it will not signify. Take care that you buy your sulphur and copper cheaply. Purchases of gold [bullion] and lead are not required. Buy and send yearly thirty *maunds* of pistachio-nuts, two hundred *maunds* of almonds, and fifteen *maunds* of *Monukkas* (1) without seeds [or stones]. Go to *Hûrmûz*, and buy there large *rolling* [*i. e.* perfectly round] pearls: small pearls are not wanted.

OBSERVATIONS.

It is uncertain whether the pistachio-nuts, almonds, and raisins, here ordered to be procured, were designed for the *Sultan's* own consumption, or as articles of trade, to be retailed in the shops, of which some account has already appeared.

LETTER CLXXIII.

To Shâh Mahommed *and* Khyrûllâh; *same Date.* (*9th December.*)

Directing them to supply themselves with the wood necessary for completing the *Rung-muhl,* (1*) in the manner prescribed in their instructions;

2 E

(1) Called also *Kishmish.* It is a small sweet raisin, with few or no stones.

(1*) *i. e.* a painted hall, or apartment.

structions; and reproaching them with assurance,[2] for repeatedly applying to the Presence on this subject, and waiting for answers to their letters.

Commands them, agreeably to their former orders, to procure wood, and all other materials they require, in whatever manner they shall think proper and practicable, and apply the same to the work in hand.

OBSERVATIONS.

This letter would seem to convey to the persons addressed, a power of procuring the articles in question, by violence, or any other means they might think fit to employ.

LETTER CLXXIV.

To RÂJAH RÂM CHUNDUR; *dated* 3d *TÛLOOEY*. (10*th December*.)

You write, "that at *Hûscottah*, and other places, the *Jowkdârs* of "the *Hûzoor* are proceeding to relieve [or change] the troops stationed "in the [several] forts, whose pay you are, in consequence, agreeably "to our orders, preparing to issue; but that, in the mean while, the "*Mûtusuddies* of the *Ehshâm Kuchurry* say, that certain stoppages are "to be made, on account of the appointments [or commissions] of "*Jumaadârs*, &c. for which stoppages, you observe, you see no authority "in our instructions [to you]."

We are amazed at the understanding and good sense [you have displayed] on this occasion! [1] Those things which are permanently fixed [or

(2) Original مشايخ properly the plural of شيخ *Shaikh*, but generally conveying the sense given in the text.

(1) This is a sneer; the *Sultan* meaning, here, the contrary of what he says.

[or standing orders alone] are inserted in our *Húkm-námehs* [or general instructions]; but such fresh matters as this, which are from time to time ordained, are notified in distinct [or separate] orders. How, then, should this new regulation be referred to in instructions delivered to you [before it was made]?

You further write, "that Syed Peer, the *Kilaadár*, demands pay for "men belonging to the *Jyshe*, *Ehshám*, and others, who have not been "regularly returned to the *Mútusuddies* of the *Kuchurry;* and that "you likewise see no authority for this in your instructions." If you contravene or exceed the same in any instance, you will have to refund what you have over-disbursed.

OBSERVATIONS.

The stoppages here spoken of, probably referred to some tax, or fees, which the *Sultan* might have ordered to be levied on new appointments, for the benefit of the government.

Râm Chundur appears, in the present instance, to have been very unjustly reproved; for, notwithstanding the decisive tone assumed on this occasion by the *Sultan*, it may be safely contended, that the *Rájah* was strictly justified, both by the general scope of his master's instructions, and the particular nature of the case in question, in what he did. Is he not told, in the very same letter, "that he will be made "to refund all disbursements unauthorized by his instructions?" And does it appear, that he was in possession of any regular, or official notification, of the innovation which he was required to carry into effect? The *Dewán* was, unquestionably, entitled to be duly apprized of a regulation, to which he was expected to conform.

2 E 2

LETTER CLXXV.

To SHUMSÛDDEEN KHÂN;[1] *dated 5th TÚLOOEY.* (*12th December.*)

DIRECTING him to air in the sun eighteen bales of worm-eaten [or moth-eaten] shawls; and after putting cummin-seed, &c. into the bales, to tie them up again, and lay them carefully by.

LETTER CLXXVI.

To BUDRÛZ ZUMÂN KHÂN; *dated 7th TÚLOOEY.* (*14th December.*)

WHATEVER we propose ordering we shall shortly order, on the subject of the rebel Moona Kool.

LETTER CLXXVII.

To SHÂH NOORÛLLAH; *dated 8th TULOOEY.* (*15th December.*)

AGREEABLY to our former orders, you are to proceed to *Mangalore;* and there obtaining from the *Aumil* of that place whatever supplies [or stores] may be required for the use of the ships, you are to dispatch the latter to *Tidry.*[1*]

You write, proposing to take fifteen hundred wax-candles, besides wax. ***Where can be the necessity for so many wax-candles?*** Get the *Aumil* to deliver what number may be [really] requisite. The latter has been already written to, directing him to supply whatsoever was required for the use of the vessels. What more?

You

(1) This person was superintendant of the *Tosheh-khâneh* at *Seringapatam.*

(1*) Name uncertain. I had, at first, read and written it *Nudry* or *Nundry,* but altered it, on the authority of Colonel Munro. It is a small harbour on the coast of *Canara,* where the *Sultan's* ships lay when unemployed.

You moreover write, "that the *Aumil* of *Mangalore* delivers to you "only old and black rice." It is known. *That rice is good. You must take it, and not engage in improper altercation.* What more shall we write?

OBSERVATIONS.

The *Sultan* having now determined on sending another embassy to *Constantinople*, and from thence to *France* (the one previously dispatched by the same route, having, as before stated, been recalled), Shâh Noorûllah was employed to make the necessary preparations for the purpose. The same person was subsequently appointed a member of this mission; which, however, proved equally abortive with that which had preceded it, and was, in its turn, succeeded by another (as will be seen hereafter) in 1787.

It has been said, that the embassies proposed to be sent to the court of France, by land, failed through the parsimony of the *Sultan*, who could not be induced to supply the funds necessary on the occasion. Whatever ground there might be for this opinion, the foregoing letter certainly announces a determination to regulate the expences of the *outfit*, at least, of the meditated embassy, on principles of strict economy. Old and black rice is declared to be good enough for his plenipotentiaries; who are likewise given to understand, that they will not be allowed to burn as many candles as they please.

LETTER CLXXVIII.

To Râjah Râm Chundur; *same Date.* (15*th December.*)

Directing him to pay monthly four *pagodas* and a half to the European *Chailah*(1) sent by Syed Mahommed Khân, the *Kilaadâr* of *Putn*, and to assign him some employment.

(1) A *Chailah* is an adopted slave. He is treated in many respects with the same tenderness as the sons of the family, of which he is considered a member. The *Chailah*, here mentioned, had of course become a *Musulman*.

LETTER CLXXIX.

To Mahommed Ghyâs *and* Noor Mahommed Khân ; *same Date.* (*15th December.*)

Your two letters, of the 16th and 19th of *Hydery* [23d and 24th November] have been received, and what you state, respecting the misconduct of the *Brahmens*, is known. That you should have suffered men, subject to your authority, to act so presumptuously, and not have put a stop to the business by scourging and punishing them well, must be owing to your great age. Let them still be immediately placed under a guard near you ; and give strict orders, that they be not allowed the least egress without permission.

You write, " that you have separately examined each of them, and " that one lays the blame on another." [Instead of this] let them be separately flogged : and then, after [duly] interrogating them, let each man write down his statement [of the matter] with his own hand. Let their names, moreover, be reported to us.

Urgent, or very particular dispatches, must be always forwarded by a pair of *Hurkârehs,* and not by the post, which will soon be discontinued.(1)

The message which you communicated to us from Unund Râo Râsta has been received, and you will give such answer to him as we shall hereafter direct.

You

(1) Meaning the post to *Poonah*, which, notwithstanding the rupture between the two governments, was still permitted by the Mahrattahs. It will be seen hereafter, that Tippoo did not yet consider himself as absolutely at war with that nation ; though, from the hint here dropped, respecting the speedy discontinuance of the post, he would seem to have thought that crisis approaching fast. It may also be inferred, from the toleration of the *Sultan's* post, the continuance of his envoys at Poonah, and their amicable intercourse with some, at least, of the Mahrattah chieftains, that the latter did not, any more than Tippoo, regard the hostilities which had hitherto taken place between the parties, as amounting to open or decided war.

You did right, in taking to Râo Râsta the [pieces of] cloth, and other customary gifts, on occasion of the marriage. But wherefore did you take, and why do you continue to take, the *Mŭtusuddies* [*i. e.* the *Brahmens* so often mentioned] along with you to Râo Râsta's house? It is owing to such folly as this, on your part, that they have become so presumptuous. You should take with you [on such occasions] none but a few *Hurkăreħs*.

The gifts from the two shrines, together with your memorandum of the counterpanes, are arrived. [See Letter CLXVII.]

LETTER CLXXX.

To the Seven Superintendants *of the* Post, *at the Seven capital Cities of the* Sultanut *(or Kingdom); dated* 9*th* Tŭlooey. (16*th December.*)

(Circular.)

We have fixed the *Coss* at six thousand *Guz*, which distance [or space] must be travelled by the postmen in a *ghurry* and a half [or thirty-three minutes and forty-five seconds]. If the letters appertaining to your province [or department] are not delivered according to this rate, and any delay arises, you must flog the *Hurkăreħs* belonging to you: and if the delay should proceed from the men of another division of the post, you must report the same to us, in writing. You are, moreover, to denote the hour, the day of the month, and day of the week, on the superscription of all your dispatches. This order is to be strictly attended to.

OBSERVATIONS.

A volume of the *Sultan's* regulations, in my possession, contains the following notice respecting the *Guz*, as established by him:

"The

" The number of letters, of which the *Kulmah* [or creed] consists being " twenty-four, it is *therefore* ordained, that twenty-four thumb-breadths shall " make *half* a legal *Guz*; a thumb-breadth being equal to the aggregate breadth " of ten grains of one kind of rice, and of seven of another kind." The *Kembâlûb*(1) [or rope] used in measuring [roads] consists of thirty-two of these *guz*.

According to this rule, the *Guz* consisted of about forty-eight thumb-breadths: but the directions for ascertaining the thumb-breadth seem too vague to admit of any certain or precise calculation. Taking, however, the *Guz*, here described, at thirty inches, or two feet and a half (which gives five-eighths of an inch for each thumb-breadth) the *coss* will amount to fifteen thousand feet, or better than two miles and three-quarters; making the rate of proceeding appointed for the postmen rather more than five miles an hour. This, though certainly very practicable, when the relays of *Hurkârehs*, or postmen, are placed at short distances, considerably exceeds, I believe, the ordinary rate of the mail in British *India*; where, happily, however, the coercive means of accelerating its progress, so familiar to the *Sultan*, are unknown.

I am not able to specify, with any certainty, the *seven* capital cities intended by the title of the present letter: but there can be little or no doubt, that *Seringapatam*, *Nugr*, and *Bangalore*, were among the number; while it is not improbable, that the other four were *Chittledoorg*, *Gooty*, *Gurramcoondah*, and *Sera*.

LETTER CLXXXI.

To Ali Râjah Beeby; *same Date.* (16*th December.*)

We have received your letter by Fukhrûddeen, who has also expatiated to us upon your situation. The custom of the world is this. Servants and dependants hold themselves [at all times] prepared for the performance

(1) Original كمبالُب which may possibly be derived from كنبار a rope made of the fibres of the cocoa-nut: the ر and ل or *r* and *l* being often interchangeable; and ن or *n*, both in *Arabic* and *Persian* words, frequently taking the sound of م or *m*.

ance of services; the execution of orders; obedience and fidelity. Many times have we written to that lady of chaste degree[1] on the subject of repairing to our Presence; in reply to which you have continually brought forward evasions and excuses, and still continue to do the same. In this case, what is to be done? Be yourself the judge.

Rooe Wurm-râj, who presented himself before us, was honored with a grant of the farm of the *Taalúk* of *Cherkul*, and with other gifts. If you [in like manner] had come [to us], agreeably to our orders, you [also] would assuredly have experienced our bounteous favour. You will learn the remaining [or further] particulars from the letter of Fukhrûd-deen.

LETTER CLXXXII.

To the Dewân *and* Buktshy *of each of the Seven* Kuchurries *of the Seat of the* Sultanut *(or* Seringapatam*); dated* 10*th* Tulooey. (17*th December*.)

(Circular.)

Directing the birth-day of the *Sultan*, or the approaching 14th day of *Túlooey* [20th December] to be celebrated, in the manner appointed in the *Húkm-námeh* [on that head].

OBSERVATIONS.

In a loose paper in my possession, containing directions for the regulation of military salutes on various occasions,[1*] there is a note, or memorandum, purporting, that the *Sultan* was born on the 14th of *Túlooey* of the year of the *Higera* 1165;

2 F

(1) Original عصمت مرتبت

(1*) I have since met with the same regulations in the *Futhúl' Mújáhideen.*

1165; on the anniversary of which day it is ordered, "that a salute[2] of thirty-one "guns shall be fired at ten o'clock in the morning, and all the people of the city "observe the same as a festival."

Whether or not this rejoicing was intended to be general throughout the kingdom, or was confined to the capital *(Seringapatam)*, I am unable to say; but I believe that it was customary for the principal officers, however distant from court, to transmit *Nuzrs* of congratulation to the *Sultan* on the annual return of his birth-day.

LETTER CLXXXIII.

To EAATIMÂDY KHOJEH FIRÂSUT;[1] *dated* 11*th* TŬLOOEY.
(18*th December*.)

THE memorandum of medicines [perhaps some prescription] which you sent has passed under our view; but the essences,[2*] therein specified, belong to the European practice, whereas Mahommed Baig is a physician of the Greek school. The conclusion to be drawn from this is, that in omitting to insert the Greek medicines, and substituting in their place those in use among the Europeans, you could have had no other view, than that of making a profit by the sale of the latter.

You must get a memorandum [or list] of Greek medicines made out by the above-named [Mahommed Baig], and send it to us, in order that we may supply you [with the articles required].

I am

(2) In the original it is "ten *ghurries*," or three hours and forty-five minutes "after sun "rise," which, at the winter solstice, answers nearly to ten o'clock in the morning.

(1) If the title of this letter be correctly given in my manuscript it may be rendered "to "the trusty (or trust-worthy) *Eunuch*, Firâsut."

(2*) Original عطريات plural of عطر *itr* (commonly pronounced *utr* or *ottar)* a perfume, essence, or essential oil.

OBSERVATIONS.

I am obliged to acknowledge, that I do not clearly understand this letter, which appears to be addressed to some eunuch, who exercised the business of a pharmacopolist; but whether under the authority, and for the benefit, of the *Sultan*, or on his own individual account, I cannot determine. The former supposition would certainly not be at variance with the practice of this extraordinary character in other cases; and, in some measure, supported by the general tenor of the letter. On the other hand, if the medicines, when compounded, were to be sold exclusively on account of the *Sultan*, there is some difficulty in comprehending whence the profit was to arise to the *Khojeh*, with the pursuit of which he is accused by his sovereign. After all, however, the difficulty may proceed from nothing but my want of due information on the subject.

LETTER CLXXXIV.

To Ali Râjah Beeby; *dated* 12*th Tûlooey.* (19*th December.*)

The humble address you sent to us has passed under our view, and the particulars set forth in it are become duly apparent.

You write, "that the villages of *Mâtmail*,(1) &c. have, from days of "yore,(2) appertained to you, and been [actually] in your possession; "but that now the revenues of the said villages have been sequestered, "on account of our *Sircar*." It is revealed; and, in consequence, we enclose a letter to Urshud Baig Khân, the *Foujdâr* of *Calicut*, in which we have given him strict orders to relinquish the villages in question, and the revenues thereof. Forward the same to him.

We have repeatedly written to you, desiring you to repair to the Presence; but, instead of coming to us, you have excused yourself

2 F 2 upon

(1) Name uncertain.

(2) Original قديم الايام

upon different pretences. For this reason, and in conformity with the policy of the moment, the settlement of the *Taalûk* of *Cherkul,* and the appointment of a separate *Aumil,* on our behalf, to the charge of the same, has appeared expedient to us.

Our consideration for the situation of that refuge of chastity, such as it is [*i. e.* such as we have always manifested it to be], has suffered no diminution. You will remain [therefore] with collected mind ; and if any of our *Taalûkdârs* should be guilty of oppression, or proceed vexatiously toward your *Taalûk,* let us know his name, and we will send him strict orders to desist therefrom.

N.B. A letter, in conformity with the tenor of the foregoing dispatch, was written, under the same date, to Urshud Baig Khân, the *Foujdâr* of *Calicut.*

LETTER CLXXXV.

To Shumsûddeen Khân *and others ;*(1) *dated* 13*th* Tûlooey.
(*20th December.*)

Directing them to deposit the produce of the revenues of *Nugr* in the *Tosheh-khâneh ;* and to carry to account [or give credit in their account for] the *value of all old cloths,* in like manner [or at the same rate] as the *Dâroghâs* of the *Jinsy* formerly fixed the same.

OBSERVATIONS.

This letter is somewhat perplexing ; nor am I clear that I understand it rightly. The word پارچه which I have rendered *cloths,* may mean either cloth in the piece, or *clothes* (wearing apparel). Then it is also possible, it may have been intended that the old cloth, or clothes, in question, should be sold, and the produce carried to account : an interpretation which, I think, the original would very well bear out.

(1) That is, other officers of the *Tosheh-khâneh.*

LETTER CLXXXVI.

To Bûrhânûddeen; *dated* 14*th* Tulooey, *at Night.* (21*st December.*)

Directing him to send for Wenkia Naig, the banker; and also to transmit a *Kowl* [engagement] and letter of encouragement to Koornath Pundit. To write to Syed Meerân, the *Kilaadâr* of *Dhârwâr*, directing him to keep a strict watch over the family of Umbâjee Râm and his nephew, and to take care that they are not suffered to go any where. Desiring him, moreover, *not to think* of putting garrisons of the *Sircar* into *Shâhpoor*, *Bulgong*, &c. as they belong to ——.

OBSERVATIONS.

In Letter CLXIX, Bûrhânûddeen is directed to place garrisons in *Shâhpoor*, *Bulgong*, and *Gokauk*, which are there declared to be dependencies of *Kittoor*. It would now appear, however, that the *Sultan* had discovered, that those places did not belong to *Kittoor*, but to some other chieftain or state, whom he did not wish to offend by seizing on them. The name is left *nearly* blank in the manuscript; the original, probably, not having been legible to the transcriber. I have said *nearly* blank, because it is not, in fact, *entirely* so; the terminating letters, or syllable, of the deficient word being preserved. This is ته which occurs at the end of many *Hindoo* words, and among others that of *Mahrattah*. If the places in question belonged to the Mahrattahs, it may seem strange, that he should not have known this when he sent the first orders for their seizure. Of the desire he might *yet* have to abstain from any directly *aggressive* proceedings against that people, and to confine himself, for the present, to mere defensive measures, some explanation has already been offered; and more will hereafter be furnished by the *Sultan* himself.

LETTER CLXXXVII.

To Budrûz Zumân Khân; *dated* 15*th* Tulooey. (22*d December.*)

Announcing to him the *Sultan's* arrival at *Tul-Cauvery*; and directing him, after deputing some person [to take the temporary charge of his government(1)] during his absence, to repair, together with his *Mûtusuddies* [or accountants] to the Presence; when such orders as should be necessary would be verbally given him.

LETTER CLXXXVIII.

To Bûrhânûddeen; *dated from* Tul-Cauvery, 18*th* Tûlooey. (25*th December.*)

The Mahrattah forces are assembling. Vigilance and [due attention to] the safety of your army are necessary. We therefore write to desire, that you will encamp your troops in a secure situation; not far asunder, but [close together] in the form [or manner] of a *rose-bud.*(1*) You must also post piquets, &c. on all sides of your army. Let it not happen that the enemy's army surprize you.(2)

You must, agreeably to our former directions, transmit to us a detailed memorandum of the effects of the *Daisye*, &c. of *Kittoor*. After receiving such memorandum, we will give our orders on the subject, according to which you will act. Let also a minute report be made to us of the followers of the *Daisye*, specifying [in particular] the number of his managers and principal men, and distinguishing them by name.

(1) I am ignorant what situation Budrûz Zumân Khân filled at this time.

(1*) Original غنچه which means a *bud* in general, but more particularly a *rose-bud.*

(2) Original دغا which usually signifies *treachery*, but is often applied to an alert, or sudden attack.

OBSERVATIONS.

The Asiatic armies are not accustomed to encamp in line, as is the practice of the more regular armies of Europe; and though Tippoo adopted many things in our tactics, this is one of the points, in which he did not think fit to depart from the established usage of the East. Whatever may be thought of the *Sultan's* military judgment in this case, it will probably be readily admitted, that the figure, by which he has expressed it, is sufficiently significant.

LETTER CLXXXIX.

To Mahommed Ghyâs *and* Noor Mahommed Khân; *dated 23d* Tûlooey. *(30th December.)*

Directing them to write all their dispatches, whether of weighty import or not, with their own hands, and not to make known the same to any of the *Münshies*, *Persian* or *Hindivy* [attached to the mission]. Announcing to them, also, the appointment of Mirzâ Uhsun, a *Persian Münshy* of the *Sultan*, to read [their] letters and write the answers to them: and concluding with an intimation, that when the subject of their dispatches related merely to the pay of the people belonging to them, they might be written in *Hindivy*.

OBSERVATIONS.

In translating the passage of the foregoing letter, which notices Mirzâ Uhsun's appointment, I have supplied the pronoun possessive, *their*, on the supposition that the dispatches of the envoys were particularly meant. But the sense may be, that Mirzâ Uhsun was appointed to read and answer *Persian* letters generally, and not those of the envoys alone. What is said of his being employed *to write* the answers, is not to be understood as necessarily meaning any thing more than his transcribing them fairly, or writing them from the *Sultan's* dictation.

LETTER CXC.

To Mohyûddeen Ali Khân *and* Urshudûllah Khân, *Dewân and Buktshy of Kurpah ; same Date.* (*30th December.*)

Notifying the *Sultan's* pleasure, that *Gurramcoondah* should, for the future, be called *Zuferâbâd*, and directing the same to be published throughout the country.

OBSERVATIONS.

I cannot positively state, whether or not *Merkerrah* of *Koorg* continued to be called *Zuferâbâd*, after the latter name was transferred to *Gurramcoondah*: but I am inclined to think in the negative; both because it is not probable that the same *new* name should have been applied to two different places, and because, whenever *Zuferâbâd* is subsequently mentioned, *Gurramcoondah* would constantly seem to be intended.

LETTER CXCI.

To Ghûlâm Ali Khân; *dated 24th Tûlooey.* (*31st December.*)

We herewith transmit a letter, which we have lately received from Mahommed Shufeea, the *Aumil* of *Munjaiser*,(1) enclosing one to his address from his brother, in which an account is given of the conferences [or negociations] going on between the *Sultan* of *Room* [*i. e.* the *Grand Seignor*] and the English ambassador. Consider well the contents thereof, and hasten to accomplish the business upon which you have been deputed.

Sometime ago Othman Khân dispatched a respectable person, with a letter from himself and Shâh Noorûllah to the *Sultan* of *Room*, containing

(1) Name uncertain.

ing a representation of the state of things in these parts; and it appears, that it was subsequently to the arrival of that person [at *Constantinople*], that the *Sultan* of *Room* began the conferences [or negociations] in question with the English ambassador.

OBSERVATIONS.

It is proper I should acknowledge, that I have found this letter extremely perplexing, and that I am far from being satisfied that my interpretation of it is accurate. The doubtful passage is that in which the name of Othman Khân occurs; for the original may be understood to mean, either that he (Othman Khân) sent a letter to the *Grand Seignor*, by the hands of "a respectable person," or that he himself was that respectable person, and had been deputed on this errand by Ghûlâm Ali Khân and Shâh Noorûllah. There are difficulties attending either construction, none of which am I sufficiently informed to be enabled to remove. The slight mention incidentally made of Othman Khân, in other parts of the correspondence, does not throw much light on the subject: yet it clearly appears, by Letter CCXXXII, that Othman Khân had himself actually proceeded to *Constantinople*.

With respect to the allusion made to the conferences or negociations of the English ambassador at the *Porte*, it is no less involved in obscurity, than the passage relating to Othman Khân. The context would seem to imply, that the representation, by whomsoever addressed to the *Grand Seignor*, regarding the situation of affairs in *India*, had given an unfavorable turn for the English to the negociation in question: but Ghûlâm Ali Khân, if still living,(2) can alone furnish a satisfactory explanation of the matter.

2 G

(2) He was living at *Seringapatam*, in 1809.

LETTER CXCII.

To MEER KÂSIM ALI KHÂN, *Post-master at* FYZE HISÂR (GOOTY); *dated* 24*th* TÛLOOEY. (31*st December*.)

YOU write, " that a thousand *Piâdehs*, five hundred regular infantry, " and three hundred horse, belonging to the *Nâzim* of *Kurnool*,(1) are " arrived at *Nundidl*, with the intention of recovering the country " sequestered [or confiscated] by us." It is known. Where is the ground for alarm [in this case]? If they should dare to take such a step, they shall see the fruits [or feel the consequences] of it.

LETTER CXCIII.

To BÛRHÂNÛDDEEN; *dated from* TUL CAUVERY, 28*th* TÛLOOEY. (4*th January* 1786.)

DIRECTING him to recall the *Risâla* of the *Sipahdâr*, Syed Ghuffâr, from *Nergûnd*, and to send thither, in its stead, two companies of the *Sipahdâr*, Syed Humeed's corps: also, desiring him to send for five hundred *Piâdehs* to Syed Meerân, the *Kilaadâr* of *Dhârwâr*, and to employ the same in the service of the *Sircar*.

LETTER CXCIV.

To BUDRÛZ ZUMÂN KHÂN; *same Date*. (4*th January*.)

YOU must first proceed to *Nelaiser* [*Neelahser*], and encamping there with Leshtia,(1*) make some delay, on pretext of looking after Sooma, the

(1) Runmust Khân, the *Patan* chief of *Kurnool*. See Letter CXCVI.

(1*) Name uncertain.

the *Tul-Cauvery* man. You will then invite Moona Kool, who, together with his nephew, went some time ago to visit Leshtia and Rooe Wurm Nâg, once more to come and see you; when you must make prisoners of himself, his nephew, and whatever followers may be with him, and report the same [immediately] to us. If a further force should become necessary, write and send for Urshud Baig and Bunkia,(2) and when the business is settled, let them return to their respective stations. We have sent the requisite orders, on this occasion, to both the above-mentioned officers. You must, *by every possible trick and contrivance*, secure the person of the aforesaid rebel.(3) The above-mentioned officers will remain where they now are till you send for them. If you should be able to do without them,(4) let them know it, in order that they may repair to their proper stations.

N.B. The letter to Urshud Baig Khân, referred to in the preceding dispatch, follows next in the manuscript; but is omitted here, as superfluous.

LETTER CXCV.

To Mohyûddeen Ali Khân;(1) *dated 29th Tûloory. (5th January.)*

You write, "that you have recently discovered a vein of lead, the ore "of which resembles that formerly found; that you have sent us seven "pieces of it by the post; and that you wish to be instructed, whether "to dispatch the lead you may obtain by hired bullocks, or to wait the "arrival of some persons from the Presence." It is known. You must collect

2 G 2

(2) Name uncertain.

(3) Original مفسد "an exciter of sedition."

(4) Literally, "to seize the rebel without them."

(1) *Dewân* of *Kurpah.*

collect the said lead in the fort of *Sidhoot.* It is an ancient custom[2] for a silver mine, that is to say, silver earth,[3] to be [always] found under a lead-mine: you must, therefore, send for the said earth [or ore], and collect it together in the before-mentioned place. Persons skilled in [such] earth [or ores] will be shortly sent from the Presence [to examine it].

LETTER CXCVI.

To RUNMUST KHÂN; *same Date.* (*5th January.*)

[AFTER acknowledging, with the usual compliments, the receipt of a letter from Runmust Khân, the writer proceeds thus]:—

Some time ago, while we happened to be making a progress, slightly attended, for the purpose of inspecting the forts of *Bangalore*, &c. the exciters of sedition in the *Koorg* country, not looking to the [probable] consequences [of such conduct], but agreeably to the nature of the children of selfishness[1] and of opportunity-watching rebels,[2*] conceiving vain hopes from the great distance of our victorious army, raised their heads, one and all, in tumult. Immediately on our hearing of this circumstance, we proceeded with the utmost speed, and, at once, made prisoners of forty thousand occasion-seeking[3*] and sedition-exciting[4] *Koorgs*, who, alarmed at the approach of our victorious army, had slunk into woods, and concealed themselves in lofty mountains, inaccessible

(2) That is to say, "it is agreeable to experience."

(3) Or, *ore.*

(1) Original ابن الغرض

(2*)
(3*) } Original تابو طلب

(4) Original فتنه انگیز

inaccessible even to birds. Then carrying them away from their native country (the native place of sedition) we raised them to the honor of *Islám*, and incorporated them with our *Ahmedy* corps.[5] As these happy tidings are calculated, at once, to convey a warning to hypocrites,[6] and to afford delight to friends, [but more especially to] the chiefs of the true believers, the pen of amity has here recited them [for your information].

We now firmly purpose repairing to that quarter [towards *Kurnool*], and shall accordingly soon arrive there with our victorious forces; when the meeting, which we have so long wished to have with that friend, will be accomplished. Râjah Dhurm Doss, and Khâjeh Lûtfûllah, shall hereafter be dismissed and dispatched to that friend. We trust you will continue, till the period of our interview, to delight and rejoice us by your letters.

OBSERVATIONS.

It will be recollected by the reader, that the *Sultan* had been recently apprized,[7] of its being the intention of Runmust Khân to attempt the recovery of some part of his country, which had been taken possession of by the *Sultan*; the present dispatch, therefore, which is in the true boastful style of a Persian *Futah námeh*,[8] or letter of victory, may be fairly considered as intended to intimidate the person to whom it is addressed; or in Tippoo's own words, "to convey "a warning to him" of what he might expect, if, by resisting the *Sultan's* will, he should compel the latter to pay him a visit. It was, moreover, well-calculated to

(5) Original زمرهٔ احمدی "Band of *Ahmedies*."

(6) Original عبرت منافقان litterally, "as an example to hypocrites," or atheists.

(7) See Letter CXCII.

(8) It is customary with the princes of the East to announce to one another the victories they obtain over their enemies. This is done in letters, which, from the subject of them, are called *Futah-námehs*, or letters of victory.

to prepare the way for the pecuniary demand which we shall presently see made upon this Patan chief.

The foregoing letter contains the only authentic record of the *Sultan's* recent expedition against the *Koorgs* that I have hitherto met with: and if we may give credit to his account of its issue, he would appear to have but too well fulfilled, on this occasion, the threat with which we have seen him dismiss the assembled chiefs of thatnation, in the year 1784.

" I have vowed to God," said he, " that if you ever again rise in rebellion, I " will make Musulmans of your whole race, and transplant you all from hence to " some other country." See Observations on Letter CLXIX.

LETTER CXCVII.

To Meer Ahmed Ali; *Taalúkdár of Nursipoor, dated 29th Túlooey.* (*5th January.*)

Your letter has been received. You write, " that the superseded " *Aumil* has, notwithstanding the guard [placed over him], escaped " from the fort." It is known. We have a just claim for thirty thousand *pagodas* on the same *Aumil:* you must [therefore] speedily discover him; otherwise you will be responsible for the sum in question.

LETTER CXCVIII.

To Shumsûddeen; *dated 30th Túlooey.* (*6th January.*)

Your letter, with the accompanying memorandum, and statement of an engagement entered into by the *Mútusuddies*, to adjust the account of the *Bárgeers* (1) in a satisfactory manner, has been received, and its contents

(1) Horsemen mounted on ordinary horses belonging to the *Sircar*. The stable horses are of a superior description.

contents are understood. The memorandum referred to is enclosed [or returned herewith]. You must, by coercive means, threats, and punishments, compel the *Mûtusuddies* of the *Bârgeer Kuchurry* to get ready, with all speed, the aforesaid accounts, enforcing their obedience by placing a *Suzâwul* over them.(2) You are to consider this as a most peremptory injunction.

LETTER CXCIX.

To Ghûlâm Ali Khân; *dated* 1st *Yoosûfy.* (7*th January.*)

The camphor tree has been [recently] discovered in this part of the *Sircar's* country.(1) We have sent two bottles of the essential oil made from it, for your use. You must rub your feet with it, and also take it [inwardly] in meat-broth, putting about a *tolah* weight of it [into a bason of broth]. Inform us what benefit you may receive from the use of it. What more shall be written?

LETTER CC.

To Meer Kâzim; *Dârogha at Muscat; dated* 6*th Yoosûfy.* (12*th January.*)

Your letter, accompanied by a sealed packet of pearls, with a memorandum of the prices at which they were bought, has been received. The pearls you have sent have, on the whole, been purchased at a very heavy price. If they can be procured cheaper in the *Buhrain* (1*) you must send

(2) Or "by proceeding against them, in the manner of a *Suzâwul;*" that is, by rigorous dunning.

(1) The *Sultan* was, at this time, in the neighbourhood of *Tul-Cauvery*. Ghûlâm Ali Khân was afflicted with some scrophulous or rheumatic complaint, which had rendered him a cripple.

(1*) Situated in the Gulf of *Persia;* and formerly famous for its pearl-fishery.

send thither for them. There is, at the same time, no objection to your buying them at Muscat, when they can be had cheap there.

Making some advance [of money] to ten divers, dispatch them to the Presence, as they are wanted for the purpose of diving or fishing[2] for pearls on the shore of *Mangalore*.

You write, "that *sandal* wood and pepper are become cheap [at "*Muscat*]." It is known. Keep them [therefore] some time by you. When they become dear [again] you must sell them. There is no necessity for selling them cheap. The *cardamums*, however, you may dispose of at the current [or market] price [of the day], if *that* should not be a losing one.[3] What you write, respecting their diminution from dryness, is understood. If it be only in weight that they are diminished, it is of no consequence. You will state [the deficiency] in your accounts.

The factory of *Muscat* has been placed under the *Aumil* [or been made a dependency] of *Mangalore*: you must, therefore, transmit to him the accounts of all sales and purchases, as well as of all other receipts and disbursements [of the factory].

We do not want any copper or lead; but you should buy sulphur, when the price of it is moderate.[4]

You write, respecting an increase to the stipend of Oba Gooler, in consequence of his being appointed to the *Churokdry*.[5] Let his stipend be augmented, to the amount of the monthly pay formerly allowed to the *Churokdr*.

The *morahs*[6] of black pepper must be weighed in bulk, and sold in that

(2) Literally "bringing up," *i. e.* from the bottom of the sea.

(3) Original کفایت مد نظر داشته literally, "keeping economy in view."

(4) Or, "when you can buy it at a saving price."

(5) I am unable to give any explanation of this word.

(6) A measure and weight equal to 80 lbs. avoirdupois.

that state. Where is the necessity of opening them, if, by that means, any loss should be incurred?

You write, recommending an increase to the allowance of Permanund Mullâh. It is apparent. Let him have an increase of five *rupees*.

The *humble addresses* of the *Imaum*, the *Khulfâr*(7) and Bheem Jee, the broker, which you forwarded to us, have passed under our view. You have been stationed there for the sole purpose of buying and selling: whenever [therefore] any occasion arises, in which you can act for our advantage, you should do so, though we may not have directed it, and without waiting for our orders on the subject.(8)

We are in great want of pearls. Purchase to the amount of ten thousand *rupees* worth, as cheaply as you can, and dispatch them to us.

You write, "that the *Dullâl* [or broker] has demanded payment of "two hundred and sixty *rupees*, advanced by him to Mahommed "Ibraheem, and of a hundred and two rupees advanced to Othman "Khân [both of them servants of our *Sircar*]." It is known. Pay the amount to the aforesaid broker, and take his receipt for the same

In your letter of the 17th of *Zilhijjeh*, A.H. 1199, you wrote, "that "the second sort of *sandal* wood, in charge of Ghous Mahommed "Khân, continued on hand, being, in comparison with the third "and fourth sorts, in little demand." Let the aforesaid *sandal* wood

2 H be

(7) I believe that the chief minister of the *Imaum* is so called. Though the *Sultan* here affects to call the letters of the *Imaum* and *Khulfâr urzies*, or "humble addresses," it is not to be credited, that these persons, and particularly the former, actually lowered themselves in the manner pretended.

(8) The *Sultan's* meaning, perhaps, is, that if any advantage was promised by the proposal, which may be supposed to have been made by the *Imaum*, Meer Kâzim should have acceded to it immediately, without any reference to the *Sultan*. But Meer Kâzim was too well acquainted with his master's character, to assume such a responsibility. The prince who could think it necessary to instruct a commercial agent, so minutely as Tippoo has done in the present and other letters, was not likely to have approved of that agent's exercising the undefined kind of power, with which he is pretended to have been invested.

be kept until purchasers are met with, and then sell it to the best advantage you can.

We want ten ship-wrights, acquainted with the construction of *Dows.* Get them together, and dispatch them hither.

You must [constanly] date your letters to us, specifying the day, month, and year, in the same manner that our orders to you are dated.

What you write, respecting your having hired a warehouse for our goods, is understood............[9] will shortly be dispatched from the Presence: upon the arrival thereof you must prepare a factory-house for the use of the *Sircar.*

Entertain a hundred *Clashies*[10] in our service, at the monthly wages of seven *rupees;* and appointing a *Surdâr* [or commander] to every twenty-five men, dispatch them to the Presence, where, on their arrival, they shall be raised to superior rank.[11] What more?

OBSERVATIONS.

I possess no information, with regard to the *Sultan's* project for establishing a pearl-fishery in the vicinity of *Mangalore*: but it may be inferred, from the silence of the subsequent correspondence on the subject, either that the requisite divers were not procurable, or that the attempt, if actually made, did not succeed. His endeavours to form a marine were somewhat more successful; but the nature of the sea coast in his possession hardly admitted of his attaining to any great importance as a maritime power. If, however, such an obstacle really existed to the accomplishment of this design, he, at least, would not appear to have been sensible of it, since it will be seen, by Appendix K, containing "Regulations "for the Marine Department," that only two or three years previously to the extinction

(9) There is a blank here in the manuscript. Possibly some materials, towards the erection of a factory-house, may have been specified.

(10) Probably, ship lascars.

(11) Literally, "shall be appointed to *oahdehs*, or commands."

extinction of his power, he had conceived the idea of creating a very formidable naval force. It may, indeed, be reasonably doubted, whether either the resources of his country, or of his genius, were equal to the realization of so bold a plan; but it is as well, perhaps, that he was not allowed time for the experiment.

LETTER CCI.

To Runmust Khân; *dated 7th Yoosûfy.* (13*th January.*)

In consideration of the friendship and regard [subsisting between us], we abated four *lacks* of *rupees*, of the eleven *lacks* justly due to us, as *Paishcush*, from that friend. Having thus fixed the balance payable to us at seven *lacks* of *rupees*, we some time ago announced the same to you. Râjah Dhurram Doss, and Khâjeh Lûtfûllah, having hereupon made an earnest representation to us of your [pecuniary] difficulties, we were induced to agree to a further remission of fifty thousand *rupees*, hereby reducing our demand to six *lacks* and a half, exclusive of twenty-five thousand *rupees*, on account of the ...... (1) of a former year. The amount was thus finally settled at 6,75,000 *rupees*, for the discharge of which the two before-mentioned persons entered into two distinct engagements; by one of which it was stipulated, that 3,75,000 *rupees* should be paid by the 5th *Jumâd ûl Ouwul*, A. H. 1200; and by the other, that a further sum of 3,75,000 *rupees* should be paid by the 20th of *Rujub* of the same year. These two persons having taken leave of us, will [we trust] reach you in safety.

With respect to our relinquishing the districts belonging to that friend, and sequestered by us, orders to that effect have been addressed(2) to the

2 H 2 *Dewân*

(1) A blank occurs here in the manuscript. The word wanting is, probably, *balance*.

(2) These orders were most probably provisional, and to be complied with only in the event of Runmust Khân's discharging the demand against him.

Dewán and *Buktshy* of *Fyze-Hisár* [*Gooty*] and delivered to the aforesaid persons [*i. e.* Dhurrum Doss and Lûtfûllah]. What friendship requires is, that the before-mentioned money should be paid, agreeably to the engagements referred to above, in order that the foundations of attachment may acquire strength and firmness. An elephant and a *Mehtáby*(3) dress are sent, in token of our regard. Always make us glad and happy by the receipt of your friendly letters.

LETTER CCII.

To MEER MOAAINÛDDEEN ; *dated 7th and 10th of* YOOSÚFY.
(13*th and* 16*th January.*)

BY the favor of the Almighty and the assistance of the Prophet, we have arranged and adjusted the affairs of the *Taalúk* of *Zufeerábád* in the most suitable [and satisfactory] manner; the tribe of *Koorgs*, to the number of fifty thousand men and women,(1) having been made captives, and incorporated with the *Ahmedy* class.

Having accomplished this object, we returned prosperously and victoriously to the seat of empire(2) at *Putn*, on the 11th of *Yoosúfy* of the year *Jullo*. This being an event calculated to give strength to the people of *Islám*,(3*) we wish *that brother* all joy on the auspicious occasion.

The advance(4) of our victorious standards is positively fixed for the 12th of *Yoosúfy* [18th January]: we therefore write, to desire that you

(3) A sort of silver tissue.

(1) In Letter CXCVI they are stated at *forty* thousand.

(2) Original دارالسلطنت

(3*) *i. e.* "the professors of the same faith."

(4) Original نهضت رايات نصرت آيات

you will march and join us, with the forces under your command [without delay].

MEMORANDUM. Three other letters, to the above effect (but to whom addressed is not said), were dispatched by the post.

OBSERVATIONS.

There is manifestly some error in one or other of the dates given in the foregoing letter, to which two different dates (*viz.* the 7th and 10th *Yoosûfy*) are assigned: for what reason I know not, unless it be to denote that it was dispatched in duplicate, one copy on the 7th, by an especial messenger, and the other on the 10th, by the post. But if these dates are correct, that one which purports, that the return of the *Sultan* to *Seringapatam* actually took place on the 11th *Yoosûfy*, must, of necessity, be wrong. It is equally certain, that at whatever time he arrived there from *Zufeerâbad,* he did not march again from thence on the 12th of *Yoosûfy* (as here stated to be his intention), since we know, from Letter CCXII, that he was still at his capital on the 23d of that month. I regret that I do not possess the means of rectifying these mistakes, which, however, are fortunately of no material consequence.

I cannot, at this moment, ascertain who Moaainûddeen was: but the circumstance of his being stiled *brother* by the *Sultan,* makes it probable that he was a kinsman of the latter.

LETTER CCIII.

To the actual and future AUMILS *of the port of* CALICUT; *dated* 10*th* YOOSÛFY. (16*th January.*)

BE it known, that in consideration of the devotion and attachment to our government of the refuge of commerce,(1) Mâo Saith, son of Râo Saith,

(1) Original تجارت پناه

Saith, *Dullál* [or broker], an inhabitant of *Muscat,* we have, at this time, [agreed to] remit the customary anchorage duty, heretofore paid to us, in favour of five *Dingies* of his [about to import at *Calicut*]: you will, therefore, on the production of a letter [or certificate] from the above-mentioned *Dullál,* [purporting that the said *Dingies* are his], refrain from demanding the aforesaid established duty [of forty *rupees* per *Dingy*] on the [five] *Dingies* in question. Consider this as a peremptory order.

LETTER CCIV.

To the actual and future Aumils *of our Ports [in general]; same Date. (16th January.)*

Be it known, that we have remitted four-tenths of the duties, levied in our ports from time immemorial, on all goods to be bought or sold [there], by the refuge of commerce, Mâo Saith, son of Râo Saith, *Dullál* of *Muscat:* you will, therefore, demand from the agents of the said *Dullál,* six-tenths of the ancient duties, *and no more.* Consider this as a peremptory order.

LETTER CCV.

To the Aumils *actual and future of the Port of* Kúriál (Mangalore)*; same Date. (16th January.)*

Be it known, that if, after selling to the agents of the refuge of commerce, Mâo Saith, &c., such rice as we may have to dispose of, the aforesaid agents should be desirous of purchasing a further quantity of that article from the inhabitants of the districts appertaining to *Mangalore,*

lore, it will be well. You must not forbid, or make any opposition to the same.

LETTER CCVI.

To Mâo Saith, *Dullál at Muscat*;[1] *same Date.* (16*th January.*)

Your letter, by Ghous Mahommed Khân and Turkem Doss, has been received, and apprized us, among other things, " of your determination " to establish a factory [or warehouse] at *Calicut*."[2] You have also represented to us verbally, by the aforesaid Khân, " that our officers at " the port of *Calicut* charge you for anchorage duty, at the rate of forty " *rupees* per *Dingy*, and this duty you request of us to remit." You have furthermore stated, " that the *Imaum* of *Muscat*, while he levies a " duty of ten per cent. on [the goods of] all other merchants, charges " our merchants no more than six per cent.; and you, therefore, solicit " a similar indulgence from us." You likewise express a desire, " that " your *Gúmáshtehs* may be allowed, as formerly, (after first buying from " the managers of our ports whatever number of *morahs* of rice the " latter have to dispose of) to purchase, without let or hindrance, from " the people of the country, such further quantities of the same article " as they may require." It is known.

[Then follows a recital of the concessions specified in the three preceding letters, which it is unnecessary to repeat here].

With respect to our establishing factories [as you propose] at *Port Mundry* in *Kutch*, and at the port of *Jámnugr*, our intention is, to dispatch, some time hence, trusty persons, with letters and the customary tokens

(1) The name is omitted in the manuscript; but the tenor of the letter sufficiently proves, that it is addressed to Mào Saith.

(2) *Calicut* is not named in the original; but the context shews it to be meant.

tokens of friendship to the *Rájahs* of both those places. On this occasion we shall require of you to introduce our agents to the two *Rájahs*, and to procure the necessary permission for the establishment of [the proposed] factories.

Agreeably to your request, we have directed Meer Kâzim to settle with you for the advances made by you of two hundred and sixty *rupees* to Mahommed Ibraheem, and one hundred and two *rupees* to Othman Khân, making together the sum of three hundred and sixty-two *rupees*.

OBSERVATIONS.

We collect, from the foregoing letter, that Tippoo Sultan had already so far accomplished his commercial views at *Muscat*, as to be considered the most favoured of the numerous traders with that port. The concessions by which he obtained that distinction (for it was hardly any thing more) are not any where distinctly stated; but it is probable, that it had been granted on a previous understanding between the *Imaum* and the *Sultan's* agent, Ghous Mahommed Khân, that the *Imaum's* vessels were to be admitted into the ports of *Mysore*, on the footing specified in the ensuing letter.

Of the particular immunities here granted to Mâo Saith, the remission of four-tenths of the customary duties (whether on imports alone, or on exports also, does not appear) would, no doubt, have been a very considerable indulgence, if the trade had been suffered to be quite free, and if Tippoo himself had not participated very largely in it. The *Sultan,* however, not only exported rice to *Muscat* in his own vessels, and imported the commodities of that country into *Mysore,* but he also obliged the *Muscat* merchant to purchase all the government rice on hand, at a price fixed probably by himself, before he allowed him to buy elsewhere. In addition to these restraints, there is reason to believe, that the most profitable branches of the commerce of his dominions, namely *sandal* wood, beetel-nut, pepper and *cardamums,* were entirely monopolized by the *Sultan.* Under these circumstances, it may be questioned, whether the encouragement ostensibly

ostensibly given to the *Muscat* traders, was, on the whole, much calculated to promote the commercial intercourse of the two countries. Of the actual extent of that intercourse, at any given period of the *Sultan's* reign, I possess, at present, no accurate means of judging; though it is probable, that ample materials for this purpose were obtained, by the gentlemen who received charge of the different sea-ports of *Canara* and *Malabar*, at the period of their falling under the authority of the English.

LETTER CCVII.

To the IMAUM *of* MUSCAT;(1) *same Date.* (*16th January.*)

YOUR pleasing letter, by Ghous Mahommed Khân, has been received. He has also represented to us, verbally, the sentiments of regard and union which you entertain for us, and the knowledge whereof has proved highly gratifying to us.

In consideration of the friendship subsisting between us, we have, at this time, remitted *half* the amount of the duties heretofore levied in our ports on your ships and *Dows*, and have, accordingly, issued the necessary orders to this effect, to the governors of all our sea-ports: do you, therefore, continue constantly to send your ships and *Dows*, laden with merchandize, to our ports. Particulars will be stated to you by Meer Kâzim.

Whereas there is a strict order in force at [all] our sea-ports, forbidding the sale of rice to any merchants coming from Portuguese, English, &c. ports, the latter have, on account of the great scarcity of grain [in their own countries], adopted the contrivance of sending other merchants, in the character of *Muscat* traders, with money, for the purpose of making purchases of rice, &c. at our ports. We have, in consequence,

2 I

(1) Though the name is here also, as in the preceding letter, omitted, there can be no doubt, that the person addressed is the *Imaum* of *Muscat.*

quence, sent positive directions to the persons in authority at all our ports, to consider as *Muscat* merchants such only as shall produce a passport, or certificate, under the seal and signature of the superintendants of our factory there. To merchants, furnished with such certificate, rice will be sold,(2) without any excuse [or evasion]. Let, then, that person of eminent rank likewise give orders to the merchants of *Muscat* proceeding to our ports, to provide themselves with the prescribed passports, for which we have strictly commanded the superintendants of our factory not to demand any fees.

OBSERVATIONS.

The remission of duties granted in favour of Mâo Saith was four-tenths. The remission of one-half, mentioned in the present letter, applies, I conclude, exclusively to the ships and merchandize belonging immediately to the *Imaum*, who, like Tippoo, was the chief merchant of his state; but a much more intelligent and enlightened one, I apprehend, than the *Sultan*.

LETTER CCVIII.

To Budrûz Zumân Khân; *dated* 13*th of* Yoosûfy. (19*th January*.)

Directing him to crucify the miscreant(1) Moona Kool, and to send for his family, and keep them confined in irons.

If the nephew of Moona Kool should be more than twenty-five years of age, to crucify him also.

Two

(2) That is, "will be sold by the *officers of government*, on the *Sultan's* account, and "from his granaries."

(1) Original شقي

Two hundred of the followers of Moona Kool to be made *Ahmedies*, and put into the...... (2) *Risâla* lately dispatched [from hence] and now arrived [at *Nugr.*]

You (3) yourself must also proceed to *Nugr*, together with the troops under your command; and, repairing to the second *Dewân* of *Nugr*, who is [at this time] at *Seo-Kullah*,(4) there make a settlement of your accounts [with him].

OBSERVATIONS.

There is no trace, in any of the documents in my possession, of the manner in which the person of the unfortunate Moona Kool was finally secured; but the instructions given at different times, regarding him, make it sufficiently probable, that the object was attained by some foul or treacherous means.

LETTER CCIX.

To Meer Moaala Khân, *the superseded* (1) *or late* Kilaadâr *of* Môdgul; *dated* 13*th Yoosôfy.* (21*st January.*)

Directing him to send one of his brothers to receive six thousand *rupees* from Ghûlâm Mohyûddeen, the *Foujdâr* of *Kunchungûddh*,(2*) and to repair with his family to the Presence.

That what he writes, of the *handsome* behaviour of the chiefs of *that*

2 I 2 *place*,

(2) The name which I have left blank is in the manuscript written *Ahmednugr*: but I know of no such place in Tippoo's dominion, and therefore suspect the right reading to have been, " and put them into the *Ahmedy* [corps at] *Nugr*."

(3) The second person being here employed, what follows is to be considered as an exact transcript of the original dispatch, and not, as in the preceding part, the mere *heads* of it.

(4) Name uncertain.

(1) In the original معزول

(2*) See Letter CCLXXV for some account of this place.

place, notwithstanding their oaths and engagements, is understood. [What follows is in the first person.]

In contemplation of the very events which have taken place, we, before-hand, desired you to repair to us. You, however, chose to exercise your foresight on the occasion; and, after all, "the same broth "remains in the pot."(3) Such is the way, in which great chiefs show their regard for their promises and solemn engagements.(4)

OBSERVATIONS.

Not distinctly knowing who Meer Moaala Khân was, and being but imperfectly acquainted with the transactions referred to, I find myself unable to interpret this letter in a satisfactory manner. If I might hazard a conjecture on the occasion, it would be, that Meer Moaala Khân (who was the same person addressed in Letter LXXX) had been governor of the fort of *Múdgul*, a place of considerable note on the south-west frontier of the *Nizám*;(5) that he had engaged in a secret correspondence with Tippoo, to whom he probably meant to deliver up the fort; but that his fidelity being reasonably suspected, he had been deprived of his government, before his plan of defection was ripe for execution. I am aware, however, that there are some passages and allusions in the letter before us, which are not sufficiently explained by the preceding hypothesis. We hear no more after this of Meer Moaala Khân.

LETTER CCX.

To MAHOMMED USHRUF; *same Date.* (21*st January.*)

YOUR letter, with the enclosed memorandum of money, &c. sent by you to the treasury at *Putn*, has been received. You write for leave to entertain

(3) This is a proverbial expression, importing "that, the very thing intended to be prevented, or avoided, had happened."

(4) Spoken ironically.

(5) *Múdgul* constituted (and perhaps still constitutes) the *Jagire* of the sister of the late Nizâm Ali Khân.

entertain ten new (or additional) *Ulgies.*(1) It is known. A hundred *Piâdehs*, of those stationed in the fort,(2) are assigned you, for the service of the collections and other affairs of the *Kuchurry*: your view, therefore, in proposing to entertain these *Ulgies*, most probably was, to *make a parade* [with them].(3) You must, at all times, employ the *Piâdehs* [and no others] in the service of the collections, &c. What more?

LETTER CCXI.

To the RÂJAH *of* PEGU; *dated*(1*) *17th* RUBIYÛL OUWUL, *A. H.* 1200. (*22d January.*)

IT will be sufficient to give the substance of this letter, which is no otherwise of any consequence, than as it adds to the other proofs which we possess, of the *Sultan's* desire to establish an intercourse, political or commercial, with the most distant nations.

The writer sets out with observing, "that a long period had elapsed, "since he had had the pleasure of hearing from the *Râjah*;"(2*) and with expressing a hope, "that the latter will, in future, frequently favor "him with the agreeable tidings of his welfare."

He then announces "that he has sent, in token of friendship, by the "hands of two of his servants, Mâhommed Kâsim and Mahommed Ibrâheem,

(1) In the original الكي of which I do not know the meaning.

(2) *i. e.* The fort of *Gooty* of the *Dewâny Kuchurry*, of which district Mahommed Ushruf appears, by Letter LXIV, to have been the *Dârogha*.

(3) Original براي جلو

(1*) The Mysore date is omitted, but, from the place which the letter occupies in the manuscript, it may be concluded to have been the 15th or 16th *Yoosûfy* (*i. e.* about the 21st January 1786.)

(2*) He possibly *never had* heard from him. The expression may be merely formal, and denote only his anxiety to hear from him.

" Ibrâheem, a present for the *Rájah,* consisting of two horses and a " *Mehtáby* dress."(3)

He states, " his view in sending those persons, to be the opening of a " commercial intercourse between the two states [of *Mysore* and *Pegu*], " whereby an exchange of the commodities of each may be established, " to the mutual convenience and advantage of both: he therefore " invites the *Rájah* to communicate to the agents in question, as also " from time to time, by letter, to himself, what articles he may wish to " be supplied with, from his [the *Sultan's*] country, in order that the " same may be forwarded to him."

He next observes, " that having heard, that rubies of high value, fine " colour, and of a superior kind [perhaps *size*], are to be had in *Pegu,* " he had, in consequence, directed his agents to purchase, through the " medium [or by means] of the *Rájah's* ministers,(4) a certain number of " stones, weighing each from ten to thirty *fanams* weight."

Then follows a request, " that the *Rájah* will accordingly order his " ministers to assist [his agents], in purchasing the rubies required, at " *as cheap a price as possible.*

OBSERVATIONS.

Whether a second mission was dispatched to *Pegu,* or the persons first intended to be sent were superseded by others, I am unable to determine : but a letter appears, under date 25th of *Bydxy* (31st March 1786) addressed, not to Mahommed Kâsim and Mahommed Ibrâheem, but to Shumsûddeen and Kûtbûddeen; in which they are told, " that their departure for *Pegu* only waits for the equipment " of the ships, which they are accordingly desired to expedite." It nevertheless appears, that the ships in question were not ready for sailing, so late as the beginning of the following June.

(3) A dress made of a particular kind of silver tissue.

(4) Original اهل کاران

LETTER CCXII.

To EHSÂNÛLLAH KHÂN; *dated from* PUTN, *the 23d* YOOSÛFY. (*29th January.*)

WHATEVER gold, silver, horses, bullocks, &c. the late Kâdir Aghâ may have died possessed of, the whole is to be delivered over to the *Kilaadâr* and *Umldâr*, from whom you will take receipts for the same. You did right, in placing the slave of the deceased in the corps of [or among] the *Usud-Ilhyes.*

OBSERVATIONS.

The character of this order cannot be determined, on account of our ignorance of the particular situation of Kâdir Âghâ, who might possibly have been a public defaulter, or have died childless.

LETTER CCXIII.

To SHÂH NOORÛLLAH;(1) *dated 25th* YOOSÛFY. (*31st January.*)

Two copies of the *Futhûl' Mûjâhideen* (2) have been sent to you under [our] seal: one by Mahommed Imaum, the *Jowkdâr* [captain] of the *Jyshe;* the other by our *Chailah*,(3) Kumâl. You must have the receipts of these books regularly entered by your *Mûtusuddies* [or accountants]. One of them you will give to be kept by the aforesaid *Jowkdâr*, who must be directed to exercise his men regularly, in the manner therein prescribed; the other you are to keep yourself: and you will likewise take good care,

(1) Proceeding on an embassy to *Constantinople.*

(2) For some account of this book see Letter XC, and also Appendix, I.

(3) This term has been explained at Letter CLXXVIII.

care, that the men [composing your escort] perform *their* exercise regularly.

LETTER CCXIV.

To Ghûlâm Ali Khân ;[1] *dated 26th Yoosûfy.* (*1st February.*)

The people who are to attend you [on your embassy], and who are enumerated in the following list, have been dispatched to you, under charge of a guard, consisting of five hundred and seven *Piâdehs,* and commanded [or superintended] by Ghûlâm Mohyûddeen Khân, the *Buktshy* of *Nugr*, and Rung Rào. Upon the arrival of the party, the *Piâdehs* are to continue to be employed in *taking care* of it, until its embarkation; after which, giving them a receipt,[2] you must dispatch them back to the Presence.

List of Persons, making altogether five hundred and one, with muskets, coats, &c.

Escort.	Men.
The *Jowkdâr*, Mûbâruk Khân, belonging to the *Ussud-Ilhyes*	71
The *Jowkdâr*, Mahommed Imaum, belonging to the *Suzâwul Jyshe.*[3]	100
The *Risâla* of Fukeer Mahommed, belonging to the *Jyshe*	250
[*Carried forward*	421

(1) The colleague of Shâh Noorûllah, and proceeding likewise to *Constantinople.*

(2) That is, an acknowledgement, or certificate, that such a number of persons had been delivered over to them by the guard.

(3) As a *Suzâwul* is a baliff or dun, this, I conclude, was a body of men, employed particularly in that kind of service.

		Men.
	[*Brought forward*	421

SERVANTS, &c. *viz.*

Kumâl Chailah........	1	
Sweepers...........	2	
*Hurkâreh*s...........	10	
Mushaalchies [or torch-bearers]........	6	
Bullahs, or *Yullahs*,(4)...........	4	
Mûnshy...........	1	
	——	24
Dobâshies...........	2	
Mûtusuddy...........	1	
	——	3
Under the command of Behrâm...........		21
Golundâzes (5)...........		31
Mahommed Ali, French and English interpreter (6)...........		1
	Total	501

OBSERVATIONS.

The only remark which I have to offer on this letter is, that it would appear from it, that the people, sent upon this distant embassy, must have proceeded on it with great reluctance, since it was necessary, in order to prevent their desertion, to keep them, till their embarkation, in custody of a military guard, of equal strength with themselves.

2 K

(4) I am doubtful as to the right reading of this word, the meaning of which I cannot guess.

(5) These are properly artillery-men; but we hear of no gun being attached to the embassy.

(6) Very probably some European, converted to the Mahommedan faith.

LETTER CCXV.

To the same; same Date. (1*st February.*)

After your arrival at *Constantinople*, you are, every third day, to serve out to the *Suzáwuls* and men of the *Usud-Ilhyes* attached [to your mission], four [blank] cartridges each man, and to see that they regularly perform their exercise.

LETTER CCXVI.

To the same; dated 28th Yoosúfy. (3*d February.*)

Your letter has been received, together with a memorandum of the remaining articles of supply, which Nursia, the *Dewán* (1) of *Nugr*, has taken upon himself to dispatch after you.

You were appointed, and have been sent from hence, for the purpose of repairingto *Constantinople, and not for that of writing to us accounts of squabbles.* Now, forasmuch as, while you are employed in narrating these disputes, the season for sailing is passing away, you must compel Nursia (2) to provide the articles you require; and, having done so, you must embark them on ship-board, and then proceed [on your voyage]. Even if there should be a small deficiency in your surplies, *you must not make that a pretence, or excuse,* for your delay, and for suffering the proper season for your proceeding to escape.

The whole of the men, who are to accompany you, have been dispatched, and will soon join you.

Agreeably

(1) He is, in other places, called the *Taalúkdár* of *Nugr*.

(2) In the original بر نرسیا محصلی نموده which is much the same as *Suzáwully*, already explained. It does not appear what means Ghûlâm Ali possessed of coercing a person of Nursia's authority.

Agreeably to the desire of that person of magnificent degree,(3) we have sent the most peremptory orders to Nursia, to expedite the remainder of your supplies.

OBSERVATIONS.

When it is considered, that Ghûlâm Ali Khân was among the most distinguished men at the court of Tippoo Sultan; that he was now proceeding on a service, to which his master attached much importance; that his appointment to such a high trust (for he was, I believe, at the head of the commission) would, at least, seem to imply, that entire confidence was placed in his zeal, talents, and fidelity; and, finally, when the frivolous nature of the offence imputed to him is adverted to, it is difficult to say, whether the *Sultan* has manifested most want of temper or of wisdom, in the harsh and degrading language here addressed to that person. Of his excessive irascibility and asperity of manner, other proofs have already appeared, and more will hereafter occur: but, on none of the occasions alluded to, did he, perhaps, so little consult, either his true dignity, or, apparently, his true interests, as in the present instance, since in proportion as he sunk the consequence of his minister, he diminished his own; while, by thus outraging the feelings of that minister, he incurred the risk of damping his ardor, paralyzing his energies, and even shaking his loyalty. It must, however, at the same time, be owned, that Ghûlâm Ali Khân was not likely to be so sensible of the indignity offered to him, or so apt to resent it, as the view here taken of the subject supposes; and it is only reasonable to conclude, that the *Sultan* knew this sufficiently well.

(3) Originally حشمت مرتبت It is not often that the *Sultan* uses this complimentary phraseology, in writing even to his principal officers. Perhaps, on the present occasion, it was meant to compensate for the severity of other parts of this dispatch. Most probably the address, or القاب as it is called in Persian, suitable to the rank of every person written to, was put at the head of the letter, though omitted in the register, or letter-book. It is very rare, however, that this address, or any part of it, is repeated by the *Sultan* in the body of his letter.

LETTER CCXVII.

To BÛRHÂNÛDDEEN; *dated 28th* YOOSÔFY. *(3d February.)*

DIRECTING him to dispatch carefully, under a trusty guard, all the gold, silver, jewels, horses, elephants, &c. belonging to the *Daisye* of *Kittoor*, together with the *Daisye* himself, and his family.

Directing, further, that such of the managers [or servants] of the *Daisye*, as were not to be trusted, should be put in irons, as formerly ordered, and dispatched to the Presence.

LETTER CCXVIII.

To SYED PEER; KILAADÂR *of* BANGALORE; *same date.* (3d *February.*)

YOU write " that about three hundred recruits have been entertained " for the *Jyshe* and *Ehshâm* [corps], and the abstracts of them regularly " made out and delivered to the *Mûtusuddies* of the *Dewâny*,(1) notwith- " standing which Râjah Râm Chundur brings forward excuses."(2) It is known. *You have* [it would seem] *laid your instructions by in the niche of forgetfulness*,(3) *or you could not engage in such an improper and senseless altercation.* What the aforesaid *Râjah* represents is perfectly right. If you would look into your instructions, there would be no necessity for your writing to us on the subject.

(1) Two or three words occur here, which are unintelligible to me.

(2) *i. e.* " evades paying the amount of the abstracts."

(3) Original طاق نسیان *i. e.* " have consigned them to oblivion."

LETTER CCXIX

To Shâh Noorûllah; *dated* 29*th Yoosúfy.* (4*th February.*)

It is owing to the whoreson tricks and roguery of the elephant keepers, that the elephants have been made to get hot: you must, therefore, flog them [the keepers] well. If, after all, one of the elephants proceeding with you should continue hot, you must separate him from the other [or others], by putting him on board a different vessel.

Then follow directions for expediting the departure of the embassy.

N. B. In a letter of the following day (or 30th *Yoosúfy*), the *Sultan* repeats his orders for separating the *must* (hot) and tame elephants, with an addition, purporting, " that the proper medicines should be given to the hot elephant for expelling his heat."

LETTER CCXX.

To Bûrhanûddeen; *dated* 29*th Yoosúfy.* (4*th February.*)

We have heard, that the enemy(1) has detached a large force, for the purpose of falling suddenly upon [or surprising] your army(2): we therefore write, to desire that you will, immediately on the receipt of this letter, take up a position at *Dhárwár*, and dispatching the whole of your baggage into the country of *Nugr* [the province of *Bidnore*], remain yourself

(1) Original مقهور " the accursed." The Mahrattahs are, of course, here meant. This is the term by which an enemy is usually designated.

(2) Original دغا نمودن which has been before explained.

yourself with your army unencumbered.(3) You must, on this point, employ the strictest precautions. Let it not be (God forbid!) that the enemy should surprise you.

LETTER CCXXI.

To Turbiyut Ali Khân; *dated Seringapatam,* 30*th Yoosûfy.* (5*th February.*)

Your letter has been received(1)........You write, "that keeping "in view [or looking to nothing else than] the proper execution of the "public business,(2) you make no distinction of persons, and labour only "to approve your zeal for our service, and to discharge the obligations of "fidelity; but that [nevertheless], owing to your evil destiny,(3*) these "circumstances have not been made known to us by the superintendants "and *Hurkârehs* of the post [or intelligence] department there [*i. e.* "*Bangalore*]."

It is comprehended. Your respectability and integrity are [duly] impressed on our mind, and, therefore, did we appoint you to your present situation. The aforesaid superintendant and *Hurkârehs* are employed to write the intelligence of that place; how is it possible, then, that they should do otherwise than represent the actual truth to us?(4)

You

(3) Original جريده the baggage of an army being sent away, the army is said to be *jureedah.*

(1) A long, but immaterial passage, relating to pecuniary details, and not entirely intelligible to me, is here omitted.

(2) Original نظر بدرستي كارسركار

(3*) Original ازنارساي طالع خود literally "from the insufficiency, or incompetency, of my fortune or fate."

(4) Literally, "what power have they *not* to represent the real truth to us"?

You moreover state, "that the circumstance of your inspecting the "accounts of the receipts and issues of the *Athouny*,(5) and examining "the same justly, and according to the rules prescribed in the regula- "tions [whereby a certain saving or advantage arises to the *Sircar*], "having rendered your interference(6) extremely disagreeable to them "[*i. e.* to the *Athouny*], they had, in consequence, misrepresented you "to us.(7)" It is revealed. Whenever, by means of a reference to the regulations, any saving [or deduction] can be fairly made in the receipts and issues of the *Athouny*, you must fearlessly carry the same into effect.

Your account of a certain person, who is extremely well versed in the affairs of that country, and who is ready to undertake the realization of the balance of eight *lacks* of *pagodas* [due from it], as well as an augmentation of two or three *lacks* on the present revenue, is fully understood. By the favor of God the Helper, our lofty standards will shortly be removed thither [*i. e.* to *Bangalore*], when we will enquire into this matter. What more shall we write?

LETTER CCXXII.

To Râjah Râm Chundur; *dated* 3d *Eezidy.* (*8th February.*)

Your letter has been received. You write, "that you were about to "issue to the eighty men of the *Nâimâr* tribe,(1) who had been incorpo- "rated into the *Usud Ilhyes*, the regulated rations,(2) and other ad- vances,

(5) I am unacquainted with this word, which may be read *Athouny* or *Athouly*, and indeed, several other ways. Perhaps the intelligence department may be meant.

(6) Literally "participation."

(7) Original لفظ ضد تعضور ظاهر میشود literally, "they set forth, or state, the words of "opposition."

(1) *Nâimâr*, usually called by the English *Nairs.*

(2) Original راتب

" vances, for their separate expences, *from the date of our orders on* " *the subject;* but that Syed Peer [the *Kilaadâr*] furthermore demanded " certain arrears of pay and rations, due to them *previously to that* " *period.*" The aforesaid *Kilaadâr* is deprived of his understanding [or has lost his wits]. The rations, and other allowances, are to be paid to the men in question, from the date of our orders [on the subject].

LETTER CCXXIII.

To RÂJAH RÂM CHUNDUR *and* TURBIYUT ALI KHÂN; *dated 4th* EEZIDY. *(9th February.)*

AT such times as new levies, or recruits, for the *Jyshe* and *Piâdehs* are to be entertained [or taken into the service], you two, and Syed Peer [the *Kilaadâr*], assembling together in the *Kuchurry*, are [to be mindful] to entertain none but proper and eligible men. You are also to take a muster of the men some time since admitted into the *Jyshe*, by the aforesaid *Kilaadâr*, and dismissing such of them as shall [appear to you to] be unfit [for the service], allow him pay for those only who are fit [to be retained].

LETTER CCXXIV.

To BUDRÛZ ZUMÂN KHÂN; *dated 8th* EEZIDY. (13*th February.*)

YOUR two letters, with the enclosed memorandums of the *Nâimâr* [or *Nair*] captives, have been received You did right in causing a hundred and thirty-five(1) of them to be circumcised, and in putting eleven of the youngest

(1) If the following numbers are right, this ought to be a hundred and five, instead of a hundred and thirty-five.

youngest of these into the *Usud Ilhye* band [or class], and the remaining ninety-four into the *Ahmedy* troop,(2) consigning the whole, at the same time, to the charge of the *Kilaadâr* of *Nugr.* You must give strict orders to the said *Kilaadâr*, to take the utmost care of these people, so that they shall not perish.(3)

N.B. There follow here some unimportant (and not very intelligible) orders, respecting certain defaulters and others, subject to the jurisdiction of Budrûz Zumân Khân.

OBSERVATIONS.

It appears from this, and some other passages, that the *Sultan*, as if pluming himself particularly on the institution of the two troops, or corps, of *Ahmedies* and *Usud Ilhyes*, was extremely attentive to every thing relating to their proper care and management. I am uncertain whether these corps continued in existence at the period of his death; but it is probable they did, as they are mentioned in documents of a recent date.

LETTER CCXXV.

To Bûrhânûddeen; *same Date.* (13*th February.*)

Your letter has been received, and its contents are comprehended. We approve of your having, for the present, with the advice and concurrence of the *Sipahdârs*, encamped with your army in the vicinity of *Kittoor*, which [it seems] is a safe and strong position. You will continue

2 L

(2) It might be inferred from this passage, that if there was any difference in the constitution of the *Ahmedy* and *Usud Ilhye* corps, it consisted partly (if not entirely) in this: that the younger converts to *Islâm* were enrolled in the latter, and the elder in the former.

(3) Original تاضایع نشود " that they may not be spoiled, or go to ruin."

tinue there, and observe the utmost vigilance, care, and precaution. Dispatch the *Daisye* and his managers, with all their effects and cattle, to the Presence, under charge of Hyder Ali Baig, one hundred horse, and two or three hundred *Piddehs.*

You have done right, in taking possession of the two villages of *Sipra* and *Jâmooty*, belonging to *Kittoor;* and in placing in the former fort a trusty *Sipahdâr*, with a garrison of three hundred *Piddehs.*

OBSERVATIONS.

The orders contained in this letter, respecting the position to be occupied by Bûrhânûddeen's army, are, it will be perceived, at variance with those transmitted to that officer about ten days before (Letter CCXX). The latter directed a retrogade movement to *Dhârwâr*, which Bûrhânûddeen and his council of war would appear to have thought inexpedient: and in this opinion we here perceive the *Sultan* acquiescing.

LETTER CCXXVI.

To the same; dated Seringapatam, *9th* Eezidy. (*14th February.*)

It is not proper or advisable, that your guns should be planted in batteries,(1) at a distance [from your lines]. You must keep them near your army, in the same manner(2) that you keep your army itself [*i. e.* in close and compact order, as directed in Letter CLXXXVIII]. You must,

(1) This is the word employed in the original, it having been very generally adopted by the natives of India.

(2) Original موافق قاعده لشکرخود which may also mean, "agreeable to the custom, or "practice, of your army:" but it strikes me, that the interpretation I have adopted is the right one.

must, moreover, continually[3] send out for intelligence of the enemy, and remain vigilant and prepared at your post.[4] Keep us, also, [regularly] informed of *these* matters [or of all occurrences].

OBSERVATIONS.

The *Sultan* appears, at this period, to have been in expectation of an early attack from the confederate forces; the commanders of which, however, did not, I believe, propose more at present than to cover the siege of *Bâdâmy*, which they undertook about this time, and of which place they finally obtained possession, in the month of May following.

It seems rather extraordinary, that the *Sultan* should have had occasion to teach Bûrhânûddeen so obvious a lesson in tactics, as that with which the present letter is introduced: but it must also be owned, that the information before us is too scanty, to enable us to form any clear notion of the subject. Much, of course, would depend on the actual distance from the camp at which the artillery was placed, as well as on the nature of the ground; and the letter throws no light on either of these points. All that is certain is, that Tippoo thought the disposition injudicious and dangerous; while it is likewise probable, that when he formed this judgment, he possessed a distinct knowledge of the different local circumstances connected with the question.

LETTER CCXXVII.

To Chishty Yâr Khân; *dated* 11*th* Eezidy. (16*th February*.)

Your letter has passed under our view. You represent, "that sensi-"ble [*i. e.* duly qualified] *Turufdârs*[1] are not to be procured at the "monthly

2 L 2

(3) Original پیهم "successively, incessantly."

(4) Original بجاي خود

(1) A petty officer, employed in the collection of the land revenue.

" monthly wages of one *pagoda*, and that the proper and faithful exe-
" cution of the public service cannot be expected from men receiving
" only a *pagoda* a month: you, therefore, propose, with our permission,
" to authorize the different *Aumils* to make some little increase in the
" monthly pay of the persons in question." Let the monthly wages of the *Turufdârs* of the *Taalûks* [or districts] under you be fixed at what you may judge proper and necessary to their subsistence, to the end that the business of the *Sircar* may be performed in the best manner.

LETTER CCXXVIII.

To the SHÂNOOR WALEH;(1) *dated* 15*th* EEZIDY. (20*th February.*)

YOUR letter by Gopâl Kishn has been received, and has given us great pleasure. What you write on the subject of the *Paishcush* is understood. What does it signify? Let the *Paishcush* in question be paid, by four instalments, to Nursia, the *Dewân* of *Nugr*. A letter, to this effect, is herewith enclosed for the said *Dewân*, to whom you must forward it. With regard to the malversations [or embezzlements], to the extent of twenty-six *lacks* of *rupees*, which have been established against the ministers, &c. of that friend, you must examine into the account of the same, and enforcing payment thereof, by *flogging* and other rigorous means, transmit to us bankers' acceptances for the amount.

OBSERVATIONS.

This letter is rather more civil, in point of style, as well as more accommodating in its spirit, than the last one to the same person (Letter CLI). Any change,

(1) *i. e.* Abdûl Hukeem Khân, the *Patan* chief of *Shânoor*. I ought to have observed before, that though I have adopted a different reading, the name is always written in the manuscript *Sânoor*. See Appendix, D.

change, in these respects, may be pretty safely referred, in the present case, to political motives, though it would be difficult, at this time, to trace such a change to any particular source of that kind. But as the operations of the belligerents began now to take a direction, which must soon compel the *Patan* to declare openly in favour of one or other of the contending parties, Tippoo's object, at this moment, might be, either to conciliate that chieftain, or to conceal, under an appearance of relaxation from his former demands, the design he had possibly already formed, of over-running his country, and of driving him from his capital; both of which the *Sultan* did, very soon after the date of the foregoing letter.

LETTER CCXXIX.

To NUWÂZISH ALI KHÂN, *Son of* SHÛJAAÛD DOWLAH; *dated* 16*th* *EEZIDY.* (21*st February.*)

[AFTER compliments.]..........Agreeably to your request we have advanced a hundred *rupees* for your expences. Undân Subhy(1) will, in pursuance of our orders, arrive [there.] After receiving the aforesaid money, repair to the Presence. We enclose a passport [for you], and also a *Purwâneh* for the above mentioned Subhy, which you will deliver to him.

OBSERVATIONS.

I am uncertain whether the Shûjaaûd Dowlah, mentioned in the superscription of this letter, be meant for the father of the present *Nabob* of *Oude*, or for some nobleman of the *Decan*, bearing the same title. It is well known, however, that the *Nabob* of that name left several sons, besides Asophûd Dowlah, his immediate successor, and Saadut Ali Khân, the present *Nabob*; who, on the death of their father, fled from their brother's court, and sought an asylum among the neighbour-

ing

(1) Name uncertain.

ing powers. Whether or not Nuwâzish Ali was one of these, I am unable to determine: but, whoever he might be, the reception here given him was certainly sufficiently discouraging. He is no where again mentioned.

LETTER CCXXX.

To BUDRÛZ ZUMÂN KHÂN; *same Date.* (21*st February.*)

CONFORMABLY with your humble request,(1) a passport has been written, and is herein enclosed. You must dispatch the necessary equipage, and send for your family [to join you]. What more?

OBSERVATIONS.

This letter is inserted, for the purpose of showing, both that no person, of whatever rank or consideration, could, when employed at a distance from the capital, have his family with him, unless by the express authority of the *Sultan;* and that the latter, occasionally, granted his servants this indulgence. His extending it, in the present conjuncture (the commencement of a war of doubtful issue), to Budrûz Zumân Khân, strongly marks his confidence in the fidelity of that officer.

LETTER CCXXXI.

To URSHUDÛLLAH KHÂN, *BUKTSHY of the EHSHÂM; same Date.* (21*st February.*)

DIRECTING him, after recovering from the *Kilaadâr* of *Kunnikgeery* the amount of the embezzlements established against the latter, to dispatch the said *Kilaadâr* to . . . . (1*)

Mentioning,

(1) Original استدعاي "imploring, supplication."

(1*) It is not said in the original to what place the *Kilaadâr* was to be sent. Another letter, on the same subject, says "to the fort;" but without specifying what fort. Perhaps *Seringapatam* is meant.

Mentioning, moreover, that, in future, he is not to take upon himself to remove or exchange any of the *Kilaaddrs* [within his jurisdiction], without the express authority of the *Sultan;* and desiring this to be considered as a most positive order.

LETTER CCXXXII.

To LŮTF ALI KHÂN *and* SHÂH NOORŮLLAH KHÂN; *dated 22d* EEZIDY. *(27th February.)*

Three *Kulgies,*(1) three *Surpaishes,*(2) and three *Puduks,*(3) of the value of thirty-six thousand two hundred and thirty *rupees,*(4) have been dispatched to you in a casket, to which our private seal [or signet] has been affixed. You must open this casket, and having examined its contents, seal the whole up again, and keep the same [carefully] by you.

The three *Kulgies,* three *Surpaishes,* and three *Puduks,* originally mentioned [or referred to] in our instructions [to you], *being afterwards considered by us of insufficient value,* have, on that account, been changed for the more valuable set now sent, and of which a memorandum is enclosed. Of this memorandum a copy must be entered in our book of instructions.

(1) The *Kulgy,* or *Kulghy,* is the plume of jewels which surmounts the

(2) *Surpaich,* or *Surpaish,* that is the *Aigrette.*

(3) I am not clear what is meant by a پدک *(Puduk.)* It seems, however, to have been a jewel, suspended from the neck. It also appears to have been worn as a badge of distinction, by officers of a certain rank, who are, in consequence, sometimes called *Puduk-wâlehs.* In this last sense it answered to our *gorget:* and it may be collected, from the *Futhûl' Mûjâhideen,* that the officers entitled to wear it, were always obliged to appear with it when on duty.

(4) Equal to about £4,500.

OBSERVATIONS.

The book of instructions, here mentioned, was among the papers found at *Seringapatam;* as was also the journal of this very embassy. I regret that I did not take copies of these curious documents, which would, no doubt, explain many points, on which we must be content, for the present, to remain ignorant.

It is a well established fact,(5) that this embassy, though ostensibly dispatched to the *Grand Seignor* alone, was ultimately to have proceeded, not only to the court of Louis XVI, but likewise to that of London; the mission to the latter being expressly designed to veil the secret negociations proposed to be opened with France. If, therefore, the jewels enumerated in the foregoing letter comprized the whole of what was destined for all the three courts mentioned, it must be allowed, that the meditated presents were not formed on such a scale of magnificence, as might have been expected from an eastern prince, desirous of impressing three of the principal sovereigns of Europe with a high idea of his power and resources. It is possible, however, that the casket, specified in this dispatch, may have constituted only a part of the jewels intended to have been presented.

The embassy was finally composed of four persons, as appears by the next letter.

LETTER CCXXXIII.

To Ghûlâm Ali Khân, Lûtf Ali Khân, Shâh Noorûllah Khân, *and* Mahommed Huneef; *dated 24th* Eezidy. (*1st March.*)

Your letters have been received, and their contents are understood. You write, "that all the stores, supplies, merchandize, &c. are laden "on board the ships, and that you only wait for the arrival of the "*Usud Ilhye* men and the jewels, when you will proceed [on your voyage]."

(5) See Colonel Beatson's Narrative, page 179.

voyage]." It is known. The men, in question, were dispatched [from hence] some time ago, and most probably have reached you before this. The jewels are now forwarded, and will arrive. As soon as you have received them, hasten your departure, and do not let the season(1) escape you.(2)

You write, " that the season for sailing to *Juddah* is passed, but that " the season for *Bussorah* and *Muscat* is not yet over ;" adding, " that " whatsoever we may please to order on this subject, you will act " accordingly." It is known. Some time since Othman Khân, a servant of the *Sircar*, being dispatched by us, reached *Bussorah*, and thence proceeded to *Baghdad*, from whence he was sent on by the *Bâsha* [of the latter place] to *Constantinople*; which, as we understand, is sixty days journey, with a caravan, from *Baghdad*. Now what appears [to us] to be most proper and advisable is, that you likewise should proceed by the same route; that is, first to *Bussorah*, from thence to *Baghdad*, and from thence to *Constantinople*.

It is our wish to obtain possession of the port of *Bussorah* in farm. Consequently, we are, for several reasons, well pleased at your going to that place.(3) Proceeding thither, accordingly, you will examine into the state of things there, and make every [necessary] enquiry respecting the port, where you will, at the same time, *dispose of your merchandize*. From thence you must repair straight to *Nujuf*, the most noble;(4) where presenting our very humble duty, you will represent in the most re-

2 M spectful

(1) Original موسم *(mosem)* from whence, probably, *Monsoon*.

(2) Original وموسم را از دست ندهند " and do not give the season from your hands;" or, " do not let it slip through your hands."

(3) *i. e.* " at its being rendered necessary, by the state of the *Monsoon*, that you should " go there, instead of to *Juddah*."

(4) Called usually *Nujuf Ushruf*. This is a place of great sanctity with Mahommedans. It is situated on the plain of *Kerbela*, celebrated for the bloody battle fought there between Yezeed and the sons of Ali.

spectful and submissive manner, that if it be agreeable [to the priests in charge of the holy shrine] to have an aqueduct brought to *Nujuf* the most noble [from the *Euphrates*], and they will signify their pleasure to that effect, we will, in the following year, send the necessary people and money for its construction. You must report to us, at length, the answer which you may receive to this proposal, together with all other particulars, in order that we may act accordingly.

You must not make any further delay, after the arrival of the party of *Usud Ilhyes* and the jewels, but proceed [immediately on your voyage]. Consider this order as positive.

OBSERVATIONS.

The *Sultan's* project of acquiring possession of *Bussorah* was, probably, as extravagant as any he ever entertained. By what means he could hope to attain such an object, it would be difficult to conceive: but it is probable, that the instructions to the embassy, and its journal, which, no doubt, are still extant, would throw some light on the subject. It has been said, that the ambassadors were empowered to offer *Mangalore* in exchange for it: but I think it unlikely that a prince of the *Sultan's* characteristic jealousy and distrust, should have consented to such an arrangement: and the letter before us certainly discountenances the notion; since, besides its not containing the most distant allusion to an exchange, it distinctly speaks of his wish "to farm" the port in question.

There is reason to believe, that the *Sultan's* project of constructing a canal from the *Euphrates* to *Nujuf*, if ever seriously entertained by him, was ultimately relinquished; since Mirzâ Abû Tâlib, who visited this sanctuary in 1803, does not mention such a work, though he has recorded a similar one, executed at the expence of the late *Nabob*, Asophûd Dowlah.

LETTER CCXXXIV.

To BUDRÛZ ZUMÂN KHÂN; *dated* 25*th* EEZIDY. (2*d March.*)

AFTER fixing a proper price on the coats which you have distributed among the *Jyshe,* you will deduct the amount from their pay.

Issue to the *Serishtedârs* of the *Ehshâm,* and to the *Gomâshtehs,* the monthly allowances specified in our instructions to you. There is no necessity for transmitting to us fresh pay abstracts [for this purpose].

You will also make a daily allowance of one *pice*(1) to such of the children of the *Koorgs,* between five and ten years old, as you may think proper.

LETTER CCXXXV.

To the same; dated 27*th* EEZIDY. (4*th March.*)

WHATEVER number of *Koorg* women and children may, at this time, be at *Nugr, Koonly-doorg,*(1*) or elsewhere, must be collected together, and the allowance formerly assigned for their support be paid to them.

LETTER CCXXXVI.

To MAHOMMED GHYÂS; *same Date.* (4*th March.*)

FIVE months ago, we sent by two *Hurkârehs* a letter, together with a dress, to Moodhojee Bhonsillah, to which we have hitherto had no answer: we have, therefore, again dispatched two more *Hurkârehs,* whom

2 M 2

(1) A *pice* is a copper coin, nearly of the value of a halfpenny.

(1*) Name uncertain.

whom you must *secretly* forward, but not directly or avowedly from yourself, with the letter which they have in charge for the aforesaid. This matter is to be kept profoundly secret. After being satisfied of the [favorable] disposition of the aforesaid, you must, from time to time, send a person to him, and privately sound his views; employing always [on the occasion] such language as may be most conducive to the improvement of [our mutual] friendship and regard.

OBSERVATIONS.

The reader will scarcely require to be informed, that Moodhojee Bhonsillah was the *Rájah* of *Berar,* and one of the principal members of the Mahrattah state. The mode adopted by the *Sultan,* of drawing this person over to his interests, would not appear to have much consulted the dignity of the latter; however it may have been demanded, by the caution necessary to be observed in such a correspondence. I possess no means of ascertaining what success Tippoo had in this intrigue; but I believe that Moodhojee Bhonsillah took little or no very active part in the ensuing hostilities.(1) It was, indeed, the uniform policy of that chieftain, in all the contests of his neighbours, to maintain, as long as possible (virtually, at least, if not formally), such a line of neutrality, as generally left it very doubtful to which side he most leaned: nor was he used to make much distinction, on these occasions, between the chiefs of his own nation, and the other circumjacent powers. His son and successor, Raghojee Bhonsillah, has not, however, adhered to his father's system, in this respect.

(1) He is said, in the Persian newspapers of this period (referred to in another instance at Letter CCXCVII.) to have quitted the Mahrattah army some time in July 1786, and to have returned to *Nagpoor,* leaving his son at the head of a body of five thousand horse behind him. Whether this apparent, though qualified, defection of the Bhonsillah was occasioned by the intrigue alluded to in the present letter, is a point which I do not possess the means of ascertaining.

LETTER CCXXXVII.

To BUDRÛZ ZUMÂN KHÂN ; *dated* 28*th* EEZIDY. (5*th March.*)

WHAT you write, concerning the death of five hundred *Koorgs* from the small-pox, is understood. The whole country [thereabouts] is covered with underwood.(1) They [*i. e.* the *Koorgs*] must be kept where the climate [literally, the water and air] may best agree with them.

N.B. Two or three letters appear about this time, containing directions for collecting *gram* (for the consumption of twelve thousand stable-horse) in the direction of *Bangalore*, *Chinroydoorg*, *Ruttungeery*, and *Sumrputn* (*Bulhâry*). These orders, which also announce the early approach of the *Sultan*, were, no doubt, preparatory to the rapid movement which he was now probably meditating against *Adoni*.

LETTER CCXXXVIII.

To ZYNÛL AABIDEEN, *Bukhshy of the* EHSHÂM *at* FYZE-YÂB HISÂR (GOOTY) ; *dated* 29*th* EEZIDY. (6*th March.*)

AGREEABLY to your request, an order has been written, and is herein enclosed, for the post *Hurkârehs* of *Hurry-hur*, to whom you will forward it.

With respect to lead and powder, do you act according to what is written in your instructions. That you should pursue your own opinion, in opposition thereto, occasions us the utmost surprise.(1*)

(1) Original همه ملک جاریست I have considerable doubt with regard to the meaning of this passage. It may signify, " it (*i. e.* the small-pox) is spread, or prevails, all over " the country." But in this case the word پر is wanting.

(1*) The word *surprise* is here supplied on conjecture, a blank having been left in the manuscript, after کمال " complete, utmost," &c.

LETTER CCXXXIX.

To BÛRHÂNÛDDEEN; *dated* 1*st* *Byâzy.* (7*th March.*)

INTELLIGENCE has reached us, stating, that Holkar, the *Guyckwâr*, and other forces of the enemy, to the number of thirty thousand horse, have set out, with an intention of falling upon(1) that light of our eyes.

It also appears, that the *Vakeels* of the *Sorapoor* man, as well as those of the *Zemindârs* of *Gunjunghur*, and other dependencies of the *Sircar*, who waited on the worthless(2) commander of the enemy, and opened negociations with him, have met with an encouraging reception, and been directed to join the enemy's army with their respective troops. This is written to that light of our eyes, by way of precaution [or, to put you on your guard].

LETTER CCXL.

To the same; dated 3*d* *Byâzy.* (9*th March.*)

Tukojee Hûlkar and the *Guyckwâr* have moved towards you with foul intentions:(1*) you will, therefore, take up a position with your army near the fort of *Dhârwâr*, and omit not a single measure of precaution in that situation. You must, moreover, enjoin all the inhabitants of that quarter to be cautious and watchful.

OBSERVATIONS.

The *Sultan* seems here to revert to his former orders (see Letter CCXX) respecting the position to be occupied by Bûrhânûddeen, but which he revoked by Letter

(1) Original ریزش نماید "pouring down," as rain.

(2) Original نامردار literally "no-leader." This is a favorite term of opprobium with the *Sultan*, when speaking of any chief or commander among his enemies.

(1*) Original به اراده باطله

Letter CCXXV, in compliance, apparently, with the suggestion of that general and the superior officers of his army. We shall soon see him wave the point again. (Letter CCXLVIII.)

LETTER CCXLI.

To Râjah Râm Chundur; *same Date.* (*9th March.*)

Notifying to him, that he must recall Sobhah Râo, the *Serishtedâr* of *Bangalore*, to whom he had, of *his own authority*, given leave of absence, or otherwise he [Râm Chundur] would be held responsible for the sum of two *lacks* of *rupees* due to the *Sircar* [that is to say, remaining to be accounted for] *by the aforesaid Serishtedâr*.

LETTER CCXLII.

To Mahommed Wâsil, *Kilaadâr of Târmurry; dated 4th Byâzy.* (*10th March.*)

Do you apply yourself to the care and defence of your fort; and if the vagabond cavalry of *Hyderabad*[1] should again appear in your quarter, chastise them.

Agreeably to your request, we enclose an order to the *Bukhshy* of the *Ehshâm* [at *Gooty*], to let you have a supply of provisions, lead, and powder, for the use of your fort. Forward the same to him.

LETTER CCXLIII.

To Meer Mohib Ali, *Bukhshy of the Ehshâm at Fyze Hisâr (Gooty); same Date.* (*10th March.*)

Dispatch to the fort of *Târmurry* a supply of provisions, lead, and powder, according to the [established] custom and regulations of the *Sircar*.

(1) Original سواران لچه حیدراباد which may also be read, "the cavalry of the vagabond of "*Hyderabad*" (*i. e.* the *Nizâm*).

Sircar. [That is to say, in the quantities or proportions of each article fixed by the regulations, either for the fort of *Tármurry* specifically, or for a fort of that class.]

LETTER CCXLIV.

To Ghûlâm Ahmed, *Kázy of Nugr; dated 6th Byázy.*
(*12th March.*)

We understand what you have represented, regarding a certain Musulman inhabitant of *Lukoty*,(1) "who was in the habit of worshipping "images, in the manner of the *Hindoos*, and whom you, in consequence, "upon hearing of the matter, seized, together with his wife and children; dispatching what money, as well as gold and silver trinkets, "they possessed, to the *Kuchurry* of the *Ehshám*, and keeping them "under a guard, till you should receive our orders respecting them."

You will deal with the aforesaid [offender] according to law, and then let him go. In matters relating to our holy law, you are authorized to act as you think proper [or, are independent].(2)

OBSERVATIONS.

The fact here recorded, supposing the *Kázy's* statement to be correct, is a very curious one, because of rare occurrence: indeed, I never heard of another instance of it. I am ignorant what punishment the Mahommedan law has appointed for this offence; but it is most probable, that the property of the present culprit, if not entirely confiscated, was, at least, heavily amerced.

(1) Name uncertain.

(2) Original درامور شرع شریف ایشان خود مختار اند

LETTER CCXLV.

To BÛRHÂNÛDDEEN; *dated* 10*th* *BYÂZY*. (16*th March*.)

You write, "that having dispatched your baggage to *Misrycotah*, our "victorious army is now light[1] and prepared for action." It is known. You must not be precipitate; but acting prudently and warily, watch for a [proper] opportunity of inflicting punishment [on the enemy]. If, moreover, they should encamp near you, you must seek for a favorable occasion, and make a night attack upon them.

LETTER CCXLVI.

To the same; dated 24*th* *BYÂZY*. (30*th March*.)

In case the enemy should encamp near you, watching for a favorable opportunity, you must make a night assault upon them, and chastise them signally. Your foragers and........[1*] must be sent into the close country of the interior,[2] on this side of you [that is, in your rear].

OBSERVATIONS.

It is curious to observe the *Sultan* directing, in this and the preceding letter, a night assault to be made on the Mahrattah army, while, on other occasions, when that mode of attack has been adopted by the English against himself, he stigmatises it as a base proceeding, worthy only of robbers.

2 N

(1) Original جريده

(1*) There is a word here in the manuscript illegible.

(2) Original درملک جهاري اندرون اين طرف

LETTER CCLXVII.

To the SHÂNOOR WÂLEH; *dated 26th* BYÁZY. (*1st April.*)

AGREEABLY to your request, we have written and enclose an order to Nursia, the *Dewán* of *Nugr*, directing him to accept payment of that friend's tribute(1) at the end of three months. Forward the same to him.

LETTER CCXLVIII.

To BÛRHÂNÛDDEEN; *dated 2d* AHMEDY, *Year* DULLO.(1*) (*7th April.*)

YOUR encamping at *Misrycotah*, as well as your dispatching of the *Kázy* of *Túrkul* to the Presence, was proper. According to your request, *Purwánehs* are enclosed for the *Aumils* of the several *Taalúks*, as likewise for the [different] *Kilaadárs*, directing them to furnish you [constantly] with intelligence of the enemy's [motions].

Let loose the marauding horse, and other predatory troops [with you], upon the enemy's army, with orders to capture and bring in [to your camp] horses *without number.*(2) Take care [at the same time] of your own army, and be always prepared [or on your guard].

LETTER CCXLIX.

To MAHOMMED ALI, *Aumil of* UFZULÁBÁDY NUGR;(1**) *same Date.* (*7th April.*)

IN like manner as you have caused two thousand *Samories*,(2*) inhabitants of *Zuferábád*, to flee [the country], even so must you send for them back [or cause them to return thither.]

(1) Original زركهندني

(1*) *Dullo*, or the fortieth year of the cycle, corresponding to A.D. 1786-7.

(2) Original اسپان بي شمار

(1**) I am not acquainted with the situation of this place.

(2*) The chief of this tribe is the person called by the Europeans the *Zamorin*.

LETTER CCL.

To Mahommed Abdûllah, *Cutwâl of the Army; dated 4th Ahmedy.* (*9th April.*)

One thousand two hundred and-forty two bullocks, belonging to the *Usud-Ilhye Kôthy*,(1) and six hundred bullocks, belonging to the powder-magazine, are appointed to be sent to pasture,(2) where you must provide for their being fed with thick milk,(3) at the daily allowance of a full *seer*(4) to every bullock. The [necessary] cowherds must be made to remain along with them at the pasturage, for the purpose of serving the curds; for which you are to take a regular receipt from them [*i. e.* from the cowherds].

OBSERVATIONS.

It is probable, that the bullocks, here enumerated, were intended to be employed on the expedition now meditated by the *Sultan* against *Adoni;* and as his movement thither was intended to be very sudden and rapid, the cattle selected for the occasion would, of course, be previously brought into the best condition possible. Thick, or curdled milk, is, I believe, considered in *India* as particularly heartening to oxen.

2 N 2

(1) *Kôthy* probably means here, " depot, or magazine."

(2) I rather think, that the name of the pasturage is given in the original; but, if so, it is illegible.

(3) Original جغرات

(4) Original دک پخته *Duk* is the term which the *Sultan* substituted for *Seer* (a weight equal to about ten pounds avoirdupois).

LETTER CCLI.

To the Dárogha of the Post-Office at Putn; dated 6th Ahmedy. (11th April.)

Such fruits as would spoil before they reached our Presence, must be taken to, and delivered at, the *Jinsy Tosheh-khâneh*, from whence they will be forwarded as may be ordered.(1)

OBSERVATIONS.

This letter is given principally for the purpose of shewing that the *Sultan* had, at the date of it, left *Seringapatam*. It does not appear on what day he actually moved from thence; but the last letter, purporting to be written from *Seringapatam*, is one dated 16th of *Bydzy*. The intermediate letters, to the date of the present one, do not happen to contain the name of the place from whence they were dispatched. On the 11th *Ahmedy* the *Sultan* writes from *Bangalore*.

LETTER CCLII.

To Shumsúddeen Khân; dated 9th Ahmedy. (14th April.)

Directing the following books, written in a good hand (not crabbed, but plain and legible) to be taken from the *Sultan's* library, and dispatched to the Presence:

IN PERSIAN.	IN DEKNY.
Gúlistán, ... 1 volume	*Khálik-Báry*
Bostán, ... 1 ditto.	*Kureemán*
Yoosúf and *Zúleekha*, 2 ditto.	*Amdun*(2)

(1) Original جاي كه رسانيدن است خواهند رسانيد literally, "they will send them where they "are to be sent to."

(2) Perhaps the *Amud-námeh* is meant.

OBSERVATIONS.

Several orders, of a similar nature with the above, appear in the present collection of letters. As the books in the foregoing list are what may be called school-books, or such as are usually put into the hands of learners, its may be concluded, that the *Sultan* was accompanied, at this time, by one or more of his younger sons.

LETTER CCLIII.

To MEER MOHIB ALI, *Bukhshy of* EHSHÂM, *at* FYZE HISÂR (GOOTY); *dated* 11*th* AHMEDY. (16*th April*.)

ON the subject of his securing the person of Râm-Râo, the *Serishtedâr* of the *Kundachâr*, who had absconded, together with the persons of all his family; and intimating to him, that he [Mohib Ali] would otherwise be made responsible [for the amount of the claims against the fugitive].

LETTER CCLIV.

To the SÂNOOR WALEH; *dated* BANGALORE, *same Date*. (16*th April*.)

[AFTER compliments]. . . . What you write, respecting the severity with which Râkhunder Nâik, &c. press the payment of the eight *lacks* of *rupees* [due to us by you], as well as your request, that we would send orders to the aforesaid *Nâik*, to desist from his rigorous proceedings in regard to this money, is understood. Agreeably to your desire, we have transmitted [the necessary] directions to the *Nâik*, whom you will send back to us, accompanied by the same persons, on your part, who formerly attended upon us; in order that, a valuation being made in [concert with them] of the gold, the trinkets, the jewels, &c. which have arrived in charge

charge of Weethul Doss, the banker, the same may be [duly] delivered into the *Sircar* [*i. e.* paid into our treasury].

You write "that the danger occasioned by the enemy's approach "having lately increased, the husbandmen, inhabitants, and others in "that quarter, have, in consequence, taken the most serious alarm; "and that this is the reason of your not having been enabled, hitherto, "to satisfy our fair claims." It is comprehended. God, the Aider, pleasing, the enemy will soon be repelled,(1) and receive the proper reward of their unjust proceedings.(2) After the confidence and tranquillity of the husbandmen, &c. shall have been restored, you must apply yourself to the discharge of our demands.

With a view to your ease and satisfaction, we have remanded the aforesaid banker, &c.(3) to our Presence; in order that all controversy and importunity, respecting pecuniary affairs, may be suspended, till the re-establishment of quiet.(4) What more shall we pen?

N. B. There follows a letter, of the same date and tenor, addressed to Dileer Khân Behâdûr Dileer Jung, whom I conclude to have been the principal minister of Abdûl Hukeem Khân, the *Nabob* of *Sânoor*.

LETTER CCLV.

To SHUMSÛDDEEN KHÂN; *dated* BANGALORE, 16*th* AHMEDY. (21*st April.*)

AFTER some directions, concerning certain gold ornaments, which the workmen belonging to the *Tosheh-khâneh* (of which Shumsûddeen was

(1) Original رفع میشود "settled, repelled."

(2) Original کردار ناهموار خود literally, "their *uneven* actions."

(3) This would appear to refer to Râkhunder Nâik.

(4) Original تارفع مجهله literally, "till the settlement of the pending dispute, or troubles."

the superintendant) were employed in making up, the letter thus proceeds :

You write, " that the druggists[1] require payment for the articles[2] " [furnished by them], and that you wait our orders on the subject." It appears by this, that you have entirely laid aside your instructions, and never peruse them. If it be written therein, that the articles purchased for our use are to be paid for, they must accordingly be paid for : if it be written, that they are not to be paid for, [then] they must not be paid for.

OBSERVATIONS.

If the foregoing letter, which is a close translation of the original, be understood in its most plain and obvious sense, we shall be obliged to conclude, that the oppressive system of requisitions, adopted some years after the date of it by the French revolutionists, was already known to, and practised by, Tippoo Sultan. It is possible, however, that his meaning might have been, that *prompt* payment was to be made for articles purchased on his account, in such cases only as were specified in his instructions ; and that, in all other instances, the tradesman was expected to submit the period of satisfying his claims to the pleasure and convenience of the *Sircar*. That the Persian reader may be the better enabled to judge how far this interpretation is admissible, I will here transcribe the original passage.

نوشته بودند که زر قیمت مصالح پساریان میخواهند در این باب هرچه ارشاد شود معلوم شد که ایشان حکم نامه‌را یک طرف داشته اند و نمیخوانند اگر در آن قلمي باشد که جنس کسیکه بسرکار خرید میشود زر آن بدهند باید داد اگر قلمي باشد که ندهند نباید داد

(1) Original پساریان who are also dealers in spices and groceries.

(2) Original مصالح This word usually means spices; but it also signifies the materials (particularly chemical) employed in various chemical operations. In this place, it probably refers to some articles of the latter kind, used by goldsmiths.

LETTER CCLVI.

To Bûrhânûddeen; *dated* Bangalore, *17th* Ahmedy. *(22d April.)*

You state, "that the *Kilaadâr* of *Dhârwâr* having dispatched to our "victorious army thirty-five thousand *pagodas*, over and above the fifty "thousand which we had ordered, you had detained the additional sum, "and waited our directions respecting it." It is known Apply the said money to the use of your army; and when, hereafter, a fresh order shall be issued to the above-mentioned *Kilaadâr* to transmit you a further supply, let the present thirty thousand *pagodas* be deducted from the amount.

You write, "that you had detached a *Risâla* of horse and a *Kushoon* "of *Jyshe* through the woods, with orders to chastise the enemy, if a "favourable opportunity for the purpose offered, but otherwise to return "to the army by the same route." It is known. In future, you must not detach the *Jyshe* [on such service], but only separate [or straggling] parties of horse, to whom you must give orders to seize and bring in all the camels, horses, and other booty they can.

LETTER CCLVII.

To Mirzâ Mahommed Khân Behâdûr Sumsâmûl Mûlk; *dated* 19*th* Ahmedy. *(24th April.)*

[After compliments]....... Your friendly letter, announcing your firm intention of repairing hither with the troops belonging to you, has been received, and afforded us the greatest satisfaction. Your [intention of] coming hither is highly approved [by us]. Proceed in the execution

of

of your purpose with the utmost confidence and security, and make us happy by an interview, for which we are extremely impatient. The distance [between us] being considerable, you should bring along with you as great a force as possible.(1) By the grace of God, we shall make you such appointments, in *Jageers* and money, as shall be entirely satisfactory to that friend.

The rosary, kneeling-carpet,(2) &c., which you sent us as tokens of friendship, arrived, and afforded us the utmost pleasure. Although, by the bounty of the Almighty, we possess an inconceivable number of *worldly* curiosities,(3) yet these, being *religious* rarities,(4) are esteemed by us equally with the richest treasures.(5)

It was our wish and intention to have sent that friend a dress, together with some jewels, &c.; but we have been prevented from doing so, by the *Hurkârehs* having declined to take charge of them, on account of the dangers of the road.

OBSERVATIONS.

I have no certain knowledge who Sumsâmûl Mûlk was. The interchange of presents, spoken of in the letter, rather discountenances the idea of his being a disaffected *Omra* of the court of *Hyderabad*; since a correspondence of that sort could hardly have escaped detection, and is not likely, therefore, to have been hazarded, during the existence of actual hostilities between the two states. The same objection applies to the supposition of his belonging to the train of Dârâjah (the son of the late Busâlut Jung, and nephew of the *Soubah*) who, at this period,

2 O held

(1) With a view to rendering his junction the more secure.

(2) Original سجده the carpet on which Musulmans kneel during prayers.

(3) Original تحايف دنوي

(4) Original تحفه ديني

(5) Original از مغتنمات دانسته شد

held *Adoni* in appenage. The former conjecture is further opposed, by the consideration, that none of the memoirs of Nizâm Ali Khân, in my possession, notice the defection of this, or any other person of distinction, from his service, during the present war. But whoever this Sumsâmûl Mûlk was, it is probable that his negociation with the *Sultan* proved abortive, since we hear no more of him after this time.

LETTER CCLVIII.

To Meer Kâzim, *Dârogha at Muscat, same Date.* (*24th April.*)

Three letters from you, accompanied by two statements of your receipts and disbursements, have passed under our view.

You have done well, in buying and lading on our ships, rock-salt,[1] instead of sapphires.[2]

For the future, you will, in like manner, send rock-salt instead of sapphires.

The carpenters [or ship-wrights] at *Muscat* construct very excellent *Dows* and *Dingies*. You must advance to four or five of these carpenters whatever money they may require for their expences, and dispatch them to the port of *Mangalore*.

The factory of *Muscat* is placed under the authority of Ghûlâm Mahommed, the *Aumil* of *Mangalore* : you are, therefore, to conduct all affairs according to his directions, and not to require our orders in any case.

Send

(1) Original نمک معدني " rock, or mineral salt."

(2) Original سنگ نيلم " sapphire stone." If this term have any other meaning than that assigned to it, I am unacquainted with it ; and yet this explanation is not free of difficulty.

Send some young date-trees,[3] with persons skilled in the management of them, to the Presence. Buy all the sulphur you can, and lading it on our vessels, dispatch the same from time to time.[4]

Ghûlâm Ali Khân, Shâh Noorûllah, &c. have, by our orders, proceeded to *Constantinople*, by the way of *Muscat*. Advise us, in due time, of their arrival.

You must take care and sell the *sandal* wood, black pepper, rice, and *cardamums*, belonging to us, to the best advantage, sending an account of your sales and purchases regularly to Ghûlâm Mahommed.

The accounts of receipts and disbursements, which you sent, are arrived. [This had been already mentioned, in the beginning of the present letter].

Saffron is the produce of *Persia*. Procure and send us some of the seed of it.

Get the *Dullâl* [broker] to write to his agents in different places, to collect silk-worms, and persons acquainted with the manner of rearing them: and [having procured them] let them be dispatched to us.[5]

Procuring, moreover, some [pearl] divers from *Bahrein* and *Hoormûz;* and making them whatever advances they may require for their expences, dispatch them hither, together with their families.

Sending, likewise, to *Rûstakh*, and getting from thence five large asses, dispatch them to us.

We have received your account of the occurrences of that quarter and of *Persia*. Continue to make similar communications.

We have given directions to Ghûlâm Mahommed [the *Aumil* of *Mangalore*] to sell rice, &c. to every merchant producing a certificate [*chitty*] from you.

2 O 2

(3) Original خرما نونهالان

(4) Original میفرستاده باشند

(5) The instructions of the *Sultan* to the *Meer-Asofs* or revenue department (issued in 1793) contain particular regulations respecting the culture of the silk-worm.

OBSERVATIONS.

It will probably have been observed by the reader, that several of the *Sultan's* former orders are repeated in the foregoing letter, for the second, and some of them for the third time. He will, hereafter, be seen to reiterate them again.

It may be inferred, from the seventh paragraph of the present letter, that the embassy to *Constantinople* had, at this time, actually departed from *Mangalore*.

LETTER CCLIX.

To Ghûlâm Mahommed, *Aumil of Mangalore ; same Date.* (*24th April.*)

We send herewith three letters, and two statements of receipts and disbursements, received from Meer Kâzim: read and keep them carefully by you.

You are to sell rice, &c. [freely] to every merchant from *Muscat*, who brings you a *chitty* [or certificate] from Meer Kâzim.

The above-mentioned [*i. e.* Meer Kâzim] instead of sapphires, has bought and sent on our vessels a quantity of rock-salt. What sort of a thing is the said rock-salt: and is there any consumption of it in this country or not? Communicate [to us] every particular regarding it. Meer Kâzim writes, that he has sent a sample of it: let the said sample be forwarded to us.

OBSERVATIONS.

It would appear, from the beginning of Letter CCLVIII, that Meer Kâzim had actually dispatched some cargoes of rock-salt; while, from the concluding sentence of Letter CCLIX it might be inferred, that he had sent only a sample of it. However this might be, it is curious enough to observe the *Sultan*, in one and

and the same moment, enquiring the nature of the commodity in question; acknowledging himself ignorant, whether or not there was any demand for it among his subjects; and yet directing it to be shipped for *Mysore*, by every opportunity.

LETTER CCLX.

To the SIPAHDÂR, SYED GHUFFÂR; *dated* BANGALORE, *24th* AHMEDY. (*29th April.*)

WE have received your application for letters from us to the *Jumaadârs* of the enemy's army. We shall arrive soon in person in that quarter, when, considering this matter duly, we will give our directions [or determine] accordingly.

You request to know our pleasure regarding the pay of your brother, who has been lately raised to the rank of a *Risâladâr*. The monthly pay of that rank, according to the former regulations of the *Jyshe Kuchurry*, is ten *pagodas*, exclusive of an allowance of twelve *annas fulmy*(1) for every man mustered.(2) Let him be paid accordingly.

OBSERVATIONS.

This letter affords another proof of the strange division of the military authority in the armies of the *Sultan*. We here perceive a subordinate officer corresponding directly with his sovereign, upon a point of considerable delicacy and importance, which apparently belonged, in a peculiar manner, to the province of the commander-in-chief (Bûrhânûddeen). It is true, that the *Sultan* does not adopt the suggestion of the *Sipahdâr*; but neither does he hint, that there was any irregularity in it.

I am

(1) Original في نفردوازده انه فلمي

(2) Perhaps *recruited* may be meant.

I am by no means satisfied, that I have correctly translated the paragraph relating to the pay of Syed Ghuffâr's brother. Either the original is extremely perplexed, or I may not rightly have understood its technical phraseology.

LETTER CCLXI.

To BÛRHÂNDÛDDEEN; *dated* 26*th* AHMEDY. (1*st May*.)

WE have received your letter, informing us, "that having detached "Shaikh Unser and Syed Ghuffâr to the relief of *Kittoor*, the former, "taking a different road [from that pursued by Syed Ghuffâr], had "fallen[(1)] upon the enemy's entrenchments, and after putting to the "sword, or taking prisoners, a thousand of their *Piddehs*, had entered "*Kittoor*: that Syed Ghuffâr, having proceeded by another route, had "attacked a small fort [or redoubt], in which the enemy had placed a "garrison of five hundred men, the whole of which were either killed "or made prisoners: that after this he surprised, in the night, a "picquet of the enemy, consisting of a thousand horse, of great part of "which he made booty,[(2)] and then got [in safety] to *Kittoor*: finally, "that having infused due confidence into the garrison, and supplied the "place with provisions and stores, both *Sipahdârs*, uniting their forces, "directed their march back by a road leading through the woods; and "that you expected them to rejoin the victorious army in the course of "twenty-four hours. You proceed to state, "that as soon as they "arrive, you will muster the horses [taken], and report the same to "us;" and you add, "that the *Kuzzâk* [or predatory] cavalry, "belonging to the *Sircar*, are constantly bringing in horses taken from "the enemy, which, agreeably to our orders, you purpose relinquishing "to them.

It

(1) Original برمورچه مخالف افتاد

(2) Original اسپان بي شمار غنيمت آورده "brought away in booty *numberless* horses."

It is known. Upon the two *Siphadárs* rejoining you, you must ascertain, and report to us in detail, the particulars of the gallant behaviour of our troops [in the recent engagements]; in order that we may give directions for their being rewarded [according to their deserts]. State, likewise, what number of horses have been taken from the enemy.

You write, "that seven hundred *Piadehs* from *Nugr*, with a *Serishtedár*, and the *Kilaadár* Hûsainy Baig, had arrived in your camp, for "the purpose of garrisoning *Kittoor*, and that you had accordingly "dispatched the men and the *Serishtedár*; but that Hûsainy Baig being "too ill to proceed thither at present, should be sent as soon as he "recovered."(3) You moreover say, "that it is your intention to send "back to *Dhárwár* Ghous Mahommed Khân, the second *Munshoor*(4) of "that place."

You must keep Hûsainy Baig with your army, and send Ghous Mahommed Khân, who has distinguished himself by his activity at *Dhárwár*, to [command at] *Kittoor*.

Report to us the particulars of all who have *exerted* themselves, in order that we may bestow rewards on them *also*.(5)

You must inform the aforesaid *Munshoor*, Ghous Mahommed, and Sheer Khân, the *Aumil* [of *Kittoor*], that if they should find the place untenable, or in want of provisions and other supplies, they must not sacrifice our troops in its defence, but evacuating it, repair through the woods to the army: *for it is but a mound of clay, the existence and non-existence of which is the same thing* [*i. e.* is of no importance either way.]

(3) The original is very obscure in this place, owing, apparently to the omission of two or three words, by supplying which the passage is rendered intelligible. Hûsainy Baig seems to have been proceeding to *Kittoor*, as *Kilaadár* of that place.

(4) A *Munshoor* would appear to have been a kind of town-major, or fort adjutant.

(5) This appears to be no more than a repetition of the order given in the second paragraph of this letter.

OBSERVATIONS.

It is uncertain whether the enemy, here spoken of, was the Mahrattah army, or only an assemblage of the adherents of the captive *Daisye*, which had attempted to regain possession of *Kittoor*. The circumstance, however, of a picquet of a thousand horse, renders the former supposition the most probable.

The *Sultan* appears to have been well satisfied with the conduct of his troops on this occasion: and if their success was really so extensive as represented by Bûrhânûddeen, he had reason to be so. But his report (as recited in the letter before us) is expressed in too vague and general terms, to be considered as decisive evidence on this point.

LETTER CCLXII.

To the same; dated 27th AHMEDY. *(2d May.)*

AFTER some orders for completing the different *Risâlas* of the army as speedily as possible, and for filling up the vacancies in the rank of *Risâladâr*, the letter thus concludes:—

A *Risâladâr* [formerly] belonging to the *Risâla* of General Matthews has been sent to join you from the Presence. What you write, with regard to our issuing orders for your being supplied with the musquets you are in want of, is understood. We shall shortly arrive in that quarter, when the necessary orders will be given.

LETTER CCLXIII.

To DILEER KHÂN BEHÂDÛR DILEER JUNG;[1] *dated 28th* AHMEDY. *(3d May.)*

[AFTER compliments]........... You write, "that it is now the "sowing season, and that, on this occasion, as well as for the purpose of

(1) The minister of Abdûl Hukeem Khân, the *Nabob* of *Shânoor*.

" of realizing the claims of the *Sircar*, the presence of Mulhâry Pundit " and of his son is a matter of the utmost consequence; and that you, " therefore, request we will revoke our orders for their attending upon " us, and allow you to send Râm Râô, Tummana Pundit, and Winkut " Râo, along with Râkhunder Nâik, in their room." It is known.

Inasmuch as it is, on several accounts, necessary, at this time, that the above named, with whom we have certain points to discuss, should repair to our Presence, we must repeat our former desire, that the *whole* of your managing servants(2) may be dispatched to us, along with Râkhunder Nâik. The negociation [or discussions alluded to] being terminated, they shall receive their dismission [*i. e.* be permitted to return to you].

OBSERVATIONS.

It may be concluded, both from the reluctance of the *Patan* chief to send Mulhâry Pundit and his son to *Seringapatam*, and the pertinacity of the *Sultan* in requiring their attendance, that these persons were particularly well acquainted with the resources of the country, and perhaps with the personal property of their master, both of which, there is reason to think, Tippoo had, at this time, devoted to confiscation. I am unable to say, whether or not the individuals in question ultimatelyrepaired to the *Sultan's* court; but as Abdûl Hukeem had most probably already determined not to wait the arrival of the *Sultan* at *Shânoor*, it may be presumed that they were not dispatched.

LETTER CCLXIV.

To Bûrhânûddeen; *same Date.* (3d *May.*)

You must relinquish [or give up] whatever horses and camels may be taken from the enemy to the captors, of whom you will buy as many of them

2 P

(2) Original اهلكاران " Men of business."

them as they themselves may not want, at a cheap and reasonable price, which is to be paid[1] to them [immediately]. They must not be allowed to sell them elsewhere.[2]

The *Jumaadârs*, who happen to have brethren[3] with them that are out of employ, should be directed to mount the latter on the captured horses, and bring them to be mustered and enrolled in our service.

We lately sent orders to you to withdraw the garrison of the small fort of *Kittoor*,[4] and direct it to rejoin your army by the road through the woods. We now write to countermand those orders, and to desire, that you will send such supplies of provisions, &c. to the said fort, as it may be in need of; for we shall shortly come in person to that quarter, and the enemy, moreover, have retired from thence.

OBSERVATIONS.

It is uncertain whether by the small fort of *Kittoor*, the *Sultan* means the principal fortress of that name, lately wrested from the *Daisye*, or only an outwork or detached post; such as that mentioned in Letter CCLXI, as having been taken by Syed Ghuffâr, on his coming to the relief of *Kittoor*; or the *small fort* noticed in the report of Bûrhânûddeen, contained in Letter CCLXI.

I rather think, however, that *Kittoor* itself is the place intended; both because it is, on other occasions, sometimes called a قلعه and sometimes a قلعچه and because the provisional order for its evacuation, contained in Letter CCLXI (and which is probably the order alluded to in the present dispatch) appears free from all ambiguity.[5]

(1) The order for *payment* may appear to be superfluous after that of *purchasing*; but it must be recollected, that *paying* did not, in Tippoo's practice, necessarily follow *buying*. See Letter CCLV.

(2) Original بیرون or, "without" *i. e.* to strangers.

(3) Original برادری or, "men of their own tribe," following them in hopes of employment.

(4) Original قلعچه the diminutive of قلعه

(5) By Letter CLXIX it appears, that *Kittoor* consisted of *two* forts (or castles), and a *Paith*, or outer town.

LETTER CCLXV.

CIRCULAR *to the following Persons; dated from* MULOONG,[1] 28*th* AHMEDY. (3d *May*.)

BUDRÛZ ZUMÂN KHÂN;
The KÂZY *of* NUGR;
The DEWÂN *of ditto.*
The DEWÂN *and* BUKHSHY *of* EHSHÂM *at* SERINGAPATAM;
The ditto and ditto, at FYZE HISÂR, (GOOTY);
The ditto and ditto, at the Presence.
The BUKHSHY *of ditto, at* BANGALORE;
NUBBY SHÂH, *Son-in-law to* AATÂ-ÛLLAH-SHAH;
BÛDHUN SHÂH, *son of* AWKIL SHÂH;
The KÂZY *of* SERINGAPATAM;
The DEWÂN *and* BUKHSHY *of* EHSHÂM *at* ZUFERÂBÂD, (GURRAMCOONDA);
The KILAADÂR *of* NUGR;
The KILAADÂR *of* SUMRPUTN BULHÂRY);
The ditto of SERINGAPATAM;
The DEWÂN, *and* DOWLUT KHÂN, *the* KILAADÂR, *of* FURRÛKHYÂB HISÂR (CHITTLEDOORG);
The KILAADÂR *of* FYZE HISÂR (GOOTY);
The BUKHSHIES *of the two* JYSHE KUCHURRIES;
The BUKHSHIES *of the five* BÂRGEER KUCHURRIES;
BÛRHÂNÛDDEEN;
MIRZÂ HYDER HÛSAIN;
DILEER DIL KHÂN;
The FOUJDÂR *and* BUKHSHY *of* EHSHÂM *at* CALICUT;
SYED AHMED SAHEB;
The KÂZY *of* BANGALORE;
The UMLDÂR[2] *of* MANGALORE.

IN the time of the seal [or last] of the Prophets (with whom be the blessing and peace of God) the divine commands were promulged. Since then

2 P 2

(1) I am not clear that I read this name rightly. No such place occurs in our maps; but it cannot be far distant from *Bangalore*, and must be situated between that place and Great *Balapoor*.

(2) In the original علم دار or "standard-bearer," which I take to be an error of the transcriber for عملدار A "collector or manager of a district."

then, owing to the decline of the true faith under the succeeding princes, they have ceased to be promulged: we, therefore, with the help of Almighty God, now issue the aforesaid commands; and, accordingly, the above mentioned commands are enclosed, herewith, under our seal and signature, to serve as a guide to the true faith.

You are, in the best [possible] manner to explain the same *to all* the people of *Islâm*, to the *Kâzy*,(3) and to the other superiors of your *Kuchurry* [or department], considering the communication thereof to the ignorant as one of the most incumbent and obligatory duties of religion: for such is the recompence of holy war.(4)

You must cause numerous copies of the commands herewith sent to be made, and must distribute the same among the people of the faith, the *Kâzies* and others belonging to your department, to the end that they may obtain the utmost publicity.

OBSERVATIONS.

Nothing can be worse written than the original of this miserable circular. Though short, it is, perhaps, as perplexed a production as any that ever proceeded from the pen of the *Sultan*, who, most probably, dictated every word of it. The proclamation to which it refers, and which immediately follows it in my manuscript, is in a better style, and was, no doubt, drawn up by some of the Mahommedan theologians of his court.

A translation of the proclamation here mentioned, appeared, in the year 1793, in the Appendix to Major Dirom's judicious and interesting Narrative of Lord Cornwallis's last Campaign against Tippoo Sultan; and if that publication were not

(3) Here, instead of the *Kâzy* being directed to explain the divine word to true believers, as might have been expected, the governors of forts, &c. are to explain it, both to the *Kâzy* and to the people at large.

(4) Original که اینچنین اجر جهاد است I confess I do not clearly perceive the connexion between this and the preceding sentence.

not now become very scarce, it would be sufficient, perhaps, to refer the reader to it, for the document in question: it is proper, however, to observe, that the Persian original, from which Colonel Read's translation was taken, appears to have differed, in some respects, from the copy recorded in the official register. Of the latter the following is a faithful version, for which I am, in a great measure, indebted to the kindness of Mr. Stewart, Persian, Arabic, and Hindostâny Professor at the Honorable the East-India Company's Oriental College at Hertford. The original abounds so much in quotations from the *Koran*, and my knowledge of the Arabic is so limited, that, without such assistance, I should have hesitated at submitting a translation of it to the reader.

Proclamation, or Manifesto, of Tippoo Sultan.(5)

" WHEREAS, in conformity with the commands of God and the Prophet " [which say], ...

" 'Fight with those who do not believe in God, and in the
" 'last day; and who do not consider those things as un-
" 'lawful, which God and his Prophet have prohibited,
" 'and profess not the true religion; and [fight] with those,
" 'unto whom the scriptures have been given, until they pay
" 'tribute by right of subjection, and be reduced low.'(6)

...." it is our constant object and sincere intention, that those worthless and " stiff-necked infidels, who have turned aside their heads from obedience to the " true believers, and openly raised the standards of infidelity, should be chastised " by the hands of the faithful, and made either to acknowledge the true religion, " or to pay tribute: particularly at this time, when, owing to the imbecility of " the princes of *Hind*, that insolent race having conceived the futile opinion, that " the true believers are become weak, mean, and contemptible; and not satisfied " even with this, but, preparing for war, have over-run and laid waste the " territories of the Moslems, and extended the hand of violence and injustice on " the property and honour of the faithful.

[Wherefore]

(5) There is no title or inscription to this document in the manuscript.

(6) Chapter IX of the *Koran*.

" [Wherefore] we, trusting to the divine power and aid, and supported by " our holy religion [according to the passage]..........................

" 'Oh true believers, shall I show you a merchandize, which " 'will deliver you from a painful torment [hereafter]? " 'Believe in God and his Apostle, and defend God's true " 'religion with your substance and in your persons. This " '[will be] better for you, if you knew it. He will forgive " 'you your sins, and introduce you into gardens, through " 'which rivers flow, and agreeable habitations in places of " 'perpetual abode. This [will be] great felicity; and [ye " 'shall obtain] other things which you desire, [namely] " 'assistance from God and a speedy victory.'(7)

...." having come to the resolution of prosecuting a holy war [against them], " deem it expedient [agreeably to the text]:..........................

" 'Command them to do that which is lawful [proper], and " 'prohibit their doing that which is unlawful; and observe " 'the ordinances of God.'

...." to make known what is the pure Mahommedan law, to all and every class " of Musulmans, both far and near, and thereby to extract the cotton of negli- " gence from the ears of their understanding: and more especially those persons " who, unmindful of the meaning of the sacred text,....................

" 'Do not obey the unbelievers and hypocrites, for certainly " 'God is omniscient and all-wise.'

...." have yielded obedience to the infidels, and engaged in the service of those " miserable tribes. It is therefore written to all those who reside in the dominions " of the infidels, ...

" 'They seek to deceive God and those who do believe; but " 'they deceive themselves only, and are not sensible thereof. " 'There is an infirmity in their hearts. May God increase " 'their

(7) Chapter LXI of the *Koran*.

" 'their infirmity! They shall suffer a grievous punishment,
" 'because they have been guilty of falsehood.'(8)

. . . " and to whose situation the [above] verse may be justly applied, that con-" sidering it to be their indispensable duty to quit the territories of the unbelievers, " they should repair, with confident hearts and assured minds, to these parts, " where, by the Divine blessing, they shall be still better provided for than they " are at present, and their lives, honor, and property, remain under the protec-" tion of God: while such as are without the means of subsistence there, shall " have a suitable allowance made to them here.

" We have accordingly issued premptory orders throughout our dominions to " this effect: 'Receive into your protection all persons seeking refuge [in our " 'territories] and report to the Presence the particulars of their situation, in " 'order that, if it please God the Aider, due provision may be made for them.'

" Whosoever shall refuse to give ear to these words, or shall contravene their " promulgation, shall be considered as destitute of [every particle of] honor [or " zeal], as a stranger to [or no participator in] the bliss derived from [a steady] faith, " and as deserving to be banished from the presence of God, to be excluded from " the circle of the faithful, and to be accounted as one of the accursed infidels.

Verse from Hafiz.(9)

" 'If you place your foot in the path of the law and of religion, Hafiz,
" 'In reward for your zeal, the Chief of Nujuf [Ali] will become your Protector.

" 'Let them not say of any thing [or on any occasion] I will " 'do so; but, if it please God [it shall be done]. Grace be " 'to him who follows this direction.(10)

Although it is probable, that the immediate object of the *Sultan*, in the foregoing proclamation, or manifesto, was to seduce from their allegiance, and draw over to his

(8) Chapter II of the *Koran*.

(9) This is not an exact quotation from Hafiz, the original having, instead of ره شرع ودین " the path of the law and of religion," ره خاندان تصدق " the path of the family or race of " alms-givers."

(10) This sentence is supposed by Mr. Stewart to be a *Hudees*, or one of the traditionary sayings attributed to Mahommed.

his standard, the Musulman subjects of the two powers, with whom he was, at this time, at open war, yet there can be but little doubt that the English, together with their dependants and tributaries, were also in his contemplation on the occasion. It is true, that the latter is not expressly named: neither are the Mahrattahs nor the *Nizám*. Indeed, with regard to the *Nizám*, he could not have been distinctly referred to without an apparent absurdity, since he was a Mahommedan as well as *Tippoo;* who, nevertheless, certainly regarded him in the light of an infidel, because he had, more than once, associated with infidels against the cause of *Islám*, that is to say, in opposition to him (Tippoo). The argument, therefore, was addressed generally to all Musulmans, in whatever manner subject to the enemies, direct or indirect, of the true faith. There was no danger of its not being properly applied and understood by those for whom it was intended: no Musulman is ever at a loss to comprehend the drift of such appeals. At the same time, if any exception had been taken to it by the English, the vague and general terms in which it is expressed would have enabled him to maintain, with sufficient plausibility, that he had only in view such Musulmans as were living under the authority of those with whom he was actually at war.

There is one passage in the foregoing production, which appears to point more particularly than any other to the English. It is that wherein he complains, not, as in Major Dirom's translation, of ravages committed in *his* peculiar territories, but (according to my copy of this paper) of the injuries and losses which the Musulmans in general had sustained at the hands of the infidels; alluding distantly (as on other occasions he has done more openly) to our establishment in *Bengal*, the *Carnatic*, and other Mahommedan states of *India*. On the whole, it must be allowed, that the extensive views of aggrandizement, entertained at this time by the *Sultan*, are abundantly developed by this curious document.

LETTER CCLXVI.

To the COMMANDANT, ABDÛL NUBBY;(1) *dated 29th* AHMEDY. (*4th May.*)

ON the subject of his repairing to the Presence, together with the *Sepoys* belonging to him (or such *Sepoys* as he may be enabled to bring with him), in perfect confidence and security: and assuring him, that he should be provided for after his arrival, agreeably to the regulations and appointments of the *Sircar*.

LETTER CCLXVII.

To ALI RÂJAH BEEBY; *same Date.* (*4th May.*)

DESIRING her to transmit incessantly intelligence of what passes at *Bombay* and *Tillicherry*.

LETTER CCLXVIII.

To GHÛLÂM MUNSOOR, *Aumil of* SILCOTAH;(1*) *dated* 1st BEHÂRY. (*5th May.*)

YOUR letter, reporting, " that the *Jumaadâr*, Syed Ameen, had " beat the *Bukhshy*, Nuwâz Baig, in such a manner, as to occasion the " death of the latter; and that you had [in consequence] secured the

2 Q " aforesaid

(1) Probably the commandant of a corps of regular *Sepoys*, either in the service of the Mahrattahs or of the *Nizâm*.

(1*) This letter serves, in some degree, to mark the progress of the *Sultan's* march against *Adoni*. He had advanced, on the 6th May, as far as *Great Balapoor*.

" aforesaid *Jumaadár*, by putting irons on his legs and arms," has passed under our view.

Our special retinue will arrive the day after to-morrow at *Great Balapoor*. Securing his [*i. e.* the murderer's] legs and arms well in fetters,(1) you must place him in a *Dooly*, and bring him along with yourself, under a strong guard, to the Presence.

LETTER CCLXIX.

To FUZL ALI KHÂN ; *same Date.* (*5th May.*)

THE report which you have sent us, of the gallant conduct of our troops, and of the men wounded [in the late actions], is known [or has been considered]. Let the wounded receive the compensation fixed by our regulations ; and let the horses, and other property taken [from the enemy], be relinquished, according to the orders of the *Sircar*, to the captors [literally, to those who *bring them in.*](2).

LETTER CCLXX.

To the SIPAHDÁR, MAHOMMED ALI ; *same Date.* (*5th May.*)

WHEN we ourself arrive in that quarter, *the Risála, wanting to complete your Kushoon,* shall be given you.

OBSERVATIONS.

This short letter is given, merely for the purpose of showing, in some degree, the constitution of a *Kushoon.* It appears, by this document, that a *Risála* was a com-

(1) This had been already done.

(2) I have no means of ascertaining who Fuzl Ali Khân was, or whether or not he was one of the commanders serving under Bŭrhânŭddeen.

a component part of a *Kushoon*: but how many of the former were contained in a *Kushoon*, I do not clearly know. I am inclined to think, however, that a *Kushoon* was a regiment, consisting of two or more *Risálas*, or battalions.(1)

LETTER CCLXXI.

To BÛRHÂNÛDDEEN; *dated* 2d BEHÂRY. (*6th May.*)

YOUR letter has been received A rupture has taken place between Nizâm Ali Khân and the enemy [*i. e.* the Mahrattahs], in consequence of some pecuniary discussions; and this has been followed by the aforesaid *Khán's* marching away, to the distance of six *coss* on the other side of [or beyond] *Báddmy*.

We shall shortly relieve both *Báddmy* and *Ramdoorg* in a fit manner [*i. e.* effectually]. Do you [in the mean while] keep your mind at ease. You did right in giving up [or resigning] the captured horses and cattle [to the captors]. You must do the same thing in future.

OBSERVATIONS.

It is certain, that the *Nizám* separated about this time from the Mahrattah army, and returned to *Hyderabad*. The measure, however, is ascribed, in such memoirs of this period as I have seen, simply to the inconvenience which his Highness suffered from the heat of the weather. He is stated to have left, at the same time, a considerable body of troops, for the purpose of cooperating with his allies.

The *Sultan* did not fulfil his promise, respecting the relief of *Báddmy*, as the Mahrattahs obtained possession of that place some time in the month of May.

2 Q 2

(1) Since writing the above, I have met with some statements of the military establishments of Tippoo Sultan, which have enabled me to give the general idea of them, inserted in the Appendix.

LETTER CCLXXII.

To Meer Kâzim, *Dârogha at Muscat : same Date.* *(6th May.)*

The rock-salt, of which you sent a sample (see Letter CCLVIII,) is very fine: you must, therefore, buy a large quantity of it, and lading it on the return *Dingies* belonging to the *Sircar*, which have carried thither rice for sale, consign the same, from time to time, to the *Aumil* of *Mangalore*, to whom you are also to transmit an account of its cost.

We are anxious to procure(1) some seed of the saffron plant, silk-worms, young date trees, almonds and pistachio plants, shipwrights,(2) and pearl divers. Get these [men] together, and entertaining them in our service, dispatch them to us, together with proper persons for taking care of the young plants, &c.

We have already written, desiring you to purchase pearls. They must be large and brilliant,(3) and [in short] of the finest kind.(4) Buy them [at as] cheap [a price as you can] and dispatch them to us.

LETTER CCLXXIII.

To Meer Moaayenûddeen ; *same Date.* *(6th May.)*

In addition to the force already attached to you, four other *Kushoons*, *viz.* Mahommed Huleem's, Rujub Ali's, Shaikh Omar's, and Ahmed Baig's, are ordered to join you At the end of to-morrow's march [and, for the future] you must encamp these four *Kushoons* in the form of a square,

(1) Original درحضورضروراند " are required, or necessary, at the Presence."

(2) Original نجاران دوساز " carpenters, who construct *dows*."

(3) Original آبدار " having a [fine] water."

(4) Original بهتر " very good, best."

square,[5] within [or in the centre of] which you are yourself regularly to take post.

We have moreover appointed Mahommed Kâzim and Yenket Râo, the *Serishtedâr* of the *Jyshe*, to these four *Kushoons*:[6] and, finally, you will be further re-inforced by the *Risâla* of *Behrâm*, and some other troops, both horse and foot, under the command of Mohyûddeen Khân.

OBSERVATIONS.

I am not certain who Moaayenûddeen was; but I have an indistinct notion that he was related to the *Sultan*. Be this as it may, he would appear, by the foregoing letter, to have been an officer of high command and trust. The order of encampment, here prescribed to him, was to be observed, it seems, from the time of the army's arriving at *Great Balapoor*. Whether or not this disposition was made with any particular view to guarding against a sudden attack, I am unable to determine. It is not probable, however, that the *Sultan* had any expectation of encountering an enemy on his present line of march.

LETTER CCLXXIV.

To Bûrhânûddeen; *dated* 5th Behâry. (9th *May*.)

Your letter, enclosing one addressed to that light of our eyes by the *Kilaadâr* of *Bâdâmy*,[1] has been received, and the particulars represented therein have become manifest. You must give orders to the country people[2] to be vigilant and careful. You, too, must conduct yourself with caution. We enclose a plan, on paper, of the manner in which your army is to encamp: let this be copied on parchment, and let your army be always encamped agreeably thereto.

(5) Original چهارسمت " on the four sides" [of your ground].

(6) It does not appear, in what capacity these two were to serve.

(1) *Bâdâmy* was at this time besieged by the Mahrattahs.

(2) Original ملکیان a phrase which I do not recollect to have met with elsewhere.

OBSERVATIONS.

It is to be regretted, that the plan, here spoken of, has not been preserved, along with the letter referring to it, as it would have illustrated the *Sultan's* ideas on the particular branch of tactics in question, better than any other document that has hitherto appeared. It is, no doubt, probable that the *Futhûl Mûjâhideen* would throw considerable light on the subject.(3)

It is remarkable, that in the foregoing short letter, the *Sultan,* though, in general, sparing of such proofs of kindness, applies no less than three different expressions of endearment to Bûrhânûddeen; whom, in the first place, he styles *Noor-chushm* (light of my eyes), in another *Saadut-nishân* (marked for happiness), and lastly, *Burkhoar-dâr* (equivalent to darling). These endearing epithets can hardly be supposed, in the instance of Tippoo Sultan, to have proceeded from genuine affection or attachment; and may, therefore, perhaps, be more safely referred, either to some temporary caprice or fit of good humour; or, otherwise, to some political consideration, which might have suggested to him, at the moment, the expediency of assuming a more conciliatory manner towards his brother-in-law, than was probably usual with him.

LETTER CCLXXV.

To MEER GHÛLÂM MOHYÛDDEEN, *KILAADAR of KUNJUNGOOD, or KUNCHUNGÛREH; dated 7th BEHÂRY.* (11*th May.*)

Do you remain, in all respects, firm and tranquil;(1) nor entertain, on any account, the least fear. Let us know, what force the enemy has in that neighbourhood, and in what situations it is posted. Be particular in stating the strength and position [of every division], and the names of the several places which they occupy. Take, also, special care, that neither

(3) Since writing the above passage, I have had an opportunity of consulting the *Fûthûl Mûjâhideen;* in which, however, I have hitherto met with nothing on the subject of castrametation.

(1) Original مطمين " tranquil, assured, confident."

neither your receipt of this dispatch, nor its contents, become known to any one.

OBSERVATIONS.

This is almost the only letter in the present collection, of those written to the *Sultan's* own servants, which has what is called an *Ulkâb*, or address. I conclude, from hence, that he was not in the habit of using this formulary, excepting on particular occasions, like the present,(2) when this sort of compliment might be intended to operate as a stimulus to extraordinary exertion; nor is it improbable, that the endearing expressions applied to Bûrhânûddeen, in Letter CCLXXIV, were employed with a similar view.

The *Ulkâb*, or address, used on the present occasion, is شوکت وتهور دستگاه which may be rendered "brave and intrepid Sir." This, when contrasted with the exhortation to courage immediately following, has rather a ludicrous effect.

It might be inferred, from the tenor of the orders contained in this dispatch, that it was in the contemplation of the *Sultan* to beat up the Mahrattah quarters in the vicinity of *Kunchungood*. Whether or not such an enterprise was attempted, I am unable to determine.

LETTER CCLXXVI.

To MAHOMMED MEHDY, *BUKHSHY of the EHSHÂM at SERINGAPATAM; dated* 10*th* BEHÂRY. (14*th May*.)

You must not suffer any one to come to your house; and whatever business you may have to do, let it be transacted in our *Kuchurry*. If, nevertheless, people should persist in coming to your house, *they shall be deprived of their ears and noses.*(1) Pay strict attention to this order.

It

(2) *Kunjungood* was, at this time, seriously menaced, if not absolutely invested by the enemy. It is situated on the east bank of the *Tungbudhra*, and about twenty miles west of *Adoni*.

(1) Original از گوش و بيني معذور خواهند شد This is a curious idiom, the words literally meaning, that the ears and noses of the offenders "should be dispensed with, or excused."

It is surprising to us, that you should act in opposition to your instructions. Perhaps you have laid them by in the niche of forgetfulness;[2] and to this may be owing your present contravention of our will and pleasure. Consider what is here said as a strict injunction.

OBSERVATIONS.

This order, if understood literally, would amount to the exclusion of every person from the habitation of the *Bukhshy,* who might occasionally have private business with him: but though the regulation, directing all *public* affairs to be transacted in open *Kuchurry,* and no where else, was rigidly enforced by the *Sultan,* it can hardly be supposed, that it was meant to extend to the mutual intercourse necessary in the conduct of personal or domestic concerns.[3] It is not difficult to comprehend the *Sultan's* motives for a prohibition of the kind under consideration: but, with respect to the punishment appointed for its infraction, it may be presumed, in the absence of any proof of its ever being actually inflicted, that it was held out only *in terrorem.*

LETTER CCLXXVII.

CIRCULAR, *dated* 10*th* BEHÂRY. (14*th May*) *to*

GHÛLÂM HÛSAIN, *at* AURUNGÂBÂD;

SUJJÂD SÂHEB *and* IBN SÂHEB, *at* HYDERÂBÂD;

The Sons of SHAIKHÛN SÂHEB, *and* MÛSEEM[1] SÂHEB *(the Nephew of the above-named) at* BEEJÂPOOR.

[AFTER compliments]..... Our mind is most anxious for the attainment of the benefit of an interview with you: but as all events have their appointed

(2) See the same expression, Letter CCXVIII.

(3) The instructions to the Intelligence Department, given in Appendix F, prove, at least, that no private visiting or conversation was suffered between men of any note or station. The prohibition did not probably extend to the lower order.

(1) Name uncertain.

appointed times, we, in the meanwhile, trouble your reverence with the present address, in the confidence that, turning your mind, in an especial manner, to the means of promoting the prosperity and advantage of the people of *Islám*, and of overthrowing the unrighteous Infidels, you will do whatever may be in your power, to encrease the lustre of the firm religion of Mahommed.

Actuated by similar motives, the persons most distinguished here for virtue and excellence, have extracted from the traditions, theological tracts, and commentaries, certain religious doctrines, a copy of which we enclose for your benevolent notice. We request of your reverence, also, to assist the cause, by your admonitions to the faithful; to all of whom we feel an earnest desire of extending that protection and support, which we possess the means, no less than the wish, of bestowing upon them.

OBSERVATIONS.

No doubt, the proclamation, or manifesto, at page 293, is the enclosure here referred to, and which, hitherto, had probably been circulated only in the territories dependent on *Mysore*. But as the chief design of the *Sultan*, in that address, was to draw to his standard the Musulman subjects of other states, and particularly such as lived under the authority of his immediate enemies, it was necessary that it should be promulgated far and near. What means he adopted for this purpose, with respect to more distant countries, or whether he made any attempt to introduce the document in question into the British dominions, does not appear: but here we see him selecting as his instruments for publishing it, and promoting its proposed effect, within the dominions of the Mahrattahs and of the *Nizám*, persons actually residing under the protection of, and owing allegiance to, those very powers; and who, consequently, could neither pray for the success of his arms, nor contribute their endeavours to supply him with recruits (which was his chief object on the present occasion), without a violation of their civil duties, or without exposing themselves to the most imminent danger. Tippoo, however, did not allow himself to be restrained by considerations of this nature. He was, at all times, in communication with the priests belonging to the different shrines, or places of peculiar sanctity among Musulmans, that are scattered over the Peninsula, but not one of which, I believe, was included within his own dominions. The only thing to be wondered at, on this occasion, is the temerity of the reverend personages who engaged in such a hazardous correspondence; for though it does not appear how the present letter was received by the individuals to whom it was addressed, the records found at *Seringapatam* afford abundant proof, that the *Sultan*, throughout his reign, stood high in the favour of this particular class. For this distinction he might, in some degree, be indebted to the gifts which he occasionally bestowed on them; but he, most probably, owed it principally to their bigotry. He fought avowedly for the glory and extension of their religion; and that, with zealots, would be a sufficient apology for treason, as well as a sufficient motive for risking their personal safety in the advancement of his cause.

LETTER CCLXXVIII.

To BÛRHÂNÛDDEEN; *dated* 11*th* BEHÂRY. (15*th May.*)

YOU write, "that Syed Ahmed, a *Jowkdâr*(1) of the *Kushoon* of.... "....(2) belonging to the *Uskur*, has recruited some men, without "advancing any bounty."(3) It is known. Let the above-mentioned be appointed to the command of one of the new *Risâlas* lately raised by Syed Ghuffâr. We have appointed and sent from hence another person to command the *Risâla* of.......(4). He will soon join you.

When

(1) A *Jowk* is a company, and a *Jowkdâr* a captain.

(2) Name not perfectly legible: but something like Shaikh Unser.

(3) Original بي مساعده

4) Name illegible.

When we shall have summoned you to our Presence, and heard [from you verbally] the particulars of the gallant services of the men belonging to the *Kushoons* of Syed Ghuffâr and Shaikh Unser, we will distinguish them[5] [in a suitable manner].

LETTER CCLXXIX.

To MEER MOAAYENÛDDEEN; *same Date.* (15*th May.*)

SEVEN sealed orders,[1] specifying [or appointing] the daily marches [of your division], are sent herewith. Keep them by you, and return those formerly [delivered to you]. Issue directions to the people of your army, to provide themselves with six days' provisions; and be prepared to execute whatever orders you shall hereafter receive.

OBSERVATIONS.

The orders, here alluded to, appear to have been of the nature of sailing orders in our navy. They were each, probably, to be opened on a stated day; when the place to which the troops were to march on that particular day would be ascertained. Secrecy, of course, was the object of this arrangement: but it does not appear upon what service Moaayenûddeen was to be employed. It was now eight days since the *Sultan* had arrived in the vicinity of *Great Balapoor;* and he was, probably, advanced, at the date of the present orders, as far as *Râidoorg,* from whence *Adoni* might be easily reached in six marches. On this point, however, we are unfortunately left entirely to conjecture, in consequence of none of the dispatches of the present period happening to specify the place from whence they were written. It is not unlikely, however, that Moaayenûddeen was pushed forward for the purpose of investing *Adoni,* previously to the arrival of the main army before it.

(5) Original سرافراز فرموده خواهد شد "shall be exalted," or literally, "shall have their heads raised."

(1) Original هفت لفافه تعین منزل سربمهر

LETTER CCLXXX.

To the COMMANDERS *of the five* BÁRGEER KUCHURRIES *and* SUWÁR KUCHURRY; *dated* 13*th* BEHÁRY. (17*th May.*)

ISSUE orders to the people under your command to provide themselves with six days' provisions, and to leave their tents, *pawls*, &c. with the baggage of the army, taking nothing with them but two horse-halters(1) each man.

LETTER CCLXXXI.

To the COMMANDERS *of the two (or both)* JYSHE KUCHURRIES; *same Date.* (17*th May.*)

ISSUE orders to your people to provide themselves with six days' provisions; and leaving the tents, *pawls*, &c. belonging to them with the baggage of the army, to keep with them [only] the *Kúndilehs*(1*) of the *Sircar*. You must [thus] remain unincumbered [*jureedeh*].

LETTER CCLXXXII.

To the BUKHSHIES *of the* EHSHAM KUCHURRY; *same Date.* (17*th May.*)

DIRECT your people to furnish themselves with six days' provisions, to be carried by themselves;(1**) and leaving their tents, *pawls*, heavy baggage, &c. with the baggage of the army, to remain light and unincumbered.

(1) Original باگلوز perhaps two *spare* halters, for securing any horses that might be taken from the enemy.

(1*) I have not been able to ascertain what a *Kúndileh* is; but I think it is some sort of cloth, or canvass, covering: perhaps for defending the arms and stores from the weather.

(1**) In the original it is برگاوان ندارند " *not* to be carried on bullocks." A slight transposition of the first diacritical point would make the sense, " let them, not keep or take, " any bullocks with them."

OBSERVATIONS.

No doubt the troops, here ordered to prepare for a rapid movement, were intended to compose part of the division proceeding under the command of Moaayen-ûddeen; whose force (if we include in it the various corps enumerated in Letter CCLXXIII) must have amounted to at least ten thousand men.

LETTER CCLXXXIII.

To SYED MAHOMMED KHÂN, *BUKHSHY of the USUD ILHYE; dated 17th BEHÂRY. (21st May.)*

(EXTRACT.)

WE enclose an order to the *Aumil* of *Sumrputn* [*Bulhâry*], directing him to forward your *Palenkeen* to you.

N.B. Then follows the order to the *Aumil* of *Bulhâry.*

OBSERVATIONS.

It is difficult to say, in what sense the foregoing extract should be understood. It may imply, either that the *Bukhshy* was not at liberty to send for his *Palenkeen*, without the *Sultan's* authority; or that, not possessing the means of getting it conveyed to him (that is, the necessary carriage), he had been obliged to solicit the *Sultan* to give directions for its being forwarded to him. The former sense would, no doubt, consist perfectly well with the despotic nature of the *Sultan's* government, and with the general system of control and restriction which pervaded every branch of it: but as the latter interpretation is equally warranted by the original, I am inclined to prefer it, on the principle of putting, in all cases of *absolute doubt,* the most favorable construction on his conduct.

LETTER CCLXXXIV.

To URSHUD BAIG KHÂN, *FOUJDAR of* CALICUT.

GETTING possession of the villain, Goorkul, and of his wife and children, you must forcibly(1) make Musulmans of them, and then dispatch the whole under a guard to *Putn.*

LETTER CCLXXXV.

To CHISHTY YÂR KHÂN *and* ZYNÛL AABIDEEN; *dated* 20*th* BEHÂRY, (24*th May.*)

YOUR letter of the 14*th Behâry* [17th May] was received this day, and has informed us of Dowlat Khân's being ill of the stone in the bladder: we have, in consequence, sent by the post an emetic [to be taken the first day], together with [other proper] medicines for the seven subsequent days. These are all separately made up in cloth and sealed.

The way of taking an emetic is this: dissolving the powder in about four *tolah* weight of hot water, let him swallow it. After this, whenever he feels inclined to vomit, he must drink eight *tolah* weight of warm water. When he has vomited five or six times, let him, after an interval of six hours, have some broth mixed with rice. In the evening, before he eats his dinner,(1*) make him take, in a little cold water, half a *tolah* weight of seed of flea-wort,(2) *softened* with some oil of almonds. By the favor of God, in one or two vomitings, the stranguary, or obstruction of urine, will be removed.

The

(1) There is some obscurity here in the original, which runs بتجدید مسلمان ساخته If the meaning be, as I suppose it is, that they were to be forcibly converted, it should have been تهدید

(1*) The Mahommedans, in *India*, make the principal meal at night.

(2) Original اسپغول

The following morning [after the vomit] a dose of the other medicine is to be taken in eight *tolahs* of syrup of *Ab-shákh*(3) and radish leaves.(4) This course is to be pursued for seven days, during which the patient need not abstain from acids, but must avoid eating black and red pepper, and other heating and flatulent things.(5) The diet should be curry of radishes with boiled rice, and his drink an infusion of musk-melon seeds, cucumber seeds, and dry thorn,(6) of each half a *tolah* weight. By this means, if there should even [or actually] be a stone [in the bladder] it will be passed.(7)

LETTER CCLXXXVI.

To MAHOMMED YOOSÛF, *CUTWÁL of the BÁZÁR*,(1) *accompanying the Presence; dated* 3d *JAAFURY*.(2) (*6th June*.)

You have represented, "that two thousand four hundred and eighty-"five bullock loads of rice, *gram*, &c. were some time ago dispatched "to the Presence [*i. e.* to the *Sultan's* army] and eleven hundred and "nine very lately [or now]." It is known, and appears very extraordinary to us, that out of fifty or sixty thousand bullock loads, the duties

(3) Original آب شاخ literally, "horn-water," of which I do not know the meaning.

(4) Original برگ ترب

(5) Original اشیاي بادي وگرم

(6) Original خارخشک

(7) Original خواهد افتاد literally "will fall or drop." This is the letter which was alluded to at Letter CXV, and the observations suggested by the latter will be found to apply, with perhaps still greater force and justice, to the present curious production.

(1) Called in the original رکاب بازار

(2) No letters appear between the 20th *Behâry* and this time, except an unimportant one of the 30th *Behâry*, which I suspect to be owing to some accidental chasm in the manuscript, as this was too busy a conjuncture for the *Sultan's* pen to have indulged in a fortnght's rest. I think that, at the date of this letter, he must have been lying before *Adoni*.

duties on which have been remitted to the *Lumbánehs*,[(3)] only one or two thousand should have been dispatched [to us]. You must give strict orders for ten or fifteen thousand loads to be forwarded [hither] at a time.

LETTER CCLXXXVII.

To MAHOMMED HYDER, *second* DEWÁN *of* NUGR; *dated 6th* JAAFURY. *(9th June.)*

YOU write, " that Nursia requires our express authority for joining " [or inserting] your name [with his own] in the [official] letters to " the *Aumils.*" It is known. When you were dispatched from the Presence, a [certain] mandate, addressed to Nursia, was delivered to you. Open and peruse the same, and conform to its contents. If it be directed therein, that you are to participate with him in the administration of the revenue business,[(1)] you will, agreeably thereto, apply earnestly and constantly, in conjunction with him, to the affairs of the *Sircar*: If [on the other hand] your participation [therein] should be forbidden,[(2)] you must act accordingly.

OBSERVATIONS.

If I rightly understand this letter, which I have translated as closely as I could, it is a very strange one. I lay no stress upon the apparently singular circumstance of Mahommed Hyder's being referred to a letter which he could not have in his possession, since he must have already delivered it to Nursia, to whom it was addressed. This difficulty is easily removed, by supposing what is most likely to have

(3) So it is written in the manuscript, but whether properly or not, they are usually called *Lumbádehs.*

(1) Original معملات which, in a restrained sense, signifies " revenue affairs."

(2) Original موقوف " discontinued, set aside, suspended."

have been the case, *viz.* that the letter referred to was only a copy (though not so called in the manuscript) with which the under *Dewán* had been furnished, for his information and guidance. But what appears extraordinary is, that the *Sultan* should have placed the question submitted to him on the hypothetical footing he has done, instead of giving a direct answer to it. We cannot imagine him to have really forgotten the orders he had transmitted to Nursia on the subject in dispute, or, if he had, that the secretary could not have produced a copy of them: hence it may be inferred, that the present letter was designed in the way of banter. It is pretty evident, from the fact of Nursia's having refused to admit Mahommed Hyder to the privilege he demanded, without the express authority of the *Sultan*, that no such authority had been conveyed in the mandate referred to: and this the *Sultan*, no doubt, very well knew. The letter to Shumsûddeen Khân,(3) at page 278, seems to have been written in the same vein.

LETTER CCLXXXVIII.

To SYED MAHOMMED KHÂN; *Third* DEWÂN *of* NUGR; *same Date.* (*9th June.*)

YOU write, "requesting of us to give directions to our secretaries to "insert your name, along with that of Mahommed Hyder, the second "*Dewán*, in the *Purwáneh*s [addressed to your department]." It is known. Who has told you (whom we had ordered to repair to the Presence) to remain there? and wherefore have you continued [till now] to reside there? (1)

2 S

(3) See Letter CCLV.

(1) The following is the original of this curious passage:

شمارا که براي رسيدن بحضور حکم شده بود جهت ماندن انجا که گفته بود چرا در آنجا سکونت ورزيده اند

LETTER CCLXXXIX.

To BÛRHÂNÛDDEEN; *dated 7th* JAAFURY. (10*th June.*)

Now that you have encamped near *Misry-kotah*, you must take up a strong position there, under the protection of the [adjacent] woods. From hence, seizing a fit opportunity, you must fall [suddenly] upon the enemy.

LETTER CCXC.

To BUDRÛZ ZUMÂN KHÂN; *same Date.* (10*th June.*)

What is the use of your fixing yourself at *Sehngah* (1)? You must shift your quarters from one place to another, such as *Urkunny*, and other dependencies of *Nugr*, and chastise the enemy [as often as an opportunity for the purpose may offer].

LETTER CCXCI.

To ALI RÂJAH BEEBY; *dated 8th* JAAFURY. (11*th June.*)

DIRECTING her to join Urshud Baig Khân with her forces, and to inflict [*i. e.* assist him in inflicting] punishment on the *Nairs*.

LETTER CCXCII.

To BUDRÛZ ZUMÂN KHÂN; *dated* 10*th* JAAFURY. (13*th June.*)

You write, "that the *Piddehs*, who had been employed to escort "provisions to the fort of *Kittoor*, wished, on their return from thence, "to

(1) Name uncertain. The expression, which I have rendered "fixing yourself," is in the original نشستن which strictly signifies "to sit, to sit down:" but here obviously used in a figurative sense.

" to be dispatched to the Presence: but that, in consequence of your " hearing of the enemy's troops being spread over [1] the country about " *Shânoor*, &c. you had [judged it best to] distribute them among the " forts of *Hurriâl*, *Ullooty*, &c.[2] for the defence of those places, and " that you had *seated* yourself [*i. e.* established your own quarters] at " *Sehngah*."[3]

It is known. In the written instructions delivered to you it is directed, that you shall keep together, under your immediate command, from ten to fifteen thousand men. Conform to these orders, and do not divide your forces; but establish yourself with them somewhere in the province of *Nugr*, as at *Hurriâl*, *Urkunny*, &c. It is now the rainy season: send for a *Risâla* of *Jyshe* from *Kûriâl* [*Mangalore*] and, agreeably to your instructions, assembling other *Jyshe* and *Piddehs*, to the amount of ten or twelve thousand men, take up a position with this force, either at *Hurpunhully*, *Urkunny*, or some other place, situated [like them] on that [*i. e.* the further,[4] or east] side of the *Tungbuddra*. Having done this, report the same to us; and afterwards proceed, according to the manner that shall be directed in the orders [you will receive] from the Presence.

LETTER CCXCIII.

To Abdûl Kureem, *Sipahdâr of the* Jyhse Kuchurry, *stationed with* Urshud Baig Khân; *dated* 10*th* Jaafury. (13*th June.*)

You write, " that the villain Goorkul, being wounded, had thrown " himself, together with his wife and children, into a fire [kindled for

2 S 2 " the

(1) Original آوارگي فوج مقهور

(2) }
(3) } Names uncertain.

(4) Reckoning, I suppose, from *Bidnore*.

" the purpose] which had consumed them [all]." You add, " that the " *Mápilahs* have all taken to flight."

It is known. You must assemble and keep your men together, and, exercising them regularly, hold them always in readiness [for service].

OBSERVATIONS.

It would appear by this letter that the unfortunate Goorkul had eluded the endeavours of Tippoo's commanders to secure his person; but that, despairing of ultimate success, and knowing the fate that awaited himself and family, if they fell into the hands of their tyrant, he had resorted to the final remedy and refuge from dishonour, so usual among the *Hindoos*. The studied indifference, as it appears to be, with which the *Sultan* mentioned this dreadful catastrophe, will not have escaped the reader's notice.

LETTER CCXCIV.

To RÂJAH RÂM CHUNDUR; *same Date.* (13*th June.*)

YOU write, " that eighty smiths are required in the musquet manu- " factory at *Khán-Khánhully*; and that, having made an application " for this number to the *Aumils* of the surrounding districts, they had " answered, that the *Ryots* excused themselves from furnishing them " just now, on account of its being tillage time."

It is known. As the tillage of the land does not depend on black-smiths, we write to desire, that the most peremptory orders may be issued to the *Aumils* within your jurisdiction, and enforced by bailiffs, for providing [immediately] the requisite number of these artificers.

OBSERVATIONS.

Whatever might be the case in *Mysore*, it is, at least, certain, that in the provinces of *Bengal* and *Behar*, the cultivation of the lands depends, in a very material degree, on the manufacturing classes and artizans; who, at the tillage season,

season, are accustomed to quit their ordinary avocations, and to resume, for the necessary time, the labours of husbandry. Even the soldiers, at this period, are in the habit of returning on furlough to their native villages, for the purpose of working in the fields belonging to their respective families. I am inclined to think, that the same practice will be found to have obtained in *Mysore*; and, indeed, the reference made to it by the *Ryots*, sufficiently establishes the fact. At this rate, the *Sultan* could not be ignorant of its existence; so that, in saying, "the culture "of land did not depend upon blacksmiths," he probably sacrificed the truth, and, what was worse, persisted in his oppression, chiefly for the sake of a conceit. Eighty men taken from the plough at such a time, would hardly fail to produce a material embarrasment in the agricultural operations of the district which was obliged to furnish them.

LETTER CCXCV.

To GHÛLÂM HÛSAIN KHÂN, *Second* MUNSHOOR *of* BANGALORE; *dated* 11*th* JAAFURY. (14*th June*.)

(EXTRACT.)

WHAT you report, of the escape of the European cannon-founder, is understood. You must, in such manner [or by such means] as you think best, and most practicable, contrive to get him back, otherwise bad consequences will follow, for which you shall be made to answer.

You write, "that instead of five or six *rupees*, which you have pro-"posed paying to the striplings[1] belonging to the *Jyshe*, they demand "nine." It is known. Let such as are very young receive the monthly pay you have fixed: when they arrive at full age, they will, according to custom, receive nine rupees.

If the gunpowder is not prepared, and the gun-barrels are not constructed agreeably to our instructions, and if every thing else, appertaining to your department, be not properly executed, you will be called to a strict account [for your neglect].

(1) Original امرد "beardless."

LETTER CCXCVI.

To BÛRHÂNÛDDEEN; *same Date.* (*14th June.*)

YOUR letter has been received, and its contents are comprehended. What you write, respecting the scarcity of grain, is known. The country of *Nugr* is near [you]. Send from thence for continual and abundant supplies of grain. What is the meaning of your loitering in one place with such an army [as you have]? You should take ten days provisions, and moving rapidly, in different directions, ten and twenty *coss* [at a time], seize an opportunity of striking some signal blow against the enemy. We have sent [similar] orders on this subject to the *Sipahdârs*, &c.

Phurnaveese [*i. e.* Nana, the Mahrattah minister] is gone [back] to *Poonah*. It is most probable that their army, too, will, by the time the river swells, break up, and return discomfited and beaten.

Remove the son of Hukeem Khân from the command of his *Risâla*, and place him in confinement.(1)

OBSERVATIONS.

It is true, that Nana Phurnaveese returned to *Poonah* some time about the end of May; and I believe that, either previously to his leaving the Mahrattah army, or immediately after his departure, the fort of *Bâdâmy* surrendered. Of this event, however, no trace is discoverable in the correspondence.

If Hukeem Khân be meant for Abdûl Hukeem Khân, the *Nabob* of *Shânoor*, (which I conceive to be the case) this passage shows, that the breach between him and the *Sultan* had now become irreparable, and that the *Patan* had, probably, declared

(1) Original ازرساله داري موقوف كرده بقيد آرند This son of Hukeem Khân is, on another occasion, mentioned by the name of Abdûl Sumud Khân. What adds to the probability of his being a younger son of Abdûl Hukeem is, that the word *Abdûl* appears to have been a common prefix to the names of this family. Thus the son and successor of Abdûl Hukeem was called Abdûl Khyr Khân (or Kheere Meer).

declared openly in favor of the Mahrattahs. We also learn from it, that a son of this chieftain actually held, at this time, a military command in one of the corps of the army under Bûrhânûddeen (possibly a battalion of an infantry *Kushoon)*; for the form of the expression in the original will hardly admit of our supposing that the *Risâla*, in question, was a body of troops furnished by the *Patan* for the service of the *Sultan.*

LETTER CCXCVII.

To Mahommed Ghyâs *and* Noor Mahommed Khân; *same Date.* (14*th June.*)

It is fifteen days since you arrived at *Furrûkh-yâb Hisâr* [*Chittledoorg*]. By your stopping in this manner fifteen days in every place, you burthen us with your own pay and that of your retinue. Then it would further appear, by the circumstance of your bringing on with you the *Hurkârehs* of the enemy, that you had no fear [or regard] for your lives and honor. It is not well. Send back the enemy's *Hurkârehs*, and hasten your arrival at the Presence.

OBSERVATIONS.

Here ends the *Sultan's* correspondence with his late ministers at the court of *Poonah,* who had probably received their dismission from thence some time in April 1786. Whatever may be thought of the diplomatic qualifications of those agents, from the faint sketches of their proceedings occasionally afforded by these letters, there would not appear to be any reason for imputing the failure of their negociations to any deficiency of talents or address on their part: for the Mahrattahs being bent on a rupture, and the *Sultan* being equally determined not to compromise his dignity, or what he deemed to be his rights, it is probable, that neither party had, from the beginning, any expectation, or indeed any desire, of accommodating their mutual differences; so that, in fact, all the envoys had to do, was to endeavour to amuse the Mahrattah government, by vague and illusory professions;

professions; to obtain intelligence of its designs; and, perhaps, to tamper with the fidelity of some of its servants. The first of these objects must have been always an hopeless one; and when the notorious parsimony of their master is considered, their success, to any material extent, in the other two, may be reasonably doubted, without derogating, in the least, from their general zeal and capacity.

The most prominent feature in the *Sultan's* correspondence with these envoys, next to the memorable manœuvre recorded in Letter LIII, is the fluctuating character of his instructions to them. There seems to have been a perpetual conflict, on this occasion, between his pride and his interest; in the course of which, sometimes one, and sometimes the other, prevailed. He appears to have been steady, only, in his ungracious treatment of his unhappy agents, whom, to the very last moment, he addresses in a style of unmitigated asperity.

Of Noor Mahommed Khân no more is heard. Mahommed Ghyâs(1) seems to have been subsequently confined to the humble sphere of superintendant of a provincial *Tosheh-khâneh*. Whether they lived to witness the annihilation of the *Khodâdâd Sircar*, I know not; but it is probable they did not, as the *Sultan* reflects on their "great age," fourteen years prior to that event.(2)

(1) My only ground for this conjecture is a letter, addressed, at a subsequent period, to a person of this name, and filling the office mentioned.

(2) The following article is extracted from an Hindostan news-paper, dated 25th September 1786, and kindly communicated to me by my valued friend, Sir John Kennaway, Bart., formerly Resident at the Court of *Hyderabad*.

" By intelligence from the *Decan*, dated about the 29th of August, it appears, that a
" report prevailed there, that Noor Mahommed Khân, and the other *Vakeels* of Tippoo
" Sultan, (who, some time before, had been sent away by Nana Phurnaveese from *Bâdâmy*,
" because that minister did not approve of their remaining any longer in the Mahrattah
" camp), were accused by the *Sultan*, on their arrival in his presence, with having betrayed
" his interests, by secretly encouraging the Mahrattahs, who otherwise would never have
" hazarded the measure, to pass the *Kishna*, and advance into his country; and that, not
" being enabled to give a satisfactory answer to this charge, the *Sultan* had caused them to
" be put to death, as a public example to others."

LETTER CCXCVIII.

To RUJUB ALI, *KILAADÂR of GUJUNDER GURRH*;(1) *dated* 15*th* JAAFURY.

BY the Divine favor, the fort of *Adoni* is on the point of being reduced. God willing, after settling matters here, the special retinue will augment the lustre of that quarter [*i. e.* we shall proceed thither]. You must [in the interim] keep your mind at ease, and attend duly to the care and safety of the fort, [by] placing [the necessary] guards, and remaining always on the alert. You may, moreover, consider us as arrived.

N.B. A letter, of the same tenor and date, was written to Jymum Khân, *Kilaaddr* of *Kopul*; and both were sent to Zynûl Aabideen, *Bukhshy* of *Ehshâm*, at *Chittledoorg*, with orders to forward them; and, at the same time, to exhort them, from himself, to be of good cheer, and to remain firm at their posts.

LETTER CCXCIX.

To TURBIYUT ALI KHÂN *and* RÂJAH RÂM CHUNDUR; *same Date.* (18*th June.*)

DIRECTING them to dispatch to *Fyze Hisâr* [*Gooty*], on hired bullocks, five thousand twenty-four-pounds shot, and the same number of eighteen-pounds shot.(1*)

2 T

(1) This is a town and fortress of considerable note, situated between *Kopul* and *Bâdâmy*. It once belonged to Ragonath Râo. It was ceded to the Mahrattahs, by the partition treaty of 1792.

(1*) Original بیست وچهار رطلي وهجده رطلي

LETTER CCC.

To MAHOMMED SHUFEEA, *DÁROGHA of the Artillery; same Date.* (18*th June.*)

AGREEABLY to the orders of the Presence, you must bring with you guns [of the *calibres*] of twelve and nine *Rutls* [*i. e.* nine and twelve-pounders].

OBSERVATIONS.

It is probable, though my manuscript is silent on the subject, that the number of guns of each kind was specified in the original, as otherwise this order would appear to leave it to the judgment of the *Dárogha,* to bring what number he pleased. A supposition utterly inadmissible.

LETTER CCCI.

To USUD ALI KHÂN,(1) *from* ALI RIZÂ *and* BÂL MUKN DOSS; *dated* 15*th* JAAFURY.(2) (18*th June.*)

WE mentioned verbally to you four articles,(3) which were submitted for your acceptance; and we now wish you to come and say, which of those four articles you will agree to, in order that we may make a suitable representation [to our master], and get the business finally settled. The honour of a world [alluding to the female part of Mohâbut Jung's family]

(1) He is called in the title, or heading, of the following letter, the "*Adoni Wáleh,*" or "*Adoni* man."

(2) This is the only occasion on which any letters, except those written by or in the name of the *Sultan* himself, have been entered in the present collection.

(3) Original چهار امر

family] is in the fort, and numberless people are collected therein. To be instrumental, with your eyes open,(4) to the ruin of people's honour, is contrary to discretion ;(5) while any further procrastination of the matter is pregnant with the most serious mischief, and must lead to the destruction of the inhabitants of the place. As to [the arrival of] succours, and the swoln state of the rivers, the case is abundantly manifest. [*i. e.* you are cut off from all hopes of relief]. Under these circumstances, it is clearly proper and most advisable, that you should set about an [immediate] adjustment, whereby you will secure the ease and prosperity of God's creatures.

OBSERVATIONS.

It does not appear from the correspondence, on what day the *Sultan* arrived before *Adoni*; but as it is probable, that he would lose no time in summoning the place, the commencement of the siege by Tippoo, in person, may be safely reckoned from the 15th June. It had, perhaps, been previously invested by Moaayenûddeen: but this is uncertain.

If the Usud Ali Khân, here addressed, be not the same person who has since made some figure (as well under that name, as by the title of Mûzufferûlmûlk) at the court of *Hyderabad*, I am unable to say who he was. However this may be, the present negociator would appear to have acquitted himself in a very able manner; since he succeeded in amusing Tippoo with expectations of the early submission of his master, Mohâbut Jung, and by this means, while he induced the *Sultan* to abstain from vigorous operations against *Adoni*, gave time to the *Nizâm* to send a considerable force, under Mûsheer ûl Mûlk and Syfe ûl Mûlk, to its relief; or rather, for the purpose of removing the ladies of Mohâbut Jung's family, who were shut up in it, to *Hyderabad*. This object, which Tippoo either did not

2 T 2

(4) Original ديده ودانسته "seeing and knowing."

(5) Original ضد مال انديشي "the contrary to considering of the future."

not suspect, or could not effectually oppose, being accomplished, those commanders left the fort[6] to its fate, which was, ere long, decided: for not being in a condition to maintain a siege, the *Sultan* soon became master of it.

The conduct of Tippoo, upon this occasion, has been said to have excited considerable surprise among his commanders, and has since given rise to some speculation, as to the causes of it, among his biographers. It has been affirmed, that the fort might have been easily carried at the same time with the *Paith*, or town; upon the storm and capture of which the garrison and inhabitants retired in great disorder to the fort, the gates of which were found wide open, and even, as pretended, unguarded. Intelligence, thereof, being conveyed to the *Sultan*, and accompanied by a request from Lally, and others, to be permitted to profit by the opportunity, thus unexpectedly offered, he forbad the attempt, observing, in effect, "that he was sure those within the fort would, in very good time, spon-"taneously place themselves in his power." The writer, from whom I take this account, and who is a very intelligent Musulman,[7] in the employ of Colonel Colin M'Kenzie, appears to infer, from this circumstance, that the *Sultan* never had any serious intention of reducing *Adoni*; and that his movement against it had no other object than that of alarming the *Nizám* for the safety of the females of his family residing there, and of detaching him, by that means, from his connexion with the Mahrattahs. But the solitary fact, upon which this opinion seems to rest, is not, I think (admitting its authenticity) sufficiently strong, to support it against the evidence leading to a different conclusion. That fact is perhaps susceptible of a more satisfactory, and less improbable explanation. The *Sultan* might have doubted the correctness of the information, upon which the expediency of attempting the fort had been rested: he might have thought the undertaking too hazardous; or he might even have been averse to exposing the women within the place to the dangers of an assault. That he hoped, by his present enterprize, to oblige the *Nizám* to forsake the Mahrattahs,

(6) *Adoni* is called, in the *Asufial* register, and by the Mahommedans of the *Decan*, *Imtiáz Ghur*.

(7) Of Meer Hûsain Ali, the person here alluded to, some further mention will be found in Appendix D.

Mahrattahs, is very likely : but this purpose would not have been effected by any proceeding, which might, in its consequences, have cast a stain upon the honor of his Highness's family ; whereas, by getting them into his power, by virtue of a capitulation, he would have been sure of attaining that object. On the whole, therefore, there would not appear to be any sufficient reason for doubting, that the end which he really had in view, from the beginning, was not the mere reduction of *Adoni*, which would have been an inadequate compensation for the exertion he had made, but the capture, in honor and safety, of the *Haram* contained within its walls.

It is to be wished, that the *four articles*, referred to in the preceding letter, had been preserved. They would, no doubt, have thrown considerable light on the present subject : yet we are not entirely destitute of other information respecting it, since the following extract from the *Sultan's* Memoirs will be found to contain, not only some notice of his expedition against *Adoni*, but also *his* statement of the origin of the war, subsisting at this time between him and the confederated powers.

" *Occurrences of the year* Busd, *or year of Mahommed* 1214.

" I had just completed the arrangements which have been mentioned,(8) when " intelligence

(8) The reader will probably not be displeased at being presented, in this place, with that portion of the Memoirs immediately preceding the one given in the text, and referred to therein by the *Sultan*, on whose extraordinary character it will be found to throw no inconsiderable light. I have translated it as closely as I could, without involving the sense in obscurity : but the original is written in such a perplexed and barbarous style, as has made this a very difficult task.

" After sending off the *Ahmedies* [in the way that has been related],* the special retinue " [or cavalcade] proceeded to the seat of the *Sultanut*, *Putn*. Here, with a view to the " [proper] arrangement of affairs, great and small, I framed various *Hŭkm-námehs* [or ordi- " nances] and numerous other *things* ; all in the very best manner, and comprehending in- " stitutes, civil and fiscal, general as well as particular rules for war and peace [literally, " for the *battle* and the *banquet*], and regulations for the government of the people at large. " They moreover treated of the [proper] mode of dealing with the noble and the ignoble " [or the high and low], of taking [or levying] tribute from the subject, and of affording " protection to the people ; of making progress through the country, and inspecting the " fortresses ; and of duly guarding the kingdom on all sides. In fine, they comprised nu- " merous

* See Observations on Letter XLII.

" intelligence arrived that the Mahrattahs[9] and Nizâm Ali Khân, forgetting their " ancient obligations [to us], whereof an account has been already written,[10] and " becoming ungrateful, had assembled together a large army, with the intention " of making a joint attack on the *Ahmedy* dominions.

" At that time, [or hereupon] several of those holding offices[11] under the " *Usud Ilhye* government humbly represented, that after providing for the " defence of the fortresses, and putting the armies in a state of preparation, it " would be proper to set about confronting [or opposing] them [*i. e.* the Mahrat- " tahs and the *Nizám*]. To this I answered: ' Six months ago, when the " ' *Vakeels* of both the chieftains were about to receive their dismission [from " ' me], I said to them [the *Vakeels*], that I had heard that their masters, " ' forgetting ancient obligations [or my ancient claims] upon them, meditated " ' upon making such a return to them, as was the practice only of the most " ' despicable of men. This [said I] is not a right thing. Fear God [and " ' know], that good should not be requited with evil. A proceeding of this " ' kind will [assuredly] draw on your masters the vengeance of the divine " ' tribunal.

" merous *new* inventions, and fresh contrivances *without measure:* and I ordained that the " same should be preserved in our elevated family, and [be transmitted through] our emi- " nent race, to the end that our sons of exalted degree, and our grandsons of illustrious " descent, generation after generation, deriving from the perusal of the abundant benefits " and ample advantages with which they are replete, may be thereby enabled to administer " the various affairs of state, and the important concerns of sovereignty, with due order " and regularity. Therefore, whatever ruler, not being of our line, shall surreptitiously " adopt these our ordinances and institutes, will, in consequence thereof, be reckoned as " one of our offspring."

The substance of the latter part of the foregoing extract has been given by Colonel Wilks (in the Preface to his History of *Mysoor)* from the *Súltáné Tuwáreekh* of Zynûl Aabideen Shoostry, the ground work of which production, as has been already observed elsewhere, was the *Táreekh e Khodá-dády*, or Tippoo Sultan's Memoirs, as written, originally, by himself.

(9) In the original مراٹک *(Murrátek);* for an explanation of which perversion of the true name, the reader is referred to the preface of Colonel Wilks's History of *Mysoor.*

(10) See observations on Letter VIII.

(11) Original عہدہ

"'tribunal.[12] [For my part] these are my intentions. The good which has "'been rendered to you by the *Usud Ilhye Sircar* is clear and evident to the "'whole world.[13] Moved by the humble supplications, as well as by the tender "'age of your master,[14] who had avowed himself to be our son, we[15] took upon "'ourselves [or willingly incurred] the evils [or dangers] which [menaced] your "'house and your life: and [hence] it is more manifest, even than the sun, that "'it was we who secured the duration of your master's house. With all this [or "'notwithstanding this] I am desirous that your misdoings [or the wrongs you "'have done me] should become still more apparent to all mankind, and "'[therefore] I will never move from hence, with hostile designs, until both "'the chieftains in question shall have entered my dominions, have ravaged "'countries to the value of ten or twenty *lacks* of *rupees*, and have laid siege to "'one or two fortified places. They should [or let them], therefore, act in "'conformity with their engagements.'[16]

"But what does it signify? With the blessing of the [divine] Helper, after "they shall have entered our dominions, we will move from hence.

"Accordingly, two months after this, the two confederated armies (on whom, "and on their parents also, be the curse of God!) laid siege to the fort of "*Bâdâmy*, and committed depredations, between the two rivers *Kishna* and "*Toongbhudra*,[17] to the amount of fifteen or twenty *lacks* of *rupees*. Hereupon "I marched

(12) Original بارگاه "court, place of audience, royal tribune."

(13) Original تمامي خلق الله "the whole of God's creatures."

(14) Here the *Sultan* speaks as if addressing the Mahrattah *Vakeel* alone.

(15) Meaning, of course, his father, in whose life-time the transaction alluded to took place.

(16) I am inclined to think, that the *Sultan's* speech to the *Vakeels* ends here; and that the short paragraph, which follows, was addressed to the persons who had advised what he deemed a premature movement against the enemy.

(17) So is the name of this river written in the original; and I have often met with it so written in other manuscripts, though the more usual orthography is, I believe, *Toombuddra*. The tract of country here spoken of is sometimes called the *Dodb* (or *two rivers*, *i. e.* the *country situated between two rivers*]. It is so designated, for instance, in the treaty concluded at *Seringapatam*, in 1792.

" I[18] marched to *Bangalore*, where I remained ten or twelve days, and [from " hence] dispatched a respectable person, together with an intelligent officer of " spies, to Mâdhojee Bhonsillah, the chief of *Nágpoor*,[19] to whom I addressed a " letter to the following effect:

" ' What is the reason that you[20] have forgotten [your] ancient obligations " ' [to us] and taken [or learned] the lesson of the whoreson?[21] Fear God, " ' otherwise your shameful actions will [assuredly] draw upon you their due " ' punishment.'[22]

" I also wrote and dispatched [letters], to the same purport, to Hurry Pundit " Phurkia and to Râo Râsta, commanders of the army of the infidels.

" I more-

(18) In the original ما بدولت the nearest translation of which that I am capable of giving is, " we happy," or " we prosperous." It is a common form of expression with sovereigns, and has been adopted by all the pseudo-princes of India. I have even known a private person (bearing, however, the title of *Nabob*, and descended from a decayed family formerly in some power) arrogate it to himself.

(19) There is here a considerable degree of obscurity in the manuscript, which I suspect to arise from the omission of some proper name. The passage in the original runs از معرفت مادهوجي بهونسليا *i. e.* through the medium, or by means, of Mâdhojee. Probably the meaning is, that the letter in question was to be delivered to Mâdhojee, through the channel of some person, whose name has been inadvertently omitted by the transcriber.

(20) Original شمايان (ye) a second plural formed from شما (you); as if the *Sultan* were addressing all the chieftains named in one and the same letter. This is, of course, either one of the anomalies so usual with the author, or an error of the transcriber. The *Sultan* here implicates the *Nágpoor* chief in the supposed ingratitude of the *Paishwa*, although Mâdhojee Bhonsillah had taken but little share in the transactions alluded to.

(21) Original مادر بخطاي as once or twice before. It is uncertain, whether the *Nizám*, or the *Paishwa*, be here alluded to; this gross appellation being sometimes given by the *Sultan* to one, and sometimes to the other. It is scarcely credible, however, that he should speak of the *Paishwa* in this offensive manner, in letters addressed to the chieftains of the Mahrattah state. If, therefore, it was actually used (which, after all, might not be the case, though so stated in the narrative) it is most probable that it referred to the *Nizám*; to whom, indeed, the implied character of a *teacher*, or giver of *lessons*, was far more applicable than to the *Paishwa*, who was at this time very young.

(22) Original به سزاي بدكرداري خود خواهند رسيد " will arrive at the due requital of their " misdoing."

"I moreover interrogated the *Sirdars* [or chief officers] of the army, respect-"
"ing the [best] mode of conducting the war, and the attack[23] [most proper] to "be made [in the first instance]; when they all, according to their [respective] "abilities [or powers], delivered their opinions: none of which, however, were "agreeable to my mind. At this time [or hereupon] calling upon God the "Bountiful, and imploring his aid, I said, 'Please the Almighty God, I will' "'proceed against *Adoni*, which is at a distance from the boundary of the *Sircar*, "'and is a strong place, where the honor[24] of Nizâm Ali Khân is lodged. "'Attacking this place, we must obtain possession of it. If, for the sake [or "'preservation] of their honor, the two *Sirdars*[25] should come [to its relief], "'we shall see [the extent of] their strength and power.' This opinion [or "plan] was *apparently* assented to by all those in attendance [upon me]; but "God [only] knows what they inwardly [or really] thought [on the occasion].

"After this, quitting *Bangalore*, I proceeded by long marches to *Adoni*,[26] "against which I opened trenches; but was [purposely] careless and dilatory in "making my approaches, in order that, hearing of the situation of Busâlut "Jung's son, and of their women, the two infidel and renegade[27] armies might "advance together [to their assistance]. Having, at the end of a month, mounted batteries

2 U

(23) Original چکونکي نمودن عزم "and in what manner to form a design," or, "what "sort of expedition to undertake."

(24) Original ناموس *(námoos)* by which is usually understood the honour of a person, as connected with, or depending on that of the females of his family. Hence the word very commonly denotes the *Haram*.

(25) There being no reason to suppose that the Mahrattahs had any women in *Adoni*, the *Sultan* might possibly mean that *their honour* was committed with that of their ally. But it is equally possible, that the expression, in question, may have proceeded solely from that perplexity of style, which so much distinguishes all the more laboured productions of his pen.

(26) This name is uniformly written ادهوني in the manuscript.

(27) The epithet مرتد "renegade," or "apostate," is here evidently designed to apply to the army of the *Nizám*, as that of مشرك "infidel" is to the Mahrattah army. The *Sultan* always affected to consider the *Nizám* in the light of an apostate, on account of the political connections he had formed with infidels, to the prejudice, as he put it, of the Mahommedan faith; or, in other words, of his own ambitious views.

" batteries near the ditch, I was employed in breaching the place, when intel-" ligence came, that the two aforesaid armies, headed by Moghul Ali Khân,[28] " brother of Nizâm Ali Khân, Sohrâb Jung,[29] Taigh Jung,[30] Tehbur Jung,[31] Gun-" naish Pundit, Apa Bulwunt, and others,[32] were arrived at the other [or opposite] " side of the river *Tungbhudra*. At that time I saw no good [or convenient] place " for intercepting the two armies ;[33] and, moreover, the army of the *Usud Ilhye* " *Sircar* was dispersed in [prosecution of] the siege of the fort. On this account " I moved from *that place*[34] [or shifted my camp] to the distance of half a *coss* " on the flank [or on one side] of the road of the aforesaid armies. By this " movement the latter were thrown into the utmost dismay and confusion ; and " in this state[35] proceeding along the skirts of the hills, [at length] reached the " aforesaid fort, near to which they remained encamped during three days. On " the fourth day they took out all the people of the fort ; but were in such " distraction and alarm [at the time], that they left behind *the whole of the wearing apparel of the females,* and every article of household furniture [be-longing

(28) I do not find this personage mentioned on the present occasion by any other authority.

(29) I think this was one of the titles of the *Nizâm's* minister, Mûsheerûl Mûlk, afterwards called Azeemûl Omra, and finally Aristoo Jàh. It is proper to observe, however, that the *Sultan* affects to write *Shoorâb* (salt-water) instead of *Sohrâb* (an eminent name in Persian history) on the principle explained by Colonel Wilks, in the Preface to his valuable History of *Mysore*, page xxii.

(30) Called also Syfûl Mûlk and Shumsûl Omra.

(31) I do not know who is here meant. The name is properly Tuhavwûr Jung, but purposely miswritten by the *Sultan*.

(32) Two words follow here in the original بانباي طلايه داران which I do not clearly comprehend. طلايه *(tiláyeh)* is a patrole, a picquet, &c. بان *(bân)* a rocket. Perhaps the persons spoken of were commanders of bodies of rocket-men, and of particular corps employed as picquets, or patroles.

(33) *i. e.* " I perceived no practicable means of intercepting them."

(34) Meaning "the position or ground" which he had previously occupied.

(35) In the original it is افتان وخيزان "falling and rising :" a phrase which, though strongly expressive in the Persian language, is difficult to be preserved in a translation.

longing to them]. In this naked,[36] condition, carrying the women along with them, they took at midnight the road of flight, and made a shameful retreat.[37]

"Immediately on receiving the intelligence [of their flight], I armed com-" pletely,[38] and, with the design of intercepting the fugitives, pursued them " with the the utmost celerity. As, however, owing to the rain, and to the miry " state of the roads, the patroles had been *on the whole*[39] very negligent [or " tardy] in making their report [of the enemy's retreat]; and, as, *on the whole*,[39*] " the artillery, owing likewise to the same circumstance, followed very slowly, " the aforesaid armies were enabled to effect their escape across the river, " *Tungbuddra*; but not without leaving behind them, in their disorder and " alarm, an elephant and some.........[40]

"At this time [or on this occasion] the power [of God] was [wonderfully] " manifested to all the world, in the following manner. While the fugitive " army was crossing the river, the water was not higher than the waist; but in " the space of six hours, at the end of which the army of the *Usud Ilhye Sircar* " arrived in close pursuit [of the enemy], it had risen to a level with the banks[41]: " and thus was that prey, which the net had [so nearly] overspread, enabled, " by the divine pleasure [or power] to escape in safety.[42]

2 U 2 "After

(36) Original جريده The term is here employed somewhat equivocally. It may be understood in its usual figurative sense of "light" or "unencumbered;" but the context would seem to imply, that the writer intended it to be taken in the sense of "naked or bare."

(37) The action, here alluded to, would appear, by an Hindostan newspaper of this period, to have taken place on the 27th June 1786.

(38) Original مسلح ومكمل شده I am not clear whether the *Sultan* meant to apply these words to his army at large, or to himself only.

(39) (39*) Original في الجمله

(40) There is a word here in the manuscript which I do not understand, but which is probably the name of some wheeled carriage. The original is, in this place, more than usually perplexed and obscure, and I have, in consequence, been compelled to take some little freedom in the translation. The *Sultan* would appear to have been conscious, that there was something in the translation he was relating, not altogether creditable to his military character, and, in his attempt to gloss over the business, he has accordingly fallen into the most bewildered style that can be imagined.

(41) Original هردولب ملبب

(42) Original جانها بدربردند "carried off their lives."

" After putting the enemy to flight, the high [or eminent] army marched [back] " to the vicinity of the fort [*i. e. Adoni*], where I lay encamped for five days, in " the course of which [I caused] the fort of *Adoni* to be entirely demolished (43). " I then bestowed the country of *Adoni* in *Jageer* upon Kûtbûddeen Khân, " Bukhshy of the *Bâr-kuchurry*, (44) to whom, moreover, I gave the *Nobut*, (45) five " elephants, and a *lack of rupees* in money; (46) directing that, after fixing [his " authority] firmly in the *Jageer*, he should leave two thousand horse, and make " such other arrangements as might be necessary for its defence, (47) and then " return himself to his attendance upon our person. (48)

" After this, marching from thence [*i. e. Adoni*], I proceeded to the banks of " the *Tungbuddra*, &c."

The sequel of the *Sultan's* brief account of this war will be given hereafter, in its proper place.

The foregoing narrative is not, perhaps, calculated to exhibit the *Sultan* to any great advantage, either as a politician or a general. If (as would seem from his own account and the correspondence of Usud Ali Khân to have been the fact) his

(43) The fort of *Adoni* appears, by the Hindostan newspapers already referred to, to have been taken possession of by the *Sultan* on the 11th of July 1786.

(44) The *Bâr-kuchurry* was the department of regular infantry. The *Bukhshy* of a *Kushoon* was an office subordinate to the *Sipahdâr* and to the *Risâladâr*: but the *Bukhshy* of a *Kuchurry*, or one of the general divisions of the army, appears to have corresponded in some degree with a general officer of our staff.

(45) The *Nobut* is the privilege of retaining a band of military musicians, who are usually stationed over the gateway of the person's house, enjoying the honor; and occasionally join his retinue in his visits of form.

(46) This *lack* of *rupees* would appear, from the manner and place in which it is mentioned, to have been a present. It is more probable, however, that this money was an advance, on account of the pay and other expences of the force to be employed under Kûtbûddeen.

(47) (48) Original مستقل بجاگیر بوده در نوکری سرکار حاضر باشد I confess myself to be quite uncertain as to the right meaning of this passage. It may import, that he was to remain with two thousand horse on his *Jageer*, but to hold himself always in readiness to join the *Sultan* when ordered; or the sense may be, that which I have given in the text. Hûsain Ali states, that Kûtbûddeen, unable to maintain his footing in the district, was compelled, some time after the *Sultan's* departure from *Adoni*, to retire to *Gooty*.

his chief aim, in the present expedition, was to get the females of Mohâbut Jung's family into his power, by means of a capitulation; it is obvious, that this end was more likely to have been attained by a vigorous and menacing attack of the place, than by the slow and feeble mode of proceeding which he adopted. In the former case, the garrison might possibly have been intimidated into an early surrender, before the allied forces could come to its relief: as it was, it had every encouragement to hold out till their arrival. The *Sultan* appears to have been betrayed into this first error, by the expectation of accomplishing his object through negociation: and this grand mistake was followed by another, of a military kind, which completely frustrated his views. He suffered the enemy, not only to reach *Adoni* without any material attempt to intercept them, but to remain in its vicinity during three or four days; and finally to remove the garrison and women in safety, without the least interruption. It is in vain that he endeavours to disguise these blunders: his endeavours, for this purpose, only prove his secret consciousness of them.

LETTER CCCII.

From the same to the same, and of the same Date. (18*th June.*)

Your note has been received, and its contents are understood. You write, " that hitherto, in pursuance of the intimation of the Presence,(1) " you have not been deficient in [your endeavours to bring] the [pending] " negociation [to a conclusion], and that, even now, nothing is gone " [or lost]."(2) You proceed to state, that you wish we would represent " the matter, agreeably to your former proposals, to the Presence; and " getting a settlement made accordingly, which would redound to our honour,

(1) This may refer either to Tippoo or to his own master, Mohâbut Jung; but I incline to think that the former is here intended.

(2) Original هیچ زفت

"honour,[3] apprize you thereof:" and you exhort us, "to exert our "most strenuous endeavours, to obtain and send you a favourable "answer."

It is known. The firmament is prepared[4] and ripe with the ruin of the house [of your master]. Pity! a thousand pities! that you, Sir, should not have opened your eyes, or contemplated the certain consequences of these proceedings; but, instead of this, should write, "that, "even now, nothing is gone [or lost]." This circumstance has excited in us the utmost surprise and amazement. That friend [or you] did lately, on the part of the *Begums*,[5] supplicate, in the most humble and earnest manner, for an accommodation and adjustment of this business. In consideration hereof, and solicitous to avert the dreadful evils which menaced the honor of *a world*, collected together within the fort (for, in any sinister event,[6] ruin to *the house* and loss of honour[7] to numberless creatures must ensue), we represented the case in such various lights [and so efficaciously] to the resplendent Presence, as brought our bountiful master to agree to a settlement. That friend, notwithstanding this, now introduces [or brings forward] excuses, respecting an adjustment of the matter: hence it would seem, that you, Sir, are desirous of bringing about the ruin of your master's house, and the misery of the people. This is an evil which no one can remedy. [Still, however, we would fain impress upon your mind] the propriety of weighing in the scales of wisdom the good and bad of this business; and, having obtained from your

(3) Or, "good name:" that is, as being the instruments of so just and humane an arrangement as the one alluded to.

(4) Original فلک مستعد *i. e.* "fate is impending" or "ready [to strike]."

(5) The superior ladies of the *Mahl*: princesses.

(6) *i. e.* "An assault of the fort."

(7) Original ناموس ریزی "a spilling, shedding, or flowing of honour," (as of blood); applied more particularly to female honour.

your master full powers for its adjustment, of your repairing hither, in order that, somehow or other, the negociation may be terminated; inasmuch as the interest and prosperity of a whole world are herein concerned [or are at stake]. Any further delay must, on the other hand, be productive of the most serious evils, which it will be no longer in your power, or in ours, to ward off. By the Divine favour, that friend is conversant in all worldly affairs, and duly acquainted with the ups and downs(8) of fortune [or life]. You have, moreover, witnessed with your own eyes, the fate of many ancient rulers; such as those of *Kurpah* and *Gooty*. With such examples [before you], to permit [this thing] is far removed from [or irreconcilable with] foresight [or prudence], as well as incompatible with [your] attachment to the interest [of your master]. At any rate, it is the imperious duty of the subdued [or powerless] to omit no means of conciliating the powerful; but, by every possible submission and demonstration of humility, to avert the ruin impending over them: it is [therefore] fitting, that that friend, accompanied by two [other] persons of weight and consideration, should repair hither to-morrow, in order that we may jointly represent matters in such a way to the Presence, as shall lead to the accomplishment of whatever may [best] conduce to the benefit of God's creatures.

LETTER CCCIII.

From the same to the same; dated 16*th* J*AAFURY*. (19*th June.*)

THE letter you sent has shown the face of arrival, and made us acquainted with the circumstances therein written. You state, "that "after obviating all difficulties(1) to day, you will come, accompanied by "the

(8) This is literal; the original being نشیب وفراز زمانه

(1) Original همه رد وبدل درست کرده "having adjusted all points in dispute."

" the persons of respectability [or credit, before mentioned] for the " purpose of putting [every thing] in a [proper] train [of adjustment]." It is known, and highly approved. The habits of friendship and mutual interest have, of old [or from former times], firmly and truly subsisted between our lord and master (long may his prosperity endure!) and your master.(2) A regard to this circumstance, joined to compassion for the situation of [God's] creatures, has disposed the blessed mind [of the former] to an accommodation; in which [disposition] he has been more especially confirmed by your humble supplications, aided by the representations of us, your friends, and others participating in the present negociation. It is, therefore, proper, that that friend, obtaining full powers to conclude a settlement, and accompanied by the persons of credit [before alluded to], should repair hither, and finally arrange the business, according to your agreement; inasmuch as his Highness, our master, has these two objects greatly at heart; namely, first, the relief of [God's] creatures;(3) and, secondly, the corroboration of the foundations of ancient friendship. What more?

LETTER CCCIV.

From the same to the same; dated Wednesday Night, 18th Jaafury.(1) *(21st June.)*

We will [punctually] attend, Sir, to your appointment for to-morrow morning. Do you come also, Sir, accompanied by your confidential [friends]; when we will proceed together to the Presence.

(2) Alluding, most probably, to the political connexion formerly subsisting between Busâlut Jung (the father of Mohâbut Jung) and Hyder Ali.

(3) Original ترحم احوال خلایق " compassion for the condition of God's creatures."

(1) This letter should properly follow the one which it now precedes; but it is inserted here, for the purpose of preserving the continuity of the subject.

OBSERVATIONS.

Nothing further is recorded in the correspondence respecting this negociation, which was probably broken off about this time, by the appearance of the relieving army. With the exception of a slight notice in Letter CCCVIII, *Adoni* is not even mentioned in any of the succeeding dispatches, till we arrive at the period when, in consequence of the peace concluded with the Mahrattahs and the *Nizâm*, the *Sultan* announces to Kûtbûddeen Khân the revocation of the grant he had made to the latter of that district in *Jâgeer*.

LETTER CCCV.

To Bûrhânûddeen ; *dated* 17*th* Jaafury. (20*th June.*)

On the subject of his chastising the enemy, and desiring him to keep moving round them at the distance of ten or twelve *coss*. Directing him, also, to procure supplies of grain from *Nugr* and to distribute the same among his troops.

LETTER CCCVI.

Circular, *dated* 18*th* Jaafury (21*st June*), *to the following* Sipahdârs.

Zynûl Aabideen,	Shaikh Imâm,
Mahommed Huleem,	Imâm Khân,
Meerân Hûsain,	Ahmed Baig,
Husâin Khânpoony,	Ghûlâm Mohyûddeen,
Rujub Ali Baig,	Shaikh Omar.

You are to retain with your *Kushoons* such young and active women, only, of those belonging to it, as may be capable of keeping pace with

2 X the

the victorious army in its [approaching] marches. The rest, who may be aged and infirm, are, with the other heavy baggage, to be sent off to *Fyze Hisâr* [*Gooty*]. In addition to your constant [or usual] stock of provisions, you must supply yourself with a sufficient quantity [to be kept in reserve] for the consumption of ten days. What more?

OBSERVATIONS.

It is probable, that the *Sultan* was now preparing to make some movement against the allied force, of the approach of which to the relief of *Adoni* he may be presumed to have received intelligence about this time. The foregoing circular is followed in the manuscript by a short note to Moaayenûddeen, desiring him to hasten to the Presence, as soon as he had finished his repast.

LETTER CCCVII.

To BUDRÛZ ZUMÂN KHÂN; *dated* 21*st* JAAFURY. (24*th June.*)

ACCORDING to your *Hûkm-nâmeh* [or written instructions], your army should consist of ten thousand men, including *Jyshe*, horse, and *Piâdehs*. Call the detached troops, or out posts, together; and do you, for the present, proceed and join Bûrhânûddeen with your army, and co-operate with him in the chastisement of the enemy.

Your appointment of Mudâra Baig to the *Kilaadâry* of *Anundpoor* is approved. You must, by means of the aforesaid, get together [*i. e.* raise for the service of the *Sircar*] as many horsemen as possible.

LETTER CCCVIII.

To BÛRHÂNÛDDEEN; *same Date.* (24*th June.*)

Two letters from you have passed under our view, and the particulars set forth in them are distinctly manifested.

What

What you write, of having chastised and defeated the enemy, is understood. Budrûz Zumân Khân has also been ordered to join you with the forces under his command, and to co-operate with you in the chastisement of the enemy. The aforesaid *Khân* will, accordingly, join you with his troops. As he possesses great practical knowledge and experience in war, you will, as a matter of course,(1) consult with him on all measures relating to the operations [you are conducting]. You must, also, keep moving round the enemy, at the distance of from two to three *coss*, in order that you may, by this means, straiten their foragers.(2)

What you write, with regard to your having relinquished to the captors the horses and camels taken from the enemy, is known; and we approve of the same.

We lately wrote to you, desiring you to turn, or pass, the rear of the enemy, and join us with your army. That, however, is not now necessary. You must remain where you are, in the districts of *Kittoor*, *Dhârwâr*, and *Shânoor*, and apply yourself to the chastisement of the enemy. Please God, we shall soon be disengaged from the business which occupies us here, when, after inflicting signal punishment on such part of the enemy's forces as may [venture to] advance on this side of *Adoni*, we shall proceed, by the route of *Hurpunhully*, and crossing the *Tungbhuddra*, pursue [from thence] our march to that quarter [*i. e.* to join you].

What you have stated, of the commendable services of Ghous Mahommed Khân, and of Sheer Khân, the *Umldâr*, and others, is comprehended, and we have, in consequence, issued orders to Mahommed Hyder and to Nursia, the *Taalûkdârs* of *Nugr*, to send you two pair of

2 X 2 gold,

(1) Original علي ضرور "A necessary point, article, consequence."

(2) So I understand the original of this passage; which, however, by the alteration of a single diacritical point, would imply, that Bûrhânûddeen's facilities of foraging would, by this means, be augmented.

gold, and thirty pair of silver *hulkahs*,(3) each pair of the weight of one *seer*.(4) The former of these you are to present to the first *Munshoor* [Ghous Mahommed Khân], and to Sheer Khân, the *Umldâr* aforesaid. The silver ones are to be given to the inferior officers, as marks of our approbation.

Of the *Coolies* attached to you, keep as many [only] as you may [absolutely] require, and distribute the rest among the four *Kushoons* [with you], for the service of the *Doolies* [or litters], in which the sick and wounded must be dispatched to the circumjacent forts.

You write, "that you have it in contemplation to make a night attack "upon the enemy." It is revealed. Where [or when] will you have an opportunity of making a night attack? You should, however, keep moving round the enemy, at the distance of three or four *coss*,(5) in order that, if a favourable occasion should present itself, you may [fall upon and] chastise them.

OBSERVATIONS.

The foregoing letter appears twice in the collection, but in different places, and with some variations. I have followed the entry which seemed to me the most perfect of the two. In the copy, however, which I suppose to have been cancelled, the following material paragraph occurs:

"What you write of the *backwardness* of the cavalry is understood. You "must give orders to their *Bukhshy* to exert himself, for the purpose of infusing "into them a proper spirit, so that they may not, hereafter, act in a cowardly "manner, at the [critical] moment of service."

(3) A *Hulkah* is a kind of bracelet or ring, worn round the wrist.

(4) In the original سیر کچا or a *light seer*, opposed to a *seer* of *full* or perfect weight. A *full seer* is equal to about two pounds avordupoise. The *light* seer does not exceed a pound and a half.

(5) In a preceding part of this letter, the distance prescribed is from two to three *coss*. In Letter CCCV it is stated at ten or twelve *coss*.

LETTER CCCIX.

To MEER TÛRÂB ALI; *dated 22d* SHAABÂN.(1) (28*th June.*)

THIS is a letter from the *Sultan*, inviting the person addressed to repair to his court, where he promises him a favourable reception, and a provision suitable to his rank and qualifications. It would not appear to be an answer to any direct overture in writing from Tûrâb Ali, but to have resulted from some verbal communication made to the *Sultan* by a *Hindoo* agent, named Lâleh Wullub Doss.

I take this Meer Tûrâb Ali to be the same person who will hereafter be found making some figure in the intrigues carried on by Tippoo, in the year 1796-7, at the court of *Hyderabad*. He was probably, at this period, a dependant of Mohâbut Jung. It does not appear from the correspondence, whether or not he accepted the *Sultan's* proposals on the present occasion; but other documents furnish reason to think he did not. It is not unlikely, that he might have satisfied the *Sultan* that he could serve him better where he then was, than by actually joining him; which, however, he ultimately did, after the lapse of some years.

LETTER CCCX.

To the SIPAHDÂR, MAHOMMED ALI; *dated 27th* JAAFÛRY. (30*th June.*)

YOU write, "that the *Dârogha* of the *Jinsy* attached to your *Kushoon* "having, without your knowledge, sent the bullocks [belonging to your "guns] to graze, the enemy's people came........"(1*) You must, after flogging the aforesaid *Dârogha*, discharge him [from our service].

With respect to the *Risâladâr*, Bubr Ali Baig, whom you represent to be very troublesome(2) to the men of the *Risâla*, and to the *Jowkdârs*, you

(1) Corresponding, I believe, with the 20th of June 1786: consequently, this letter should properly have followed Letter CCCIII.

(1*) Either the *Sipahdâr* left the rest to be guessed by his master, or the transcriber omitted what should have followed, namely, the words "and carried them off." The latter is the most probable, as will appear from Letter CCCXXIII, where the same subject recurs.

(2) Original شرارت which is not less vague in its signification than the word by which I have been obliged to render it.

you must give him such strict orders [or admonish him so severely] as shall prevent him from repeating his improper practices.

LETTER CCCXI.

To BÛRHÂNÛDDEEN; *same Date.* (30*th June.*)

You write, "that some of[1] the *Kilaadârs* and *Ryots*, of the [adja-" cent] *Taalûks* [or districts], having thrown off their allegiance[2] to us, " convey intelligence to the enemy, and, moreover, supply the latter " with provisions." It is known. You must seize upon the [offenders], punish them,[3] and hang them upon trees, as examples to others.

LETTER CCCXII.

To ZYNÛL AABIDEEN; *BUKHSHY of EHSÂM at FURRÛKH-YAB HISÂR, (CHITTLEDOORG); same Date.* (30*th June.*)

Your letter, enclosing one [to your [1*] address] from the *Kilaadâr* of *Kopul*, has been received. You state, " that you had [some time before]

(1) Though this restriction of the sense is not authorized by the manuscript, yet it seems more probable that the words which I have ventured to supply should have been omitted by the transcriber, than that the disaffection, or disloyalty, referred to, should have been so universal, as the original, without this correction, would imply. The *inhabitants* of a frontier province might waver in their attachment; but as all the *Kilaadârs* must have been of the *Sultan's* own appointment, it would be difficult to believe that they should all have proved unfaithful to him.

(2*) Original باغي شده " having revolted, or rebelled."

(3) The sense may be, and punish them by hanging them, &c.," or " that some were to be punished (perhaps flogged) and others to be hung." The original is تنبيه ساخته بردرختان آويزان نمايند

(1*) Original معه خط قلعدار كوپل where the word خط *(khutt)* sufficiently denotes that the enclosure referred to was addressed to Zynûl Aabideen; since, if it had been addressed to the *Sultan*, it would have been called an *urzee*, instead of a *khutt*.

" before] written to us, on the subject of providing for the security of the " fort of *Kopul*, and of dispatching [thither] a thousand or five hundred " trusty men [to reinforce the garrison], but that no answer had [yet] been " sent by us to your letter." It is known. Some time has elapsed since we gave orders for the dispatch of the trusty men [in question], and also replied to your letters.(2*) We will now, however, send people [or a reinforcement] to the aforesaid fort [directly] from the Presence.

LETTER CCCXIII.

To BÛRHÂNÛDDEEN; *dated* 2d *DÂRÂEY*. (5*th July*.)

WE have learned of the flight of the enemy's army from *Hoobly* (1); and that that light of our eyes has encamped at *Kulhungy*,(2) a very strong and [well] protected situation. The rains, however, are violent at that place: you must [therefore] encamp on [or move to] some spot, where the rain is more moderate, in order that your horses, &c. [or your cattle] may not perish, or your people suffer inconvenience.

You write, on the subject of confining Abdûl Sumud Khân,(3) the son of Hukeem Khân, " that Dileer Dil Khân having represented him to " be attached to the *Sircar*, and as entertaining no dangerous views of " any kind, you propose waiting a repetition of our orders for his " arrest." It is known. You must secure his person, and send him [a prisoner] to *Nugr*.

Agreeably to your desire, we have written [and enclosed] orders to the *Taalûkdâr* of *Nugr*, and to the [several] *Aumils* of that district, to

(2*) The answers referred to had probably miscarried.

(1) Original هبلي which circumstances make probable is designed for *Hoobly*.

(2) Name uncertain; but perhaps the *Kuilkunda* of Captain Moor.

(3) See Letter CCXCVI.

to dispatch supplies of grain to you. You must forward the said orders to them, and apply for the grain [you require].

LETTER CCCXIV.

To RÂJÂH RÂM CHUNDUR; *dated 4th DÂRÂEY. (7th July.)*

YOU have represented to us, "that Syed Peer, the *Kilaadâr* of that "place [*Bangalore*], requires a separate order from us to himself [as a "warrant], for his dispatching to the Presence the cannon-shot [for "which we lately wrote to you]." It is known. Cannon-shot are not now wanted: they must, therefore, not be sent.

OBSERVATIONS.

As Syed Peer was not reproved for declining to obey an order not addressed to himself, it may be concluded, that he was justified in what he did by the regulations of his department; and, consequently, that the *Sultan* had issued his orders in an informal manner.

It moreover may be inferred from the foregoing letter, that the *Sultan's* operations against *Adoni* had now terminated.

LETTER CCCXV.

To RUNMUST KHÂN, *FOUJDÂR*(1) *of* KURNOOL; *same Date. (7th July.)*

[AFTER compliments]......... A long period has elasped, during which you have not delighted or gladdened me with the joyful tidings of your

(1) This term literally signifies, "one having charge of an army;" but, in its ordinary acceptation, it means an officer of government, exercising the civil and military jurisdiction of a district, to which is sometimes added the administration or collection of the revenues, though this is usually a distinct employment, and held by an *Aumil*.

your health and happiness. This neglect is very distant from the established rules of friendship, since friendship renders it incumbent [on you] to afford me regularly the satisfaction of receiving letters [from you], containing accounts of your welfare.

The victorious army being arrived in these parts,(2) it is fitting that that friend should afford me the pleasure of an interview [with him], in order that the foundations of mutual regard and amity may be strengthened, and that various points, which can only be properly discharged in a personal intercourse,(3) may be finally adjusted [between us].

OBSERVATIONS.

I am unable to say, whether the interview, here proposed by the *Sultan*, took place or not. It is probable, that Runmust Khân would endeavour to evade it, if for no other reason than because he could not consent to such a meeting, without rendering himself obnoxious to the suspicions and displeasure of the *Nizâm*, whose feudatory he was.

It must not be concluded, from the circumstance of the *Patan* chieftain being designated *Foujdâr* in the title of the foregoing letter, that he was actually addressed by this disparaging appellation. Such an affront could not be reconciled with the general style of the letter, which is not deficient in courtesy. It is very possible, however, that the *Sultan* might have been in the habit of speaking of him, to his secretaries and others, as the *Foujdâr* of *Kurnool*, and that term, like that of *Sânoor Wâleh*, might, in this manner, have come to be adopted by the transcribers, or registers, of the correspondence.

2 Y

(2) This letter was probably written while the *Sultan* was in the vicinity of *Adoni*, which is only about seventy miles from *Kurnool*.

(3) Original هم بزمي An expression which, if used by any other person but Tippoo, might be construed as meaning "a convivial meeting;" which, of course, could not have been in his contemplation.

LETTER CCCXVI.

To Râjah Râm Chundur; *dated* 6*th Dârâey.* (9*th July.*)

Directing him to issue the pay of the men raised by Syed Peer, the *Kilaadâr* [of *Bangalore*], according to the return transmitted; with an intimation, that if the aforesaid *Kilaadâr* should entertain any infirm, useless, or old men, he would be compelled to refund the advances made to them. Ordering, moreover, a receipt to be demanded of the above-named *Kilaadâr*, for all articles delivered to him; and signifying, in short, that Râm Chundur was not to supply him with any thing, without taking his receipt for the same.(1)

LETTER CCCXVII.

Circular, *same Date*, (9*th July*), *to*

Khâjeh Ibûd Khân,	Mahommed Kûli Khân,
Khâjeh Uzeemûllah Khân,	Ishmâel Baig Humdâny and

Ishmâel Baig Isfahâny.(1*)

Inviting them to repair, with collected minds [*i. e.* with confidence], to the Presence, and to bring with them as many horsemen as possible: promising that the whole shall be provided for, according to their merits and to the regulations of the *Sircar*.

(1) Literally, "*there is no necessity* for delivering any articles to him without a receipt."

(1*) It is probable that all these were officers in the service of the *Nizâm*, or of Mohâbut Jung.

LETTER CCCXVIII.

To MEER MAHOMMED SÂDIK, *DEWÂN of the HÛZOOR*[(1)] *(or Presence); same Date.* (9*th July.*)

DIRECTING him to ascertain and trace the goods and furniture[(2)] in the possession of the inhabitants of that place [meaning *Seringapatam*] and to make a report of the same.

OBSERVATIONS.

The phrase سراغ بهم رسانیدن which I have rendered "*to trace*," is usually applied to the recovery of things *concealed:* the order, therefore, implies, that a strict search, or examination, was to be made. What the *Sultan's* object, in this inquisition, was, does not appear; but it was most probably directed with a view to some contribution, which he might have had in contemplation to levy on his subjects, in aid of his finances. There is no authority, however, that I know of, for supposing that any such contribution was actually levied at this period.

LETTER CCCXIX.

To BÛRHÂNÛDDEEN; *dated* 9*th DÂRÂEY.* (12*th July.*)

DIRECTING him to station a *Risála* of the *Jyshe*, under Shaikh Boodhun (brother to Shaikh Unser), at *Dhárwár;* and to dispatch, with great care, to *Chittledoorg*, the *Daisye* and other hostages.

2 Y 2

(1) "Minister of the Presence:" such it seems was the official designation of Meer Sâdik at this period. Whether or not any change subsequently took place in it, I am unable to state positively. He was afterwards, at the institution of the *Meer Asofs*, placed at their head; but, probably, still continued to be styled "*Dewán* of the *Húzoor*."

(2) Original اجناس و سامان This expression does not usually, I believe, include the idea of money: and yet the context would here seem to imply as much.

OBSERVATIONS.

The *Daisye*, here mentioned, is, no doubt, the unfortunate chief of *Kittoor*, of whom the last notice was taken in Letter CLXX. Another dispatch, on the same subject, makes it rather uncertain, whether the *Daisye* himself was to be removed to *Chittledoorg*, or only such of his servants or dependants as were deprived of their liberty at the same time with him; and who are distinguished in the original by the term *Ool*, or hostages.

LETTER CCCXX.

To Shumsûddeen Khân *and* Ghûlâm Hyder, *Dâroghas of the Tosheh-Khâneh, (at Putn) ; dated* 14*th Dârâey.* (17*th July.*)

A Book, entitled *Fukhrû's Shûyookh* [or "the glory of the *Shaikhs*"], has been dispatched to you by the post. Of this book you are to get forty copies correctly and plainly written by the transcribers there [*i. e.* at *Seringapatam*], leaving fifteen blank leaves at the beginning and end of each copy. Let this be expeditiously done,(1) and let the several copies be forwarded to us as they are finished, and an entry be made of the same in the register of your department.

You must compare the books, which were sent to you [lately] by the post, with the catalogue forwarded [at the same time], and depositing them in our library, make an entry thereof in the register of the [proper] department. Of the books in question we have retained seven volumes.

OBSERVATIONS.

The book here directed to be copied is mentioned in Major Stewart's catalogue, at page 157; where it is stated to be a treatise on the duties of pious Musulmans.

So

(1) In the original جلد تیار گردانیده which may possibly mean, "let them be *bound*."

So many copies were doubtlessly ordered, with a view to the general dissemination of the doctrines inculcated in the work, which, of course, corresponded with the *Sultan's* own intolerant and bigotted principles.

It is not improbable, that the books, mentioned in the last paragraph of the preceding letter, were part of the booty acquired at *Adoni*.

LETTER CCCXXI.

To RUNMUST KHÂN, *Chief of* KURNOOL; *dated* 12*th* RUMUZÂN, *A. H.* 1200. (*or* 9*th July* 1786.)

MENTIONING the dismissal of Dhurum Doss, who would verbally communicate matters circumstantially; and recommending to him to continue to cultivate the union subsisting of old [between the two families or states], as this [line of conduct] would be productive of salutary ends.

N.B. This letter should properly have followed Letter CCCXVIII.

LETTER CCCXXII.

To BÛRHÂNÛDDEEN; *dated from* KURGOOR, 14*th* DÂRÂEY. (17*th July*.)

ON the subjects of stationing the *Risâla* of Shaikh Boodhun, according to former orders [see Letter CCCXIX] at *Dhârwâr*; of sending for the *Aumil* of that place, Yenkut Rungia, and keeping him *carefully*(1) with himself; of appointing Sheer Khân, the *Umldâr* of *Kittoor*, to the *Umldâry* of *Dhârwâr*; and of dispatching Mahommed Ghous Khân to *Dhârwâr*.

Announcing

(1) It would seem by the context, that Yenkut Rungia was in disgrace.

Announcing to him, moreover, that the *Sultan* was about to cross the river(2) at *Gung-Kurknât*,(3) and would soon arrive [*i. e.* would soon join him]; and enjoining him [in the mean while] not to give battle precipitately.(4)

Informing him, finally, that the special retinue was arrived at *Kurgoor*; and directing him to send orders for the demolition of the fort of *Kittoor*, and for the return of the garrison to his army.

LETTER CCCXXIII.

To the SIPAHDÂR, MAHOMMED ALI; *same Date.* (17*th July.*)

Two *Urzies* [or humble addresses] have been received from you, wherein you mention "that the *Dârogha* of the *Jinsy* of your *Kushoon* "had, without your knowledge, sent [your] bullocks to graze; that "the enemy's horse came and carried them off; that you had, [in consequence] placed him [the *Dârogha*] under a guard; and that "Mahommed Kâzim, interceding for him with Bûrhânûddeen, had "procured his release."

We formerly wrote, and we now again write to say, that the abovementioned *Dârogha* must be dismissed from our service, and another appointed in his place.

Our

(2) I conclude the *Toombuddra* to be here meant. I am not certain, however, that

(3) *Gung-kurknât* is the right name of the passage spoken of, though it is so written in two or three places. It does not appear in any of our maps. I take *Kurgoor* to be the *Kergoade* of Colonel Wilks' map, placed about twenty-five miles south-west of *Adoni;* though *Kurgoor* would appear, by the next letter, to be situated on, or near, the bank of the *Toombuddra*, from which *Kergoade* is, at least, fourteen miles according to the map.

(4) As in a few other instances, this part of the abstract is in the words of the original letter ما هم عبور ندي نموده ميرسم "We, too, crossing the river, will soon arrive;" where it is remarkable, that the *Sultan* employs both the pronoun personal ما (we), and the verb in the first person, of which I doubt whether there are two other examples in the whole correspondence. One more occurs in Letter CCCLVI, to Mûlâim Jung.

Our most holy camp[1] is pitched on the banks of the *Tungbuddra*, and you may reckon on the special retinue speedily reflecting splendor on that quarter.

OBSERVATIONS.

If any orders were sent to Bûrhânûdden, respecting the *Dárogha* of Mahommed Ali's *Jinsy*, they do not appear. It is not improbable, however, that under the loose system, by which the military authorities were regulated in the *Sultan's* armies, the present directions to the *Sipahdár* were deemed sufficient for the occasion.

LETTER CCCXXIV.

To GHÛLÂM HÛSAIN KHÂN, *MUNSHOOR of BANGALORE; dated* 18*th* *DÁRÁEY.* (21*st July.*)

DIRECTING him to employ the *Kumáties*, or labourers, belonging to the fort, in erecting habitations for the *Ahmedies;* to attend, in due time, to the provisioning of the place; to write his *Urzies* [to the *Sultan*] conjointly with the *Kilaadár;* and to examine carefully into all affairs relating to the fort, as business was in progress, that made attention necessary in all things, great and small.[1*]

Ordering him, finally, to make his written instructions the rule of his conduct.

(1) Original مخيم اقدس This is the language of royalty, which the *Sultán* occasionally uses in writing to his own subjects and dependants. حضور پر نور "resplendent presence;" and ما بدولت "our prosperous person," are of the same nature. These forms do not, however, occur very frequently in the present correspondence. The Memoirs furnish rather more examples of them. It is probable, that in his oral intercourse with his people, he constantly employed the style of majesty.

(1*) Original جزوي وكلي "particular and general."

LETTER CCCXXV.

To Kûtbûl Mûlk; *same Date.* (21*st July.*)

Directing him to circulate among the Musulman inhabitants of that place [meaning *Adoni*] the mandates containing the *arguments, explanations, and statements*;(1) and also to transmit [copies of] the same to *Hyderabad* and *Aurungabad.*

OBSERVATIONS.

There can be no doubt, that the documents referred to in this brief entry, or memorandum, under the designation of *arguments,* &c. are the circular letter and proclamation inserted at page 291, and which the *Sultan* appears to have been anxious to disseminate, wherever there was any chance of their procuring him partizans, or of inducing Musulman adventurers to repair to his standard. We shall, accordingly, presently see him transmitting the same persuasions to the extremities of *Hindostan,* in which quarter, however, his success was not likely to keep pace with his wishes, (whatever might be the case in the dominions of his immediate neighbours); inasmuch as the contest for power between Mâdhâjee Saindeah and the Moghul chieftains of *Hindostan* had not yet terminated; and because, while that contest continued, the inducements to the Musulmans to emigrate from thence were not so strong as they subsequently became, upon the complete establishment of the Mahrattah authority throughout the provinces lying between the *Chumbul* and the *Ganges.* But even in this last conjuncture, when there did not any longer exist, to the northward of the *Toombuddra,* a single Mahommedan leader, capable of affording employment to the scattered bands of Moghuls and Patans, who were now left without a master, the *Sultan* would not appear to have obtained any material accession of strength from the side of *Hindostan:* the chief reason of

(1) Original احکام دلایل و افادیت و احوال "mandates containing arguments and explanations with accounts or expositions [of the actual circumstances or state of *Islâm* in India]."

of which, most probably, was, that there was no access to *Mysore*, excepting by countries in the possession of his enemies, or of states jealous of his power, who were not likely to have permitted any bodies of armed men to pass through their territories, for the purpose of reinforcing his armies. If, therefore, he received, at the period alluded to, any recruits at all from this quarter, it could only be such straggling individuals as might, from their insignificance, be enabled to proceed unnoticed.

The Kûtbûlmûlk,[2] to whom the foregoing letter is addressed, is the same person elsewhere called Kûtbûddeen Khân, which last is a name by no means uncommon among Musulmans. Kûtbûlmûlk, on the other hand, is a *title;* and one, indeed, of considerable eminence, the affix of *ulmûlk* to a title denoting the highest that is, in general, bestowed. I say, *in general,* because it was rarely that any title of a superior degree was conferred by the court of *Dehli.* Sometimes we meet with *ulmumâlik* added to, or substituted for *ulmûlk,* of which it is the plural; and this would appear to have been a step higher than what was denoted by the same term in the singular number.

The usual gradation of titles is in the following ascending scale. 1, *Behâdûr;*[3] 2, *Jung;*[4] 3, *Uddowlah;*[5] and 4, *Ulmûlk;*[6] which the reader may, if he pleases, fancy to resemble, 1, Baronet; 2, Baron; 3, Viscount; 4, Earl. The addition of *Khân* was also considered as an honorary distinction, and is still occasionally bestowed, as such, by the imperial and some of the pseudo courts. It is, how-

2 Z ever,

(2) I believe that this Kûtbûlmûlk was the father of Hûsain Ali Khân, who was killed on the 6th April 1799, in an attack made by the English on the post of *Sultanpet.*

(3) Etymologists pretend that this word is compounded of بها "price, value," and در "a pearl;" *i. e.* "precious as a pearl." It figuratively signifies "a champion, warrior, or "brave man."

(4) *Jung.* This title, to be rendered significant, must be preceded by some other word, expressing some quality or characteristic of a warrior: as *Shokût Jung,* "formidable in "battle;" *Dilâwur Jung,* "valiant in battle, or in war, &c.

(5) *Uddowlah.* This word may be rendered "of the state;" as

(6) *Ulmûlk* may be "of the kingdom," and *ulmumâlik* "of the empire." Thus *Nizâmûddowlah* signifies "regulator of the state," or "one who contributes to the order or regula-"tion of the state;" as *Mûsheer ûlmûlk* does "counsellor, or minister, of the kingdom."

ever, in such very general use, as a component part of proper names, among the Mahommedans, and particularly those of the *Patan* or *Afghan* tribes, that it is not always easy to distinguish, when it occurs, in what sense it is meant to be applied, that is, whether as a title or a proper name.

The first title generally conferred is that of *Behâdûr*, then *Jung*, afterwards *Ud-dowlah*, and lastly *Ulmûlk*. On some occasions, however, all four are bestowed at once. At least such has been the practice since the decline of the Moghul empire: but there is reason to believe that, in its more flourishing days, these distinctions were less lavishly distributed than has been latterly the case. They have, at all times, been conferred by patent, and were never considered hereditary.

Such are the titles ordinarily granted by the imperial court; but the *Soubahs* of the *Decan*, as if ambitious of surrounding themselves with superior splendor, have added to them the more eminent distinction of *ul Omra*; or rather extended the application of this title, which, I believe, was usally restricted by the emperors to the single individual occasionally elevated to the rank of *Emirûl Omra*, or " lord " of lords." At the court of *Hyderabad*, however, we meet with *Aazumûl Omra*, " grandest of lords;" *Shumsûl Omra*, " the sun of lords;" *Tâjûl Omra*, " the " crown of lords," &c.

I have no where been able to discover any clear or distinct proof, that Tippoo Sultan ever conferred titles of any sort upon his subjects; and yet there are some passages in the correspondence, which would seem, in some degree, to authorize such a belief. In a letter, for instance, to Râjah Râm Chundur, " he directs him " always to affix his *title seal*(7) to his *Urzies*." We meet also with one dispatch addressed to a Mûlâim *Jung*; and another to a Shaikh Abdûl *Mûlk*, *Kilaadâr* of *Houscottah*. With respect, however, to the former of these titles, there is reason to suspect that it was no other than a ludicrous one, or kind of nick-name, since it signifies " *gentle*, or *soft*, in battle," and appears to have belonged to the leader of the *Sultan's* musical band. Besides these titled persons, it is certain that there was an officer of considerable distinction in the *Sultan's* service, called *Bubr Jung*, or " the tiger of war:" and Mahommed Riza, another commander of rank, who was

(7) Original خطابي مهر

was killed at the battle of *Sedaseer*, was also known, to Europeans at least, by the title of the *Binky Nabob*. It is proper to observe, however, that though Bubr Jung is, on one or two occasions, spoken of by the *Sultan* under that title, Mahommed Riza is no where mentioned, in the official documents, by the appellation of the *Binky Nabob*.

It is possible, that the different persons here mentioned, including Kûtbûl Mûlk, may have been in possession of the titles by which they were distinguished, at the time of their becoming subjects of the *Sultan*, or of his father: and, indeed, on no other supposition can the matter be satisfactorily explained; since, if the *Sultan* had ever bestowed titles, it is natural to conclude, that he would have decorated his principal servants with them: whereas the fact is, that not one of these, nor even a single individual of his own family, would ever appear to have received any distinctions of the kind in question.

It remains to be considered, what could be the reason of the *Sultan's* abstaining, during a reign of sixteen years, from assuming a privilege, so freely exercised by the *Soubah* of the *Decan* and other upstart rulers, and generally deemed an essential appendage of sovereignty. It could not be, that he entertained any doubts of his right to bestow titles of honour; since there are abundant proofs that he was never under the influence of any scruple respecting the authority of the imperial court, none of whose nominal vassals showed so little deference to it as he did. His conduct, therefore, in the instance under examination, is, perhaps, to be referred solely to that jealousy or mistrust, which formed a prominent feature of his character. He was, probably, afraid of making his servants too great; and might think the splendor of a titled retinue, more calculated to eclipse, than to exalt his own personal importance. Titles of honour might breed in those, on whom they were conferred, ambitious wishes and views, which would not otherwise be excited: they would also give the possessors of them too much consequence with the people, and thus might prove a source of various evils, more or less dangerous to his authority. The history of the rise of his own father's power would tend to confirm the prudence of this reasoning: which in a mind, naturally prone to suspicion, as that of the *Sultan* was, may easily be conceived to have led to the conclusion, that "his security would be best promoted by the political insignificance of his agents."

LETTER CCCXXVI.

To Mahmood Ali Khân; *dated 20th Dâráey.* (*23d July.*)

(Extract.)

We wrote some time since, and we now write again, to desire that the ship [you are now fitting out] may be coppered, as coppering [the bottom of] vessels renders them strong and durable. You must ascertain from the shipwrights whether coppering the....... (1) conduces to the strength [of the ship]; and if that should be the case, let it be done: but if [the ship] should be stronger by not having the....... coppered, then [that part] must not be coppered. In fine, that method, of the two, must be adopted, by which the ship will be rendered strongest, and made to last *a thousand* or *two thousand years.*

OBSERVATIONS.

I believe the ship, here mentioned, was one fitting out at *Calicut* for a voyage to *Pegu.*

I am not clear that I have rightly understood every word of the foregoing extract, the sense of which is rendered the more obscure by the blank which I have been obliged to leave. The general import of it is, however, sufficiently manifest.

Though there are some remarkable instances upon record of the great durability of *teek-built* ships, of which kind those constructed in Tippoo's dock yards, no doubt, were; yet the *Sultan* is not to be understood as literally meaning, in this place, that he expected the ship in question to last one or two thousand years. It is a figurative mode of expression, denoting that the vessel was to be constructed in the strongest manner possible, and resembles the metaphor employed in Letter XCVIII, to Râjah Râm Chundur.

(1) The original is پهور which I do not understand. It comes nearest to the *Hindivy* word *Putwár*, a rudder.

LETTER CCCXXVII.

To Bûrhânûddeen; *dated* 23*d* Dárâey. (26*th July*.)

You must, after some days, when the road shall have become safe [or the communication is opened], dispatch the *Risála* of Shaikh Boodhun, which is one that may be depended on,(1) to *Dhárwár*, and send for the *Risála* of Shaikh Humeed [to supply its place]. The *Kiladár* of *Dhárwár* is, at the same time, to be directed to dispatch to you, under charge of the said *Risála*, Yenkut Rungia,(2) of whom you must take good care. You must also be mindful to encamp with your army in a good situation, where little rain falls [or lays]. The special retinue will speedily arrive in that quarter from *Kurk-náth*.

LETTER CCCXXVIII.

To Kûtbûl Mûlk Kûtbûddeen Ali Khân Behâdûr; *dated* 25*th* Dárâey.(1*) (28*th July*.)

There is a little business [going on] in our high *Sircar*.(2*) Dispatch to the Presence, for a short time,(3) a seal-engraver.

OBSERVATIONS.

Although there is an air of mystery in this short note, it might possibly only mean, that the *Sultan* had occasion to employ a seal-engraver, and therefore desired

(1) Original اعتمادیست

(2) Besides Yenkut Rungia, twelve other persons appear to have been ordered to be sent in custody; but there is some obscurity in the original, which I am unable to dispel.

(1*) A letter of the 24th *Dárdey* (not inserted) is dated from *Durrojee*, which I take to be he *Daroje* of Colonel Wilks's map, placed about twelve miles west of *Kurgoade*, or *Kurgoor*.

(2*) Original در سرکار علي اندکي کاراست

(3) Original بالفعل "for the present," or "at present;" also "actually, in fact." The sense, however, seems to require the construction which I have given.

desired one to be sent him from *Adoni*, where, perhaps, this branch of business might be better understood than at *Seringapatam*. Thus, about thirty years ago, every one on the northern side of *India*, who was desirous of having his name or titles engraved in a superior manner, employed, for this purpose, an eminent seal-engraver of *Fyzabad*, in the province of *Oude*, named Mahommed Sâleh, whose exquisite execution of the most beautiful *Nustalikh* character on the hardest stones, was certainly unrivalled, excepting by his own son, who succeeded him in his occupation. The charge for engraving depended on the stone employed. If that was a cornelian, the price was a *rupee* a letter; but if an emerald, or other stone equally hard, it amounted, I think, to six *rupees* a letter.

LETTER CCCXXIX.

To Meer Moaayenûddeen; *dated 26th Dárâey.* (*29th July.*)

To-morrow you will halt at this place;(1) and distribute the pay [of your people], &c. The day after to-morrow you will march, and encamp at some place affording [plenty of] water and grass; and, on the following day, you must proceed, with the forces under your command, to *Huss Paith*.(2)

LETTER CCCXXX.

To Runmust Khân;(1*) *dated* 16*th Rumuzân*, *A. H.* 1200. (13*th July* 1786.)

We have, at this time, assigned the *Foujdâry*(2*) of *Adoni* to the charge of Kûtbûddeen Khân. The aforesaid Khân, in conformity with the

(1) That is *Daroje*, where the *Sultan* still was on the 29th *Dárâey*.

(2) Name uncertain.

(1*) The *Patan* chief of *Kurnool*.

(2*) Kûtbûddeen's new government is elsewhere called a *Jâgeer*.

the orders of the Presence, will keep one or two respectable persons established at *Kumr-nugr*,[3] for the purpose of collecting together [or recruiting] horsemen, &c. Let that kind friend [therefore] enjoin his principal officers[4] to be assisting to the persons deputed by the aforesaid Khân, in order that no one may obstruct this business. What more?

LETTER CCCXXXI.

To Kûtbûddeen Khân; *dated 29th Dârâey.* (1*st August.*)

What you have written, on the subject of the *Khûtbah*[1] being read in our special name,[2] is understood. The case is this.[3] The first thing in the *Khûtbah* is the praise of God; the next, the praise of the Prophet (on whom be the blessing and peace of God); and after this [should follow] the name of such prince[4*] of the faith, as, being a [true] protector of the Mahommedan religion, keeps in view, on all occasions [*i. e.* in every respect], the honour and interest[5] of *Islâm*, and exerts himself for its increase and diffusion.[6] To introduce the names of such, and to offer up prayers for them in the *Khûtbah*, is among the [most] indispensable

(3) *Kurnool* is so called by the Musulmans of the *Decan.*

(4) Original کارپردازان "transactors of business," "managers of affairs."

(1) The *Khûtbah* is a form of prayer used in Mahommedan mosques, wherein the reigning sovereign is prayed for.

(2) Original نام خاص

(3*) Original کیفیت اینست

(4*) Original نام سلطان دین literally, "the name of the *Sultan* of the faith," &c.; where, by applying the word *Sultan* for prince or sovereign, he doubtlessly meant to point indirectly to himself. Tippoo was fond of this sort of conceit.

(5) Original رعایت اسلام

(6) Original ترویج

sable duties.(7) As to those ideots, who at this time introduce the name of Shâh Allum into the *Khûtbah*, they act through ignorance; since the real condition of the *above-mentioned*(8) is this: he is actually enslaved, and a mere cypher; being the servant of Saindeah, at the monthly wages of fifteen thousand *rupees*. Such being the case, to pronounce the name of a dependent of infidels, in reciting the *Khûtbah*, is a manifest sin, and repugnant to the laws [usages] of the Muselmâny faith. For these reasons it is written, that the *Khuteeb*(9) of that place [*Adoni*] must be directed to introduce our name constantly in the *Khûtbah*.

OBSERVATIONS.

Whether or not the *Sultan* had, prior to the date of this letter, caused his own name to be substituted in the *Khûtbah* for that of Shah Allum, I have no means of clearly ascertaining: but it may, I think, be inferred, from the general tenor of the present document, that this was the first occasion on which he thought proper to adopt that practice; since, if it had been already established by him, he would hardly have deemed it *now* necessary to justify and explain it, as he has here formally endeavoured to do.

This letter, if contrasted with Letter CCCXXXIV, written nearly at the same time, will exhibit, not only the duplicity, but the inconsistency of the *Sultan*, in striking colors. He here, throwing off all disguise, openly declares his contempt of the reigning Emperor of *Hindostan*, and, in the most unequivocal manner, asserts his independence of the imperial authority. Yet he will be presently seen professing an earnest solicitude for the re-establishment of that very authority, and an ardent desire to contribute his utmost efforts towards the accomplishment of that end. There is no difficulty in comprehending, why the *Sultan* should, at this

(7) Original از جمله واجبات ضرور است

(8) Original مومي اليه This is a term by which none but persons of mean or ordinary consideration are referred to, and was probably never before applied to a crowned head.

(9) The person who reads or pronounces the *Khûtbah* is called a *Khuteeb*.

this conjuncture, have wished to cultivate a good understanding with the Mahommedan powers of the north of *India*: and had he, steadily and judiciously pursued that object, he might have found his account in such a policy. What is most extraordinary and unaccountable in his conduct, on this occasion, is, that he should, in one and the same moment, labour to make common cause with those powers, and utterly set at nought the sovereign whom they recognized, and the authority which they at least affected to respect and uphold. Is it possible, that he should have presumed upon their probable ignorance of the transactions of *Mysore*? This is difficult to suppose; since the tenor of the public prayers delivered in the *Mosques* must necessarily be a matter of notoriety, neither requiring nor being susceptible of concealment. On the other hand, if his conduct, in this and similar cases, should be known at the court of *Dehli*, how could he expect that any credit would be given there to his professions of zeal and attachment? Hence we may venture to conclude, either that he actually did proceed under the notion that that court was not likely to be apprized of the arrogance of his pretensions; or that, bestowing no thought on this point, he was prompted to address the chieftains in question, rather by the desire of displaying his religious enthusiasm, and of impressing those persons with a high idea of his power and resources, than by any deliberate view to a political connexion with them, or with any serious expectation of inducing them to co-operate with him, either in the war which he was at this time waging against the Mahrattahs, or in that which, there is abundant reason to believe, he already meditated against the British nation.

LETTER CCCXXXII.

To BUDRÛZ ZUMÂN KHÂN; *same Date.* (1*st August.*)

OUR special retinue will soon cross the river at *Gung Kurknâth*, and arrive in that quarter. It is now the rainy season. Taking all your army with you, apply yourself to the chastisement of the rebels of *Soopeh*, &c. The superintendant of the post at *Suddasheoo-ghurr* and *Soandeh* will be shortly removed, and another be sent in his place.

3 A

OBSERVATIONS.

Although it appears, by Letters CCCVII and CCCVIII, that Budrûz Zumân Khân was directed to join Burhânûddeen, there is reason to think, that this order was subsequently revoked; since, besides the different destination here assigned him, it is pretty certain, that he was not present at the general action which took place between the Mahrattahs and Tippoo near *Shânoor*, the beginning of the following December.

LETTER CCCXXXIII.

To Moal Chund *and* Soojân Râe, *(Agents at* Dehli*); dated 1st* Hâshimy. *(2d August.)*

Two letters, accompanied by your accounts, and dispatched in charge of Hoomajee, Tolârâm, and other *Hurkârehs*, have passed under our view, and the particulars therein set forth are comprehended.

The special *Shûkkeh*,(1) which you obtained and dispatched to us, in answer to the *Urzdâsht* and *Nuzr*,(2) presented, on our part, to the most sacred Presence by Shâh Nizâmûddeen Saheb,(3) has been received, together

(1) Original شقه خاص *Shúkkeh* is properly applied only to the letter of a person of rank and a superior. From the letter here alluded to being called a *Shúkkeh-khâss* (a special *Shûkkeh)* it may be inferred, that if not written in the Emperor's own hand, it was, at least, signed by him, and bore his private seal. A more public one would, probably, have been styled a *Firmaun*.

(2) The *Urzdusht*, or "humble address," is that forming Letter LXXI of the present collection, which was accompanied by the exceptionable *Nuzr* mentioned in the text.

(3) This person affected to be of the order of religious or devotees, called *Fakeers*, as is implied by the title of *Shâh* prefixed to his name. This holy character, however, did not prevent his taking an active part in the management of the court of *Dehli*, under the direction of the Mahrattahs; who found him as subservient to their views in that quarter as they could desire.

together with the letters addressed to us by the latter; through whom you must represent to the Presence, "that the newly struck "gold *Mohrs* were sent by us, merely for the purpose of ascer-"taining the pleasure of his Majesty concerning them; which being "now known to us, we have, in conformity with the royal com-"mands, inserted his Majesty's blessed name in the new coin [in "question]." It must, moreover, be stated, "that the manner in "which we heretofore chastised the Nazarenes [*i. e.* the English] "is too well known to require to be recapitulated; and that now, "again, we are earnestly occupied in punishing certain rulers and "nobles,(4) who have engaged in measures of evil tendency, and been "guilty of acts utterly repugnant to [the prosperity of] *Islâm.*" All these particulars you must get communicated to the sublime Presence, through the medium of the Shâh Saheb; by whose means you will also [endeavour to] procure imperial mandates to be written and dispatched to the *Nabob*, Nizâm ûd Dowlah Behâdûr, and the other Musulman rulers [in this quarter] directing them to unite together in support of the *Ahmedy* faith.

Here follow some uninteresting details, respecting the pay of the two agents addressed, and of the messengers employed in conveying the dispatches between *Seringapatam* and *Dehli*, of which a sufficient specimen has already been given in Letter LXXIII. To defray these, and other charges, a bill for one thousand nine hundred *rupees* was transmitted with the present letter. Of this sum, nine hundred *rupees* were directed to be applied to the purchase of five *Khilaats* (or complimentary dresses) which were ordered to be distributed as follows (each dress being accompanied by a letter, in the terms of that addressed to Mahommed Baig Khân Humdâny, for which see next letter)—

3 A 2 To

(4) Original رکنات, which may be meant for the plural of noble رکن though the regular plural is ارکان *(urkán)*. Possibly, however, some other word may have been intended.

To Mahommed Baig Khân Humdâny, Budl Baig Khân, and Shâh Nizâmûddeen, each a *Khilaat* of the value of two hundred *rupees*,

To Kâsim Khân and Siddeek Baig Khân, each a *Khilaat* of the value of one hundred and fifty *rupees*.

After these details, the dispatch proceed thus:

The five *Khilaats*, above-mentioned, must be delivered *secretly*, and *at night*, together with this message, *viz.* "that Nizâm ûd Dowlah, "having united with the Mahrattahs, and engaged in war against us, "and this proceedimg being manifestly contrary to [the interests of] "*Islám*, it is due to the support of [our] religion, that you, who are "near the person of his Majesty, the Divine Shadow,(5) and are more-"over Musulman leaders, should pursue such effectual measures as may "[at once] bring the............(6) to ruin and disgrace, and impart "additional strength to the true *Ahmedy* faith."

The letter concludes with directing the agents to send off a pair of *Kâsids*(7) once a month; and with stating, that the present dispatch consists altogether of seven letters, namely, the five already specified, an *Urzdásht*(8) [to the address of the Emperor], and a letter to Munsoor Ali Khân(9)

A note, or memorandum, follows next, of the different *Ulkábs*, or addresses, used in the five letters to the persons enumerated above; as also of the particular sort of paper on which each was to be written, and the kind of bag in which they were severally to be enclosed. On this occasion, the precedence appears to be assigned to Mahommed Baig Humdâny, to whom the *Sultan* writes in terms of entire equality. The others, though honorably addressed, are not equally distinguished.

For

(5) Original ظل سبحاني a title appropriate to crowned heads.

(6) Two words here occur, of which I can make no sense. Whatever they are, they of course refer to the Mahrattahs, or the enemies of *Islám*. One of them may be read موبدان (*moobidán*) or *guebres*.

(7) *Kásids* are couriers.

(8) Which does not appear.

(9) I suspect that this should be Munzoor Ali Khân, the chief of the eunuchs, the same to whom Letter LXXII is addressed.

For the gratification of those curious in such matters, I subjoin the directions relative to the paper and bags.

To Mahommed Baig Humdâny, the paper used was of the kind called *Zur-afshâny*, or "sprinkled with gold:" the *Khureetah*, or bag, was of *Mehtâby*, a sort of silver tissue.

To Budl Baig Khân and Kâsim Khân, silvered paper and *Kumkhâb* bag.

To the rest, *Kumkhâb* bags; but paper not specified.

OBSERVATIONS.

It is evident, from the foregeing letter, that the *Nuzr* formerly sent by the *Sultan* to Shâh Allum (see Letter LXXI) had been objected to, because the inscription on the coin, of which it was composed, did not contain the Emperor's name, which, it seems, was inserted in the gold *mohrs, now* transmitted. The words, in which the *Sultan's* apology for the disrespect alluded to is conveyed, imply that the second *Nuzr* (or that forwarded with the present dispatch) consisted of the *new coinage,* with the addition of the Emperor's name: but if this was actually the case, there is reason to believe that the die was formed expressly for this occasion, and that no more gold *mohrs* were struck from it, than were required for presentation to his Imperial Majesty.

The apology here tendered by the *Sultan,* for the affront which he had offered to the Emperor, in the instance of the *Nuzr* formerly sent to his Majesty, though too flimsy to impose on the Imperial Court, was probably accepted as a sufficient atonement for the offence; since it was now no time for the reduced representative of the royal house of *Timur* to assume a lofty or inflexible tone in the assertion of any of its rights.

I am unable to say, whether or not the application, here directed to be made to the Emperor, for mandatory letters to the *Nabob,* Nizâm ûd Dowlah, and the other Musulman chiefs of the *Decan,* enjoining them to co-operate with the *Sultan* against the Mahrattahs, was actually submitted to his Majesty; but, considering the situation of Shâh Allum at this time (as described, only the day before, by Tippoo Sultan himself, in his letter to Kûtbûddeen Khan), it is not likely

likely that any attention was paid to it. Indeed, the absurdity of such a proposal to a prince, so completely in the power of Saindeah as the Emperor now was, and who was placed so much out of the reach of any assistance from the proposer, could only be equalled, by the infatuation of employing two *Hindoo* agents in a negociation, the object of which was to exalt the *Mahommedan* at the expence of the *Brahmenical* religion. It was as if a Catholic state or sovereign were to depute a Protestant ambassador to the Pope, for the purpose of engaging his Holiness to exhort all the princes of the Romish persuasion to unite together, for the purpose of making a crusade against some neighbouring power of the reformed religion. So egregious a blunder could be committed only by such an eccentric character as Tippoo Sultan.

The great distance, joined to the difficulties of communication (arising from that and other causes) between *Seringapatam* and *Dehli,* sufficiently accounts, perhaps, for the circumstance of the *Sultan's* directing the presents, which he thought proper to make to the nobles of the Imperial Court, to be purchased at the metropolis, instead of sending them immediately from himself; which would, no doubt, have been the greater compliment. From the more than usual respect with which the *Sultan* mentions the Emperor in this dispatch to his agents, it appears probable, that he intended such parts of it as related to his Majesty, to be communicated, if not directly to himself, at least to his ministers.

Mahommed Baig Humdâny had been one of the principal commanders under the celebrated Nujuf Khân; after whose death he obtained, amidst the distractions which followed that event, still greater consideration and authority. He opposed, for some time, a firm resistance to the encroachments of Saindeah in the *Dehli* quarter; but at length fell, in one of the battles which took place between the Moghul and Mahrattah powers. Budl Baig Khân, Kâsim Khân, and Siddeek Baig Khân, were likewise leaders who had risen to distinction, while Nujuf Khân exercised the chief military authority under the court of *Dehli.*

LETTER CCCXXXIV.

To MAHOMMED BAIG KHÂN HUMDÂNY ; *same Date.* (*2d August.*)

NOTWITHSTANDING that, owing to various causes, it has so happened, that no epistolary correspondence has hitherto taken place between us, yet having, at this time, heard from the lips(1) of Bâl Mukn Doss, of your highness's(2) laudable qualities, and [particularly] of your courteousness, eminent courage, and political knowledge; my friendly mind(3) has derived therefrom the highest satisfaction and most abundant delight. Hence, agreeably to [the saying], " that all true believers are " brethren," the fervor of religious affection(4) has moved me [to the present attempt] to form an intimate and amicable connexion [with you].

The manner in which your friend [or I] punished the Nazarenes is so well known as not to require any [further] statement. No doubt you must have learned all the details [thereof] from common report.(5) I am now employed in chastising certain Musulman rulers; who, engaging in measures contrary to the rules of *Islâm* [or the institutes of the faith], are become the allies and supporters of the reprobate(6) infidels. In consequence hereof, I have lately caused to be drawn up and dispatched to all quarters, an abstract of God's ordinances, and of the commands of

(1) Original زباني literally, " by the tongue."

(2) Original سامي (*sámy*) : but though this word signifies " high, exalted, sublime," it is proper to observe, that the term is applied too generally to correspond strictly with our phrase of " your highness." It comes nearer, perhaps, to the expressions, " your worship, your " honour."

(3) Original خاطر دوستي مآثر

(4) Original جوشش اتحاد ديني

(5) Original ازخارج literally, " from without or abroad."

(6) Original بد انجام " whose end is bad or calamitous."

of his Prophet [on this article]; of which a copy is enclosed for your perusal. It is requisite, for the support of [our] religion, that all Musulmans should unite together; and, considering the annihilation of infidels as a sacred duty, labour, to the utmost of their power, to accomplish that object: to the end that the *Ahmedy* faith may, day by day, acquire fresh lustre; that the weakness of the empire of *Hindostan* may be changed for efficient dominion and power; that the abominations of the wicked may find neither habitation nor retreat(7) within the kingdoms of his Majesty (the Shadow of the Divinity), who is the chief of the vicegerents of Mahommed; and [finally] that the rulers of *Islám* may not be put to the blush(8) before the holy Prophet, on whom be the peace and blessing of God!

In token of my cordial regard [for you], I have written to Moal Chund and Soojân Râe, desiring them to deliver you a [complimentary] dress, which you must do me the pleasure to accept. You must, likewise, constantly make me happy, by the receipt of your delightful epistles.

LETTER CCCXXXV.

To Zynûl Aabideen, *Bukhshy of* Ehshâm *at* Furrûkh-yâb Hisâr (Chittledoorg); *dated 4th* Hâshimy. (*5th August.*)

We have received your letter, representing, "that if of the two "*Dufturs*,(1) attached to the *Ehshâm Kuchurry*, one be transferred to "the *Dewân Kuchurry*, the consequence must be, that while the ac-"counts of the latter department cannot be completely and properly "kept

(7) Original نفره و فجره مقر وماوا نيابند

(8) Original شرمسار نشوند

(1) *Duftur* here means a register, or book-keeper. In its more general acceptation, however, it signifies the office where accounts, &c. are prepared or registered. In this case the word خانه *(khâneh)* is usually added to it. A *Duftury* is an office-keeper, whose business it is to take care of the books, stationary, &c. belonging to it.

" kept [with such incompetent assistance], neither can the business of " the former be rightly managed [by the remaining one]." It is known. Whatever is written in your *Húkm-námeh* [or instructions], do you act conformably thereto. Too much self-conceit is needless.(2)

LETTER CCCXXXVI.

To the RÁJAH of the FRENCH; dated 5th HÁSHIMY. (6th August.)

NOBLE-MINDED and elevated in rank,(1) of powerful and exalted degree,(2) chief(3) of the sovereigns of the realms of Europe, and eminent among rulers, the peace of Almighty God be with you!

After presenting the customary compliments of regard and affection, and [after tendering] the due observances of friendship and union, it is made known to your odoriferous [or noble] mind.(4)

Some time since two letters, with *Khilaats* [or dresses], were forwarded [to you], by [the hands of] Monsieur Souriac,(5) which, no doubt, have been received. After that, Ghúlám Ali Khán, Lútf Ali Khán, and other *Sirdars* [or commanders] of the *Sircar*,(6) were dispatched in the ship.........,(7) with letters and rarities, by the way of *Bussorah*, to

3 B that

(2) Original زيادة خودراي ضرور نيست

(1) Original شهامت وعوالي مرتبت

(2*) Original بسالت ومعلي منزلت

(3) Original سرآمد "leader, foremost, uppermost, pre-eminent."

(4) Original خاطرمعطر

(5) In some places written Souliac: but whether either is the proper name of the person intended (who had been Governor of *Pondicherry*) I have not, at present, the means of ascertaining.

(6) *i. e.* my subjects.

(7) The name of the ship is omitted in the manuscript.

that [personage] of noble rank, [at whose court] they will [in due time] safely arrive.

At this time I have learned, from the communication of Monsieur Cossigny,(8) the Governor of *Pondicherry*, that *that kind* friend has written to him, directing him to settle the accounts of the advances of money made by the *Sircar* [*i. e.* me], for defraying the expences of the troops belonging to you, which were under the command of Messieurs Du Chemin and Souffrein, and of Monsieur Bussy; and [having done so] to repay the amount to the *Sircar* [or to me]. *This circumstance has occasioned me the utmost surprise.*(9) It was purely from motives of regard, and a desire to improve the friendship subsisting of old between us, that I sent to the *Mauritius* for the troops of that friend, and expended *crores* [of money], and sacrificed *lacks* of my people, in the course of five years that I was engaged in chastising the English; whom, at last, I was on the point of expelling from this country [or *India*]. During this period, the English repeatedly made overtures of peace to me; to which, however, I would not agree, returning [always] for answer, that I would make no peace, excepting in concert with the French, and never separately. Notwithstanding this,(10) Monsieur Bussy, the commander of the forces of that [personage of] noble rank, did, without my knowledge, conclude a peace [with the enemy]. The fact is known to every Frenchman in this country [*i. e. India*]. Thus I incurred all these expences, and made all these exertions, for the purpose of increasing our mutual friendship and renown;(11) and if such be still the desire of that friend, his

(8) I think, but cannot be certain, that this is the name intended by the original.

(9) Original ازاين معني خيلي تعجب روداد

(10) Original درابن اثنا properly, "in the mean while," or "during this;" but the context appears to require the construction which I have adopted.

(11) Original نام آوري "name-bringing."

his enemy shall [again], if it please God the most high, be signally chastised.

A double-barrelled gun, made in the arsenal[12] of the *Sircar*, together with an embroidered dress, is sent for that [personage of] noble rank, and will arrive[13] [in due season].

I[14] frequently indulge an inclination for the arts,[15] and am fond of collecting artists together [or about me]: if [therefore] that friend, out of his ancient regard, would dispatch [to me] some persons skilled in every art, I should esteem it as [a proof of] the most perfect friendship.

Ghûlâm Ali Khân, and the other *Sirdars*, will arrive [at your court] in due season;[16] and it is in my mind to dispatch another confidential person, on one of that friend's ships. If, therefore, you will write orders on this subject [or to this effect], to your [different] governors,[17] another confidential person shall be deputed on one of that friend's ships.

OBSERVATIONS.

Exclusively of the gross impropriety of designating the King of France by the title of *Rájâh* (on which I have already had occasion to animadvert) it may be observed

(12) Original کارخانجات "workshops or manufactories."

(13) Original خواهد رسید This form of expression is not uncommon in the Persian, and frequently occurs in these letters. It implies, that the thing or person sent will arrive in due course or time.

(14) Original اینجانب literally, "this side, part, or quarter." A phrase used by persons of rank, when speaking in the first person, instead of the pronoun personal.

(15) Original مزاج اینجانب اکثر برصنایع و فراهمی صنعت کثران راغب است The arts meant by the *Sultan* are of the handicraft kind; and those skilled in them, artizans. For the higher, or more liberal arts, Tippoo probably had little taste.

(16) Original بمرور "by degrees, progressively."

(17) Original تعلقداران *(taalûkdârs)*: a word which is obviously unsuitable to the occasion if meant to apply to M. Cossigny, with whose station it by no means corresponded. Possibly, however, the persons designed might be the governors or intendants of such places in *France* as the proposed mission would have to pass through, in its way to *Paris*. However this may be, a fitter term than *Taalûkdâr* might have been employed.

observed of the present letter, that it is extremely deficient in the forms of respect and complimentary phraseology, invariably observed in the correspondence between Eastern princes. Of the justice of this remark, the Oriental reader will be sufficiently satisfied by its general style and contexture, as preserved in the translation, which I have made as literal as I could. The expression of آں مهربان "that "friend," is, in particular, extremely exceptionable in an address to a crowned head, as being too familiar and common. Neither is the "*Ulkáb*," or address, free from objection, since the phrases of شهامت مرتبت "of noble rank," بسالت منزلت "of powerful degree," &c. are very usually applied, not only to dependent or subordinate chieftains and rulers, but even to distinguished servants of a certain class. Thus Tippoo himself occasionally addresses one of his *Sirdars* by the style of حشمت مرتبت "of pompous or magnificent degree;" another, by that of بسالت منزلت "of powerful degree," &c.

These deficiencies cannot, I think, be reasonably attributed to ignorance; since it would be difficult to believe, that there was not a *Múnshy*, or secretary, or other literary person, at the court of the *Sultan*, of sufficient learning to frame a letter, in a proper style, to a monarch of the rank and consideration of Louis XVIth. It is much more probable, that the *Sultan* himself dictated, or drafted, this epistle; and that, in doing so, he permitted the same spirit of animosity and aversion towards all the professors of Christianity, which led him to bestow the degrading title of *Rájah* on his royal correspondent, to regulate its general construction. It is also possible, that he might, on the present occasion, have been actuated, in some degree, by the notion, that his own importance was raised, in proportion as that of the French monarch was lowered: a notion which, in fact, has given rise to the well-known practice at Eastern courts, of taking every opportunity of assuming what may be called a technical superiority, in their epistolary intercourse with each other. But it is not in the style of their letters, alone, that they exercise this sort of address, and labor to obtain this paltry species of advantage, though the nice and numerous distinctions of language, depending on the gradations of rank, are more particularly favorable to the attempt. It is pursued, with equal industry and perseverance, in the presentation of complimentary gifts, and in the performance of visits of ceremony.

It

It may appear strange, that the *Sultan* should, for the gratificationof his spleen or his pride, have run the hazard of giving offence, by this proceeding, to a prince, with whom, if it was not his real interest, it was, at least, his apparent wish, to establish an intimate political connection. But Tippoo was not accustomed to look deeply into any subject; he was content to view things superficially: and hence it is probable, that it never occurred to him, that there was any danger of the disparaging style of the letter being detected in France; and that, even if any exception had been made to it, he would not have found it difficult to satisfy his royal correspondent, that no slight, or disrespect, to him, had been intended. In the meanwhile, his importance would be magnified in the eyes of those, among his own subjects, who should be admitted to a knowledge of the letter in question.

Judging by the context of the fourth paragraph, and especially by the words, " this circumstance has occasioned me the utmost surprize," it might almost be inferred, that the proposal of the French King, to reimburse Tippoo for the advances which the latter had made, for the use of the French forces, during the second war in the *Carnatic*, proved offensive to the *Sultan*, and that the payment, thus honourably tendered, was actually declined. What the *fact* was, I do not possess the means of ascertaining, for none of the documents found at *Seringapatam* (at least to my knowledge) throw any light upon the subject. I incline to believe, however, that the offer of the French government to liquidate its debt was not accepted, and that the *Sultan* was led to the adoption of this liberal proceeding, by the hope that it might conduce, with other motives, to make the French monarch consent the more readily to the renewal of hostilities against the English in *India*; an object which, as is abundantly shown by the foregoing letter, the writer had very much at heart at this time. His wishes on the subject were, no doubt, more fully stated through Ghûlâm Âli Khân and the other embassadors, dispatched to *France* by the way of *Constantinople*, as well as by those whom he sent thither by sea, subsequently to the date of the present letter; towards the close of which he intimates his having the latter deputation in contemplation. Fortunately, perhaps, for the British interests in *India*, these invitations to a new effort for their destruction arrived in *France*, when that nation was no longer able, however willing it might have been, to enter into the *Sultan's* views.

It

It must be acknowledged, that the *Sultan* complains, in this letter, of his desertion by the French, in the year 1783, in terms sufficiently moderate. He, however, indulges his natural resentment, on the occasion, more freely in his Memoirs; where, in his account of the siege of *Mangalore*, he thus expresses himself on the subject:

"Carrying on a mine by a double shaft to the foot of the wall, I only waited "the proper moment for springing it. I had also erected a battery opposite to "the gate, and on the edge of the ditch, in so elevated a situation, that not being "able to stand the fire of musquetry and cannon, which was kept up from it, not "a single Nazarene dared to appear on the walls or bastions of the fort. Thus "circumstanced, the Nazarenes demanded a capitulation, and were disputing "respecting the article of delivering up their arms, when letters reached me from "*Cuddalore*, written by the worthless commander(18) of the French, and by Meer "Moaayenûddeen, whom I had left at the head of a division of my army to assist "the aforesaid worthless commander. These dispatches purported, 'that in a single "'[or in the only] action(19) which had taken place between the French and English "'before the fort of *Cuddalore*, the former, to the amount of five thousand men, "'had been defeated, with the loss of fifty guns; in consequence of which they "'had been compelled to flee, and shut themselves up within the fort: that the "'army of the *Sircar*, though placed at the disposal of the French for their "'assistance, had not been required to join them upon this occasion, but were "'left *standing*(20) four or five *coss* in the rear of the English: that the second "'day following this defeat, the English had sent into the fort of *Cuddalore* a "'letter of peace(21) from the French *Râjah:* that Bussy, the worthless comman-"'der of the French, who was very old (being eighty or ninety years of age), "'and

(18) Original ناسردار "no-commander."

(19) Original یک بار بر قلعه مذکور جنگ واقع شد

(20) Original بر پچھاڑي انگریز ایستاده کرده بود where پچھاڑي is a Hindivy word signifying "the rear."

(21) Original خط صلح Probably orders for the cessation of hostilities, and a copy of the treaty of peace between the two nations in Europe.

" 'and being in his dotage, had lost his wits (at least, two-thirds of them),[22] " 'immediately at sight of his *Rajah's* letter of peace complied with its contents: " 'and that, finally, the two *accursed* ones had discontinued hostilities, and " 'concluded an accommodation.'

" These advices were accompanied by an order from the worthless French com- " mander to Cossigny,[23] who was, at this time, at the head of three hundred " French *Fringies*, serving immediately with myself, directing him and his party " to leave me, and repair to [*Cuddalore*]. At the same time, several Nazarenes, " who had served during twenty years with the *Usud-Ilhye* army, quitting me " without any notice, at the instigation [or hint] of the accursed and worthless " commander, set out with the rest. It was to no purpose that I remonstrated on " the occasion with Cossigny, and the faithless set so long in the employ of the " *Sircar*. Nay, they were ripe for sedition [or treachery].[24] No doubt, there " would have been but little difficulty in putting Cossigny and his companions to " death; but, inasmuch as they had eaten [my] salt, I did not think proper to " act by them[25] in that manner.

" Two days after this, the aforesaid Nazarenes, procuring passports from the " English, and supplying themselves with some few necessaries, set out from " *Kúridl* [*Mangalore*] for *Mahe*, a sea-port belonging to the French, which they " reached in five or six days. They left behind them in their camp about a " hundred sick, whom I furnished with provisions, and embarked on a ship, which " conveyed them to the place of those accursed ones *(i. e. Mahe)*."

The *Sultan* then proceeds to state, that disregarding the ungrateful and perfidious conduct of the French, he determined to add to the obligations they already owed him, by consenting, at the instance of their *worthless* commander, Bussy,

(22) The perplexity of the original, in this place, is such, as to make it very difficult, if not impossible, to give a close translation of it. The passage runs thus بهوسي نام ناسرنار فرانسیس که بسیار پیر وهشتاد نود سال بود از ممر خرافت عتل وهوش باخته بود در حقیقت دوحصه از شکست عقل وهوش راکم کرده بود

(23) So I read the name given in the manuscript.

(24) Original بلکه مستعد حرام نمکي شدند

(25) This passage is likewise obscure in the original. I suspect the text to be corrupted.

Bussy, to make peace with the English: and that, in consequence hereof, he discontinued the war in the *Carnatic*, and relinquished his design upon *Mangalore*, at the moment that he was about to reduce the place; contrary to the advice of his *Sirdars*, who strongly urged him [to prosecute the siege and] to put the garrison to the sword.

The circumstance of the *Sultan's* sending a double-barrelled gun in a present to Louis XVI is worthy of notice; because it strongly marks his desire to impress the French monarch with a high opinion of the military establishments and resources of his country.

This letter, it will be observed, places, beyond all doubt, the fact of the ostensible mission of Ghûlâm Ali Khân to *Constantinople* having been actually destined for the court of *France*: and it may hence be safely inferred, that the preceding deputation of Othman Khân to the *Sublime Porte* was, in like manner, originally intended to proceed to *Paris*, whatever was the reason of that object's being afterwards relinquished. The same Othman Khân made one of the subsequent embassy announced in the present letter, and finally sent to *France*, in 1787

LETTER CCCXXXVII.

To Monsieur Cossigny, *Governor of Pondicherry; dated* 14*th* Hashimy.(1) (15*th August*.)

We have received the letter you sent us by Pierre Monneron, requesting that we would cause an account to be drawn up, and delivered to him, of the advances made by us, whether of money or general supplies,(2) to Monsieur du Chemin, Monsieur Suffrein, and Monsieur Bussy, in order that you might, in pursuance of your *Râjah's* commands, discharge the amount.

We

(1) If this letter is not misdated, it is here inserted out of its place: but, however this may be, I have thought it right that it should immediately follow the one addressed to the King of France, on account of their mutual connection.

(2) Original جنس

We have long[3] entertained the most cordial regard for the *Râjah* of the French, whose honor we have always considered as our own. Accordingly, during a period of five years, we expended *crores* of *rupees*,[4] and lost *lacks*[5] of men; proposing, by these sacrifices and this labor, nothing else but the increase of our mutual friendship and renown. God pleasing, we will, hereafter [or still], make the most strenuous efforts for the same purposes.

The five hundred musquets, which you sent us by the way of *Nuzr*,[6] are arrived; and, in consideration of our friendship for the *Râjah* of the French, and of your good will[7] towards us, they are accepted.

Some time since we dispatched Ghûlâm Ali Khân, Lûtf Ali Khân, and others of our principal officers, (charged with several rarities, and an elephant with a silver canopy) to the French *Râjah*. They will proceed, by the route of *Juddah*,[8] to *Constantinople*, and from the latter place to *France*. We are about to send another deputation, consisting of certain persons of rank, and also charged with presents. These embassadors will, in the first instance, proceed to *Pondicherry*, from whence it is our request that you will send them by sea to *France*, accompanied by Pierre Monneron.

3 C Agreeably

(3) Original ازقديم الايام "from old times," or "of yore."

(4) A *crore* is a hundred lacks, or ten millions.

(5) A *lack* is a hundred thousand.

(6) If Monsieur Cossigny applied the term *nuzr* to his present, he forgot what he owed to the dignity of his station: but it is very possible that the French governor may not have so called it, though the *Sultan* has done so. If the expression escaped notice, a point would be gained: if complained of, it would not be difficult to offer some plausible excuse for it.

(7) Original خيرخواهي "well-wishing." This expression is, however, usually employed to denote the sentiment of good will entertained by an inferior towards a superior, and is equivalent to attachment, devotion, &c.

(8) This is, I suspect, an error of the manuscript, since the embassy proceeded by *Muscat* and *Bussorah*, and not by *Juddah*.

Agreeably to the representation of the above named [*i. e.* Monsieur Monneron] we have written and enclose an order to the *Taalúkdár* of *Calicut*, commanding that no molestation be given to the villages depending on *Mahé*. We have likewise instructed the *Taalúkdár* of *Selim* to attend strictly to such passports, written in the French and *Arwi* languages, and having your signature to them, as you may grant. These passports, besides the names of the merchants receiving them, must specify the number of the bullocks [laden]. Let your passports be regularly made out in the foregoing manner.

Certain secret particulars, of a nature conducive to the interests of the French *Rájah*, have been stated to Pierre Monneron, who will communicate them to you. A dress and a horse (9) have been sent to you, in token of our friendship.

OBSERVATIONS.

Of Pierre Monneron, I am unable to give any other account, than that he was a French merchant, employed either by the Governor of the *Isle of France*, or by the Governor of *Pondicherry*, in the transactions which took place, about this time, between Tippoo and the French nation. He appears, on the present occasion, to have had a personal interview with the *Sultan*.

Notwithstanding the proposed embassy by sea is thus early announced, it did not actually proceed from *Pondicherry*, according to Major Stewart, till the month of July in the following year (1787); that is to say, about eleven months after the date of the present letter.

(9) Before the word خلعت "dress," in the original, a blank occurs, preceded by the word یک *(yuk)* or one, which shews that the present consisted of something else besides the horse and dress.

LETTER CCCXXXVIII.

To the D*ároghas of the* J*insy* (probably Shumsûddeen Khân and Ghûlâm Hyder); *dated from* H*emsâgur*,(1) *6th* H*áshimy*. (*7th August.*)

Directing them to dispatch ten copies of the *Múfurrihúlkúloob*. Five of them containing the work at large,(2) and to have silver locks [or hasps]: the other five to be abridgements,(3) without silver locks [or hasps].(4)

OBSERVATIONS.

The book here mentioned is, according to Major Stewart (Catalogue of Tippoo Sultan's library) a collection of fables, in imitation of *Pilpay's*. It may be inferred, from the *Sultan's* sending for so many copies of this book, that they were designed as presents. If I understand the original rightly, there must be two editions of the work in question: one containing the fables at large, or complete; the other an abridgement.

3 C 2

(1) I have here given the reading which seems most countenanced by the manuscript, as the true name of this place is rather doubtful. Our maps of this part of *Mysore* are nearly a blank; which, joined to the meagre information on the subject afforded, whether by the correspondence, or the *Sultan's* own Memoirs, makes it impossible to trace with accuracy the course of his present march. This, therefore, I have not attempted to do.

(2) Original مفصلي "at length, at large, in full."

(3) Original مُجملي "in abstract, an abridgement."

(4) Original قفل نقروي where قفل probably means a *hasp* rather than a *lock*, in its usual sense.

LETTER CCCXXXIX.

To Bûrhânûddeen ; *dated* 10*th* Hâshimy. (11*th August.*)

Our special retinue is arrived at[1] *Kurknâth,* and we shall presently[2] cross the *Tungbuddra.* Send some men to procure intelligence[3] of the enemy's army; and communicate, occasionally, to the Presence, such accounts as you may receive.

LETTER CCCXL.

To Shâh Abdûllah Sâheb ; *same Date.* (11*th August.*)

Versed in theology and in the sciences, the peace of Almighty God be with you!

Our special retinue happening, at this time, to come into the vicinity of *Kurknâth,* we have dispatched Abubekr Khân, with a *Dooly,*[1*] for [the conveyance of] that [person] conversant in the sciences, who must afford us the pleasure of an interview.

OBSERVATIONS.

My information does not enable me to state, whether or not there is any *Durgâh,* or shrine, of particular sanctity, within the neighbourhood of *Kurknâth*: but it is not improbable that there is, and that Shâh Abdullâh Sâheb was the presiding priest of it. But whatever his office might be, it may be inferred, from the circumstance of the *Sultan's* sending a *Dooly,* instead of a *Palankeen,* for him, that he did not hold the first rank among the order of the religious.

(1) Original بر كركناته جلوه افروز شده است "has shed splendor on *Kurknâth.*"

(2) Original متعاقب "hereafter, following."

(3) Original باطني "private or secret information." Literally, "the interior, or inside:" hence, figuratively, "accounts of what passes within" any place, person, &c.

(1*) A *dooly* is a conveyance carried in the same manner as a *palankeen,* but of a meaner and different construction.

LETTER CCCXLI.

To EHSÂNÛLLAH KHÂN; *dated from* KURKNÂTH, *12th* HÂSHIMY. (*13th August.*)

REDUCE the monthly wages [or pay] of Shaikh Ali; take back the bounty[1] of a hundred *pagodas* [advanced to him]; and giving the same to [or distributing it among] those who shall raise men, fill up [by this means] the vacancies in your corps.

LETTER CCCXLII.

To BUDRÛZ ZUMÂN KHÂN; *same Date.* (*13th August.*)

YOU write, "that Moosa Khân, *Risâladâr* of *Jyshe*, and Abdûl "Ruheem, *Kilaadâr* of *Soândeh*, who were dispatched, for the purpose "of chastising the insurgents[1*] of *Soopah*, had seized upon a place in "the possession of the latter, who had [thereupon] taken to flight."

It is known. Ten years ago, from ten to fifteen thousand men were hung upon the trees of that district; since which time the aforesaid trees have been waiting for [or been in expectation of] more men. You must [therefore] hang upon trees all such of the inhabitants of that district, as have taken a lead in [or been at the bottom of] these rebellious proceedings.

OBSERVATIONS.

The dreadful executions, here spoken of with so much levity by the *Sultan*, must refer to the time of his father, in the year 1776: but if the latter was actually

(1) Original مساعده "assistance, aid." Shaikh Ali had probably failed in his engagements to raise recruits.

(1*) Original مشروران I take this to be an irregular plural of شرير "a wicked or mis-"chievous person."

actually guilty of the cruelty indirectly imputed to him by his son, it is more than any of his biographers (at least to my knowledge) have recorded of him. It must, however, be allowed, that it would not be easy to assign any satisfactory reason for Tippoo's purposely exaggerating the fact in question.

LETTER CCCXLIII.

To the SHÂNOOR WÂLEH (*i. e.* ABDÛL HUKEEM KHÂN); *dated* 14*th* HÂSHIMY. (15*th August.*)

YOUR letter, conveying the account of your welfare, and containing certain particulars, together with two other papers [which accompanied it], has adorned the face of arrival, and afforded me delight.

Forasmuch as the requisites[1] [or reciprocal duties] of union and concord are firmly established between us, how is it possible that our mutual regard should give way to estrangement and misunderstanding? That friend must, in all respects, keep his mind at perfect ease: nor imagine that, in any shape whatsover, the least diminution can take place in our friendship. With the blessing of God, your friend will presently arrive in that quarter, and apply himself to the chastisement of the enemy.[2]

OBSERVATIONS.

This is, perhaps, the most civil of all the letters addressed to the Patan chieftain by the *Sultan*; who, however, as there is reason to believe, was at this very time firmly resolved upon his destruction.

(1) Original لوازم

(2) Original اشقيا "miserable or wretched men." A term commonly applied to enemies.

LETTER CCCXLIV.

To the Bukhshy *of the* Ehshâm *at* Chittledoorg; *dated* 13*th* Hâshimy. (14*th August.*)

You must send for the families of all the *Aumils*, who are natives[1] of the *Payen-Ghaut*, and, together with the *Aumils* themselves, keep them at *Chittledoorg*.

LETTER CCCXLV.

To Meer Futah Ali, Taalûkdâr *of* Chik *(or little)* Balapoor; *dated* 17*th* Hâshimy. (18*th August.*)

There are heavy balances [of revenue] due from the country [*i. e.* from your district]. These must be realised; and, with the produce, you must procure provisions for the *Ahmedies* from some other district.[1*] In case you should have no assets [for the purpose], apply to Râjah Râm Chundur, who will give an assignment to the amount he may judge proper.

LETTER CCCXLVI.

To Meer Jaafur Wuffa Khâny; *dated* 14*th* Hâshimy. (15*th August.*)

The account of Gunaish Bhyroo's arrival in hell[1**] has been received. We [only] require the blessing of God to attend us, in order to the [speedy]

(1) Original سکنه "inhabitants," *i. e.* "who were formerly, or *originally*, inhabitants "of the *Carnatic*." This order was probably occasioned by some distrust recently conceived by the *Sultan* of this class of his subjects.

(1*) There was, probably, a scarcity, at this time, of the necessary provisions in *Little Balapoor*. This letter affords one, among numerous proofs, of the constant attention of the *Sultan* to the interests of this favourite corps.

(1**) Original داخل جهنم شد This is a common mode of expression with Mahommedans in announcing the death of an enemy, and particularly of an unbeliever.

[speedy] removal of whatever superfluous hairs are remaining.(2) Many such are [always] coming, and many going. The favour of God constitutes our aid and support.

OBSERVATIONS.

I can give no account of the Gunaish Bhyroo, whose death is here so exultingly noticed by the *Sultan*. He may either have been an insurgent *Polygar* or a Mahrattah commander. If the official designation of Meer Jaafur had been given, it might have thrown some light on this point. The addition of *Wuffa Khâny*, which follows the proper name of this person, is, if I am not mistaken, an appellation, by which a particular tribe, or family, of Moghul descent, was distinguished.

LETTER CCCXLVII.

To Bûrhânûddeen; *dated* 18*th* Hâshimy. (19*th August*.)

You must not be in a hurry to give battle; but if the enemy should advance upon your army, you must chastise them effectually.(1) Our special retinue will shortly cross the *Tungbuddra*, and arrive at that place [*i. e.* will join you]. Abdûl Ahmed Khân,(2*) together with his family, must be taken into custody, and dispatched to *Nugr*.

(2) I am rather doubtful, whether I have succeeded in giving the exact sense of the original in this place. The passage runs thus: فضل الهي شامل حال ميبايد چندين پشم ها که زياده ميشوند انرا ميبرند وچندين ميايند و چندين ميروند فضل حق مدد و معاون ما است *Pushm* strictly means the *hair*, or *wool, of animals*; also *nap* or *down*. The word is clearly applied in contempt.

(1) Original واقعي " truly, really, signally, soundly."

(2*) I suspect that this is the same person elsewhere called Abdul Sumud Khân, and that one of the sons of Abdûl Hakeem Khân is meant.

LETTER CCCXLVIII.

To Syed Ghuffâr; *same Date.* (19*th August.*)

The chastisement of the enemy's cavalry is approved. We, too, shall shortly cross the *Tungbuddra*, and arrive [or join you]. What is the amount of the enemy's forces? Mere hearsay is not entitled to credit.(1) You must view them with your own eyes, and report what you see, without addition or diminution. We some time ago wrote to Bûrhânûd-deen, directing the punishment of the *Jowkdar* [or captain] of the *Jyshe*.

OBSERVATIONS.

The task here assigned to Syed Ghuffâr would appear to have been no easy one. Indeed it is inconceivable, how he could execute it with the accuracy required. The difficuly would, no doubt, have been less, if he had had to estimate, by inspection, the amount of an European army, the regular array of which is favorable to such computations. But, even supposing an army, constituted like that of the Mahrattahs, to be viewed, under every possible advantage, by a distant observer, such as Syed Ghuffâr must necessarily have been, it would hardly be in his power to determine its numbers with any degree of exactness. A judgment formed, in the manner prescribed by the *Sultan*, would seem to be, at least, as liable to error, as one founded on the "hearsay intelligence" alluded to by him; and by which he probably meant the reports of neighbouring villagers, of casual travellers, and of the itinerant *Fakeers* or *Jogies*, who are usually permitted to pass unmolested from one army to another.(2)

Here follows in the manuscript a letter addressed to the *Dároghas* of the *Tosheh-khâneh*, containing directions for the composition of a particular dentifrice, with

3 D which

(1) Original مسموعي اعتبار ندارد

(2) It is owing to the immunity enjoyed by the *Fakeers* and *Jogies*, in this respect, that spies most commonly assume those characters.

which the *Mahls* or *Harams* at *Seringapatam* and *Bangalore* were to be supplied, for the use of the ladies occupying them. I am prevented from translating this curious document, by my inability to give the names of the ingredients specified, in English. Some of the composition is ordered to be sent to the *Sultan*.

LETTER CCCXLIX.

To BÛRHÂNÛDDEEN; *dated* 23*d* *HÁSHIMY*.[1] (*24th August.*)

By the Divine favour, the passage of the *Tungbuddra* is effected; and in two or three days, please the Almighty, we shall summon you and your army to the Presence. Proceeding by the road of *Nushapoor*,[2] and arriving in the vicinity of your camp, we shall send for you. If, in the meanwhile, any other force besides *Holkar's* [as that under Hurry Pundit, &c.] should make its appearance in any considerable numbers, with a view to attacking you, you must withdraw three or four *coss*, and take up a position among the woods: but if a superior force should not advance against you, and Holkar's only should present itself, you must remain where you are; and procuring constant intelligence of the enemy's army, keep on the alert, and write regularly [of what passes] to the Presence.

OBSERVATIONS.

Another letter appears, dated 29th *Hâshimy* (30th August) directed to "Bûr-"hânûddeen, Budr ûl Âman Khân,[3] and the *Sipahdârs*," announcing, in like manner

(1) This letter is dated from a place written نذي which may be variously read. It is probably situated on the west bank of the *Tungbuddra*, over which river the *Sultan* would seem to have passed about this time: perhaps this very day.

(2) Name uncertain.

(3) This is not the only place in which this name (so like that of Budrûz Zumân) occurs: yet I am not without a suspicion that it is an error of the transcriber for Budrûz Zumân.

manner as the preceding one, the passage of the *Tungbuddra*; so that either there is some mistake in the dates, or this operation must have occupied the *Sultan* during the period between the 23d and 29th of *Hâshimy*: in which case the letter of the 23d may be supposed to have been written on the passage of the van of the army, and that of the 29th when the whole of the army had crossed the river. In the latter dispatch the *Sultan* says, "We shall proceed from hence to-morrow or the "next day, and soon arrive with you." And yet he would appear, by another letter, to have been still encamped on the banks of the *Tungbuddra* as late as the 7th of *Wâsaaey* (or 6th of September). Possibly, the line of his march, after crossing the river, might have been for some days in the direction of its course.

Tippoo, in his Memoirs, plumed himself considerably on the military operation in question, and, apparently, not without reason; since besides being undertaken at a time when the river was at its greatest height, it was performed, according to his account, in the face of the main body of the enemy's army, which, nevertheless, would not seem to have offered any opposition to this bold movement. The following is the manner in which the *Sultan* states this occurrence:

"Marching from thence [*i. e. Adoni*] I arrived on the bank of the *Tungbuddra*. "It was now the rainy season, and the river was at a great[(4)] height. I sent for "boats from the country of *Nugr*, and consulted with the commanders of the "*Usud-Ilhye* army on the subject of crossing [the river], when all of them stated "it to be their opinion, 'that the attempt was on no account advisable, inasmuch "'as Hurry Pundit Phurkia, and the commanders of the army of Nizâm Ali "'Khân, to the amount of a hundred thousand horse, besides numberless foot "'forces, were posted on the opposite side, for the purpose of preventing our "'passage.' To this they added, 'that the river was at its greatest height; that "'the rains were extremely violent; and that, as the army of the *Sircar* would "'be obliged to cross in small bodies at a time, [it was to be feared that] the "'enemy, apprized of this circumstance, would bring a heavy [*i. e.* superior] "'force against [the divisions as they crossed].'

3 D 2 "Disregarding

(4) Original تغیانی which, I believe, strictly implies, that state of a river in which its banks are overflowed. The expression is figurative, the word تغیان meaning "passing "bounds."

" Disregarding[5] these opinions, and collecting all the boats together, I embarked, early in the morning of the second day [after my arrival on the banks of the *Tungbuddra*], with two *Kushoons*, with which I crossed the river, and took post in a favourable situation, where I caused the standards of the army to be erected. By evening, the passage of all the remaining *Kushoons*, together with their guns and stores, was accomplished. On the following day, the boats being distributed among the cavalry, the rest of the army began to cross, and in three or four days the whole were over. Hereafter, let whosoever shall happen to be similarly circumstanced,[6] proceed in the same manner, *viz.* by first crossing the infantry in force, and afterwards the cavalry and others.

" Hurry Pundit Phurkia, and the other commanders [of the enemy], on hearing of the passage of our army, retired with their forces to the distance of four *coss*, and encamped on the skirts of the [adjacent] hills and woods; from whence, at the end of three or four days, they came and drew up before our army, with their guns and other appurtenances of war, [apparently] with the intention of offering us battle. Whereupon, giving orders to the eight *Kushoons* that were with me to hold themselves in readiness [for action], I advanced, in person, with a *Kushoon* of *Usud-Ilhyes* and another of *Jyshe*, towards the infidel forces: before which movement, however, a picquet, which had been pushed on in front, was obliged, by superior numbers of the enemy, to fall back. Just at this moment I arrived, and opened a fire upon the enemy from some guns and rockets, which soon made them flee in disorder.[7] After an interval of a day, the infidels once more advanced with the intention of attacking us: when the *Usud-Ilhye* army met them as before,[8] and they, according to " their

(5) Original این سخنان را بگوش نیاورده " not giving ear to these words."

(6) This advice is to be understood as addressed to the *Sultan's* own family, for whose exclusive benefit these Memoirs would appear to have been written.

(7) Original روبفرار مثل بنات النعش نمودند " turned their face to flight, like the constellation of the bear," *i. e.* scattered like the stars composing that constellation.

(8) Original بدستور " according to custom."

" their usual practice, turned their backs, and withdrew in confusion to their " camp.(9)

" On the following day, about five o'clock in the afternoon, making ready three " *Kushoons*, and placing them under the command of Mâh Mirzâ Khân, I " directed a night assault to be made [on the enemy], and proceeded myself " with this detachment halfway towards their camp. Here I halted, keeping " with me [only] a few men and a [single] gun, for the purpose of making " signals. The *Sircar's* troops [*i. e.* the detachment under Mâh Mirzâ Khân] " advanced; but on approaching the enemy's army became alarmed,(10) and " stopping short, opened a fire from their guns. I concluded, from the circum- " stance of my troops keeping up this cannonade, that they did not mean(11) to " advance farther [to the attack of the enemy], and therefore I fired the gun, as a " signal for them to rejoin me, which they accordingly doing, I returned with " them to our camp, which we reached the following morning.

" The next day, in order to strengthen the hearts(12) of my people, I distributed " presents of horses, money, gold and silver wrist-rings, &c. to the value of near a " *lack* of *rupees*, among the officers and men of the three *Kushoons*, according to " their respective merits.

" The following day the Mahrattah army, with a train of artillery, came and " presented itself in order of battle before the *Usud Ilhye* tygers, on whom they " commenced

(9) Original تکثیف فرمودند *i. e.* withdrew "in a mass, or pell-mell;" where, by the bye, the verb فرمودند seems improperly used, since, if I am not mistaken, it should never be employed in any but a good or favourable sense. It is possible, however, that as the *Sultan* is here speaking contemptuously of the Mahrattahs, the word may be used ironically, and perhaps as a jingling antithesis to the common expression of تشریف فرمودند.

(10) Original فوج سرکار نزدیکي لشکر مخالفان رفته اندیشه فوج آنها نمودند

(11) Original پنداشتم که آنها قصد سبقت ندارند

(12) Original جراکه دل مردم قوي کردد If I understand these three several passages rightly, they plainly denote some backwardness on the part of the *Sultan's* troops to attack the Mahrattah camp: and yet it seems somewhat strange, that he should have taken such an occasion to *reward* his troops. This apparent inconsistency makes me very doubtful, if not of the correctness of the manuscript, at least of the accuracy of my interpretation.

"commenced a distant fire from two or three guns. The men of our victorious "army hereupon placing themselves in a state of preparation, received the enemy, "with the same kind of cry [or noise] that is employed to frighten [or drive "away] hogs and the like; upon hearing of which, the enemy returned shame- "fully by the same road they had come. After remaining another day in their "burial place,(13) they marched the ensuing morning, like so many ill-omened "owls, and took up a position at the distance of eight or ten *coss* from their "former camp."

The *Sultan* next proceeds to relate his further operations against the enemy, in the same barbarous and perplexed style, which distinguishes the narrative from whence the preceding extract has been made. Nothing, however, of any moment, or indeed very intelligible, appears, till the period of his arrival at *Shânoor*; when he gives an account of the general engagement which was fought in the neighbourhood of that city, and of which I will, in its proper place, present the reader with a translation.

LETTER CCCL.

To Budrûz Zumân Khân; *dated* 29*th* Hâshimy. (30*th August.*)

The list of Soandeh and other captives has been received. The aforesaid captives must be dispatched to *Nugr*, and [there be] incorporated with the *Usud Ilhyes*; to such of whom as are without wives, the females among the prisoners are to be given in marriage.

Entrenching yourself strongly,(1) you will remain [at all times] in readiness to co-operate with Bûrhânûddeen in the chastisement of the enemy.

(13) Original مدفون گاه by which metaphor the *Sultan* means to intimate, that the camp of the enemy was to be considered, owing to their ill-fortune, as the place of interment.

(1) Original بتریہا مستحکم تیار کرده where I conceive the word "batteries" (adopted from the English) to mean "entrenchments."

LETTER CCCLI.

To the KILAADÂR *of* PUTN *(i. e.* SERINGAPATAM*) ; same Date. (30th August.)*

ON the subject of getting four intelligent children [1] of the *Usud Ilhye* band [or body] instructed in the encomiastic *Raikhtehs* [or odes], otherwise called *Bhât*. Desiring copies of the collection of the said odes to be made from the set transmitted with the present letter, and delivered to them. Another copy to be given to Uzeemûddeen, the *Taalûkdâr* [or superintendant] of the dancers [2] there [*i. e.* at *Seringapatam*], in order that the latter may teach the same to the said dancers.

OBSERVATIONS.

Of the encomiastic odes here spoken of, I think I am in possession of a copy; for which I am indebted, as for many other interesting communications, to the kindness of my friend, Lieutenant Colonel Ogg. With the exception of the concluding distich of each ode, which is in Persian, the rest of the composition is in the *Hindivy* dialect, which is, indeed, denoted by the term *raikhteh*. These odes are ninety-six in number; and consist, on the one hand, of the most fulsome and hyperbolical praises of the *Sultan*, and on the other, of disparaging allusions to the English, the Mahrattahs, and the Nizâm. The style is extremely unpolished; and though I will not pretend to have given them more than a superficial and cursory perusal, or to understand perfectly all that I have read, I have no hesitation in affirming, that they are utterly destitute of every kind of poetical merit.

Of these curious compositions, which were set to music, and sung, or recited, at appointed seasons and hours of the day, the following extracts may suffice as a specimen.

"When

(1*) Original چهار طفل اسد الهي باهوش

(2) Original رقاصان, under this general term was included singers as well as dancers.

* * * * * *

" When the *Rústum*-hearted king rushed forward [or charged] on the *Rukhsh*[3]
" of his anger, then did the hearts of the lions of Europe [*i. e.* the English] quake
" with dread.

" The flash of his sabre struck the army of Bailey like lightning: it caused
" Munro to shed tears, resembling the drops distilled from spring clouds.[4]

" On Lang's heart was fixed a stain, like that of the tulip: Coote was made,
" by this calamity, to lament like a hyacinth."[5]

There follows here an allusion to General Matthews, who is distinctly named, the nature of which I do not comprehend. Bussy and Lally are likewise mentioned; but I am too doubtful, regarding the sense of the passage in which they are introduced, to offer a translation of it.

* * * * * * *

" When the Mahrattahs behold this army of our King, the dread thereof
" causes them to flee like deer.

" The *Fringy* [*i. e.* the European] and Nizâm ûl Mûlk pass night and day
" together trembling with fear of our King.

* * * * * * *

" The kingdom flourishes, and the army increases daily, through thy muni-
" ficence and justice.

* * * * * * *

" The *Hujjâm's*[6] army flees through dread of thee, as the hunter does when
" he beholds the lion.

" The

(3) *Rukhsh* was the name of the horse of the Persian hero, or champion, *Rústum*.

(4) I am not certain that I have rightly understood the first hemistich of this verse. The ابرنیسان *i. e.* April or spring clouds, are fabled by the Persian poets to distil a vapour, which is converted into pearls on alighting in the oyster, so that the expression might be rendered " pearly drops or tears."

(5) I am equally doubtful whether I have here correctly rendered the original, which, indeed, is not perfectly legible in this place. Thus the word, which I read سنبل may be meant for something else. The stain of the tulip refers to the black spots on its inside.

(6) Though the *Nizám* is distinguished by his title in the preceding verse, that was only the because it happened to suit the measure. He is generally, as in this place, called *Hujjâm* (barber) and *Hujjâm Nulli*, being a play on his proper name, Nizâm Ali.

" The Nazarenes, on contemplating from the sea shore the sagacity of our king, " forget their own schemes and counsels [*i. e.* despair of their success].

* * * * * *

" When mankind behold the liberality and munificence of our king they " exclaim with one accord, " Hâtim was an absolute miser [7] compared to him."

" Socrates, Hippocrates, all the sages of the earth, appear before him like to " the most ignorant children.

" Mars dwindles before the valor of our king to a mere infant: Sâm, Nureemân, " and Rûstum,[8] are of no account."

* * * * * *

But, perhaps, none of the flights, with which this extraordinary performance abounds, are equal in extravagance to the following one, with which I will close these extracts.

" Owing to the justice of this king, the deer of the forest make their pillow of " the lion and the tiger, and their mattress of the leopard and the panther."

LETTER CCCLII.

To BÛRHÂNÛDDEEN; *dated 4th WÁSAAEY. (3d September.)*

YOUR humble address has passed under our view, and the account [therein given] of the enemy's force, and of the issue of two months' pay to the *Jyshe* troops stationed [in garrison] at *Nergúnd*, from the produce of the collections of that place, is understood.[1]

You write, also, " that in addition to the month's pay already issued " to the above mentioned troops, you have since [2] sent orders to the

3 E " *Kilaadár*

(7) Hâtim was an Arabian Prince, celebrated in story for his munificent spirit.

(8) All of them celebrated champions of ancient *Persia*.

(1) Original ظاهر گشت "became visible, clear, manifest, known:" that is, the account or statement "became known," or "is understood;" for the verb گشت is postponed to the close of the sentence, agreeably to the established Persian idiom.

(2) Original حال "now, at this time."

" *Kilaadâr* of *Nergûnd* to give them another month's pay, and [at the " same time] have desired a small advance to be made to the *Ehshâm* " troops: but as the latter belong [properly] to *Nugr*, you suggest to " us, that Budrûz Zumân Khân should be directed to transmit the " pay of these people to them."

It is known. *Nugr* and *Nergûnd* are one and the same.(3) Let the troops of the *Ehshâm* be paid out of the collections made from the districts depending on *Nergûnd*, in the same manner as the *Jyshe* have been paid.

Our special retinue has passed the *Tungbuddra*, and will shortly shed lustre on that quarter.

LETTER CCCLIII.

To the same; dated 7th WÂSAAEY. (6th September.)

A PIECE of *Bubry* has been [or is herewith] sent for that light of our eyes. You must get a vest made of it for yourself.

N.B. A similar letter follows here, addressed to Meer Moaayenûddeen Khân.

OBSERVATIONS

The *Bubry* was a kind of printed cotton, of a particular pattern; consisting of a stripe, resembling in form, and sometimes in color, the stripe on the skin of a tyger, one of the names of which animal is *Bubr*. Tippoo Sultan is well known to have considered the tyger as emblematical of his own family or government: probably on account of its affinity to the lion, by which appellation the *Caliph* Ali has been distinguished. Indeed the tiger and lion are so often called in *India* by the same name, that it would have been quite uncertain which of the two animals

(3) Original حکم واحد است literally, " is one command." It is an idiomatical or figurative expression, answering to our phrase of " one and the same thing."

animals in question was meant by the *Sultan*, under the appellation of *Bubr*, if the distinctive mark of the *stripe* had not placed the matter out of doubt. This stripe, in short, may be said to have constituted the crest, or armorial bearing, of Tippoo; who caused it to be introduced into almost every article belonging to him. Hence it was found stamped on the binding of his books, engraved on his plate and his fire-arms, woven in his standards, &c. It even formed the water-mark of the paper manufactured for his use.

Orders for the fabrication and distribution of *Bubry* cloths appear in several of the letters forming the present collection. I believe it constituted the uniform dress of a considerable portion of the *Sultan's* regular troops.

LETTER CCCLIV.

To Ghous Mahommed Khân *and* Mahommed Akâ, *Dároghas of the Jinsy Tosheh-khâneh; same Date.* (*6th September.*)

It has come to the knowledge of the Presence, that the *Dároghas* and *Mútusuddies*, as well as Suddanund, and other servants of the jewel office, do not attend [there properly], in consequence whereof the business of one day is protracted to ten. Those [persons] must be strictly enjoined [or severely admonished]: nay, they must be scourged, and made to give [due] attendance, so that the jewellery article (1) [upon which they are employed] may be speedily finished.

LETTER CCCLV.

To Monsieur Cossigny; *dated 18th Wásaaey.* (*9th September.*)

We have heard, that a Mahrattah *Vakeel* has resided, for some time past, at that place [*i. e. Pondicherry*]. As this circumstance is not suitable

3 E 2

(1) Original رقوم plural of رقم which is applied to jewels and the like, in the same manner as نفر in the enumeration of *men*, راس in that of *cattle*, &c.

suitable to the friendship subsisting between the *Sircar* [*i. e.* us] and the *Rájah* of the French, we therefore write to desire, that the aforesaid [*Vakeel*] may be dismissed, and not allowed to remain [there any longer]. What more shall be written?

OBSERVATIONS.

The style of this letter must be admitted to be sufficiently arrogant and peremptory; and was, certainly, but ill calculated to conciliate the good-will of the French governor, however it might serve to impress others with a high notion of the power of the writer. Either the *Sultan* must have trusted greatly to M. Cossigny's ignorance of the Persian language, as well as of the respect due to his rank and station; or else so deep and inveterate must his dislike to Europeans or Christians of every denomination, whether friends or foes, have been, that he could not always abstain from letting it appear in his intercourse with them, even when it was palpably (as in the present case) his interest so to do. It may indeed be doubted, whether he hated the French less than the English: and however he might wish and hope to render the former subservient to his views against the latter, still he would never seem to have forgotten, that they were both Nazarenes, and enemies of the true faith; and, consequently, alike the just objects of his abhorrence and contempt.

I do not possess the means of ascertaining what degree of attention, if any, was paid by the French governor to the extraordinary demand contained in the foregoing letter.

LETTER CCCLVI.

To MÛLÂIM JUNG; *dated* 12*th* *WÂSAAEY*. (11*th September*.)

You have humbly stated, "that you have instructed five youths of the "*Usud-Ilhye* band [or corps] in the royal praises.(1) It is known and approved.

(1) Original ثناي شاهنشاهي These are most probably the odes mentioned in Letter CCCLI.

approved. Herewith is sent a copy of encomiastic odes, which you are likewise to teach to those five youths.

LETTER CCCLVII.

To BÛRHÂNÛDDEEN; *dated* 11*th* *WÂSAAEY*. (10*th September*.)

You write, "that you have determined to stop a month's pay, by way "of amercement, from those concerned in the late brawl[1] [or disturb-"ance] of the two *Kushoons* commanded by the *Sipahdâr*, Syed Hu-"meed, and the *Sipahdâr*, Syed Ghuffâr." You moreover state, "that "the *Jowkdâr* who excited the quarrel, and over whom a guard had "been placed, made his escape the second day after, being the day on "which you had the engagement with the enemy,[2] accompanied by his "guard, whom he had contrived to seduce."

It is known. Where are the women, the relatives, and brethren of the persons in question? Ascertain this point, and report accordingly to us. Take a muster also of the troops, muskets, and other stores, and specify distinctly, in a memorandum to be transmitted to the Presence, the number of muskets, of men, and of cartouch-boxes. You were, some time ago, directed, and we now write again to direct you, to transmit the aforesaid memorandum.

OBSERVATIONS.

Neither the cause, nor the nature, any more than the extent of the disturbance alluded to in this letter, is any where stated: but there is no reason to suppose, that

(1) Original قضيه

(2) No particulars of the engagement here alluded to appear.

that it was any thing more than a private dispute between some individuals of the two *Kushoons* in question, fomented by one of their officers. A mutiny of the troops would not have been expressed by the word *kuziah*.

But of whatever kind the disturbance was, the punishment of those concerned in it was not light; and a still more rigorous course was probably adopted in regard to the fugitives, whose offence it appears to have been the *Sultan's* intention to visit, in some way or other, upon their innocent families. In this instance, however, no particular injustice is imputable to him, since similar proceedings are but too usual with all the native governments of India.

It is not quite clear, whether or not the muster, or inspection, directed to be taken in the foregoing letter, had any reference to the disturbance mentioned in the same letter; but the following dispatch, to Budrûz Zumân Khân, makes it most probable that it was unconnected with that occurrence.

LETTER CCCLVIII.

To Budrûz Zumân Khân ; *same Date.* (10*th September.*)

We have received your humble address, wherein you solicit the favour of some muskets, for the use of the *Uskur* troops[(1)] [under your command]. That eminent person must remain vigilant and careful.[(2)]

We wrote some time ago, and we have now written again, to our beloved son,[(3)] Bûrhânûddeen, desiring him to transmit to us a return of muskets, cartouch-boxes, men, and stores, &c.[(4)] After receiving the aforesaid return, the muskets [you require] shall be granted you, from such

(1) *i. e.* the regular troops.

(2) Original باید که آن رفعت نشان بحزم و احتیاط باشند This seems to be meant reprovingly, as if he had said " look to the security of your post, and do not agitate other matters."

(3) Original برخوردار which has been already explained.

(4) This is the order in which each article occurs in the original

such place [*i. e.* store] as shall appear expedient.[5] At present there are no superfluous [or spare] muskets with the victorious army.

LETTER CCCLIX.

To Râjah Râm Chundur; *same Date.* (10*th September.*)

(Extract.)

Two *Urzdâshts* [or humble addresses] transmitted by you have passed under our view. You write, "that, agreeably to our directions, the "rations and monthly pay of the *Ahmedies* belonging to *Little Bala-* "*poor*, *Hûscotah*, and *Khân Khânhully*, are issued, at the computation "of thirty days [to the month]; but that having heard that Pitumber, "the *Aumil* of *Yoosûfâbâd*, had [lately] received orders to issue the pay "of the *Ahmedies* [depending on his jurisdiction] at the computation "of thirty-six days [to the month], you were, in consequence, doubt- "ful whether to issue the same [for the future] at the rate of thirty or "thirty-six days, and would act therein as we should command."

It is known. Do you act conformably with the directions which you have received. What business have you with [the orders given to] others?

OBSERVATIONS.

In regulating the monthly pay of servants and others in *India*, the length of the month is not necessarily determined, either by the lunar or solar reckoning. Indeed, it is very rarely that either domestics or military persons, in the country service, are paid at so favorable a rate. On the contrary, the month is sometimes arbitrarily

(5) Original ازجاي كه بنادیق دهانیدن است مرحمت خواهد شد literally, "from the place "where the muskets are, or may be, to be given, [thence] shall they be graciously be- "stowed." This is a very usual idiom of the Persian, the scope of which I have expressed as well as I could in the text, but without being satisfied that I have entirely succeeded.

arbitrarily made to consist of forty days, and very commonly of thirty-five. By this means the actual falls far short of the nominal pay; the difference, when forty days are assigned to the month, being no less than three months in the year. Thus a *Sepoy*, apparently rated at twelve *rupees* a month, would, in fact, receive only nine.

This practice, which does not obtain among the English in *India*, enables a master, when he wishes either to reduce or raise the pay of his dependants, to do so, without making any alteration in its established or nominal amount: and though there is, in truth, no delusion in the device, there is something in it that appears to gratify the vanity, both of the servant and of his employer; the importance of each being supposed to be increased, in a certain degree, by the ostensible amount of the regulated salary.

However officious or supererogatory the representation of Râjah Râm Chundur might have been, it hardly merited the sharp reproof which it received from his master; especially as its tendency was to effect a reduction of the public expence. But this is only one, among a variety of similar instances, of the excessive irritableness and austerity of the *Sultan's* disposition, which seems to have rendered him, at all times, more prone to censure than to commend his servants.

LETTER CCCLX.

To MAHOMMED IBRÂHEEM, *AUMIL of NÂGMUNGUL; same Date. (10th September.)*

YOU write, " that Poonia [or Pootia], the *Serishtedâr* of that place " [*i. e. Nâgmungul*] is an unfaithful person,(1) and that the *Ryots*, owing " to him [*i. e.* to his mal-practices], will [assuredly] turn their faces to " flight [or abandon the country]." It is known. Whatsoever you have to write [on this subject], let it be written to the *Dewân* of the mansion of sovereignty, *Putn.*

(1) Original نمک حرام literally, "unlawful or prohibited salt," *i. e.* not deserving the salt one has eaten: making a bad, or ungrateful, return for favours or protection granted. Hence, figuratively, "faithless, fraudulent, ungrateful," &c.

OBSERVATIONS.

It must not be inferred from this letter, that the affair to which it relates was intended by the writer to be referred to the *decision* of the *Dewân*. The *Sultan* was far from being in the habit of delegating his authority on such occasions: nor does he, in general, appear to have had any objections to being addressed directly on matters of business. On the contrary, he seems to have encouraged this practice, which was calculated to operate as a check upon his official servants. His object in the present instance was, probably, to obtain fuller information, preparatory to the enunciation of his pleasure on the subject.

It is not certain who was meant by the *Dewân* of *Seringapatam*; but I am inclined to think that the designation could apply only to Meer Sâdik.

LETTER CCCLXI.

To Bûrhânûddeen; *dated* 12*th* *Wâsaaey* (11*th September*.)

Your letter, containing an account of the victory obtained by our triumphant army, and of the flight of the enemy to the distance of a *Fursung*,(1) has passed under our view. You must, hereafter, whenever the enemy makes his appearance, and an opportunity offers, chastise him effectually, in the same manner that you have now defeated him. By the favor of God the Aider, the infidels here(2) shall also receive the due reward of their misdeeds.(3)

3 F

(1) The *Fursung* (or *Fursukh*, as it is also written) is usually considered equal to three *coss*.

(2) That is, those immediately opposed to the *Sultan* himself.

(3) Original بد كردار

LETTER CCCLXII.

To BÛDRUZ ZUMÂN KHÂN; *dated* 13*th WÂSAAEY.* (12*th September.*)

WE have received your three letters, together with those addressed to you by Ali Râjah(1) and the *Kâzy* of *Nugr*, and also the statement of the peculations of the *Kilaadâr* of *Bullaraedoorg*.(2) You write, "that the "aforesaid *Kilaadâr* is a cheat(3) and an oppressor;(4) and that, with "our permission,(5) you will appoint and send [thither] Kureem Khân, "who, agreeably to our orders, has [lately] joined you from *Lud-*"*dasheoo-ghurr*."

It is known. It is well.(6) Displace the aforesaid *Kilaadâr*; and, according to your proposal,(7) appoint and dispatch the above named [Kureem Khân] to [take charge of] the fort [in question.]

On the night(8) of the 13th of the month *Wâsaaey*, we detached two *Kushoons* [with orders] to make a night-attack upon the enemy. The detachment accordingly surprized the enemy,(9) poured such a discharge of cannon and musquetry among them, that the reprobate crew,(10) unable

(1) That is, the *Beeby* of *Cannanore*.

(2) Probably the *Bullalraedoorg* of Colonel Wilks's map.

(3) Original خاين "dishonest, fraudulent."

(4) Original متاذي from اذيت "vexation, oppression," &c.

(5) Original اگرحکم شود literally, "if order be:" *i. e.* "if it be ordered."

(6) Original بهتر است literally, "it is better," or "it is very well."

(7) Original معروضه خود "your own humble representation."

(8) By the night of the 13th is here meant the time between the preceding midnight and the morning of the 13th. *Shâm*, or evening, comprizes the time between sun-setting and midnight.

(9) Original برسرمقاهیررفته "going, or falling upon, the head of the enemy:" by which expression a sudden or unexpected attack is meant.

(10) Original فرقه خباله

unable to support [it], fell into the utmost disorder, and dispersed(11) with cropped ears and tails.(12) This is written for your information.

LETTER CCCLXIII.

To the Kázy of Bangalore; same Date. (*12th September.*)

Write out, and send to the Presence, a copy of the *Hûkm-námeh* [or instructions] with which you have been graciously furnished, the same being wanted, for the purpose of bestowing [*i. e.* transmitting] it to the *Kázy* of *Zuferábád*. Observe that the name of the *Kuchurry* of *Zuferábád* is to be inserted in the [first] line of the first page [of the copy], instead of the name of *Bangalore*, and that the name of the *Kázy* must be omitted.(1) For the rest, all that relates to fees, &c., and whatever else is written therein, must be copied *verbatim*,(2) and transmitted to us.

Let the copy of the *Hûkm-námeh* [herein-mentioned] be bound,(3) previously to its being dispatched to us.

N. B. There follows next a letter to Syed Peer, the *Kilaadár* of *Bangalore*, informing him of the orders sent to the *Kázy*, and desiring him to see that they were duly complied with. The document in question was, when ready, to be forwarded to the Presence by him (Syed Peer.)

3 F 2

(11) Original تاربتارگردیده

(12) Original دم علم وگوش قلم شده رفتند which I am far from pretending to understand perfectly. The word علم in particular, standing, as it does, in construction with دم involving the passage in an obscurity that I am unable to dispel.

(1) *i. e.* "a blank must be left for it."

(2) Original بعینہ "as it is," or "just as it is."

(3) Original مجلد ساخته The instructions in question consisted, perhaps, of several leaves or pages, as many of those documents did. In this case, it was usual to *bind*, or, at least, to *stitch* them.

OBSERVATIONS.

It might be inferred from the foregoing letter, that no copy of the instructions to the *Kázy* of *Bangalore* had been preserved, and that hence arose the necessity of calling upon that officer to furnish one: but, considering the great regularity with which official documents, in general, appear to have been registered under Tippoo Sultan's government, it can hardly be imagined, that an entry of the instructions in question should not have been duly made among the records of the proper department. Nor is such a supposition at all requisite, in order to account for the present directions; since there is no difficulty in conceiving, that the register, containing the document wanted, might have been left at *Seringapatam*, in which case, no doubt, a copy would be more easily and speedily obtained from *Bangalore* than from the capital. The thing chiefly remarkable, therefore, in the letter before us, is the direction which it contains, for sending the instrument specified, in a form which should save the trouble of preparing in camp any other copy for the *Kázy* of *Zuferábád*: for such would seem to have been the sole object of the minute instructions given on this head. By this means, nothing more would be necessary, on the receipt of the document in question, than to fill up the blanks left in it, and to affix the usual seal and signature to it. Such an expedient, for the economizing of time and labour, would scarcely occur to any but a very eccentric mind.

It might have been expected, considering the particular design which the *Sultan* would appear to have had in requiring the document in question, and adverting to the minuteness of his directions respecting it, that he would not have forgotten to order a blank to be left for the *date* of the instructions, as well as for the name of the *Kázy* to whom they were to be transmitted. But this omission is only one of various instances of similar inadvertency and inconsistency, with which all the productions of his pen abound, and which may be safely referred to the indistinctness of his views, and the crudeness of his conceptions on the generality of subjects. To the same causes (originating in an understanding naturally contracted) still more, perhaps, than to caprice and levity, are to be ascribed most of the trivial and indigested regulations, as well as many of the incongruous and vacillating measures, which marked the course of his bustling but ruinous reign.

LETTER CCCLXIV.

To the Kilaadár *of* Putn (Seringapatam); *dated* 15th Wásaaey. (14th September.)

The abstract of this letter, as given in the manuscript, appears to have been inaccurately copied, for which reason I have not attempted a regular translation of it. The subject of it, however, is too remarkable to be entirely passed over. It relates to the establishment of a kind of school in certain of the *Risálas* composing the garrison of *Seringapatam:* and from the context I infer, that the *Risálas* in question were some of the *Usud Ilhye* or *Ahmedy* corps. The number of pupils in each *Risála* was fixed at twenty, who were ordered to be selected from the most promising youths belonging to it. Besides being taught to read the *Koran,* they were to be instructed in the Persian language and in accounts.

There is reason to conclude, from a curious memorandum among the *Sultan's* papers, in which the qualifications of several of his principal servants are specified, that those of the military class were, for the most part, utterly illiterate. It was probably, therefore, with a view to the correction of this evil, and to the formation of a more intelligent and respectable description of officers, that he instituted the schools here spoken of. I am unable to state, what effects resulted from this regulation, or whether, indeed, it continued in force long enough to lead to any. It was, no doubt, well calculated, if steadily pursued and duly executed, to produce a considerable improvement in the character of the superior ranks of the army; and particularly, if it was extended, or intended to be extended, to all the garrisons, among which the *Ahmedies* and *Usud Ilhyes* were distributed. But whether or not this was the case I have no means of judging.

The letter, which we are now considering, contains also a paragraph to the following effect:

" You did right, in committing five youths to the charge of Uzeem-
" ûddeeen,(1) for the purpose of their being taught the encomiastic odes;
" but

(1) See Letter CCCLI, where it appears that this Uzeemûddeen was superintendant of the dancers and singers.

" but there is no need for adding four more to the number.[2] The former
" are sufficient."

LETTER CCCLXV.

To NUBBY SHÂH, *at* BANGALORE; *same Date.* (14*th September.*)

You write, " that agreeably to [our] orders, the *Pagoda* which was " in front of the blessed *Durgâh* [or shrine] has been demolished, but " that the *Aumil* will not resign [to you] the ground [on which it stood]." It is known. The *Aumil* will make over the aforesaid ground [to you], when you must annex the same to the premises of the *Durgâh*.

You have requested of us " to issue our orders to the *Aumil* of *Selim* " ....[1] to put you in possession of [or continue to you] the [usual] fees,[2*] &c." It is known. Whatsoever was thought proper to be directed on the subject of fees, &c. has been directed. It is not our custom to repeat our orders.[3]

OBSERVATIONS.

Whatever might have been the bigotry of the *Sultan*, it would appear, from the general style and tenor of the foregoing letter, that his respect for the priesthood was not of a nature to prevent their experiencing, occasionally, together with the other orders of his subjects, that acerbity of manner, which so much distinguished

(2) It is probable that Uzeemûddeen had applied for the additional youths, here mentioned, through the *Kilaadár*, Syed Mahommed.

(1) Name uncertain.

(2*) Original براي جاري داشتن رسوم و غيرة The application may have been for the *restoration* of some particular fees or endowments which had been abolished.

(3) Original اين دستور نيست كه باربارزيب نكارش نمايد " it is not customary [with us] to write over and over [on the same subject]."

guished his character. Nubby Shâh is one of those, to whom the circular proclamation, or manifesto, against the infidels (inserted at page 293) was forwarded; and was, probably, the governing priest of the principal *Durgâh* at *Bangalore.*

Although the present collection furnishes several instances, in which the *Sultan* is seen to *repeat* orders already issued, yet it is certain, that he was not in the *habit* of doing so; and that is probably all that he meant, by saying that "it was "not his custom." His commands were, in general, too peremptory, and the consequences of disobeying them too well understood, to make it often necessary to reiterate them.

LETTER CCCLXVI.

To MÛSHEER ÛL MÛLK; *dated* 19*th* WÂSAAEY. (18*th September.*)

[AFTER compliments].......... A long period has elapsed, during which I have not had the happiness of hearing the glad tidings of the health and welfare of the *Nabob*, Nizâm ûd Dowlah, and of that exalted [person]. May the cause which has prevented it be no other than good.

It is a [just] ground of wonder and amazement,(1) that at this time, the above described(2) *Nabob* should unite himself to the rulers at *Poonah*, and without any cause proceed to the infraction of the treaties and friendship subsisting between us, and determine upon committing hostilities against me. Some time ago I dispatched Mahommed Iftikhâr Khân, after personally explaining to him various particulars, calculated to promote and preserve the mutual friendship and interests of both our states, as

(1) Original تعجب وتحير These words, though usually considered as synonymous, have a shade of difference in their meaning; the latter including, in some degree, the idea of alarm, uneasiness, or consternation, as well as that of surprize.

(2) Original نواب موصوف where though موصوف is a polite expression, it is hardly suited to the relative situations of the *Nizâm* and the *Sultan*: the former of whom claimed to be addressed as superior by the latter; who, in general, I believe, acquiesced in the pretension. ممدوح (praised) would have been a more respectful phrase.

as well as that of *Poonah.* If the aforesaid Khân had faithfully detailed these particulars, there can be no doubt that the above described *Nabob,* who is a great lord[3] [or nobleman] and a profound statesman,[4] would have acquiesced therein ;[5] and have applied himself to reconcile the differences which have arisen at this time between me and the people of *Poonah,*[6] to strengthening the foundations of union between the three states, and to promoting their joint prosperity and splendor.

The case, with regard to *Adoni*, is briefly this. How much soever I made pacific propositions founded in reason and sincerity, the ministers on that side [or the court of *Hydrabad*] constantly returned harsh answers, calculated [only] to embroil[7] [matters further]. The business would require a long explanation, and is beyond the limits of a letter. All the particulars will be made known to you verbally, by the *Mûtusuddy,* Luchman Râo, who is a man of understanding, and a person possessing my confidence. You will be pleased to make him acquainted with the views and wishes of the above described *Nabob,* and send him [back] speedily hither.

A *Mehtâby* dress is herewith sent, in token of our abundant regard. For the rest, may joy and happiness be yours !

OBSERVATIONS.

Mûsheerûl Mûlk was, at this period, and continued to be till his death, in the year 1805, the principal minister at the court of *Hydrabad*; having been confirmed in that office by the present *Nizâm*, Secunder Jâh, on the accession of the latter

(3) Original امیر کبیر

(4) Original داناي صايب تدبير literally "knowing in difficult counsels."

(5) Original پذيرا فرموده

(6) Original اهل پونه

(7) Original جواب بدرشتي و برهمي ميفرستادند

latter to the *Musnud*, in 1804. During the whole of his long administration, which though in the main prosperous, was, nevertheless, considerably checquered by untoward events, he steadily and successfully cultivated a good understanding with the British Government in *India;* between whom and his own court he had finally the credit and satisfaction of establishing the strict alliance now happily subsisting between them, and which is the more likely to prove permanent, inasmuch as it is erected upon the basis of reciprocal advantage and security.

It is not pretended, that the views of Mûsheer ûl Mûlk, in this instance, were influenced by any feelings arising out of private partiality for the English; though there wants not ground for believing, that this minister not only duly appreciated the character of our nation, but also entertained sentiments of personal regard for many individuals of it. But, on the occasion at present under consideration, he was guided solely by the suggestions of his political sagacity, which taught him that, placed as the state of *Hyderabad* was, between two powerful and encroaching neighbours,[8] both of them watchful for the opportunity of acquiring a predominancy in its councils, or, in other words, of rendering it entirely subservient to their interests, there was no security, either for the integrity of its dominions, or the independence of its sovereignty, but in the protection of the British government. This, then, was the object of his constant solicitude: an object of which he never appears to have lost sight, though repeatedly disappointed in his endeavours to attain it; and to which, it is probable, that the events of the war in which his master was engaged, at the date of the foregoing letter, more than ever disposed him.

Of that letter it may be remarked, that it seems to indicate a desire in the writer to open a negociation for a separate peace with the court of *Hyderabad;* for which purpose it is also not improbable, that Luchman Râo was charged with some specific propositions. If such, however, was the object of the *Sultan*, in the mission of that agent, it certainly failed; since the *Nizâm*, though, perhaps, now become rather lukewarm in the common cause, did not absolutely abandon it, or make peace with the *Sultan*, but in conjunction with the Mahrattahs.

7 G The

(8) Namely, the Mahrattahs and Tippoo Sultan.

The Mahommed Iftikhâr Khân, mentioned in the foregoing letter, was the *Vakeel*, or minister, of the court of *Hyderabad*, residing with Tippoo, at the period of the negociations at *Mangalore* in 1784. The *Sultan*, in his Memoirs, calls him Mûftukhir Khân; and on occasion of his dismission (which took place at the same time that the majority of the English prisoners were released, in consequence of the treaty of *Mangalore*) speaks of him in the following terms:

" At this period Mûftukhir Khân, the *Vakeel* of Hujjâm Nully, solicited an " audience of leave. Sending, in consequence, for the aforesaid, I presented him " with a *Khilaat* and five thousand *rupees* in money, and gave him his dismission. " On this occasion I demanded of him what Hujjâm Nully Khân[9] was at that " time employed about? To this Mûftukhir Khân replied, that as it was then " the season of the *No-roze*,[10] his master was most probably seated at that " moment [in *Durbar*]. Hereupon I rejoined: ' does your master, on occasion " ' of the *No-roze*, sit, *all standing*, or is there any elevated structure upon which " ' he is seated during nine days? State every particular at large.'[11] The afore- " said not comprehending what I said, repeated his former answer. In this man- " ner we two or three times bandied the subject about: when, at length, the " *Vakeel* perceiving my drift, and being covered with shame and confusion, said, " that he wished for an answer to the propositions which he had delivered to me " from his master, on his first arrival in my Presence at *Mangalore*. To this I " replied, by desiring him to state again what his master had proposed. Here- " upon he said, that his master was ready, on learning my wishes, to give me the " most satisfactory proofs of his pacific [or amicable] disposition, and to bind " himself to the performance of his engagements by oaths: in return for which " he entertained the hope, that I would join with him in chastising the Mahrat- " tahs. As soon as I heard this, I said, ' I give you full power to decide for me

" ' on

(9) This appellation has been explained before.

(10) The festival celebrated at most Mahommedan courts at the commencement of the vernal equinox. It was instituted by the ancient Persians.

(11) Original تمام ایستاده شده آقاي شما نو روز مينشيند و يا چيزي بلند باشد كه بر آن نه روز مينشيند. I have rendered this passage as closely as I could; but it was not more unintelligible to Mûftukhir Khân than it is to me. I suspect, however, that there is some indecent allusion in it.

" 'on this occasion, and to say how I am to trust to the pacific professions of your
" 'master, who has in so many instances violated his solemn engagements with
" 'others.' To this Mûftukhir Khân, who was a man of strict veracity and pure-
" breasted,(12) replied, 'that [there was no doubt] his master was an established
" 'liar,(13) and evil-minded [person], who, though he should give one or two of
" 'his sons as hostages [for his good faith], would not be restrained [by that
" 'consideration] from acting ill. Never should you pay the least regard to, or
" 'put the smallest confidence in, any of his words or actions.' Upon this I
" demanded, 'how, when such was the estimation in which his master was held
" 'by all the world, I could place any faith in him?' Finally, having had this
" conversation with Mûftukhir Khân, I dismissed him."

However, difficult it may be to believe that Iftikhâr Khân should have so far betrayed the trust reposed in him, as to have expressed himself, regarding his master, in the gross terms ascribed to him by the *Sultan*, it must, on the other hand, be owned, that it would not be easy to assign any satisfactory reason for the latter's absolute fabrication of so extraordinary a story, which somewhat resembles the account he has been seen to give on another occasion, of the declarations of the Mahrattah *Vakeel* with respect to the rulers of the state. However this may be, it does not appear probable, from what is here related, that Iftikhâr Khân should have been charged with any communications to the court of *Hyderabad*, of a tendency much calculated to conciliate its good will, or " to promote and " preserve the mutual friendship and interests of the two states."

LETTER CCCLXVII.

To SYED MOHYÛDDEEN, *AUMIL of HUSCOTAH; dated* 21*st WÂSAAEY.* (20*th September.*)

YOUR letter, representing " that the *Risâladârs* of the *Ahmedy* " [corps stationed in your jurisdiction] refuse to receive any other sort " of

3 G 2

(12) Original صاف سینه

(13) Original كاذب مقري and بد ذات مشخص

" of *Dál* than [that called] *Toor*," has passed under [our] view. You must serve out to the *Risáladárs* of the *Ahmedy* such *Dál* as may be procurable, whether it be *Toor, Moong*, or *Mâsh*.(1)

LETTER CCCLXVIII.

To SHUMSÛDDEEN KHÂN *and* GHÛLÂM HYDER, *DÁROGHAS of the TOSHEH-KHÁNEH at SERINGAPATAM; dated 22d WÁSAAEY.* (21*st September.*)

DIRECTING them to advance to three certain *Usud-Ilhyes* the sum of three hundred *rupees* [*i. e.* one hundred to each], on occasion of their approaching marriage; and, moreover, instructing them to give strict injunctions to the *Dárogha* of the Mint to furnish every thing necessary for the celebration of their nuptials.

OBSERVATIONS.

This letter furnishes an additional proof of the lively interest taken by the *Sultan*, in whatever related to this favorite corps, the establishment of which he appears to have always considered with peculiar self-complacency, as bearing indubitable testimony to his zeal for the propagation of the Mahommedan religion. The same observation is applicable to the *Ahmedies*, for whom he manifested, on various occasions, an equal partiality. Even Letter CCCLXVII, affords an instance of this favorable disposition towards them: for it is highly probable, that if any other description of his troops had presumed to express the same dissatisfaction with the rations served out to them, which was declared by the *Risáladárs* of this body, they would have received a similar answer to that given to Shâh Noor Ullah, when the latter ventured to represent the badness of the rice delivered for the use of his retinue (see Letter CLXXVII). Here, on the contrary, the *Sultan*,

(1) These are the names of different kinds of dry pease.

Sultan, so far from reproving the complainants, seems to have been sufficiently willing to indulge their preference for *Dál* of *Thor*, provided that article happened to be in the market or in the public store.

LETTER CCCLXIX.

To Syed Ahmed Sâheb;[1] *dated* 22*d* *Wásaaey.* (21*st September.*)

Desiring him to offer up his prayers for the prosperity of the faith, and for the destruction of its enemies.

LETTER CCCLXX.

To Runmust Khân Behâdûr, *Chief of Kurnool; same Date.* (21*st September.*)

In conformity with your wishes, orders have been sent to the *Foujdár* of *Adoni*,[1*] desiring him to give particular instructions to the persons employed by him in collecting horsemen [for our service, within your territories], to proceed in the business with all possible secrecy. Be you, Sir, likewise aiding and assisting on this occasion.[2]

OBSERVATIONS.

It appears by this letter, that though the chief of *Kurnool* had found himself under the necessity of permitting the *Sultan's* officers to recruit within his territories, he was not without apprehensions of incurring thereby the displeasure of the court of *Hyderabad*, whose vassal he was. While, however, Tippoo seemingly

(1) This was a *Durweish*, or devotee, with the place of whose residence I am unacquainted.

(1*) Meaning, of course, *Kútb úl Múlk.*

(2) Original ممد ومعاون rendered literally in the text.

ingly concurs in the reasonableness of the Patan's desire to guard against any suspicion of acting collusively in this affair, he, in the same instant, calls upon that chieftain to promote its success, by his personal authority and influence; which, with whatever secrecy it might be employed, could not fail to expose him, still more, to the imputation which he was so anxious to escape. Whether this was merely one of those inconsistencies, or contradictions, which so often marked the conduct of the *Sultan*, and so frequently occur in his writings; or whether it proceeded from a latent design of embroiling Runmust Khân with the *Nizâm*, and, by that means, compelling the former to throw himself upon his (the *Sultan's*) protection, is a point, which it is now, perhaps, impossible to determine.

LETTER CCCLXXI.

To Meer Ghûlâm Hûsain, *Dârogha (or Superintendant) of the Fleet*;[1] *dated 25th Wâsaaey. (24th September.)*

Your letter, reporting, among other things, "that four months had "elapsed without Mahommed Ali Khân's making his appearance at "*Onore*,[2] whither, however, he had sent his brother," has been received. What business is it of that asylum of nobleness,[3] whether the aforesaid *Khân* comes or stays? Do you apply yourself diligently to the discharge of the trust reposed in you, and see that the ships are equipped with the utmost dispatch. You must, moreover, take care that they are coppered, agreeably to our former orders.

(1) Original آرماد or *Armada*; a word adopted, probably, from the Portuguese.

(2) There is reason to think, that this Mahommed Ali Khân had been ordered to prepare to proceed to *Pegu*, and that the vessels proposed to be employed on this expedition (which was subsequently relinquished) were at *Onore*.

(3) Original آن نجابت پناه which is a common *Ulkâb*, or form of address, from a superior to a person of good birth.

OBSERVATIONS.

I am ignorant of the amount, as well as of the nature, of the *Sultan's* naval force, at this period. If we were to judge by the designation *(Armada)* which he has thought proper to apply to it, we might be led to conclude, that it was of considerable strength. But no inference can be safely drawn from so slight a circumstance; while, on the other hand, there is more than one reason for believing, that his marine must have been very insignificant at the time referred to. In the first place, it is pretty certain that Hyder Ali had bestowed little or no attention on this object; and it is equally clear, that his successor had not hitherto had either time or means to do much in pursuit of it. Besides, nothing was either known or seen of his *Armada*, during the war which ended in the partition treaty of 1792; and though, after that event, he applied himself seriously (as will appear by Appendix K.) to the formation of a respectable navy, he had, happily, not been enabled to effectuate his purpose, before his restless and impatient spirit plunged him into another premature war; in the short course of which, as little was heard of his navy as during that which preceded it.

LETTER CCCLXXII.

To Bûrhânûddeen *and* Budrûz Zumân Khân *(of the same tenor); same Date.* (*24th September.*)

In a letter which we dispatched to you by Eeeroo Pindâreh,(1) and the *Hurkâreh*, Munchajee, you were furnished with a route. You must, accordingly, proceed, either by the route indicated in that letter, or by some other road, leading through a [close or] woody country; and taking up a position within six or seven *coss* of *Deogurry*,(2) where our victorious

(1) *Pindâreh* is a term chiefly in use with the Mahrattahs, and is of the same import as *Kuzzâk* and *Looty*.

(2) This place is situated about twelve miles S.S.E. of *Shânoor*, and very near the *Wirda*, which is, perhaps, the river alluded to in the next letter.

victorious army is [at present] encamped, report your arrival to the Presence.

Ghâzy Khân[3] is a person of extensive knowledge and experience, and [particularly] well acquainted with the roads [of this country]. He has, on this account, been sent with his *Risâla* to join you; upon his doing which, you are to regulate your march by his advice and opinion.

LETTER CCCLXXIII.

To BÛRHÂNÛDDEEN; *dated 26th* WÂSAAEY. *(25th September.)*

FOUR *Kushoons* have *likewise* been dispatched [to you] with Ghâzy Khân. You must *leave all the women and other rubbish,*[1] together with the superfluous baggage belonging to your army, at *Unwutty*,[2] and crossing the river with the above-mentioned [Ghâzy Khân], repair directly to the Presence, instead of halting [as directed by our letter of yesterday], at the distance of six or seven *coss* from the victorious army. You will bring on with you, however, your light baggage, as well as all your warlike apparatus,[3*] with the exception of one of your three great guns. This, with whatever spare wheels you may have,[4] you must leave with your heavy baggage: with which, such of your bullocks as are in bad condition must, likewise, remain. The two *Lumchurs*[5] are to accompany you.

(3) Ghâzy Khân was the principal *Pindâreh* commander in Tippoo Sultan's employ.

(1) Original اناث وغیره خس وخاشاک

(2) Name uncertain.

(3*) Original اسباب جنگی *i. e.* guns, tumbrils, ordnance stores, and the like.

(4) I think, but am not certain, that this is the meaning of the passage, which is not perfectly legible.

(5) I take the *Lumchur* to have been a long gun, calculated for distant cannonading.

OBSERVATIONS.

On the 25th of *Wásaaey* (or 24th of September), the *Sultan* had determined to send Ghâzy Khân, with no more than his own *Risála* of *Kuzzáks*, or *Looties*, to join Bûrhânûddeen's division: but, either in consequence of some intelligence of the enemy's motions, received subsequently to the dispatch of Letter CCCLXXII, or with a view to render the junction of his brother-in-law with his own army more secure and easy, he next day changes his plan, and resolves on re-inforcing the latter, to the extent which has been seen. It does not appear, either from the correspondence or from the *Sultan's* own Memoirs, where Bûrhânûddeen was at this time, or when his junction with the "victorious" army was effected.

LETTER CCCLXXIV.

To RÂJAH RÂM CHUNDUR; *dated 27th WÁSAAEY.* (*26th September.*)

YOUR letter, acknowledging the receipt of our orders for putting Meer Ali, the second *Bukhshy* of the *Ehshám*, into possession of a spacious dwelling-house [at *Bangalore*], has passed under [our] view. You state "that the aforesaid *Bukhshy* has pointed out the house of the "*Khidmutgár Behádúr*, as being, on account of its size, well suited to "the accommodation of his numerous family, and that he has accordingly "applied for the same."

You must inform us, [previously to our giving our orders on this subject], in which ward, and what street, the house in question stands; as well as how many fountains, and how many apartments it contains.

N.B. A letter, requiring the same information with regard to this house, was written to Peer Khân, the *Kilaadár* of *Bangalore*. It may hence be inferred, that the *Sultan*, however willing he might be to accommodate the *Bukhshy* with a suitable residence, suspected the one pointed out by the latter himself to be too good for him. It also appears, that the *Sultan* did not think proper to rely on the single report of Râm Chundur, even in so trivial a matter.

LETTER CCCLXXV.

To Syed Mahommed, *Kilaadâr of* Seringapatam*; dated 28th* *Wâsaaey. (27th September.)*

Buhâûddeen and Kustoory Runga, who were sent [some time since] to *Bengal*, for the purpose of procuring silk-worms, are now on their return [to *Seringapatam*], by the way of *Sedhout*. On their arrival, you must ascertain from them the proper situation in which to keep the aforesaid worms, and provide accordingly. You must, moreover, supply for their food [leaves of] the wood or wild mulberry-trees, which were formerly ordered to be planted [for this purpose]. The number of silk-worms brought from *Bengal* must likewise be distinctly reported to us. We desire, also, to know, in what kind of place it is recommended to keep them, and what means are to be pursued for multiplying them.

There is a vacant spot of ground behind the old palace, lately used as a *Tosheh-khâneh*, or store-house, which was purchased some time ago with a view to building upon it. Prepare a place somewhere near that situation, for the [temporary] reception of the worms.(1)

OBSERVATIONS

When the peculiar circumstances, under which the foregoing letter was written, are adverted to, it will, no doubt, be allowed to furnish a striking proof, both of the

(1) I have here introduced the word *temporary*, though not authorized by the original; because we must either conclude this to have been the *Sultan's* meaning, or suppose him guilty of the absurdity of first desiring to be informed what was the proper situation for the silk-worms, and, in the next moment, determining upon it, without waiting for the communication he had required.

the coolness and activity of the *Sultan's* mind. He was, at the date of it, not only deliberating on the measures to be pursued with respect to *Shânoor*; in planning the future operations of the war in which he was engaged; and in providing for the safety of Bûrhânûddeen's army; but he was, in fact, on the eve of a general engagement with the Mahrattahs. Yet all these important and urgent considerations united, were not capable of diverting his attention from any of the minor objects of his interest. Thus, in the bustle of a camp, and in the face of an enemy, he could find leisure, and was sufficiently composed, to meditate on the rearing of silk-worms. This, indeed, was a very favorite, though, I believe, an unsuccessful pursuit with the *Sultan*; who actually established, or proposed to establish, no less than twenty-one principal stations within his dominions, where the breeding of the silk-worm was directed to be attended to with the utmost care and diligence. These stations are specified in one of the sections of the instructions issued to the *Meer Asof*, or revenue department, in the year 1794.

LETTER CCCLXXVI.

To Bûrhânûddeen; *same Date.* (*27th September.*)

We hear that, besides Holkar, another body of the enemy's force is in motion towards you: you must, therefore, be extremely vigilant. We have dispatched Ghâzy Khân with four *Kushoons* to re-inforce you. Uniting this detachment to your army, you will come on [towards us] with the utmost circumspection.

LETTER CCCLXXVII.

To Meer Ali, *Second* Bukhshy *of* Ehshâm *at* Bangalore; *dated* 2d Zuburjudy. (1*st. October.*)

(Extracts.)

Your two letters, accompanied by a sample of the provisions laid in at *Sâwundy-doorg* [*Sevendoorg*], and by an inventory of the same, have

3 H 2 been

been received. The answer, however, to all the long and tedious stories[1] contained in those dispatches, is to be found in the written instructions to your *Kuchurry* [department]. Peruse, and act in conformity with them.

. . . .

You write, " that the *Piddehs* who arrived there [at *Sevendoorg*], " wounded, from *Badâmy*, are without arms." It is known. Direct the *Kilaadâr* to buy arms for them, and let the price of the same be deducted, by instalments, from their pay. This, too, is contained in your instructions.

. . . .

After inspecting *Sevendoorg*, you must hasten back to *Bangalore*, and there apply yourself, conjointly with the First *Bukhshy* [of *Ehshâm*], Turbiyut Ali Khân, to the examination and settlement of the accounts of the several forts, &c. How can these accounts be adjusted, while you go about singly to the forts.

LETTER CCCLXXVIII.

To Syed Mahommed, *Kilaadâr of Seringapatam*; *dated 6th Zuburjudy.* (*5th October.*)

By the favor of the Divine Aider, what you related respecting Roopa is about to take place. Almighty God has always governed, and will continue to govern, the seven climates[1*] of the earth, by the hands of his own [true] worshippers. The *Nuzr* of five *rupees*, which you sent on occasion of the aforementioned omen, has been received.

(1) Original قصه‌ها طول وطويل

(1*) Original هفت اقليم the geographers of the East dividing the globe into seven climates, this term is, of course, employed to denote the earth at large.

OBSERVATIONS.

Tippoo Sultan is well known to have been extremely superstitious, and to have placed great faith in dreams and omens; and Syed Mahommed was, probably, no less prone to believe in them than his master. The omen here alluded to was, of course, an auspicious one; and, accordingly, the prognostic, whatever it was, would be supposed to have been in part fulfilled, by the victory which had been obtained over the Mahrattahs, only a few days before the date of the present letter,[2] and of which we shall soon have occasion to take more particular notice.

LETTER CCCLXXIX.

To Mahommed Ushruf, *Dewán of Fyze-Hisár (Gooty); same Date. (5th October.)*

What you mention, respecting your having advanced fifty thousand *rupees* to Kûtbûddeen Khân, the *Jagiredár* of *Adoni*, as well as what you state with regard to your having seventy thousand *rupees* more ready, in your *Tosheh-khâneh* [or treasury], and to the dispatch of your people [into the country], for the purpose of collecting the revenues, has afforded us satisfaction, and meets our approbation.

You write, "that, owing to the want of rain, it is to be apprehended "that there may be some delay in realizing the revenue." It is known. You must write to the *Aumils* of the several *Taalûks*, and direct them to distribute grain, &c. in charity. Almighty God will, in his great goodness and mercy, bestow the rain of his bounteousness [upon us].

(2) Namely, the 7th of *Zilhijjeh*, or 1st October.

LETTER CCCLXXX.

To Monsieur Cossigny; *dated* 11*th* Zuburjudy. (10*th October.*)

At this time, the rulers of *Poonah*, notwithstanding the innumerable favors [for which they are indebted to us], uniting with the forces of Nizâm Ali Khân, came and confronted our victorious army. With the aid and power of God, we were enabled, in a single assault, to establish our camp on the ground which they had occupied, and to give them a signal defeat. Upon this they took to flight, and we are now engaged in a close pursuit of them.

OBSERVATIONS.

It is probable, that the action, here alluded to, was brought on by an attempt, on the part of the Mahrattahs, to prevent the junction of Bûrhânûddeen with the army of the *Sultan*. However this may have been, it seems pretty clear, from the words, "*came* and confronted our army," which occur in the foregoing brief notice of this engagement, that the Mahrattahs had advanced to meet the *Sultan*, in the position which the latter had taken up near *Shânoor*.

In a letter addressed to the Governor of *Madras*, under the same date as the preceding one to M. Cossigny, and written on the same occasion, the *Sultan* affirms, "that his quarrel with the Mahrattahs and the *Nizâm* had arisen without "any cause:" that is to say, without any provocation on his part. He likewise (speaking of the battle which had recently taken place) observes, "that, actuated "by the hope of being enabled to accommodate matters with the enemy, he "would fain have restrained his troops from attacking them; but that, when two "armies are brought to confront each other, this is a thing absolutely impracti- "cable." The former of these assertions is not, perhaps, entirely destitute of foundation: but it will be difficult to give credit to the latter, on any other supposition, than that of his being anxious to conclude a speedy peace with the Mahrattahs, in order that he might be the sooner in a condition to make war upon the English. This suggestion, indeed, derives considerable support from the following

ing passage of a letter written by the *Sultan*, soon after settling his differences with the enemy.

" In the end, by the divine power and strength, and through the aid of the " firm faith of Mahommed, joined to the auspicious intercessions of the sages [of " our holy religion], the enemy, after sustaining repeated defeats, and being " driven to the banks of the *Kishna*, implored peace of us, in the most earnest and " humble manner. Upon this, having in view the ease and security of mankind, " I granted them such terms as were agreeable to me: *and now* my fixed determi- " nation is, to proceed to the *chastisement and extermination of those, who pro-* " *hibit the calling to prayer* [from the *Minarets*], *and who are the most inveterate* " *of Infidels. It is on the utter extirpation of these that my mind is now intent.* " Such being the case, do you, reverend Sir, employ yourself in prayer for the " success of the champions of the faith, and the destruction of the wicked un- " believers; to the end that the Mahommedan religion may flourish."

The following letter, though dated nearly a month later than the foregoing one to M. Cossigny, is inserted here (and consequently out of its proper place), because it contains a more particular account of the engagement in question, and of its immediate consequences, than that given in the dispatch to the French governor. It was addressed, *mutatis mutandis*, to Mahommed Baig Khân Humdâny, and several others, to whom he thought it fit to announce his recent successes; among which number was the Emperor Shâh Allum. It bears date the 9th *Hydery*, or 6th of November 1786, and is to the following effect.

LETTER CCCLXXXI.

To Mahommed Baig Khân Humdâny *and others; dated 9th* Hydery. *(6th November.)*

(Circular).

Not long since, the ministers[(1)] of the state of *Poonah*, forgetting their innumerable obligations to me,[(2)] and joining with Nizâm Ali Khân, advanced

(1) Original کاربردازان literally " transactors of business.

(2) Original دوستدار " your friend," or, " this friend."

vanced with a hundred thousand horse, and [a numerous train of] artillery, into the country belonging to me, spreading destruction wherever they came. Upon this I marched to repel the aggression; proceeding, in the first instance, against *Adoni*, a strong place in the possession of Nizâm Ali Khân, to which I laid siege. About the same time, Nizâm Ali Khân, apprehensive for the security of his nephew, and of the females of his late brother's [Busâlut Jung's] family, who were then shut up in the fort [of *Adoni*], dispatched his *whole* army, under the command of his [youngest] brother, Moghul Ali Khân, for the purpose of removing them from thence. This army proceeded accordingly by a route leading along the skirts of the mountains, which served to cover their march. In this manner they reached *Adoni* [in safety], and taking from thence Mohâbut Jung(3) and the women, hastened with them, night and day,(4) and [as before] under the protection of the mountains, to *Hyderabad*. I pursued the fugitives to the banks of the *Tungbuddra;* much of their baggage and cattle falling, by the way, into the hands of my people. The fort of *Adoni* was likewise captured on this occasion.

I next marched to chastise the ministers of *Poonah*, who, together with the forces of Nizâm Ali Khân,(5) had established themselves

(3) Mohâbut Jung, called also Dârâ Jah, was the son of Busâlut Jung. *Adoni* and *Rachoor* constituted his appenage, which on his death passed to Mohâbut Jung. Upon the death of the latter, however, the *Nizám* did not think proper to confirm his son, Ghûlâm Husain Khân, in the whole of his inheritance, but confined him to the possession of *Rachoor*. This led to the open rebellion of Ghûlâm Hûsain Khân, in 1796, against the government of *Hyderabad*. If this work should be hereafter continued beyond the present volume, it will appear how much this rebellion was secretly fostered by Tippoo, notwithstanding his being then at peace with the Nizâm. Ghûlâm Hûsain was, however, after standing a siege in *Rachoor*, compelled, in the end, by an English detachment, under the command of the late Lieutenant Colonel Dalrymple, of the Madras Establishment, to surrender that place, and to throw himself upon the clemency of his great uncle.

(4) Original شباشب which strictly means "all the night."

(5) The *Sultan* has here fallen into one of those self-contradictions, so usual with him. He had just before said, that the *whole* army of the *Nizám* had proceeded to the relief of *Adoni*, after

selves[6] at [or near] *Shánoor.* On this occasion I crossed the *Tungbhudra* with my whole army and artillery in boats, and proceeding with rapidity against the enemy, suddenly appeared before them. On the 7th *Zilhijjeh* [1st October 1786] an engagement ensued. Before, however, my troops could come to close action with them,[7] the fire from our guns sent such numbers of the infidels to the abode of perdition [or hell], that leaving their camp standing, and abandoning great part of their baggage, they took the road of flight. *Shánoor* became, in consequence, an [easy] conquest. Please God, the Aider, I shall again apply myself, after the celebration of the *Mohurrum,* to the chastisement of the enemy. All these particulars have been communicated to give delight to your odoriferous [noble] mind.

The following passage from the *Sultan's* Memoirs will be found to contain some further particulars, respecting his operations against the Mahrattahs at the present period. It is in immediate continuation of the extract formerly given under Letter CCCXLIX.

" Having, in this manner, put the enemy to flight, I moved, at three o'clock " in the afternoon [of the same day], and encamped three *coss* in advance of my " former ground. On the following day I proceeded three *coss* farther; and, pur- " suing my march, on the third took up a position on this side, and within one " *coss,* of *Shánoor.*

3 I " By

after effecting which they had returned to *Hyderabad.* Here the *Nizám's* forces are indefinitely stated to have been at *Shánoor,* to which point they could hardly have advanced from *Hyderabad* in that interval. In both cases, his evident object was to magnify the number of his enemies.

(6) Original رخت ادبار داشتند " who had fixed their miserable equipage," " taken up " their wretched quarters."

(7) Original هنوز کار بشمشیر و سنان نرسیده بود literally, " the business had not yet arrived at " sword and bayonet."

" By this movement, the death-devoted Mahrattahs, who, favored by the *Shâ-*
" *noor*-man,[8] had established themselves behind a stream which passes close to
" *Shânoor*, were placed in the situation of an ill-fated bird, caught in a snare,
" whose own feet may be said to conduct it to its doom;[9] the fact being, that
" *Shânoor* [where they had voluntarily cooped themselves up] did actually prove
" such a snare to them.

" It being an established rule under my government, for every *Kushoon*[10] to
" cover its camp with batteries,[11] I, in pursuance of this system, caused en-
" trenchments to be thrown up around and in front of my position near *Shânoor*.
" Having done this, I proceeded to attack the enemy,[12] with which view, after
" allotting two *Kushoons* of regular, and ten thousand *Ehshâm* infantry, for the
" protection of my lines and camp, I formed the remainder of my army (consist-
" ing, besides six *Kushoons* of regular infantry, of [a considerable force in] regular
" and irregular cavalry, *Ehshâm* troops,[13] &c.) into four divisions, one of which
" I placed under the command of Mâh Mirzâ Khân,[14] whom I directed to charge
" across the river. Another division, conducted by Bûrhânûddeen, was to fall
" upon the enemy's left flank; while Meer Moaayenûddeen, at the head of the
" third, was to attack their right. A fourth division[15] was led by myself.

" Every

(8) Meaning Abdûl Hukeem Khân.

(9) I have been obliged to depart, in some measure, from the letter, though, I trust, not from the spirit, of my original, according to which the bird's own feet are made to conduct it to the kitchen مطبخ where its destiny is obvious. In like manner, *Shânoor* is represented to have proved a kitchen, or, in other words, a slaughter-house, to which their own steps had led the Mahrattahs.

(10) That is, as I suppose, *when marching on actual service*, or *in time of war*.

(11) This is the word employed in the original, by which probably is meant field-redoubts or entrenchments.

(12) This account is at variance with that given by the *Sultan* in his letter to the Governor of Madras, and referred to under Letter CCCLXXX.

(13) No number is here specified.

(14) I suppose this to be the same person to whom Letter CXIX is addressed. I am ignorant of his fate, as well as that of Moaayenûddeen; but conclude, that neither of them was living at the period when *Seringapatam* was captured, their names not appearing among those of the commanders who survived that event.

(15) Forming, probably, the principal attack.

" Every thing being thus prepared, and the third night after my arrival at " *Shánoor* being dark and rainy, and therefore favorable to my purpose, I put my " troops in motion for the assault of the enemy's position. The distance between " the two armies not exceeding a *coss* [or two miles], the advanced picquets of " each were posted close to one another. Upon my reaching those of the enemy, " the latter, to the amount of about two hundred horse, came forward, and " demanding who we were, and what we wanted, forbad our advancing. I was " myself, at this time, in front of the column thus challenged. To these ques- " tions no one presuming to reply without my authority, those scorpions advanced " still nearer[16] to us, and repeated their enquiries. Upon this I directed a com- " pany of my advanced guard to reply to them *with fire*;[17] when a volley was " instantly discharged amongst the scorpions by the foremost company of the " victorious army, which sent numbers of the said scorpions to hell. Of the " remainder, some escaped to their own camp, while others of the infidels were " made prisoners.

" I followed the fugitives till I approached very near their camp, when I made the " [appointed] signal by gun[18] for the other three divisions of the army to advance " with speed [to their respective attacks]. To this signal, however, no answer " being given, I concluded they must have encountered some [unforeseen obstacle, " such as a] river or mirey road, which had occasioned their present failure. I " continued, nevertheless, my way to the enemy's camp; on reaching which I " repeated the signal to the three other divisions, which was now answered by one " of the commanders, but still no notice was taken of it by the other two. Under " these circumstances, I became apprehensive lest the opportunity [of attacking " the enemy] should slip through my hands:[19] exclaiming, therefore, *Allah-yár!*

3 I 2 [or,

(16) Original عقربان اقربتر آمدند where there is that kind of play upon the words *Ukrubán* (scorpions) and *Ukrubtur* (nearer) of which the *Sultan* was very fond.

(17) Original از آتش

(18) There is some difficulty in understanding how a signal by gun, made during the confusion of a night attack, could be distinguished from any other firing of cannon.

(19) This is nearly literal, the original being که وقت از دست میرود

" [or, God is our friend!] I rushed forward into the camp of the infidels, and " opened upon them a [brisk] fire from my artillery.[20] Soon after I had thus " penetrated into the enemy's camp, the commanders of two of the other divisions " likewise arrived there, at the points respectively assigned to them.

" It was just day-break when I entered the camp of the infidels, at which time I " had only about three hundred *Jyshe* and a single gun with me. I was soon after, " however, joined by others. The flight of the unbelievers resembled that of " kites and crows; and, after some time, they stood viewing from the summits " of the distant eminences, the plunder of their deserted camp.

" An hour and a half after the victorious army had taken possession of the " enemy's camp, the fourth division, under the the command of Mâh Mirzâ Khân, " which, proceeding from the vicinity of *Shânoor*, had fallen upon and routed the " army of Holkar, likewise joined me.

" About nine o'clock in the forenoon, the whole of the unbelievers, re-assem-" bling like so many gnats and flies, advanced towards us, and drew up, as if with " an intention of offering us battle; commencing, at the same time, a distant " cannonade from six pieces of artillery. On my part, I forbad my people to " throw away their ammunition in this manner, directing that the short light guns " attached to the different divisions should alone fire upon such of the enemy as " approached extremely near: and, even in this case, they were ordered to dis-" charge only a single shot at a time, and that very deliberately. My object, in " this manœuvre, was, to make the infidels believe that I had none but short field " pieces with me. This notion would encourage them [I thought] to draw nearer " to us, when, suddenly opening a heavy fire upon them from our long guns, we " should be sure to put them completely to the route. It happened exactly as I " foresaw. The infidels came close up to our line, in the manner of crows; when " all four divisions of the army opening their long guns together, gave them, " agreeably to my instructions, such a general discharge, as instantly made them " disperse

(20) This must have been when he had collected the whole of his division together, as when he first entered the enemy's camp he had only one gun with him.

" disperse on all sides, and fly in despair,[21] like a flock of the same crows, in the " midst of which a stone has been thrown.

" In this action[22] the enemy lost about two thousand horse and three elephants, " killed by cannon shot: great numbers of their people, horse and foot, likewise " speeded on this occasion to hell.[23] The remainder of their army, turning their " faces to flight, retreated to the distance of four or five *coss*, where they again " encamped. I also, with my whole army, returned to my [entrenched] camp, " where I continued two days, till I could ascertain where the infidels were. At " length I received intelligence, that they had moved to a new position, near " *Shánoor*, where they were encamped, with the river on their left flank. Upon " this I also shifted my camp, and took up a fresh position directly in their front.

" Here, the festival of *Zilhijjeh* being at hand, I halted two or three days, for " the purpose of celebrating it: and having accordingly done so, I prepared the " following day for action. For this purpose, drawing up my army with the " whole of the *Behropeahs*[24] in front of the different *Kushoons*, and throwing my " right flank upon *Shánoor*, I advanced against the enemy. The moment the " infidels perceived this movement, they withdrew what troops they had placed in " *Shánoor*, and then, taking the *Shánoor*-man along with them, fled, without " fighting, to the distance of six *coss*, when they again halted. In the meanwhile,

" I encamped

(21) Original مثل گله زاغ سنگ خورده پشت دست بدهان زده پراگنده شدند which would not bear a literal translation: for though " biting the back of the hand" is a common action with the natives of India, to denote despair or disappointment, the expression would not so well apply to a flock of crows.

(22) Though the *Sultan* has not given the date of this action, the context sufficiently establishes that it was the one referred to in Letter CCCLXXXI, as having taken place on the 7th *Zilhijjeh*, A.H. 1200, or 1st October 1786.

(23) Original اسفل السافلین literally, " the meanest of the mean," or " the lowest of the " low." In this last sense it is sometimes employed to denote hell, or " the lowest pit of " hell," according to Mr. Gilchrist, the first Hindoostany philologer of this or any other period, and one to whom the students of that language are under similar obligations, to those which the Persian scholar owes to the oriental labors of Sir William Jones and of Sir John Richardson.

(24) I am not clear with respect to the meaning of this word (supposing it to be correctly written), but think it likely that it may be another term for *Bánddrs*, or rocket-men.

" I encamped near the ground which the enemy had occupied, still covering my
" right flank with *Shánoor*.

" It was on this occasion that the destitute chief of that place, who had allowed " himself to be seduced [from his allegiance to me] by the insidious representa- " tions of the Mahrattahs, experienced the nature of the protection he had to " expect from these perfidious friends, to whose camp he had lately removed, to- " gether with his family and effects. Of the latter of these he was now openly " plundered of the chief part, by the people of the Mahrattah army, who even " carried off some of the women belonging to him. The next day, this senseless " creature,[25] together with what remained of his property and women, and with " no other clothes than those which they wore at the time, was sent off, under a " guard of five thousand horse, to *Mirich*. The Mahrattahs themselves made, at " the same time, two or three successive marches [in a retrograde direction].[26]

" After this, breaking up my camp at *Shánoor*, and leaving a small garrison in " that city, I proceeded to the [adjacent] town of *Bunkapoor*, near which I lay " encamped during the first fourteen days of *Múhurrum*, performing at this place " the mournful ceremonies of the season. Here also the commanders of the " Hydery army presented me with three *Nuzrs*: one on occasion of the birth " of the prince[27] Nizâm ûd deen; another, for my late victory; and the third, on " account of the *Eed* (or festival).

" It was at this time that I came to the determination of communicating with " the infidels, on certain points which had suggested themselves to my mind. In " pursuance of this design, I sent a person of respectability,[28] accompanied by one " of the chief of my spies, to Tukojee Holkar, who had the reputation of being

" the

(25) Original معذور العقل

(26) The exact line of their retreat is not indicated. As, however, they subsequently appeared in the quarter of *Kopul*, where another engagement took place between the two armies, it is probable that they retired in that direction.

(27) Original شاهزاده That is, " king's son." This, I believe, is the first instance of the *Sultan's* so plainly laying claim to the royal title.

(28) Original مردي آدمي

"the most valiant among the infidels; and to whom I directed the following "message to be delivered.

"'Nizâm Ali Khân, to whom, if he had been here, I should have addressed "'myself, is not present. It is for this reason I send to you to say, 'wherefore "''should we any longer suffer hundreds of thousands of men to be killed and "''wounded in battle? What is most desirable is, that you and I should draw "''up our respective armies in two lines............''"

* * * * * *

* * * * * *

The sequel of this curious and interesting passage is unfortunately wanting, having, as already alluded to in the Preface, been torn out at this place. My recollection of what followed the words with which the preceding extracts ends, enables me, however, to state generally, that the message in question conveyed such another challenge to Tukojee Holkar, as that which was sent by the *Sultan* (according to his own account) to General Macleod, during the siege of *Mangalore*, in 1783, and of which a translation has been given by Colonel Wilks, in the Introduction to his valuable History of *Mysore*. The two armies were to be drawn up opposite to each other, for the purpose of witnessing the combat; in which, however, they were, on no account, to interfere. The questions in dispute between the contending states were to be decided according to the result of the battle; that is to say, the vanquished party was to accede to such pretensions, or demands, as had been previously set up by the adversary. Holkar, as might be expected, treated the proposal with derision; observing, on the occasion (among other things), "that "it was not the custom of his nation to refer their claims to the issue of a single "engagement, but, on the contrary, to attack and retreat, retire and advance, as "the nature of circumstances required." Such is the substance of what I remember of this singular occurrence, as related by the *Sultan* himself: the deficiency in my account of which will, it may be hoped, be supplied in due season by Colonel Wilks, from the *Sûltân ût Tuwâreekh*, referred to by him in his Preface, and which is very likely to have recorded the transaction in question, as well as the similar bravado already noticed. At all events, there can be little doubt, that there are other copies of the *Sultan's* Memoirs in existence, besides the mutilated one in

my

my possession. In the case here supposed, it may still be reasonably presumed, that this curious document will, at some future period, be offered to the public, in a more perfect and connected form, than that in which I have judged it convenient to exhibit it in the present work.

I have not, at this moment, the means of ascertaining what credit is due to the *Sultan's* account of the treatment experienced by Abdûl Hukeem Khân at the hands of his Mahrattah allies. The probability of the fact is, no doubt, supported, in some degree, by the general character of that people for rapaciousness and bad faith. It is, at the same time, very possible, that the prejudices of the writer may have betrayed him into some exaggeration on the occasion.

The *Sultan* would not seem, even by his own narrative, to have followed up the advantage which he states himself to have obtained over the Mahrattahs at *Shânoor*, either with the celerity or the vigour which might have been expected. Besides the delay occasioned by the celebration of the festival of *Zilhijjeh*, he remained stationary during a great part of the ensuing month, for the purpose of fulfilling the customary rules of the *Mûhurrum*. Though not acknowledged, it is, nevertheless, not unlikely, that some other considerations, as well as those of superstition, may have led to this extraordinary inactivity; which, if it had not a tendency to damp the zeal of his own army, at least afforded time to that of the enemy, to recover from the effects of their recent discomfiture.

LETTER CCCLXXXII.

To MEER ALI, *Second* BUKHSHY *of* EHSHÂM *at* BANGALORE; *dated* 18*th* ZUBURJUDY. (17*th October.*)

YOUR going about to the forts by yourself, and your investigating the accounts of the same, without being accompanied by the first *Bukhshy*, is not proper. Repair to *Bangalore*, and after finally settling the accounts of that fort, proceed with the first *Bukhshy*, and in conjunction with him, examine minutely into those of the other places [within your jurisdiction].

N. B. Several

N. B. Several letters appear at this period, acknowledging the *Sultan's* receipt of *Nuzrs* transmitted to him, in compliment to his recent victory over the Mahrattahs. In one of these, addressed to Râjah Râm Chundur, the *Dewân* of *Bangalore*, he approves of that officer's having distributed sweet-meats on that occasion, and desires him *to do the same thing in future.*

LETTER CCCLXXXIII.

To Budrûz Zumân Khân ; *dated* 23*d* Zuburjudy. (22*d October.*)

Do you remain on the borders of *Soandeh, Kittoor, Dharwâr, &c.* and there apply yourself to the effectual chastisement of the turbulent wretches who infest those parts.

N. B. There follows here an order to Budrûz Zumân Khân, directing him to examine and make a report on a certain spot, situated in a part of the country comprehended in his government (but the name of which I am unable to make out), where the *Sultan* seems to have been desirous of erecting a fort. Besides possessing great natural strength, the position was further recommended by its proximity to the frontier of the *Kokun.* Indeed it is intimated to be the proper route for an army proposing to penetrate into that country. Budrûz Zumân Khân is accordingly instructed to procure and transmit to his master, the fullest information in his power on the subject.

This letter then proceeds as follows:

Demolish the fort of *Kittoor.* Seize upon the disturbers of the country, and incorporate them with the *Ahmedies* [*i. e.* make Musulmans of them]. Write letters of peace [or amity], in the first instance, to the *Polygar* of . . . . ,(1) and afterwards, sending a person of

3 K respectability

(1) Name not legible.

respectability to him, bring him over to the interests of the *Sircar*. Having done this, you must ascertain [through him] what strong forts there are in the *Kokun*, and what villages occur in the road leading thither. You are to be very particular in your enquiries [on this subject]; and you are to keep the matter quite secret. You are, moreover, to make your communications to us, regarding it, in the Persian language.(2)

OBSERVATIONS.

Whether Budrûz Zumân Khân joined the *Sultan's* army at the same time with Bûrhânûddeen, and was now sent back to his government; or whether he had, all along, continued there, I am unable to determine. The circumstance, however, of his not being named by the *Sultan*, in the latter's account of the battle of *Shânoor*, strongly indicates, that he did not participate in the honors of that day, since, if he had been present, it is most probable that he would have had a conspicuous station assigned to him on the occasion. I am equally ignorant, where Kumrûddeen Khân was at this period: but as it may be presumed, that, if he had been employed on a separate command, some letters to his address would have appeared in the collection, it is most likely, that he had remained in attendance upon the *Sultan* since the time of his return from the siege of *Nergûnd*. There is, indeed, reason to believe, that although he was occasionally placed at the head of an army, he was never much trusted by the *Sultan*, who appears to have entertained no very favorable opinion of his talents. This is particularly evinced in some minutes of a consultation, dated in 1794, in which the *Meer's* incapacity is pretty plainly insinuated by the majority of the subscribing counsellors.

(2) It appears, by this and other passages of the correspondence, that even those persons, who were capable of writing Persian, did not always address the *Sultan* in that language.

LETTER CCCLXXXIV.

To Monsieur Cossigny; *dated* 24*th* Zuburjudy. (23*d October.*)

The persons to be dispatched to Europe have been fixed on by *the Presence*, and will accordingly soon proceed from hence, and arrive [at *Pondicherry*]. When they arrive [there], you must send them to Europe, along with M. Perron,[1] who [we understand] is about to repair thither.

LETTER CCCLXXXV.

To Syed Ahmed Saheb, Boodhun Shâh, Nubby Shâh, Kuleem-Ûllah Shâh, *and others* (Peer-zâdehs *or Devotees*); *dated from* Shânoor, 24*th* Zuburjudy. (23*d October.*)

[*All of the same tenor.*]

By the blessing of God and the aid of the Prophet, the forces of the accursed having experienced a signal defeat and chastisement, have turned their faces to flight, leaving the troops of Islâm victorious over the enemies of the faith. Thus has the army of the accursed infidels been trodden under foot by the hoofs of the horses of Islâm, and rendered vile and miserable; while the religion of Mahommed has been thereby made to flourish.

You, Sir, are one of the elders [of the faith], and will therefore apply, with all your heart, to the best means of advancing the religion of Mahommed, and of administering to the support of Islâm.

3 K 2

(1) Though this name is very distinctly written, I am inclined to think that it was meant for Monneron.

N. B. Here follows an inventory of the presents, respectively, sent to the persons addressed; by which it would appear, that the highest in the *Sultan's* estimation were Boodhun Shâh and Nubby Shâh.

LETTER CCCLXXXVI.

To MOHYÛDDEEN ALI KHÂN, *DEWÂN of KURPAH,* CHISHTY-YÂR KHÂN, RÂJAH RÂM CHUNDUR, NURSIA, *and others; dated from SHÂNOOR, 26th ZUBURJUDY. (25th October.)*

(CIRCULAR.)

A PAPER, containing the *Khûtbah* [or form of prayer to be read in the mosques], is enclosed. Give strict orders to the *Khûtibs* [or reciters of the *Khûtbah*] belonging to your *Kuchurry*, to recite the *Khûtbah* regularly, after the praises of God and the Prophet, according to the accompanying form.

OBSERVATIONS.

The form of prayer here referred to does not appear; but it is most probable, that it appointed the *Sultan's* own name to be substituted in place of Shâh Allum's. If such was the case, it may be presumed, that, although this measure seems to have been determined on by Tippoo, so far back as July 1786,(1) he had not hitherto carried it into effect; at least not throughout the whole of his dominions. Being now elated with his recent successes against the Mahrattahs, he might, perhaps, think the occasion peculiarly favorable to the complete and final execution of his purpose.

(1) See Letter CCCXXXI.

LETTER CCCLXXXVII.

To the SHÂNOOR-*Man* (*i. e.* ABDÛL HUKEEM KHÂN); *same Date.* (*25th October.*)

YOUR intention of coming [hither] has been verbally communicated to us by Kureem Khân, and the account has afforded us pleasure: notwithstanding, the ungracious proceeding(1) of which you have [recently] been guilty is such, as I could never have imagined to be possible. It is well. My friendly disposition towards you still continues: repair hither, therefore, with a confident mind. The house and place are both yours.(2) The remaining particulars will be imparted to you by the bearer of this letter.

OBSERVATIONS.

Whatever message Abdûl Hukeem Khân may have sent to the *Sultan*, it is difficult to believe, after what had passed, that he should have entertained a serious intention of putting himself again in the power of the latter. He may, indeed, have been disappointed in his expectations from the Mahrattahs; but he probably knew the *Sultan* too well, to hope for any better treatment, in the event of his return to *Shânoor*. Be this as it might, it is certain that he did not return thither till the conclusion of the war.

(1) Original امرنا ملايم

(2) This is the usual answer giving to a person proposing to visit another. It may here, however, be understood, and was, perhaps, meant in a literal sense.

LETTER CCCLXXXVIII.[1]

To RÂJAH RÂM CHUNDUR; *dated* 1*st* HYDERY. (29*th October.*)

DIRECTING him to issue strict orders to the different *Aumils* within his jurisdiction, to enroll [or impress] all such *Piadehs*[2] and *Coolies* as might be found concealed in the dress [or under the disguise] of peasants.

OBSERVATIONS.

This letter would seem to show, that it was not unusual with Tippoo Sultan's government to press into the public service, not only labourers and carriers of burdens (a custom, by the bye, very generally obtaining throughout India), but also fighting men, for the purpose of recruiting the army. It might likewise be inferred from this document, that neither of the oppressive practices in question was liable to affect the real peasant. I am, nevertheless, doubtful, how far either of these conclusions would be correct; and am, indeed, rather led to think, from various passages in the correspondence, that there was no period of the *Sultan's* reign, in which the peasantry, or *Ryots* (as they are called in the original), were *bonâ fide* exempt from compulsory service, as laborers or artizans. It is, on the other hand, not impossible, that the present order for impressing soldiers might be no more than a temporary expedient, suggested by the exigencies of the war: and, at any rate, it would appear to have extended only to such persons as had formerly borne arms, but were become, from whatever motives, averse to the resumption of them.

LETTER CCCLXXXIX.

To the BUKHSHY *of* EHSHÂM *at* GOOTY; *same Date.* (29*th October.*)

DIRECTING him to chastise the turbulent [or seditious] wherever they raised the head of revolt; and after making them prisoners, to place those

(1) This letter is preceded in the original by two others, dated 29th *Zuburjudy* (or 28th October) addressed to two *Peer-zâdehs*, or devotees, and requiring, in the usual terms, their prayers for the destruction of "the rejected infidels" and the prosperity of Islâm.

(2) That is, *Peons*, or foot soldiers, of the irregular classes.

those under age [or of tender years] in the *Ahmedy* band, and to hang the remainder.

LETTER CCCXC.

To RÂJAH RÂM CHUNDUR; *dated* 4*th* HYDERY. (1*st November.*)

WHAT you have represented, regarding the flight of the *Ryots* belonging to the district of *Great Balapoor,* on account of the increase of six or seven thousand *pagodas* produced in the revenue, in consequence of our having fixed the exchange of the royal *pagoda*(1) at twelve *Cantarai fanams,* together with the excuse which you have offered for the *Ryots* on the occasion,(2) is understood. Where is the hardship or difficulty in a *Ryot* [or renter, having] to pay an additional *fanam* or two upon his rent, which is the most that can fall upon the individual, when the tax [complained of] is divided among the whole?

LETTER CCCXCI.

To MOHYÛDDEEN ALI KHÂN, *DEWÂN of KURPAH; dated* 7*th* HYDERY. (4*th November.*)

YOUR letter, praying to be allowed the use of ten *Bândârs* [rocketmen] for the services of your house and gardens, has passed under our view. *Bândârs* are entertained for fighting, not for looking after houses and gardens. You must employ the *Piâdehs* stationed with you in the services you mention.

(1) Original هن بادشاهي by which was probably meant the *Súltány pagoda.*

(2) This passage is rather obscure in the original.

LETTER CCCXCII.

To Meer Moaayenûddeen Khân ; *same Date.* (*4th November.*)

Send and station the bullocks belonging to the great guns, and also those attached to your own *Kushoon,* together with their *Dároghas* and drivers, into the rear of our special tents [or of the head-quarters], where, at the extremity of the army encampment, there is a spot abounding in grass, which will afford the cattle [good] pasturage. In that friend's present situation, there is no grass but what is at a great distance. Here it is at hand; by which means the cattle will [soon] get into good condition. When you march again, or if you should want them for any particular purpose, you can send and order them to rejoin you.

N.B. A similar order appears to have been addressed, at the same time, to Bûrhânûddeen; but afterwards revoked, in consequence of its being ascertained and reported to the *Sultan,* that the situation occupied by Bûrhânûddeen afforded sufficient pasturage for the cattle of his division.

LETTER CCCXCIII.

To Mahommed Ushruf ; *dated 9th* Hydery.(1) (*6th November.*)

Your letter, enclosing a statement of the demands against the superseded *Aumil* of *Sumrputn,*(2) has been received, and has made us acquainted with the particulars of his embezzlements. Let the claims of the *Sircar* upon the aforesaid *Aumil* and others be realized, by means of flogging.

(1) Two letters of the same date with this are omitted, it being sufficient to mention, that one of them directs some elephants belonging to Abdûl Hûkeem Khân, and which had been seized at *Shânoor*, to be sent to the *Sultan's* camp, and the remainder to *Seringapatam.* The other letter announces the abandonment of the intended embassy to *Pegu.*

(2) *Bulhâry.*

LETTER CCCXCIV.

To Zynûl Aabideen, *Taalûkdâr of Gûlshumâbâd; same Date.* (*6th November.*)

(Extract.)

In compliance with your application for an order to the *Aumil* of *Khan-Khanhully*, to furnish you with two more iron boilers,(1) which you represent to be necessary, on account of the increase in the number of horses under your charge, we have written, and now enclose, the requisite letter to the aforesaid *Aumil*, to whom you will forward it. The boilers in question must, however, be *paid* for, at the time of their being delivered to your people.

OBSERVATIONS.

There appears to have been a great iron-foundery and manufactory established *Khan-Khanhully*,(2) the business of which was, I believe, conducted on account, and for the exclusive benefit of, the *Sultan's* government. There is, no doubt, some difficulty in understanding why an article, purchased, in fact, *of* the *Sultan*, and *for his* service, should be actually paid for in money, when a simple order to the directors of the works to furnish such articles, would apparently have answered the purpose as well. A similar practice, however, seems to have prevailed in other departments of the government; and the object of it might possibly have been to preserve the accounts of the proceeds or profits of the monopolies in question, as distinctly as possible.

3 L

(1) Used in boiling the *Grâm* (a kind of horse bean) with which horses are fed in *India*.

(2) Usually written *Kan-Kanelly*.

LETTER CCCXCV.

To Soojân Râe *and* Moal Chund, *Agents at* Dehli; *same Date.*
(*6th November.*)

After a similar account of the battle of *Shânoor* with that given to Mahommed Baig Khân Humdâny and others, under the same date (see Letter CCCLXXXI), the present letter proceeds to give some immaterial orders, respecting the periodical dispatch of *Kâsids* (or messengers) from *Dehli.* Then follows an explanation of the new notation, according to which the *Sultan* had recently named the months and years of the Malabar cycle, and of which this is the substance.

The letters to which numerical powers are assigned are stated to be thirty; being the number, including لا *(lâm-alif)* and ء *(humza)* which occur in the *Koran.* Of the two last mentioned letters, the former, or لا, represented a *half*, and ء *(humza)* a *quarter.* The powers of the remaining twenty-eight letters were regulated according to their order in the alphabet; the first nine, to ذ *(zal)* inclusive, representing units; the next nine, to ع *(ain)* inclusive, tens; the third series to ه *(hé)* inclusive, hundreds; the last letter, or ي *(yé)*, standing for a thousand.

The foregoing rule is conveyed in the following verses, which are inserted here for the gratification of the Persian reader. Whether they may be considered as a specimen of the *Sultan's* poetical talent I cannot affirm; but, however this may be, they do no great credit to their author.

جو سازي نظر در كلام الله
كه سي حرف هستند با سلسله
بطبق حروف مسلسل حساب
بفرمود سلطان علي جناب
احاد است نه حرف اول بدان
بود عشر نه حرف ديكر از آن
مايه حرف بعد از آن در شمار
بود يي الف بشمر اي مردكار
كه هست لم الف نيم و همزه دكر
بود ربع نامش نهادند زر

It

It would appear by these verses, that this scheme of notation was invented, or, at least, first established, by Tippoo Sultan, who may possibly have given it the name of *Hisáb e Zur*, or the golden computation, in allusion to the circumstance of its being composed of the letters used in the *Koran;* which is not so exactly the case in the *Ubjud* scheme, as by that both *Lám-alif* and *humza* are rejected.

The remainder of this letter is occupied by an enumeration of the names of the months and years, according to the new nomenclature. The former of these, and as many of the latter as were deemed necessary, have been already given in another place.

LETTER CCCXCVI.

To Mahommed Ushruf; *dated* 11*th* Hydery. (8*th November.*)

Your humble address has passed under our view, by which we perceive that you have dispatched the account [of sales] of the shops(1) belonging to the *Sircar* [*i. e.* to us].

You write, that " there is no *Mútusuddy* appointed for keeping the " accounts of the *Tosheh-kháneh*, and that, with our leave, you will " employ a *Serishtedár*(2) for the purpose; otherwise, you request that " some one may be nominated and dispatched from the Presence." It is known. If you will refer to your *Húkm-námeh* [or instructions] you will find it written there, " that a separate *Mútusuddy* for keeping the " accounts of the *Tosheh-kháneh* is unnecessary, and that this duty is " to be performed by one of the numerous *Serishtedárs* of the *Muháls* " [or revenue officers]." That you should propose, notwithstanding this [regulation], to employ a separate *Mútusuddy*, can be attributed to no other cause than ignorance and want of understanding. Look into your instructions, and act agreeably to them.

3 L 2

(1) See Letter XCVIII, to Rájah Rám Chundur, on the subject of these shops.

(2) Revenue accountants.

LETTER CCCXCVII.

To Râjah Râm Chundur; *dated* 19*th* *Hydery.* (16*th November.*)

Your letter, enclosing one to you from the *Aumil* of *Kunucky*, on the subject of the disturbances excited by the fugitive *Polygar* of that district, has been received. What are you and Turbiyut Ali Khân about, that you do not issue the most rigid orders on this occasion, and see this business properly settled?

LETTER CCCXCVIII.

To Boodhun Shâh; *dated from* *Shânoor*, 22*d* *Hydery.* (19*th November.*)

The names of the chiefs of the enemy, who are, at this time, suffering under the wounds inflicted upon them by us, are Bâlâjee Phurnuweese(1) and Mâdho Râo(2). Be your reverence earnestly intent on [praying for] the confusion [or disgrace] of the enemy, and the splendor and increase of the true religion of Mahommed.

LETTER CCCXCIX.

To Monsieur Moneron, *Fringy*, *at* *Pondicherry*; *same Date.*

The humble address which you sent [to us] has passed under our view; and what you represented therein has been comprehended. Your account of passing occurrences, and of your having written, and dispatched to *Europe*, all particulars relating to our friendly disposition [towards the French nation], as well as your information regarding the ships of war coming to these parts, are all made known.

You

(1) The celebrated Mahrattah minister, Nana Furnaveese, and
(2) The *Paishwa*.

You write "whenever the chiefs of the *Sircar*, selected for the em-"bassy to *Europe*, shall arrive at *Pondicherry*, M. Cossigny will dispatch "them thither, with all the respect and honor [due to their rank and "station]." It is known. In conformity with the orders which we issued in your presence, and agreeably to what you have written, Mahommed Durwaish Khân, Akbar Ali Khân, Mahommed Othman, and other chiefs, charged with letters and presents, have set out [for *Pondicherry*], where they will [in due time] safely arrive. We have no doubt that you will take care that the above mentioned chiefs are properly supplied with whatever they may want, payment being made for the same; and that, providing in the best manner for their accommodation, you will convey them in perfect ease and comfort, along with yourself, to *Europe*.

We have learned by letters from Ghûlâm Ali Khân, Lûtf Ali Khân, Noorûllah Khân, and other *Sirdârs* [or chiefs] formerly sent [to *Europe*], of their safe arrival at the port of *Bussorah*, and of their departure from thence [in prosecution of their journey].

You write, "that during the stormy weather which prevails at sea "[about this time], and which may be expected to continue for two "months longer, ships cannot remain at their [usual] anchorage [on "the coast]; but that M. Cossigny having [some time since], with a "view to this circumstance, given you orders to prepare and bring a "good ship from the *Mauritius*, you should accordingly arrive from "thence at *Pondicherry* with one by the first of.........."(1) It is known: and we assure ourselves, in consequence, that you are by this time arrived at *Pondicherry* with a good ship.

We observe the desire you have expressed, that we would write to your *Râjah* in recommendation of M. Cossigny's confirmation in the government

(1) The name of the month is not quite legible, but is, apparently, intended for *Choiter* (April).

ment of *Pondicherry;* and we have, accordingly, in the letter which we have sent to your *Rájah* by the *Sirdárs* of our *Sircar*, not only made the request suggested by you, but have, moreover, taken that occasion to speak [in due commendation] of the courage and knowledge of business[2] which distinguish the said Monsieur.

We received the copy which you sent us of M. Cossigny's letters to Nizâm Ali Khân and to the Mahrattahs, and all the particulars thereof are become known [to us].

You write, "that five thousand soldiers' musquets will arrive imme-"diately, either at *Calicut* or *Mangalore;* and that you will bring five "thousand more along with yourself, when you return [to *Pondicherry*] "from the *Mauritius*." It is understood. We have written to the *Taalúkdárs* of *Calicut* and *Mangalore*, directing them to receive the musquets you may send, whenever they arrive, *provided you shall have fixed a proper* [or just] *price upon the same.*

LETTER CCCC.

To SHUMSÛDDEEN, *and others (DÁROGHAS of the* TOSHEH-KHÁNEH *at* SERINGAPATAM*); dated from* SHÁNOOR, 22d HYDERY. (19*th November.*)

(EXTRACT.)

YOUR humble address, accompanied by a statement of the quantities of gold and silver remaining in the *Tosheh-khâneh* and mint, together with an account of receipts and balances, has passed under our view. We wrote to you, some time since,[1] directing you to prepare and keep together, in a separate coffer, the sum of five *lacks* of *rupees*, which it was

(2) Original شجاعت و كارداني

(1) It has not been thought necessary to insert the letter here referred to, which was written about a fortnight before the present one.

was our intention to appropriate to the construction of a canal [or aqueduct] at the holy *Nujuf*. This money was to consist of such *Hyderies*, half *rupees*, and quarter *rupees*, as were in the treasury or the mint, or might come in with the collections from the country. We now repeat those orders; and also direct that, having placed the money in question in a distinct coffer, you affix a label on the said coffer, containing these words. "In this chest are deposited the *rupees* composing the *Nuzr* to "be appropriated to the construction of an aqueduct [from the *Euphrates*] "to the sepulchre of the holy Ali." Not a single *Dâm* [or farthing] of this money is to be expended [for any other purpose than the one which has been indicated].

OBSERVATIONS.

Notwithstanding these ostensible, and, perhaps, sincerely-meant preparations for executing the pious work alluded to, there is reason to believe, as has been elsewhere stated, that it was never carried into effect.

LETTER CCCCI.

To Ghûlâm Ali Khân, Lûtf Ali Khân, *and* Shâh Noorûllah; *same Date.* (19*th November*.)

Your humble address was received [by us] on the 5th of *Hydery* [2d November] of the year *Dullo*. You write, "that, by the blessing of "God, you were well, and at *Muscat*, on the 22d of *Jaafury* (A.H. "1200), and that you were to proceed onward to *Bussorah* on the 25th "of the same month."(1) You refer us, in the same dispatch, "for "further

(1) In Letter CCCXCIX, to M. Moneron, of the same date as the present one, the *Sultan* tells the latter, that he had learned from Ghûlâm Ali Khân of their arrival at *Bussorah*.

" further particulars, to a separate letter, addressed to us by Shâh Noor-" ûllah; and moreover mention, your having, some time before, trans-" mitted to the Presence, by a pair of *Hurkârehs*, an account of your " arrival at *Muscat*, together with two other packets, containing copious " details [of your journey and proceedings]." It is known. The aforesaid *Hurkârehs* have not hitherto arrived.

We desire you to let us know what persons you have sent by the ship [which is on its return hither]. It is astonishing, that notwithstanding the written instructions [which you have received on this head], you should, instead of writing to us in detail, refer us to a letter from Shâh Noorûllah. It appears by this, that you never look at your instructions; agreeably to the saying, " the epistles of lovers [are hung or placed] upon " deer's horns."(2) Do not again lose your wits in this manner, but act according to your instructions.

You have written, " that Mûbaruk Khân, the *Jowkdâr*, is dead; and " that you will, with our permission, promote Mahommed .... " in his room." It is understood. We have invested you with full powers; you should, therefore, act in all matters according as you may think best suited to the circumstances of the moment, and not wait for our orders.

We have, at this time, in consequence of the late period to which your arrival in *France* will be protracted, dispatched Mahommed Durwaish, Akbar Ali Khân, Othman Khân, and other *Sirdârs*, to the *Râjah* of the French, for whom they are charged with letters and presents. They are to proceed in a French ship from *Pondicherry*. This is written for your information.

We

sorah. These accounts seem to be at variance, since the letters, referred to in the dispatch to M. Moneron, were most probably those acknowledged above. The contradiction is not material, and is, most probably, an error of the transcriber.

(2) Original برات عاشقان برشاخ آهو I am obliged to acknowledge my ignorance of the meaning of this allusion. *Burât* also signifies a draft, or order, for money.

We have learned from report, that one of the elephants which you took with you died on your way to *Muscat*. It is astonishing that you should not have mentioned this circumstance.

N.B. There was added to the foregoing letter a similar account of the battle of *Shánoor* with that given in Letter CCCLXXXI and others.

OBSERVATIONS.

It is remarkable, that although the *Sultan* had, at this time, dispatched another embassy, by sea, to *France*, he does not, on the present occasion, intimate any intention of recalling Ghûlâm Ali and his associates. On the contrary, he speaks of their arrival in *France* as an event still in his contemplation, though apparently distant. The reason, perhaps, of his not yet revoking the mission of the latter, was, that the new embassy, though appointed and now actually on its road to *Pondicherry*, was likely to be detained a considerable time at that place, and might, by a variety of accidents, be eventually altogether defeated. In fact, it did not take its departure from the *French* presidency till the middle of the year 1787.

LETTER CCCCII.

To Urshud Baig Khân, *Aumil of Calicut; dated 25th Hydery.* *(22d November.)*

Enclosed is a letter which we have received from Gopa, the *Aumil* of *Koorumnád*, relating to the depredations of the robbers and highwaymen [who infest that district]. Peruse the same, and settle the business. Such of the authors of[1] [or principle actors in] these flagitious proceedings *as have been already killed, are killed.* But why should the remainder of them, on being made prisoners, be put to death? Their proper punishment is this. Let the dogs, both *black and white*, be regularly dispatched to *Seringapatam*.[2]

3 M

(1) Original مایه فساد و شرارت پیشگان

(2) Original آن سگان سفید و سیاه را

OBSERVATIONS.

As we may be pretty certain, that it was not the object of the present order to extend any lenity to the offenders in question, it would not be easy to guess what sort of punishment was intended for them upon their arrival at *Seringapatam.* It is equally difficult to explain, what the *Sultan* meant by *black and white dogs*; since the solution of the matter which occurs to me (namely, that of the European settlers on the coast of *Malabar* being alluded to by the latter term) would not seem to be admissible in the present instance. Is it possible that, by the *white dogs,* he could intend the native Christians of *Malabar?* This supposition is, it must be owned, opposed by a strong fact; which is, that the Christians in question are as black as any other people in *India:* so that, if they were in the contemplation of the *Sultan,* he must have employed the words " white dogs " in the way of metonymy, or as another designation for *Nazarenes* or Christians.

LETTER CCCCIII.

To MAHOMMED EESAU, *AUMIL of UFZULÂBÂD NUGR; dated 27th HYDERY. (24th November.)*

THE account of the cardamum reaping is fully understood. When we [some time since] gave [*i. e.* made over to] you a [numerous] body of the sect of *Shaikhs,* and others, our intention, in that measure, was purely this: that lands should be assigned to the people in question for cultivation, and that the business of the cardamum reaping should be entrusted to them [exclusively.]

It would seem, by the account you give of the excesses committed by the robbers in your district, that the latter were become very desirous of being incorporated with the *Usud Ilhye* band. It shall be as they wish.

OBSERVATIONS.

It appears by another letter in the collection, which I have not thought it necessary to insert, that the class of people usually employed in reaping or gathering the cardamums, had been recently detected in embezzlements of the produce to a considerable amount. This circumstance had probably led the *Sultan* to transplant a colony of *Shaikhs*, and other Mussulmans, into the district in question, with a view to their superseding the ancient laborers in this particular branch of agriculture, which constituted one of the principal monopolies of the government. What effect was produced by this expedient I do not know: but there is no reason to believe, that the Mahommedan reaper proved at all more faithful to his trust than the Hindoo, whom he displaced. On the contrary, it has been affirmed by a very respectable authority, that "although all the *Asofs* and "*Amuldárs* under the *Sultan's* government were Moormen, who were seldom "chosen for any other reason than their being Mahommedans, and although the "whole of them had an oath of fidelity administered to them, the embezzlement "of public revenue, by the several classes of servants, is supposed to have "amounted annually to fifteen or twenty *lacks* of *Cantarai pagodas*."(1) Colonel Beatson has also informed us, that "notwithstanding the severity and minuteness "of the *Sultan's* regulations, no prince was ever so grossly imposed upon."(2)

LETTER CCCCIV.

To the DEWÁNS *of* ZUFERÁBÁD (GURRAMCOONDAH); *dated* 1st TÚLOOEY. (28*th November.*)

INFORMING them, that the management [or chastisement] of the *Polygars*, and other turbulent and contumacious tribes, belonged to

3 M 2 the

(1) See letter from Captain (now Lieutenant Colonel) William M'Leod to the Commissioners for the Affairs of *Mysore*, in Colonel Beatson's View of the Origin and Conduct of the last War with Tippoo Sultan, page clxx of the Appendix.

(2) Vide Colonel Beatson's View, page 150.

the province of the *Bukhshy* of *Ehshâm*, and not to theirs; that the above mentioned *Bukhshy* was accordingly engaged in that business; and that the charge of the defence of the forts and of the district [in general], likewise appertained [exclusively] to the same officer.

LETTER CCCCV.

To Mahommed Durwaish, *and the other* Vakeels *proceeding to* France; *dated 2d* Tûlooey. *(29th November.)*

We have lately dispatched to you, in the joint charge of Yunkut Rumna, an *Hurkâreh* of the brotherhood(1) of Pota, and of Kumâl Mahommed, of the brotherhood of Shaikh Mudâr, a casket, having our special seal affixed to it, in which is enclosed a diamond ring. You must open this casket, and taking from thence the ring which it contains, deposit the same in the box of jewels intended for the *Râjah* of the French, which you took with you from hence, and which has also our special seal affixed to it. You are, at the same time, to take out from the said box the ruby ring which you will find in it, and placing it in the casket now sent to you, to which your seals must be affixed, return the said ruby ring to us by the two aforesaid persons.

Having deposited the diamond ring, now sent, in the box with which you were originally charged, you are to affix your seals to it, and take great care of the same.

As there was from the beginning a diamond ring in the box [which you took with you], there will now, including that which has been just sent to you, be two, which is the number of diamond rings specified in your *Hûkm-nâmeh* [or instructions], as you will perceive on a reference to the latter.

(1) Original برادري rendered literally in the text. It is equivalent to *clan*.

LETTER CCCCVI.

To Ghûlâm Ghuzunfur; *dated 4th Tûlooey.* (*1st December.*)

(Extract.)

What you write, respecting the promise of Wunkeish Doob, the banker, to fulfil his engagements in the course of fifteen days, is understood. The aforesaid has, for six years past, constantly given the same assurance at the end of every fifteen days. He is a great liar, and you must not mind his promises; but, at the expiration of the time appointed for his settling, compel him to do so, by proceeding very vigorously against him.

It has come to our knowledge, through the channel of the Canarese newspapers, that Mohyûddeen Ali Khân, notwithstanding his great age,(1) and his experience, during his recent visit to us, of our disposition in this respect,(2) has forgotten himself so far as to resume his former passion for the exhibition of dancing, which he knows to be highly repugnant to our pleasure. *This is a sign* [or *proof*] *of superfluous wealth.* But wherefore have you remained silent on this occasion; and why have you not forbidden his pursuit of this amusement?

LETTER CCCCVII.

To Budrûz Zumân Khân; *same Date.* (*1st December.*)

We some time since wrote to you with our own hand, and we now again write, to desire that, after properly arranging the business of your army,

(1) Original با وصف بي دنداني literally "toothlessness."

(2) Original با وصف ديدن نشيب و فراز حضور كه حال ديده رفته است i. e. "notwithstanding "his having himself very lately witnessed (or beheld) the *ups* and *downs* of the Presence;" meaning, the particular manners of the court, and especially the sort of conduct most consonant with the sentiments and wishes of the *Sultan*.

army, you will leave the same in charge of your son, and repair to our Presence, through the interior of the country, and by a close or woody route, in company with Khizr Khân,[1] whom we have sent with two hundred horse to join you. You must proceed with expedition, but [at the same time] with care and vigilance. Our special retinue is about to remove from hence to the pass of *Kurk-nâth*.

LETTER CCCCVIII.

To Turbiyut Ali Khân ; *dated 5th Túlooey.* (*2d December.*)

(Extract.)

Your representation, with regard to our not honoring your letters with [regular or early] answers, is understood. That great person [1*] [meaning Turbiyut Ali Khân] eats two or three times a day, sits at his ease, and amuses himself with conversation. We, on the other hand, are occupied, from morning to night, with business. Whenever we have leisure, we attend to the answering of your dispatches.

LETTER CCCCIX.

To Mahommed Durwaish *and others ; dated 6th Túlooey.*

(*3d December.*)

Directing them to *speak* to the *Rájah* of the French, and [through his means] to procure [and bring with them from France] a skilful physician ;

(1) I believe that this Khizr Khân was a commander of *Kuzzâks*, or *Looties*.

(1*) Original آن عظمت نشان which though a common form of address from a sovereign to a servant, or other person of superior rank and consideration, seems, in this place, to be meant somewhat sarcastically.

physician; a pharmacopolist, thoroughly acquainted with, and capable of preparing, every kind of medicine known in *Europe*; and lastly, an able surgeon.

LETTER CCCCX.

To the DEWÂN *of* CHITTLEDOORG *and others; dated from near the* TUNGBUDDRA, *14th* TÛLOOEY. (*11th December.*)

DIRECTING them to send an intelligent agent to the *Payen-Ghaut*, with instructions to invite into the *Sultan's* dominions [such] well-born, and other unprovided persons [as might be found disposed to remove thither]. Enclosing, moreover, a passport for the agent proceeding [on this service] to the *Payen-Ghaut*, and desiring a particular account of every individual agreeing to repair to *Mysore* to be transmitted to the Presence.

LETTER CCCCXI.

To MONSIEUR LALLY[(1)]; *same Date.* (*11th December.*)

YOU must allow no more than a single shop to be opened in your camp for the vending of spirituous liquors; and over that you must place a guard, for the purpose of preventing the sale of spirits to any but the Europeans belonging to you; it being a rule in our victorious army, that no shop of this kind shall be permitted to be established in it.

(1) M. Lally commanded, at this time, the party of Europeans in the service of the *Sultan*.

LETTER CCCCXII.

To Monsieur Cossigny; *the Governor of Madras;* Ghûlâm Ali Khân; *the Imâm of Muscat; and others: dated* 18*th Tûlooey.* (15*th December.*)

(Circular.)

The [main] body of the accursed ones,(1) joined by the forces of Nizâm Ali Khân, and amounting together to nearly a hundred thousand horse and foot, accompanied by [a train of] artillery, having lately approached, with hostile intentions, within ten or twelve *coss* of our victorious army, which lay encamped near *Shânoor:* we no sooner received intelligence of this movement, than taking all our guns and baggage with us, we advanced rapidly against the enemy, whom we completely surprized.(2) The engagement which took place upon this occasion was fought on the 11th of *Sufur*, A.H. 1201 [or 2d December 1786]. The action, however, had not yet arrived at [the clashing of] swords and bayonets, when the enemy, no longer able to support the fire from our guns, involuntarily(3) took the road of flight; upon which they were closely pursued for two or three *coss* by our victorious army, who slew and took prisoners great numbers of the fugitives, besides obtaining possession of the whole of their baggage. In addition to this, three thousand camels, laden with various articles, twenty thousand bullocks, five elephants with canopies, twenty standards and kettle-drums, and seven or eight thousand horses, fell into our hands.

Our

(1) Original مقهور

(2) Original دفعتا بر سروقت اشقيا مزبور رسيديم

(3) Original بي اختيار that is, "had no other choice;" or, "were irresistibly compelled "to fly."

Our victorious army is still in close pursuit of the enemy, and, with the blessing of God, the Aider, having driven them as far as *Poonah* and *Hyderabad*, which are the places of their residence, we shall communicate the same to you. That eminent person being among the number of our friends, we have thought it proper to give him the present detailed account of this battle.

OBSERVATIONS.

It may be presumed, that if the *Sultan* had taken any guns upon this occasion, he would not have omitted so material a circumstance in the present *Futah-nâmeh*, or "letter of victory," which, for this reason, may be suspected to have somewhat exaggerated his general success; though, on the whole, it is certainly less inflated and pompous, in point of diction, than is usually the case in similar productions. It would, at any rate, appear, that the advantages which he obtained over the enemy in this last action were of a more decisive character than those which had resulted from the battle which preceded it. It is probable, that the *Sultan*, in his Memoirs, entered into a fuller relation of the engagement of the 11th of *Sufur*, than that contained in the foregoing letter; but, unfortunately, that part of his narrative was included in the portion of the manuscript destroyed by the accident already alluded to. This, however, as well as many other defects of the present work, considered in an historical light, will, no doubt, be amply supplied hereafter, by the able and elegant historian of *Mysore*.

In addition to the foregoing account of the battle of the 11th *Sufur*, the *Sultan's* letter to the *Imâm* of *Muscat* contains the following paragraph:

"Enclosed is a letter to Ghûlâm Ali Khân, and the other *Sirdârs*, [proceeding "to Constantinople], which you will forward to them.

"Agreeably to your own proposal, you must send a *Vakeel* [or minister] to "our Presence at the beginning of the ensuing season. You must likewise not "fail to establish factories at our different sea-ports; and as we have come to the "resolution, that not a single grain of rice shall be sold [in our country] to any

" Nazarenes coming from *Muscat*, or to any others but the [*bonâ fide*] merchants " of *Muscat*, you, therefore, must give orders to the merchants of that place " bound to our ports, to bring with them certificates from our *Vakeel* there, in " order that they may be enabled to purchase and carry away [without obstacle] " whatever commodities they may require.

" Procure and dispatch to us some saffron seed, and also some mules, with the " breed of which you are acquainted [*i. e.* which you can recommend as being of " a good breed].

N.B. Wrote to the same effect as the above to Meer Kâzim, the commercial agent at *Muscat*, who was also desired to buy and send more pearls to the *Sultan*.

LETTER CCCCXIII.

To GHÛLÂM ALI KHÂN; *same Date.* (*15th December.*)

WE have learned by letters which we have received from the *Imâm* and from the *Khulfâr* [or minister] of *Muscat*, that one of the vessels which proceeded with you from hence has been burnt. It is very astonishing that you should not have mentioned any thing of this matter. Communicate to us all the particulars of it. We conclude that you have proceeded onwards from *Bussorah*. Let us know. Let us likewise know, what things you stand in need of, that they may be sent to you.

LETTER CCCCXIV.

To CHISHTY YÂR KHÂN, *DEWÂN, and* ZYNÛL AABIDEEN, *BUKHSHY of the EHSHÂM of CHITTLEDOORG; dated 19th TÛLOOEY.* (*16th December.*)

YOUR letter, congratulating us on our [late] victory over the enemies of the faith, and accompanied by a *Nuzr* of twenty *rupees*, has passed

passed under our view. It behoves all Mussulmans humbly to address themselves to the Almighty Presence, and to implore, that the forces of the accursed may be always confounded and disgraced, and the army of Islâm be always victorious and triumphant.

LETTER CCCCXV.

To MOHYÛDDEEN ALI KHÂN, *DEWÂN, and* GHÛLÂM GHUZUNFUR, *at KURPAH; dated 24th TÛLOOEY.* (21*st December.*)

YOUR relation of your late encounters with the enemy's horse [1] is become duly known; and we are much pleased with the account you have given of their chastisement, and of your having taken six prisoners and twelve horses from them. This behaviour was worthy of your noble descent and of your fidelity to us.

Let the prisoners be strangled,[2] and let the twelve horses, after being valued according to custom, and paid for to the captors,[3] be taken into the service of the *Sircar*.

N.B. By some letters which follow here, but which are not deemed sufficiently interesting to be inserted, it appears, that the *Sultan* was, at this period, much occupied in dedicating shrines, &c. to the principal Mahommedan saints. Whether as an expression of his gratitude for the benefits which he might suppose himself to have recently derived (in the instance of his military successes) from their intercession in his behalf, or in order to render them propitious to his ulterior views

3 N 2

(1) Most probably alludes to some irruption of the *Nizâm's* troops into the province of *Kurpah*, during which they would appear to have plundered the *Paith*, or outer town, of *Kurpah*; but the passage relating to this point being somewhat obscure, I have omitted it in the translation.

(2) Original اسرارا کل باید داد

(3) Original اردل on which word see Letter XXXII.

views and wishes, is not stated. It is probable, however, that he was actuated on the occasion by both considerations.

LETTER CCCCXVI.

To SHUMSÛDDEEN KHÂN; *dated 29th Tŭlooey.* (*26th December.*)

YOU represent, "that the people of the jewel office and of the "goldsmith's workshop have applied to you to be supplied with the gold "and silver necessary for making up the *Puduks*, and other articles of "jewellery, which have been ordered, but that no receipts coming in at "this time, either on account of the collections, or from the *Surrâfs* [or "money-changers] superintending the *Dŭkâns* [or retail warehouses] "of the *Sircar*,(1) you do not possess the means of answering the de- "mand: besides which, twelve hundred *pagodas* weight of gold has "been already furnished for this service by the mint, which has not yet "been replaced."

It is known. In the *Tosheh-khâneh* [or treasury], and in the department where the elephants' teeth(2) are kept, there is gold and silver, to the amount of several *lacks* (3) weight of *pagodas*, appropriated [some time since] to the coinage of gold *mohrs*, *pagodas*, &c. Is not, then, that gold and silver still in the same place; or do you imagine it to be something else? This is, truly, a subject for wonder! You must take from this apartment whatever gold and silver may be required for the purpose in question; and after seeing that it is carefully assayed, deliver the same to the workmen.

(1) On the subject of these warehouses, or shops, see Letter XCVIII.

(2) Elsewhere called "the ivory apartment."

(3) A *lack* is a hundred thousand of any thing.

OBSERVATIONS.

Notwithstanding the wonder here expressed by the *Sultan,* at his treasurer's not having taken upon him to break in upon a hoard of bullion, distinctly stated to have been appropriated to a specific purpose, it may be fairly doubted, whether if that officer had presumed to do so, his conduct would have escaped animadversion. It is true, that if we were to judge by the occasional intimations of the kind here conveyed, and which occur in the course of the correspondence, we might infer, that the public functionaries under Tippoo Sultan were invested with considerable discretionary powers: but, on the other hand, how many are the instances, in which the slightest exercise of such a power has brought upon them the severest reproofs of the *Sultan,* who was for ever directing them "to mind "their instructions, and to abstain from pursuing their own conceits." The trust reposed in Shumsûddeen Khân was of a peculiarly delicate nature; and if he had ventured to act in the manner which his master affects to insinuate he should have done, and had so acted with impunity, it must be admitted, that such a fact would have materially altered our view of the *Sultan's* character, in one important particular, at least; since it would have shown him to have been of a far more confiding and unsuspicious disposition than the general tenor of his actions imply. The safest guide, however, to our judgment, on the present occasion, is the evident backwardness of the treasurer to exceed the letter of his orders. No doubt, he had very sufficient reasons for this cautious conduct.

The *Sultan* appears to have distributed, about this time, various marks of his favour among his principal commanders. These tokens of approbation consisted chiefly of gold chains, rings, and what are called in the original *Puduks* or *Pudugs.* To some he gave seal-rings, with the names of the persons thus distinguished engraved upon them. Among these was a cornelian, with the inscription "Budrûz Zumân Khân Behâdûr;" being the first instance, if I am not mistaken, in which the title of *Behâdûr* is applied by Tippoo to any of his servants. He presented, at the same time, to certain *Kuchurries,* or divisions of the army, official seals, some made of gold and others of silver, and having inscriptions engraved on them, alluding to their services in the cause of Islâm. The *Kushoons* composing

composing these *Kuchurries* (namely, the second and third *Kuchurries* of regular infantry, and the second and third *Kuchurries* of *Bârgeer* cavalry) had probably particularly distinguished themselves in the late actions with the Mahrattahs.

LETTER CCCCXVII.

To Monsieur Cossigny; *dated 2d* Yoosŭfy. *(28th December.)*

What you wrote, respecting the departure of M. Monneron, on the 12th October, from the port of *Pondicherry* for the *Mauritius*, is understood. A month has elapsed since the persons appointed by us to proceed to *France* were dispatched from hence. Accordingly, having reached *Bangalore*, they afterwards pursued their journey from thence, and will [in due time] arrive [at *Pondicherry*].

You write recommending, " that we should direct the aforesaid persons " [*i. e.* the *Vakeels*] to remain at *Selim* or *Eeloor* till the arrival of the " above-mentioned Monsieur." It is understood. With the blessing of God, the said Monsieur will soon return in safety from the *Mauritius*. We have, in the mean while, agreeably to your humble suggestion,(1) sent orders to the aforesaid persons to remain [for the present] at *Anŭntgeery*. They will proceed [to *Pondicherry*] whenever you shall desire them to do so.

You write, " that a strict friendship subsists between the Hollanders " and the *Râjah* of the French; and that is is expedient that we, also, " should establish a good understanding and correspondence with that " people." It is comprehended. Whosoever is united with the French, is, in fact, united with us.

The

(1) Original حسب معروضه شما .

The barometer[2] which your humble attachment[3] prompted you to send us has been received. No doubt, you will, also, after getting it prepared [or made up], dispatch to us the .... of ....[4] which you have promised us.

You engage [a great share of] our attention: be [therefore] in all respects easy in your mind.

N.B. A letter, of the same date as the above, directs Mahommed Durwaish, and the other *Vakeels*, to halt at *Anúntgeery*, till desired by M. Cossigny to proceed to *Pondicherry*.

The following passage, though inadvertently inserted in the letter to the *Vakeels*, appears to belong properly to that addressed to M. Cossigny.

The barometer which [you] sent us in charge of [your] *Hurkáreh* is in all respects very complete, excepting in the article of the quicksilver, which, owing to its *oldness*, does not move up and down. It is, therefore, returned [to you]: and you must send another good one in its stead, that has been made in the present year.

LETTER CCCCXVIII.

To Urshud Baig Khân, *Foujdár of Calicut; same Date.* (*28th December.*)

Abandon your vain idea of proceeding [on a pilgrimage] to the Holy Temple, and apply yourself, according to custom, to the affairs of the *Sircar*. This is the most advisable thing you can do.

(2) This is the word employed in the original, which has برامیتر

(3) Original به مقتضاي عقیدت where عقیدت denotes the attachment of an inferior to a superior.

(4) The original is written کارت دژد کراني which I take to be intended for French words. Perhaps, the first is meant for *carte*, or map.

OBSERVATIONS.

This officer appears, from other parts of the correspondence, to have formed some improper female connection, which the *Sultan* had insisted upon his renouncing. The lover resented this interference, by announcing his resolution to proceed on a pilgrimage to *Mecca.* This sort of declaration is often made under the influence of temporary chagrin or disappointment, and sometimes without any serious intention of fulfilling it, and with no other view than that of intimidation. Whatever the case might be with regard to Urshud Baig Khân, he ultimately relinquished his purpose (whether real or pretended), although the object of his irregular attachment had, by order of his sovereign, been publicly banished from the town of *Calicut.* The following letter will show in what manner the *Sultan* was accustomed to proceed on occasions of this kind.

LETTER CCCCXIX.

To the DEWÂNS *of* CALICUT; *same Date.* (*28th December.*)

DISSUADE Urshud Baig Khân from his vain purpose of repairing to the House of God [*Mecca*]. Try, at first, as far as you may be able, the effect of fair persuasion; and if this should not succeed, you must, of necessity, confine him. You must, likewise, imprison the courtezan, who has been the cause of this affair.

N.B. Upon Urshud Baig's "coming again to his senses," as it is expressed in the original, he was restored to his office; and the woman in question was released, and "*driven*" from Calicut.

LETTER CCCCXX.

To MONSIEUR COSSIGNY; *dated* 3d YOOSÛFY. (*29th December.*)

THERE is a book which comes from Europe, and which treats of the barometer,(1) wherein it is written, that at certain [stated] times the quicksilver

(1) Original هوانما literally, "showing [the state of] the air.

quicksilver rises a certain number of degrees; and that if, at such times, a person afflicted with any one of certain [stated] disorders shall, during a paroxysm of his complaint, place his hand on the barometer, the degree to which the quicksilver may, in consequence, ascend, will indicate the state [or height] of such person's disorder. Get this [book] translated into Persian, and send it to the Presence.

LETTER CCCCXXI.

To Shumsûddeen Khân; *dated from near* Kopul, *5th* Yoosûfy. (31*st December* 1786.)

(Extract.)

The leather basket, containing [our several] treaties with the Mahrattahs, which you sent by the post, has reached us [safely] from *Hurry-hur*.

OBSERVATIONS.

The *Sultan* appears to have sent for the treaties here mentioned, either in consequence of some overtures of peace made to him by the Mahrattahs, or preparatory to the discussions which he might expect to take place soon on that subject.

LETTER CCCCXXII.

To Mûsheer ûl Mûlk; *dated 4th* Rubee ûl Ouwul, *A.H.* 1201.(1)

The *Mûtusuddy*, Luchman Râo, was sent by me, merely for the purpose of ascertaining why the *Nabob*, Nizâm Ali Khân Behâdûr, notwithstanding

3 O

(1) Corresponding, as well as I can compute, with the 24th December 1786. If this calculation be correct, the present letter is not exactly in its place.

withstanding the contract of mutual union which took place between us, through the medium[2] of Mahommed Iftikhâr Khân,[3] had suddenly confederated with the people of *Poonah*, and without any cause [or provocation on my part], advanced into my dominions. He was not dispatched with any other view.

I have, at this time, indirectly learned,[4] that that friend has placed a guard over the above-mentioned *Mûtusuddy*. This circumstance is very surprising: and though I find it difficult to believe the account, seeing that such conduct is not usual with great persons, yet if it should really be the case, [I desire you will] dismiss the said *Mûtusuddy*.

LETTER CCCCXXIII.

To GHÛLÂM HYDER, *AUMIL of BANGALORE; dated* 9*th* YOOSÛFY. (4*th January* 1787.)

THE account, stating you had strictly prohibited the distilling and vending of spirituous liquors, and had, moreover [in pursuance of the same object], made the whole body of vintners enter into written engagements [to desist from selling such liquors], is understood. You must make the distillers execute a similar engagement, and then oblige them to take up some other occupation.

LETTER CCCCXXIV.

To SYED MAHOMMED, *KILAADÂR of SERINGAPATAM; dated from KATURKY, near KOPUL,* 10*th* YOOSÛFY. (5*th January*.)

A SHIRT, formerly belonging to the Holy Prophet (on whom be the peace and blessing of God!) and which was first discovered at *Kurpah*, from

(2) Original زباني literally, "by the tongue."

(3) See Letter CCCLXVI.

(4) Original ازخارج "from without," *i. e.* not immediately from Luchman Râo himself.

from whence, in process of time, it came into our possession, has been dispatched to you. This precious relic must be delivered in charge to the priests, to whose care the [other] holy traces [or remains] of the prophet have been already consigned, with instructions to place and keep it along with those.

LETTER CCCCXXV.

To Yâkoob, *and other Armenian Merchants; dated* 16*th* Yoosúfy. (11*th January.*)

(*Entitled a* Kowl-nâmeh, *or Engagement.*)

The duties upon [such] goods [as you may import into our dominions] are, without exception,(1) [hereby] remitted. Bring, therefore, with entire confidence to our ports, and into our kingdom, either by sea or land [as you may think proper], your silk stuffs and [other] merchandize, and there [freely] buy and sell. Wheresoever you may [choose to] bring your goods, there a place shall be assigned for your residence: and if you should, at any time, be in want of workmen or laborers, the same shall be furnished you, on hire, by our *Taalúkdárs*.

OBSERVATIONS.

I am not enabled to account for the sudden and extraordinary encouragement here held out to the Armenian merchants; nor do I know how far it succeeded in alluring that industrious race of men to *Mysore.* The immunities offered to them were, no doubt, apparently tempting, since they greatly exceeded whatever had been hitherto granted, either to their fellow countrymen, or to any other foreigners. Still, however, the promised advantages were but loosely and generally expressed: and certainly were not intended to admit the adventurers to a participation in those

3 O 2 branches

(1) Original درویست "completely, entirely."

branches of the trade of *Mysore* (as sandal-wood, pepper, &c.) which were rigorously monopolized by the *Sultan*, as constituting the chief commercial resources of his kingdom. It does not appear, of what country Yâkoob was a subject or resident,

LETTER CCCCXXVI.

To MEER MOAAYENÛDDEEN, BÛRHÂNÛDDEEN, MÂH MIRZÂ KHÂN, *and* HÛSAIN ALI KHÂN; *dated the Night*[1] *of the 17th* YOOSÛFY. *(12th January.)*

(CIRCULAR.)

DIRECTING them to prepare two batteries[2] in [front of] their respective divisions, according to a plan transmitted to them, and to place two guns and a company of regular infantry in each.

N.B. A few words follow here, of which I am unable to make any sense. Something appears to have been omitted.

LETTER CCCCXXVII.

To SHUMSÛDDEEN KHÂN, &c. *DÂROGHAS of the* TOSHEH-KHÂNEH, *or Treasury, at* SERINGAPATAM; *dated 22d* YOOSÛFY. *(17th January.)*

(EXTRACT.)

IN addition to the camels which were some time ago sent to you, for the conveyance hither of certain articles of our special camp equipage, we have now dispatched fifty others, for the purpose of bringing treasure. You must, accordingly, dispatch the tents on the former, and on the latter the treasure.

(1) There are no less than five different dispatches dated on this night.

(2) Battery is the word used, as formerly, in the original.

OBSERVATIONS.

The treasure here mentioned was, most probably, designed for the Mahrattahs; and appears, by a subsequent letter, to have consisted of 3,88,971 *pagodas* of sorts, and 72,000 *Pondicherry rupees*, making together about thirteen *lacks* of *rupees*, which agrees pretty nearly with the sum stated (as will be presently seen) by the *Sultan* himself, as the amount of what he paid to the Mahrattahs at the conclusion of peace.

LETTER CCCCXXVIII.

To the Dewâns *of* Zuferâbâd; *dated* 29*th* Yoosûfy. (24*th January.*)

Having made up, according to the established system of our government, the account of pay due to the *Jyshe*, the *Piâdehs*, *Coolies*, &c. you must issue the same in the manner prescribed in your instructions: that is to say, the whole body are to be paid, *man by man*,(1) in your own presence. There is no necessity for your consigning the amount of their pay to the *Kilaadâr* [to be distributed by him]. If you do so, you shall be punished in the manner specified in your *Hukm-nâmeh*.

LETTER CCCCXXIX.

To Râjah Râm Chundur; *dated from* Anagoondy, 3*d* Eezudy.
(28*th January.*)

Authorizing him to take [from the public money] two thousand *rupees*, as a gift from the *Sultan*, to enable him to celebrate the marriage of his nephew, and to send for his connexions and relations from the *Carnatic*.

(1) Original دست بدست "from hand to hand."

LETTER CCCCXXX.

To BUDRÛZ ZUMÂN KHÂN; *same Date.* (*28th January.*)

HAVING read, we transmit for your perusal [two] letters, brought to us by a pair of camel couriers, from Râo Râsta and Holkar. We have likewise sent to you the two camel couriers [in question]. You must, after looking at these letters, proceed thither [*i. e.* to the Mahrattah camp] with the couriers above-mentioned.

A cornelian seal, with your name engraved upon it, has arrived from *Putn*: but as it was not set for a ring, we have ordered it to be properly mounted as such, and when ready it shall be dispatched to you.

OBSERVATIONS.

It would appear by the foregoing letter, and is confirmed by the *Sultan's* Memoirs, that Budrûz Zumân Khân was chosen to conduct the negociations now pending with the Mahrattahs. It may even be inferred, from the terms of this dispatch, that if he was not named in the letters of Râsta and Holkar, as the most eligible person that could be employed by the *Sultan* on this occasion, he was, very probably, mentioned as the individual who would be most agreeable to the Mahrattah chiefs. Similar suggestions often proceed in *India* from a hostile power: but when this is the case, it generally denotes either an actual, or an assumed superiority in the latter. If Tippoo tacitly yielded, in the present instance, to such a pretension, it is not unlikely that he was led to do so, as much by his impatience to prepare for a fresh contest with the English as by any other consideration. Except with some motive of this nature, he would hardly have consented to a measure so liable to be construed into an act of submission, as the deputation of a person of Budrûz Zumân's rank to the Mahrattah camp would be.[1]

(1) For some additional observations on the above Letter, the reader is referred to the Postcript subjoined to Letter CCCCXXXV.

LETTER CCCCXXXI.

To Meer Ibraheem ; *dated* 6*th* Eezudy. (31*st January*.)

You must not, in future, form the design of chastising either the Nâirs or Moplahs. This business appertains to the *Foujdâr* of that quarter. Yours is to apply yourself earnestly to the collection of the revenue, and other fiscal matters.

LETTER CCCCXXXII.

To Urshud Baig Khân, *Foujdâr of* Calicut; *dated* 8*th* Eezudy. (2*d February*.)

You must give the most strict orders to all the merchants, and other inhabitants of that place [*Calicut*], neither to buy any goods of the English factor who is come thither, nor sell grain, or any other articles whatsover, to him. How long [in this case] will the above named remain ?(1) He will, in the end, despair of making either sales or purchases, and depart from thence.

OBSERVATIONS.

It will be sufficient to remark on this letter, that the order contained in it amounts to a gross infraction of the eighth article of the treaty of *Mangalore*, concluded between the English and Tippoo in March 1784.

(1) That is, "He will soon, in this case, be compelled to depart."

LETTER CCCCXXXIII.

To Kureem Sâheb ; *same Date. (2d February.)*

Your humble address, accompanied by a *Nuzr*, on account of our chastisement of, and [late] victory over, the enemy, has passed under our view. What you write, respecting your intention of repairing to our Presence, and the re-establishment of your health, is understood, and has afforded pleasure to our mind. With the blessing of God, our special retinue will soon shed lustre on that place [*Seringapatam*] when we shall have a meeting.

OBSERVATIONS.

Kureem Saheb was the second son of Hyder Ali by a concubine, but was adopted by Medina Begum ;(1) who, I believe, was a lawful wife of Hyder, as well as Fukhurûn Nisa Beeby, the mother of Tippoo Sultan. Kureem Saheb survived his brother, after whose death he came under the protection of the British government, together with the other branches of his father's family, and was still living in 1808. He is represented to be of weak intellects ; and would not, at any period, appear to have been entrusted with authority by his father, or to have been an object of jealousy to his brother. The foregoing letter is not the only one to his address which appears in the present collection. There is another of a prior date, acknowledging, as this does, the receipt of a *Nuzr* on occasion of a former victory.

(1) It was a daughter of Medina Begum, by Hyder, who was married to Abdûl Khyre Khân, the *Nabob* of *Shânoor*, and not an own or full sister of Kureem Saheb, as elsewhere erroneously stated. I have been enabled to correct this mistake, by means of a genealogical table of the family of Hyder Ali, obligingly communicated to me by Colonel Marriot, since this work went to press.

LETTER CCCCXXXIV.

To Mahommed Durwaish, &c. *dated* 20*th* Eezidy.[1]
(14*th February*.)

You did right in apprizing Monsieur Cossigny, the Governor [of *Pondicherry*], of your arrival at *Anuntgeery*; and must, hereafter, act as the aforesaid Governor shall recommend to you. [When you resume your journey] you must proceed to *Pondicherry*, without stopping by the way.[2] How are the English people[3] to open and search any thing belonging to you ?[4]

OBSERVATIONS.

It would appear by this letter, that the *Vakeels* had, in their dispatches to the *Sultan*, expressed some apprehensions of being stopped and searched by the English, in their passage through the territories of the *Nabob* of *Arcot*. The *Sultan* affects to treat their fears as chimerical; but, nevertheless, seems to have thought it advisable that they should elude the observation of the English as much as possible, and with this view, directs them to travel by night to *Pondicherry*. He had previously, as the context leads me to suspect, caused their dispatches to be concealed in some part of their apparel, or bedding.

3 P By

(1) No letters of any particular interest occur between the 8th and 20th of *Eezidy* (2d and 14th of February 1787). It is probable that the *Sultan* was much occupied in this interval with the negociations of peace, the conclusion of which is announced in the next letter. On the 14th *Eezidy* (or 8th of Febuary) the *Sultan* appears to have been encamped at *Kunuckgheery*.

(2) Original شباشب به پهلچري برسند *i. e.* "you must proceed all night to *Pondicherry*"

(3) Original مردم انگريز which may mean the persons belonging to the English.

(4) That is, "they will not presume to search." This passage is not very clear in the original.

By a subsequent letter it appears, that M. Cossigny recommended, that the *Vakeels* should remain at *Anuntgeery* till the arrival of M. Monneron from the *Mauritius.* On this occasion the *Sultan* observes, that M. Cossigny "has coun-"selled well, and is a good man, to whose opinion it will be proper in them "always to conform." He concludes the dispatch, here alluded to, with exhorting them to approve their zeal and fidelity in the execution of the commission entrusted to them, and with promises of high reward and favor on their return from their embassy.

LETTER CCCCXXXV.

To KÛTBÛL MÛLK MAHOMMED KÛTBÛDDEEN KHÂN BEHÂDÛR ;(1) *same Date.* (14*th February.*)

THE enemy, after flying, in consequence of the successive chastisements they have received [from us], as far as the banks of the *Kishna*, found themselves in the end reduced to such a helpless state, as compelled them to sue to us for an accommodation in the most humble and earnest manner.(2) The result is, that a treaty of peace, entirely conformable to the wishes of the *Usud Ilhye Sircar*, has been concluded between us. In consequence [of this treaty], we shall have to relinquish the possession of *Adoni :* but we will bestow some other country upon you in its stead.

It is therefore written, that you must, with the utmost expedition, collect all the money you can from the country. *You must, moreover, completely encompass two or three towns, and getting together five or seven thousand people, report the particulars to us ; as men are wanted*

[*at*

(1) The form of *Ulkáb*, or address, used in this letter to Kûtbûddeen, is شهامت ومعلی مرتبت بسالت و عوالی منزلت being exactly the same with that employed in Letter CCCXXXVI. to the King of France.

(2) Original آخر الامر لاچار شده بسیار بعجز والحاح بدست و پا افتاده

[*at this time*] *for the Usud Ilhye corps*. A further reinforcement is about to be dispatched to you. Whatever hostile force may appear in that quarter,(3) you must chastise it effectually, and level it [with the earth].(4)

OBSERVATIONS.

Although the treaty, recently concluded between the *Sultan* and the Mahrattahs, would seem to have provided for the restoration of *Adoni* and its dependencies to the *Nizâm*, yet it is, nevertheless, probable, that the latter might not yet have formally acceded to it; or even have had time to do so. Here, then, we see Tippoo, with his characteristic perfidy, eagerly endeavouring to avail himself of the short interval which might be expected to elapse before the completion of the general peace, in order to impoverish and depopulate, as much as possible, the country he was about to relinquish. I am ignorant of the success of the *Sultan's* barbarous policy upon the present occasion. It appears, however, but too probable, that the inhabitants of *Adoni*, and of the surrounding country, would have reason to deplore, for a long time, his temporary occupation of it.

A few other letters follow here to different persons, announcing, in terms nearly similar to the preceding part of the dispatch to Kûtbûddeen, the termination of the war. It is only, however, in a circular letter of the same date, to the *Peer-zâdehs*, Boodhun Shâh, Kuleem Ûllah Shâh, Syed Ahmed Sâheb, and Nubby Shâh, of which an extract has already been given at Letter CCCLXXXI, that he announces his determination to turn his arms against the English, or "those who "forbid the practice of calling to prayers from the *Minarets*:" in which terms Christians in general are frequently described by other Musulmans, as well as by Tippoo.

3 P 2

(3) The hostile force here alluded to was, of course, one belonging to the *Nizâm*.

(4) Original تنبیه واقعی نموده برابر سازند

HAVING brought the correspondence of the *Sultan* to the close of the war, with the early operations of which it commences, I cannot, perhaps, better conclude this work, than with the only remaining fragment of his Memoirs, which it is to my purpose to lay before the reader. Owing to the chasm which has been already accounted for, the present extract will not throw so much light on the progress of the war, subsequently to the action of the 2d of December, as could be wished; but what is still more to be regretted is, that after reciting the first article of the treaty by which the war was terminated, and preparing the reader for a continuation of this interesting document, the original abruptly passes to an exaggerated picture of the miserable condition to which the Mahrattah army was reduced, at the period of the pacification.

The operations which followed immediately after the rejection of the *Sultan's* challenge by Tukojee Holkar are wanting, the remnant of the manuscript beginning as follows:

"On the following morning they rejoined the victorious army, bringing with "them the whole of their booty.(1) I now halted for four or five days on the "ground which had been occupied by the enemy, during which time I sent out "some *Kuzzâk* [or *Looty*] horse, to procure intelligence of the infidels. This party "returned with an account that they were posted on the other side of *Kopul* and "*Behâdûr-bundeh*, in the latter of which they had placed a [strong] garrison. "On receiving this information, I proceeded by long marches to *Behâdûr-bundeh*, "near to which I encamped; sending forward, at the same time, a division of the "army, so close to that side of the place [which communicated with the country] "as to prevent its receiving succours from the unbelievers. After this, I made the "circuit of *Behâdûr-bundeh*, and [narrowly] viewed the place, which I found "to be small, but of most difficult access, there being no [visible] path by which "a human

(1) The Sultan had probably been describing some partial attack upon the enemy.

" a human creature could ascend to the top of it. I now caused two batteries to " be erected, one against each angle of the face next to us, and placed six batter- " ing guns in each. I then had ladders prepared for scaling the opposite side of " the fort."

The Sultan here proceeds to detail the means (2) by which, in the course of the night, he made a lodgement at the foot of the fort, from whence he was enabled to fix his ladders. Previously, however, to attempting an escalade, he tried the effect of his batteries, but apparently with little success, the walls of the place having been hewn out of the rock, and rendered by himself, before its capture by the Mahrattahs, extremely strong. This case, the *Sultan* observes, furnished a verification of the proverb, which says, " there is no help for the evil of one's " own creating." In the mean while the Mahrattahs were encamped at the distance only of three *coss*, watching for a favorable opportunity of relieving the place. " Under these circumstances," continues the *Sultan*, " not thinking a further " delay of two or three days advisable, I determined on an immediate assault; " with which view I prepared three hundred men, composed of regulars, of *Jyshe*, " and of *Ehshâm*, who being placed over night in the lodgement made at the foot " of the fort, were directed to rush forward at the hour of morning prayer, when " a rocket signal would be made for the purpose. In aid of this enterprize, " besides the fire from the batteries, I caused eight pieces of light artillery to be " placed in the plain before the fort, upon the walls of which they were ordered " to keep up such a close fire, as should prevent the garrison from manning them, " and thereby facilitate the progress of the storming party. Agreeably to this " arrangement, the latter commenced the assault exactly at dawn of day; but " were opposed with great firmness and courage by the infidels, who planting them- " selves at the part of the wall which had been breached, and by which the " assailants advanced, hurled upon them from thence large stones, besides pouring " amongst them, from all sides, a heavy discharge of musketry. On this occasion " a *Teepdâr* [colonel] who had mounted the wall, as well as several others, tasted " the sherbet of martyrdom. All this time the besieged, notwithstanding the " heavy

(2) The reason of my omitting these details is, that there is some part of the account given of them which I do not clearly understand.

" heavy fire which poured upon them like rain from our guns, continued to defend " themselves, wherever they could find any cover: at length, I myself taking the " direction of two guns, fired from them at every man who made the least " movement. At this time the governor of the place stood concealed [as he " thought] behind one of the bastions, from which situation he viewed what was " going on. Here a shot striking him on the head sent him to hell; (3) upon " which the whole of the garrison immediately demanded a capitulation.(4) They " were [in consequence] removed from the fort, which was taken possession of " by the *Sircar*. The following day I sent the garrison back to their own army.

" Two days after the capture of this fort, the whole army of the infidels, " preparing for battle, advanced against us. The cavalry picquets having an" nounced the approach of the enemy, the vanguard of my army proceeded to " meet them; but it had only fired a few guns at them, when the accursed crew, " contenting themselves with what they had done, returned to their camp. Two " days after this I marched and took post two *coss* beyond *Kopul*, the enemy " being, at this time, encamped at the distance of four *coss* from thence. Here " I formed four parties of cavalry, each consisting of fifty horse and four rocket " men, to whom I gave orders to proceed and show themselves severally on the " right and left flanks, and in the rear and front of the enemy's position; and " after throwing some rockets among them, to cry out, 'behold the victorious army " 'is arrived! If you value your safety, fly speedily from hence.' This order " was accordingly exactly executed: the consequence of which was, that the " whole force of the infidels, commanders as well as men, *obeying the directions* " of the horsemen of the victorious army, took instantly to flight, and proceeding " all night, did not stop till, cursed both by God and man,(5) they had got to the " distance

(3) The *Sultan* appears to have been so enamoured of this phrase, that he immediately repeats it, saying, " in the same instant that he was sent to (or arrived in) hell, the garrison " demanded," &c.

(4) Original قول خواستند That the garrison were granted a capitulation may be fairly inferred, from the circumstance of their being sent the next day to their own army. Thus it appears, that the place was not taken by storm, but surrendered, in consequence of the death of the governor.

(5) Original ملعون خالق و خلق گردیدند

" distance of ten *coss*. They left behind them in their camp [6] various stores to " a great amount, and among the rest a quantity of shot and powder.

" It had been the constant practice of the enemy, during the last four months, " to pack up the baggage, and load their cattle with them, every day, an hour " and a half before sun-set. In this situation they would continue mounted on " their horses all night: and if, while they slumbered, any one gave an alarm of " the approach of the victorious army, they would immediately take to flight. " This they would frequently repeat ten or fifteen times in the course of a single " night. All this vigilance, however, did not prevent their plundering one " another, as often as a convenient occasion for the purpose occurred.

" At length Tukojee Holkar, who held a superior rank among the worthless " chiefs of this people, together with Râsta, who was, in fact, not inferior, in " point of birth, to Mâdho Râo himself, conceiving a just alarm at their [perilous] " situation, addressed *Urzies* [7] to our sublime Presence, which they sent us by " two horsemen."

Tippoo then proceeds to give the substance of the letters in question, making the writers, as usual, humble themselves to the dust, and speak of their own sovereign (the *Paishwa*) in terms of disrespect, utterly incredible. They are made to conclude by imploring his compassion for themselves and his *unworthy son*,[8] and intreating him to send a confidential person to them, to receive their representations and proposals.

" Accordingly," continues the *Sultan*, " in compliance with their desire, I sent " Budrûz Zumân Khân, Ali Rizâ, and other great men,[9] to negotiate with them. " On the arrival of the latter in the enemy's camp, the Mahrattah leaders ad- " dressed them, saying, ' our master stands in the place of a son to yours, and " ' we are servants. Pardon us for the evils which we have, by our own fault, " ' brought

(6) The camp is here, as on other occasions, called their مدفن گاه or " burying-place." Probably the affair here spoken of is the battle of *Kopul*, alluded to in the *Futhûl-Mûjahideen*. (See Appendix I.)

(7) The letter of an inferior to a superior; an humble address; a petition or memorial.

(8) Original فرزند نا لایق و نا شایسته alluding to the pretended adoption of the *Paishwa* by Tippoo, or rather by Hyder Ali.

(9) Original عمدها

" 'brought upon the country; and let your sovereign, by way of sweetmeat, " 'present our master, according to custom, with a little money, and one or two " 'villages: this being no more than such a favor as a son is entitled to claim of " 'his father.'[10] To this they added a declaration, that they were the victims " of Nizâm Ali Khân's seduction. In fine, they made many humiliating pro- " testations of this kind."

In proof of the constant terror which the Mahrattahs were under, of being surprized by the *Sultan's* army, Tippoo proceeds to relate, that during the negociations for peace, intelligence happening to be conveyed to them by some of their spies, that he was preparing to make a night attack upon them, Holkar and the Râstas instantly sent for Budrûz Zumân Khân and Ali Rizâ, and telling them of the intelligence which had been received, conjured them to dispatch two camel couriers immediately to their master, to intreat that the intended attack might be relinquished, declaring, at the same time, that they were ready to comply with whatever demands the latter might make on them. " It was in vain," pursues the *Sultan*, " that the aforesaid persons [his *Vakeels*] assured the chiefs in question, " that there was no truth in the report which had been brought to them, and that " it was impossible for such a thing to take place while they continued in the " Mahrattah camp. The aforesaid chiefs, nevertheless, persisted in their in- " stances, beseeching my people, for the love of God, to do as they required, and " by this means save them from the ruin which must otherwise fall upon them. " Thus importuned, the aforesaid persons at length agreed to comply with the " wishes of the Mahrattah commanders, saying, that they would return to their " tents, and immediately write the necessary letters on the occasion. Upon this " the others observed, that much time would be lost in writing letters, and in- " treated my people to dispatch at that moment, and in their presence, a verbal " message on the subject, as nothing else could set their minds at ease. My " confidential servants perceiving that the fears of the Mahrattah chiefs made " them distrust the promise which they had given to write, determined, in the " end,

(10) Original براي شيريني خوردن It is not improbable that this might be the footing upon which the Mahrattahs were willing, at this time, to place the pecuniary demand, as well as the territorial claims, which they still continued to make upon the *Sultan*.

" end, to satisfy them in their own way; and, for this purpose, sending for a pair " of camel couriers, they delivered to the latter, in the hearing of the chiefs, a " message to us, purporting that the enemy was in the utmost distress, and humbly " begged that we would not assault their camp that night. These couriers being " conducted by a party of the enemy's horse beyond the Mahrattah camp, " pursued their way with great speed to our camp, where they arrived at three " o'clock in the morning, and delivered to us the message with which they had " been charged. I sent them back at day-light with a satisfactory answer, and the " same morning moved, as I had previously determined, about three *coss* from " *Kunuckgheery*, to a new position along the banks of the *Tungbuddra*, where there " was abundance of pasture.(11)

3 Q The

(11) The circumstance, which gave rise to the false intelligence conveyed to the Mahrattahs on this occasion, is related by the *Sultan* in terms to the following effect. Contrary to his established custom, he had given orders, over night, that no foragers should go out the following morning, as it was his intention to march. This order coming to the knowledge of the Mahrattah spies, who were harboured secretly in the camp of the Mahrattah *Bárgeers*, or hired cavalry, in the service of Tippoo, they converted it into a notice to prepare for a sudden attack upon the Mahrattah position, and hastened thither, accordingly, with the information. The *Sultan* had with him, at this time, about seven thousand of these horse, who had served himself and his father upwards of fifteen years; all of whom he disbanded soon after the occurrence which has been related. "Since that time," observes the *Sultan*, " the infidels have ceased to receive intelligence respecting my movements."

It was said above, that the *verbal* order issued by the *Sultan*, on the occasion in question, was "contrary to his established custom." This is the *Sultan's* own admission; for he expressly says, that, excepting in the instance mentioned, it had been his uniform practice to communicate the orders of march in *writing*, and never *verbally*. These orders, which were written in the Persian language, were sealed, and directed to the several commanding officers of divisions and corps, to whom they were always delivered at nine o'clock the preceding night. This was their tenor: "To-morrow the army marches. Parade at such an " hour; and falling into your proper station on the line of march, follow our special caval" cade [or retinue]." The general, it seems, was accustomed to beat at three o'clock in the morning, and the assembly at five.* After the inadvertency, of which he confesses himself to have been guilty in the above-mentioned instance, the *Sultan* became more strict and particular on this point than ever. Among other regulations which he framed on this occasion, one was (as stated in his Memoirs) to give *sealed* routes to officers in the command of marching corps.

* Though I do not know that any terms were applied by the *Sultan* to these signals, corresponding with our "general," and "assembly," yet there is no doubt that the two distinct notices mentioned (and which were given by the kettle-drum) were intended to answer the same purpose.

The *Sultan*, after giving the foregoing account of the alarm occasioned to the Mahrattahs by his intended movement, and of the reflections and regulations which it suggested to him, proceeds in the following manner:

" It was not my intention, in the beginning, to have gone to war with the " Mahrattahs; but when they, thinking proper to requite the favors they had " received from us, by a conduct entirely the contrary [to what I had a right to " expect], had advanced [into my country], I consequently judged it necessary " to repel their aggression, by *just so much chastisement as should suffice to satisfy* " *them, and make them solicit peace.* Having brought the business accordingly " to this point, I agreed to an accommodation, and *to give* them twelve *lacks* of " *rupees.* The treaty being concluded, I wrote [a letter] to Lewai Mâdhee Râo,(12) " which I sent to him, together with a *Kulgy* and *Surpaish* of precious stones, " and an elephant. I also sent an elephant, with a dress and jewels, to Tukojee " Holkar; and the same to Râo Râsta and to Hurry Pundit. These presents I " forwarded by the hands of confidential *Vakeels.*

" The treaty concluded on this occasion by the embassadors of the *Sircar*, with " Nizâm Ali Khân and Mâdhee Râo, consisted of three articles to the following " effect. The *first* stipulated, that *on this side* the *Nurbudda*, Nizâm Ali Khân, " Pundit Purdhân, Mâdhee Râo, and the *Usud-Ilhye Sircar*, should all three " remain united together, each ruling over his proper territories: and that if any " fourth person should make an [hostile] attempt upon the country of any one of " the allies, all three were, in such case, to join in repelling the same, whatever " disagreement might happen to subsist between them at the time; it being " provided, that the disagreement in question should be suspended [during the " continuance of the external danger or aggression].

" The second article was as follows:........"

Here,

corps. These routes were numbered on the outside, 1, 2, 3, 4, &c. the first specifying the place to which the corps was to proceed on the first day; the second, its destination on the following day, and so on. These routes, or orders, were not to be opened till the troops had moved off their ground, and, in fact, commenced their day's march. As, by this contrivance, even the commanding officer himself was kept in ignorance of the point to which he was to march till he was actually in motion, there was the less danger of a premature discovery of his destination by an enemy's spies.

(12) The *Sultan* every where calls the *Paishwa* Mâdhee (feminine) instead of Mâdhoo.

* * * * * * *

Here, as before said, the manuscript abruptly passes to a description of the miserable condition to which the Mahrattahs were reduced by the war. On this subject the *Sultan* asserts, that the Mahrattah chiefs themselves assured his *Vakeels*, that independently of those who had fallen in battle, they had lost near a hundred thousand men by sickness, since the commencement of the campaign.

Here my copy of the *Sultan's* Memoirs at present ends: but it originally consisted of four or five leaves more, in the course of which the narrative was continued for a short period beyond the termination of the Mahrattah war. I apprehend that the *Sultan* never completed the work; though, if I recollect rightly, some memoranda for the purpose were found among his papers. If this should have been actually the case, no doubt those documents will, at some future season, be communicated to the public.

POSTSCRIPT.

AFTER the preceding sheets had gone to press, I was favored by Sir Charles Warre Malet with some communications, relating principally to the peace announced in the foregoing dispatch. These, though received too late to be applied, in the proper places, to the elucidation of those parts of the *Sultan's* correspondence which they would have served to explain or illustrate, appeared to me of too much value to be altogether suppressed. I considered that the diligent reader might still, if he pleased, convert them to the use just adverted to; and that they would, at least, form a record, of which the future historian of the period in question might avail himself. I have, for these reasons, thought it proper, with the permission of Sir Charles Malet, to insert them in this place.

The documents, here spoken of, consist of translations of five curious letters from Tippoo Sultan to Budrûz Zumân Khân, and of an extract from the private journal of the Resident, commencing the 20th December 1786, about which time the *Sultan* appears to have made some overtures of peace to his adversaries, which were rejected by the latter; but of which no trace is discernible, either in the correspondence or the memoirs. Indeed, it is clearly shown by the journal, that the mission of Budrûz Zumân Khân to the Mahrattah camp, mentioned in Letter CCCCXXX, must have been the *second* on which that officer was employed, although of his *former* fruitless embassy no notice is any where taken

Of

Of the five letters to Budrûz Zumân Khân,(1) mentioned above, I have given only one (which, in the order of time, immediately follows Letter CCCCXXX); the others, though not less interesting, belonging to a much later period than that embraced by the present publication. There being no reason to doubt the authenticity of the letter in question (which, on the contrary, is strongly confirmed by its conformity, in point both of matter and manner, with other productions of the *Sultan's* pen), I can no otherwise account for its not appearing in my collection, than by supposing that it may have been deemed by the writer of too delicate (or rather indelicate) a nature, to be entered in the usual registry of his correspondence. It must, at the same time, be allowed, that many things are preserved in that record, of which the *Sultan* had still greater cause to be ashamed.

LETTER *dated from* HUGLY, *near* KOPUL, *4th* EEZIDY, *year* DULLO *(or 29th January 1787.)*

" In these days some of our cavalry have taken prisoners Hunmunt Râo, a " person of palankeen rank, and three others belonging to the Mahrattahs. " Hunmunt Râo was sick; but has had due attendance, both in medicine and " provisions, and was then sent back. He says he has two brothers in Pursaram " Bhâo's service. Tell Holkar and Râo Râsta, that princes and great chiefs act " thus; while *they*, on the contrary, have carried off from *Surhutty* the *Kilaadâr* " and *Aumildâr*, who being old are of no use to the *Sircar*, but being of a noble " origin, I would advise them to get some of their offspring.(2) Also a *Kilaadâr*, " named Ghûlâm Mohyûddeen, who is young; but, being wounded in the foot " is become useless. It is the custom with them [*i. e.* the Mahrattahs] to get the " breed

(1) Although Sir Charles Malet has forgotten by what means these letters came into his possession, it is not improbable that the originals were found among the effects of Budrûz Zumân Khân, at the time that that officer, after the surrender of Dhârwâr, in 1791, was so shamefully pillaged by the Mahrattahs. In this case, it is easy to conceive how either the originals themselves, or copies of them, might reach the hands of the British resident.

(2) That is, from the Mahrattah women.

" breed of horses; therefore it is right that they have kept these people also for a " breed. Doubtless their offspring will be good. One Kishun Râo, likewise, has " been detained by the above. He likewise, being old, I do not want. Let the " *Brahmens* employ him in getting children: and as I have a great many other " useless people, I will, if they please, send them also, who may be employed in " the same way." (Written by Mirzâ Husan.)(3)

Although, if rigidly understood, the preceding letter would warrant a belief, that the *Sultan* really intended that his embassador, employed in negociating a peace, should actually hold the offensive language here prescribed, to the persons with whom he had to treat, yet the supposition seems too extravagant to be admitted: I am, therefore, inclined to think, that if the letter before us proceeded from any thing else but a mere ebullition of spleen, it was probably meant to display that talent of coarse raillery, in the exercise of which he was particularly fond of indulging.

EXTRACT *from the* JOURNAL *of* SIR CHARLES WARRE MALET, *Bart., Resident at* POONAH.

" 20th December 1786. *Mahrattah Camp.*—On the 17th Budrûz Zumân " Khân arrived at Tukojee Holkar's camp, in this army, as embassador from " Tippoo, with a retinue of five hundred horse and a company of *Sepoys*. The " 18th Hurry Pundit gave him an audience. An express was immediately sent to " *Poonah*: and if a favorable answer arrives to Tippoo's proposals, Bûrhânûddeen " will come to settle the conditions of peace.

" 30th December. *Mahrattah Camp*, five miles east of *Kopul*.—The proposi- " tions made by Tippoo Sultan being rejected by the Mahrattah Government, the " 28th instant his *Vakeel* had his audience of leave. The *Vakeel*, however, is " still here; but expected to depart, unless his master consent to the terms offered " by the Mahrattah government and Nizâm Ali Khân. Tippoo is encamped on " the *Tungbhuddra*, six or seven leagues off.

" 14th

(3) Many of the *Sultan's* letters, as well as other papers, are subscribed, like the present one, by the *Mûnshy*, or secretary, employed to pen it.

" 14th January 1787. *Mahrattah Camp.*—Tippoo having attacked *Behâdûr* " *Bundeh* while his *Vakeel* was in the Mahrattah army, Hurry Pundit Furkia, " the commander of the Mahrattahs, was very much displeased; and on the 7th " instant, at midnight, dismissed the *Vakeel,* who was escorted within sight of the " enemy's camp by a body of horse. On his arrival, the trenches were withdrawn " from *Behâdûr Bundeh.* On the 10th an express arrived from Tippoo: but it is " supposed the answer was unfavorable, as on the 12th Tippoo renewed his fire " on *Behâdûr Bundeh,* which was taken by assault the 13th, though our army " was within four or five leagues of it. A pestilential disorder prevails in this army.

" 21st January. *Mahrattah Camp.*—The enemy having advanced with inten- " tion to attack our camp, we broke up about eight or nine o'clock at night, and " retreated to *Kunuckgheery,* thirty *coss* from *Adoni* and ten from *Moodgul,* where " we now are. There is no talk of peace at present. The sickness still prevails. " The enemy is about eleven *coss* from us.

" 4th February. *Poonah.*—I am inclined to think, that what with the jealousies " that prevail among the Moghul and Mahrattah chiefs, the ravages of the pesti- " lence, and the incompetency of Hurry Pundit's authority over the great num- " bers of the vast army assembled under his command, no great exertion is to be " expected from it. At the same time I do not think Tippoo will be able to make " much progress to the northward, or move far from the banks of the *Tungbhuddra;* " by which he would give the allies an opportunity of interrupting his convoys, " and render them masters of all the advantages arising from their great superiority " in cavalry.

" *Poonah.* 10th February. *Mahrattah Camp.*—1st February. Notwithstanding " the late rejection of Tippoo's proposals, he still promises himself to bring the Mah- " rattahs to an agreement; and having (as evidently appears) concerted matters with " Holkar, his ambassador, Budrûz Zumân Khân, arrived in camp again on the " 23d ultimo, with Ali Rizâ, formerly of *Arcot.* On the 24th he was, through " Holkar's mediation, admitted to an audience of Hurry Pundit, and has permis- " sion to remain till the further determination of government can be signified on " the present proposals; and, contrary to expectation, reports were prevalent " yesterday, of an approaching pacification. The sickness is abated.

" 17th

"17th February. *Mahrattah Camp.*—The Mahrattahs having accepted Tip-
"poo's last offers, his ambassador has left camp, and is returned to his master to
"settle the conditions. It is announced, that Tippoo is to pay three *crores* of
"*rupees* for all arrears due, the country he has taken from the Mahrattahs for
"these ten years past, and for the expences of the campaign. The pestilence,
"with which we have been afflicted for three months past, has subsided, and is
"reported to have now broken out in Tippoo's army.

"5th March. *Poonah.*—On the second instant I was, by message from
"Nâna, informed, that he had just received a letter from Hurry Pundit,
"mentioning that since Tippoo's *Vakeel* left the camp, he had received a letter
"from him, advising that he should soon return, with the necessary documents
"for the conclusion of peace, as they were all drawn up and prepared for his
"master's signature, which he expected would soon be affixed to them. That
"the principal articles were the surrender of *Nergûnd*(4) and *Kittoor*, the payment
"of the arrears of tribute, and the confirmation of *Bâdâmy* and *Gujundur*
"*Ghur* to the *Paishwa*, and the restitution of *Adoni* to Nizâm Ali Khân.
"That after being sent to Hurry Pundit, they would be forwarded for the final
"consideration and ratification of the *Durbâr* [*Paishwa's*]; but, for his own
"part, as they were not yet signed by Tippoo, he could place no reliance on the
"*Vakeel's* communication to Hurry Pundit, and had thus mentioned the present
"state of the negociation, only as a mark of his confidence and friendship.

"*Poonah.* 7th March. *Mahrattah Camp.* 26th February.—This day, be-
"tween the hours of twelve and one, Tippoo's *Vakeel* returned, with three ele-
"phants and several camels, loaded with money. It is reported, the army will
"shortly march to the *Kishna* to await the second payment.

"14th March. *Mahrattah Camp.* (No date).—Five miles South of *Moodgul.*
"The treasure that arrived with the ambassadors is thought to be no more than
"fifteen *lacks.*

"24th ditto. *Poonah.* To Governor General.—Nâna has not yet thought
"proper to inform me of the terms of the treaty; and all that I can collect, with
"any degree of certainty, is the payment of the tribute for four years, at eighteen
"*lacks*

(4) The *Nergûnd* of the Correspondence.

" *lacks* per annum, including *Durbâr* charges, and the surrender of *Nergünd*, " which was reduced by Tippoo two years ago." (N. B. This peace seems to have been mediated by Holkar and Râsta, and was reported not to be approved of by the Sindian party at the *Durbâr*.)

" 10th April. *Poonah.* To the same.—On the 8th instant I received intel- " ligence from Behro Pundit, that half of Tippoo's stipulated payment had " arrived in camp, but that the ratified treaties were not yet exchanged.

" 17th April. *Poonah.*—On this day Nâna assured me, that to the 13th " instant the definitive treaty with Tippoo was not exchanged, though Tippoo " had written on the 8th of February to Nizâm Ali and to the Governor of " *Madras*, that all was settled to his satisfaction.

" 21st April. *Poonah.* To Governor General.—The army [Mahrattah] has " certainly commenced its march from the South towards this place.

" 5th May. *Poonah.* To Governor General.—On the 30th ultimo the minis- " ter formally acquainted me, that after much prevarication on the part of Fut- " tah Ali Khân(5) (Tippoo), peace was at length made with that prince, and the " ratified treaties exchanged, including, in one part, the *Paishwa* and Nizâm Ali " Khân, and on the other Futtah Ali Khân. The conditions of which were, that " Futtah Ali Khân was to pay four years' arrears of tribute due to the *Paishwa*, " part of which had been already paid, the balance to be discharged in six " months; that *Adoni* was to be restored to Mohâbut Jung; *Nergünd* and *Kittoor* " to be surrendered to the *Paishwa*, who is also to retain *Bâdâmy*. Here the " minister paused; and I was surprised, on enquiry, to find that this communi- " cation was to be understood as comprising the whole of the treaty; the more " so, as the *Paishwa's* surrender of *Gujundur Ghur*, some circumstances concern- " ing *Shânoor*, and the discussions relative to Futtah Ali Khân's titles and address, " were matters of public notoriety, and which, I, of course, expected would be " noticed in this formal communication. He also declined any formal congratula- " tion to the *Paishwa*, on my part, on the occasion, as too unimportant, not " scrupling to express his want of confidence in Tippoo for the observance of the " peace thus concluded. I subsequently, by message, on the 3d, applied for " further information, but without effect."

3 R " 5th May.

(5) This was, I believe, a title conferred upon Tippoo by Shâh Allum.

"5th May. *Poonah.*—Received this day from Secretary Hay, copy of a letter "from Tippoo to Governor of *Madras*, dated 8th February, from which the "following is extract.

"The *Poonah* army being pursued by mine has crossed the *Krishna*, and peace "has taken place between us in the manner I wished. They have, accordingly, "returned to their own country, and I purpose returning to my capital in about "a week, after quieting the disturbances raised by some *Polygars* in these parts."

"N. B. This letter contained applications relative to some refractory boundary "chiefs.

"3d June. *Poonah.* To Governor General.—In reply to my enquiries relative "to the late discussions on Tippoo's titles, the minister has informed me, that "hitherto the *Paishwa* used to address him by the name of Futtah Ali Khân, "that he had now desired to be stiled Tippoo Sultan Khân Behâdûr. To the "first of which, as it had no relation to royalty, but was actually the name given "to him at his birth by his mother, in consequence of a vow to name her child, "if a male, after a famous Mahommedan *Peer,*(6) at *Colar*, in the *Carnatic,*(7) whose "name was Tippoo Sultan, no objection could be made. That Khân, as it had "formerly joined to Futtah Ali, was nothing new, and, in fact, did away any "royalty that might otherwise be imputed to the word *Sultan*; and that the "appellation of Behâdûr was the only word of additional dignity to be used in the "*Paishwa's* future addresses to this prince, who is not even styled *Nabob* by this "*Durbâr*."

(6) The *Peer*, among the Mussulmans of *India*, is a kind of ghostly father, or spiritual guide. The word properly signifies an aged person, an elder.

(7) That is, the *Balaghaut*, or higher *Carnatic*, in which *Mysore* is comprehended.

APPENDIX.

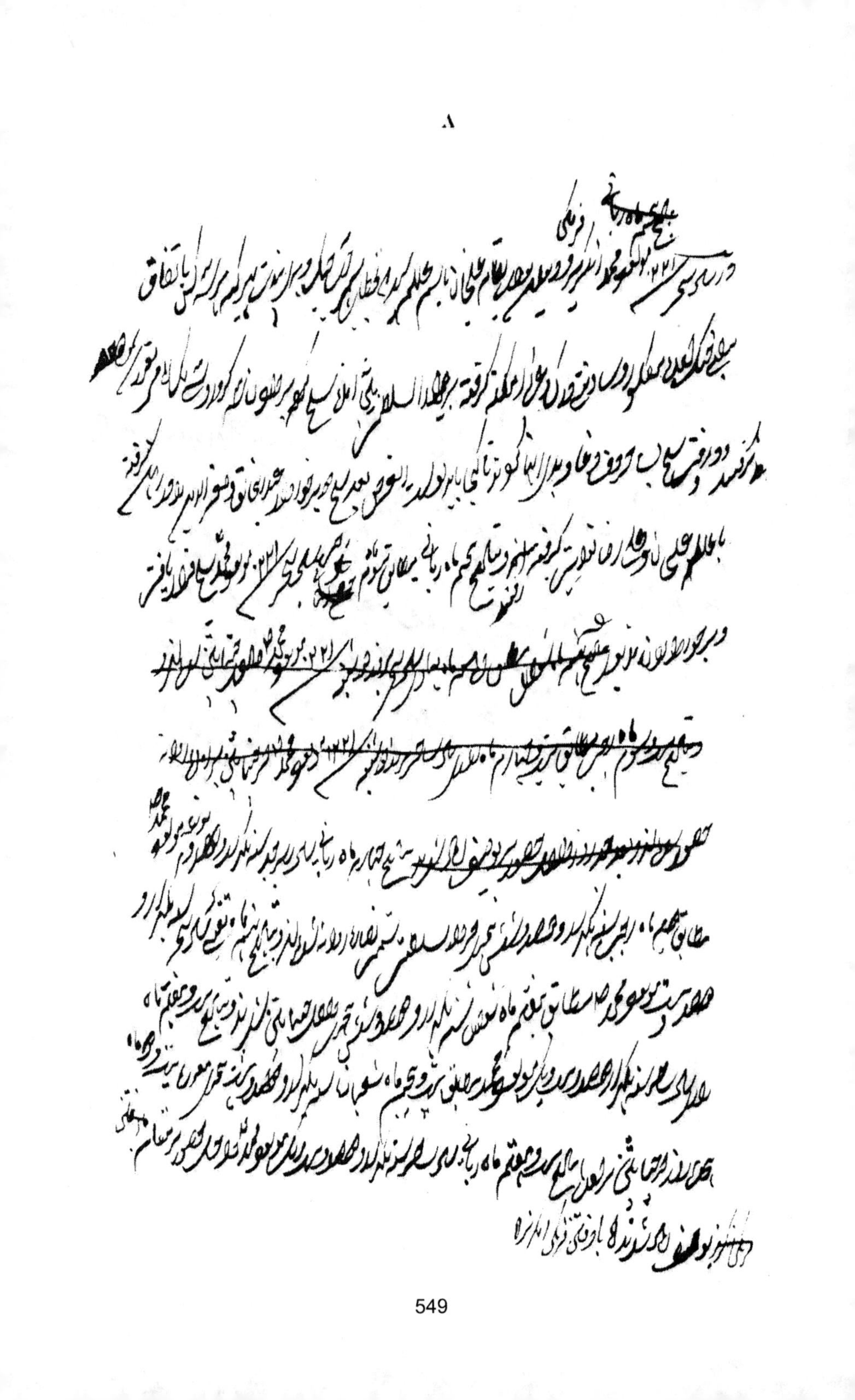

[illegible]

ر

عرض غلامان اینست اگر از نصارا یکی هم گاهگاه شاهزادها بجای مضایقه ندارد هست

بملاقات هم سرفراز فرمود نظر باینکه سخنهای شیخی هم باید فرمود و در دل آنچه که

و ملاقات در بنگلور یا بجای دیگر باشد مضایقه ندارد در صورت موقوفی آمدن او

نوعی در خاطر او خلل گذشت معروضه غلام علی و سید فضل علی

APPENDIX.

APPENDIX, A.

(Referred to in the PREFACE.*)*

TRANSLATION *of No.* 1 *of the annexed Plate, being the* MEMORANDUM *of* TIPPOO SULTAN.

“ In the year *Sehr,* 1220 of the *Mowloody* [*i.e.* the birth] of Mahommed,[1] the
Fringy
“ English ‸ and the *Dewán* of the *Nábob,* Nizâm Ali Khân, named Ghûlâm “ Syed [and also called] by the title of Sohrâb Jung, and Hurry Pundit “ Phurkia, all these three persons came together [or united] to make war; and “ [after] taking *Bangalore, Sawantydoorg,* and other places, came to the royal “ residence of *Putn,* when peace, upon the condition of [my] giving three *crores* “ and thirty *lacks* of *Imaumies* [*i. e. rupees*] was settled, of which [sum] two “ parts [*i. e.* two-thirds] were taken in money. And, at the time of [making] “ peace, they did abundance of deceitful and bad things,[2] of which there would “ be no end to the recital.[3] In fine, after the peace, [they] took two of my “ sons, Aabdûl Khâlik and Moizûddeen, in pledge [*i. e.* as hostages] and, toge- “ ther with Ghûlâm Ali Khân and Ali Rizâ Nurwâil, took them away. And on “ the 5th of the month *Rubbány,* corresponding with the 3d of the month *Rujub,*

a . “ year

(1) If the year *Sehr,* A. M. 1220, was meant to refer to the event stated immediately after, namely, the appearance of the allies before *Seringapatam,* the memorandum set out with a mistake; since the event in question did not take place in *Sehr* 1220, but in *Zuburjud* 1219. The *Sultan* however, when he took up his pen, might intead to begin with the mention of some transaction of the year *Sehr,* or 1220, but changing his mind, have passed abruptly to the subject which occupies the commencement of the memorandum. With regard to the interlined and erased date, “ 5th of the month *Rubbány,*” it may be observed, that that was the day (corresponding with the 26th of February, 1792) on which the hostage princes quitted *Seringapatam,* and were delivered into the hands of Lord Cornwallis. It is probable, therefore, that the *Sultan* was, at first, about to mention that circumstance; but, changing his mind again, proceeded to relate the previous appearance of the allies before his capital.

(2) Original بسا حروف دغا وبدي آنها كردند “ they used abundance of bad and deceitful words.”

(3) Literally, “ to where must we write? ”

" year *Sehr*, 1220[4] birth of Mahommed, peace was concluded [or settled].
" And the above-mentioned sons, ~~on the 9th of *Shuwwal*, corresponding with the~~
" ~~10th of the month *Behâry*, year *Sehr*, being Monday, 1220 of the birth of~~
" ~~Mahommed, entered *Chinaputn*~~ [*i. e. Madras*]~~, and on the 23d of the month~~
" ~~*Rujub*, corresponding with the 24th of the month *Kâzy*, year *Sâhir*, being~~
" ~~Monday, year 1221 of the birth of Mahommed, coming forth from *Chinaputn*,~~
" ~~proceeded to the Presence, and after some days arrived in the Presence at~~
" ~~*Yoosûfâbâd*,~~ on the 4th of the month *Rubbâny*, year *Zuburjud*, 1219
" of the birth of Mahommed, corresponding with the 2d of the month *Rujub*,
" A. H. 1206, proceeded from the royal residence towards the *Nusâra* [*i. e.* the
" *Nazarenes*]; and on the 9th of the month *Tukky*, year *Sehr*, 1220 of the
" birth of Mahommed, answering to the 7th of the month *Shuwwâl*, A. H.
" 1206, entered [or arrived at] *Chinaputn* [*i. e. Madras*]: and on the 27th
" of the month *Râzy*, year *Sâhir*, and 1221 of the birth of Mahommed,
" corresponding with the 25th of the month *Shaabân*, A. H. 1208, being
" altogether twenty-two months and eighteen days, they came forth from
" *Chinaputn*; and on the 27th of the month *Rubbâny*, year *Sâhir*, and of the birth
" of Mahommed 1221, arrived in the Presence~~, with Doveton, the English *Fringy*,~~
" at *Yoosûfâbâd*, with Doveton, the English *Fringy*."

The foregoing memorandum is followed by a minute (also in the *Sultan's* hand-writing) wherein the *Sultan*, after stating his own opinion pretty fully, calls upon his counsellors to deliver their sentiments, with regard to the measures proper to be pursued at this period (*viz.* the return of the hostages); after which follows a note of dates, furnished by Ali Rizâ Khân, and apparently designed to set the *Sultan* right, with respect to some of those given in the engraved memorandum. The dates in question relate, 1st. to the arrival of the hostages at *Madras*; &c., 2d. to their departure from thence; specifying precisely the day and hour of each occurrence, and differing considerably, in both articles, from the *Sultan's* statement.

TRANSLATION

(4) Here the *Sultan* deliberately and explicitly states the peace to have been concluded in the year *Sehr*, or A. M. 1220, whereas it should unquestionably be *Zuburjud*, A. M. 1219. By *the peace*, the *Sultan* clearly means the preliminary articles; to which, however, he does not give the date assigned to them in the definitive treaty, where they are distinctly stated to have been signed on the 22d February 1792, corresponding to the 28th of *Jumâdûssâny*, A. H. 1206 (and 1st of *Rubbâny*, year *Zuburjud*, or A. M. 1219). He probably reckoned the peace from the day on which his sons proceeded to the English camp, and not from that on which the preliminaries were actually executed.

Translation *of No. 2 of the annexed Plate, being a* **Minute** *or* **Note**, *containing the joint opinion of* **Ghûlâm Ali** *and* **Syed Fuzl Ali**, *on the question respecting* **Colonel Doveton's** *reception.*

"The humble representation of your slaves is this. If one person of the "*Nazarenes* come along with the princes,[1] it is of no consequence. He may be "both honoured with an interview, and amused[2] with the words of friendship. "Whatever is in the heart, it may [nevertheless] remain there:[3] and whether "the interview takes place at *Bangalore*, or elsewhere, does not signify. [On "the other hand] in case his coming should be set aside, it will excite some "mistrust in their minds.[4]

"The humble representation of Ghûlâm Ali and Syed Fuzl Ali."

The manuscript, from which the two foregoing articles have been taken, is composed of forty leaves of European paper, of the size of quarto post: and though several whole leaves and some pages are blank, it contains, besides the minutes here inserted, many other curious and interesting documents, chiefly questions proposed by the *Sultan* to his ministers, on political subjects, with their answers subjoined, in their respective hand-writings.

APPENDIX B.

(Referred to in the Preface*).*

The account of the *Sultan's* march from *Seringapatam* to *Bidnore,* and of his first operations against General Matthews, is unfortunately wanting; that part of the manuscript, which contained those details, having been destroyed by the accident noticed in the Preface. Some previous skirmishing between the hostile armies had been described; but what remains of the narrative commences as follows:—

a 2 "A discharge

(1) Original شاه زادها There are numerous proofs, besides this, of the *Sultan's* having assumed, in a certain degree, the title of *Shâh*, *Bâdshâh*, or *King*. It is true he did not insert it on his coin, or on his seals, but he allowed himself to be addressed by it.

(2) Original بظاهر سخنها دوستي هم بايد فرمود

(3) Original ودردل انچه كه هست هست "whatever is in the heart is in it."

(4) نوع درخاطر او خواهد گذشت "will pass into the mind in a manner," that is, "an unfavourable manner.

" A discharge of artillery and musquetry succeeded, which occasioned the loss " of a few of those who looked on.(1) Then the troops of the *Usud-Ilhye*,(2) and " the French people, advancing on each side of the road, gave another discharge " of musquetry. Immediately on hearing this discharge, I (being then seated " at the distance of a hundred yards) advanced rapidly with a division, when " about sixty of the English people were sent to hell. The rest being pursued left " behind them the two guns they had previously seized on: and thus the aforesaid " *Nazarenes* were driven back, discomfited and disheartened, to [the position " occupied by] their worthless leader, who thereupon, with all his forces, sought " [refuge in] the fort and batteries. Writings of the said worthless leader were " found in the pockets of four of the English *Sirdars* [or officers] who were among " the slain.(3) On this day about three hundred *Nazarenes* were made prisoners " and twenty guns taken. On the second, or following day, I myself, taking two " thousand light troops with me, attacked and gained possession of a large powder-" magazine at some distance from the fort, and of a magazine of grain close to it. " Six hours after the capture of these two places, the enemy sent about four " thousand men to attack us. This force advancing by a concealed route [or " secretly], an action ensued between them and the *Usud Ilhye* army, in which " both parties, passing from the fire of musquetry, fought with the bayonet and " sword. On this occasion, also, about two hundred of these good-for-nothing " people were sent to hell. A few persons, too, of the army of the *Ahmedy* " *Sircar* tasted the sherbet of martyrdom; and one *Risáladár*, after being " wounded, was carried off by the *Nazarenes*.

" The third day I had all the powder and grain removed from the said maga-" zines, and lodged in a place of safety. On the same day, the *Nazarenes* set " fire to the palace of the *Rájah*, and to ten or twelve other noble buildings; " keeping up, also, such a fire [from their guns], that there was not a span's " space of the wall [of the outer town] which was not reached by their shot.

" On

(1) Original تماشا بينان " beholders of the spectacle or diversion." By this expression the writer probably meant to convey the idea, that the resistance made by the English, on this occasion, was trifling.

(2) This term seems to imply, throughout these Memoirs, not the particular body composed of converts to the Mahommedan faith, elsewhere called *Usud Ilhyes*, but the troops in general.

(3) Tippoo would not appear to have derived any information from the intercepted letters of the English. Great numbers of dispatches, to and from English officers in command, were found at *Seringapatam*, the seals of which had never been broken. Either he had no persons about him who were capable of reading and explaining their contents, or, if he had, he did not chuse to trust them. Whether he ever endeavoured to obtain a translation of any of these letters, by means of his English prisoners, is unknown: but it is probable, that if he had fallen on this expedient, and had found it to answer, so many of them would not have remained unopened to the day of his death.

"On the fourth day, carrying on my approaches in front of the *Dárúl*
" *Imáret*,[4] and in front of the mosque, and by two other sides, I erected
" batteries close to the fort, in which I placed some large guns, which I had caused
" to be removed from the walls of the city.

" The *Nazarenes* had conveyed into the fort, from the different magazines [of
" the city], about fifty thousand shot, and a vast quantity of powder. The
" remainder, consisting of about two hundred thousand shot, one hundred
" thousand *utls* of lead, and five hundred thousand *utls*[5] of powder, besides an
" innumerable quantity of other stores, fell into our hands.

" Having next fixed on a high spot, I caused batteries to be constructed and
" mounted with guns, at sight of which the *Nazarenes, without religion*, opened
" a very heavy fire. When the said *Nazarenes* became tired [of firing], the
" batteries of the *Usud Ilhye* opened their fire, discharging from four to five
" thousand shot; and in this manner did the firing continue, on the part of the
" *Usud-Ilhye Sircar*, for five or six days. As to the *Nazarenes*, they did not fire
" a single shot from the fort on the second day. What fire they kept up was on
" the first day: the reason of which was this. The fire from without was so hot,
" that no creature within the fort durst approach their guns [for the purpose of
" working them], while General Matthews (the name of their worthless leader)
" causing a....... [6] to be made, crept or slunk into the same. There was
" not, in short, a span's space throughout the fort, which the shot of the *Usud*
" *Ilhye* guns did not reach, or where the blood of the *Nazarenes* was not spilt.

" On the fifth day the *Nazarenes*, during a storm of rain, rushed from a
" concealed place, and attacked our intrenchments: but the *Ahmedy* troops being
" on their guard, the infidels were repulsed at the point of the sword and bayonet,
" many of them being seized by the legs, and in that condition thrown by the
" people of the *Sircar* into the trenches. The rest, leaving their wounded behind
" them, fled in confusion into the fort.

" After

(4) *i. e.* "the house, or place, of nobility." Probably, the principal edifice in the fort.

(5) I have elsewhere supposed, that by the word اطل *utl*, a *maund* (or 82 lbs.) was meant; but either a much smaller weight was intended by that term, or there must be some error in the numbers here given, since these carry the quantities of lead and powder beyond credibility. Perhaps for اطل we should read رطل *rutl*, a weight equal to eighteen ounces avoirdupois; or, possibly, by an *utl* might be meant not the *Bengal Bazar maund*, of forty *seers*, or eighty pounds avoirdupois, but the *Mocha maund* of two *rutls* and three quarters, or three pounds avoirdupois: I incline, on the whole, to the latter explanation.

(6) The word which I have left untranslated is not legible: at least I can make nothing of it.

" After this, I pushed on my approaches before the gate of the fort, and on " every other side, still nearer; and caused such a fire of musquetry to be kept " up, that not a single man of the *Nazarenes*, within the fort, durst ascend the " walls, or come near their guns. In this manner did the *Nazarenes* altogether " make three sallies, in considerable force; but were each time repulsed with great " loss, and compelled to slink back, like mice, into the fort. Thus did hostilities " continue during ten days. On the eleventh day the *Nazarenes* begged for " quarter, and sent me the draft of terms of capitulation, consisting of the seven " following articles:

" ' Article 1. Neither the troops of the *Sircar* of the *Usud-Ilhye*, nor the " ' inhabitants [*Ryots*] of the country of the *Sircar*, shall, after we evacuate the " ' fort, spit in our faces,(7) or abuse us, or wound us.

" ' Article 2. Let our private property be left to us; and let guns, musquets, " ' money, goods, military stores, &c. be taken by the *Sircar*.

" ' Article 3. Whatever money, goods, or cattle, belonging to the *Sircar*, may " ' be in our possession, we will deliver up the same: and if we should take with " ' us to the value of a *Daum* or *Dirm*(8) of money or goods; and if, upon search " ' by the people of the *Sircar*, any thing of the kind should be found upon us, " ' we consent to be considered criminal. Inflict [in that case] whatever punish- " ' ment you please upon us.

" ' Article 4. Let us have a safe-guard to the sea-side.

" ' Article 5. Let some ships of the *Sircar* be lent to us [for conveying us " ' home]: and let us be favored with grain, and other articles of provision, by the " ' *Sircar*, at a fixed price. After we arrive at our own place, the amount of the " ' price of the same shall be sent.

" ' Article 6. Ships to be furnished for the conveyance of whatever number of " ' men shall [chuse to] embark. But those who may not consent [or like] to " ' embark on board of ship, shall be dispatched by land to *Bombay*, under an " ' escort.

" ' Article 7. Two *Sirdars* [*i. e.* officers of rank] of the *Sircar* shall remain " ' with us, as hostages, until our embarkation; and two *Nazarene Sirdars* to " ' remain with the *Sircar*. Whenever the *Sirdars* of the *Sircar* shall return to " ' the Presence, the two *Nazarene Sirdars* shall be dispatched [or sent back to us.]'

" I agreed

(7) Of this strange stipulation it may be sufficient to observe, that it is much more credible that it should be an exaggeration or mistatement (not to say an absolute invention) of the *Sultan*, than that it should have actually proceeded from General Matthews. We have abundant proofs, in the course of this volume, that the *Sultan's* regard to truth was far from being very strict: and perhaps there was no occasion on which he was so likely to deviate from it as in speaking of the English.

(8) The lowest denomination of money.

" I agreed to these proposals, and, according to the request of the *Nazarenes*, " caused two treaties, one in Persian, and the other in English, to be drawn up: " to which were affixed my seal and signature, and, in like manner, the seal and " signature of the *Nazarenes*. One of the treaties was kept by the *Sircar*, and " the other was given to the *Nazarenes*. The following morning the *Nazarenes* " preparing [or assembling] all their people within the fort, loaded such parts of " the *Tosheh-khâneh* of the *Sircar* as consisted of specie, on mules, horses, and " bullocks, bearing the mark(9) of the *Sircar*, and distributed the rest of the " articles amongst their people; after which they came out of the fort. On " passing the gate, the worthless chief of the *Nazarenes* first, drawing his " sword, delivered up the same with his own hand: after which, all the rest, " amounting to about two thousand two hundred *Nazarenes*, and ten thousand " infantry, native troops, grounded their arms, and proceeded to the encamp- " ment assigned them without the city. The next day, sending for Matthews " (the name of their worthless leader) and their other worthless commanders, I " demanded of them, whether the treaty which they had executed the preceding " day was right [or valid] or not right. To this they all answered, that on that " point there was not any doubt, and that the treaty was right [or valid]. Here- " upon I sent to them about twenty principal men and *Sirdars* of the *Sircar*, " through whom I thus interrogated them.

" 'What is the reason that, contrary to the treaty, you have taken with you " 'the money and goods [of the *Sircar*], and also the prisoners made by you in " 'the *Sircar's* country, dressing them up in your own apparel? What is the " 'reason that you have loaded cattle, bearing the mark of the *Sircar*, with " 'specie, and carried the same away? Finally, why, at the time of your evacu- " 'ating the fort, did you distribute among your people the *Tosheh-khâneh* of " 'the *Sircar*?'

" Their answer [to these demands] was, 'that they had no knowledge of the " 'matter; and that if the *Sircar* had any suspicions, and did not put trust in " 'their declaration, a search might be ordered by the *Sircar*.' To this I replied, " through the *Sirdars*, 'that it would be best for them to issue positive orders to " 'their people to deliver up to the *Sircar* whatever coined money of the *Sircar*, " 'captives made in the territories of the *Sircar*, or cattle, goods, &c. they had " 'taken with them.' In reply to this they declared, 'that neither themselves, " 'nor any of their people, had a single *daum* or *dirm* [farthing], or retained a " 'single hair of any inhabitant of this country;' proposing, at the same time, " that

(9) The mark here alluded to probably consisted either of the tyger stripe or the letter ح (the initial of حيدر Hyder), both of which were employed by the *Sultan* for such purposes.

" that a guard of the *Sircar* should be placed over them, and that a search should " be made, and [every thing] taken [that might be found]. After much " altercation on their part, the *Sirdars* of the *Usud-Ilhye* took from them, and " brought [to me] a writing to the above effect. Hereupon I dismissed the " accursed, worthless, *Sirdars:* and on the second [or following] day, having " surrounded them with guards, I caused them to march from the encampment " they then occupied to the vicinity of another spot [which had been appropriated " by them] as a burying ground.(10) The *Sirdars* of the *Sircar*, placing themselves " in the road, examined them, one by one, as they passed. The accursed ones " were, in consequence, found to have concealed in every seam of their clothes, " *Hydery Hoons* [*pagodas*] and jewels. They had also made holes in sheep's " heads, which they had filled with *pagodas.*(11) Some had concealed *pagodas* in " loaves of bread; others within *Húkkah* snakes, and *Húkkah* bottoms; while " several had even resorted to the most indelicate means of concealment:(12) all of " which were detected by sweepers, and other *Sámries,* appointed for the purpose " by the *Sircar.*(13) Many young people, also, male and female, natives of the " country of the *Sircar*, were found disguised in the dress [of the *Nazarenes*]. " These captives, of their own accord, set up a loud cry, [by which means] about " five hundred were discovered. The search being over, I had the worthless " *Sirdars* placed separately, the *Nazarene* people separately, and the other infidels " separately; and as they had not acted conformably with their written engage- " ments, I made the whole prisoners, and distributed them throughout the " country. During the investigation, ten or twelve Musulman women *(Syeds* and " *Shaikhs)* who had been made captives, or slaves, by the infidel *Nazarenes*, at " *Surat* and in *Bengal*, were found among their people. These persons being " likewise separated from the *Nazarenes,* and restored to their freedom, were " permitted to depart.

" After this, passing the *Ghauts,* I proceeded, by five or six days' marches, to " fort *Kúridl-bunder* [*Mangalore*], which is an excellent fortress, erected by(14) the " *Ahmedy*

(10) Original نزديک ديگر يک جاي براي مدفون گاه شان مقرر کرده کوچانيديم

(11) This is a doubtful passage. The original is ودر کله گسفندان سوراخ نموده در آن هونها پر کرده بودند

(12) That is, according to the original, ومخصوص در مواضع مخصوصه خود هم هونها پوشيده کرده بودند

(13) He means to say, that the outcasts only were employed in this service, as any others would have been defiled by it.

(14) Original نو احداث literally "*newly* erected;" which, however, not agreeing very well with the period mentioned immediately after, I have, in my translation, omitted the adverb. The *Sultan* meant by the expression, not (as might be supposed) that the fortress in question had been *recently* built by himself, but since the acquisition of *Canara* by his father.

C

ادوار نامه

بدون مرضی مبارک حضرت خداوند نعمت بیگ کار نخواهم کرد
اگر کنم که جرم در خاطر همین بکند او سزاوار باید بلعنه الله قلم بیگ

در امری که رد دارد و تعلقی که در تقصیر کنم سزاوار است و نکال
باید بلعنه الله قلم بیگ

خلاف قول و دعا بار کنم سزاوار این همین حال گشت
بلعنه الله قلم بیگ

بدون حکم حضرت خداوند کسی نذر و عهد نخواهم گرفت و خزانه از
کسی نخواهم گرفت اگر کنم سزاوار لعنه الله قلم بیگ

با هر کس سوای از موالات که در روز دیگر قلم و کلام و دعا بار کنم و ...
کنم سزاوار الله سردار باید کشید قلم بیگ

هرگاه از کرم [illegible] متعین [illegible] سوال و جواب
آن با استصواب شخص معتبر از کرم حضور خواهم معروض [illegible] سوال
و جواب خواهم کرد و سوال [illegible] سوال و جواب [illegible]
والله
قلم بیگ

اگر [illegible] نوشته [illegible] و تحریر [illegible] داده باشند و [illegible] از [illegible]
به استصواب شخص از حضور [illegible] است به صلاح او خواهم
کرد والله
قلم بیگ

این چند قلم از روی [illegible] الدوام [illegible] دل یار
داشتن هر یک کار خواهم [illegible] از [illegible] موافق
از روی صدور [illegible] باید والله
قلم بیگ

" *Ahmedy Sircar*, and on which, in the course of five and twenty years, about " twenty *lacks* of *rupees* have been expended. An ungrateful rogue, who had " been honored with the government of it, had invited the *Nazarenes*, and " delivered it up to them. Here I arrived; and on the second [or following] " day, after crossing another *Ghaut* [or pass] situated two *coss* on this side of the " said fort, encamped near the city. The worthless *Nazarene*, who commanded " in the fort, had erected a battery of heavy guns on an eminence near the fort, in " which were placed about three hundred *Nazarenes* and a thousand other troops. " After I had taken up my position, I dispatched a *Kushoon* to occupy the town. " This division, passing the outer-wall, was attacked by a body of *Nazarenes*, " posted there by the enemy: between whom and my people a sharp conflict was " maintained till evening. Having, during the same day, collected the necessary " materials for the purpose, I erected a battery in the night, opposite to that of " the *Nazarenes*, in which I placed fifteen guns: and sending a storming party " of two *Kushoons*, I posted them in a hollow, where they remained till the hour " of morning prayer; when, after firing a volley [from our battery], and crying " out '*Allah yâr*,'(15) they rushed forward, and with great slaughter drove the " *Nazarenes* without religion, from the eminence they occupied; taking also " many prisoners, and pursuing the fugitives to the very gates of the fort, in front " of which my people maintained themselves, till such time as, with the divine " assistance, I was enabled to entrench them. In the course of the two next " days, every thing being prepared for the purpose, I invested the place, and " mounted two batteries. A very hot fire was kept up on both sides the first day. " On the second day the gunners of the *Hydery* army served the batteries in such " a manner, that ten guns of the fort were dismounted and shattered to pieces, and " a great number of *Nazarenes* sent to hell. In the end, the *Nazarenes* abandoned all their guns, and were no longer able to appear on the walls; while I " had two or three other batteries erected, in which placing six mortars, I caused " large stones to be thrown from them. Hereupon the *Nazarenes* without religion " dug trenches within the fort, into which they slunk [for shelter].

" In this conjuncture the rains of that country, which continue for six months, " set in. At the end of two months, I had carried my approaches, notwithstanding the violence of the rains, to the ditch of the fort; in the course of which " time the besieged had made two sallies, at the hour of midnight. On one of " these occasions I happened to be seated near the trenches, in a house in which " I had taken up my residence, when hearing a more continued report of musquetry than usual, I hastened, in the midst of the rain and darkness of the

b " night,

(15) God is our friend.

" night, to the support of the people in the trenches; and said to the *Sirdars* of " the *Usud Ilhye* army, ' that, with the divine aid, I would the following day, " ' when the sun was in the meridian [or at twelve o'clock] cut off the heads of " ' the infidels within their own ditch and batteries, by the hands of my foot " ' troops;[16] and, in this manner, retaliate their *thief-like* action of coming " ' against us in the night.' Accordingly, under God's assistance, and the pro- " tection of our Prophet, I formed a party of thirty *Ehshâm* soldiers[17] and " twenty other persons of approved courage;[18] which dividing into two bodies, " I sent one of them, consisting of twenty-five men, in noon-day, against the " gate-battery, and the other twenty-five men into the ditch; where each party " falling upon the infidels without religion, they cut off the heads of about forty " of those impure-minded [people].[19] Such as escaped the edge of the sword,[20] " falling into the ditch and other places, fled like chickens, and crept [for " concealment] into the nearest holes. The *Usud-Ilhye* men, resembling lions, " returned with the prisoners they had made in safety. In fine, the *Nazarenes* " were reduced to such straits by our fire, that they no sooner saw one of the " *Hydery* people lift a musquet to his shoulder, than they would take off their " hats, and bow to him like an ape.[21]

" One day the *Nazarenes*, at break of day, attacked and penetrated into the " trenches at the edge of the ditch. I was seated, at the time, in my quarters, " having just performed my customary exercises,[22] when hearing the noise of " musquetry and of men, I took a company of *Usud-Ilhyes*, and ran on foot to " the trenches, where I found the *Nazarenes* standing. The *Usud-Ilhye* people, " instantly attacking them with sword and bayonet, sent several of them to hell, " and made some of them prisoners. The remnant of the sword took to flight.

" In

(16) Original پیادهاي احشام meaning, I suppose, as if in contempt of his enemy, that his irregular infantry would be sufficient for the purpose.

(17) The *Ehsham* were sometimes employed for the purposes of parade, constituting a sort of guards. They were most commonly, I believe, stationed in garrison, but occasionally acted with the army in the field.

(18) Original مردي آدمي literally, I believe, " manly man," a respectable person.

(19) Original نا پاک طینتان

(20) Original بقیه السیف " the remnant (or remains) of the sword."

(21) This ludicrous representation is, no doubt, founded on the practice, not uncommon with soldiers at sieges, of *bobbing*, as it is called (*i. e.* dropping the head) to avoid shot or shells: and as a hat presents rather a conspicuous object to a marksman, it may be easily conceived, that this might have been occasionally taken off with the same view.

(22) Original بعد فراغ ورزش

"In short, during three months, such was the slaughter *on both sides*, that the "trenches exhibited nothing but a mixture of mud and clay with the blood and "flesh of men. The toes of many were completely rotted, in consequence of the "excessive rains, and owing to the mire [in the midst of which they were con-"stantly forced to stand]. Often of a dark night, and [wading] through the "floods occasioned by the heavy rain and wind (which here always exceed any "thing known in other parts of our kingdom), I say, often during this time, "have I, both by night and day, gone the rounds, to see that the necessary "works were properly carried on, and that the *Ahmedy* people were duly watchful. "In consequence, it happened that two or three *Sirdars*, and others, fell, in the "darkness of the night, into wells, which were then quite full, and became "martyrs, without any one's knowing of the accident. Moreover, at this time, "the water lay on the ground knee-deep."

What immediately follows here, in the original, has already been given, in the observations on Letter CCCXXXVI, to the King of France, beginning with the words "Carrying on a mine, &c." and the passage following that appears in the observations on Letter VIII, to Mahommed Ghyâs Khân and Noor Mahommed Khân, beginning with the words "Previously to the resolution, &c."

APPENDIX, C.

(Referred to under LETTER *I.)*

A FAC SIMILE *of* TIPPOO SULTAN'S ENGAGEMENT *with his* FATHER.

See Plate annexed.

APPENDIX, D.

(Referred to under LETTER *XVI.)*

An HISTORICAL SKETCH *of the* PATAN PRINCIPALITY *of* SHÂNOOR.

INTRODUCTION.

The following memoir is taken from a Persian manuscript, kindly communicated to me by my friend, Lieutenant Colonel M'Kenzie. The author is Meer Hûsain Ali,

Ali, a very intelligent Musulman, in the employ of that ingenious and indefatigable explorer of the history and antiquities of the *Decan*. If it be little more than a genealogical sketch of the distinguished family of which it treats, it possesses, at least, the merit of being derived, as far as it goes, from information obtained chiefly on the spot, and therefore the more likely to be authentic. Its principal defect consists in the total want of dates throughout the earlier part of the narrative; the first one with which we meet being that of the succession of the fourth chieftain, Bhûlool Khân, to the government of *Bunkapoor*, in A.H. 1022. And though, after this time, the number of years that each chieftain ruled over the principality is uniformly expressed, yet neither the commencement nor the close of the respective administrations, nor any of the few events recorded regarding them, are marked by the specification of the year in which they severally occurred; while even the few dates, deducible from the general narrative, are liable to considerable doubts and difficulties. I have endeavoured to supply this omission as well as I could; but have not always been able to do so entirely to my own satisfaction. When I may happen, therefore, to differ, with respect to dates, from preceding writers, I beg to be understood to do so with suitable diffidence, and not to pledge myself for the accuracy of my author.

It may be proper to observe, that with regard to the manner of writing the name of Shânoor, I have, throughout the present article, conformed to the orthography of Meer Hûsain, which I believe to be that in most general use. For though sometimes written in the Persian سانور or *Sánoor*, شانور or *Shánoor*, may nevertheless be meant; the difference consisting merely in the diacritical points of the ش or *sh*; the occasional omission of which, in the hurry of transcribing, may be easily supposed to happen. As to *Savanore*, it is evidently an European corruption of *Sánoor*.

I have only another observation with which to detain the reader. Perhaps, strictly speaking, the term *Principality* may not be properly applicable to such a state as that of *Shánoor*; since its chieftains have never, I believe, been distinguished by the appellation of princes, though as well entitled to it as many individuals among the *Nabobs* and *Rájahs* of *India*, on whom Europeans have bestowed it. As, in most respects, however, they exercised sovereign power, and virtually, at least, transmitted their possessions to their descendants, I have thought it allowable to follow the example of other writers who have spoken of them; and to give the name in question, not only to their fief, but likewise to the two other *Patan* chiefships of *Kurnool* and *Kurpah*.

The

The *Patan* family, of which it is here proposed to give a brief account, and which, during a period of nearly three centuries, make a conspicuous figure in the annals of the *Decan*, affect, in common with every *Afghan*[1] tribe throughout the East, to derive their origin from Khâlid-bin-Wâlid, who was one of the most celebrated of the companions of Mahommed. What is more certain, however, than this boasted descent, is, that they justly reckon among their ancestors some of the principal nobles of the Musulman kingdom of *Beejapoor*. Of these, the acknowledged founder of the dynasty, was

1. *Jân-nisâr-Khân*,

who first distinguished himself during the reign of Ismâel Adil Shâh,[2] by whom he was raised to the dignity of an *Omra* of one of the higher orders. Being of a remarkably swarthy complexion, as well as of a savage appearance and nature,[3] the Decanese gave him the name of Kâlâ-puhâr, or *the black mountain*. After attaining, under Ali Ibrâheem Adil Shâh,[4] the successor of Ismâel, to some of the first offices of the state, he lost his life at *Ahmed Nugr*, in a battle with the army of Nizâm Shâh.[5] He was succeeded by his eldest son,[6]

2. *Uzeez Meea*,

who, under the title of Futah Lushkur Khân, acquired great celebrity, during the reign of Ali Adil Shâh;[7] from whom he received, besides the *Musnud*, or dignity, of an *Omra* of one thousand five hundred, the much coveted distinctions of the standard and kettle-drum.[8] He closed a brilliant career, in the course of which

(1) The nation, or people, here spoken of, are indifferently denominated *Patans* or *Afghans*. Though fond of being considered the descendants of Khâlid, they are not satisfied with so modern a pedigree, and therefore derive themselves from the still higher source of Judah: nor are there wanting circumstances in their history and manners, that strongly favour their claim to Jewish origin.

(2) Ismâel was the second of the Adil Shâhy Kings of *Bejapoor*, and reigned from A.H. 916 to 941, or from A.D. 1509 to A.D. 1534, being cotemporary with Henry VIIIth of England.

(3) Original دیوحبشه which may be read so as to signify either "an Ethiopian dæmon" or "a man of a wild or savage nature."

(4) He reigned from A.H. 941 to 965, or from A.D. 1534 to 1559.

(5) This was another Mahommedan dynasty of kings of *Decan*. The reader, who is desirous of knowing more of them, is referred to Scott's *Ferishta*.

(6) Jân-nisâr Khân had another son, named Nubby Khân, who was also known by the title of Run-must Khân.

(7) He reigned between the years 965 and 988 of the Higera, corresponding with A.D. 1557 and 1580.

(8) That is, the privilege of carrying a standard and of beating a kettle-drum.

which he was no less eminent as a statesman than as a warrior, by falling honourably in battle, as his father had done. He was succeeded by his son,

3. *Jubbâr Meea Meeâneh,*

who was so favoured by fortune, that he is said to have never failed in any military enterprize in which he engaged. No doubt he owed much of this extraordinary success to the enthusiastic attachment of his followers: an attachment which would appear to have been inspired, in the first instance, by their confidence in his valor and prudence, and subsequently confirmed by his earnest care to provide, on all occasions, for their ease and comfort. By these means he soon outstripped, in reputation and influence, the most eminent of his cotemporaries at the court of *Beejapoor.*

This was manifested in his appointment to the government of *Bunkapoor*, and in his elevation, at the same time, to the dignity of an *Omra* of five thousand, with the command of four thousand horse. The *Soubah*(9) of *Bunkapore,* as it was then called, comprized twenty-two *Mahals*, and was estimated to yield an annual revenue of fifty-four *lacks* of *rupees.* It does not distinctly appear, upon what footing the *Patan* received this important charge; but the Narrative affords sufficient grounds for believing, that the tenure by which he held it was of the nature of a military *Jageer*, or fief.(10)

However this might be, Jubbâr Meea, remaining himself in attendance on his sovereign, dispatched his son, Bhûlool Khân, to take possession, and administer the affairs, of his new government in his name. This Bhûlool Khân was, like his great-grandfather, of a sable complexion: and being, moreover, of a huge stature, and remarkable for the squalidness of his usual dress, he received from his subjects the appellation of Rugty Kâlâ Puhar, or "the dirty black mountain;" the word *rugut* signifying, in the Canarese dialect, *dirty or filthy*. He was a man of extraordinary intrepidity, but of a sanguinary and cruel disposition. Hateful, however, as his character was, it would appear to have conduced considerably, by the universal terror which it inspired, to the early and advantageous settlement of the country committed to his care.

Jubbâr Meea is stated to have fallen in battle, like both his predecessors, and to have been succeeded, in the year 1022 of the Higera, by his son.

4. *Bhûlool*

(9) *Bunkapoor*, although denominated a *Soubah*, or province, under the *Adil Shâhies*, ranked only as a *Sircar* (or subdivision of a *Soubah)* after the Moghul conquest.

(10) Which consists of lands, granted partly as a mark of personal favour, and partly for the purpose of enabling the holder to maintain a specific military force for the service of the state. They are resumable at the pleasure of the sovereign.

4. *Bhûlool Khân,*

who would, hereupon, appear to have removed the seat of his government from the town and fortress of *Bunkapoor*, to a place in the vicinity thereof, called *Sânoor*, or *Shânoor-hully*; to which he is said to have been attracted by the beauty of its environs and the salubrity of its air. Here he founded and peopled a large city, to which he gave the name of *Shânoor*; erecting in it a handsome palace for his own residence, and several commodious *bazars* (or market-places) for the convenience of the inhabitants. *Bunkapoor*, being thus abandoned by its chiefs, fell rapidly to decay, so that there is hardly a trace of it to be seen at this day. The fate of *Shânoor* itself has been little better, " that delightful city being now " reduced," says our author, who wrote only about ten years ago, " from an " earthly paradise, surrounded by pleasant gardens, abounding in fruits of various " sorts, and fertilized by numerous canals, to the condition of the meanest of all " mean places."

Nothing further is recorded of Bhûlool Khân, till the period when Aurungzebe appearing in the *Decan*, at the head of the Moghul forces, many of the nobles of the now declining kingdom of *Beejapoor* began to swerve from their allegiance, and to consult their own personal interests, at the expence of those of their natural sovereign and native country. Among these was Bhûlool Khân, who, no longer keeping any terms with his court, but repairing openly to the camp of the prince, presented the latter with a *Nuzr* of three *lacks* of *rupees* and other costly gifts, in return for which he obtained an imperial patent of confirmation in the *Soubahdâry* of *Bunkapoor*; for the protection of which from any attempts that might be formed against it by his justly incensed sovereign, he now proceeded to raise an adequate force. He appears, about the same time, to have successfully employed his credit with the prince, in favour of an old friend and fellow student, named Khizr Khân Beeny; who obtaining, through the recommendation of Bhûlool, the *Sircar* of *Kurnool* in *Jageer*, together with the dignity of an *Omra* of the empire, became the founder of the *Patan* dynasty of *Kurnool*, of which a succinct account is given in Appendix G.

Bhûlool Khân, exclusive of the term of his administration as his father's deputy, is stated to have ruled over the principality of *Shânoor* during a period of forty-nine (lunar) years; upon his death he was succeeded by his son,

5. *Duleel Khân,*(11)

otherwise called Dileer Khân; the latter being a title conferred on him by the Emperor

(11) Supposing my author's dates to be correct, it follows, that Duleel Khân succeeded his father in A.H. 1071 (A.D. 1660) or in the first year of the second Ali Adil Shâh.

Emperor Allumgeer, on the occasion which will be presently noticed. In the mean while, he is said to have applied himself, with unwearied diligence, to the improvement of his *Jageer:* and though his father had, long since, renounced his allegiance to his legitimate sovereign, the present chief thought it expedient to make a show of submission to the feeble authority of that prince. Whether he adopted this line of conduct immediately on his accession to the *Musnud,* and during the remainder of the second Ali Adil Shâh's reign, does not distinctly appear; but it is certain, that he maintained an epistolary correspondence with Secunder Adil Shâh,(12) which was deficient in nothing but sincerity. In the end, however, throwing off all further disguise, he repaired with two thousand Afghan horse, and from three to four thousand well-armed infantry, to the standard of the Emperor Allumgeer, by whom he was received with distinguished honour. He subsequently consummated his treason and ingratitude towards the royal race, through whose unbounded favor himself and family had attained to their present eminence and power, by assisting in the reduction of *Beejapoor,* and in the consequent extinction of the dynasty of Adil Shâhy.

The Emperor's son, Sultan Moaazim, being sent, after the fall of *Beejapoor,* to reduce *Ahmedâbâd Beder,* that place soon opened its gates to him, in consequence of the sudden death of its governor, Mirjân Hubshy, occasioned by the explosion of a powder-magazine.(13) Here this weak prince, yielding to the suggestions of a wild ambition, and to the interested advice of evil counsellors, formed the extravagant project of wresting the reins of government from the hands of a parent, whom he was taught, by his flatterers, to consider as superannuated, and no longer fit to rule. He announced this rebellious purpose by causing the *Khûtbah*(14) to be read in his own name at *Beder,* and by attempting to establish his authority in *Ahmed nugr, Jûnair,* &c. The Emperor, upon being informed of these proceedings, assembled together his principal *Omras,* and stating to them what had occurred, demanded, at the same time, if there was any one among them who would undertake to bring the deluded prince (for whose personal safety, notwithstanding his outrageous conduct, his father was still anxious) alive and unhurt before him. All present at this audience, with the single exception of Duleel Khân, appearing to shrink from the arduous task proposed to them, maintained

(12) He was the last of the Adil Shâhy kings of *Beejapoor.* His reign began A.H. 1083 (A.D. 1672) and terminated with the fall of *Beejapoor* to the Moghul arms, in A.H. 1097 or A.D. 1685.

(13) *Beder,* upon this occasion, received the name of *Zuferâbâd,* by which it is still occasionally distinguished.

(14) That is, in fact, caused himself to be proclaimed emperor. I give this, and the account immediately following, entirely on the authority of Hûsain Ali, who probably derived his information from some of the local annals and family memoirs, collected under the direction of Colonel M'Kenzie.

tained a profound silence. He alone, without the least hesitation, declared his readiness to fulfil the Emperor's wishes; whereupon Allumgeer, in admiration of his zeal and intrepidity, immediately saluted him by the title of Dileer Khân (or the valiant Lord), and dispatched him, without delay, on the service which he had so promptly undertaken.

Dileer Khân (as he must now be called), putting himself at the head of his followers,(15) proceeded the same night from the imperial camp, and taking the road to the rebel army, addressed a plausible letter to Moaazim Shâh; in which he pretended "to be disgusted at the neglect which he had experienced from Allumgeer, and to be desirous of attaching himself to the cause, and of participating in the fortunes of his Highness." The credulous prince, ignorant of what had recently passed at the imperial court, and unsuspicious of treachery, joyfully accepted the insidious overture of the *Patan*, to whom he immediately wrote, urging him to hasten his arrival. Dileer Khân, having, by these means, introduced himself into the camp of Moaazim Shâh, contrived, in the course of the interview to which he was soon admitted, to make such progress in the prince's good graces, that the latter gave directions for the Afghan quarters to be established contiguously to his own. The following day being appointed for the march of the rebel army, Dileer Khân repaired, at an early hour, to the tent of the prince; who was easily persuaded, in order to do honour to the new favourite, to mount the elephant of the *Patan*, by whom it had been pre-concerted that Moaazim Shâh's personal retinue, together with his baggage, should be completely encompassed by his own troops. In this array, Dileer Khân himself being seated behind the prince in the *Khuwâsy*,(16) the party proceeded for some time, without the least distrust, either on the part of Moaazim Shâh, whose attention the *Patan* took care effectually to occupy, or of any of his immediate attendants. The elephant on which he rode being remarkably swift footed, and the driver being directed in his route by occasional signs from his master, the army of the prince was quickly left far in the rear. At length some of the royal retinue, perceiving that they had entered upon the road leading to *Beejâpoor*, proclaimed the treason of the *Patan*, and attempted to impede his progress: the latter, however, instantly causing the most active of them to be put to death, all further resistance to his design immediately ceased. The *Patan* now applied himself to console and encourage his captive, with whom he proceeded, by rapid marches, to *Beejâpoor*, where he

c

(15) Consisting, as has been seen, of two thousand Afghan horse and from three to four thousand well armed foot.

(16) The *Khuwâsy* is so called, from its being the part of the *Umâry* or *Howdeh* (i. e. the litter fixed to the back of the elephant) assigned to the *Khuwâs*, or attendant. The *Umâry* is the canopied litter; the *Howdeh*, the plain open one.

he soon delivered him, in perfect safety, and surrounded with his usual state, into the hands of the overjoyed monarch. It is scarcely necessary to add, that the latter amply requited the delicate and important service rendered on the present occasion by Dileer Khân; on whom, indeed, he is said to have heaped such unprecedented honours, as excited considerable jealousy in the breasts of the other *Omras* of the imperial court.

After this, Dileer Khân distinguished himself, in an eminent degree, at the sieges of *Golcondah* and *Dowlutâbâd*, as well as on various other occasions. He displayed, in particular, considerable talents and address, in the course of the operations which he was employed to conduct against Yunkut Naig, the *Polygar* of *Shoolapoor;* whom he reduced to such straits, as at length compelled that stubborn chieftain to acknowledge the imperial authority, after he had firmly and successfully resisted, for three years, every effort of Allumgeer to subdue him.

Dileer Khân now retired to the seat of his government; nor would either he, or the other *Patan* chieftains of the *Decan*, appear to have taken any part in the succeeding troubles, excited by the various intrigues and factions which distinguished the period in question. Dying, at length, in the thirty-second year of his rule over the *Shânoor* principality,(17) he was succeeded by his son,

6. *Abdûl Ghuffâr Khân*,

of whom nothing in particular is recorded, till the death of Allumgeer, at which period he paid his court so effectually to Khân Jehân, the foster-brother of the late emperor, and governor in chief, or viceroy of the *Decan*, on the part of the new emperor, that he soon obtained from him the requisite patents of confirmation in his *Jageer*, or principality.

After some time, taking offence at the great state assumed by Khân Gooreh, the *Daise-pândeh*(18) of *Serhutty*,(19) who was a tributary of the *Shânoor* government, he

(17) Or in A.H. 1103, corresponding with A.D. 1691.

(18) This is an office, corresponding, I believe, with that of *Puttail*, and not differing materially from the *Mûkuddum*, or head man of a village, in *Hindostan*.

(19) As the chiefs of *Serhutty* make some figure in the history of the *Decan*, and as both *Serhutty* and *Lukmaiser* (the latter of which depended upon *Serhutty*) were included within the dominions of Tippoo Sultan, the reader may not be displeased with the following short account of them, extracted from the collections of Meer Hûsain Ali:

" At the period when Enkus Khân, a distinguished nobleman of the kingdom of *Beejapoor*, was " invested with the charge of the *Soubahdâry* of *Bunkapoor* and its dependencies, *Lukmaiser** being a " populous and flourishing town, he chose it for the seat of his government. Not far from thence stood " the village of *Serhutty*, whither the governor occasionally resorted, either on business or for pleasure. " On

* *Serhutty* is situated, according to the map prefixed to Colonel Wilks's History of Mysore, about twelve miles north-east of *Lukmaiser*, which is placed about twenty miles north of *Shânoor*.

he sent a numerous force against that chieftain, under the direction of his nephew, Khân Meea; who, allowing himself to be surprised and shamefully defeated by very inferior numbers, fell wounded into the hands of the enemy. This misfortune did not, however, prevent Abdûl Ghuffâr from assembling another army, with the avowed purpose of redeeming the credit of his arms, and of effectually chastising

c 2

his

" On one of these occasions he happened to receive a trifling service from the *Puttail* of the village " (who was a *Lingayet*, named Soampa) which some superstitious notion appears to have led him to " requite in the most absurd and extravagant manner; since, sending for him the following day, he " publickly adopted him, in open *Durbâr*, conferred upon him the office of *Daise-pândeh* of *Lukmaiser*, " with a *Jageer* of five thousand rupees, and gave him the title of *Khân-gooreh*, or, as it may be " interpreted, *Lord of the village*.* He continued in high favour with Enkus Khân during the life of " the latter, who did not forget him at his death, but bestowed upon him, at that moment, his own " state elephant, together with his standard and *Nobut*.† These honourable pledges of their patron's " esteem, constituted, henceforward, the chief pride and most valued distinction of the *Khân-gooreh's* " family; who, to this day, hold the memory of their original benefactor in such reverence, that they " never light a lamp or candle of an evening, without invoking his name.

" The *Khân-gooreh*s (who are also sometimes called *Kunchun-gooreh*s) continued in the undisturbed " possession of their office and lands, from the time of the transfer of the *Soubah* of *Bunkapoor* to the " *Patan* chieftain, Jubbâr Meea, till the administration of Abdûl Ghûffar Khân; who, as above related, " involved himself in a frivolous quarrel with

" 2. *Dud Khân Gooreh*,

" the eldest son, and successor of the first Khân or *Soampa*; who vainly endeavoured, through " the medium of agents deputed for the purpose, to prove to the *Patan* the unreasonableness of " his displeasure; and as vainly sought every practicable means (except that of discontinuing the " use of the standard and kettle drum, bequeathed to his family by Enkus Khân) to appease and " conciliate his offended superior. At length, urged by despair, the *Daise-pândeh*, fixing the " *teekah* ‡ of *sandal* on his forehead, waving the interdicted banner, and invoking the assistance " of its lamented donor, rushed suddenly, at the head of no more than five hundred horse and " a thousand foot, upon the Afghan forces, over whom he obtained the signal victory mentioned " in the text, and thereby reduced the Patan chieftain to the ultimate necessity of granting him an " honorable peace.

" Dud Khân Gooreh was, some time after this, succeeded by

" 3. *Chuk Khân Gooreh Behâdûr*,

" the fourth son of Soampa, who attaching himself to the Mahrattah chief, Balajee Râo, ob- " tained from the latter the farm of the entire district of *Serhutty*, yielding a yearly revenue of " two *lacks* and sixty thousand *rupees*, of which he agreed to pay one *lack* of *rupees* annually to " the Mahrattah government. This arrangement continued in force till the year 1764, when the " successes of Hyder Ali Khân obliged, not only the *Patan* chief of *Shânoor*, but most of the

" *Polygars*

* I am by no means confident that this is the sense in which the appellation in question was employed, my author not having given any explanation of it.

† The *Nobut* consists of the kettle-drum, and other musical instruments, which an *Omra* may be privileged to use.

‡ The *Teekah* is the line which Hindoos draw, on certain occasions, across their foreheads. It is made sometimes with a consecrated earth, sometimes with a preparation of sandal; the latter being used only on very particular occasions, like the present.

his successful adversary: but learning, in the mean while, that the Mahrattahs, whose power had, by this time, become extremely formidable to their neighbours, were preparing to march to the *Gooreh's* assistance, he determined, with more prudence than spirit, to retire from the contest; and accordingly, in consideration of a trifling sum of money, agreed to be paid by his vassal, he not only receded from all his late arrogant pretensions, but, together with an honorary dress, accompanied by corresponding assurances of future favor and protection, conferred upon the *Daise-pândeh* the additional title of *Behâdûr*.[20]

Khân Jehân dying about this time, was succeeded in the government of the *Decan* by Meer Hûsain Ali Khân, the younger of the two ambitious brothers, celebrated, in the history of this turbulent period, under the appellation of the the *Siyuds* of *Bârheh*. Hereupon the *Patan* chieftain dispatched his son, Ghufoor Meea, to *Bûrhânpoor*, with a considerable *Nuzr* in money, and other valuable presents for the new viceroy, who, in return for this seasonable complement, confirmed him in the possession of his *Jâgeer*, as well as of the other dignities enjoyed by his predecessor. After this he gave himself up to a life of ease and dissipation, and at length dying, in the twenty-eighth year[21] of his government, was succeeded by his above-mentioned son,

7. *Ghufoor Meea*,

who was scarcely seated on the *Musnud*, before he was called upon to repel an invasion of the Mahrattahs, headed by a chieftain of the Râsta family, by whom great

" *Polygars* of the surrounding country, to submit to the conqueror's authority. At this period, the " *Daise-pândeh* of *Serhutty* was

" 4. *Dud Kunchun Gooreh*,

" a grandson of Chuk Khân Gooreh; who throwing himself on the protection of Hyder, the latter, " on condition that he remitted in future to *Seringapatam* the same tribute he had hitherto paid to " the Mahrattahs, allowed him to retain possession of his *Taalûks*. Hyder moreover, with a view to " encourage the neighbouring *Polygars*, treated him, while he remained in the Mysore camp, with " considerable distinction, and finally dismissed him with various flattering marks of his favor.

" The *Daise-pândehs* of *Serhutty* continued, from this time until the year 1792, under the protection " of the Mysore government. They then became once more subject to the authority of the " Mahrattahs; who, by virtue of the partition treaty of *Seringapatam*, acquired possession of all the " country situated to the northward of the *Tungbuddra*. Since this period, no further change would " appear to have taken place in their condition."

(20) It appears to have been somewhat early for the *Nabobs*, or governors, of such districts as that of *Bunkapoor*, to have exercised the prerogative of bestowing titles of honor. It must, however, be admitted, that the imperial authority of the court of *Dehli* was already on the decline, and that even the more immediate powers of the local *Soubahdârs*, or viceroys, were neither uniformly acknowledged nor respected, by their nominal deputies or subordinates.

(21) That is in A.H. 1131, or A.D. 1719.

great ravages were, for some time, committed in the *Patan* territories. At length Ghufoor Meea, encountering the enemy in the environs of *Misry-Kotah*, gave them a considerable defeat; which, however, only obtained him a temporary respite from hostilities, since the fugitives, having procured a reinforcement from Gopaul Râo Ghoarpurreh, the *Nâzim* (or governor) of *Mirij*, were soon in a condition to renew their depredations on the *Shânoor* districts, immediately adjoining to their own frontier, which they accordingly continued to harass for nearly two years longer. At the end of this period the *Patan* was glad to avail himself of the mediation of Gopaul Râo, in order to effect an accommodation with the invaders, who, upon his paying them about a *lack* of *rupees*, in goods and money, and ceding to them the fort and district of *Misry-Kotah*, agreed to withdraw from his dominions.

From this time Ghufoor Meea remained at peace until his death, which took place in the ninth year of his government,[22] and during the *Nawâb*, Asof Jah's,[23] viceroyalty of the *Decan*. He was succeeded by

8. *Abdûl Mujeed Khân*,[24]

who already aspiring to complete independence, omitted paying his court to Asof Jah, and rashly assumed the management of his patrimony, without applying for, or obtaining, the customary patent of confirmation from the viceroy. By this conduct he drew upon himself, as might be expected, the displeasure of Asof Jah, who had, about this period, transferred the seat of his government from *Aurungabad* to *Hyderabad*, and who lost no time in preparing to chastise the contumacy of the *Patan*. With this view, after having dispatched his grandson, Hidâyet Mohyûddeen Khân (better known afterwards by the title of Mûzuffer Jung) to take possession of *Beejapoor*, he marched himself directly against *Shânoor*, many of the districts of which he resigned to the depredations of his army. He was, on this occasion, eagerly joined by the disaffected *Daise-pândehs* of *Serhutty*, *Guduk*, and other *Polygars*; who, stimulated by their habitual hatred of the Afghans, omitted no means of inflaming his resentment against Abdûl Mujeed. Asof Jah, however, was too wary and experienced, to allow himself to be swayed by the interested representations and suggestions of these people; and having nothing in view but to bring the *Patan* to a proper sense of his

(22) That is in A.H. 1140, or A.D. 1728.

(23) More commonly called Nizâm ûl Mûlk.

(24) On other occaions, as well as the present, my author has omitted to mention the degree of consanguinity subsisting between the successor and his predecessor. In such instances, it may be safely presumed, that the successor was the son of the person he succeeded.

his duty, he readily admitted of the mediation of the chief of *Kurnool* for that purpose. Thereupon hostilities ceased, and the negociation terminated in Abdûl Mujeed's paying two *lacks* of *rupees* to the *Nizám*; to whom he also made various valuable presents, in return for which he obtained patents of confirmation in all his possessions. It being thought proper, on this occasion, that the *Patan* should make a visit of form to the Viceroy, he only consented to do so, on the express condition of being received in a manner suitable to the high rank which he held among the *Omras* of the empire. Accordingly, Nâsir Jung, the second son of Asof Jah, was deputed to conduct him to the *Durbâr*; where, on his arrival, the Viceroy seated him on the *Musnud*, with himself. He was even permitted to smoke his *Húkkah* during this interview: and when he did homage to Asof Jah, as his official superior, by presenting him with the usual *Nuzrs*, the Viceroy condescended to receive them standing. In short, Asof Jah omitted no attention towards him, which could gratify his pride or vanity: "having" (as our author observes) "the wisdom to think, that the attachment of so powerful a chieftain "would be cheaply purchased at the price of such trivial concessions." Nor was he mistaken in his calculation; since the *Patan* was so highly pleased with the gracious and flattering behaviour of the Viceroy towards him, that, from a contumacious vassal, he was suddenly converted into one of the most useful and zealous adherents of that celebrated personage. This was soon after evinced, by his accompanying Asof Jah, in the year of the *Higera*(25) 1157 (or A. D. 1744) in the expedition of the latter to the *Payen Ghaut Carnatic*; where himself and followers acquired considerable renown for their valor on several occasions; particularly at the attack of *Nuthurnugr* (or *Trichinopoly*), at that time in the possession of Murâr Râo Ghoarpurreh.

Asof Jah was occupied nerly three years in the settlement of the *Carnatic*, during the whole of which period Abdûl Mujeed Khân continued in his train. At length having reduced *Trichinopoly*, and made a satisfactory adjustment with the several *Polygars* of the *Carnatic*, the viceroy returned to *Hyderabad*; at the same time permitting Abdûl Mujeed, and other *Patan* chieftains, who had attended him in his expedition, to repair to their respective homes.

Asof Jah dying about four years after this,(26) was succeeded, as *Soubah* of the *Decan*, by his second son, Meer Ahmed, better known by the title of Nâsir Jung; who being shortly after directed to repair to the court of *Dehli*, appointed his nephew,

(25) Or, according to other authorities, in A. H. 1156, or A. D. 1743.

(26) He died the 4th of *Jumâdûs Sâny*, A. H. 1161 (or 24th March 1748), not at the extraordinary age of one hundred and four, as Dow and others have inadvertently stated, but in his seventy-seventh year.

nephew, Hidâyet Mohyûddeen Khân (more commonly called Mûzuffer Jung) to the temporary charge of his government. It is foreign to the object of the present memoir to enter into a detail of the events which followed: it may suffice to say, that Hidayet, availing himself of his uncle's absence, and yielding to the persuasion of traitors, assumed the title of *Soubah;* and that Nâsir Jung, on being apprized of his nephew's proceedings, excused himself from complying with the imperial summons, and hastened back to *Hyderabad.* From thence he lost no time in advancing against the rebels; being previously joined, on this occasion, by the different feudatories of the *Decan,* who either sincerely espoused his cause, or only pretended to do so, for the purpose of betraying him. Among the latter were the *Patan* chieftains of *Shânoor, Kurnool,* and *Kurpah.* The former, however, did not himself accompany the *Soubah* in this fatal expedition; declining to do so (whether truly or not) on the ground of sickness, and sending his son, Kureem Meea, at the head of a suitable force, in his stead.(27) Nâsir Jung, as is well known, soon after fell a victim to the treachery of the *Patan* commanders: of whom, however, only one lived to return to his capital; both Kureem Meea and the chief of *Kurnool* being slain, in the sanguinary feud which arose among the conspirators, within two months from the murder of Nâsir Jung. Hence it appears, that these writers were mistaken, who have represented the actual ruler of *Shânoor* as an immediate accomplice in the treason of the *Patans.* It is even uncertain, whether he was, in any measure, privy to the designs of the conspirators.

Abdûl Mujeed would not appear to have taken any share in the troubles which followed the transaction just related, and which continued to disturb the tranquillity of the *Decan* for five or six years after: nor do we hear further regarding him, till his death, which took place in the thirty-second year of his government, (28) when he was succeeded by

9. *Abdûl Hukeem Khân Meeâneh,*(29)

not long after whose accession Nizâm Ali Khân (who had, by this time, seized upon the government of the *Decan)* in conjunction with the Mahrattahs proceeded against *Shânoor,* with the avowed intention of overturning that state, and avenging the murder of the former's brother, Nâsir Jung. In pursuance of this purpose, the

(27) The author of the *Maasir ul Omra* (a biographical work of the first estimation and authority, and a judicious translation of which is among the principal Oriental desiderata) calls the son of Abdûl Mujeed, who commanded the *Shânoor* contingent on this occasion, Bhûlool Khân; and adds, that Abdûl Mujeed was, from the beginning, privy to the design formed against the life of Nâsir Jung.

(28) That is in A. H. 1172, or A. D. 1759.

(29) Here, again, our author has omitted mentioning, in what relation Abdûl Hukeem stood to his predecessor: but it is most probable that he was a younger brother of the Kureem Meea, who was engaged in the conspiracy against Nâsir Jung.

the confederates entered and laid waste the *Patan* territories for the space of three months; in the course of which the Mahrattahs also possessed themselves of *Serhutty, Misry-cotâh, Gudduck,* and other places depending on the *Shânoor* principality. Abdûl Hukeem, being of an indolent character, and addicted to pleasure, and despairing, moreover, of being able to cope successfully with such superior forces as now encompassed him, determined, if possible, to save himself by submission. With this view, he solicited and obtained the mediation of Busâlut Jung, the brother, and of Rûknûd Dowlah, the *Dewân* (or minister), of the *Nizâm,* who was prevailed upon, at their instance, to accept of two *lacks* of *rupees* from the *Patan,* as an atonement for what had passed. The Mahrattahs, however, though with less cause of complaint, were not so easily satisfied; Abdûl Hukeem been obliged to relinquish to them, in perpetuity, the sixteen *Mahals,* of which they had made themselves masters in the course of the late irruption.

"The heavy misfortunes," observes my author, "which thus befel, and had "nearly overwhelmed, the *Patan* state, were, at the moment of their occurring, "very generally regarded (and especially by all devout Musulmans) as a judgment "of heaven upon that tribe, for the treacherous murder of Nâsir Jung;" of which atrocious deed they appear to have been almost universally considered as not only the actual perpetrators, but likewise the chief promoters. The same reflection would be as naturally suggested (and probably was) on occasion of the rapid decline, after this time, of the two other *Patan* governments, of *Kurnool* and *Kurpah*; one of which was, ere long, completely subverted, and the other reduced to a similar state of dependence and insignificance with that of *Shânoor,* which however, had not yet fallen so low as it was destined to do, at no distant period.

Hyder Ali Khân, having gained possession of the fort of *Dhârwâr,* through the treachery of its governor, Rûstum Khân[30] (who, on this occasion, engaged in the service of Hyder) proceeded from thence against *Shânoor;* where Abdûl Hukeem, hastily collecting together what forces he could, dispatched them, under the command of Jubbâr Meea, with orders to oppose the enemy's advance. The two armies met in the environs of *Anwutty;* where Hyder completely routed the *Patans,* and followed up his success so closely, that both *Shânoor* and *Bunkapore* were presently invested. Abdûl Hukeem, alarmed at the rapid progress of the invader, determined to seek an accommodation with him; and, for this purpose, made overtures, to which Hyder, "moved," says our author, "by respect for the "honourable ancestry of the *Patan,* readily assented." This sentiment may seem somewhat at variance with the general character of Hyder, if not, indeed, with the usual nature of upstart power: but the issue of this very negociation evinces, that he

(30) He was governor of *Dhârwâr* on the part of the *Soubah* of the *Decan.*

he really did hold nobility of descent in some estimation, since it was one of the conditions of the treaty concluded on this occasion, that a double union, by marriage, should be formed between his own family and that of the *Patan*.(31) It may be thought, that Hyder was actuated in this proceeding solely by considerations of policy, grounded on the notion, that such a connection was calculated to conduce to the consolidation of his usurped authority. It would be difficult, however, to show, how such a purpose could be promoted by an union with a state, now so depressed, as to require, instead of being enabled to afford, assistance. Be this as it might, it is certain, that no benefit ultimately resulted to either party from this contract.

Our author has not communicated any of the minuter articles of the treaty in question; nor have I been able to supply the omission from any other source of information. It may be presumed, however, that the *Patan* government bound itself, on this occasion, both to pay a certain annual tribute, or *paishcush*, to the Mysore chieftain, and to furnish him, when required, with a specific military force. The former supposition is rendered probable, by the allusions, which we have seen made in Tippoo Sultan's correspondence with Abdûl Hukeem, to his pecuniary claims on the *Patan*: while the latter conclusion is also, in some measure, warranted, by the fact of Hyder's having been accompanied, in most of his subsequent expeditions, by a body of *Patan* troops. Thus Kheera Meea, with five hundred horse and a thousand infantry, was present at the reduction of *Gooty*, *Bulhâry*, *Kurpah*, and other places, which submitted, about this time, to the authority of his father-in-law; and though he was prevented, by sickness, from attending the latter, during his invasion of the *Carnatic*, yet on that occasion, also, did the stipulated contingent of the *Patan* state, headed by another commander, appear among the auxiliary forces of the Mysorean.

Previously to his departure from the neighbourhood of *Shânoor*, in prosecution of his ulterior plans of conquest, Hyder (whether in conformity with any private article of the treaty, which has been alluded to, or merely at the subsequent solicitation of his new ally, is uncertain) undertook to put the latter, once more, in possession of the greater part of the districts, which, as has been seen, had been wrested from him, a few years before, by the Mahrattahs. This object he accordingly accomplished to a certain extent, recovering some of the districts in question by force, and others by bribery. Nor is it, by any means, necessary, in order to our admitting the probability of this statement, to suppose, that Hyder

d and

(31) Abdûl Hukeem, on this occasion, gave his daughter in marriage to Hyder's second son, Kureem Sâheb, whose sister (by the same mother) was bestowed upon Kheera Meea, the eldest son of the *Patan* chief.

and the Mahrattahs were, at this juncture, still at war; since aggressions, of the kind here spoken of, frequently take place among neighbouring states and chieftains in *India,* without leading to a positive rupture, or to general hostilities between them. They are considered, perhaps, as mere border disputes, and are not uncommonly adjusted without any serious or formal appeal to the sword.

We hear nothing further of Abdûl Hukeem till the death of Hyder Ali, at the close of the year 1782, and the consequent accession of Tippoo Sultan to the *Musnud:* on which occasion, though the commander of the *Patan* contingent, serving with the Mysore army, took upon him to present the *Sultan* with the *Nuzr* and other compliments customary in such cases, no letter of congratulation came from Abdûl Hukeem himself. This omission gave great offence to Tippoo: who, however, did not judge it convenient to take any immediate notice of the affront.

It was about this period, that the famous Dhoondy Jee Wang (or Wâgh) first rendered himself conspicuous in the *Decan.* He had previously contented himself with petty depredations, in the course of which he had fallen into the hands of the Mahrattahs, who, after some time, were prevailed on (probably by bribes) to restore him to liberty; a favour of which it was not long before he gave them cause to repent. In the mean while, joining the expedition of Hyder Ali to the *Carnatic,* he served, during the whole of the war in that quarter, in the Mysore army, under the banners of an old associate of his, called Bâdâmy Bhishtâpâ. On the termination of hostilities in the *Carnatic,* Dhoondy Jee, accompanied only by about seventy or eighty adherents of the same desperate character as himself, hastened to *Shânoor;* where suddenly appearing at the gate of Abdûl Hukeem's palace, he declared that chieftain in a state of *Dhurna,* or siege,(32) and proclaimed his determination not to quit his position, until the *Patan* either consented to take himself and his followers into his service, at the yearly allowance of a *lack* of *rupees,* or otherwise to bestow upon him the *Dewâny* of such of the *Shânoor* districts as were still in the possession of the Mahrattahs. To the generality of readers, it will, no doubt, appear extraordinary, if not incredible, that a handful of men, insulated and unsupported as these were, should be able to give the law (as may be said) in his own capital, to a chieftain, surrounded by guards and vassals, who, it may be supposed, could have easily and signally punished the temerity of the intruders. By those, however, who are conversant in the customs of *India,* or who have perused the singular report referred to at the bottom of the page, the fact, here related, will not be thought irreconcileable with experience or probability. Be this as it may, our author proceeds to say, that Abdûl Hukeem, impatient

(32) For a very particular account of the singular practice of *Dhurna,* the reader is referred to a most curious communication from Lord Teignmouth, in the Asiatic Researches.

impatient to get rid of his importunate and daring suitor, and, of the two evils proposed to his choice by Dhoondy Jee, considering the latter as the least, consented to invest him with the office he demanded. Dhoondy having, accordingly, obtained from the fears of the *Patan* the *Sunuds* (or patents) necessary for his purpose, hastened, with what followers he could suddenly collect together, in addition to his original party (and in such a country, the temptation to plunder would not fail to procure him many), surprized two or three of the districts in question, seized upon the fortress of *Misry-cotah*, and finally acquired so considerable a booty, in money and effects, as enabled him to send a *Nuzr* of two *lacks* of *Shânoory pagodas*, together with other valuable presents, to Abdûl Hukeem; who appears to have ratified all his violent and irregular proceedings, not only by accepting a share of the plunder, but by bestowing on the plunderer, in return, an honorary dress, accompanied by other marks of distinction and approbation. After this, Dhoondy Jee, augmenting his force to five or six hundred horse and two thousand foot, continued, for a considerable while, to levy contributions, and to commit every sort of depredation, on the frontiers of the Mahrattahs: and though it is not expressly stated, that he respected, on these occasions, the territories of *Shânoor*, there is some ground for believing that he did. On the whole, it must be admitted, that there are circumstances in the conduct of Abdûl Hukeem, with regard to this famous free-booter, which, if the *Patan* did not appear to have been actually of a timid and wavering character, might well warrant a suspicion of collusion between them in the affair of the *Dhurna*.(33)

d 2 Things

(33) It is well known, that the famous adventurer, spoken of in the text, became still more conspicuous, at a later period, during which he furnished considerable employment to the British forces in *Mysore*. It was on this occasion, that Lord Viscount Wellington (then the Honorable Colonel Wellesly) gave that earnest of the consummate military skill and enterprizing spirit, of which he subsequently afforded so many eminent proofs, in the course of the Mahrattah war of 1803-4, but of which the most brilliant evidence was reserved for another period, and a still more arduous theatre.

Among the papers found at *Seringapatam*, there is a curious document, in the hand-writing of Tippoo Sultan, on the subject of Dhoondy Jee Wâg, of which the following is nearly a literal translation.

" The question [or case] proposed by the *Khodâdâd Sircar*, for the consideration of all the four " departments of government, and of Bishna Pundit, and relating to the robber, Dhoondy Jee, is " this:—first, the aforesaid robber has many times humbly represented, through the medium of " Bishna Pundit, and once or twice in *Urzies* from himself [to us], that he was the servant of the " *Sircar*, and that, if a little help were afforded him by the *Sircar*, he would [engage to] take all the " country of *Shânoor*; and [again], that he was the servant of the *Khodâdâd Sircar*. In answer hereto, " that person was told, once or twice, by letter from ourselves, and furthermore by different verbal " communications, that as it was [a time of] peace, we should [or could] positively afford him no " assistance. To the same effect we sent him word, about two months ago, by Futah Shâh, saying, you " ' are a servant of the *Khodâdâd Sircar*, and our well wisher: you must [therefore] never enter the " ' territories of the *Khodâdâd Sircar*, as, by your doing so, the peace would be disturbed [or broken];

" ' but

Things remained in this situation in the principality of *Shânoor*, till Tippoo, having made peace with the English, and established his authority in *Bidnore*, *Mangalore*,

" 'but you may remain in the territories of others, and do therein what you will.' This message " being delivered to him, he sent back, along with Futah Shâh, an Afghan of the name of Omar " Khân, to whom he gave in charge a horse and an *Urzee* for us. On the arrival of these two persons " in the Presence, we demanded of them an account of the situation of affairs in that quarter: to " which Futah Shâh answered, that this was the intention of the accursed Râo; namely, to introduce " himself, by whatever means might be [practicable], into the Presence, and there labour, after being " admitted to the honor of Islâmism, to attain distinction and renown; and that he had, accordingly " sent his confidential [friend or servant], Omar Khân, for the purpose of representing these particulars " to us in detail. The following day we summoned Omar Khân, together with Futah Shâh, to our " Presence, where we desired [the former] to state truly to us, *and without lying*, what Dhoondy Jee had " said. Hereupon the aforesaid [Omar Khân] made a similar communication to us; namely, 'that the " 'real wish of Dhoondy Jee was to obtain an introduction to the Presence, and by approving (after " 'his admission to the honor of Islâmism) his zeal and devotion in our service, to secure to himself " 'an honorable name.' The communication of this wretch being concluded, we [being still doubtful of its " accuracy] made him repeat it, which that *nobody* accordingly did. After this we said [to him], 'well, but " 'wherefore does he come hither?—By his coming, displeasure will arise between us and the *Poonah* people. " 'Let him remain there; and we will secretly supply him with what money and other articles he may " 'require.' To this, *that ass* [or Omar Khân] rejoined, 'that he had [already] stated to us what the " 'utmost wish and object of Dhoondy Jee was, and could only add, that he was actuated by no other.' " Hereupon we further said: 'it is well: do you go back to Dhoondy Jee, and say to him, that the " 'first condition [prescribed by us] is, that he shall agree to embrace the faith: the second, that he " 'shall marry [under our direction] into some respectable family: furthermore, that upon his " 'receiving the honor of Islâmism, he shall be put in possession of one or other of these two forts, " 'namely, the fort of *Murugsera* or *Husmungy*, together with a *Jâgeer* [adequate to the maintenance] " 'of a thousand horse. If (we added) he does not agree to these things, his coming hither will not " 'be proper.' To this effect did we three or four times, sending for Omar Khân, signify our " pleasure to him. We even desired him to repeat aloud what we had stated to him, in order that " we might be satisfied whether or not he [perfectly] remembered, or had rightly comprehended, the " same; whereupon *that dog* repeated the whole, word for word. What is here stated took place " three or four times. After this, giving *that dog* a horse to ride, we dispatched him, with directions " to be expeditious, and to inform the *catamite* * (his employer), that on condition he embraced the " faith, he might repair to the Presence; but that, otherwise, it would be needless for him to come. " Accordingly, this *accursed dog* proceeding from hence [soon] returned, accompanied by Dhoondy " Jee: The aforesaid *dog* [*i. e.* Omar Khân] was no sooner arrived, than sending for him we said to " him: 'having brought the *catamite* along with you, you have, of course, got him to engage to " 'embrace the faith, and have, moreover, made him acquainted with all our other orders.' Hereupon " that *accursed dog* humbly set forth, that by the blessing of God, Dhoondy Jee had not only agreed " to embrace the faith, but to comply,† heart and soul, with every thing required of him, and, in " this disposition, had repaired to the Presence. On hearing this we were highly delighted, and said, " 'we have ordained, that his name shall be *Shaikh Ahmed*. Let a time be fixed for his repeating the " '*Kulmah* [or Mahommedan creed].' To this the infidel [meaning Omar Khân] answered: 'it will

" 'be

* Original مبرتة or مرتة which I take to be the word alluded to by Colonel Wilks, at page xxiii of his Preface.

† Original سروچشم " head and eyes."

Mangalore, and other parts of his dominions situated to the westward of *Seringapatam*, which had manifested a disposition to revolt, he now proceeded on his return

" 'be better if his repeating of the *Kulmah* be delayed till after two or three visits to the *Durbár*; but,
" 'if it be required of him, he will repeat it this moment.' Hereupon we said, that it did not
" signify. But on sending for them the next day, the same reply was given [by Omar Khân]. Being
" again sent for on the third day, we caused Meer Sâdik to enquire of [Dhoondy Jee himself] when
" he meant to be admitted to the honor of the faith, and to urge him to embrace it speedily, in order
" that he might repair to his *Jágeer*. Hereupon the *accursed dog* [*i. e.* Dhoondy Jee] plainly denied
" every thing, declaring that he did not know, and had never heard, a word of the matter. After this
" we had *the catamite* examined by the *Asof*, by the *Sudoor*, and by others; to all of whom *this*
" *nobody* affirmed, that the Afghan [*i. e.* Omar Khân] had never communicated these things to him,
" and that he heard them now for the first time.

" The remaining particulars [of this affair] will be verbally made known by Meer Sâdik, Mahommed
" Rizâ, and Purnia. If the above-named be kept [here], no doubt strife [or enmity] will arise [in
" consequence] with the *three* infidels; * and if we send him away, still will enmity ensue; you will,
" therefore, write down, what shall appear to you advisable and beneficial on this occasion. It was
" owing to the confidence which we placed in the communications of the *reprobate dog* [Omar
" Khân] that we sent for Dhoondy Jee to the Presence, in order that we might have an interview
" with him."

Then follows the opinion of the counsellors referred to, and of which a translation is subjoined. It appears to be in the hand-writing of Mahommed Rizâ (the *Binky Nabob)*:

" The humble representation (or opinion) of the slaves of all the *three* † departments of government,
" that is to say, of the *Meer Meerân*, ‡ the *Asof*, and the *Sudoor*, is this:—

" With respect to the keeping, or sending away, of Dhoondy Jee, as directed to be considered by
" the Presence, there is no doubt, or question, that the keeping of him will be attended with complete
" evil, and give rise to enmity [or disagreement] with all *the three infidels*. On the other hand, if
" he be sent away, the same enmity will be produced. Therefore, what we, your slaves, humbly
" suggest, is, that Dhoondy Jee be kept imprisoned, and never be released. The humble representation,
" this 14th day of the month *Tukky*, year *Râsikh*, and of the birth of Mahommed 1222,§ of

" MEER MAHOMMED SADIK, *Asof*.
" || * * * * * *
" GHULAM ALI, *Sudoor*,
" MAHOMMED RIZA."

Next follows, in the Mahrattah language, the opinion of Bishna Pundit; to which a Persian translation, in the hand-writing of Mahommed Rizâ, is subjoined. Here is the opinion of the Pundit.

" Dhoondy Jee is not a person of [good] faith: he is without faith. He is not fit to be retained,
" nor ought he to be released: he should be put to death."

The milder judgment, however, of the majority prevailed. Dhoondy Jee was retained in prison, and did not recover his liberty, till the day on which *Seringapatam* was stormed and taken; when, availing

* Meaning the English, the Mahrattahs, and the Nizâm.

† In the Sultan's reference to them they are said to be *four*.

‡ That is, Mahommed Rizâ.

§ Corresponding to the 10th June 1794.

|| The original signature, in this place, appears, in the Canarese character. It is, probably, that of Purnia. There is another signature rather obscurely written, which may be read Budrûz Zumân. It is not the least curious circumstance attending this opinion, in which the Mahrattahs are called *infidels*, that it should have been subscribed (as there is reason to believe it was) by a Hindoo!

return to his capital, by the route of *Rány Bidnore.* His arrival at the latter place, which is not far distant from *Shánoor*, was the signal of alarm to Abdûl Hukeem, who now began to anticipate the effects of Tippoo's resentment of the slight he had put upon the latter at his accession to the *Musnud.* In order, therefore, to avert the storm which he thought ready to burst upon him, he hastily dispatched his son, Kheera Meea, with a *Nuzr* of forty thousand *rupees* and several rich presents for the offended *Sultan*, to whom he also sent the best apology he could devise for his past neglect. The experiment succeeded, probably, beyond the *Patan's* expectations; for Kheera Meea not only met with a very gracious reception from his brother-in-law, but obtained from him, before they separated, the usual *Sunuds*, or letters patent, confirming his father in all his possessions. Whether or not the *Sultan* exacted, at this period, any new concession from Abdûl Hukeem, is not stated by my author, who is also entirely silent, with regard to the probable motives of Tippoo's moderation on the present occasion.

But whatever these motives might be, Abdûl Hukeem, who had always, during the life-time of Hyder, entertained an equal dread and dislike of Tippoo, did not feel entirely re-assured by the issue of his son's negociation. When, therefore, Bûrhânûddeen was dispatched, in the beginning of the year 1785, against *Nergúnd*, it is not to be wondered at, that the fears of the *Patan* were again awakened, by the arrival of so considerable a force in the vicinity of his capital: especially, as the pecuniary discussions, which took place about the same time between him and the *Sultan*, were but ill calculated to remove his distrust. It was, accordingly, under these impressions, that Abdûl Hukeem thought he should best consult his safety and interests by joining the coalition, formed at this period by the courts of *Poonah* and *Hyderabad*, for the purpose of checking the ambitious projects of the *Sultan.* He did not, however, openly renounce his dependence on Tippoo, or seek the protection of the allies, till the *Sultan* appeared to be in full march for *Shánoor*, when he suddenly and secretly fled from thence, accompanied only by a few of his most attached followers; and of all the riches and valuable property, accumulated, during so many generations by his predecessors, taking with him nothing more than an inconsiderable sum of money, and the equipage which conveyed him to the Mahrattah camp; and leaving behind him the chief part of his family, including Kheera Meea and his wife, the half-sister of the *Sultan.* The date of this precipitate flight has been commemorated by

availing himself of the confusion of the moment, he effected his escape, and collecting together a numerous force, which the recent subversion of the Mahommedan dynasty of *Mysore* made particularly easy, made head for a considerable time against the British army. He was in the end, however, defeated and slain, in an action with Colonel Wellesley, on the 10th September 1800.

by the following satirical chronogram, composed on the occasion in the Hindivy dialect. حکیم خان میانہ سب کو چھوڑکی آپ بہاگا (34)

that is, "Hukeem Khân Meeaneh, abandoning every thing, ran away himself," or "saved himself by flight."

Tippoo, not a little astonished (or, at least, pretending to be so) at the flight of the *Patan*, immediately dispatched Meer Sâdik into the town, with orders to sequestrate the whole of the fugitive's property, which was, of course, done without opposition or difficulty, and, no doubt, with sufficient rigor. Whether the private property of the inhabitants at large was respected on this occasion, is not mentioned; but as no blame was imputable to them, it is reasonable to suppose that it was spared. In the mean while, Kheera Meea, mounted on the only horse he possessed, and accompanied by no more than two or three attendants on foot, hastened to make his submissions to his brother-in-law; who is stated to have received him kindly, and to have asked him what could have induced his father to abandon himself, as he had done, to ruin and disgrace. "I had in no shape," said the *Sultan* "offered him the slightest molestation, but, on the contrary, was "daily giving him new proofs of my favor and regard. Alas! that notwithstanding our affinity, and my uniform forbearance and good faith towards him, he "should have thus united himself with my enemies! Never can such a man "behold the face of prosperity." To this harangue Kheera Meea is reported to have replied, "that it was but too true, that his father had acted wrong, and "sacrificed both the fortunes and honor of his house in a fit of despair:" to which he added an assurance, "that he had been kept to the last moment in entire "ignorance of his father's intentions." After this, the *Sultan* had tents erected near his own, for the accommodation of Kheera Meea and the females of his family, who were likewise daily supplied with provisions from his own table. These attentions, however, did not prevent him from adopting the necessary precautions for guarding against the future escape of his voluntary prisoner.

Peace being concluded, soon after this, between the confederates and Tippoo, the places taken on each side, in the course of the war, were, for the most part, mutually relinquished. It was not, however, without considerable difficulty(35) that Pursaram Bhen and Râsta, who are said to have exerted themselves strenuously on the occasion, succeeded in procuring the restoration of *Shânoor* to its fugitive chieftain, who, it may easily be conceived, did not obtain this boon, but at the price of many fresh and humiliating sacrifices.

From

(34) Which, according to the *Ubjud* notation, amounts to 1199 A.H.

(35) It is not stated by my author, on what side the difficulty, here spoken of, lay: but it was, of course, on that of Tippoo Sultan.

From this time we hear nothing more of *Shánoor* or its chieftain, till the year 1791, at which period the Mahrattahs, in pursuance of the engagements which they had recently entered into with the English, for the purpose of reducing the power of Tippoo Sultan, advanced against the capital of the latter; but not before they had seized, in their way thither, upon the whole of the *Patan* territory, in the possession of which they were formally confirmed, the following year, by the partition treaty of *Seringapatam*. In the meanwhile, Abdûl Hukeem dying,(36) after a long but unprosperous administration, was ostensibly succeeded by his son,

10. *Abdûl Khyre Khán*,

commonly called Kheera Meea, whose inheritance was now reduced to a single *Mahal*, which the Mahrattahs had the generosity to assign him for his maintenance, and of which, if still living, he probably continues in possession at this day. His wife, I believe, had been withdrawn some years before from his protection, by her brother, in whose *Haram* she was found, if I recollect rightly, at the capture of *Seringapatam*; when, I am also inclined to think, that she was pensioned, along with the rest of the late *Sultan's* family, by the British government.

(36) Meer Hûsain Ali says, that he lived five years after his restoration to his principality; which would place his death in the early part of the year 1792. It would also appear, from the same authority, that the actual Chief of *Shânoor*, at the period of the peace of 1792, was Abdûl Khyre Khân. I am unable to reconcile these statements with the account given by Captain Moore (in his interesting narrative of the operations of Captain Little's detachment) of his interview, in April 1792, with the *Nabob* of *Shânoor* whom he designates Abdûl Hukeem Khân. It is possible, that he may have mistaken the name of the ruling chief; and what favors this conjecture is, the circumstance of his calling that chief, on the same occasion, the *brother* (*i. e.* the brother-in-law) of Tippoo; an appellation which, it is evident, belonged not to Abdûl Hukeem, but to his son, Abdûl Khyre.

In the "Historical and Political View of the *Decan*," of which I am not in possession, but which is quoted by Captain Moor, Abdûl Hukeem Khân is said to have been "the *seventh* in lineal descent, as "*occupant*, and the *fourth*, as *sovereign ruler* of *Shânoor* and its dependencies. The former part of this statement agrees exactly with the detailed genealogy given in the present article, Abdûl Hûkeem having been the *seventh* in descent from Jubbâr Meea, the first occupant of the principality in question. What is meant by his being the *fourth sovereign* ruler of it, is not equally apparent; since Hûsain Ali says nothing of Abdûl Ghuffâr Khân's (who must have been the *first* of those rulers) having attained to, or assumed, a state of absolute independence. But there is a passage in his account of Ibraheem Khân, the fourth chief of the *Patan* dynasty of *Kurnool*, which may serve to explain this point. That chief is there said to have obtained from Khân Jehân Kokeh, the viceroy of the *Decan*, instead of the usual patent of confirmation in his *Jâgeer*, a new grant, in which the former stipulations,* whatever they might have been, were wholly omitted. Now, as Abdûl Ghuffâr Khân is stated to have paid his court to the same viceroy, it is not improbable that he was equally successful on that occasion with his countryman. But however this might be, it is certain, that the claims of these chiefs to absolute independence or sovereign rule, if ever advanced, were far from being recognized by the subsequent viceroys of the *Decan*.

* Original مشروطه

APPENDIX, E.

(Referred to at LETTER XIX.)

COMMERCIAL REGULATIONS.

The *Sultan's* regulations for the commercial department of his government, of which it is proposed to give an outline in the present article, were issued at two different periods; one section of them being dated the 14th of *Akmedy* of the year *Sâhir*, or A.M. 1221,[1] and another, the 3d of *Ahmedy* of the following year, *Râsikh*.[2] They are introduced by two passages from the *Koran*, headed in the following manner:—

" Two verses from the Word of God, which descended [or were delivered] in
" honor of maritime commerce, are here transcribed."

Then follow the verses in question, the first of which (taken from the chapter entitled the *Bee)*, is to this effect:

" It is he who hath subjected the sea [unto you] that ye might eat fish there-
" out, and take from thence ornaments for you to wear: and thou seest the ships
" plowing [the waves] thereof, that ye may seek [to enrich yourselves] of his
" abundance by commerce; and that ye might give thanks."

The second is from the chapter entitled the *Greeks*, and is as follows:

" Of his signs one is, that he sendeth the winds bearing welcome tidings [of
" rain], that he may cause you to taste of his mercy, and that ships may sail at
" his command, that ye may seek [to enrich yourselves] of his abundance by
" commerce, and that ye may give thanks."[3]

It might be inferred from this preamble, that the design of the *Sultan*, in the present regulations, was to provide *exclusively* for the promotion and encouragement of the *maritime trade*: but though this was, no doubt, at all times, his principal object, it will, nevertheless, appear, that he was not altogether unmindful of, or indifferent to, the benefits of *inland* commerce. Whether his manifest preference of the former was founded on the distinction apparently conferred upon it by the quoted passages of the *Koran*, or arose from a desire of becoming a maritime power, or was a natural consequence both of the local position of a large portion of his dominions, and of their particular produce, I will not take upon me to determine. It is probable, indeed, that each of these considerations had more or

e less

(1) Corresponding with 25th March 1793.

(2) Corresponding with the 2d April 1794.

(3) See Sale's *Koran*, Chapters XVI and XXX.

less weight with him; besides which, an intercourse with strangers, separated from him by the ocean, was not liable to suggest to his jealous and distrustful mind, the same apprehensions of danger, as were likely to be, and actually were, incessantly created, by whatever tended, in any degree, to a free communication with the countries immediately contiguous to his own.

The regulations in question set out with describing the general duties of the officers at the head of the commercial department, which the *Sultan* designated by the term فرقه ملک التجار or the *Mulikût Tûjár* department.(4) These officers were nine in number, and appear to have constituted a sort of permanent board, or college.

The following were the principal objects to which the attention of this board was more especially directed.

1. They were to see that the various articles required for commercial purposes, such as silken stuffs, sandal-wood, pepper, cardamums (great and small), cocoa-nuts, rice, sulphur, elephants, &c. were duly provided [according to the nature of the commodity] as well for importation as for exportation.(5)

2. They were to draw foreign merchants to *Mysore*, by transmitting to them, for that purpose, the most solid and encouraging assurances [of favour and protection].

3. They were to seek out and engage in the service [of the state] trust-worthy and economical *Mûtusuddies*, and able and experienced *Gúmáshtehs*, skilled in accounts and commercial affairs, and of approved integrity and disinterestedness: and having procured such, were to employ them in the several *Kohties*, or factories, [whether at home or abroad].

4. They were to pay the most minute attention to all the concerns of their department; to investigate the various accounts thereof, in the most rigorous manner; and to be careful, that no frauds, or embezzlements, were committed by any of those employed under them, whether in the foreign factories or in the home depôts.

5. The heads of the departments, as well as the various officers under them, were to pledge themselves in the most solemn manner, according to the forms of their respective religions, to discharge the duties of their several stations, with the utmost diligence, concord, and fidelity.

6. If any of the principal officers of the department should violate, or in any instance

(4) The term *Mulikût Tûjár* properly signifies "Prince of merchants," and is a title given in *Persia*, exclusively, I believe, to the chief, or, at least the most favoured merchant of the kingdom.

(5) Thus, in the above enumeration, sulphur and silk stuffs were among the articles to be imported, the rest being articles of exportation. For a more detailed list of the exports and imports of *Mysore*, the reader is referred to Colonel Beatson's View, page 171 of the Appendix.

instance swerve from, the duties of his station,[6] all the rest were to unite in exposing the offender to shame and disgrace, and in representing his conduct to the Presence, in order that he might be signally punished for the same, and a useful example be thereby afforded to others.

7. If any of the inferior persons, attached to the different *Kohties*, or factories, should be guilty of fraud, or other misdemeanors, they were to be punished for the same, agreeably to the law of God.

8. In all cases of difficulty, or of particular importance, the heads of the department (excluding the *Mútusuddies* and others from their meetings) were to sit and deliberate together on the same; each person writing down, in a book to be provided for the purpose, his opinion on the point under consideration, and subscribing his name thereto. The book, containing these minutes or consultations, was to be deposited in a box, which was to remain under the seal [of the office], till there might be occasion to refer to it, for the justifications or explanation of the proceedings, or resolutions, of the meeting; which, in case of any difference of opinion, were to be determined by the majority of voices.

9. They were to report their proceedings fully and regularly to the *Sultan*, whose pleasure on the occasion would be signified in writing, at the back, or at the bottom of the said report.

10. In any transaction relating to large pecuniary advances, or being of such importance as to require particular secrecy, the written documents, necessary to be submitted on the occasion, were to be written in the hand-writing of some member of the board, or of one of the heads of the department,[7] and delivered to the *Sultan* by such member himself; when a written answer, duly authenticated by the *Sultan's* own signature, would, in like manner, be secretly returned to him.

11.[8] *Nubby Mális* [the Prophet is Lord]. All *Húkm-námehs* and other papers bearing the seal and signature of the Presence, must be deposited in a box, to which the seal [of the department] is to be affixed. This box shall be lodged in the treasury at the seat of the empire [*Seringapatam*], where it will be taken charge of by the *Meer Meerán*. Copies [only, of these documents] are to be [taken, and] retained by the proper officers. *Nubby Málik* [as before].

12. Care was to be taken, that all the Mahommedan officers of the department, such as the *Mirzáey Duftur*, &c. should be selected from the tribe of *Koreish*, and the

e 2

(6) This case is qualified by the usual deprecatory expression "which God forbid!"

(7) That is, not by any clerk or secretary.

(8) This article is in the hand-writing of the *Sultan*. Here the *Sultan's* usual signature is *prefixed* as well as *added* to the article. It appears at the *end* of all the other articles. This signature consisted of the words *Nubby Málik*, written in the contracted form of a cypher.

the sect of *Siyuds*, following the tenets of Hunifah, to the end that they might agree the better together

Next follow the more specific or detailed directions for the guidance of the department of trade.[(9)] These are distributed into separate sections, which though numbered, are not titled or headed. They, however, treat briefly

I. Of the marine force.

II. Of the *Kohties*, or factories, of *Muscat* and *Kutch*.

III. Of the appropriation of the fund, or capital, allotted for commercial purposes.

IV. Of the commercial depôts or marts established in *Mysore*; and of provincial factors, and other officers of commerce.

V. Of the means to be pursued, with a view to the opening and establishing of commercial intercourse with foreign countries.

VI. Of commercial deposits; or a plan for admitting the people at large to a participation in the benefits to accrue from the trade of the country.

VII. Of field *Mulikût Tûjârs*.

VIII. Miscellaneous regulations.

I. *Of the Marine Force.*

Before proceeding to communicate the substance of this article, it is proper to apprize the reader, that although, at the date of the following regulations, the marine department was placed under the control and superintendance of the *Mulikût Tûjârs*, or board of trade, yet it was erected, a few years after, into a separate and independent branch of the government, under the denomination of the *Meer Yumm*, or admiralty department; of which a more particular account will be found in Appendix K, including a detailed statement of the naval force at that time in the *Sultan's* contemplation.

1. You must set about building a hundred ships.[(10)] In the mean while, ten sail, completely manned, and equipped with warlike stores, have been placed under your orders.

2. It

(9) Besides the instructions addressed directly to the *Mulikût Tûjâr* department, other orders, relating to the same branch of the public service, are contained in the regulations for the revenue department. These I have incorporated with the present article.

(10) In the original خضري والياسي *Khizries* and *Eliâsies*, here meant for ships: but of what particular class, or whether there was any difference between them, does not distintly appear. *Khizr* is the name of a prophet, sometimes confounded with *Elias*: and as the tradition, or legend, respecting the former, respresents him as a sort of tutelary guardian of the waters, this is probably the reason of both of their names being used by Tippoo to denote ships of war, which I suppose to be exclusively intended in this placo.

2. It is expected, that you will exert yourselves to collect together [as many] trusty men, experienced in [naval] warfare [as may be procurable], as well as others conversant in the affairs of trade; and that you will labor, with one accord, to promote the prosperity of the commerce of our dominions.

3. The wood, iron, rope, and other articles, which may be required in the construction of the ships ordered to be built, are to be bought [in the countries adjacent to the docks, with the assistance of the *Asofs* of the districts in question, who will receive the necessary directions for this purpose].(11)

4. The workmen of every description [employed on this service] must be paid with the utmost regularity, and the ships be completed with all possible dispatch.

5. If the necessary warlike stores should not be procurable for money [or at market], the same is to be represented to the Presence, when we will direct you to be supplied with such articles as you may require [from our own magazines].

The four following articles are extracted from the instructions to the *Meer Asof*, or revenue department.

6. The merchants established at *Jumálábád*, *Májidábád*, and *Wájidábad*,(12) are to engage to build, with all possible expedition, thirty-one three-masted and two-masted vessels, for the purposes of commerce. Eleven of these to be built at *Jumálábád*, and ten at each of the other places named.

7. The merchants building these vessels shall be allowed to lade them with rice, cocoa-nuts, and any other articles [not reserved for the exclusive trade of the *Sircar*].

8. After the vessels, here specified, are built, the merchants building them shall discontinue employing the small craft which they now use, and which, at any rate, they are not to be suffered to send to sea after the expiration of a year from this time. All other merchants are immediately to cease from employing the small craft in question.(13)

9. Whereas the ships of *China* are precluded, by the circumstance of not being armed,(14) from resorting to these seas,(15) some of ours must be sent to that country; where due encouragement and assurances being given to the merchants thereof, and the protection of our vessels being afforded them, they will be induced to repair hither, with an abundant supply of the rare productions of that region. These being

(11) Which, accordingly, appears in the instructions to the *Meer Asof*, or revenue department.

(12) That is, *Mangalore*, *Suddashooghur*, and *Buscorajee*.

(13) On account, it may be presumed, of the danger from pirates.

(14) Literally, "not mounting guns."

(15) On account of the pirates which infested them.

being disposed of, the vessels, so importing, are to be permitted to depart, whenever the owners or merchants please, and are to be safely conducted, under a proper convoy of our ships, to the borders of our dominions.(16)

II. *Of the Kohties, or Factories, of Muscat and Kutch.*

Though not stated in the instructions to the commercial department, it appears by an article in those addressed to the *Meer Asofs*, that there were *two* factories established by the *Sultan* at each of the ports of *Muscat* and *Kutch*. One of these, belonging to *Muscat*, consisting of fifty of what are called *Chushmehs*, was placed under the orders of the *Asof* of *Jumálábád*: the other, consisting of thirty-four *Chushmehs*, was given in charge to the *Mulikút Tújár* department. Again, of the two factories of *Kutch*, one, consisting of twelve *Chushmehs*, was committed to the superintendance of the *Asof* of *Wájidábád*: the other, containing twelve *Chushmehs*, being subjected, like the inferior factory of *Muscat*, to the authority of the commercial board. What is meant by *Chushmehs* (springs or fountains) I cannot at present state with any confidence; but I think it probable, that the term may have a reference to the number of the commodities, in which the dealings of the respective factories consisted.

The same instructions to the *Meer Asofs* contain the following additional articles, relative to the factories of *Muscat* and *Kutch*, not inserted in those addressed immediately to the *Mulikút Tújárs*.

1. Of the six thousand *Utls* of sulphur, ordered to be annually sent from *Muscat*, eight hundred *Utls* are to be delivered to the *Asof* of *Jumálábád*, and seven hundred to the *Asof* of *Nugr*, for the manufacture of gunpowder.(17) The remaining four thousand five hundred *Utls* are to be dispatched to, and delivered to the charge of, the *Kilaadár* of *Seringapatam*.

2. The *Dároghas* and *Mútusuddies* employed at the aforsaid factories are to be changed every three years.

The instructions relative to the factories in question, addressed directly to the *Mulikút Tújár* department, were as follow:

1. The factories of *Muscat* and *Kutch* are hereby placed under your control and direction; and you are, accordingly, to take charge of all the *Húkm-námehs*, as well as the official seals,(18) appertaining thereto.

2. You

(16) The meaning is, that they were to be escorted till out of the reach of danger from the pirates, "who," says the *Sultan* in another place, "float on the waters of our coasts like so many air "bubbles, and for the destruction and capture of whom every possible stratagem must be employed."

(17) For the same purpose, 810 *utls* were directed to be sent annually by the *Asof* of *Seringapatam* to *Jumálábád*, and 7200 *utls* to *Nugr*: I suspect, however, that for 810 we should read 8100. For some account of the *utl*, the reader is referred to Note 5 of Appendix B.

(18) The official seals, here mentioned, are described in one of the *Sultan's* letters, not included in the present volumes. They were constructed and transmitted to the factories some time in

2. You will, moreover, dispatch thither trusty and able persons, selected by yourselves, to receive charge of the aforesaid factories from the agents now there, who will be directed to deliver over the same, together with all the stores, &c, appertaining thereto, to the officers whom you shall nominate to supersede them, taking from the latter the necessary receipts for the articles so delivered.

3. You are to report unto us the quantities of round (or black) pepper, sandal-wood, cardamums (great and small), cocoa-nuts, beetle, rice, wax, and honey,(19) that you may require [for exportation], in order that the necessary directions may be issued to the *Asofs* of the Presence for assisting you in the purchase of the same.

4. The profits arising from the sale of the aforesaid articles are to be regularly and faithfully accounted for, and entered in the books of the respective factories.

5. No persons but your *Gúmáshtehs*, or agents, at the aforesaid factories, are to be allowed to deal in the articles specified.(20)

6. You are annually to procure from the factory at *Muscat* six thousand *Khám Utk*(21) of sulphur of the first quality, and to dispose of the same according as you shall be directed by us, upon your reporting its arrival.

N. B. Most of the articles composing the preceding, as well as the following instructions, are subscribed at the end of each with the words *Nubby Málik* (or, the

the beginning of year of the *Higera* 1201 (1786-7): but they were without a date, as usually inscribed on all seals, "because," as the *Sultan* says in the letter alluded to, "the year being indicated by "the numerical value of each inscription, reckoned according to the *Zur* "notation,* its insertion is unnecessary." Thus the inscription on the seal of the *Kutch* factory was ظرف ذهب (the golden vase or vessel) the letters of which gave 1201: that belonging to the *Juddah* factory † contained the words دارسراسرمال (the mansion, or city, abounding in wealth), which also yield the year 1201. The inscription on the official seal of the remaining factory of *Muscat* is not perfectly legible: the words کان زر (mine of gold) being alone distinct. These letters amount to 1131. The next word appears to be خصر (equal to 67); and this is followed by an indistinct mark, which may be supposed to have been meant for a ت This would complete the number 1201: but though it were allowable to read خصرت I do not know that any sense could be made of it.

(19) The two last articles (viz. wax and honey) are added from the instructions to the *Meer Asofs*, or revenue department.

(20) The merchants building *large* ships would, of course, agreeably to the stipulation contained in the seventh article of Section I, be exempted from this prohibition.

(21) That is, an *utl* of light, in contra-distinction to one of *full*, or complete weight. The terms *khám* (unripe) and *poakhteh* (ripe) when applied to weights or measures of the same denomination, denote respectively *small* and *great*. Thus a *poakhteh* (or *pucka*) *seer* means a large *seer*, and a *khám* (or *kucha*) *seer* a small one.

* See Prefatory Remarks, on the *Sultan's* Kalendar.

† Thus it appears that, at this time, the *Sultan* had a factory at the port of *Juddah*, which, however, must have been subsequently withdrawn, as no mention is made of it in the present regulations.

the Prophet is Lord), written in the *Sultan's* own hand, and formed in the manner of a cypher. This was the signature by which he always attested his orders.

III. *Of the Appropriation of the Fund, or Capital, allotted for Commercial Purposes.*

1. The sum of four *lacks* of *Râhities*[22] has been committed to you, in trust, for commercial purposes. With this money you are to make the necessary purchases of gold and silver bullion,[23] cloths, elephants, &c.[24] and to hold the same in readiness [for exportation]. With the blessing (or aid) of God the most high, *countless profit* shall be hereby acquired.

2. Having stated to the Presence the number of elephants, as well as the several quantities of sandal-wood, cardamums (great and small), round (or black) pepper, rice, beetle, cocoa-nuts (dry and moist), and cinnamon,[25] required for commercial purposes [*i. e.* for exportation], and having thereupon received from us the necessary orders to the *Asofs* for assisting you in the purchase thereof, at such prices as shall be regulated by them, you will pay into the hands of the said *Asofs* the value, as so settled, of every article with which you shall be supplied, taking their receipts for the same.

3. All purchases of gold and silver, coined or uncoined, and of silken stuffs made of your department, whether on account of the Presence, of the *Asof Kuchurry*, or of the *Sudoor Kuchurry*, shall be paid for in money; and you must, in like manner, pay in money for whatsoever articles you may purchase of the said *Kuchurries*. If, however, the payments in question should be postponed for three or four months, it will be of no consequence.

4. Gold and silver bullion, jewels, silks, and other valuable articles, may be received as pledges for the payment of goods sold by your agents: thus for goods valued at one thousand *rupees*, a pledge of the value of 1200 rupees may be accepted.

5. You are to pay the established duties or imposts on all articles,[26] in the same manner as is done by the *Ryots* in general.

IV. *Of*

(22) A *râhity* was the name given by Tippoo to the *Cantarai pagoda* of ten *fanams*; consequently, four lacks of *rahities* were equivalent to 3,20,000 *star pagodas*, or £128,000 sterling.

(23) Original طلا و نقره مسکوک و غیر مسکوک that is, "gold and silver, coined and uncoined." What was meant by purchasing "coined gold and silver," I do not clearly comprehend. Perhaps coins suited to foreign markets might be intended.

(24) There is a fuller enumeration of the articles in question in other places.

(25) By cinnamon must be meant here, I conclude, the cassia lignea; as the true cinnamon is not, I believe, produced in *Mysore*.

(26) Meaning, most probably, both exports and imports.

IV. *Of the Commercial Depots, or Marts, established in Mysore; and of Provincial Factors, and other Officers of Commerce.*

1. You are to entertain in our service, and to station at the thirty places within our dominions, hereafter enumerated, the necessary *Gúmáshtehs* and *Mútusuddies*, for carrying on, to the extent suited to the place, a trade in such articles as shall yield a proper profit.

2. The following are the places within our dominions, where you are to establish factories or commercial depôts:

The Capital or *Putn*,
Sulámábád or *Sattimungalum*,
Viziemungul or *Arivacoochy*,
Bangalore,
5. *Bágloor*,
Colar,
Murwágul,
Muddunpilly,
Zufurábád or *Gurramcoondah*,
10. *Punganoor*,
Rachouty,
Fyze-Hisár or *Gooty*,
Dhurumwár,
Furrúkh-yáb-Hisár or *Chittledoorg*
15. *Bay-nuzeer*[27] or *Hurriál*,
Nugr or *Bidnore*,
Shikárpoor,
Soondeh,
20. *Kooriál* or *Mangalore*,
Khooshálpoor,
Barkoor,
Gurwár or *Kurwár*,
Jumálábád,
25. *Bhut-Kullah* or *Butcul*,
Futahábád,
Kuroor or *Guroar*,
Gurrup or *Kurrup*,
Bunwásy,
30. *Gurdoon-Shikoh* or *Nundy-doorg*.

3. Other subordinate agents are to be employed, for the like purpose, at such places in our dominions (yielding proper produce for trade) as are not comprehended in the foregoing list. These agents are to be changed every year.[28]

4. There is no objection to your disposing of the articles heretofore enumerated, and being the produce of our dominions, to private merchants, who may be desirous of speculating in the same on their own account.[29]

5. Besides the *Gúmáshtehs* to be employed in the different depôts above enumerated, you are to station with every *Asof* throughout our dominion, a *Náib*, or deputy, who must be a trust-worty person, and a man of respectable character and condition. He is to have a *Mútusuddy* for an assistant. Before dispatching

f these

(27) This is one of the *Sultan's* new names. I do not know to what place it was applied.

(28) Something is added, respecting the emoluments of these agents, which I omit, because I do not clearly understand the passage.

(29) That is, the *Gûmâshtehs*, or agents, of the board of trade, might dispose of the commodities in question, to such merchants as chose to deal in them, and were precluded from procuring them, in any other manner, by the restrictive regulations of the *Sultan*.

these persons, however, to their stations, you must obtain sufficient security for their good behaviour, and then producing them in the Presence, procure our special signature to their nomination.

6. The subordinate agents, mentioned in Article 3, are to be placed under the control and authority of the *Náibs*, or deputies, stationed with the *Asofs*.

7. The aforesaid *Náibs* and *Mútusuddies* are to accompany the *Asofs*, in the annual attendance of the latter on the resplendent Presence, for the purpose of celebrating the *Eed*, or festival, of *Zilhijjah*. Immediately on their arrival [at court], you must examine their accounts of receipts and disbursements, and prepare an abstract thereof for our information.

8. On a certain day, to be occasionally appointed, all the Musulman officers belonging to your department shall be entertained, at the charge of the *Sircar*, with a public repast, to consist of *Púlláo* of the first sort. The *Mútusuddies* and others, being Hindoos, shall, at the same time, have a separate repast provided for them, to consist of rice, and such other articles as usually compose their food. The whole of them, after this, are to be brought into the Presence, when the above-mentioned accounts are to be produced and examined; and they are to make such verbal communications, relative to their respective concerns, as may be judged requisite. This business being concluded, they are to receive the *pawn* leaf,(30) to make their obeisance, and to withdraw.

9. You are to procure the special signature of the Presence to the afore-mentioned accounts, and to preserve the same in your office.

10. You are [periodically] to receive back from the *Náibs* and *Mútusuddies* above-mentioned, all such letters and receipts [or acknowledgements] whether formal or informal,(31) as you have previously written or sent to them. Of these you are to make a list [or abstract], which, after affixing a seal and signature to it, your are to deliver to the said *Náibs*, in lieu of the original documents, which last are all to be destroyed.(32)

V. *Of*

(30) It is usual to present *pawn* to the inferior classes of public officers and servants, on dismissing them to their stations. The superior orders receive, on such occasions, dresses and other marks of approbation.

(31) Original سندي و غيرسندي " attested and unattested, regularly signed and sealed, or otherwise."

(32) The object of this regulation is not very obvious. It might be, to prevent an inconvenient accumulation of documents, no longer useful.

V. *Of the Means to be pursued, with a view to the opening and establishing of a Commercial Intercourse with Foreign Countries.*

1. You must address *Urzies* to the *Sirdárs* [or chiefs] of foreign countries,(33) and send the same, together with [suitable] presents for the said *Sirdárs*, by the hands of persons of respectable character and condition. After applying to, and obtaining from, those *Sirdárs*, the necessary *Kowl*(34) for the purpose, you will proceed to establish factories in their countries, by appointing and sending thither the requisite officers, duly provided with money.

2. These officers [or *Náibs*, as they are called in the original] are to be instructed to purchase and send hither all the rare and curious productions of those countries, which, on arriving here, are to be sold [on our account, or for our benefit]. In like manner are the rarities and commodities of this country to be sent to the aforesaid factories, and there sold [on our behalf].

3. The factories to be thus established in foreign countries are to be seventeen in number (including those of *Kutch* and *Muscat*, already existing) agreeably to the following list:

Kurnool,
Cheena-putn or *Madras*,
Pondicherry,
Poonah,
Kurpah,
Nagore (in *Tanjore*),
Wyrág (depending on *Poonah*),
Máligong (ditto on *Hyderabad*),
Págar Koteh (belonging to the *Rásta*,)
Utnee (belonging to the *Rásta*),
Nándair (depending on *Hyderabad*),
Humnábád (ditto),
Rachore (Adoni),
Muscat,
Kutch,
Kurachy-bunder of *Sinde* belonging to *Nuseer Khán Buloche*,
Mahé-bunder, to *France*.

4. You are authorized to expend such sums as shall appear necessary and proper to you, for the purpose of establishing the aforesaid factories.

5. Proper agents must be stationed at those places in our dominions, where silken stuffs, of a superior quality, are fabricated, whose business it shall be to make œconomical contracts for the provision thereof. The stuffs, so provided, are then to be exported to the places where they may be in demand.

f 2 6. Agents

(33) It is by no means clear, who are meant, in this place, by *Sirdárs*. If the sovereigns, or chief rulers, of the countries in question, had been intended, it is probable that the *Sultan* himself would have addressed them on such an occasion. But whether the chiefs themselves, or only their principal officers or ministers, were to be applied to, on this occasion, the difficulty of reconciling such a proceeding with the usual policy of the *Sultan*, will remain the same.

(34) That is to say, the necessary encouragement and assurance of protection.

6. Agents must, also, be sent to those foreign parts noted for their silken manufactures; which being purchased, are to be brought hither, and sold at an advantageous price.[35]

7. Sending, in charge of your deputies or agents, to other countries, the produce of our dominions, and disposing of the same there, the produce of those countries must be brought hither in return, and sold at such prices as will afford [good] profit.[36]

VI. *Of Commercial Deposits*; or *a Plan for admitting the People at large to a Participation in the Benefits to accrue from the Trade of the Country.*[37]

1. All praise and glory be to the most high God, who, breathing life into a handful of clay, which was before inanimate, gave it the form of man; and who has raised some chosen individuals [of the species] to rank and power, riches and rule, in order that they might administer to the feeble, the helpless, and the destitute, and promote the welfare of their people.

In pursuance of this duty, we now decree as follows:

2. That whosoever shall deposit with you any sum, from five to five hundred *Imaumies,*[38] for the purpose of being employed in traffic [on his account], such person shall be entitled to receive [from you], at the end of a year, together with the principal amount of the said deposit, a profit, or increase, of half an *Imaumy* on every *Imaumy* so deposited or advanced.[39]

3. That whosoever shall make a similar deposit, of from five hundred to five thousand *Imaumies,* such person shall, in like manner, be entitled to receive, at the end of a year, together with the principal amount of his advance, a profit thereon of a quarter *Imaumy* on every *Imaumy* so deposited.[40]

4. That for every sum exceeding five thousand *Imaumies* which shall be so deposited, the person making such deposit shall be entitled, at the end of a year, to receive, together with his principal, a profit, or increase, to be calculated at the rate of twelve *Imaumies* on every hundred *Imaumies* of such principal.[41]

5. That this regulation shall remain in force from generation to generation.

6. That

(35) Original فروخت بکفایت باید کرد

(36) Original فروخته منافع بهم باید رسانید

(37) Although the present section does not bear, in the original, the title here given it, its tenor will nevertheless, be found to agree sufficiently with that title.

(38) *Imaumy* is the term which Tippoo Sultan thought proper to substitute for *rupee*. Three of them made a *râhity*, or *cantarai pagoda*.

(39) That is, a profit of fifty per cent.

(40) Being a profit of twenty-five per cent.

(41) Or an increase of twelve per cent.

6. That whenever any person, making a deposit of the nature above described, shall think proper to apply for the restoration of any part of such deposit, together with the proportion of profit which may be due thereon, the same shall be immediately paid to him, without hesitation or dispute, and a receipt for the amount be taken from him.

7. That in the event of the death of any person making a deposit of the nature aforesaid, the heirs and successors of such person, shall, on producing the certificates (bearing the seal of the *Sircar)* which were granted by the *Mulikût Tújâr* department to the deceased, at the time of his making the deposit in question, and on due proof being obtained of their being the rightful claimants, be entitled to receive the amount of the same [principal and profit], without demur or delay.(42)

Here follow some subsidiary regulations, respecting the mode in which the accounts of these transactions were to be kept, which it is not thought necessary to insert.

VII. *Of Field Mulikût Tújârs.*

1. As often as three or more *Kushoons* of the *Meer Meerân* department, together with two or more *Kushoons* of the *Meer Sudoor* department,(43) are sent upon any service of the *Khodâdâd Sircar*, there are to be attached to such force one *Meer Meerân* [or general officer in command], one *Meer Sudoor*, one *Meer Asof*,

(42) It is sufficiently clear, that the profit, or increase, spoken of in the foregoing regulation, was, in fact, a stated interest, which he agreed to pay on certain loans, proposed to be raised on the ostensible footing of a commercial transaction. As a rigid Musulman, however, it would not have become him to pay or receive *byâz*, or *interest*, and therefore the word *profit* was substituted for this obnoxious term. But though the deposits in question should have been really intended for interest loans, it would not appear, that the *Sultan*, supposing him to deal by his creditors with good faith, could have had any view to personal advantage in the transaction, since the nett profits of the trade in question would hardly amount to the interest stipulated to be paid to the two inferior orders of lenders, whatever the case might be with regard to the superior class, to whom no more than the ordinary rate of interest in *India* was to be allowed. On the whole, therefore, it may be safely admitted, that with respect to the humbler description of subscribers, at least, the accommodation, thus placed in their reach, was sufficiently encouraging; and that, even in the case of the more opulent of them, it may be fairly doubted, whether it was possible for them, under such a government as that of *Mysore*, to have employed their capital in a more beneficial manner, than the one here offered to their acceptance. Although the extraordinary difference in the rates of interest assigned, respectively, by this regulation, to the small and great, is at utter variance with the principles which usually govern public loans in other countries, yet there can be no doubt, that the *Sultan* intended it as a practical proof of his obedience to the divine law, alluded to in the preamble of the present ordinance. Whether, however, rich or poor had sufficient confidence in his good faith, to avail themselves of the indulgence held out to them, or whether he did not, with his characteristic caprice, soon abandon the plan, I am equally unable to say.

(43) The *Meer Sudoor* department superintended the forts and garrisons, the latter of which were, for the most part, composed of the troops called *Ehshâm*.

Asof,[44] one *Meer Khâzin*,[45] and one *Mulikût Tûjâr*, who are conjointly to order all issues of pay and other disbursements, and to consult together on all matters relating to the interests of the state, such as war, revenue, the state of garrisons, &c.; on which occasions the result of their deliberations is to be committed to writing, according to which they are to act.[46] The record, containing the aforesaid deliberations, is to be deposited in a box, which is to be sealed up, and lodged as directed in Article 21 of the first section of these Regulations.

2. When one or two *Kushoons* are detached on any service, under a *Bukhshy* or *Sipahdâr* of the *Meer Meerân* department, or when one *Kushoon* from the *Meer Sudoor* department is so detached, there must be sent with such *Bukhshy* or *Sipahdâr*, from each of the departments of state above enumerated, a person of respectable character and condition, and properly qualified for the situation; whose duty it shall be to assist in all deliberations on the affairs of government, in the same manner, and with the same authority, as prescribed in the case of a *Meer Meerân*, &c. employed with a superior force.

3. You must accordingly provide five men of respectable family, and duly qualified for the occasional discharge of the trust in question, and present them [for our approval]: after which you must give them the necessary instructions for their guidance in the service for which they are designed, and hold them in readiness to proceed on the same whenever required.[47]

VIII. *Miscellaneous Regulations.*

1. Every possible encouragement was to be given to the culture of sandal-wood and black pepper; the *Ryots'* share of which articles of produce was constantly to be bought up, on account of the *Sircar*.

2. The commercial *Nâibs*, stationed with the several provincial *Asofs*, were authorised to employ *Gûmâshtehs*, throughout their respective districts, for the purpose of trafficking in all articles, excepting those exclusively reserved for the account of government (among which sandal-wood, and coined and uncoined gold and silver, are particularly specified). With the exception of such articles, they might deal freely [48] in all others, without let or hindrance from the *Asofs*, who, on

(44) The *Meer Asofs* were at the head of the revenue department, as the *Meer Meerâns* were at the head of the military department.

(45) The *Meer Khâzins* had charge of the treasury, mint, &c.

(46) Although not expressly stated in this place, yet it may be inferred, from other passages on similar occasions, that this record was to contain each individual's opinion.

(47) The use of a *Mulikût Tûjâr*, or any other commercial agent, with a military expedition, is not very obvious. Perhaps the *Sultan* had no other view in the measure, than that stated in Article 4 and Note 51 of the following Section.

(48) That is (as I understand the passage) on their own account.

on the contrary, were directed to be aiding to them in their commercial pursuits. No other persons (except those to be presently mentioned), were, on any account, to be suffered to exercise the same free trade.

3. The several *Asofs* and *Aumils*, throughout the country, were allowed to employ *their own property*(49) in trade; and were, moreover, exempted from the payment of duties.

4. Whenever a *Durbár*, or court, was to be held, notice thereof was to be given to the chief officers of the several departments of state; and, among the rest, to the *Mulikút Tújárs*, one of whom, accompanied by a *Mirzáey Duftur*,(50) and a *Hindooy Duftur*, was always to attend the *Durbár*, on such occasions, and to remain there till it broke up: as well in order that the said *Mulikút Tújárs* might, in succession, acquire a knowledge of the general transactions of the government,(51) as that they might be enabled to state verbally to the *Sultan*, such matters, concerning their own particular department, as might require his attention.

5. Elephants, required for exportation, were to be bought of the *Sircar*;(52) and such as might be wanted for the immediate use of the *Sultan*, were to be procured from *Mahmood-bunder*,(53) and other places.

6. The *Mulikút Tújárs* were to collect all the gold and silver bullion they could from the various factories under their direction, and to send the same to be coined to the fourth mint,(54) at *Seringapatam*, which was to be paid the established mintage on the amount.

(49) Original اکر اصفان و عمال از مال خود تجارت نمایند مضایقه ندارد which may either mean, that they might employ their own *money* in commercial speculations, or traffic in such commodities as they possessed.

(50) The *Mirzáey Duftur* was a Musulman, and kept his accounts in Persian.

(51) This implies, that the officers, so attending, were to be present at all discussions and deliberations which might take place. Indeed, the *Sultan* himself observes of this regulation, "that the advantage to be expected from all the different departments of the government being assembled together, "was, that, by this means, each department would obtain an insight into the business of the others, "*and mutual counteraction and opposition be, for the future, prevented.*

(52) That is, were to be supplied from those caught on account of government.

(53) This is a sea-port town, in the district of *Palamcoteh*.

(54) There were five mints, one of which was appropriated to the coining of gold and silver: at the other four, the copper currency was coined. The first of these mints was established within the walls enclosing the palace. The whole was placed under the direction of the *Meer Khâsins*, or lords of the treasury.

APPENDIX F

(Referred to at LETTER *XL.)*

COPY *of* INSTRUCTIONS, *relative to* INTELLIGENCE, *directed to the* DÂROGHAS *of* HURKÂREHS, *and others.*(1)

[*In the Sultan's own hand.*] The *Dároghas* and *Náigs*, together with the spies, are to go the rounds; to see with their own eyes; and to report [all occurrences] in writing.

INSTRUCTIONS directed to Ghûlâm Ahmed *Dárogha* of *Hurkárehs*, and Syed Ali, *Dârogha* of Couriers, and Meer Bâker, *Dárogha* of the *Paish-kheema*, (2) and Shama Nâig, and Shaisa Nâig, and Sadaseo Nâig, as follows:

You, the above mentioned *Hurkáreh Náigs*, must, during the space of one month, place spies throughout the whole fort, in the town of *Gájam*, and in the two camp *huzars*, &c. and also over the doors of the great *Meers'* houses, and [by these means] gain intelligence of every person who goes to the dwelling of another, and of what people say; and acquire knowledge of the true state of things.

You three *Dároghas* must write the occurrences of every day in three separate Persian reports, with your own hands; and you three *Náigs* must, with your own hands, write three separate Canary reports, and bring and deliver them to the Presence. But first you must give intelligence to all persons, that it is the order of the Presence, that no one shall go to the house of another to converse; but that whatever they may have to say must be communicated in their respective *Kuchurries.* If, notwithstanding this order, any person should go to the house of another, you must, upon his returning out of the same, bring him that moment to the gate of the palace, and report [the circumstance] to the Presence.

During one month, you, together with your *Hurkárehs*, shall perform the duty of spies; and the next month you must communicate these orders, regarding intelligence, to Akibut Mahommed, *Dárogha* of *Hurkárehs*, and Kâdir Ali, *Dárogha* of Couriers, and Meer Yoosif, *Dárogha* of the *Paish-kheema*, and Singa Nâig, Poota Nâig, Nubby Yâr Khân, Chik Nâig, and Hully Narâin, and put them on the duty of spies. You will then remain in [the execution of] your functions at the gate of the palace.

After

(1) For the original of the present article, as well as for the following translation of it, I am indebted to Lieutenant Colonel Ogg.

(2) The *Paish-kheema* is the establishment of tents, &c. sent in advance, for accommodation when marching.

After one month, the aforesaid will report to you again the orders regarding intelligence, and you will again perform the duty of spies. In this manner you must relieve each other monthly: and the orders of the Presence are not again necessary [on this subject].

Written the 25th of the month *Rubbâny*, year *Shâd*, 1223 from the birth of Mahommed, with the hand of Syed Hûsain.

To this purport other instructions have been written, directed to Akibut Mahommed, *Dârogha* of *Hurkârehs*, and Kâder Ali, *Dârogha* of Couriers, and Meer Yoosif, *Dârogha* of the *Paish Kheema*, to Singa Nâig, Pootah Nâig, Nubby Yâr Khân, Chik Nâig, and Hully Narâin.

The following is a translation of a note addressed to Tippoo, by no less a personage than Mahommed Mukhdoom, the son of Lala Meea. This document shows, that the *Sultan* employed spies of all ranks.

"Cherisher of the World! Health be unto you!

"Your slave, as he was coming from the house of his brother, happened to "meet in the way with Ghûlâm Hyder. Sitting down together, he told me that "the household effects of Husun Ali were about to be sent off that very day. I "answered, that I had heard the same thing, but not from any authority to be "depended upon. Now, however, that your slave has received the orders of the "resplendent Presence for the purpose, he will be careful to obtain every possible "information, and to report to the sublime Presence such authentic intelligence as "shall reach him."

APPENDIX F.*

(Referred to in LETTER *LXVII.)*

I am indebted for the following explanation of the cypher, alluded to in Letter LXVII, to Mr. Stewart, the Arabic, Persian, and Hindoostany Professor at the Honorable the East-India Company's College at Hertford. Not having received it till after that Letter had gone to press, it is inserted in this place.

The verse, containing the key to the cypher in question, is read by Mr. Stewart, as follows:—

احد رسد بنغط بمد نميرسد عشرات
مايه بسمت يمين كم الف بسوي يسار

g

which

which may be thus rendered:

> The Units reach just to the line;
> The Tens not quite so low are seen:
> The Hundreds to the right incline;
> While Thousands to the left do lean.

Thus  Stand for 1, 2, 3, 4, 5, 6, 7, 8 & 9.

 Stand for 10, 20, 30, &c. to 90.

 Stand for 100, 200, &c. to 900.

 Stand for 1000, &c.

Or the Hundreds and Thousands may be thus denoted:

Hundreds 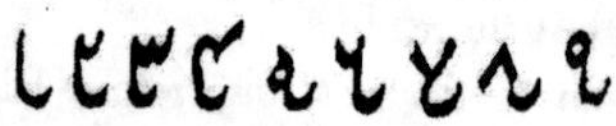

Thousands 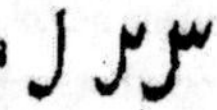 &c.

But the *Ubjud* notation (according to which the several letters of the alphabet are to be denoted by figures, and, *vice versa*, the latter to be reduced to letters) not going beyond 1000, by which number the letter غ is expressed, the foregoing scheme is applicable no farther: what follows a thousand, therefore, can be employed only to denote numbers. Thus س or ٣ might be used for 3000; but would not convey any other meaning.

The following example is added, for the better illustration of the cypher in question.

Ghûlâm Hyder (غلام حیدر) would be thus written

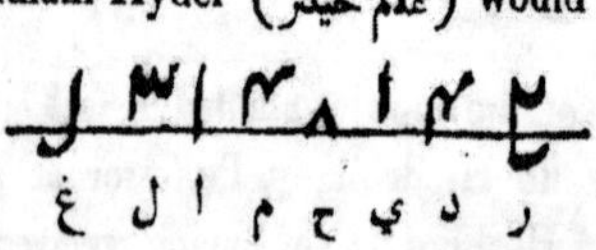 or instead of ل this \ may be used.

And Tippoo Sultan (تیپو سلطان) thus,

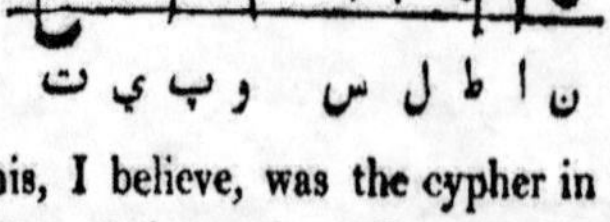 or instead of 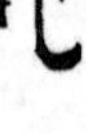 this  may be used.

This, I believe, was the cypher in which (as mentioned at Letter LIII) the description of the works of Fort St. George was written by Tippoo's *Vakeels,* during their residence at that presidency.

APPENDIX, G.

(Referred to at Letter CII.)

An Historical Sketch *of the* Patan Principality *of Kurnool.*(1)

Kurnool, or, as my Persian original has it, *Kunnool*,(2) is by some authorities described as a *Muhul*, or *Purgunnah*, of the *Sircar Adoni*; while others call it a *Sircar*, giving, at the same time, the title of *Soubah* (as in the case of *Bunkapoor*) to *Adoni*. But however this might be, it is certain that, as well during the existence of *Beejapoor* as a separate kingdom, as subsequently to its degradation to the rank of a province of the Moghul empire, both the districts in question were included in its jurisdiction.

Kurnool is not particularly noticed in the annals of the *Decan* till the period of Aurungzebe's appearance in that quarter of *India*. Since then, however, the active part taken by some of its chiefs, in the subsequent transactions of that busy scene, has conferred upon it a considerable degree of distinction.

The founder of the Patan dynasty of *Kurnool* was, as has been elsewhere incidentally mentioned,(3)

1. *Khizr Khân Punny*,(4)

an Afghan, of the tribe called *Poory-Zye*.(5) He had already attained to some rank in the Moghul army, when the latter was joined from *Shânoor* by Bhûlool

g 2 Khân,

(1) The following article is chiefly derived from the same source as the memoir relating to *Shânoor*, given in Appendix D. If the chronology, however, of the latter be in general defective, and often uncertain, that of the present sketch is, on the whole, still less satisfactory. Inattention to dates unfortunately constitutes too common a fault in most of the productions of the minor annalists of *India*. I am free to own, indeed, that both the chronology and the narrative of Meer Hûsain, when at variance, either with Scott's *Decan*, or with the *Moasir ül Omra*, should be received with caution.

(2) Meer Hûsain informs us, that this town (to which Allumgeer gave the name of *Kumr-nugr*) derives its Hindoo name from the beautiful cotton fabrics, such as *Sailahs* and others, for which it was formerly, and may be still, noted: *Kundnool* signifying, in the language of that country, "fine "spun, clear thread." Hence came *Kunnool* and *Kurnool*: the *n* and *r* being permutable in most of the dialects of *India*. *Kurnool* is not less celebrated, according to my author, for the beauty of its women than for that of its muslins.

(3) See Appendix D, under "Bhûlool Khân."

(4) I am uncertain whether this word is *Punny* or *Beeny*, the original being susceptible of both readings: and, therefore, I have followed the orthography which I find adopted by Captain Jonathan Scott, the learned translator of *Ferishtah*.

(5) It is thus written in my manuscript;

Khân, between whose family, and that of Khizr Khân, a great friendship had always subsisted. The young men having, in consequence, been educated together, had contracted a strict intimacy, which was now renewed, and closely cultivated by both. Bhûlool Khân happening, at this conjuncture, to stand high in the favour of Aurungzebe, as well as in that of his chief counsellor, Khân Jehân Khân, employed his credit with them so effectually in behalf of his friend; that Khizr Khân, besides an augmentation of his immediate *Munsub,* soon obtained the government of *Kurnool* in *Jágeer,* upon the condition of his maintaining, for the imperial service, a body of three thousand horse, and seven thousand foot. The limits of the *Sircar* of *Kurnool* (as it is on this occasion called) have probably fluctuated greatly, in the course of the various revolutions which that district has experienced. They must, at least, if the information before me be accurate, have been considerably more extensive, at the period just now referred to, than they are at this time, since the revenue, of which Khizr Khân became master, is rated at a sum exceeding thirty-four *lacks* of *rupees.*

The fortress of *Kurnool* had not yet submitted to the Moghul arms, but was still occupied on behalf of the reigning sovereign of *Beejapoor:* Khizr Khân, therefore, had to reduce it, before he could enter upon his new government. For this purpose, accompanied by Bhûlool Khân, he immediately proceeded against that place, the commander of which was soon convinced, by the joint force of bribes and threats, of the necessity of surrendering it. After this, he would not appear to have experienced any serious difficulty in establishing his authority throughout the rest of the district. When this object was completely effected, and not before, Bhûlool Khân, taking leave of his friend, returned to his own *Jágeer.*

We hear nothing further of Khizr Khân, till several years after this time, when he is said to have distinguished himself greatly at the siege of *Aurungabad,* conducted by Allumgeer in person. It was at this juncture that, while proceeding one day to pay his respects to the Emperor, he happened to encounter, at a gateway leading to the Imperial residence, Shaikh Minhâj De Rany, an *Omra* formerly of the first rank at the court of *Beejapoor* (which, with several other nobles of that declining kingdom, he had some time before quitted in disgust), and no less celebrated for his bold and unguarded language on all occasions, than for his intrepidity in the field. Whether any rivalry or ill-will had previously subsisted between these two great men does not appear; but meeting now in the situation which has been mentioned, they engaged in a violent dispute regarding precedence, which soon terminated in the death of Khizr Khân, who fell by a wound

wound, inflicted during the contest, by his adversary's own hand.[6] The latter, nevertheless, utterly fearless of the consequences of his sanguinary rashness, instantly repaired to the Imperial Presence; where, with a levity but ill suited, either to the place or to the occasion, he scoffingly related, "that having met, in "his passage through the portal of the palace, with a kicking ass,[7] he had "presently removed the nuisance."[8] The Emperor, astonished at this address, was still considering what it could mean, when the *Urz-baigy*[9] appearing, explained the allusion of the *Shaikh*, by a circumstantial report of what had happened. The murderer, in the mean while, remained perfectly unmolested: for such was the weight and credit which he enjoyed, at this time, at the imperial court, that Allumgeer judged it expedient to wink at his conduct on the present occasion. It was not thus, however, with

2. *Dâood Khân Punny*

the son of Khizr Khân, who no sooner learned the fate of the latter, than, quitting the government of the *Payen Ghaut Carnatic*, which had been some time before confided to him by Allumgeer, he hastened to *Kurnool*; from whence, after collecting together a considerable body of troops, and leaving his brother, Ali Khân, in charge of his *Jâgeer*, he proceeded by rapid marches towards *Aurungabad*, with the avowed purpose of avenging his father's death. The desperate step thus taken by the Patan excited no small uneasiness in the mind of the Emperor, who was justly apprehensive, lest it should produce a division, and perhaps a tumult, in the imperial army, in which both Shaikh Minhâj and his adversary had numerous friends and partisans. If he sent a force to oppose the progress of the latter, or to chastise his temerity, it would be to proclaim the contempt entertained for his authority; and if, on the other hand, he suffered the Pâtans, in the present disposition of their leader, to join the imperial camp, he anticipated the confusion and bloodshed which were too likely to ensue, from the impetuous spirit, and deep-rooted hatred of the contending chiefs, acting on the fierce and turbulent character of their respective adherents. From this dilemma he was, however, for the present, relieved, by Zoolfkâr Khân, the *Khânsâmân* (or house steward) of the *Vizier*, Asud Khân, who had been the intimate friend and sworn brother of Khizr

(6) A different account is given of Khizr Khân's death in the second volume of Scott's *Decan*, page 38.

(7) In the original خرلکدکوب

(8) Original ازمیان برداشت or literally, "lifted from the midst," an expression usually denoting extermination, or putting to death.

(9) The master of requests or of ceremonies.

Khizr Khân; by whose sons he had been, in consequence, always considered in the light of an uncle. Zoolfkâr Khân, availing himself of this title to the deference of the Patan (and which, by Mahommedans in general, is deemed to be little or nothing inferior to the claims derived from absolute consanguinity), proposed to write to his adoptive nephew, exhorting him to submit himself entirely to the justice of the Emperor, and dismissing the chief part of his followers, to repair, in perfect confidence, to his (Zoolfkâr's) quarters; whence he promised to conduct him to an audience of his Majesty, and to procure for him all the satisfaction he could desire. Dâood Khân, yielding to the advice and entreaties of his friend, was immediately presented to the monarch; who, besides a most gracious reception, gave him some wholesome counsel for the regulation of his conduct, which he concluded, by assuring him that, in regard to his father's death, the law should take its course. The following day was accordingly appointed for the public hearing of the cause. In the mean while, however, desirous, either for personal or political reasons, of skreening the culprit, if possible, from punishment, Allumgeer sent privately for Shaikh Minhâj; and telling him that as, agreeably to the law, he could not be convicted of the offence imputed to him, except upon his own admission, he (the Emperor) trusted that he would feel no hesitation, when confronted with his accuser, in asserting his innocence. To this the *Shaikh* is said to have apparently assented: but however that might be, he was, no doubt, very far from entertaining such an intention; since the next morning, when publicly interrogated on the occasion, instead of denying the crime laid to his charge, he loudly exclaimed, "that it was most true that he had slain the whoreson[(10)] in "question, with the identical poignard which he then held in his hand, and that he "was, in like manner, prepared to kill any other whoreson, who should seek to "avenge his death." So saying, he quitted the *Durbâr*, leaving the whole assembly in utter amazement at his temerity. Nor was it at any future period in the power of Dâood Khân to wreak his meditated vengeance upon the murderer of his father; who, after this time, was always surrounded by a body of three hundred well armed and desperate Decanies, whose particular duty it was to watch the motions of the Patans, and whose vigilance and courage constantly frustrated every attempt of the latter upon his life.[(11)]

It

(10) Original مادر قحبه which has nearly the same signification as the مادر بغطاي so frequently used by Tippoo Sultan. The former is said by Meer Hûsain to be a very common term of abuse with the Decanies.

(11) It is a remarkable fact, that the death of this turbulent nobleman was at last occasioned, when least to be expected, by his bestowing on one of his own servants the same foul epithet which he had till

It is not stated by our annalist, what means were taken by the Emperor, in this perplexing predicament, to reconcile Dâood Khân to the disappointment of those hopes of public satisfaction for the murder of his father, which he had been confidently taught to entertain. It appears, however, that the Patan continued with the imperial army till the death of Allumgeer; some time after which event he was slain in a sanguinary tumult, excited, as Meer Hûsain says, by the jealousy and hostility of a faction at court, who spared no means to effect his disgrace and removal from thence. By other accounts, however, it would appear that he fell in an attempt which he had made to cut off the Viceroy of the *Decan*. What is certain is, that many *Omras* of distinction, besides Dâood Khân, lost their lives upon this occasion. He dying without issue, was succeeded by his only brother,

3. *Ali Khân Punny*,

who ruled between five and six years, during which period nothing is recorded of him. Upon his death, the government devolved upon his son,

4. *Ibraheem Khân*,

who is stated to have filled the office of *Soubahdâr* of *Adoni*, during the life-time of his uncle, Dâood Khan; but whether on the part of the latter, or under an immediate nomination from the Viceroy of the *Decan*, is not mentioned. I incline to think, however, that he must have held it as a separate government, since their is no authority, that I know of, for believing that *Adoni* constituted at any period, a dependency of *Kurnool*. However this may be, Ibraheem Khân, soon after ascending the *Musnud*, set about rebuilding with masonry the citadel of *Kurnool*, the wall of which, before this time, appears to have consisted only of mud. He also made considerable additions and improvements to the town; and applying sedulously to the augmentation of his military force, and particularly to that part of it composed of Afghans of his own tribe, soon found himself at the head of a respectable

till then so often used with impunity, both to high and low: for it is related of him, that having, on some occasion, discovered a slight error in an account submitted to his inspection, he passionately taxed the clerk, who had prepared it, with negligence, applying to him, at the same time, his customary term of abuse. This drawing from the insulted clerk a respectful, but spirited remonstrance, the *Shaikh*, exasperated at what he conceived to be the insolence of his servant, not only repeated the offensive appellation, but accompanied it with a slap on the face. The poor *Mûtusuddy*, rendered frantic by this aggravation of the disgrace already put upon him, and (as my author expresses it) "washing his hands "of life," suddenly plunged the pen,* with which he was writing, into the side of his master, who died of the wound thus inflicted. It is scarcely necessary to add, that his murderer fell, at the same instant, a sacrifice to the fury of the surrounding attendants.

* When it is recollected, that the pen spoken of was formed of a strong sharp-pointed *reed*, it will not, perhaps, appear incredible, that such an instrument should have inflicted a mortal wound.

respectable army, with which he was enabled to subject to his authority, and to exact tribute from, many of the surrounding *Polygars*, who had, for some time past, paid a very reluctant obedience to their Mahommedan rulers.

After this, leaving his son, Alif Khân, in charge of his *Jágeer*, he proceeded himself, by the advice of his principal counsellors, to *Aurungabad*, for the purpose of paying his court to Khân Jehân Khân, who was at that time Viceroy of the *Decan*. This he did so successfully, that in return for a *Nuzr* of five *lacks* of *rupees*, which he presented to the Viceroy, he obtained, instead of the usual patent of confirmation for his *Jágeer*, a new grant, in which the former stipulations, whatever they might have been, were wholly omitted. Having accomplished this object, he returned to *Kurnool*, where he occupied himself in the affairs of his *Jágeer*, till the appointment of the *Nábob*, Asof Jah, to the government of the *Decan*, upon which occasion the Patan hastened to do homage to the new Viceroy; which he did while the latter was still encamped, after his recent victory over Aalum Ali Khân (the nephew of the *Umeer ûl Omra*, Syed Hûsain Ali Khân) in the vicinity of *Burhanpoor*.[12] Here he met with a distinguished reception from Asof Jah, who, according to my author, renewed the patent for his *Jágeer* in the terms of that which had been granted him by Khân Jehân Khân. Being seized, about this time, with a severe indisposition, he left his son, Alif Khân, in attendance upon the *Názim*, and repaired to *Kurnool*, where he died, at the end of three or four years, after having ruled over the principality of *Kurnool* somewhat more than fourteen years. He was succeeded by his son,

5. *Alif Khân Punny*,

who contriving to ingratiate himself with Nâsir Jung, the second son of Asof Jah, is said to have had a principal share in seducing him from his duty and allegiance to his father, at the time that the latter, being obliged to repair to *Dehli*, left him in the temporary charge of the government of the *Decan*. What followed, on this occasion, does not belong to the present narrative. It may suffice to say, that Nâsir Jung was, in the end, reconciled to his father, who contented himself with manifesting his displeasure against those who had been most instrumental in exciting him to rebellion, by prohibiting their appearance in his presence. It is probable, however, that some of these, and particularly Alif Khân, were indebted for this impunity, less to the lenity of the *Nizám*, than to considerations of policy, which might have suggested the inexpediency, if not the impracticability, of punishing such powerful offenders in a more signal manner.

Alif

(12) This victory was obtained, according to the *Maasir ûl Omra*, on the 6th *Shuwwál*, A.H. 1132, or some time in A.D. 1720.

Alif Khân continued in disgrace with his superior, till the period when Asof Jah, turning his thoughts to the settlement of the lower *Carnatic*,[13] summoned the various *Munsubdárs* and *Jágeerdárs*, subject to his authority, to repair to his standard, with their respective military contingents. On this occasion, the Patan, in the first instance, dispatched his son, Behâdûr Khân, to join the *Názim*, to whom he transmitted, at the same time, a considerable *Nuzr* in money, together with suitable apologies for his past misconduct. These submissions being seconded by the good offices of the chiefs of *Shánoor* and *Kurpah*, who were, at this period, in attendance upon Asof Jah, had the effect of subduing the resentment of the latter, or, at least, of inducing him to dissemble it. Alif Khân obtained a formal pardon; and Behâdûr Khân, after an honourable reception and dismission, hastened back to *Kurnool* with the joyful intelligence. The father, hereupon, leaving his son in charge of his *Jágeer*, proceeded in person to the camp of the *Nizám*, by whom he was received in a manner sufficiently gracious, and with whom he appears to have continued till the termination of the expedition to the *Carnatic*, when he was permitted to return to his *Jágeer*. Here he shortly after died, having ruled thirteen years, and was succeeded by his eldest son,

6. *Behádúr Khán*,

known also by the title of Himmut Behâdûr,[14] of whom Meer Hûsain reports, that he was distinguished for his extraordinary intrepidity, and for the prudence with which he carried on the internal affairs of his government, in the management of which he steadily followed the example, and conformed to the practice, of the wisest of his predecessors. But whatever his character, in these respects, might be, his conduct (as well as that of the other Patan chieftains of the *Decan*) towards Nâsir Jung, subsequently to the accession of the latter to the *Musnud* of *Hyderabad*, and soon after with regard to Mûzuffer Jung (a *Názim* of their own creation), exhibits nothing but a tissue of the blackest perfidy and ingratitude.

The particulars of the transactions, here alluded to, are already too well known to require to be recited in this place. It will be sufficient to state, that, according to Meer Hûsain, it was by the immediate hand of Behâdûr Khân[15] that the unfortunate *Názim* perished; and that the detestable traitor did not long survive the victim of his treason, being himself slain, about two months after, in a sanguinary tumult which took place at *Raechooty*, between the ever-

h turbulent

(13) That is in A.D. 1743.

(14) It does not appear by whom, or upon what occasion, this title was conferred upon Behâdûr Khân.

(15) This event took place near *Gingee*, on the 5th December 1750: other writers, however, make the *Nabob* of *Kurpah* the assassin. The *Maasir úl Omra* agrees with the account in the text.

turbulent Afghans and their late accomplices in the atrocious assassination of Nâsir Jung.[16]

Behâdûr Khân ruled over *Kurnool* between seven and eight years,[17] and was succeeded, at his death, by his brother,

7. *Mûnuwer Khân Punny,*

who happening to reside, at this period, at *Nundîdl*, the *Polygar* of *Gudduck*, encouraged thereto, and assisted by the French, took advantage of his absence from *Kurnool*, and the confusion which prevailed there, in consequence of the sudden and disastrous death of Behâdûr Khân, to surprize and seize upon that place. Mûnuwer Khân hereupon hastened to *Kurpah*, where he solicited the aid of its chief, Abdûl Nuby Khân, towards the recovery of his inheritance. Abdûl Nuby, who could not feel himself very secure on his own *Musnud*, so recently after the tragic events of *Gingee* and *Raechooty*, is nevertheless said to have afforded him some assistance in money. By this means Mûnuwer Khân was enabled to collect together about seven hundred foot soldiers and three hundred horse, with which small force he did not hesitate to advance against *Kurnool*. The attempt to recover his capital with such a handful of men appeared little short of desperate, and would, probably, have proved so, if the garrison left in it by the *Polygar* of *Gudduck* had prudently remained within the walls. Instead of this, however, they unwisely came out, and giving battle to the Patan, were defeated with great slaughter. Hereupon the *Polygar's* commander, being panic struck, immediately surrendered the place. According to Meer Hûsain, however, this extraordinary success of Mûnuwer Khân was not so much owing, either to the indiscretion of the enemy, or to the valor of his own followers, as to the powerful aid which he derived from the presence and prayers of a celebrated *Peer*,[18] established in the neighbourhood of *Kurnool*, and called Shâh Mustân, whom he had had the good fortune to encounter on his march, and to propitiate in his favor. It was (if our author may be believed) the appearance of this holy personage, at the head of the Patan's little band, which, by striking unusual terror into the enemy, principally contributed to the victory obtained over the latter.

Mûnuwer

(16) This tumult occurred on the 17th of *Mûhurram*, A.H. 1164, or about the end of January 1751.

(17) This account would place his accession to the *Musnud* about the middle of A.H. 1156, or towards the latter part of A.D. 1753. See note at the end of the present article.

(18) This term is applied by the Mahommedans to those superiors of the religious orders, most eminent for their sanctity and piety They are the ghostly fathers of the Musulmans, and many of them are pretended to have performed miracles.

Mûnuwer Khân remained, from this time, in quiet possession of his country, until the period when Shahnuwâz Khân[19] being raised to the office of chief minister to Sulâbut Jung (the brother and successor of Nâsir Jung) dispatched an army from *Hyderabad*, for the declared purpose of reducing *Kurnool*, and of punishing, in the person of the ruling chief, the treason and ingratitude of his predecessor. The Patan, however, not only had the address to avert the impending danger, but, by means of the proper application of bribes, and of suitable submissions, to obtain a confirmation of his *Jâgeer*, on condition of paying a certain annual tribute to the government of *Hyderabad*. The amount of this tribute is not stated: but it was, probably, the same which was, some time after, exacted of him by a new adversary, still more formidable than the one whom he had lately appeased.

The enemy who now disturbed the repose which Mûnuwer Khân vainly flattered himself he had secured, by his recent pacification with the *Soubah*, was the celebrated Hyder Ali Khân; who, some time after he had made the Patan Chief of *Shânoor* submit to his authority, advanced against *Kurnool*, with the professed determination of reducing the latter place also to subjection. Mûnuwer Khân prepared, as well as he could, to repel the invader, whom, however, he could not prevent from investing his capital. In these perilous circumstances, as on all other critical occasions that had arisen, since his memorable overthrow of the troops of the *Polygar* of *Gudduck*, and his subsequent establishment in his principality, he sought the council and assistance of Shâh Mustân (already mentioned in the relation of those events) and one of whose most steady and zealous disciples he had now become, if he had not been always so. The holy man, presuming, perhaps, on the remarkable effects attributed, by his superstitious admirers, to his former interposition in behalf of the Patan, boldly desired him to be of good cheer, and to rely on the speedy discomfiture of his enemy. Whether this enthusiast had actually persuaded himself, that he possessed any supernatural means of realizing the hopes he raised, or depended, for producing that result, on some secret correspondence which he might have entered into with the invader's army, is not mentioned by my author. However this might be, he mounted the following morning, bare-headed and bare-footed, on an elephant provided for the occasion, and taking with him a select body of Afghans, proceeded, with great rapidity, in the direction of Hyder's camp. Hereupon, some of the principal persons in the confidence of that chieftain, observing the movement of the *Peer*, and probably apprized of

h 2 his

(19) This was the author of the *Maâsir ûl Omra*, to which a supplement was added, after his death, by his son Meer Abdûl Huyi Khân, afterwards raised to the title of Sumsâmûd Dowlah, the same by which his father was distinguished.

his purpose, were induced, either by superstitious considerations, or by motives still less excusable, to represent to their master the obloquy and danger to which he would expose himself, by persisting in the attack of a place, which was evidently under the protection of so venerable and powerful a saint as Shâh Mustân. They concluded with earnestly exhorting him, as he valued his own interest and safety, or the prosperity of his house, to desist from a purpose so pregnant with evil. Hyder, who was but little subject to the influence of superstition, offended, either at the freedom or the folly of this advice, sharply demanded of those from whom it proceeded, " whether *his* state was not under the protection of a saint, as well " as that of *Kurnool?*" To this reasonable interrogatory, the others, being, of course, obliged to reply in the affirmative, Hyder sneeringly observed, " that " such being the case, he would leave the two saints to settle their own quarrel as " they pleased, while, at any rate, he was determined to bend the neck of " Mûnuwer Khân to the yoke of obedience." During this conversation, the *Shâh* continued to advance towards the Mysorean camp: but whether it was owing to his observing any movements in the latter, which indicated a resistance he had not reckoned upon, or to any intelligence conveyed to him from thence, or, finally, to a sudden conviction of the extravagance and hopelessness of his enterprize, he thought proper, while still at some distance from the enemy's lines, to turn short round, and hasten back to *Kurnool;* where, on his arrival, he instantly advised Mûnuwer Khân " to give some money to his visitor, and to " send him away:" adding, " that as things were then circumstanced, he could " answer for the preservation of nothing beyond the walls of the fort." Whether the prowess of the *Shâh* would have been adequate for the defence of these, was not put to the proof; for the Patan wisely dispatched a *Vakeel* to Hyder, with such proposals of accommodation as the latter judged it expedient to accept, although, according to Meer Hûsain, they amounted only to the payment of an annual tribute of a *lack* of *rupees,* and the immediate delivery of a large supply of provisions: to which, however, were added abundant assurances of future attachment and submission. Perhaps the chief motive of Hyder, in granting such easy terms to Mûnuwer Khân, arose from his impatience to proceed against *Kurpah,* which he appears to have done directly after his departure from *Kurnool.*

Mûnuwer Khân continued subject to the pecuniary contribution imposed upon him at this juncture (but which, as may be collected from Tippoo Sultan's correspondence with Runmust Khân,[(20)] was not very punctually discharged) till the partition

(20) It is proper to observe, in this place, that either Mûnuwer Khân must have been also called Runmust Khân, which is by no means impossible, or Meer Husain must have overlooked, in his enumeration of

partition treaty of *Seringapatam*, in 1792, which at once transferred this tribute to the *Nizâm*, and released the principality of *Kurnool* from all future dependence on the ruler of *Mysore*. During the war which preceded the treaty, Mûnuwer Khân had been required to repair to the standard of the *Nizâm*, with the military quota, which, as a feudatory of the *Soubah* of the *Decan*, he was bound to furnish: and though he was himself, at this period, too old and infirm to undergo the fatigues of the field, he nevertheless sent his contingent, headed by his son, Alif Khân, along with Secunder Jah,(21) when the latter joined the British forces under Lord Cornwallis.

On this occasion was exemplified the curious, but anomalous nature, of the tenure, by which many of the petty states and chieftains of the *Decan* hold their territories, being, at the same time, the feudatories of one, and the tributaries of another, superior lord. Thus, Mûnuwer Khân was at once subject to Tippoo Sultan and to Nizâm Ali Khân: yet the former's claims upon the Patan were not considered as any way impairing those of the latter, who was still supposed to possess the right of summoning him to his standard, and of demanding his services, no matter against what power, whenever he thought proper. It is true, that this right being derived from a source which, in point of fact, no longer existed,(22) rested chiefly on what might be called a mere political fiction: but, nevertheless, similar pretensions continue, in various cases, to be respected by prejudice and habit, and, in others, to be enforced by power.

Mûnuwer Khân died, according to my author, soon after the conclusion of the peace of *Seringapatam*, that is to say, some time in the year 1792, having ruled over *Kurnool* during a period of forty-one lunar years. He was succeeded by his son,

8. *Alif Khân*,

who, by the treaty concluded in 1800, between the British Government in *India* and the *Nabob*, Nizâm Ali Khân, was placed, in a certain degree, under the protection of the East-India Company, to whom the tribute, which he stood engaged to pay to the government of *Hyderabad*, was then transferred by the latter.

Meer

of the chiefs of *Kurnool*, one of the dynasty; an omission which will be allowed to be very unlikely. That the person who ruled over that principality, in 1786, was named Rustmust Khân, admits of no doubt; yet if he bore two names, it might have been expected that our biographer would have mentioned both of them.

(21) At that time the second son of Nizâm Ali Khân, and now nominal *Soubah* of the *Decan*.

(22) Because, strictly speaking, there is no longer a *Soubahdâr*, or viceroy, of the *Decan*.

Meer Hûsain concludes his brief account of the Patan dynasties of the *Decan* by observing, that the reputation of their chiefs, for courage and manly enterprize, would appear to have begun to decline from the period of Dâood Khân's death, and to have finally expired with Behâdûr Khân.

The following table has been formed with the view of fixing, as far as was practicable, the periods at which the several chieftains of *Shânoor* and *Kurnool* succeeded to their respective principalities. Being deduced, for the most part, from the imperfect data furnished by Meer Hûsain, and these being too vague to be confidently relied on, it follows, that it can be offered as no more than an attempt at an approximation to the truth.

Shânoor Dynasty.	Began to Rule.	Ruled.	Died.
1. Jân Nisâr Khân	......	..	1531
2. Uzeez Meea........	1531	..	......
3. Jubbàr Meea Meeâneh	......	..	1612
4. Bhûlool Khân	1612	47½	1659-60
5. Dulail Khân, or Dileer Khân	1659-60	31	1690-1
6. Abdûl Ghuffàr	1690-1	28	1718-9
7. Ghufoor Meea	1718-9	9	1727
8. Abdûl Mujeed Khân.	1727	31	1758
9. Abdûl Hukeem Khân.	1758	34	1792
10. Kheera Meea	1792	..	......

Kurnool Dynasty.	Began to Rule.	Ruled.	Died.
1. Khizr Khân	.....	..	1674
2. Dâood Khân	1674	38	1712
3. Ali Khân	1712	5½	1717-8
4. Ibraheem Khân	1717-8	14½	1731
5. Alif Khân..........	1731	13	1744
6. Behâdûr Khân, or Himmut Behâdûr	1744	7½	1751
7. Mûnuwer Khàn	1751	40	1792
8. Alif Khân..........	1792	..	......

APPENDIX H.

(Referred to at LETTER *CXIV.)*

ENGAGEMENT *entered into by* MEER SÂDIK.[1]

He is the Sultan:[2]
In the name of the most merciful God,
May God preserve our gracious Sovereign!

I, Meer Mahommed Sâdik, Son of Meer Ali Nuky, servant of the *Khodâdâd Sircar*, do swear by God, and engage (to which engagement God and his Prophet, and the word of God, which is the *Imâm* of true-believers, are witnesses) to perform my duty to my Lord and Master faithfully, with all my heart,[3] and with my four members;[4] that is to say, with my eyes, my ears, my tongue, and my hands:[5] that I will study nothing but obedience to my Lord and Master, and never act, in any instance, contrary to my duty or to his interests. And [I moreover promise] to communicate whatever I shall hear or see to the resplendent Presence.

If, however, (which God forbid!) I should happen to be guilty of a breach of any of the four obligations[6] [above mentioned], or of the obedience which I owe, may God, the most holy and omnipotent, and whose name is the Avenger, overwhelm me and mine with his wrath, and utterly destroy us!

According to the prohibitions in the holy word of God, the Almighty has forbidden eight things: those [eight] crimes, by the blessing of the confession of faith I will reprobate and put from me, even as [I would] the devil. I will, moreover, in comformity with the holy word, not only zealously discharge my duty, on all occasions, to his Majesty, my Lord and Master, but also labor to promote

(1) The original document is in my possession; for which, as well as for the translation, I am indebted to Colonel Ogg.

(2) This is meant of God, who is sometimes so called.

(3) Original برناقت دل

(4) Original از چهار عضو خود

(5) After the hands, the original has the words ودل "and my heart," which I think are meant to connect with what follows.

(6) Meaning what his eyes, ears, tongue, and hands, are bound to perform, and all which are afterwards enumerated.

promote and maintain the concord and union of the people of *Isldm*, or those who [are accustomed to] repeat the confession of faith.

If (which God forbid!) any act, forbidden by the holy word, should come to my knowledge, I will drive the unworthy person, committing the same, from among the people of *Isldm*; for the most glorious and high God has declared, that whosoever commits one of the eight sins, abovementioned, is the son of rejection. And I am descended, on both sides, and through three generations, from nobles and *Siyuds* of the tribe of *Koreish*, and of the Mahommedan religion, and am true and faithful both in tongue and hand.

And I declare, under the aforesaid solemn sanctions, that except the wealth of my Royal Master, the Shadow of God, at the time of his becoming a servant of the *Khodádád Sircar*, your slave[7] was possessed of three *pagodas*. After becoming the servant of the *Sircar* (the centre of bounty) I sent for my family, who possessed in *jewels*, &c. about three thousand *rupees*. Since that time your slave, who is always ready to sacrifice his life[8] in your Majesty's service, swears by the book of God (witness God, and the Prophet of God!) that all he has acquired in cattle, arms, effects, clothes, and vessels of brass, jewels, money, and presents, from his Lord and Master, including profit and original property, as above stated, amounts, in all, to about 1,08,200 *rupees*: out of which sum he expended, during the three years that he laboured under your Majesty's displeasure, and confined himself to his own house, about 15,000 *rupees*. There consequently remain 93,200 *rupees*, as detailed in the subjoined statement.

I swear by the book of God, and by the words[9] of the Prophet, that your slave represents his true situation; but if he should [be suspected to] have embezzled any of the *Sircar's* property, or to have taken bribes from any *Asof*, *Mútusuddy*, *Amuldár*, or *Serishtedár*, or to have done injury to any inhabitant of the *Sircar*, let orders be issued from the Presence full of splendor (the Shadow of God) for enquiry to be made therein; and if your slave shall be found guilty, let a severe punishment be inflicted on the unfaithful offender [*i. e.* on me]. Let him be rolled up in a mat, and burnt, and let his dwelling and family be destroyed; but though your sacred Majesty should forgive, God will surely punish that wicked doer.

From

(7) Original خانه زاد "born in the house."

(8) Original جان نثار *jánnisár* (life-devoting, or life-sacrificing) an expression from which I should have been inclined to derive the Turkish term janissary, if a different etymology had not, on good authority, been assigned to it.

(9) Probably the *Hudees*, or traditions, are here meant.

From the beginning of his service, your slave has not given a farthing to any of his relations; and in your slave's house, marriage ceremonies have seldom exceeded five and twenty *rupees*, and at no time one thousand *rupees*. Your slave's pay was twelve hundred *rupees* per month: in lieu of half of which your Majesty graciously conferred upon him a *Jágeer* of three thousand *pagodas*. Of this, whatever I have spent, I have spent: the remainder is ready to be laid, together with my life and heart, an humble sacrifice at your sacred and august feet.

All former crimes of this devoted slave, my royal Lord and Master has, through his abundant generosity, favour, and protection, forgiven: but if, hereafter, I should receive any bribes, or commit any [other] misdemeanor in the [management of the] country of the *Khodádád Sircar*, the aforesaid oath will be binding on me. And I will perform the duties of my station, with heart, soul, and fidelity; and never be neglectful of, or deficient in, the same. To this engagement God, and the Prophet of God, are witnesses: and if I act contrary thereto, I shall be obnoxious to the wrath of the throne of vengeance. And the specification of my duties, according to the four above-mentioned members, is as follows:

1st. As to the duty of the eyes. I will not authorize, by any sign made by my eyes, any embezzlement of the property of the *Sircar*: and if any one should, to my knowledge, do any thing prejudicial to the affairs and property of the *Sircar*, I will not wink thereat, but will forbid the same, and report it to the exalted Presence.

2d. As to the duty of the ears. If any person should utter expressions of a treasonable nature, or prejudicial to the wealth or affairs of the *Khodádád Sircar*, or act seditiously, and the same should come to my hearing, I will not remain silent, but will forbid and punish the offence, and also report it to the exalted Presence.

3d. As to the duty of the tongue. That is to say, in all matters relating to the due management of the affairs of the *Khodádád Sircar*, whether now or hereafter, and in which the interest, glory, and prosperity of your Majesty may be concerned, it (*i. e.* my tongue) shall be ever actively employed, as long as it retains motion: nor shall it fail, at any time, to make all necessary communications to the Presence, full of splendor.

4th. As to the duty of the hands. That is to say, the enemies of my royal Lord and Master I will kill with sword and pen,[10] and most certainly will never neglect any opportunity of destroying his enemies with sword and pen. I will, moreover, communicate all such transactions to the resplendent Presence, in my

i own

(10) If the *Sultan's Dewán* could write no better than he did upon the present occasion, the enemies of his master had but little reason to dread the threatened execution of his pen. Nothing can possibly be worse written than the original of this curious document, which abounds, also, in false spelling.

own hand-writing; and I will, likewise, write out all abstract accounts with my own hand. I will, in fine, in all affairs, be loyal with my four members, and omit or neglect nothing which can be accomplished by them.

Particulars [or Inventory] of the above-mentioned sum of one lack eight thousand two hundred rupees.

Deduct expended during my disgrace and retirement to my own house.......... .... *Rupees* 15,000

Remains.... 93,200

Viz.

In jewels, being presents graciously bestowed by the *Khodâdâd Sircar*, about...... .... *Rupees* 20,000

Furniture of the *Ashoor-khâneh*,[11] carpets, lamps, &c. about 5,000

Jewels and pearls of your majesty's female slaves,[12] about 3,000

Gold ornaments (weight 2,000 pagodas), value..........................8,000

Silver plate, 4,000 *rupees'* weight, value.................................3,500

Copper and brass vessels, &c. about................. 2,000

Arms, one hundred and fifteen articles, *viz.* for *Bârgeers*, one hundred firelocks: your slave's own arms [as swords, pistols, &c.] fifteen: value.. 2,000

Tents, and new wearing apparel (exclusive of old clothes) about..........4,000

Horses, camels, cattle for the plough, sheep, &c........................30,000

Ready money in specie, about..15,200

Price of timber in store... . 500

N. B. The foregoing articles have been set down at about twelve *rupees* above their real value.[13]

Written on Wednesday, the tenth of the month *Hydery*, year *Shûdâl*, 1226[14] from the birth of Mahommed, in the hand-writing of Meer Sadik.

(11) That is, the *Imâm-bâreh* erected during the *Ashoorah*.

(12) Meaning his own women.

(13) Meaning, probably, for the sake of preserving round numbers.

(14) Corresponding to the month of July 1798.

APPENDIX, I.

(Referred to at LETTER CXXXVII.)

EXTRACTS *from the* FUTHÛL MÛJÂHIDEEN.

It is proper I should here premise, that the copy of the *Futhûl Mûjâhideen*, with which I have been favoured by Colonel Marriot, is unfortunately extremely imperfect; for though the work is stated in the beginning to consist of eight chapters, my manuscript contains only three (*viz.* the third, fourth, and fifth), and even these are in some disorder. The following abstract of this curious performance is, therefore, less complete and satisfactory than I could have wished to render it.

The work commences with the usual invocations to God and the Prophet, which are followed by a high-flown eulogium on Tippoo Sultan, in which last, however, nothing new occurs. Next comes a long and bitter invective, apparently levelled at Europeans in general, but evidently intended to apply more immediately to the English, whose various possessions in the *Carnatic*, in *Bengal*, and on the west side of the Peninsula, are particularly noticed and stigmatised, as the acquisitions either of fraud or of violence.

The author then passes to some slight observations on the military tactics of the Europeans; mentioning, more especially, their early superiority in point of artillery, together with their dexterity in the use of small arms; and contrasting these acquirements with the extreme ignorance of the natives of *India* in those essential branches of war.

But whatever advantages the Christians might, at first, have possessed in these respects, they could, it is observed, be no longer boasted of; at least by those among them who were opposed to Tippoo Sultan: since the latter is stated to have improved so greatly on the European tactics, as to have left his masters in the art at an infinite distance behind him. But it was, most of all, in the ordnance department, that he is pretended to have surpassed his rivals: a circumstance the more remarkable, according to our author, "because the *Nazarenes* "pass all their lives, like the salamander, in the fire."(1)

i 2 The

(1) I do not understand how this allusion applies to the *Nazarenes*, or Christians.

The order for the compilation of the present work,[2] which was expressly designed "for the instruction of true believers in general in the art of war, to the "end that they might thereby be enabled more effectually to subdue the enemies "of the faith," appears to have been issued in the year of the *Higera* 1197,[3] (A.D. 1783), and was, probably, among the earliest measures of the *Sultan's* reign. It is not stated by the writer, what assistance he received in the composition of it; but it may be safely presumed, from the characteristic style of various passages in it, that Tippoo himself contributed largely to it. Neither is it, perhaps, unlikely, though it is not acknowledged, that M. Lally, the commander of the European party in his service, had some share in its production.

The work appears to be divided into eight chapters, and each chapter into several sections. The copy in my possession being, however, as already stated, imperfect, and not containing either the two first,[4] or the three last chapters, I can only describe the general contents of those before me.

The third chapter treats of the various manœuvres of a body of regular infantry on actual service, and is divided into twenty-one sections. The eleventh and fourteenth sections describe the mode of fighting in a close or woody country, and form the particular part of the work, with his inattention to which the author is reproached by the *Sultan*, in Letter CXXXVII.

The two sections referred to are very short, both together not exceeding sixteen lines. Being, however, expressed in technical language, some parts of which I do not clearly understand,[5] I decline attempting a regular translation of them, lest I should do injustice to the original. It may suffice to say, that a corps is supposed to be advancing by Indian files, of two men abreast, through a wood, in which situation it is assailed, on each flank, by the enemy. In this case, the troops in question, having been previously formed into platoons, the rear platoon, after facing to the right and left outward, and giving fire, was to divide, and advance to the head of the corps, the right hand files taking the right, and the left hand files the left, of the platoons in their front. In this manner was each platoon successively to advance, till the enemy was dispersed, or the wood was passed.

The

(2) It has been elsewhere mentioned, that the compiler of this work was Zynûl Aabideen Khân Shoostry. (See Letter CXXXVII.)

(3) Colonel Marriott's copy of the work must be a later edition than the original one, as it refers, on a certain occasion, to the battle fought near *Kôpul*, in A.H. 1200, with the Mahrattahs.

(4) From a passage in the Introduction, I think it likely that one, at least, of these two missing chapters, treated of the obligations of true believers to wage war against the infidels.

(5) Thus the terms کهکشان (galaxy) and ثریا (Pleiades) are applied, I do not know how, to different evolutions.

The third chapter is introduced by some general observations on the different modes of attack; in the course of which, notwithstanding all that has been elsewhere said against it by the *Sultan* himself, the *Shub-khoon*, or night-assault, is declared to be *the best*, when the situation of the enemy is favourable to it; that is, when he is encamped on a plain, or in an open country. Particular directions are accordingly given for conducting this species of attack.

It is in the same place directed, that if, in the hour of battle, any soldier fall back out of his station, he shall be instantly put to death; and that if any *Risáladár* turn his back to the enemy, he shall be put to death, *by his Sipahdár's own hand.*

Any *Sipahdár* disobeying the orders herein given, or abandoning his guns to the enemy, or seeking his safety in flight, was, on due proof of the same, to be hung in public. On the other hand, if he distinguished himself, he was to be advanced in [rank and] *Jágeer,* and to have an elephant bestowed on him.

When a *Sipahdár* was killed in action, or died, he was to be succeeded in his station by the *Risáladár* in command of the first *Risála.* The first *Risáladár* was to be succeeded by the second; the second by the third; and the third by the fourth.(7) The latter was to be succeeded by the first *Jowkdár* of the senior *Risála.*

All soldiers and others were strictly to obey their respective *Sipahdárs* and *Risáladárs,* on pain of being punished, at the discretion of the said superior officers.

In the introductory part of the third chapter, the author likewise describes the manner of attacking the *Nazarenes* (*i. e.* the English) in a plain. It is stated to be of infallible success; and triumphant allusions are made, on the occasion, to the actions with Colonels Baillie and Braithwaite, during the last irruption of Hyder into the *Carnatic.*

By the twelfth section of this chapter, "on charging with the bayonet," the commanding officer was directed to exclaim, at the moment of charging, "the "*Sultan* of the Faith is living and well;" which words were to be repeated aloud by all the troops. This mode of attack is highly commended by the author, *as being that in which the assailant suffers least and the enemy most.*

The nineteenth section (which is a very long one) treats of the performance of the

(6) Though not stated in this its proper place, it is elsewhere mentioned, that the promotion of a *Sipahdár* was to be to the rank of *Sipah-sálár,* or commander (as it is explained) of two or three *Kushoons.*

(7) It would appear by this passage, that a *Kushoon* consisted, at this time, as well as in 1793, of four battalions, here called *Risálas,* but, at the latter period, *Teebs* or *Teeps.* See Appendix L.

the manual exercise by signals made with the sword and drum, instead of the word of command. The chief advantage of this mode consists, according to our author, " in its binding the mind, hands, eyes, and ears of the soldiers, to their " commanding officer;" that is to say, in its obliging them to attend carefully to him: " by which means," it is observed, " they learn the exercise much " sooner than by the other method."

The fourth chapter is divided into eighteen sections, which describe the duties of the variousranks of the army.

I. *The Sipahdár.*

1. The *Sipahdár* was to understand writing and accounts. He was to inspect narrowly into the conduct of all those under him, from the *Risáladár* to the *Yuzukdár*, or common soldier: to punish and remove such as misbehaved, and to promote such as merited advancement.(8) If a *Risáladár* appeared to him to deserve promotion, or the contrary, the *Sipahdár* was to make a faithful report of the circumstance to the *Sultan*. Other officers, to the *Jowkdár*, or captain, inclusive, when guilty of any offence, were to be brought to trial before *all* the officers of the *Risála* to which they belonged, and to be dealt with according to the decision of the assembly on the case. A *Risáladár*, on being convicted of any offence, was to be deprived, in the presence of all the officers of his corps, of his sword, which was to be lodged in the guard [room] of the corps, and the circumstances of the case to be reported to the Presence.

2. It was likewise the duty of the *Sipahdár*, in conjunction with the *Bukhshy* and *Mútusuddies* attached to his *Kushoon*, to take a muster, once in every month, of the men, firelocks, and accoutrements, belonging thereto. He was also, personally, to inspect into the state of their clothing and other necessaries; and, conjointly with the *Bukhshy* and *Mútusuddies*, to make a report of the same to the *Sultan*.

3. He was to pay particular attention to the state of the ordnance branch, as well as that of the firelocks of his *Kushoon*, and to take care that all the necessary and warlike apparatus and stores were kept in good order, and ready for service.

4. A *tolah* weight of oil was, every fifteen days, to be served out to the private men, for the purpose of enabling them to keep their arms in good condition.

5. When the *Kushoon* had a field day, the *Sipahdár* himself was to attend the parade, and give the word of command. He was constantly to exert himself to perfect

(8) I take the meaning of this passage to be, that the *Sipahdár* was to recommend those under his command for promotion, or otherwise, according to his opinion of their merits. Many things concur to throw considerable doubt on the fact of his having actually possessed the powers here apparently delegated to him.

perfect his men in their excercise, and was to be responsible for any deficiency which might appear in his corps in this respect.

6. If, on actual service, any material difficulty occurred, he was to consult his *Risáladárs* on the occasion; and, in the first instance, to state his own opinion, on the case. In the event of their differing from him, he was to require the opinion of each in writing, and to act according *to the general will.*

7. The standard of the *Sircar* was not to be moved backward and forward, but to remain on a march constantly under the immediate eye of the *Sipahdár,* and in charge of a guard belonging to the first *Risála.* When the corps took up its ground after a march, the standard was to be erected in the most secure part of the encampment.

8. He was to take care, that the troops under his command encamped in regular order, and that the proper guards were placed and relieved every twenty-four hours.

9. He was to give the guns, tumbrils, and ammunition stores, belonging to his *Kushoon,* in particular charge to the *Risáladárs,* who were to take care that every thing appertaining thereto was in constant readiness for service. If any repairs of the articles in question should be wanting, or if there should be any other deficiency in them, the said *Risáladárs* were immediately to report the same to their *Sipahdár,* who was to give directions for supplying what was necessary, and for the execution of the requisite repairs.

10. The guns and tumbrils were, on a march and in action, to be attached to the *Sipahdár's* own *Risála.*(9) When the corps was encamped, they were, in like manner, to be stationed, the guns in front, and the tumbrils in the rear of his *Risála.*

11. The *Sipahdár* was to recommend to the Presence a person properly qualified (and particularly in point of reading and writing) to fill the office of *Sur* (or *Head) Yusákchy* (or brigade-major). The duty of this officer will be described in the proper place.

II. *The Bukhshy and Mútusuddies.*

To each *Kushoon* was attached a *Bukhshy* and two *Mútusuddies,* one of whom (generally called a *Mirzdey Duftur)*(10) kept his books and accounts in Persian, and the other in Hindooy. Their duties were:

1. To muster the *Kushoon* on the twenty-seventh day of every month, in the presence

(9) It would appear, by this passage, if I have rightly understood it, that one of the *Risálas* of the *Kushoon* (probably that elsewhere called the first) was nominally commanded by the *Sipahdár.*

(10) The *Mirzáey Duftur* was always a Musulman. The *Bukhshy* seems, at this time, to have been nothing more than a paymaster or commissary. At a subsequent period the appellation was differently applied. See Appendix L.

presence of the *Sipahdár*, to whom they were, at the same time, to make a full report of every thing relating to the corps.

2. To take a separate muster of the *Kushoon* every two months in their own *Kuchurry;* which muster, however, was to be attended by the *Sipahdár*.

3. To make out, on the last day of every month, a just and faithful account of the pay due to the *Kushoon:* to deliver in the same on the following day (or first of every month) to the *Húzoor Kuchurry:* to receive the amount thereof from the said *Kuchurry:* and there to pay the same, in the presence of their *Sipahdár*, to the troops, delivering each man's pay into his own hands.[11]

4. It was also the duty of these officers to return, at the end of five days, to the *Húzoor Kuchurry*, the pay of all such men as had been drawn for, but had not been claimed (owing to the absence or neglect of the party entitled thereto) within the specified period.

5. Any failure in these duties was to be punished by removal from office.

III. *The Sur-Yusákchy (or Brigade Major) and the Yusákchies (or Adjutants).*

The duty of the former of these officers was to visit daily, but at no fixed hour, each *Risála* of the *Kushoon*, and to enquire of the adjutants *(Yusákchies)* and *Risáladárs* of the different *Risálas*, into the state of their respective corps. Having committed all the accounts, thus obtained, to writing, he was to wait upon his *Sipahdár*, and, *sitting down*, to communicate the same to him. He was then to attend the Presence, where he was to make a similar report: and, after that, he was required to repair to the *Jyshe Kuchurry* of the Presence, and there also *sitting down*, to furnish the same details, for the information of that office. The *Yusákchies*, or adjutants of *Risálas*, were to make their reports *standing;* but, on other occasions, might sit in the presence of their *Sipahdár* and of the *Húzoor Kuchurry*.[12] The several Adjutants were to accompany the Brigade-Major, when he attended the *Sultan* with his report. It was, furthermore, the duty of the *Sur*, or head *Yusákchy*, 1st. to convey daily the sign, or parole, to the *Sipahdár* and *Risáladárs* of his *Kushoon*. 2d. to attend parades and field days, and see that the men stood properly to their arms, and went through their exercise correctly, setting those right who might happen to be wrong. He was, 3dly, the channel of all orders from the *Sipahdár* to the different *Risáladárs* and *Jowkdárs* of the *Kushoon;* and,

(11) Original دستا بدست that is, "from hand to hand," or "man by man." It seems here supposed, that the *Kushoon* is stationed at the same place with the *Sultan*.

(12) That is, the *Kuchurry* of the Presence.

and, on service acted as an aid-de-camp to the former. 4th. When a *Yusákchy*(13) merited advancement, he was to be made a *Jowkdár*:(14) and when, on the other hand, he was to be degraded, it was to be to the rank of *Surkheel*.(14) 5th, and lastly, the *Yusákchy* (or adjutant) was to go round the quarters of the *Risálas* at unexpected times, and examining closely into the state of the men and arms, was, at the established orderly hours, to make his report of the same, *standing*, to his *Sipahdár*, to his *Risáladár*, and to the *Húzoor Kuchurry* of the *Jyshe*: after doing which he was at liberty *to seat himself*.

IV. *The Risáladár*.(15)

1. The *Risáladár* was, at all events, to be able to read and write: but in the selection of persons for that station, a preference was to be given to men of approved courage and prudence, and conversant in accounts.

2. During six days of the week, he was to consider himself as on constant duty, and to appear accoutred accordingly. He was to put his *Risála* through their exercise at the stated times. He was himself, also, to look closely into the conduct of those under him, and not to trust, in this matter, to the recommendations or complaints of the other officers. Having formed his own judgment of the merits and demerits of every one, he was to make his report accordingly to his *Sipahdár*, in order that the due rewards might be distributed, and the necessary punishments inflicted.

3. When the punishment, or removal, of any one (*i. e.* any officer) appeared necessary to him, he was to assemble all the officers of the *Risála* together, and direct them to examine strictly and impartially into the imputed charge: after which he was to report the result to the *Sipahdár*, who was to act accordingly.

4. There was to be no exercise on a Thursday, that day being set apart for an inspection of arms and necessaries.

5. A *Risáladár*, when deserving of promotion, was to be raised to the rank of *Sipahdár*. On the other hand, if it became necessary to degrade him, he was to be reduced to the station of a *Jowkdár*.

k V. *The*

(13) It is not clear whether the *Sur-yusákchy* or the *Yusákchy* (adjutant) be here meant. Perhaps both were intended.

(14) These ranks are explained, under articles 5 and 8.

(15) This is the order in which this officer stands in the original; but he certainly ought to have preceded the *Yusákchy*. The appellation of *Teebdár* was, at a subsequent period, substituted for that of *Risáladár*. See Appendix L.

V. *The Jowkdár.*[16]

He commanded a *Jowk* (or company) consisting, according to the original, of fifteen *Yuzuks*, which, from other passages, I conclude to be equivalent to ninety men; a *Yuzuk* appearing to have been composed of six rank and file. His rank corresponded with that of the *Soubadár*[17] of our *Sepoy* corps, and his duties were as follows:

1. He was to take a survey of his company once in every fifteen days.

2. When on guard, he was to take care that his men were constantly at their post, with the exception of two hours in the twenty-four, during which they were allowed to attend to their own concerns.

3. He was to report to his *Risáladár* the conduct of the officers under him; to point out those who were deserving of punishment or removal, and to recommend such as merited advancement.

4. He was to appoint a *Jumaadár* of the *Week*, or bell-tents,[18] who was to have the immediate superintendance of the arms and accoutrements of the company, which he was carefully to inspect [from time to time], and to keep in proper condition.

5. Whatever part of his company might be on guard, or on other duty, he was to visit the same once in twenty-four hours, and to see that the centinels and others were alert and vigilant.

6. In case of being guilty of any neglect of duty, his sword was to be taken from him, and lodged in the [quarter] guard, till such time as the charge against him should be duly enquired into: nor was the same to be restored to him without the orders of the *Sircar*.[19]

A *Jowkdár*, when sentenced to be degraded, was to be reduced to a *Surkheel*; and when promoted, was to be raised to the rank of a *Risáladár*.

VI. *The Surkheel.*[20]

This officer would appear to have answered, in point of rank, to the *Jumaadár* of our native corps in *India*. He was subject, however, to corporal punishment, which

(16) This officer was afterwards called *Yoozdár*. See Appendix L.

(17) It would not be easy to account satisfactorily for the name given to this officer, which properly signifies the governor or viceroy of a province. That of *Jowkdár* (the keeper or commander of a troop or body of men) is sufficiently appropriate. By *Yoozdár*, too, the *Sultan*, no doubt, meant to intimate that his soldiers resembled panthers.

(18) Original نجم (or *nujm)* which appears to have been a tent, in which the arms of the company were lodged. The men in charge of these tents were called *Nujm-wáleks.*

(19) It appears by this, as well as by other passages, that notwithstanding the power ostensibly vested in the *Sipahdár*, he, in fact, possessed very little. Thus he could not release an officer under him from arrest.

(20) Which means, "the head of a troop or body of men."

which the *Jumaadár* of *Sepoys* is not. When a guard to the amount of twenty-four men was on duty from his *Jowk*, he was to visit the same twice during the day, and as often during the night, and to see that the men did their duty properly. If he failed in his own, he was to receive fifty strokes of a cane,[21] and to be reduced to the rank of a *Jumaadár*. On the other hand, when deserving of promotion, he was to be made a *Jowkdár*.

VII. *The Jumaadár.*[22]

He seems to have answered, in most respects, with the *Havildár* of our *Sepoy* corps. If he neglected his duty, he was to be reduced to the rank of *Dufaadár*, and to receive two hundred and fifty strokes of a cane.[23] When deserving of promotion, he was to be raised to the station of *Surkheel*.

VIII. *The Dufaadár.*[24]

He may be compared with the *Naig* of the British native infantry of *India*. If he neglected relieving the centinels regularly every two hours, he was to be punished with two hundred strokes of a cane, and to be reduced to the ranks. It was his duty, when he placed sentries, to take proper notice of the nature of the ground, where they were posted, and particularly of the different avenues leading to it, to the end that, in case of any alarm or disturbance, he might not be at a loss how to proceed.[25] If he omitted this precaution, he was to receive one hundred and fifty strokes of a cane, and to be broke. He was to pay strict obedience to the orders of his *Jumaadár*; and, failing herein, he was to receive a hundred strokes, and to be reduced to the ranks. When meriting promotion, he was to be made a *Jumaadár*.

IX. *The Yuzukdárs.*

The word یزک *(yuzuk)* properly signifies a guard: it is also applied, in Tippoo Sultan's regulations, to a centinel's post, as well as to a specific number of men; that is, as I suppose, six rank and file. The word *Yuzukdár* would strictly mean a centinel;

k 2

(21) Original ضرب چوب literally, "strokes of a stick," but it is probable that a bamboo was used on these occasions.

(22) That is, "the keeper, or commander, of an assemblage of men."

(23) There is, probably, some mistake in the number of strokes mentioned in this place; since there is no reason why the *Jumaadár* should have been more severely punished than his inferior officer, the *Dufaadár*.

(24) Meaning, perhaps, "the commander of repellers."

(25) The original is not, in this place, perfectly intelligible to me. I have given the best interpretation of it I could.

centinel; but it appears to have been likewise used to denote a private soldier, or rank and file in general.

If the *Yuzukdár* sat down, or neglected to move about, while posted as a centinel, he was to receive a hundred strokes of a cane. If he was found sleeping, or if any thing under his charge was stolen during his guard, he was to be punished with five hundred strokes. He was to render strict obedience to the *Dufaadár*; and, failing herein, he was to receive a hundred strokes. When judged deserving of promotion, he was to be made a *Dufaadár*.

The five following sections treat of the manner of mounting and relieving guards, and other ordinary details.

The fifteenth section specifies the salutes to which the different officers of the army were entitled from guards and centries. On this occasion, a *Meer Bukhshy* is for the first time mentioned, and he appears to have taken precedence of the *Sipahdár*. Thus, when the *Meer Bukhshy* passed either the advanced or rear guard, a *Surkheel*, at the head of four *Yuzuks* (or twenty-four rank and file) was to turn out and salute him: whereas, to a *Sipahdár*, a *Jumaadár* and two *Yusuks* (or twelve rank and file) only, were to turn out. Neither of them was to be saluted upon coming on parade. The *Risáladár* was entitled to no more than presented arms from sentinels. No officer whatsoever was to be saluted after sunset: nor were the superior ranks, above-mentioned, to receive the specified compliments, if they appeared without their gorgets *(puduks)*.

The sixteenth section relates to the furloughs to be granted to the men and officers when in quarters. The furlough was not to exceed two months. Desertion, in time of peace, was to be punished with a thousand strokes of the cane; but in time of war, the culprit was to be shot, in front of the *Risála* to which he belonged. If a soldier deserted to the enemy, and was afterwards taken, he was to be hanged. A soldier running away in face of the enemy, was, on being apprehended, to be punished as above (that is, I suppose, to be hung). If through any neglect of the *Sipahdár*, *Risáladárs*, or *Jowkdárs*, the fugitive escaped, *the punishment appointed for him was to be inflicted on those officers.*[26]

The eighteenth section specifies the different occasions on which salutes of ordnance were to be fired. The anniversary of the *Sultan's* birth-day (14th *Tálooey*, A. H. 1165), and of his accession to the *Musnud* (or the 3d of *Beháry*, A. H. 1197), were each to be celebrated by a salute of thirty-one guns, which seems to have constituted the royal salute. The several *Eeds*, or holy festivals, were

(26) It is hardly credible, that this rigorous regulation was meant to be actually enforced. It was probably made only *in terrorem*.

were honoured with no more than twenty-one guns, which was also the number appointed to be fired on any victory obtained by the *Sultan* in person.

The fifth chapter treats chiefly of the different establishments of the army; and among the rest, of the *Uskur* (or regular) cavalry, and the artillery branches: for both of which various rules and manœuvres, of no particular interest, are given.(27) It is introduced by some regulations regarding promotion, which are little more than a repetition of what is stated in the fourth chapter. There is one article, however, on this subject, which deserves to be noticed. It is expressed in words to this effect: "whatever any person's reputation for gallantry or talents may be, "it is not proper that he should be at once advanced to high station: it is necessary that he should arrive thereat step by step. This difference may, however, "be made between men of superior endowments and those of ordinary merit: "while the latter must be suffered to remain a long time in their respective "stations, let the former be advanced rapidly through the established ranks of "the service."

I reserve what I have to offer on the various establishments of the army for the Appendix L.: because they are by no means so minutely or so clearly detailed in the *Futhûl Mûjâhideen* as in some other documents of a later date, which I had only cursorily examined, when the former part of the present work went to press, or I should have been enabled to give a more satisfactory explanation of several military terms occurring in the correspondence, than it was in my power to do at the time I translated the latter.

APPENDIX, K

(Referred to at LETTER *CC).*

MARINE REGULATIONS

The *Hûkm-nâmeh,* or ordinance, for the marine department, of which I propose, in this place, to give an abstract, is addressed, generally, to the *Meer Yumms,* without any specification of the persons so denominated, but stating their number to be eleven.

The *Meer Yumms,* (or marine lords, as the term may be rendered) composed a board of admiralty, ordinarily resident at the capital; but, together with all the other

(27) No account, however, is given of the number of corps (of either description) composing the army.

other public boards, ambulatory, I believe, with the court.(1) This department was instituted in the month of *Jaafury* of the year 1224 from the birth of Mahommed (or in September 1796), before which time the naval establishments of the state appear to have been placed under the direction of the *Mulikût Tújârs*, or board of commerce.

Next in rank to the *Meer Yumms* were the *Meer Buhrs*, which last term is, in fact, synonimous with the other. The *Meer Buhrs*, however, were officers destined to serve afloat, two of them being assigned to a squadron of four ships of war: they corresponded, therefore, with our admirals or commodores. I have said that they were *destined* to serve at sea, because, fortunately, perhaps, for the security of the British possessions in *India*, the *Sultan's* project, as detailed in the present article, for creating a great naval force, was nipped in the bud by the sudden subversion of his throne, within less than three years from the date of its conception. It may possibly be thought, that, even if he had remained at peace with the English, the resources of his country would have proved utterly inadequate to the formation and maintenance of so extensive a marine as was in his contemplation; and that, at all events, opposed to *Great-Britain*, he could never have become formidable as a maritime power. Without stopping to examine the grounds of the former supposition, and entirely admitting the justness of the latter, it may nevertheless be contended, that in proportion as the *Sultan* might have been able to realize his alarming plan of a marine establishment, we should, as a measure of necessary precaution, have been compelled to augment, at a heavy expence, our naval force in *India*, for the purpose of duly watching his armaments, and of keeping them in constant check. This evil, at least, was averted, by the issue of the war of 1799.

The ordinance which we are at present considering sets out with anouncing, "that forty ships of war were thereby consigned to the care and superintendance "of those to whom it was addressed." But it appears, from the sequel, that nothing more was meant by this, than that the *Meer Yumms* were to have charge of the ships alluded to, as soon as they should be built; for, as yet, they were not in existence. They were, however, to be constructed with all possible dispatch; and, when finished, were to be named agreeably to a list contained(2) in the instructions, but with which it would be useless to trouble the reader.

The

(1) Some of the members of this board, as will be presently seen, were occasionally stationed at the principal sea-ports, or dock-yards.

(2) According to the list here referred to, there were to have been forty-one instead of forty ships: the model, mentioned in the text, being, perhaps, included in the number. One was to be called *Sultan bukhsh*; another *Ali bukhsh*; a third, *Mohammed-bukhsh*, &c. but no *Hyder-bukhsh* appears among them. All the names terminate with the word *bukhsh*, signifying, in composition, "the gift "of," or "bestowed by."

The ships were formed into three divisions, under the denomination of *Kuchurries*, or departments, namely: 1. The *Kuchurry* of *Jumálábád*; 2. The *Kuchurry* of *Wájidábád* (or *Buscoraje*(3)); and 3. The *Kuchurry* of *Májidábád* (or *Sudásheeoghur*).

The *Kuchurry* of *Jumálábád* (sometimes called, also, the *Kuchurry of Kúriál* or *Mangalore*) was to consist of .... 12 ships
that of *Wájidábád* of .... 14 d°.
and that of *Májidábád* of .... 14 d°.

With a view to expediting the formation of this embryo fleet, two *Meer Yumms*, assisted by a *Mirzdey Duftur* and a *Mútusuddy*, were to be established at *Mangalore*, from whence they were to superintend the building of the vessels intended to be attached to the *Jumálábád* station. Two other *Meer Yumms*, together with a *Mirzdey Duftur* and a *Mútusuddy*, were to be resident, in like manner, at or near *Mirján Creek*,(4) for the purpose of directing the construction and equipment of the ships of the *Wájidábád* and *Májidábád* divisions. The places (or docks) to be fixed on for the building of the different ships were to be near, but not absolutely contiguous, to each other.(5)

The board of admiralty was furnished with the model of a ship of war,(6) having a lion or tyger head: according to which model all the vessels allotted to the different naval stations were to be built. The whole of them were, moreover, to be coppered; and the utmost care was to be taken, to render them complete in all respects.

The timber which might be required in the construction of the vessels in question, was to be cut down, under the direction of persons appointed for the purpose, by the *Meer Yumms*, in the forests where ship timber was usually procured:

(3) This is the name given by Colonel Beatson as the synonyme of *Wájidábád*. I am ignorant of its situation.

(4) Sometimes called *Mirjee* or *Merjee*. It is situated about thirty-four miles S. S. E. of *Shudásheeoghur*; but its distance from *Buscoraje* I cannot ascertain, the latter place not appearing in our maps.

(5) Original نزديک نزديک عليحده جاي مقرر كرده of the right meaning of which I am extremely doubtful. The sense may be that which I have given in the text: but the words may also be understood to import, that though the docks for the three different divisions were to be near each other, they were, nevertheless, to be considered as entirely distinct and separate.

(6) Original يک جهاز خورد شيردهان براي نمونه از حضور داده شده است literally, "a little ship, with "a lion mouth, has been given by the Presence, for a pattern or model;" which may either mean, a miniature model in ivory or wood, or a vessel constructed on a small scale, for the double purpose of going to sea, and of serving as a model for the ships ordered to be built.

procured: from whence it was to be floated, by means of the adjacent rivers, to the respective dock-yards.

Of the ships to be built, twenty were to be line of battle, and twenty large frigates, according to the following detail.[7]

I. *On the Jumálábád Station.*

6 Line of battle Ships, *viz.*

3 of 72 guns each, and
3 .. 62 .. d°

The 72's were to mount 30 guns, twenty-four pounders
30 .... eighteen.... d°
6 .... twelve...... d°
6 .... nine ...... d°

The 62's were to mount 24 guns, eighteen.... d°
24 .... twelve...... d°
4 .... twenty-four.. d°
10 .... six .... d°

6 Frigates, of 46 guns each, *viz.*

20 guns, twelve pounders
20 .... nine.... d°
6 .... four.... d°

II. *On the Wájidábád Station.*

7 Line of battle Ships, *viz.*

3 of 72 guns each } as before.
4 .. 62 .. d°.... }

7 Frigates, of 46 .. d°.... as before.

III. *On the Májidábád Station.*

7 Line of battle Ships, *viz.*

4 of 72 guns each
3 .. 62 .. d°

7 Frigates, .. 46 .. d° .. as before.

The

(7) Two years before the date of the present ordinance, or some time in 1794, the *Sultan* had directed the following ships to be built: at *Jumálabád*, six, from eighty to eighty-five guns, and six (two masted) grabs, of from twenty-five to thirty guns; and at *Wájidábád* and *Májidábád*, each seven, from eighty to eighty-five guns, and seven grabs as above: total line of battle ships, twenty; grabs or small frigates, twenty. Possibly the alteration now made in his original plan may have been suggested by Ripaud, or some other French adventurer.

The establishment of officers to the foregoing fleet was to be as follows:

11 *Meer Yumms* (Pay to be according to their respective qualifications.)

30 *Meer Buhrs, viz.*

Stationed to ships (being two to every *Fouj*, or squadron, of four ships.).... 20

At the Presence, for instruction, ... 10

The first class (or twenty) of the *Meer Buhrs*, were to receive a monthly pay of 150 *Imaumies*, or *rupees*, including an allowance for a horse.(8)

The *Meer Buhrs* attending the Presence, for the purpose of instruction, were to be paid according to their respective merits.(9)

The land establishment of the *Kuchurries* was fixed as follows:(10)

		Ráhities, or *Pagodas.*	*Fanams.*
3	*Mirzáey Dufturs*, (including horse) each	20	0
3	Hindooy Writers ...... d°. .... d°.	20	0
12	*Gúmáhstehs* .... d°.	15	0
1	*Kázy*	12	0
2	*Nukeebs* (11) .... d°.	12	0
11	*Házirbáshies*(11) .... d°..	3	3
11	*Sherbashurns*(11) (able to read and write) d°.	10	0
1	*Furrásh* (12)	3	0
1	*Mushálchy* (or link-boy)	2	0
1	*Sárbán*, or *Surván*, in charge of two camels, allotted for the carriage of the stores or baggage of the *Kuchurry*	3	0

The establishment of officers to each ship of the line was fixed as follows:

4 *Surdárs* (or officers), denominated first, second, third, and fourth.

1

2 *Teepdárs*

(8) Original معه راس Horse allowance to a naval officer seems so strange a thing, that I should feel doubtful of understanding the term rightly, if it did not occur frequently in stating the allowances of land officers, and every where appears to bear the signification assigned to it in the text.

(9) It does not appear by what means these admirals were to be instructed in naval tactics, or other duties, at *Seringapatam*.

(10) There is a want of distinctness in the statement which follows here; for it is doubtful whether the establishment detailed was intended for one *Kuchurry* only, or for all three. As, however, one *Kázy*, one *Furrásh*, one *Mushálchy*, &c. could not have sufficed for three *Kuchurries*, I conclude that the establishment in question, as far, at least, as related to those employments, was that of a single *Kuchurry*.

(11) I am ignorant of the nature of these employments.

(12) The *Furrásh* has charge of the camp equipage and carpets.

2 *Teepdârs*[13]

6 *Yoozdârs.*[14]

The inferior officers will be stated hereafter.

Of these, the first *Surdâr* was to command the whole.

The second officer,[15] with one *Teepdâr*, and two *Yoozdârs* under him, was to superintend the great guns, and gunners, belonging to the ship. He was, moreover, to have the care of the powder magazine, of the shot, and, in fine, of every thing appertaining to the guns. He was also to have charge of the provisions, which he was to see served out at stated times.

The third officer,[16] with one *Teepdâr* and two *Yoozdârs* under him, was to have the direction of the marines and small arms, and whatever related to this branch of the equipment. To his charge, moreover, were to be consigned all the spare tools, implements, &c.[17] or those kept in store for future use or consumption.[18]

The fourth officer[19] was to have particular charge of the *Khulâsies,* or sailors, and of the artificers belonging to the ship, as the smiths, carpenters, &c. It was also his business to superintend the cooking of the victuals of the crew, and to see the same duly distributed among them. The navigation of the ship appears to have been immediately entrusted to him; since it is said, that the orders for hoisting and trimming the sails, &c. were to proceed from him. He had likewise charge of all the tools and implements in immediate use, which he was to keep in good condition and repair. He was also, occasionally, to place under the orders of the second officer, whatever number of sailors the latter might require, for the purpose of assisting in the management of the guns. He was to employ the carpenters and smiths in making up such articles in their respective departments as were likely to be required, at some future time, for the ship's use. "If, on any occasion," continues the ordinance "*which God avert!* a cannon shot should "strike the ship," it was the business of the fourth officer to see the damage instantly repaired. He was, finally, to superintend the pumps, &c.[20]

All

(13) I am uncertain whether this word should be pronounced *Teeb* or *Teepdâr.*

(14) The number of *Yoozdârs* has been inadvertently omitted in the original; but I have supplied it from the subsequent detail.

(15) He corresponded, in point of rank, with the first lieutenant of our ships of war.

(16) Or second lieutenant.

(17) Original آلات و اوزار by which, perhaps, the general furniture or equipage of the ship is meant.

(18) Original آلات و اوزار و غيره عاقبتي يعني زيادتي

(19) Answering to our third lieutenant.

(20) The duties of the several officers belonging to the frigates, though not stated in the original, may be presumed to have been the same as those assigned to the officers of the line of battle ships.

All the foregoing officers were to be selected with care; and none but such as were well descended on both sides, were to be employed. It was, moreover, required, that they should all be able to read and write.

The *Sepoys*, or troops, serving on board, were, on no account, to be suffered to trade, "*not even to the extent of a single Imaumy* (or *rupee*)."

I. *Detailed Establishment of each line of battle Ship.*

Twenty ships, each having 346 men of all denominations on board, Total 6,920

1st Musqueteers:

(1 *Teep* of *Uskur*, of 124 men, or 4 *Yooz*.)

Staff:

		Pagodas	Fanams
1 *Teepdár*, pay 7 *pagodas* 8 *fanams*: subsistence calculated on 120 men, at 1 *fanam* each[21]	Pagodas 12 =	19	8
1 *Shurbashurn*		4	8
1 *Nufeer-nuwdz*[22]		3	6
1 *Shahndey-nuwdz*[22]		3	6
Monthly pay of the staff		31	8

4 *Yooz*, each *Yooz* consisting of 30 men, *viz*.

1 *Yoozdár*, pay 4 *pagodas* 2 *fanams*: subsistence 3 *pagodas* $6\frac{1}{4}$ *fanams*, calculated on 29 men		7	$8\frac{1}{4}$
1 *Surkheel*		4	8
4 *Jumaadárs*, pay 3 *pagodas* 6 *fanams*: subsistence 6 *fanams*, calculated on 6 men	P. 4 P. 2 =	16	8
24 Privates, pay 3 *pagodas* 6 *fanams* each		86	4
One *Yooz*		115	$8\frac{1}{4}$
Four *Yooz*		463	3
Staff		31	8

	Pagodas	Fanam
Total pay of one *Teep*	495	1

I 2

(21) The subsistence (or *rusud*, as it is called in the original) was an extra allowance granted to the officers, and calculated upon the number of men actually on the strength of their respective divisions. It varied from half a *fanam* to two *fanams* per man. This allowance operated as a stimulus to the officers to keep their corps as complete as possible.

(22) I am not clear whether *both* these are meant for trumpeters of different kinds, or whether one of them may not have been a fifer.

	Pagodas	Fanam
Brought forward	495	1

2d Gunners:

(1 *Teep* of 79 men, or 2 *Yooz* of 39 men each, each to carry a musquet.)

	Pagodas	Fanams
1 *Teepdâr*, pay 9 *pagodas* 1½ *fanam*: subsistence 7 *pagodas* 8 *fanams*, calculated on 78 men, at 1 *fanam*	16	9½

2 *Yooz*, each 39 men, *viz.*

	P. F.	Pagodas	Fanams
1 *Yoozdâr*, pay 4 *pagodas* 4 *fanams*: subsistence 4 *pagodas* 7 *fanams*, calculated on 38 men, at 1¼ *fanam*		9	1½
2 *Surkheels*, pay 4 *pagodas* 8 *fanams* each (23)		9	6
4 *Jumaaddrs*, pay 3 *pagodas* 6 *fanams* each: subsistence 8 *fanams*, calculated on 8 men	4 4	17	6
32 Privates, at 3 *pagodas* 6 *fanams* each		115	2
One *Yooz*		151	5½
Two *Yooz*		303	1
Add *Teepdâr*		16	9½

	Pagodas	Fanams
Total pay of 1 *Teep* of gunners	320	0½

3d Seamen:

(2 *Jowks*, or *Gangs*, of 61 men.)

	Pagodas	Fanams
1 *Jowkdâr*, pay 3 *pagodas*: subsistence 3 *pagodas*, calculated on 60 men, at ½ *fanam* each	6	0
6 *Dufaadârs*, pay 3 *pagodas*: subsistence 9 *fanams* each	23	4
54 Privates, from 21 to 30 *fanams* each, calculated at 3 *pagodas* each	162	0
One *Jowk*	191	4

	Pagodas	Fanams
Two *Jowks*	382	8
Carried forward	1,197	9½

(23) It is observable, that the *Surkheel* (or lieutenant) received only four *fanams* a month more than the *Jumaadâr* (or serjeant), and the latter only eight *fanams* a month more than the *privates*.

	Pagodas.	Fanams.	Pagodas.	Fanams.
Brought forward			1,197	9½
4th Artificers:				
1 Head carpenter, pay 3 *pagodas:* subsistence 1 *pagoda*	4	0		
1 d.° smith, pay 3 *pagodas:* subsistence 6 *fanams*	3	6		
5 Carpenters, 3 Smiths } pay 3 *pagodas* each	24	0		
			31	6
5th Officers of the Staff;(24)				
First *Sirdár* (or officer), pay 80 *Imaumies,* or *rupees,* of three *fanams* each (including horse); being *Ráhities,* or *Cantarai pagodas*	24	0		
Second *Sirdár,* 60 *rupees* (no horse allowed)	18	0		
Third .. d.° .. 50 .. d.° .... (d.°)	15	0		
Fourth .. d.° .. 50 .. d.° .... (d.°)	15	0		
Staff:				
3 Pilots, from 100 to 150 *rupees* each, calculated at 150 *rupees* (or 45 *pagodas*)	135	0		
2 *Dároghas,* viz.				
1 in charge of the water, provisions, &c. of the ship: pay 7½ *pagodas.*				
1 in charge of tools, implements, and articles in store: pay 7½ *pagodas*	15	0		
1 Physician and surgeon (in one)	9	0		
1 *Mirzdey Duftur,* to keep the accounts of the ship, and also of the troops or marines	11	0		
			242	0
Total monthly expence of a line of battle ship, while in port, including 346 persons of all denominations			1,471	5½
Expence of twenty line of battle ships			29,431	0

II. *Establishment*

(24) This is the order in which the pay and allowances of this class are stated in the original ordinance (now before me), and which, though, according to our practice, out of place, I have not thought it necessary to disturb.

II. *Establishment of each Frigate.*

	Men.
Twenty ships, each having 180 men, of all denominations, on board. Total	3,600

1st Musqueteers:

(1 *Teep* of *Uskur*, of 64 men) *viz.*

	Pagodas.	*Fanams.*		
1 *Teepdár*, pay 7 *pagodas* 8 *fanams*: subsistence 6 *pagodas*, calculated on 60 men, at 1 *fanam* each..	13	8		
Staff:				
1 *Shurbashurn*........................	4	8		
1 *Nufeer-nuwáz*........................	3	6		
1 *Shahnaey-nuwáz*........................	3	6		
			25	8
The above *Teep* being composed of 2 *Yooz*, of 30 men each, *viz.*				
1 *Yoozdár*, pay 7 *pagodas* 8¼ *fanams*....	7	8¼		
1 *Surkheel*........................	4	8		
4 *Jumaadárs*, 4 *pagodas* 2 *fanams* each...........	16	8		
24 Privates, 3 *pagodas* 6 *fanams* each	86	4		
One *Yooz* -	115	8¼		
Two *Yooz* -			231	6½

2d Gunners:

(1 *Yooz* of 29 men, *viz.*)

1 *Yoozdár*, pay 4 *pagodas* 4 *fanams*: subsistence 3 *pagodas* 5 *fanams*, calculated on 28 men, at ¼ *fanam* each	7	9		
1 *Surkheel*, pay........................	4	8		
3 *Jumaadárs*, pay 3 *pagodas* 6 *fanams*: subsistence 8 *fanams*, or 4 *pagodas* 4 *fanams* each.........	13	2		
24 Privates, at 3 *pagodas* 6 *fanams* each	86	4		
			112	3

3d Seamen:

(1 *Jowk*, or Gang, of 71 men.)

1 *Jowkdár*, pay 3 *pagodas*: subsistence 3 *pagodas* 5 *fanams*, calculated on 70 men, at ½ *fanam* each	6	5		
7 *Dufaadárs*, pay 3 *pagodas* each: subsistence 9 *fanams*, calculated on 9 men, at 1 *fanam* each........... } P. 3 F. 9 ea. =	27	3		
63 Privates, from 21 to 30 *fanams* each: calculated at 3 *pagodas*........................	189	0		
			222	8
Carried forward			592	5½

			Pagodas.	Fanams.
Brought forward			592	$5\frac{1}{2}$
4th Artificers:				
2 Smiths } 2 Carpenters }			19	0
5th Officers and Staff:				
First Officer, pay 80 *Imaumies,* or *rupees,* (including horse)..	24	0		
Second d°. .. 60 *rupees* (without horse)............	18	0		
Third d°. .. 50..d°. ......(d°.)	15	0		
Fourth d°. .. 50..d°. ... ...(d°.)	15	0		
			72	0
Staff:				
2 Pilots, at from 100 to 150 *rupees,* or 45 *pagodas* each	90	0		
2 *Dároghas,* at $7\frac{1}{2}$ *pagodas* each	15	0		
1 Physician and Surgeon (in one)..................	9	0		
1 *Mirzdey Duftur*................................	11	0		
			125	0
Total monthly expence of a frigate while in port			808	5

Expence of twenty frigates.....................	16,171 *pagodas*
Add twenty line of battle Ships.................	29,431
Total monthly expence of forty ships in port, exclusive of wear and tear, ammunition, stores, &c.	45,602 *Cantarai pagodas*
Or nearly..........................	38,000 *Star pagodas*
Being, at eight shillings the *Star pagoda,*.....	£15,200 *sterling*
Or, per annum	£182,400 (25)

The above pay and allowances were to be received by the men and officers when on shore. When afloat, or embarked, they were, in addition thereto, to receive the rations to be presently stated.

As a *Meer Yumm* might be occasionally employed with the fleet, it was ordered, that, in such cases, " a particularly good dinner, together with fruit," should be daily provided; the expence of which was to be defrayed by government.

All

(25) The most striking defect in the foregoing establishment consists in the insufficiency of the number of seamen allotted to ships of such force; as it would not appear that any augmentation of the crews was intended during actual service.

All the officers were to eat together. The following were the persons to whom rations were to be issued when afloat:

1 *Meer Yumm*,
1 *Meer Buhr*,
4 *Sirdárs*,
1 *Mirzdey Duftur*,
3 Pilots,
2 *Dároghas*,
1 Physician and Surgeon.
—
13
—

To the above officers the following daily rations were to be served out:

Rice.................... ¾ of a full *Duk*, or *Seer*.
Dál (or split peas)........ ¼.... d°.
Ghee.................... 8 *Jouz* weight.(26)
Meat .... ½ short *Duk*, or *Seer*.
Salt..................... 3 *Jouz* weight.
Tamarinds .... 2.... d°.
Turmeric.......... ..... ½. .. d°.
Dry Garlic............... ½.... d°.
Onions .... 1½ .. d°.
Coriander seed........... ¼. .. d°.
Black pepper............. 1.... d°.

The following were the rations to be issued to the Musqueteers and Gunners; no distinction being made between men and officers:

Rice..................... 1 *Duk*, or *Seer*.
Dál..................... 6 *Jouz* weight.
Ghee .... 4.... d°.
Salt........ .... 2.... d°.
Tamarinds .... 2.... d°.
Turmeric .... ½.... d°.
Dry Garlic............... ½ .. d°.
Onions .... 1½ .. d°.
Coriander seed .... ¼.... d°.
Black pepper............. 1.... d°.

Besides

(26) That is, the weight of eight nutmegs.

Besides the above rations, it would appear that meat prepared with spices, and roasted (or made into *Kubábs*), was to be kept in store, and served out once in every fifteen days, at the rate of a quarter of a *short Seer* per man.[27] The meat in question was to be cured or prepared with salt, ginger, turmeric, and black pepper.

The seamen were each to be allowed daily

¾ of a full *Seer* of Rice,
¼ of .... d° .... *Dál*,
2 *Jouz* weight of *Ghee*,
2....... d° .... Salt.

They were to supply themselves with spices. Whether they were to partake, every fifteen days, of the *Kubábs* above-mentioned, is uncertain.

The several officers of the marines and seamen were to see that their men had their appointed meals, *before they took their own.*

Prayers were to be performed every day, at the five appointed times. The first officer, or commander, was to officiate as priest on such occasions, and to deliver the appointed *Waaz*, or discourse; and the *Dároghas* to recite the five prayers.

During the rainy season, the ships were to be laid up in the creek (probably *Mirján Creek)*, where they were to be placed under cover of sheds to be constructed for the purpose; the necessary materials for which sheds were to be furnished by the *Asofs* of the adjacent districts. The seamen were to be employed in this service.

After mentioning that orders had been issued for the erection of two forts and some batteries at *Háfiz-Hisár* (commonly called *Beed-kole*, or *Batcul)*, the *Meer Yumms* were directed, by the present ordinance, to examine carefully the ground in the vicinity of the aforesaid place, and having pitched upon proper spots for the works in question, to make a plan or drawing of the same, and transmit it to the Presence. They were to direct their particular attention to the two hills, or rocks, which would appear to form the entrance of the creek, or harbour, and to ascertain the exact distance between them, as well as the extent of the channel, or strait, formed by them. The depth of water, and the number of ships which might lie at anchor *between these hills*, were likewise to be ascertained and reported; when, "*with the blessing of God,*" forts and batteries were to be erected there.

A ship, named the *Fukhur úl Murákib*, is stated to be then lying in *Mirján Creek*; and another, called the *Futah Múbáruk*, in the creek at *Hunáwar*

m (*Onore*):

(27) Original گوشت را مصالح داده کباب تیار کرده باید داشت

(Onore): both of them past repair. These ships were directed to be broken up with due care, and the iron, and other materials, obtained from them, to be used in the new ships ordered to be built.

Twelve small vessels, denominated *Nugs*, or *Nuks*, were, moreover, delivered, on the present occasion, in charge to the *Meer Yumms*. Of these, ten were galliots; five of them being at *Mangalore*, and five at *Onore*. Of the remaining two, one is called an *Usud-Ilhye* grab; and the other, a small *Usud-Ilhye* ship. The marines, and *other people*, belonging to the ships (*i. e.* I suppose, the crews which were destined for the vessels ordered to be built) were to be embarked upon these *Nugs*, which were to sail about the coast, in order that the men might thereby be duly trained in their respective duties. With the same view, it was directed that a kind of buoy should be anchored in some convenient situation, and a flag erected thereon, to serve as a mark for practising with great guns; in the management of which those attached to them were to be carefully instructed.

It is next observed, that if green wood be cut up according to the required dimensions, it will, when dry, be found to fall short of those dimensions. To avoid this inconvenience, it was directed, that the timber, after being felled and barked, should be kept one or two years; and when perfectly seasoned, be cut up, agreeably to the proposed standard.

The men required for the service of the fleet were, after being mustered *in the Presence*,(28) and *duly sworn*, to be dispatched to their respective destinations, as fast as they were entertained.

The accounts of the expenditure of the ships and crews, and of whatever related thereto, were to be carefully and minutely kept by the *Meer Yumms* and the *Asofs* of the provincial *Kuchurries* (having any connection with this branch of the service) in conjunction with each other. The movements and warlike operations of the fleet were, likewise, to be directed conjointly by the *Meer Yumms* and the aforesaid *Asofs*. If the *Sultan* should, at any time, wish to employ the ships on any particular service against an enemy, he would issue his orders for the purpose in full council, or assembly, of the ministers of state.(29)

The *Meer Yumms* had it in charge to station two *Yuzuks* (or twelve men) with a *Yoozdár* of the regular troops belonging to their department, at each of the *Kohties*, or factories, established, " by the favor of God," at *Muscat* and *Kutch*; and which are

(28) It would seem by this passage, if strictly understood, that no men were to be entertained for the service of the navy but at *Seringapatam*. It is not certain, however, that this was the meaning of the original.

(29) Original رو بروي هر شش فرقه رياست حكم و احكام فرموده خواهد شد literally, " the orders [for " the purpose] will be delivered in face [or presence] of all the six departments of government:" meaning, as I conclude, 1, the Military; 2, the Revenue; 3, the *Sudoor*, or Ordnance (including garrisons and fortifications); 4, the Commercial; 5, the Treasury; and 6, the Marine.

are said, on this, as well as on a former occasion, to be *four* in number, namely, two at *Muscat* and two at *Kutch*. The pay of these guards was to be issued by the *Mirzdey Dufturs* of the aforesaid factories, to whom the *Meer Yumms* were to make the necessary remittances for the purpose. The guards in question were to be relieved annually.[30]

The *Meer Yumms*, *Meer Buhrs*, and *Serishtedárs*, attached to the three several *Kuchurries* (or naval stations) of *Jumálábád*, *Wájidábád*, and *Májidábád*, were to repair, in the month of *Ziljhijjeh* of every year, and ten days before the *Eed*, or festival, celebrated in that month, to *Seringapatam*; there to deliver to the Presence an account of their respective receipts and disbursements, and to report the progress made at their respective stations, in the preparation of the vessels ordered to be built. The officers belonging to the ships, together with the several *Teepdárs*, the *Mirzdey Dufturs*, and the *Dároghas*, were, in like manner, to repair every year, ten days before the *Eed* of *Rumuzán*, to the capital, for the purpose of delivering their respective accounts, and of reporting the state of their respective departments to the Presence.

To the foregoing ordinance is subjoined a supplementary section, dated 24th of *Tukky*, year *Sáz*, or A.M. 1225,[31] containing a detailed statement of the establishment of artificers appointed for the service of the three dock-yards of *Jumálábád*, *Wájidábád*, and *Májidábád*, of which the following is an abstract.

	Men.	*Monthly Pay and Subsistence. Cantarai Pagodas.*
Carpenters (including three *Chowdries* and twelve *Dufaadárs*, and divided into twelve gangs of ten men, inclusive of one *Dufaadár*	123	316
Smiths (including two *Chowdries* and four *Dufaadárs*) and divided in like manner into four gangs of eight men each, inclusive of one *Dufaadár*..	34	94
Total artificers to each dock-yard........	157	410
Three dock-yards	471	1,230
Being per annum .... *Cantarai pagodas*		14,760
Or *Star pagodas*		12,300

m 2

(30) The twelfth section of the present ordinance follows here; and, though having no apparent relation to the general subject of that ordinance, is too curious to be passed unnoticed. Its object is to prohibit the practices of rising, for the purpose of receiving or saluting any one; of shaking or kissing hands; and of embracing upon meeting: all of which are declared to be odious customs, and contrary to the commands of the Prophet. It concludes with directing, that as all reciters of the *Kulmah* (*i. e.* all true believers) were brethren (or equal), they shall desist from these unlawful practices (excepting in the case of sovereigns, whom it is always fitting to approach with reverence), and to confine their mutual salutations to the compliment of *Us-sulám ulee kúm*, "peace be with you," and its response, *Ulee kúm us-sulám*, "to you be peace."

(31) Corresponding with June 1797.

which, at eight shillings the *Star pagoda*, makes .... £4,920 sterling
If this sum be added to £182,400
the annual amount of the pay and allowances of the officers, marines, and seamen, we shall have, for the total annual fixed charges of the marine (exclusive of provisions, and the salaries of the *Meer Yumms*, not specified.) .... } £187,320

APPENDIX, L.

(*Referred to at* LETTER CCLXX.)

An OUTLINE *of* TIPPOO SULTAN'S MILITARY ESTABLISHMENTS.

I propose, in the present article, to give such a general idea of the formation and amount of the late Tippoo Sultan's army (but particularly of the regular part of it) as the materials in my possession enable me to furnish: and although the scantiness of these does not admit of my rendering the account so complete as I could wish, I nevertheless trust, that it will, on the whole, be found to be tolerably accurate, as well as sufficiently minute, for the gratification of literary curiosity; which is now the chief, if not the only, purpose it can answer.

The documents from which I have formed this statement consist of: 1, A *Húkmnámeh*, or ordinance, dated the 14th of *Ahmedy*, year *Sáhir*, or A.M. 1221,(1) and addressed to the *Meer Meerán*, or military department;(2) and 2, Some rough memoranda

(1) Corresponding with the 25th of March 1793.

(2) Consisting, at this time, of, 1, Budrûz Zumân Khân; 2, Mahommed Rizâ (the Binky Nabob); 3, Syed Mahommed; 4, Purnia; and 5, Meer Násir Ali. The name of the latter is inserted in the *Sultan's* own hand-writing.

The *Húkm-námeh*, here mentioned, is bound up, together with five others, addressed to as many different departments of the government, in a thick volume, the cover of which is curiously stamped with the names of Mahommed and of the four *Caliphs*, his immediate successors, surmounted by the words "*Sircar e Khodádády*," or "the state founded or bestowed by God." Many parts of the manuscript are in the *Sultan's* own hand; and every article of the regulations or instructions of which it consists, is separately attested by his usual signature, "*Nubby Málik*," which has been already explained. It likewise contains a great number of blank leaves, designed for the insertion of occasional additions to the articles forming the several ordinances. Many such additions accordingly appear, under the title of "supplement to such an article." The document, here described, appears to have been a record, which the *Sultan* kept constantly by him, for the purpose of easy reference. The first page of the first four ordinances bears the impression of his small ring seal (dated A.M. 1215). The other two are not sealed; but, in the place of the seal, the usual invocation of "Bism Allah," &c. appears, in his own handwriting.

memoranda, relative to the military establishment, written, for the most part, in the *Sultan's* own hand, and dated in the month of *Jaafury*, of the year *Sâhir*, or about five months subsequently to the ordinance. There is no essential difference between these two statements, excepting in the article of irregular cavalry, in which branch of his army the *Sultan* appears, during the intermediate period, to have made a reduction of six thousand men; namely, five thousand *Silâhdâr*, and one thousand *Kuzzâk*, or *Looty*, horse.

I have not the means of ascertaining what reduction, if any, was made in the military force of *Mysore*, in consequence of the diminution of its resources produced by the partition treaty of 1792. It is probable, however, considering the hostile views which the *Sultan* never ceased to entertain, from the moment in which he was compelled to surrender half his country into the hands of his enemies, that he disbanded no other part of his army on the occasion, than the number of cavalry specified above. Indeed, the great marine establishment which he resolved to form about the same period, sufficiently proves, that nothing was less in his contemplation, than any material abridgment of the means, by which he still hoped to repair his losses, and to recover his military reputation. The irregular horse, now dismissed, could at any time be replaced: and, in the meanwhile, the money saved by their discharge would go far towards defraying the expence of his proposed navy.(3)

The copy of the *Futhûl Mûjâhideen*, now before me, containing merely the formation of a single *Kushoon* of infantry, without either stating the total number of such *Kushoons*, or furnishing any other data for estimating the aggregate strength of the army; and this being the only document in my possession, relating to the military establishments of the *Sultan*, during the early part of his reign, it is not in my power to ascertain what changes, if any, took place in those establishments, between the date of the work in question and the year 1793, when they were formed on the model to be presently shown. I am alike unable to determine, whether the force brought by Tippoo Sultan into the field, in the war of 1799, exceeded or fell short of that contained in the following enumeration. Adverting, however, to the vindictive projects which he conceived and pursued in this interval, it may be safely presumed, that it was, at least, equal to the establishment

(3) The annual expence of six thousand horse, reckoning at the rate of thirty *rupees* a month for each man and horse (the usual average pay of خود اسپه *Khood-uspa*, or men riding their own horses) would amount to about £240,000, which exceeds the pay or fixed allowances of the naval establishment in the sum of nearly £60,000.

establishment of 1793.[4] Indeed, the official papers, of the time here alluded to, afford numerous proofs of his unceasing anxiety, not only to complete, to their full extent, the various corps of his army, but also to draw to his standard the greatest possible number of followers, and particularly those of the Mahommedan religion.

Establishment *of* Tippoo Sultan's Army *in* 1793.

1. *Piddeh Uskur* or (*regular infantry.*)

Divided into five *Kuchurries,* and composed of twenty-seven *Kushoons.*

Specification of the five Kuchurries.

1*st. Kuchurry Ahmedy,* or the *Ahmedy Kuchurry.*

Two *Bukhshies* commanding the whole,[5] and having a *Teep* of *Uskur,* consisting of 346 men, attached immediately to them.[6]

Six *Kushoons* of *Uskur* and one *Teep* of *Uskur* (of the strength above mentioned).

The men of the *Koreish* tribe and of the *Sûny* sect. With twelve field pieces.

2d. *Kuchurry Hûzoor Uskur*

Six *Kushoons* of *Uskur,* composed of men of the same tribe and sect as the preceeding *Kuchurry.* Twelve field pieces.

3d. Second *Kuchurry* of *Piddeh Uskur.*

Five *Kushoons* of *Uskur,* and one *Teep* of *Uskur* attached to the *Bukhshies.*

Men of the tribe of *Koreish, Siyuds, Moghuls,* and *Patans* of the *Sûny* sect. With ten field pieces.

4th. Third

(4) According to Colonel Beatson (page xciii of the Appendix to his book), the *Sultan's* army amounted, in 1799, to forty-eight thousand fighting men. If, by this designation, he meant men bearing arms; and if the garrison troops, throughout *Mysore,* were not included in the number, the difference in the efficient forces of the two periods in question will be found to be very inconsiderable.

(5) Though not so stated in the original, there would appear to have been two *Bukhshies* attached to each *Kuchurry* of regular infantry, and the same number to a *Kuchurry* of cavalry. The *Ehshâm* troops had also their *Bukhshies;* but I do not know of what number, or of how many *Kuchurries,* they consisted.

(6) I am unable to state for what purpose these independent *Teeps,* or battalions, were assigned to the *Bukhshies;* or why they were not attached to all the *Kuchurries* as well as to the three specified in the text. If they were designed as guards of honour (which, however, seems rather unlikely), it may be presumed, that the particular *Kuchurries* to which they belonged were commanded by officers in whom the *Sultan* placed more than usual confidence.

4th. Third *Kuchurry of Piddeh Uskur.*

Five *Kushoons.* Men of the *Koreish* tribe, *Siyuds, Patans* and *Moghuls* of the *Súny* sect; with one *Teep* of *Uskur* (as before) attached to the *Bukhshies.* Ten field pieces.

5th. The *Usud Ilhye Kuchurry.*

Five *Kushoons*, viz: three *Uskur*, composed of men of the *Koreish* tribe, and of *Siyuds* of the *Súny* sect; and two *Kushoons* of *Usud Ilhyes.*(7) With ten guns.

Total twenty-seven *Kushoons*, with three independent *Teeps* of *Uskur* and fifty-four field pieces.

Besides the guns belonging to the *Kushoons*, there was a park of artillery attached (apparently) to the whole body of infantry, and consisting of a heavy train of

10 battering guns
6 long guns (for distant cannonading), and
6 howitzers

The staff of each *Kuchurry* seems to have consisted of

2	*Bukhshies*	pay according to their repective merits.
1	*Mirzáey Duftur*	
1	*Hindooy* d°. ..	

		C. Pagodas.	Fanams.	
16	*Gúmáshtehs*, from .... 18 0 to	16(8)	0	each
2	*Sur-yusákchies*	17(8)	0	do.
2	*Nukeebs*	12(8)	0	do.
5	*Házirbáshies*	3	6	do.
4	Standard bearers..............................	1	5	do.
1	*Furrásh*	2	7	
2	*Surwáns* (in charge of three camels)	2	7	do.
1	*Mushálchy*	2	1	

Establishment of a Kushoon.

Staff:

1 *Sipahdár* (pay according to his qualifications.)

2 *Mútusuddies*

(7) Here the two *Kushoons* of *Usud Ilhyes* are distinguished from the *Uskur*, or regular troops, as if they were considered in the light of irregulars. This, however, I believe, was not the case.

(8) These sums included an allowance of five *Cantarai pagodas* for a horse.

	Pagodas.	Fanams.
2 *Mútusuddies*(9)	16	0 each.
1 *Yusákchy*	7	0
1 *Hukeem* (or physician)	5	0
1 *Jurráh* (or surgeon)	3	0
1 *Mushálchy*	2	1

Each *Kushoon* was composed of four *Teeps* (10) of *Uskur*; of which the first, second, and third were denominated *Ouwuls* (or of the first class), and the fourth *Dooem* (or of the second class).

Staff of a Teep.

	Pagodas.	Fanams.
1 *Teepdár* of the first class, or first, second, and third *Teeps*, pay (including horse) (11)	30	0
1 *Shurbashurn*	7	5
2 *Gurdóon-nuwáz* (drummers) providing their own drums	4	2 each
1 *Shahnáey-nuwáz* (or trumpeter) including trumpet	4	2
1 Standard bearer	7	5
1 *Munshoor*	3	6

Each *Teep* consisted of four *Yooz*,(12) and each *Yooz* was composed as follows:

	Pagodas.	Fanams.
1 *Yoozdár*	16	0 (13)
2 *Surkheels*	7	0 each

(9) Including four pagodas for a horse: It is here observable, that the *Bukhshy*, who, according to the formation of a *Kushoon* given in the *Futhûl Mûjáhideen*, ranked apparently as the second officer of it, was not included in the *Kushoon* establishment of 1793, at which period the title was confined to the heads, or commanders, of *Kuchurries*.

(10) Formerly called *Risálas*: this last term seeming to be limited by the regulation of 1793 to the *Kushoons* composing the *Usud Ilhye Kuchurry*,

(11) If the *Teep* was short of the full compliment, the *Teepdár* was to receive no more than the pay of a *Yoozdár*. This regulation was, of course, designed to stimulate the *Teepdár*, or *Risáladár*, to exert himself in keeping his corps complete. The same regulation appears to have applied to the subordinate officers.

(12) The *Yooz* appears to have been what is elsewhere called a *Jowk*, or company. The latter term (like that of *Risála*) was now confined, I believe, to the *Kushoons* forming the *Usud Ilhye Kuchurry*, and to the companies of rocket-men, gunners, &c.

(13) It ought to be observed, that the pay of the fourth *Teep* was fixed through all the ranks on a reduced scale. Thus the *Teepdár's* pay (including horse allowance) was only twenty-seven *pagodas* per month; the *Yusákchy's*, seven *pagodas* and a half; the *Yoozdár's*, fifteen *pagodas*; the *Surkheel's*, six *pagodas*; the *Jumaadár's*, five *pagodas* and one *fanam*; and the Private's, four *pagodas* and two *fanams*. The men and officers of the fourth *Teep* were probably removed occasionally, and when meriting advancement, to the senior *Teeps*.

Pagodas. Fanams

8 *Jumaadárs*.. 6 0 each

64 *Yuzukdárs*, or privates[14]........................ 5 1 d°

1 *Bheesty*... 2 1

9 *Nujm-wáleh*, for bell tents, &c.

Strength of one *Yooz*.................. 87 men[15]

D° of one *Teep* or four *Yooz*...... 348 d°

Strength of a *Kushoon*, or four *Teeps*, 1392 men, (of which, however, only 1056 are stated to have carried musquets).

The following were likewise attached to each *Kushoon*.

One *Jowk* of rocket-men, *viz.* Pay per man. Pagodas. Fanams. Total number of men.

1 *Jowkdár* (including horse)........................17 0

1 *Surkheel*.. 6 0

4 *Jumaadárs*.... each 4 2

32 Privates...... each 3 3

1 *Nujm-wáleh*

Each man carrying 2 rockets, or (with *Jumaadárs*) 72 rockets.

—— 39

One *Jowk* of *Durkhshundáz*, or gunners, for the service of the two guns attached to the *Kushoon*.

N. B. Each gun was in length two *dirais* (or *guz*) and a half [about seven feet], and carried shot weighing four short *duks* or *seers*: *i. e.* about six pounds weight.

2 *Surkheels* (one to each gun) each armed with a pair of pistols[16] pay each............................ 9 0

28 Gunners. . . at each.................................. 5 4

2 *Nujm-wáleh*

—— 32

Two *Jowks* of *Burkundáz*, or matchlock-men, each consisting of:

1 *Jowkdár*, pay 3 *pagodas* 6 *fanams*: subsistence 10 *pagodas*, calculated at 2 *fanams* on 50 men...... 13 6 ——

Carried forward..71

n

(14) This pay considerably exceeded what the privates of the East-India Company's Sepoy corps receive.

(15) The detail gives only 85; but, as there can be no doubt of the total (87) being right, it follows that there is some omission: possibly of a drummer and trumpeter. A similar discrepancy occurs in the specification of an *Usud Ilhye Kushoon*, on the formation of which the *Jowk* corresponded with the *Yooz*, and the *Risála* with the *Teep*.

(16) Original تفنچہ

	Pay per man. Pagodas.	Fanams.	Total number of men.
Brought forward			71
5 *Jumaadárs*, pay 3 *pagodas* 6 *fanams*: subsistence 9 *fanams*, calculated at 1 *fanam* on 9 men.	4	5	
45 Privates. . . . at each	3	6	
5 *Nujm-wáleh*s			
—— The two *Jowks*			112
Two *Jowks* of *Khulásies*,[16] each *Jowk* consisting as follows:			
1 *Jowkdár*, pay 2 *pagodas*: subsistence 12 *pagodas*, calculated on 60 men at 2 *pagodas* each	14	0	
6 *Dufaadárs*, pay 2 *pagodas* 7 *fanams*: subsistence 9 *fanams*, calculated on 9 men at 1 *fanam* each	3	6	
54 Privates. . . . at each	2	4	
—— The two *Jowks*			122
The guns were drawn each by twelve bullocks having three men (drivers) attached to them			6
The two tumbrils were drawn by forty bullocks, having ten drivers attached			10
There was, besides, an ammunition cart to each *Kushoon*, drawn by twenty bullocks, having five drivers attached to them			5
To twelve spare bullocks, drivers			2
Spare cart drawn by eight bullocks, with drivers			2
Two *Chowdries*[17] of bullocks, with their assistants[18]			23
To the whole of the bullock-drivers belonging to the guns were attached four *Dufaadárs*			4
A *Dárogha* over the whole			1
One camel-driver to two camels, carrying 108 rockets			1
One *Moallum*, or teacher of the *Koran*			1
			360
Add			1,392
Total strength of the *Kushoon* (including all descriptions of men)			1,752

(16) I am doubtful what the employment of these men was; but I think it likely that they answered to our own *Lascars*.

(17) A kind of officer, or superintendant.

(18) Besides the regular establishment of bullocks attached to a *Kushoon*, the *Meer Sudoor* department was directed, by the ordinance of 1793, to furnish a thousand extra bullocks, for the service of every *Kushoon* employed on any expedition conducted by the *Sultan* in person.

Those carrying firelocks amounted to.......... 1,146
Total of twenty-seven *Kushoons*.................................47,304
and of firelocks 30,942

It appears by the foregoing statement, that a considerable change had been made in the formation of a *Kushoon*, since the period when the establishment given in the *Futhûl Mûjâhideen* was formed; the strength of a *Kushoon* consisting then (including all descriptions, as above) of 2,928 men, of which number 2,400 appear to have carried muskets.

It is not, however, to be inferred from this circumstance, that the aggregate amount of the *Sultan's* infantry in 1783, exceeded that of 1793, because, though the *Kushoons* were stronger at the former period, they may have been, and probably were, fewer in number; and such an alteration as this may be easily supposed to have been adopted, with the sole view of rendering these corps less unwieldly than formerly.

In order to arrive at the total amount of the regular foot forces of Tippoo Sultan,

at the period immediately in question (or 1793), we must	*Men.*	*Firelocks.*
make the following additions to the foregoing enumeration	47,304	30,942
Monsieur Vigie's[19] (formerly Lally's) corps, 500 Europeans and 500 *Sepoys*..................	1,000	800
N.B. To this corps (the monthly expence of which is stated by the *Sultan* himself at 8,179 *Cantarai pagodas)* were attached two guns.		
Three independent *Teeps* of regular infantry *(Piâdeh Uskur)* attached to the *Bukhshies* of the first, second, and third *Kuchurries*,[20] each 348 strong	1,044	864
Staff of the five *Kuchurries*	205	
Drivers, and others, to 1,935 bullocks attached to the heavy park, *viz.* 1,664 draft and 271 carriage......	719	
Bildars, or pioneers	735	
Elephant-drivers to seven elephants attached to the heavy guns	7	
Carried forward	51,014	32,606

n 2

(19) In the original ویژی

(20) These *Teeps* are thus posted, according to the *Sultan's* memorandum of August 1793. By the ordinance of March 1793, they were placed under the *Bukhshies* of the first, third, and fourth *Kuchurries*.

	Men.	Firelocks.
Brought forward	51,014	32,606
Khuldsies (or gun lascars) to the heavy park, fourteen *Jowks* including *Jowkddrs*.	714	
Add also the following establishment of artillery men:		
To the four long brass guns (*viz.* two long eighteen-pounders and two long eight-pounders).		
4 *Surkheels* and 56 *Gunners* } (Pay the same as those of the *Kushoons.*)	60	56
To the 10 iron battering guns (*viz.* six twenty-four pounders and four ten-pounders):		
10 *Surkheels*, pay 9 *pagodas* each; 140 Gunner, 3 *pagodas* 9 *fanams* }	150	140
To the six howitzers:		
6 *Surkheels*, pay 6 *pagodas* each; 36 Gunners .... }	42	36
Drivers to one hundred carts, drawn by three hundred bullocks, and appropriated to the carriage of the *Sultan's* baggage....................	100	
For bringing in forage to the above, forty-eight bullocks and fifty-two bullock-men, including *Ddrogha* and three *Chowdries*	52	
Chowdries and *Dufaaddrs* to 636 hired carts attached to the heavy park.................................. ..	—	
Artificer's yard	625	
One General in Chief of Infantry (at the monthly pay of 240 pagodas) 1 *Yusdkchy* or aid de camp to ditto, and 1 *Mutusuddy* to ditto..............................	3	
In all ..	52,760	(21) 32,838

The total of the foot forces amounted, however, according to an abstract in the *Sultan's* own hand, to 52,774 men, making a difference in the two statements of fourteen men: which may either be referred to the omission (on account of the great obscurity of the passage in the original) of the *Chowdries*, &c. attached to the hired carts, or to some other petty error in the detail.

The *Kushoons* composing the fifth, or *Usud Ilhye Kuchurry*, of regular infantry, differed a little in their formation, as well as in point of pay, from the other *Kuchurries*, as will appear by the following specification. The reason of this difference

(21) This total exceeds that given in the *Sultan's* own memorandum by sixteen firelocks.

difference I am unable to explain, otherwise than by supposing (what, indeed, there are some grounds for believing) that, in addition to their pay, both the *Ahmedies* and *Usud Ilhyes* received rations of *Dál* (dry peas), and perhaps other articles of provision, from government.

	Pagodas.	Fanams.
1 *Sipahdár* (pay according to his merits).		
2 *Mútusuddies* { one at	16	0
{ one at	6	0
1 *Sur-yusákchy*	6	0
1 Physician	5	0
1 Surgeon	3	0
1 *Mushálchy*	2	1
1 *Moallum* (or instructor in the *Koran*)	5	0

The *Kushoon* was divided into four *Risálas* (instead of *Teeps*), each consisting of 348 men, *viz.*

1 *Risáladár* (including horse allowance)	25	0
1 *Yusákchy*	5	1
1 Drummer and 1 fifer, each	3	9
1 Standard bearer	4	5
1 *Munshoor*	3	6

Each *Risála* was composed of four *Jowks* (instead of *Yooz*), each *Jowk* consisting of:

1 *Jowkdár*	12	0
2 *Surkheels* each	5	7
8 *Jumaadárs* each	4	2
64 *Yuzukdárs*, or privates, each	3	9
9 *Nujm-wálehs* each	2	1
1 *Bheesty*, or water-carrier	2	1

——Total of a *Jowk*	85 men
Of four *Jowks*	340 d°
Staff of the *Risála*(22)	8
Total of a *Risála*	348

and of four *Risálas* 1,392; being the same strength as the *Kushoons* of the other *Kuchurries*.

The

(22) The specification gives only six; but either two of the staff have been inadvertently omitted by the *Sultan*, or I have not rightly understood the original.

The *Ehshâm*, or garrison troops, are stated, in the ordinance of 1793, addressed to the *Sudoor* department, at 25,000 men.[23] I have no means of estimating the amount of *Kunduchâr*; that is, the provincial troops, or militia.

I now proceed to a summary statement of the cavalry, according to the establishment of 1793.

I. *Suwâr Uskur (or regular cavalry).*

Three *Kuchurries.*[24]

Each *Kuchurry* consisting of six *Mokubs* (or regiments), of 389 horses and 376 men each.[25]

Total of one *Kuchurry*, (with a *Syse* or attendant to each horse).... 2,334 horses

Of three *Kuchurries*.. 7,002 d°

The detail of the *Mokub* is not given in the original; but the latter appears to have been divided into *Teeps* and stables, each stable consisting of twenty-two horses. The strength of a *Teep* is not stated.[26]

To each *Kuchurry* of regular horse two guns were attached, with a proportionate number of gunners, &c.

II. *Silahdâr*

(23) Of these twenty-five thousand *Ehshâm* troops (armed, I believe, with swords and matchlocks) fifteen thousand were distributed among the several forts throughout the country. These were ordered to be relieved *annually*, and were paid at the computation of forty days to the month, and at the rate of two *pagodas* per man. The subsistence to their officers was fixed at two *fanams* and a quarter per man. The remaining ten thousand *Ehsham* were stationed at *Seringapatam*, or with the *Hûzoor*. The pay of the latter was two *pagodas* four *fanams*: and the subsistence of the officers, three *fanams* per man.

(24) By the ordinance of March 1793, the regular cavalry was formed somewhat differently from the establishment of August 1793, as stated above. It then consisted of four *Kuchurries*, composed each of four *Mokubs*, the latter being of the same strength as those given in the text: consequently, the aggregate amount of the latter establishment exceeded that of the former by two *Mokubs*, or about seven hundred and fifty men.

(25) It does not appear, why the number of horses exceeded that of men. Perhaps the difference might arise from some of the officers being allowed more than one horse.

(26) But although neither the ordinance of March 1793, nor the *Sultan's* memoranda of the same year, furnish the details of a *Mokub*, or regiment, of regular cavalry, as then constituted, I find, in a regulation dated in February 1797, a specification of a *Kuchurry* of regular cavalry, of which an abstract follows. The *Kuchurry* in question is called, in the *Hûkm-nâmeh* here referred to, "*Hafiz Sawâr e* "*Uskur*." Whether this was a newly formed corps, or an old one to which a new name was now given, I have not the means of ascertaining.

The *Kuchurry* is stated to have consisted (including all descriptions) of 1,619 men and 1,582 horses: of the latter of which 1,562 were stable horses; the remaining twenty belonged to the persons mounted on them. The whole were commanded by two *Bukhshies*, with the usual staff.

The *Kuchurry* was divided into four *Mokubs*; and each *Mokub* into four *Teeps* or *Teebs*. The *Teep* was composed of two *Yooz*; and each *Yooz* divided into two stables.

DETAIL

II. *Silahdâr Cavalry, (or Cavalry mounted on their own horses).*

Two *Kuchurries,* composed of Musulmans and unbelievers.

Each *Kuchurry* commanded by two *Bukhshies,* and divided into eight *Risâlas,* of 250 horse each, besides the usual staff:

1 *Kuchurry*............. 2,000 horse.
2 D°.................. 4,000 d°

III. *Kuzzâk (or Predatory) Cavalry.*

Three *Kuchurries,* of 2,666 horses each, divided into *Risâlas* of 260 each.

Total

Detail of a Mokub.

	Men.		Horses.
Sur e Uskur, or *Mokubdâr*	1		2
Shurbâshurn *	1		1
Trumpeters	2		2
Teepdârs	4		8
Yoozdârs	8		16
Surkheels	16		16
Jumaadârs	48		48
Privates	288		288
Standard-bearers	4		4
Shurbâshurns attached to *Teeps*	4		4
	376		389
Staff, *viz.*		One *Kuchurry*	1556
Four *Mûtusuddies;* a *Sâlotry,* or Veterinary Surgeon; a Farrier, &c.	16	*Bukhshies,* &c.	6
One *Mokub*	392		1562
Four ditto	1568	Exclusive of *Syces,* horse-keepers, and Drivers to 1300 Bullocks, attached to the *Kuchurry.*	
Bukhshies and *Kuchurry* Staff	30		
Burkundâzes, or matchlock-men, attached	21		
Total	1619		

General Abstract.

1 Stable........21 Troopers.†
2 Stables........ 1 *Yooz,* or 42, including *Jumaadârs.*
2 *Yooz* .... 1 *Teep,* or 84, including ditto.
4 *Teeps* .... 1 *Mokub,* or 336, including ditto.
4 *Mokubs* ...... 1 *Kuchurry,* or 1344 men carrying arms.

* I take the *Shurbâshurn* to be another name for the *Yusâkchy.*

† The number of *Horses* composing a Stable would appear, by some documents, to have been twenty-two. This would make the number of Stable Horses to a *Kuchurry* no more than 1,408; which I do not know how to reconcile to the preceding detail.

Total of the three *Kuchurries* stated at eight thousand horse, which appear to have been officered in the same manner as the *Silahdár* cavalry, the officers receiving a regular pay, like those of the latter body. It may be presumed, that the men composing this predatory corps must also have received pay during peace, whatever might be the case in time of war.[27]

The foregoing seems to have been the establishment of *Kuzzáks*, or *Looties*, in time of peace. They would, of course, be augmented during a war. In addition to the above, a *Khás*, or special *Risála*, of *Kuzzaks*, is mentioned. It was composed of Musulmans of various denominations, and amounted to fifty men and horses, commanded by a separate *Bukhshy*.

(27) The *Lootie*, or *Kuzzák* cavalry, are said to receive no pay: in lieu of which they are allowed to retain whatever booty they can acquire.

INDEX.

THE END.

DIRECTIONS TO THE BINDER.

Plate A. to face Appendix A., page i.

..... C................., C., page xi.

LONDON:
Printed by Cox, Son, and Baylis,
Great Queen Street.

ERRATA, &c.

Page.
18 line 1 *for* capitulations, *read* recapitulations.
19 ....17 — we lay, *read* we will lay.
20 note — نابیکاران *read* نابکاران
28 .... 7 — تنیه *read* تنبیه
31 .... 2 *after* پرده *insert* غیب
50 line 3 *for* on separate, *read* in separate.
58 note 8 *after* Usud ûllah ul Ghâlib, *insert* This was one of the titles; *and dele* viz.
66 line 13 *for* approaches, *read* parallels.
67 ....17 *and wheresoever occurring, for* Bukshies, *read* Bukhshies.
99 note 12 *for* A. H. 1147, *read* A. H. 1197.
109 line 5 — Dalwâr, *read* Dulwye.
112 last line — Bubi Ali, *read* Bubir Ali.
126 line 12 — Mukhun Zaal, *read* Mukhun Laal.
130 note — a shilling, *read* from four to five shillings.
150 .... 5 The sentence which follows the word "circumcised," and beginning "If this," has been accidentally transposed. It should follow at line 11 page 151 the words "title of Letter CXLV."
152 line 6 *for* subsisted, *read* subsists.
165 .... 9 — Mânâyâr, *read* Mânâwâr.
168 ....21 — gram, *read* grain.
185 .... 8 — brother-in-law, *read* relative.
— ....21 The words "at Muscat" should follow "Commercial Consul," instead of following "Hydery."
202 note 13 *for* A. D. 1764, *read* 1759-60.
— — Ubjee, *read* Ubjud.
208 .... 1 — want of encouragement, *read* want of arrangement.
212 .... 1 *dele* name uncertain.
233 line 5 *for* Khulfâr, *read* Khulfân.
235 .... 3 — realization, *read* execution.
244 ....16 — reasonably, *read* seasonably.
275 note 4 — ten, *read* two.
296 line 4 — the latter is, *read* the latter are.
326 note 8 line 4 *for* the perusal, *read* their perusal, *and dele* of.
— ...12 put the bracket after "them," instead of after "claims."
331 ....40 line 5 *for* translation, *read* transaction.
342 line 5 The words "some of," should have stood between brackets, thus [some of].
345 .... 9 *for* discharged, *read* discussed.
347 .... 9 — recovery, *read* discovery.
349 ....21 *dele* himself, *and substitute* his (Bûrhânûddeen's) army.
371 note 15 *for* کشران *read* گران
391 .... 2 — was, *read* are.
395 ....19 — article, *read* articles.
402 note 10 — خبالة *read* نبالة
411 line 12 *dele the comma after* however.
— ....18 *for* the state, *read* that state.
420 ....14 At the end substitute a note of interrogation for the full stop.
431 ....10 *for* extracts, *read* extract.
432 .... 16 — customary rules, *read* customary rites.
437 note 2 — giving, *read* given.
441 line 2 — Gûlshumâbâd, *read* Gûlshunâbâd.
— ....13 *after* established, *insert* at.

Page.
448 note 1 line the last, *for* and is most probably an error, *read* and arises, perhaps, from an error.
453 line 9 *for* rigorously, *read* rigorously.
458 ....14 — Khulfâr, *read* Khulfân.
460 ....15 — department, *read* apartment.
461 ....18 — imply, *read* implies.
479 .... 4 *after* pack up, *instead of* the baggage, *read* their tents and baggage.
481 .... 4 *for* begged, *read* begging.
— note 11 line 3, *after* given, *insert* verbal.
482 line 11 *for* Lewai Mâdhee, *read* Sewâi Mâdhee.
489 ....17 — in one part, *read* on one part.

APPENDIX.

1 penult. *for* Nurwail, *read* Nuwâyet.
2 line 6 — Kâzy, *read* Râzy.
13 .... 3 from the bottom, *for* Musnud, *read* Munsub.
— note 4 *for* 1559, *read* 1557.
15 line 9 — Beeny, *read* Punny.
23 ....19 — these writers, *read* those writers.
24 ....12 — been obliged, *read* being obliged.
26 ....14 — Wâng, *read* Wâg, *or* Waug.
31 .... 4 from the bottom, *for* Bhen, *read* Bhow.
34 .... 5 from the bottom, *dele the s in* departments.
35 ....14 *dele the final s in* justifications.
38 note 18 *dele the s in* volumes.
41 line 23 *after* Bay-nuzeet or, *insert a — to denote a blank*; *and read* Hurriâl *at the sixteenth of the towns enumerated.*
48 ....12 *for* Gûjâm, *read* Gunjâm, *usually called* Shehr Gunjâm.
— ....13 — Huzârs, *read* Bâzârs.
— — Meers', *read* Men's.
52 .... 8 from the bottom, *for* De Rany, *read* Decany.
66 penult. *for* Shudâl, *read* Shâdâb.

ALTERATIONS AND ADDITIONS.

141 note 2 This is an idiom, or rhetorical figure of the Persian language by which a word, necessary to the sense, but thought to be of ill omen, is dropped, and some other, of a very different (perhaps, as in the present instance, of quite an opposite) meaning, is substituted in its place. Thus, instead of saying "the Nabob is ill," the polite or respectful phrase is, "the Nabob's *enemies* are ill."
230 note 1 Dele this note, *Bârgeer* being only another name for *Silahdâr* cavalry.
329 note 26 After اُدھونی insert Udhôny, Udhoony, or Udhowny — for the second syllable admits of being thus variously read. At Hyderabad I think it was invariably pronounced Udhowny, *i.e.* with *futha* before و
373 line 7 Cancel the words "and that even if any exceptions had been made to it, he would not have found it difficult," and substitute for them, "or he might think that if any exception should be taken at it, it would not be difficult," &c.